3 1257 00146 4204

W9-BRO-358

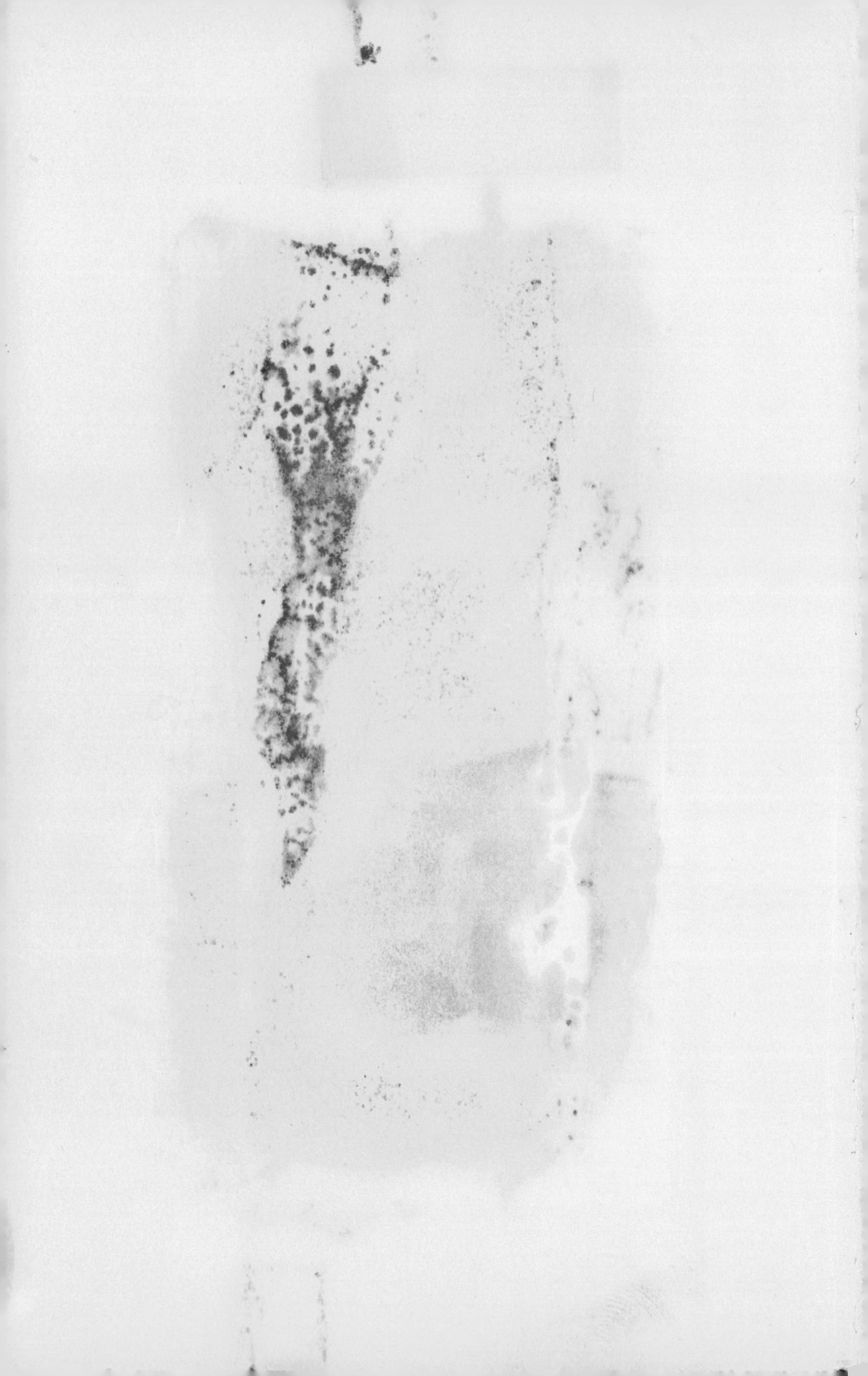

BY THE SAME AUTHOR

A History of the Swedish People:
From Prehistory to Renaissance

A History of the Swedish People

From Renaissance to Revolution

A History of the Swedish People

From Renaissance to Revolution

TOLD BY
Vilhelm Moberg

Translated from the Swedish by
PAUL BRITTEN AUSTIN

PANTHEON BOOKS
A Division of Random House, New York

First American Edition

 Published in the United States by Pantheon Books, a division of Random House, Inc., New York. Originally published in Sweden as *Min Svenska Historia II* by P.A. Norstedt & Soners, Forlag, Stockholm, and in Great Britain by William Heinemann Ltd., London.

Library of Congress Cataloging in Publication Data

Moberg, Vilhelm, 1898-
A History of the Swedish People.

Translation of *Fran Engelbrekt till och med Dacke,* which is pt. 2 of the author's *Min svenska historia.*
1. Sweden—History. I. Title.
DL648.M613 1974 948.5'01 73-11252
ISBN 0-394-48973-X

Manufactured in the United States of America

Contents

'Every true history must, by its human and vital presentation of events, force us to remember that the past was once real as the present and uncertain as the future . . . it enables us, by the light of what men once have been, to see the thing we are, and dimly to descry the form of what we should be.'

G. M. Trevelyan, in *Clio, A Muse*, 1955

Foreword

IN THE FOREWORD to the first part of my *History of the Swedish People* I motivated its motto 'The history of Sweden is the history of her commons' by emphasizing that the word *allmoge*, in the original Swedish, was being used in its pristine sense of 'the whole people'. This has not prevented many people from understanding it in its modern, restricted sense of 'peasantry' and quite unjustifiably saddling me with the view that the history of Sweden is exclusively the history of her peasants, and that it is their history I have set out to write. Concerned to dispel this misunderstanding, I find I must reiterate what I wrote in my foreword to Volume I: *My history's main theme is the Swedish common man.* This comprehends for me all groups and classes of people who, down the centuries, have lived in our country, from the kings at the summit of the social pyramid, to the peasants, the outcroppers, the rank and file in our armies, the servants, the bondsmen and the unpropertied, at its base. Since this base consists of more than nine-tenths of the population of Sweden, it must necessarily dominate my narrative.

And it is for the commons of Sweden, in the sense of the whole Swedish people, I have written my *History*.

Since the first part was published I have – much to my surprise – received a wide variety of historical source materials from readers offering them to me for use in future parts of this work. Most of my correspondents are amateur historians, laymen and persons interested in local history. But some, too, are academics and professional historians. I have carefully filed away all these items of information and will go through and examine them in detail. Some will certainly prove useful as I proceed. Here I can only gratefully acknowledge their receipt.

My first book was published in 1921; that is to say I have been an author for fifty years. But to find my readers offering me their help for the work's continuation has been an entirely new experience. It is both remarkable and symptomatic. My compatriots' interest in their own history is apparently a great deal stronger than I had ever imagined. And this is above all true, to judge from these readers' letters, of the youngest generation.

To my good friend and Swedish publisher Ragnar Svanström, finally, I must proffer my warmest thanks. He has been the author's best imaginable adviser and support in the work's creation. In checking my facts and historical sources I have had the greatest possible use of his expertise. And his never-failing interest in my *History of the Swedish People* has been an invaluable stimulus to me.

V.M.

A History of the Swedish People

From Renaissance to Revolution

Engelbrekt—a Great Man who was Small of Stature

The man

ONE CHILLY EVENING IN APRIL 1436 a murder was committed with an axe on an island in Lake Hjälmaren. Today, more than five hundred years after the event, Swedes still refer to the victim in daily speech (but more especially on solemn or festive occasions) as the very symbol of our Swedish liberties. Only the other day I was reading in a newspaper that his name had been invoked at the annual meeting of the Centre Party, the speaker saying he could not pronounce it without feeling 'the wing-beat of history' above his head.

Everyone agrees that the man who met his death on the island in Lake Hjälmaren was a great liberator. Since freedom is a word which figures in the political programmes of all our parties it is a name which is in high degree serviceable as a rallying point. When Swedes speak of Engelbrekt it is without affectation, almost as if they were speaking of a contemporary. No other mediaeval personage enjoys so honourable a status. Together with Gustav Vasa, Engelbrekt would seem to be the figure from our Swedish past who appeals most vividly to our imagination.

Yet there is a paradox. As an individual, no historical personage from the Swedish Middle Ages is less known to us than Engelbrekt Engelbrektsson.

I have tried to absorb all available research into his life and achievements and as far as I know I have hardly overlooked any work of importance that deals with him. But when all the propaganda of the chronicles and annals has been sifted, and after cutting a path through the thickets of myth and legend, the sum total of substantiated and incontestable source materials that remains is meagre. Certainly they do not add up to a living portrait. Of his own writings only two summary letters are extant. The sources leave us in the lurch. Engelbrekt, as he really was, eludes investigation; he vanishes into the jungle of mythology.

The man who was to become the very symbol of Sweden's liberties and of our national freedom emerges from the darkness of the 15th century and dominates events for a brief – and fleetingly brief – while. All he achieved, he achieved between midsummer 1434 and the end of April or early May 1436, a period of only one year and ten months. In the ocean of time it seems but an instant. But the events of that instant have filled more pages in Swedish history books than any equivalent period in our past.

As to his person, historians are agreed on two points: Engelbrekt was a great man, of small stature. In his *Song of Freedom* (*Frihetsvisa*) Bishop Thomas calls him '*then litsla man*' – 'that little man'; and Ericus Olai, who wrote a Latin history of Sweden in the 15th century, describes him as *statura pusillus*, 'of boyish stature'. An epitaph, possibly the work of Bishop Thomas, presents the dead man as *parvus corpore*, 'small or insignificant of stature'. Olaus Petri, too, our famous 16th-century church reformer and historian writes that Engelbrekt '*war en liten man till wext*' – 'was in stature a little man'. A latter-day biographer, Henrik Schück, wonders whether the expression '*then litsla man*' has not been wrongly interpreted: may it not mean Engelbrekt was of low estate? But in point of fact Engelbrekt can hardly be said to have been of low estate: he came from the lesser aristocracy (*lågfrälse*), had a coat of arms, and sprang from a family of prosperous miners in Kopparberget, as the hill region in Central Sweden now known as Bergslagen was then called.

In his own part of the country, then, we may assume that Engelbrekt was a prominent personage. When the men of Bergslagen wished to complain to the King of the Union in Copenhagen of their distresses, the man they sent as their spokesman was naturally the one in whom they felt they could repose most confidence – they sent Engelbrekt.

Schück calls Engelbrekt 'the first Swede'. This is a rhetorical expression, more in place in a novel than in a biography. Undoubtedly men existed before Engelbrekt who could have been called Swedes, but we have every reason to doubt whether his peasants were nationalists. This 'first Swede', at all events, was of German extraction. Admittedly, a modern expert, Bertil Waldén (*Engelbrektsfejden*, 1934) is of the view that the documents 'provide no conclusive proof whatever' that he was of German origins. But in *Svenskt Biografiskt Lexikon* Professor Gottfrid Carlsson has gone into the question deeply and shows conclusively that a German by name Engelbrekt was a citizen of Västerås – the heart of Bergslagen – as early as 1367. Probably he was the great-grandfather of our national hero. That Engelbrekt was of German extraction is something this writer concludes from his name and its orthography.

Usually I find research into the ancestry of great men tedious to the point of boredom. Mostly they are no more than speculations on hereditary characteristics. But in Engelbrekt's case his German origins *are* of importance. It has been suggested that they were connected with Bergslagen's commercial transactions with the Hanseatic League, which could mean that there was a link between these transactions and the outbreak of the great rebellion. But proofs are lacking.

And already we are on shaky ground. We do not know, for instance, *when* Engelbrekt was born. But since at the time of his revolt he was obviously a middle-aged man, at least forty and probably older, he must have been born somewhere in the 1390's. In 1434, at all events, the year when he steps forward as the leader of the propular insurrection, he is already a man in the prime of life.

Nor do we know *where* he was born. Olaus Petri speaks of him as 'living in Kopparberget', but this could mean anywhere in the whole of Bergslagen, the country's oldest industrial region, where mining had already been in full swing in the 13th century. Dalarna and Västmanland each comprise a part of Bergslagen, and have competed for the honour of his birthplace. For a long while he was known as '*Engelbrekt dalkarl*' – 'Engelbrekt from Dalarna'. In our own century, however, the people of Västmanland have begun to lay claim to him. They assert that his birthplace lay in the Norberg mining district, a claim based on a court record from Norberg, dated January 23, 1432, concerning legal proceedings attended by a miner named Aengelbraeth, of that place.

Whether Engelbrekt came from Dalarna or Västmanland is thus a topic of local dispute, which we may ignore. Homer was born in seven different cities of Greece, and in the Middle West of the pioneer period in the United States fourteen log cabins can be seen, in all of which Abraham Lincoln first saw the light of day. So doubtless it is also quite in order that Sweden's great rebel should have more than one birthplace.

Engelbrekt, then, has neither a childhood nor a youth. When he first comes to meet us it is as a mature man. All his days up to the outbreak of the insurrection pass in obscurity. Every authority agrees that he was married, and tradition says his wife's name was Karin, and that she was his second. But he appears to have left no children, 'at all events none who reached maturity' (G. Carlsson), a childlessness which has not prevented quite a few Swedes from claiming descent from him. In his play *Engelbrekt*, Strindberg provides him with a Danish wife – poetic licence, the dramatist says, taken in order to find in the breach of sympathies between Swedes and Danes a source of the marital wrangling indispensable to his dramas. Strindberg also endows Engelbrekt's murderers with a hitherto unheard-of motive. He has Måns Bengtsson Natt och Dag declare: 'Engelbrekt took from me the bride of my youth'. On the Hjälmaren island he wreaks his revenge – just one more instance of how unhistorical Strindberg's historical dramas can be.

So much for what we know of Engelbrekt's private life. As to his social standing it has been established that as a member of the so-called '*bergsfrälse*' – i.e. those landed gentry of the mining regions who were exempt from taxation – he was entitled to a nobleman's coat of arms, with three demi-fleurs-de-lys set in a triangle. But the gap between this lower gentry and the Swedish nobility was a wide one, and the magnates certainly did not regard this Norberg mine-master as one of themselves. He was not a 'lord'. Perhaps we could even use a modern expression and call him middle-class, a man who would today simply be called the proprietor of an iron-works. For someone to have risen from this class to the highest position in the realm is unique in Sweden's mediaeval history.

Nor can the epoch show any counterpart to a situation where a propertied man comes forward as a leader of the oppressed common people. A contemporary German chronicler, Hermann Korner, bears witness that Engelbrekt did not initiate his revolt 'out of any overweening pride or lust for power, but out of compassion for those who were suffering'. Engelbrekt's actions, too, strongly suggest that if he sought power it was not for his own sake but to obtain justice for his people. Himself in no straits, he became the leader of a people who were. I am sceptical in principle of great men, place no faith in history's haloes and laurels; yet I cannot help conceding Engelbrekt his probity and altruism. Nothing in the sources blotches his escutcheon. The only men ever to denigrate him were King Erik of Pomerania and Måns Bengtsson, who murdered him.

Otherwise the sources are one long hymn of praise for the stumpy little mine-master. Noble, high-minded, heroic, resolute, a plain-dealer, eloquent, such are the epithets they use of him. And even if the real Engelbrekt did not perhaps exactly exemplify all these qualities, the man who, at the head of an exasperated and tormented population, went to the attack against the royal bailey of Borganäs around Midsummer 1434, was unquesionably a genuine man of the people.

The Insurgent

Engelbrekt's insurrection can only be fully understood against its European background. The late Middle Ages were an era of great popular risings. Peasants' revolts broke out in France, England, Germany and Denmark, all over Western Europe. The causes of these insurrections, which swept across the countries like a tidal wave, were mainly social. But they were also religious. The papacy and the universal Roman church were in a state of acute crisis.

As early as 1356 a revolt of the French peasantry against feudal oppression, the 'Jacquerie', had been crushed with appalling ferocity by the upper classes' well-equipped and war-seasoned legionnaires. In 1381, as a result of an agricultural crisis which was a consequence of the Black Death, severe disturbances broke out among the English peasantry. The English workers found an able leader in Wat Tyler; his fall meant their defeat. By his doctrinal ardour Wycliffe, an Oxford don, incited people's minds against the Church of Rome and precipitated an English revolt against its pretensions. As a reformer, Wycliffe anteceded Luther by a century and a half. On his own authority he quite simply excommunicated the Pope, whom he declared to be Anti-Christ.

At this time God had acquired two earthly representatives, one in Rome and another at Avignon, who were mutually excommunicating each other. The existence of two popes naturally meant a loss of prestige for the holy see in the eyes of the faithful. Which pope was the rightful one? But matters were to deteriorate still further. A General Council of the Church, held at Pisa in 1409, deposed not only God's representative in Rome but also his colleague at Avignon, and elected a pope of its own. Both the deposed pontiffs refused to recognize the validity of the Council's decision, and clung to their office. So now there were three popes, a trinity which immediately set about excommunicating one another. Confusion in Christendom was complete. Finally, another church council was held at Constance in 1414 and succeeded in prevailing upon all three popes to abdicate. In 1417, Martin V was elected sole pope, whereafter ecclesiastical law and order was considered to have been re-established.

But the Great Schism had loosened the Church's hold on the souls of all sensible and independently-minded people. It was the first tremor of the Reformation. The popes only had their own behaviour to thank if excommunication, that monstrous threat hovering over the head of every Christian, had now lost some of its terrors. Perhaps, after all, it was not so dangerous to be excommunicated as people had believed? The Church's grip on the rank and file of her followers had been loosened. And the proof came with the popular revolts. Men now had the audacity to rebel not only against worldly but also against spiritual oppression.

The greatest of these popular insurrections, and the one which lasted longest, was the so-called Hussite Rising in Bohemia. Breaking out in 1419, it lasted until 1436. Huss himself, whose doctrines had been inspired by Wycliffe, had been burnt as a heretic at Constance in 1415. According to Halvdan Koht, the Norwegian historian, the Bohemian conflagration sent sparks flying even into the remote North. Among peasants at Setesdal, in Norway, he has come upon German catchwords which clearly once incited them to rebel. And Swedish bishops went in fear that there might be some connection between the revolt of the commons in Sweden and the Hussite rising, still in full blaze at the time of Engelbrekt's insurrection.

The causes of the Engelbrekt rising have so often been described by Swedish historians that I have only dealt with them briefly. What Erik of Pomerania's régime was like we already know. As Erik XIII, he could not have had a more appropriate number to his name. The Kalmar Union, Queen Margareta's brilliant idea, had been thrown away by her niece's son. Only rarely did Erik ever visit his Swedish domains, which he left in the hands of his bailiffs. Yet at the same time he introduced into Sweden a novel system of taxation, requiring his subjects to pay cash. In converting the peasants' stores of grain, butter, meat, hay and other commodities into currency, the royal bailiffs had a free hand and naturally did not hesitate to under-value these products and put the profits into their own pockets. Here was a new chance for them to 'pill and poll' a peasantry already staggering under a grievous burden of taxation. One of Erik's new impositions obliged the peasants, in the teeth of all law and custom, to carry out days of compulsory labour on his royal estates.

At this juncture a general revolt would appear to have been inevitable. If ever a popular rising was spontaneous, it was this Swedish rising of 1434. The amazing thing is that it had not broken out earlier, for instance during Albrekt's German régime in the 1370's and 1380's. During the quarter-century when they had been subject to Albrekt, the Swedes had been probably more sorely tried than at any other time during the Middle Ages. These burdens had been relieved by Margareta's reduction of the noble estates. Schück is of the view that she saved the liberties of the Swedish peasant – that time. Perhaps he exaggerates slightly. Anyway, under Albrekt the tyranny had been even harsher and the peasants' existence even more intolerable than it was now under Erik's Danish rule. And indeed several insurrections had been attempted. Stifled at birth, these peasant revolts have been only summarily noticed by historians. Unfortunately they have been the object of very little research and, for the time being at least, we must be content with the indisputable fact that they did break out. My own view is that, if they failed, it was chiefly for lack of the right leader. This man had as yet not been found.

Not until 1434 did the peasants find him. The right man, in the right place, at the right moment. Engelbrekt Engelbrektsson.

On Midsummer Day, the contemporary *Rhymed Chronicle* tells us, the bailiff's castle at Borganäs was stormed and burnt to the ground. Borganäs lies in Southern Dalarna, near the present-day town of Borlänge, where there is a memorial tablet to the event. But the firewood for this great midsummer bonfire, as we have seen, had been gathering for a long time; and just how dry it was can be judged from the swiftness with which the conflagration spread throughout the kingdom.

A revolutionary state of affairs, as one can only call it, had long existed. Such a situation cannot be artificially brought about by writings or speechifyings. Nor can it be provoked from without. It can only spring from fertile soil; grow, like the grain in the fields, according to natural laws. 'Revolutions begin in men's stomachs', is a much later saying, but one which I believe to be applicable to the situation in Sweden in 1434. Only when their daily existence had become utterly insufferable did Engelbrekt's hosts take up their primitive weapons, their poleaxes, spiked clubs and bows and arrows. Most insufferable of all their torments was famine.

What the peasants wanted, the sources tell us, was the restoration of Sweden's ancient laws and customs, 'as in St Erik's day'. Like a popular refrain the memory of that monarch's reign was recalled by the people as a lost paradise, no little enhanced (no doubt) in a retrospect of three hundred years.

That the revolt should have broken out just in Bergslagen was not a mere matter of chance; it was a consequence of King Erik's unlucky war against the Hanseatic League and Holstein. Rich seams of Osmund ore and copper had been discovered in this part of Sweden, where mining was an ancient industry, and many vagrants, footloose men of no fixed abode, were finding their way up to Bergslagen and worked in its mines. During the war the Hanseatic cities had effectively blockaded Sweden's commerce; ore exports had been brought to a standstill, and unemployment was rife. Not that any real class structure is to be discerned in Bergslagen at this time: mine-owners and miners are more or less indistinguishable. What is certain is that they had common reasons for revolting. According to unverified statements, the revolt had been preceded by disturbances among the workers. If this was really so – it is a subject for future research – this would be the first strike of miners in Swedish history. We know that as early as the autumn of 1432 a rebellious crowd had made their way down to the bailiff's residence at Västerås. In the spring of 1433, too, there had been a march of dissatisfied and disgruntled folk to the same castle. Waldén, in his above-mentioned work, calls it 'the first demonstration known in our history'.

But, as transpires from Magnus Eriksson's charter for Kopparberget, granted on February 17, 1347, the workers of the famous copper mine at Falun were allowed no weapon but their knives: 'We further graciously forbid, under pain of our royal vengeance, any of the commons to bear whatsoever weapon may do harm to others, namely dagger, bow, club, spear, sword or broad axe, on pain of a fine of three marks a man; except at the utmost the knife wherewith he eateth. Masters are permitted to own a sword, shield, iron hat and gauntlet. If, however, it be so, that the commons cause any disturbance that do harm to the mine, then may those of the masters as may be appointed by our bailiff be fully armed, until such time as they shall bring the commons back to order and each man goeth about his work without causing damage to other.'

The 1347 document further contains regulations stipulating severe punishments for 'troublemakers'. From which it seems likely that insurrections had been attempted in Kopparberget long before the outbreak of Engelbrekt's rebellion.

Västerås Castle was the seat of the Danish bailiff Jösse Eriksson, lord of Bergslagen. For me, ever since I first read about him in my school history book, Jösse Eriksson has embodied the concept of a bailiff. His cruelties to the 'poor peasants of Dalarna' threw me into a state of violent indignation. He 'hanged them up to smoke' and harnessed their pregnant wives to ploughs and haywains, so that their babes were stillborn. From childhood up, bailiffs of all sorts and sizes were hateful to me. They led my thoughts infallibly to Jösse Eriksson.

As a boy, of course, I swallowed my school books whole; took every word for gospel. Not until many years later did I realise that they were merely echoing the 15th-century *Engelbrekt Chronicle*, whose author wished to stir up hatred for the Danes and the Kalmar Union.

In this chronicle – which is a section of the *Karl Chronicle* – the misdeeds of Jösse Eriksson are detailed for posterity. Peasants hung up to smoke, pregnant women dragging heavy hay carts – here was propaganda with a vengeance! In the Bergslagen countryside, however, such sights cannot have been an everyday affair. Perhaps a few sporadic atrocities sufficed to inspire the chronicler's verses. But that peasants who rebelled or talked back at their masters were made an example of and subjected to gross maltreatment is historical fact, cannot be disputed. The question is, how frequent were such occurrences? In the name of historical truth it must be stated that the Danes had no monopoly of cruel behaviour. Swedes indulged in it too.

Mediaeval legends about the inhumanity of bailiffs abound, but just how much truth they contain no one can say. Some were committed to paper several centuries after the Engelbrekt rebellion, after being passed down through many generations of narrators. Probably these tales underwent successive changes; the bailiffs became steadily more cruel and inhuman. At the point where the Gullspång River flows out into Lake Vänern some large stones known as Plågan ('Torment') are to be seen. Here a bailiff by name Olov Stut is said to have obliged insubordinate peasants to sit on the stones in the icy lake water, naked as the day they were born, until they died of exposure.

For rebels and heretics, however, the penalty was usually the stake. Leaders of mediaeval rebellions commonly ended their days in flames. Neither hanging nor beheading were frightful enough to root out such evil – only fire sufficed. For this we have the word of

Archduke Leopold of Habsburg, in the true feudal spirit. Forcing his way into Switzerland in 1386 to suppress the freedom-loving people of the Alps who had taken up arms against him, he declared: 'I'll boil and fry this pack of rebellious peasants.'

The Union king's bailiffs undoubtedly followed continental practice. What the *Engelbrekt Chronicle* omits to mention, however, is that the leader of the Swedish nationalist party did exactly the same. In six known instances, Karl Knutsson, Earl Marshal and later King of Sweden, sent insurgent leaders to the stake. In 1437, four men of the commons of Västmanland, described as 'reputable', mounted the faggots outside Västerås Castle. And later, on the suppression of a revolt in Värmland in February 1438, two of its leaders, Torsten Ingelsson and Jösse Hansson, were burnt alive. Two Swedish historians, Gottfrid Carlsson and Kjell Kumlien, mention them by name.

But since the *Engelbrekt Chronicle* says not a word about these events, neither did any of my school history books; with the result that when I was at school I was never informed that this Swede, who thrice became King of Sweden, treated his own Swedish peasant just as ferociously as the Danish bailiff, Jösse Eriksson had done before him.

An eloquent instance, drawn from Swedish history, of E. H. Carr's thesis that facts do not speak for themselves until historians lend them a voice!

To posterity Jösse Eriksson's rampage has been made to appear the spark that lit the blaze. But his authority after all was limited to a single district – Dalarna and Västmanland – and therefore it cannot have only been this tormentor of peasants who was responsible for the revolutionary situation so soon to arise throughout the land. Several factors must have coincided.

All major Swedish histories describe the insurrection in detail. The best account, in my opinion, is that of Bertil Waldén. Here I shall only summarize.

Throughout the summer and early autumn of 1434 the skies of Sweden were darkened with smoke. Armies of peasants were marching through the land, leaving a trail of 'fire-blackened' ruins –

the bailiffs' castles. According to my reckoning, twenty-five famous castles, most of them in the south, were burnt to the ground. Probably the total number was greater. Most were no more than timber forts surrounded by palisades and earthen ramparts, and therefore easy enough to set fire to. Some were even smaller and more primitive. Thinly garrisoned, it seems they fell an easy prey to Engelbrekt's men, many times more numerous. After a brief resistance many of these fortresses simply surrendered on terms.

In his *History of the Nordic Peoples* written a century later, Olaus Magnus instructs us in the art of burning down castles. His lesson is probably based on a popular tradition dating from the Engelbrekt rebellion. The simplest way of setting fire to a castle, he says, is to fling red-hot iron balls over its walls. But there were also other admirable methods. Like foxes from a lair, the defenders could be smoked out. Great quantities of burning firewood piled up outside walls and ramparts could be used to fill the castle with smoke – whereupon the occupants would prefer capitulation to suffocation.

In his *Art of War* (*Stridskonst*) Bishop Peder Månsson, who died in 1534, tells us how the firebrands and fireballs used for setting wooden castles and fortresses ablaze were manufactured. There were four ingredients: willow wood, saltpetre, petroleum and brandy. There is no mention of brandy in Swedish annals until the 15th century, and then not as a drink but as a component in the manufacture of fireballs and gunpowder.

So Engelbrekt's rebellious army of peasants – a new phenomenon in Sweden's military history – were not only armed with axes, spiked maces and crossbows, but also with fire. Their leader, however, seems to have preferred to settle matters peacefully with the enemy, only resorting to force when all other arguments failed. In a number of instances Engelbrekt simply bought castles outright, paying large cash sums to their commanders, for whom capitulation became a smart stroke of business. We have descriptions of such proceedings, at Örebro Castle and elsewhere.

In the province of Halland, in the south, Engelbrekt purchased Laholm Castle, known in those days as Lagaholm. Reaching the Lagan River, his army had arrived at the frontier of Skåne, then part of Denmark. On the other side he found himself faced by an army in battle array. Immediately an armistice was concluded between the two peasant armies. This peace, concluded between two provinces, is historically remarkable; a forerunner, one might say, of many such peasant treaties afterwards concluded along the Swedish-Danish frontier. The last was reached as late as 1676.

Nothing succeeds like success. Engelbrekt was everywhere victorious. Soon other social classes and the lords spiritual and temporal supported him. They too had reasons for revolting against King Erik. Feeling themselves discriminated against as compared with the Danes who were really ruling Sweden, the Swedish nobles saw in Engelbrekt and his peasants a means of recovering their lost power. The Church, too, had long been in conflict with the Union king, notably concerning its right to appoint bishops – the most recent bone of contention had been the Uppsala archbishopric – and the lords spiritual were able to lend Engelbrekt military support. Some bishops were themselves military officers, commanding whole companies of men-at-arms, hundreds of soldiers. Gradually, well-equipped knights, squires and men-at-arms were absorbed into the ranks of the untrained and crudely armed peasants and supplied the need for officers. Little by little, from having been a genuine peasant insurrection, Engelbrekt's rising loses its original character. Nobles and commons participated in the revolution for quite different reasons, and were inspired by quite different aims. This became abundantly plain at its tragic dissolution. At Vadstena on August 16, 1434, the struggle took a dramatic and decisive turn. Here, in St Bridget's town, the lords of the council had met to confer. Among them were the highest potentates of the realm, including its leading bishops. Like a stupendous natural force the revolt's general dissemination throughout the realm had put them in an exceedingly sensitive position. Now they had to take sides. Which side?

At this juncture the little mine-master comes riding into Vadstena at the head of a great swarm of peasants – 'to the lords would he ride'. And a famous, dramatic scene is played out. The *Rhymed Chronicle* describes it vividly. As the lords are in the midst of their deliberations, there, unexpected and unannounced, he stands among them; the leader of the great revolt. Peremptorily, he demands that the highest personages in the realm shall join his struggle against King Erik's régime. Right now, on the spot, they must write a letter revoking their oath of fealty and obedience.

The lords refuse. Whereupon Engelbrekt, seizing Bishop Knut of Linköping and Bishop Sigge of Skara 'fast by the throat', threatens to throw them out to the furious peasants swarming and shouting outside in the market place. In the same way he threatens Bishop Thomas of Strängnäs. These are ungainsayable arguments, they prove decisive. Fearing for their lives, lords and bishops compose the required letter – but contrive to formulate it in such a fashion that King Erik will realise that they are acting under duress. Had they not bowed to Engelbrekt's will, writes Olaus Petri in his *Chronicle*, he and his men would have slain them and pillaged their estates.

Engelbrekt has been called 'the first democrat in Swedish history'. This honourable title, however, is a complete anachronism.

Throughout his brief career Engelbrekt showed himself to be a resolute man of action of the first order. Of this his behaviour at Vadstena is an instance. But the decision he then exacted from the council was certainly no majority decision, reached by a regular vote. Failing to move the lords by eloquence, he resorts to threats. It was his only recourse. In a revolution democratic law and order are suspended, and this was no action of a democrat but of a revolutionary. In the circumstances it was only natural that Engelbrekt should resort to violence.

This important historic confrontation between Engelbrekt and the lords of the council occurred on August 16, 1434 at Vadstena. But in which of its ancient buildings did it take place? In the days when I was working at Vadstena as a journalist I looked into this question and came to the conclusion that it must have been in the town hall where the city court still sits, and where I have often reported its proceedings. Vadstena's town hall, said to have been built in the early 15th century, is supposed to be the oldest still in use. At the time of the Engelbrekt rising it must have been new-built. Today its dark furnishings and low ceiling all seem heavily mediaeval. Outside is the little market place where, on that August day, 1434, the furious peasants are said to have stood shouting and clamouring. Sitting in the room, I have imagined the scene. There is another building on the market place, known as the Engelbrekt House; but since it dates from the 16th century it cannot come in question. In all likelihood it was in the old Council House that Engelbrekt threatened to fling the senior bishops of the realm to his peasants.

After three or four months' campaigning, Engelbrekt's work of liberation was in all essentials complete. Erik Puke, his faithful follower and second-in-command, brought out the commons of Northern Sweden, and it was not long before Finland, too, had declared for him. Yet the strongest fortresses still lay in King Erik's hands. Most such places, Stockholm, Stegeborg, Stäkeholm and Kalmar, lay along the east coast. The lord of Fågelvik in Tjust, on the south-east Baltic coast, young Karl Knutsson Bonde had joined forces with the peasant leader but failed to take Stäkeholm, which lay in his home district. Timber forts could be burned to the ground; but the castles at Stockholm and Kalmar had stone walls. They could only be taken by storm. Peasant armies were not storm troopers. In a later age Gustav Vasa and his Dalesmen, too, were to stand equally powerless before the walls of Stockholm Castle.

Marching through the countryside, Engelbrekt's host proceeded circumspectly. No outrages were committed against non-combatants; and there was no plunder. 'None suffered insult, none was deprived of his property, none lost so much as the value of a hen.' This touching and most unusual account of a mediaeval campaign, however, does not quite tally with the truth. There is evidence of another kind: Bishop Thomas of Strängnäs, namely, accuses Engelbrekt of stealing church property. In a letter to Karl Knutsson he calls the leader of the revolt, *ad hominem*, a thief: 'Engelbrekt, a ship's pound of pork in Romtuna church, that stole Johan Andersson on his behalf.' A ship's pound ('*skeppund*') was equal to about 400 ordinary pounds ('*skålpund*'), or upwards of two hundred kilos. This theft of pork conjures up a vivid picture of camp life during the Engelbrekt rising. By their camp fires a flock of famishing peasants sit roasting a few pounds of pork taken from a bishop. In view of the urgent business they had in hand one would hardly have thought that the Bishop of Strängnäs, the author of the famous *Song of Freedom*, would have begrudged them their supper.

Other contemporary documents imply that persons of rank were in fact plundered. Indeed it seems unlikely that the peasant host did not now and again eke out its meagre diet with food taken from others who were better supplied with it.

Yet this was no ordinary passage of men-at-arms feeding themselves by the forcible exaction of 'hospitality'. The peasant armies came to the countryfolk as their liberators, and were willingly given board and lodging. These were no mounted mercenaries in the service of great men and bishops, demanding to be fed and billeted with their horses. They were brothers and comrades in arms, welcome in the homestead. And probably Engelbrekt maintained what is called good military discipline among his folk; for as he was well aware, he exerted over them a magical influence, knew how to speak to them in their own language.

'He carried sword and club through the land.' This miner from Bergslagen, unknown outside his own part of the country until his middle years, suddenly appears as a successful commander-in-chief, a natural military genius. He also showed himself a political leader of substance. To enjoy the confidence of one's own parish by carrying out tasks equivalent to those of a county councillor or chairman of the local council is one thing; to lead an entire people in war, both militarily and politically, is quite another. Engelbrekt did both.

How can he have acquired these qualities? Here we have historical enigmas.

No one becomes a great commander overnight. Before appearing as leader of this rising the little man from Bergslagen must presumably have acquainted himself with the art of war. In his *Chronica regni Gothorum*, Ericus Olai, who had himself lived through the insurrection in his boyhood, writes that in his youth Engelbrekt had stayed in the houses and courts of great men and there been trained in the use of arms, in the manner usual among young noblemen. He is also mentioned as a squire. 'He had been abroad and stayed in many Courts,' writes our 18th-century author Olof von Dalin, without, however, producing any further evidence on this point.

Several historians assume that Engelbrekt had done military service under King Erik in his German war. Research has therefore sought Engelbrekt's name among Swedish gentlemen who had served under the King of the Union; but has not found it. Thus we know nothing with any certainty of Engelbrekt's military career prior to 1434. But that he lacked all previous experience of warfare is most unlikely.

Another and even more interesting question is: how did Engelbrekt finance this, his first great campaign? As yet he had no access to public funds, and his private fortune cannot possibly have sufficed. As far as I know, no expert has looked into this question, either.

Yet this peasant leader had to provide for an immense host, hitherto the largest ever to appear on Swedish soil. When he was about to blockade Stockholm his army is stated to have amounted to 100,000 men. Since this figure would mean that one in five of the entire population (then about half a million) had gone into the field, this can only be a gross exaggeration. Even an army of 40,000 or 50,000 (according to another statement) must also be excessive. Furthermore, the 1434 campaign was undertaken in haymaking and harvest time, when fields and meadows were crying out for peasants to reap them. But even if these figures must be greatly reduced, the number of troops who had to be equipped, fed and supplied, was still huge. That the leader of the revolt must have had a substantial war-chest at his disposal is also evident from his cash payments to a number of bailiffs, in exchange for their castles. But where did the money come from? How could Engelbrekt keep his great army supplied for four whole months as it marched through the kingdom?

Gustav Vasa, when his turn came, borrowed the necessary money from the Lübeckers; his war against the Danes was waged on credit. In Engelbrekt's rising, too, the name of Lübeck crops up. The insurgents were fighting the same foe as the Hanseatic League, namely King Erik of Pomerania. So the obvious question arises: did Engelbrekt receive economic support from the League?

Professor Erik Lönnroth (*En annan uppfattning*, 1949) finds a remarkable coincidence between the time of the insurrection's outbreak and an exceedingly sensitive juncture in the Union king's peace negotiations with the Hanseatic cities. For him the Swedish rising came at a most inconvenient moment. In fact it turned the tables against him. Was this pure coincidence? Or had it been agreed in advance?

There is evidence to show that Lübeckers owned mines at Norberg, in Bergslagen. Letters from German residents there have been found in the Hanseatic archives. As far as we can see from extant documents, however, no meetings were held between the men of Bergslagen and the Hanseatic League, other than those necessary in the normal way of business. There is no evidence whatever of any political links between Lübeck and the insurgents.

That a popular Swedish rising should have been financed by the great German capitalists of those days is an intriguing theory; but it can be nothing more. Research into this question has probably got as far as it ever will. So the historical enigma remains. Where did Engelbrekt obtain the money for his rising?

The Captain-General

After his war with the Hanseatic League had been brought successfully to a close, King Erik sought to open negotiations with his rebellious Swedish subjects. An armistice between the two parties followed, and thereafter compromise succeeded compromise. Soon the two parties were joined by a third: the Swedish aristocracy. By devious manoeuvres the nobles did all they could to get rid of Engelbrekt. As we have already surmised, the nobility and the commons had had entirely different motives for supporting the revolution. And now the popular leader finds himself seated beside the young Earl Marshal, Karl Knutsson Bonde, in the country's councils. From now on until Engelbrekt's death the sequence of events becomes so involved and complex that I shall not even attempt to survey it.

The meeting of the Estates of the Realm at Arboga, in 1435, had elected Engelbrekt Engelbrektsson 'Captain-General in Sweden' (*rikshövitsman*). This merely meant that he became in form what for more than six months he had already been in reality: commander-in-chief of all military forces in Sweden. As to Engelbrekt's other powers, experts disagree. There are two schools of thought. Lönnroth is of the view that his political importance dwindled swiftly after the Vadstena meeting, and that the country was thereafter ruled by the Council of State. Nils Ahnlund, however, is of another opinion, one which is shared by Gottfrid Carlsson. In the view of these two historians Engelbrekt remained 'the country's standard-bearer'. For a mere amateur to try to settle matters under dispute among professors of history would be presumptuous. Nevertheless I cannot see it in any other light than that, up to that fateful evening in April 1436, the popular leader continued to be the greatest single factor in the struggle for power. Having the commons behind him and pre-eminently enjoying their confidence, he could presumably at any time have led them to revolt against the Council of State and the aristocracy.

That Engelbrekt did not desire the end of the Kalmar Union is evident from the fact that he was party to the signature of a settlement with the Union king. But agreements with Erik XIII were not worth the paper they were written on. He kept no promises and abided by no agreements – behaviour quite normal in mediaeval potentates who, though they had not yet read Machiavelli, had no need to. They knew all his arts already. And when Erik, on his way home from Stockholm to Denmark, burned and ravaged the east coast of Sweden, his own kingdom, the revolt broke out a second time.

Early in 1436, therefore, Engelbrekt had to begin a second war of liberation. His second campaign passed through Southern Sweden. Being, unlike the first, a winter campaign, it was more troublesome. Yet it turned out fully as successful as its forerunner, and as brief. Once again the mine-master from Bergslagen showed himself a consummate field commander. Probably it was these months of winter warfare and this campaigning life during the cold season of the year, most of which Engelbrekt spent on horseback, which cost him his health. In the *Engelbrekt Chronicle* we read that he contracted 'a great sickness'. During his siege of Axvall Fortress in south-west Sweden, he had fallen sick and was 'rather ill'. What the nature of this illness may have been no one can now say, but we know that afterwards he could only get about on crutches. Probably it was some acute rheumatic disorder, contracted from the snows and freezing temperatures of his winter war.

At the end of April he left Axvall to recuperate at Örebro Castle, the province of Närke having been given him in fief. But there was to be no rest for the invalid. The question of a new agreement with King Erik was to be discussed, and the Council of State summoned him to a meeting in Stockholm. That the Captain-General could not absent himself from so important a meeting was obvious.

So Engelbrekt had to go up to Stockholm. What happened then we are informed not only by the *Rhymed Chronicle*, but also in other writings. All these accounts of the matter seem more or less to agree. By this time Engelbrekt's physical powers were so reduced that he could no longer even sit his horse and therefore it was decided to travel by water. Evidently in a crippled condition and accompanied by his wife and some servants, he was carried down to the boat. After the first day's voyage across Lake Hjälmaren the party decided to pass the night on one of its islets. The early spring evening was chilly. A fire is lit to warm them. Just then a boat with a number of men on board draws into sight. Among its occupants is Måns Bengtsson of the noble Natt och Dag family, son of Bengt Stensson, the lawman of Närke and lord of the nearby castle of Göksholm. Bengt Stensson and Engelbrekt had been enemies but had recently resolved their differences. Engelbrekt takes it for granted that the son of his former enemy is approaching on some peaceful errand, perhaps to invite him and his party to pass the night in his father's castle, and sends one of his servants down to the shore to show Måns Bengtsson the best spot to land.

The boat 'struck hard against the land', and Måns Bengtsson jumped ashore. Running up to Engelbrekt, who, on crutches, stands there awaiting his guest, he shouts: 'May I have peace from you in Sweden!' Engelbrekt refers to his reconciliation with Bengt Stensson. But Måns Bengtsson 'struck straightway at him with an axe'. With one of his crutches Engelbrekt tries to ward off the blow. The axe strikes his hand and cuts off three fingers. Turning, with his assassin at his heels, he tries to flee. With 'wrathful hands' Måns Bengtsson cuts a deep wound in Engelbrekt's neck, and then, with another blow of the axe, cleaves his skull. As Engelbrekt, his skull crushed, lies on the ground Måns Bengtsson is joined by his men, who shoot the corpse through 'with many arrows'. Wife and servants are taken prisoners to Göksholm. Later they are released.

The assassination of Engelbrekt who, completely defenceless, unsuspectingly had gone out to meet his murderers on crutches, was a crime of the first order. No other mediaeval event caused so loud an outcry. In popular fantasy and tradition it has survived for more than five centuries. As for its propaganda value, in the form it was disseminated in by the *Engelbrekt Chronicle*, it is beyond exaggeration.

The local peasantry 'in tears' took the people's leader's corpse to a nearby church, whence 'for greater honour sake' it was moved to the city church in Örebro. After his martyrdom Engelbrekt became a popular saint. At his tomb in Örebro church God caused many miracles to occur, and the lame and the halt were cured. In an entry in the Stockholm city records for 1487 mention is made of a pilgrimage to Engelbrekt's tomb. As Bishop Thomas's *Song of Freedom* bears witness:

> Many a pilgrim seeketh it out
> and there of his ill is quit,
> and harmless goeth home.

The subsequent fate of the popular leader's relics is a problem no one has ever been able to solve. At all events they have totally disappeared. Even his tomb is no longer to be seen in Örebro church, nor even any trace of it. But there is a chapel to his memory in one of the side-aisles. The fate of his original grave is an unexplored subject. Probably his relics were removed from the church as early as the 16th century at the time when the Lutheran faith was trying to extirpate the peasantry's worship of saints. A parallel may be drawn with the bones of St. Bridget which, as we have seen, were moved several times over. When the ground was being dug up for the construction of a new chapel in 1898, says Nils Finnhammar, director of Örebro Museum, numerous craniums and parts of skeletons were brought to light, and the rumour went round that some of them had belonged to Engelbrekt. But none of the craniums showed traces of an axe-blow.

What was the date of his murder? Research has had two Fridays to choose between: April 27, and May 4, 1436. It has settled for the former. But the site of Engelbrekt's murder has proved impossible to determine with any certainty. A promontory in Lake Hjälmaren, some six miles or so from Örebro, has long been known as 'Engelbrekt's Holm', the general rising of the land-level having joined it to the mainland. Here, in 1818, three hundred and eighty-two years after the murder, a monument was erected. It bears the legend: 'Here fell Engelbrekt Engelbrektsson, the Bulwark of Swedish Liberty, Gustav Vasa's forerunner, and Victim of a Vile Murder, April 27, 1436.' This memorial was put up by the then owner of Göksholm, G. M. von Rehausen. According to popular belief, no grass would ever again grow in this place; all the islet's vegetation was doomed to wither away. The ground was accursed for ever for having drunk Engelbrekt's innocent blood.

But today this promontory on the shore of Lake Hjälmaren is a lovely leafy grove with lush grasses and fresh and exuberant greenery. One day in June 1970 I saw how the most delightful lilies-of-the-valley were blooming there, like a white chaplet about the monument to the champion of our national liberties.

Popular belief thought a curse would rest for all futurity on the Natt och Dag family, one of whose members had done the deed. Yet Måns Bengtsson's real motives for his act are obscure. Probably it was some deep personal resentment against Engelbrekt. Between the murderer's father and Engelbrekt there had been a long-standing enmity. Olaus Petri tentatively suggests that father and son were in league, had jointly planned the murder. There are those who opine, he writes, 'that it was Herr Bengt who counselled him (Engelbrekt) to take boat.'

The Swedish 19th-century historian Anders Fryxell tells how the murderer was afterwards smitten by the bitterest remorse: 'But all his remorse did not suffice to wipe out his deed. The people always regarded Måns Bengtsson with deepest loathing.' For the commons, whom this act had deprived of their beloved leader, this reaction was most natural. But it was not shared by all classes of the country. Olaus Petri writes, briefly, that 'some counted it but small harm that Engelbrekt had been rid out of the way' – a mild way, to say the least of it, of describing the real state of affairs. The Danish historian Erik Arup, on the other hand, does not mince his words. In *Danmarks Historia* he writes that Engelbrekt

Engelbrektsson was murdered 'to the great relief of the Swedish nobility' – words which I believe to be the historical truth.

Presumably the man who drew the deepest sigh of relief was the young Earl Marshal, Karl Knutsson Bonde. After Engelbrekt's death, Karl Knutsson, his most dangerous rival out of the way, became the chief man of the realm. And therewith events took a new course. Wishing to be all-puissant in Sweden, the lords of the council and the rest of the nobility wanted to be quit equally of King Erik and of Engelbrekt. Thereafter the character of the Engelbrekt rising changed. It became a civil war. Engelbrekt's peasants had served their turn and were no longer needed.

Symptomatic is Karl Knutsson's immediate protection of the murderer. According to the usually reliable Ericus Olai, Knutsson issued a proclamation protecting Måns Bengtsson. It decreed that none might 'persecute, denigrate or libel him for his deed,' an injunction issued 'for the sake of peace and quiet in the realm.' Undisturbed by any considerations of justice, the murderer was to be allowed to continue his career. A member of the Council of State, one of the most important and respected men in Sweden, at the coronation of King Kristoffer in 1441 he was dubbed a knight. Finally, in 1451, Måns Bengtsson succeeded to his father's position as lawman of Närke. Thus the murderer of the Captain-General became the supreme representative of justice in the very assize where, seventeen years earlier, he had committed his own heinous crime. Had our present twenty-five year proscription period for murder then been in force, and Måns Bengtsson been prosecuted, he would have had to pass sentence on himself!

These latters patent, protecting Måns Bengtsson, implicated Karl Knutsson in the suspicion of being involved in Engelbrekt's murder. Undeniably, he had a strong motive for it. His family relationship to the murderer has also been pointed out: Måns Bengtsson's paternal uncle, Nils Stensson, a councillor of state, was Karl Knutsson's brother-in-law. But the connection was a distant one and most great 15th-century Swedish families were more or less related by marriage. So this is no valid evidence of his complicity; and for lack of evidence he must be acquitted. What is obvious is that he protected a murderer, who went scot-free. Current Swedish law metes out two years' imprisonment 'for protecting a criminal'. The parallel merely illustrates the difference between Swedish justice now and five hundred years ago.

No portrait of Engelbrekt exists; but his assassin can be viewed in a mediaeval wooden sculpture showing the descent of Christ from the cross. The work is part of an altar cupboard, now in Örebro Museum. Only about a fifth the size of the sculptor's other figures, Måns Bengtsson is a little figure down in one corner. His hands clasped, he kneels at the Redeemer's feet, imploring the crucified one to forgive him his sins.

Whether repentant or not, one thing is certain: the 'vile murder', as it is called on the monument, went unpunished. On the contrary, it seems to have been rewarded; a fact of historical interest.

The Living Engelbrekt: his achievement

The life of Engelbrekt Engelbrektsson was in high degree of the stuff of myths and legends. Therefore I must distinguish between Engelbrekt as he was when alive, and as a mystical figure. First, his living achievement.

As I have said, modern research, chiefly represented by Erik Lönnroth, has sought to reduce Engelbrekt's influence on political developments considerably. Further, the traditional view of his work, based mainly on the 19th-century historian Geijer, has been re-evaluated on two important points:

1. Engelbrekt's rising was not aimed at the Kalmar Union as such; its goal was therefore not the foundation of a national Swedish state.

2. The Arboga meeting of January 1435 'can in no circumstances be called Sweden's first parliament'; and consequently Engelbrekt is not the originator of the Swedish Diet.

Socially conditioned, the Engelbrekt rising had been a violent outbreak of fury and despair, fomented by starvation, oppression and general misery. If the peasantry had taken to their spiked clubs and followed their leader against the Danish bailiffs it was because their families' daily bread had been at stake. That is to say, the commons had not been incited by any hatred of the Danes, as such. Their hatred had been for particular individuals, as we see from the case of Jösse Eriksson who in due course was seized by resentful peasants in Östergötland, and beheaded at the town of Motala. Not that there were not other foreign bailiffs who had distinguished themselves by their decency and justice. Prominent among these was the German-born Hans Kröpelin of Stockholm Castle, of whom it has been said: 'The local population appreciated his just and humane administration and regarded him as virtually one of themselves.'

Nowhere in the sources does Engelbrekt appear to have been an opponent of the Kalmar Union. On the contrary, it must have in the highest degree lain in the peasants' interest to preserve a Union which, for more than forty years, had brought the Nordic peoples the blessings of continuous peace. Proof exists that in the provinces of Southern Sweden, which profited greatly from the free trade across the border, the commons were strongly pro-Union.

The second point which has been clarified is the question of the origin of the Swedish parliament. In 1935 the Quincentenary of the Arboga Assembly was celebrated with much official pomp and circumstance as the birthday of the Diet. Historians and poets were mobilized, publications came out in time for the jubilee praising Engelbrekt to the skies as the father of Sweden's five-centuries-old parliament, so deeply revered. Swedes felt they had every reason to be proud of themselves.

The jubilee, however, turned out to have been premature. The 1935 event lacked any historical basis. It had all been due to a misunderstanding, an erroneous reading of the *Karl Chronicle*. Something had been read into its pages which is not there: namely that the commons of Sweden had been represented at Arboga in January 1435. For this there is no evidence. Some nine-tenths of the Swedish people were in all probability *not* represented at it, hardly a cause for rejoicing.

Actually the Swedish parliament has no definite birthday on which historians can agree. Some of them are of the view that the Riksdag was founded at the election of King Magnus Eriksson on Mora Mead in 1319; while another scholar thinks it may have occurred at the 1464 meeting of the whole realm in Stockholm. As far as a layman can determine, the institution slowly grew into being as the result of a long process, from the meetings of the High Middle Ages to the definite establishment of the Estates of the Realm by Gustavus Adolphus' Parliament Act of 1617.

Engelbrekt's liberation movement also spread to Norway. The Norwegian peasants followed their Swedish brothers' example and flew to arms. But the Norwegian insurrection did not turn out so happily as the Swedish. Within a very short space of time it had ended in crushing defeat. Simultaneous disturbances among the Danish peasantry came to the same unhappy end.

In Sweden, Engelbrekt had had all classes of the population behind him and had been completely victorious in two campaigns. Yet even this did not suffice for his peasants' demands to be met. There were some changes in their conditions of life, of but little significance. Instead, the fruits of victory fell largely to the upper classes, a fact admirably expressed by a Norwegian historian: 'And, sure enough, the victorious insurrection was exploited by the indigenous aristocracy to its own advantage.'

And that, in a few words, was the final outcome of Sweden's first great popular rising.

The profound tragedy of Engelbrekt's insurrection has many parallels in world history. A revolution breaks out spontaneously, and for a while enjoys great success. But gradually it passes into new phases. The revolutionaries, it turns out, have been fighting for different goals; are therefore unable to unite; and their internecine strife is exploited by reactionary forces which finally gain the upper hand, whereupon the insurrection only leads to renewed oppression, sometimes harsher than the old.

When Engelbrekt's life was terminated, his achievement was still incomplete. Just how much he had meant to the commons in their struggle for freedom, however, was soon to become plain. The Council of State and the privileged classes rejected the peasants' social demands. What had been a general rising of the whole people was forthwith turned into a class war within the splintered structure of the Swedish community. From now on, Engelbrekt's folk had to turn their weapons against their own native lords. The country had been liberated from Danish rule. But from now on, as far as I can see, we are obliged to describe the rising as an *out and out class war within Sweden;* a sanguinary contest among Swedes.

The man who had been the peasant leader's right-hand man and his most capable commander and who now took up the dead man's mantle and attempted to bring his achievements to fruition, was Erik Nilsson Puke. Before long, open hostilities broke out between Puke and Karl Knutsson. Puke summoned the Dalesmen and the men of Västermanland to arms and for a while his fresh insurrection met with success. Over and above his class allies Karl Knutsson had on his side the city burghers, notably the citizens of Stockholm. With intent to deter the rank and file of the peasantry in other provinces from revolting, he behaved toward them with the utmost ferocity, causing as I have already said, four peasants to be burnt at the stake outside Västerås Castle.

After a preliminary settlement, Puke too fell into the hands of his enemy, by treachery. Breaking a promise of safe conduct, Karl Knutsson had him beheaded in Stockholm, in February, 1437. Bishop Thomas, the man who had guaranteed the safe conduct, bore witness to the Earl Marshal's treachery, and it aroused in him the profoundest indignation.

What the sources tell us about Erik Puke is little enough, and I should like to know more. He appears as an upright man of action, a lover of liberty and, after his death on the scaffold, a deeply tragic figure. In the *Karl Chronicle*, inspired by Karl Knutsson, he is for obvious reasons depicted as a scoundrelly rebel and an inciter of rebels. Gottfrid Carlsson writes of him: 'His epitaph was written by the hand of an enemy; having been deprived of his life, he was thereafter denied the honourable obituary he undoubtedly deserved.'

Now Engelbrekt's successor, too, had been disposed of. Once again the peasants lacked a leader. For the time being the insurrection had been crushed. The well-off and the privileged had triumphed. Måns Bengtsson's axe had cleared the Swedish aristocracy's road to power, personified now by Karl Knutsson Bonde. Up to 1441 he remains the most powerful man in Sweden.

On Palm Sunday 1437, about a year after the murder of Engelbrekt, a meeting of the lords, which can only be called a reactionary epilogue to the great popular rising, was held at Strängnäs.

At this meeting the Council of State issued an edict, known as the Strängnäs Decree. It gives us a reliable picture of the state of affairs in Sweden after the rising. Certain improvements are proclaimed in the commons' lot. Days of compulsory labour are to be reduced by one-third. They are also granted certain minor relief from other burdens. But this was their total gain. The so-called lawful tax (*laga skatten*) was still to be exacted as before. Another paragraph of this decree, though it may seem to imply an improvement, is, as an image of the times, horrific: children brought up by peasants and countryfolk may no longer be taken from their fathers and mothers against the latters' wishes. 'None shall have power so to do', we read. Which can only mean that, earlier, someone had: peasants' children had been taken from their parents and forced into service. Just how common this malpractice had been in reality is impossible to assess. The explanation is the usual one: 'detailed studies are lacking'.

Peasants who had fled to the cities during the Engelbrekt rising and were there wandering about as 'litherers'* were to be forced back to the countryside and there be degraded to the lowest class of servant ('*legohjon*'). But the most serious threat to the peasants' personal freedom was contained in a paragraph which reads: 'No peasant or countryman or their servants shall bear cross-bow, armour or the like weapons to church or council, market town or banquet; let those swords which are thus borne be forfeited.' Engelbrekt's peasants had inspired respect. The nobility, the upper classes, now wished to disarm them.

Karl Knutsson and his fellow nobles had made up their minds; there were to be no more peasant risings. Henceforward peace and quiet should reign in the land. But hardly six months after the lords' meeting at Strängnäs, in the summer of 1437, matters again came to a head. Once again, disturbances broke out. First, among the Dalesmen; then among the men of Värmland. The insurgents killed the bailiffs whom Karl Knutsson had sent to govern them.

Against these quarrelsome and rebellious peasants the Earl Marshal prepares to take new deterrent measures. The time has

* '*lättjades*' = 'lazed about'—the old English word about fits the bill.—*Transl.*

come for someone to be made an example of. At a meeting of the Council at Arboga, at Christmas 1437, Karl Knutsson defines the nature of these measures. It is his intention to march up to Dalarna and there chop a hand and a foot off every Dalesman. Whereafter he will go on to Värmland and inflict on the peasants of that province 'the same pain'. The *Rhymed Chronicle* devotes eleven whole lines to Karl Knutsson's recipe against peasant risings, culminating in a declaration of principle, based on experience:

> For if the commons be not whipped full sore,
> None will obey us more.

Let no one suppose that Karl Knutsson Bonde was crueller than other men in his position in that century of peasant insurrections; perhaps he was even less so. I believe Bertil Waldén's assessment, in his work on the Engelbrekt rising, is correct: 'To deprive . . . rebellious subordinates of a hand and a foot would have been regarded as a fairly humane disciplinary measure for the age.'

In the upshot the Dalesmen were not exposed to a general crippling. Perhaps the mere threat sufficed. Anyway, the Dalesmen made peace with the Earl Marshal, and had to pay heavy fines for slaughtering his bailiffs. But the men of Värmland did not throw in their hand. In the person of Torsten Ingelsson, earlier one of Karl Knutsson's lieutenants, they had found a leader of military skill, and under his command threatened Närke. A host of cavalry had to be sent against them, and a pitched battle had to be fought in north-west Värmland, in Jösse hundred, before the insurgents could be quelled. Cruel reprisals were then exacted from the Värmland countryside. In the late winter of 1438 the whole of the Fryksdal and Älvdal valleys were laid waste, and Torsten Ingelsson, together with another leading insurgent, Jösse Hansson, were burnt alive.

Both in Västmanland and in Värmland Karl Knutsson used fire to extirpate the evil dwelling in factious and disobedient peasants. Further on we shall see how this evil nevertheless survived and found its outlet in renewed risings.

One of the most widely read of Swedish historians, Carl Grimberg, sums up his older colleagues' erroneous assessment of the Engelbrekt rising: 'By their participation in the struggle for freedom the lower estates also freed themselves for all futurity from the threat of serfdom'. This statement would be good history if it said '*for the moment*' or '*for this time*', instead of '*for all futurity*'. Unfortunately, as it stands, the statement is false. The threat of servitude remained latent for centuries to come. It again became imminent a century after Engelbrekt, under Gustav Vasa's régime which was influenced by his German advisers, and again during the hegemony of the nobles in the mid-17th century, two hundred years after the 'little man's' revolt.

In the history of the Swedish people many dramatic events still await us.

The Myth

It is my belief that Engelbrekt, as a myth, achieved a good deal more than was ever achieved by the real Engelbrekt in the course of a mere two years.

After his martyrdom he became, as we have seen, a popular Swedish saint, hardly yielding pride of place even to Saint Erik at Uppsala. In the chroniclers' narratives his revolt was exploited to whip up hatred for the Danes; the suspected complicity of the national Swedish party's leader in his death was expunged from the records. During the latter part of the 15th century a regular cult grew up of the popular leader's memory. In the course of a dispute with his fellow-nobles Sten Sture the Elder* conjured up the bogey that the peasants might find a new Engelbrekt – 'cast up an Engelbrekt on to the neck of the realm'.

In the Reformation period the liberator was denigrated. The new Swedish Church accepted no Catholic saints. In his *Chronicle*, even Olaus Petri is critical of Engelbrekt; he exhorts the common people to be loyal to that authority which God has placed above mankind, and reproaches the Bergslagen miner for his rebelliousness 'against his rightful lords'. Olaus Petri's view was that from time to time men must 'suffer one tyrant, thereby to void themselves of many'. Even the strictly Lutheran Charles IX, who had himself revolted against Sigismund, the rightful King of Sweden, called Engelbrekt 'a

* See p. 86 et seq.

somewhat rebellious fellow'. But we cannot expect absolute monarchs to show understanding for any revolutions except their own.

But if Engelbrekt's name and deeds lived on down the centuries this was above all thanks to Bishop Thomas's *Song of Freedom*. Erik Lönnroth's admirable monograph of this poet (*Biskop Thomas av Strängnäs*, 1966) places him in his correct historical context and exhaustively explores his relation to the liberator.

Bishop Thomas of Strängnäs and Bishop Sigge of Skara had been staying with King Erik in his castle of Vordingborg, in Denmark, when the news of Engelbrekt's rising reached them. The two Swedish prelates were panic-stricken. In a still extant letter to their colleagues they give vent to their terror. For them this rising of the peasantry is 'a fire of evil and destruction' which had been lit by 'the blind commonalty of our realm'. In their letter both bishops pray to God Almighty that He of His gracious mercy will 'put out this perilous fire, that it grow not endlessly'. Clearly they had the long-standing Hussite Rebellion in mind.

A couple of months later Bishop Thomas was one of the lords spiritual who, at the Vadstena meeting, at first declined to despatch the letter rescinding their oath of fealty to King Erik. At this juncture Thomas was still opposed to the insurrectionary leader; as we have seen, he accuses him of plundering church property during the revolt. But before long Bishop Thomas joined the liberation movement and was sitting together with Engelbrekt in the Council of State. A few years after Engelbrekt's death it was he who wrote the remarkable song, which was to survive down the ages, acclaiming his memory. In 1434, Engelbrekt and his 'blind commonalty' had been, in the eyes of Bishop Thomas, the very personification of evil. Five years later, in 1439, in his *Song of Freedom*, he was lauding Engelbrekt to the skies as a saint and a worker of God's miracles, as God's instrument on earth.

'What sort of a man was this, who could make such an about-face?' Lönnroth wonders.

The sources do not suffice for a definite answer. We must seek purely psychological explanations, not to be found in the documents. It may be that his personal acquaintance with the popular leader caused Thomas's volte face. The bishop makes a somewhat opportunist impression. But in the matter of Engelbrekt his conversion was probably sincere. Further, it should be borne in mind that the *Song of Freedom* was written at a juncture when it had become crucial at all costs to incite the Swedes to resist the king of the Union, whom its verses depict as 'a tyrant and an enemy of God'.

From the sources it is obvious that Bishop Thomas of Strängnäs was a wealthy man, who had an eye to his worldly goods – a trait by no means unusual among lords spiritual. Among other things he owned smelting-huts in the very district of Bergslagen where the great insurrection had begun. In the autumn of 1437 he complains of not having received the mining monies due to him, because of the troublous times. Bishop Thomas, according to what we know from the sources (writes Kjell Kumlien, an expert on these problems), 'was deeply interested in matters to do with economy, and was naturally concerned to exact the Bergslagen taxes due to his see and whose collection was being seriously impeded by this rising centred in the mining districts of Västmanland. This circumstance, hitherto overlooked by research, should be taken into account in any study of Bishop Thomas's attitude toward Puke's rebellion – perhaps also to Engelbrekt's.'

That is to say, the bishop may have had purely personal and financial reasons for his extreme anxiety on hearing of the rebellion. From the outset, his attitude to Engelbrekt's war of liberation was ambivalent. But however we choose to see his tergiversation, in writing his *Song of Freedom* Thomas gave both Engelbrekt and himself a permanent place in our annals. His work has survived its first half-millenium, and whatever interpretation we place upon it this timeless poem remains a living flame, burning in the darkness of the Later Middle Ages: exciting words in the struggle to achieve a state of affairs which has so far nowhere been permanently established in our world.

At Vadstena the little miner had seized the Bishop of Strängnäs by the throat – an act of assault and battery against a church dignitary which in normal times could have brought him to the block – but by the irony of history it was just to this very Thomas of Strängnäs that Engelbrekt was to owe his posthumous fame.

Underblown by the Gothic movement, by romanticism and by the nationalistic view of history taken by another of our Swedish poets, Geijer, the Engelbrekt cult reached its apogée in the mid-19th century. Now the mine-master is made to appear a liberal nationalist, and thus a personality very much in the spirit of that age.

Geijer and his epigones make Bishop Thomas appear to be deeply read in the ideological doctrines of 19th-century liberalism. At this time the liberator also conquers the Swedish theatre, where his star burns brilliantly. Engelbrekt also becomes the favourite hero for authors of historical novels. In 1865 'the king and people of Sweden' erect an imposing statue to 'that little man' in the market place at Örebro, where the 'faithful defender of Sweden's freedom' now stands. In his hand he holds an axe, and from his belt hangs a huge two-edged sword.

In the reign of Karl XV (1859–1872), this Engelbrekt-romanticism bursts into full flower. The mine-master becomes 'the first Swede', creator of Swedish nationalism. As for his Dalesmen, they are made out to be a sort of nobility among the commons, bolder, more courageous, more liberty-loving and in every way superior to other Swedish peasants. Yet Dalarna, we know for a fact, was colonized later than the provinces which lie to the south of it.

As recently as the beginning of this century when a wave of opinion in favour of strengthening the national defence swept the country, the term '*allmogefrälse*' – 'a nobility among the commons' – which sprung from this Engelbrekt myth of the dalesmen, was revived by the celebrated ultra-nationalistic politician and explorer Sven Hedin and exploited politically during the campaign for the so-called *bondetåget*, when thousands of peasants marched on Stockholm in February 1914. Even later, in the critical years of the Second World War, the Engelbrekt myth was invoked in word and print, for instance by the historian Nils Ahnlund to fight Nazi sympathisers. And earlier, when Natanael Berg's opera *Engelbrekt* had its première at the Royal Opera in Stockholm in 1929, it drew a big public.

But the 19th-century image of Engelbrekt is baseless. Even the great Harald Hjärne, the conservative historian, objected strongly to this theatrical apotheosis of the popular leader: 'If Engelbrekt and his Dalesmen loved their fatherland, which is by no means altogether certain, it was not to give vent to such feelings in gaudy boastful rhodomontades'.

Certainly not. And I should like to add: when, late in the evening, these peasants got home from a heavy day's work, they were surely so weary that they lost no time in stretching out their limbs to rest. They can hardly have had the energy to sing Bishop Thomas's *Song of Freedom* or other patriotic ditties. Still less, compared with Hjärne, am I convinced of their patriotism. To the commons, whose view of affairs was so strictly confined to their own province, the very word 'Swede' must have been a vague concept. Often the provinces' interests differed widely and any sense of common interests ended at the boundaries between them.

This is why I assume that Engelbrekt's folk primarily regarded themselves not as Swedes but as Dalesmen, Värmlanders, Västergötlanders or Smålanders. What united them, probably, was not any nationalistic feeling, but sheer hatred of the oppressor. And it was among these people that Engelbrekt's memory lived on silently, while the literary myth about him was being created by the educated upper classes.

I have shown how our national hero has been exploited for political, literary, dramatic and musical ends. In art, too, he assumes various guises. This rebel with the immense mediaeval battleaxe in his hand was a favourite motif with our Swedish 19th-century painters; but his destiny has also captivated some modern artists of consequence. The great sculptor Bror Hjorth (1894–1968) has depicted Engelbrekt as the genuine rugged popular leader he was, a powerful figure, a man capable of seizing dignitaries 'fast by the throat', a furious spokesman for the common man, a man who threatened to drag out the bailiffs 'by the hair' and who, when they refused to parley, burned their castles. Little or nothing is left, here, of the saint. In this sculpture Engelbrekt has been given the traits of character which I believe historically to have been his. I think that it is in Bror Hjorth's sculpture we come closest to Engelbrekt the man.

Sven Erixson (1899–1970), one of our best-known contemporary artists, has painted the murder of the liberator in oils. As far as I know it is his only work with a historical motif. Executed in naïvist style, it shows some resemblance to our old peasant paintings. Here the image, surviving in the imagination of the Swedish peasantry, is of the popular saint. Already felled by the first blow of Måns Bengtsson's axe, Engelbrekt has fallen to his knees. With one hand he steadies himself on his crutch, with the other – which has lost three of its fingers – he points at his assassin, who raises his axe for the *coup de grace*. Måns Bengtsson Natt och Dag is strikingly youthful, a mere stripling, wearing a red knightly garb with a lace collar and baggy breeches. In one corner we see Göksholm, his family seat. In the background a woman in black, the victim's wife, is falling on her knees, imploring mercy of the assassin. A great fire casts sparks across the whole painting, like stars gleaming in a night sky. As a painting it is a fascinating image of man's defencelessness in the face of overwhelming violence. Obviously Sven Erixson was deeply moved by the terrible event.

More statues, it should be added, have been raised to Engelbrekt than to any of our Swedish kings.

The achievement of the miner from Bergslagen can be re-evaluated and reconsidered and given another content than that given it by posterity. But in one crucial respect it can never be denigrated. Engelbrekt lit a flame of self-assurance in the people whom he led. Until he appeared on the scene they had been unconscious of their powers. Thanks to him they had begun to realise that they could defend themselves against the threat of serfdom. Not until Engelbrekt does the Swedish peasant appear as a powerful factor in mediaeval society, a factor which can no longer be ignored. From now on his rulers are obliged to take him seriously. The war of liberation's immediate gains were minimal. But its victories had awakened a will to resist, which legends about the popular leader were to keep alive for centuries. For the common people's future struggles for their own liberation the myth became an inestimable asset.

The work of Engelbrekt, dead, was to be more durable than his achievements when alive.

Our Daily Bark-Bread

BREAD IS THE SYMBOL of life's bare neccesities, of all that man needs in this earthly life. 'Give us this day our daily bread', says the Lord's Prayer. Elsewhere in the Bible it is called 'the bread of life'. One of the sacraments, through which the worshipper becomes a participant in the body of Christ, is a piece of bread. But the symbol is older than Christianity. Homer calls it the 'marrow of men'. An old Byzantine proverb says: 'He who has bread may have many troubles; he who lacks it has only one. But it is a great trouble'. One of our old Swedish laws agrees: 'Unhappy beyond all others is the breadless'.

Many other Swedish expressions use the same symbolism. That bread should have been held sacred seems only natural. He who showed it disrespect was punished – witness the story of the girl who, to protect her elegant shoes when crossing a bog, stepped on a piece of bread which she had brought with her. The earth swallowed her up. I have even seen farmers in the field carefully avoid treading on broken ears of wheat – instinctively fearing the desecration of that which is holy.

Our Swedish word for bread (*bröd*) was a 12th-century modification of the German *Brot*. But bread's earliest history is linked with the worship of the gods and their mysteries. To our forefathers the breaking of bread was a religious act. Mediaeval kneading troughs sometimes bore religious inscriptions, prayers to God to bless the dough. The women made the sign of the cross over the kneading trough and prayed for the loaves as they put them into the oven. The outcome could vary with the heat of the oven, both above and below. More especially, there was always a danger that the bread might separate itself from the crust.

Bread-making was exclusively women's work. At meals the

peasant's wife, known as *matmodern* (lit. 'the food-mother'), cut the bread up into slices and distributed it among her 'family': in smaller farms the servants and other employees always ate at table with their master and mistress.

Swedish peasants have cultivated four types of grain: barley, rye, wheat and oats. Depending upon the nature of the soil and the length of the growing season, which in Skåne is very different from what it is in Norrbotten, the type of crop varies from one province to another. Prehistoric remains show that the earliest bread known to us was corn-bread. Later came rye and oats, which, after the climate had deteriorated and the weather had become wetter and chillier, came into general cultivation. In *Egil's Saga* wheat is mentioned as being imported into Iceland. But long ages were to pass before wheat, which requires heavy soil, became a common sight on the fields of Sweden. Even as late as the 19th century it was still mainly being cultivated in the plains, our real agricultural districts.

But as early as the Middle Ages wheat bread formed part of the upper classes' diet, and after the triumph of Christianity it also came into general use for the new religion's chief ceremony – the Mass. No other flour except wheat flour was good enough for the oblation, the body of Christ, consumed at the Lord's Table. And our old provincial laws stipulate that bishops who are to consecrate a church shall be given wheat bread to eat: superior food, that is, suited to the solemnity of the occasion.

When I was growing up, wheat bread was chiefly known to me as the bread of the gentry. For other people, rolls of white bread were festive food, suited to weddings, christenings, funerals and the church festivals. It was never baked on ordinary days. Not until some way into the 20th century did white bread become the Swedish people's daily bread. And, indeed, one may ask whether this transition from rye to wheat has really been good for our health. Important elements are excluded from white bread, so we are told. Be that as it may – our Swedish white bread tastes dry and unappetizing in my mouth, and I always prefer rye bread as more succulent. As a boy there was no more wonderful smell in my nostrils than the odour of rye loaves, freshly baked and steaming hot from the oven.

Like all countrymen, I have grown up eating bread as the most important part of my diet; I am accustomed to it and do not really feel I have had enough to eat unless I have had some bread with my meal. Anyone who does hard physical work can hardly manage without it. During the last hungry years of the First World War, in 1917–18, when food was severely rationed in Sweden, the authorities realised this; they gave manual labourers an extra ration. At that time I was working as a lumberjack, felling trees. My 'extra bread card' gave me 50 grams more bread a day than a clerical worker received, altogether 250 grams.

In the Middle Ages a variety of breads were baked in Sweden. In the southern and eastern parts of the country and in Finland people chiefly ate a fermented and leavened rye bread, baked in an oven; whilst in Western and Northern Sweden they made a bread known as 'flat bread' or 'thin bread', made from corn and oats and baked on an iron slab over an open fire. Even up to our own day the Dalesmen have regarded rye bread as a special delicacy. In the brief summers of the far north, so-called 'ninety-day grain', corn and oats which ripened in three months, was cultivated.

In his *History of the Nordic Peoples* Olaus Magnus devotes several chapters to this crucial factor in their existence, which followed them from cradle to grave. He cites immemorial notions about the divine origin of bread. It was Ceres who invented the cultivation of grain, he says, and Pan who hit on the manner of grinding it and turning the flour into bread. Olaus Magnus had an encyclopaedic mind. He gives us detailed instructions in various ways of 'forming bread', indeed his account is so detailed that one forms a distinct impression that Sweden's last Catholic archbishop – because of Gustav Vasa's intervention, he was never permitted to take up his office – had himself kneaded dough and baked loaves with his own hands. Certainly he must have visited the women in the baking-huts and studied their way of going to work.

Olaus tells us how in the great farms of Västergötland the women folk baked rye-loaves 'large as warriors' shields, thick and round', a reference of course to the great roundels of 'crisp-bread' still made in Sweden. The men of Östergötland offered wayfarers – their honoured guests – saffron bread, which they also gave their departing guests, 'to refresh their spirits' on the way. Olaus Magnus describes a rare kind of bread which remained fresh and edible for more than 20 years: 'if baked at a child's birth, it can keep quite well without going mouldy until the day of that child's bethrothal'. But it had to be made according to certain instructions. The dough had to be made with water possessing certain qualities it only has in the month of March; and certain rules had to be observed when baking and storing it. But, providing all was done according to these rules, a bread is obtained which 'keeps for 16 to 20 years or even longer, if it be but kept under roof, against rain and snow.' The baking was done on their iron plates, round and wide as 'a warrior's shield'. A fire is lit under each such plate, and must be kept burning ceaselessly and slowly. In the hilly parts of Sweden women used to 'gather in the light spring days at a particular place and in particular numbers, to assist each other in the work'. Olaus' assertion that the bread will keep fresh for twenty years seems dubious. But it is true that in many peasant homesteads bread used to be baked which was afterwards buried in the rye and oat bins, where it would keep for several months without going mouldy. In this way the Christmas bake could be kept until Easter.

Olaus Magnus paints for us an idyllic and charming picture of the way in which the women collectively baked their bread. He stresses that it is 'a woman's art'.

One of women's great contributions to history.

Olaus Magnus, as far as I can see, makes no mention of the sort of bread which forms the main topic of this chapter – a bread which did not come from the field, but from the forest; which, not growing in the soil, was scaled off the trunks of trees: *bark bread.* For long periods at a time and at ever-recurring intervals bark bread has been the Scandinavians' famine bread. Food when the harvest failed, it is also part of our history, and therefore repays study.

In a country whose population consisted so largely of farmers, people helplessly exposed to the forces of nature, were utterly dependent on the weather. Each crop-failure – caused either by long drought or persistent rain – constituted a deadly threat. Each heavy spring thaw was followed by floods which delayed the spring-sowing. The crop would also be ruined by early autumn frosts. Every outbreak of cattle disease was followed by a shortage of milk, butter and meat. Nor was it possible for a province staggering under such disasters to obtain help from another which had escaped them. In our days a local catastrophe to the harvest in one part of the country can be offset by aid from another; but in the Middle Ages, and for centuries to come, any part of the country where the harvest had failed simply starved, abandoned by all the others. The population was sparse, roads were almost non-existent and effective means of transport lacking. To shift any significant quantities of grain from one province to another was simply impossible. Two or three sacks of corn could be loaded onto a crude ox-cart, or a bag of it slung across a horse's back – but what help was that?

In any isolated part of the country, therefore, a year of crop-failure meant outright catastrophe. We do not know just how many victims starved to death in such years, the source materials are too scanty. From the last famine years in Sweden, 1868–69, the parish books speak of parishioners who starved to death; but it is not until 1750 that we have any real parish registers, and the Middle Ages have left us no statistics of these tragedies. So we cannot even guess how many people died of hunger or its consequences. Representatives of a nameless suffering, they faded out of life, silent and unnoticed.

Not until the 18th century did the authorities seriously begin to do something about getting grain to districts where the grain-harvest had been inadequate: and even in the 1860's the problem was not properly solved. Where crop failure had been really serious, starvation still followed.

We know little about how people experienced those times of famine. The sort of help they begged for in times of prolonged drought or rainfall transpires from the psalms they sang in their churches. But here and there, too, a secular voice makes itself heard. The experiences of a peasant whose gleanings from his field had been minimal are ironically summed up in an old rhyme. I have written it down verbatim:

Of corn I sow ten parts,
And then I nine do reap;
A tenth I give to the priest,
And am happy the rest to keep.

In such years the peasant turned to the forest for his bread.

As far into the past as research can probe, bark bread formed part of our ancestors' diet, and for long periods at a time it was the daily bread on their tables. In his great work on everyday life in 16th-century Scandinavia, the Danish historian of culture, Troels-Lund, says of its consumption in Norway: 'In certain districts of northern Norway, where the grain often freezes before it can be reaped, bark bread was the finest nourishment'.

Certain years of Torgils Knutsson's regency, in the 1290's,* were among the most catastrophic in our mediaeval history. From 1291 we have contemporary records of 'hard times and great pestilentia'. The state of affairs was still further aggravated by the frequent coincidence of plague and famine. Semi-starvation greatly reduced people's resistance to disease.

One of our oldest reliable items of evidence on famine times in Scandinavia is to be found in a bishop's letter from 1232. It is Archbishop Uffe of Lund who, writing to the Pope, gives vent to his grief at the misery prevailing in his diocese. The previous year, cattle disease had destroyed the stocks of animals. In 1232 an even more terrible torment had befallen the province: 'a fierce famine which hath taken away the lives of a great part of the people.' Not knowing how many people lived in mediaeval Skåne, we cannot estimate what is meant by 'a great part'. The archbishop was writing to the Pope to explain why the Peter's Pence had not been despatched to Rome.

A severe winter, too, was another blight on the commons. Then icy temperatures joined forces with famine. In the harsh northern climate the winters were the testing-time of men. It was a question, quite simply, of keeping body and soul together until the spring. The coldest mediaeval winters have left certain traces in the sources. In 1296 and 1306 the Swedes had a 'severe winter'. In 1331 the word 'severe' (*svår*) is supplanted by 'hard'. That year five cubits of snow had fallen. In a country where distances between one cottage and another and from one village to the next were so great, so unique a winter, with snow covering the ground to a depth of three metres, must have been well-nigh intolerable.

* Moberg, *A History of the Swedish People*, Vol. I, pp. 95 et seq.

In some annals relating to January 1346, again, we are told that 'folk and cattle perished from the cold and bad weather'. During the Twelfth Night holiday in 1402 there was so great a fall of snow 'that one could hardly fetch needful firewood from the forest'. In 1405, it rained without ceasing from the feast of St Olof in July until Christmas, destroying all crops. In 1408, again, there was a famine winter. That year, among other catastrophes, 'much cattle died on Gotland'. (This information on times of famine has been supplied me by the distinguished historian Dr Ingvar Andersson.)

From Kristoffer of Bavaria's reign in the 1440's, too, we have repeated note of years of severe famine. His enemies sarcastically dubbed Kristoffer 'the Bark King'. Such a famished state of affairs, with people eating bark bread, was an admirable argument against his régime. But we also know of crop-failures and hungry times in the years when the Swedish nationalist Karl Knutsson was responsible for our Swedish weather, namely 1437 and 1438. In 1439, King Erik of Pomerania sharply accuses the Swedish Earl Marshal, maintaining that under his overlordship the peasants had been obliged to eat bark, 'like other soulless beasts'. And it is true, there were disturbances among the commons in the above-mentioned years, presumably because the peasants were starving.

In the first years of the 1440's, Finland was smitten by a dire catastrophe: the crops failed repeatedly. The rye, the Finns' main source of bread, was ruined by drought or frost. Dry weather in spring and summer reduced the sowing, and early frosts in the autumn hindered the harvest work. The documents bear witness to many deserted Finnish farms uncultivated as a result of 'these hard years'.

A century later, during the Dacke rising, 1542–43,* Småland suffered from an extended period of bark bread, long remembered by the population as a trial past enduring. The fact is, Gustav Vasa, in order to force them to their knees, had arranged an efficient blockade of all grain supplies to the rebellious Smålanders. No grain, no foodstuffs of any sort whatever, were allowed into Småland

* See pp. 42 et seq.
* See pp. 219 et seq.

from other provinces. People were obliged to resort to a diet of bark for their daily bread.

Fortunately Småland was a thickly wooded province.

During the three years 1596–98 our forefathers were plagued by what is perhaps the longest famine ever to befall them in historical times. It seems to have comprehended the entire realm and its neighbours, and is known to us from contemporary descriptions which give us a good idea of the state of affairs then prevailing. These accounts, written down in four different provinces, Västergötland, Värmland, Dalarna and Hälsingland, are largely unanimous, and accounts from Finland, the eastern part of the kingdom, tell the same story.

In 1596, this people who lived wholly on the fruits of the soil had been overwhelmed by a general crop failure. Spring had come early that year, sowing could take place in favourable weather and everything pointed to a good harvest. But then came a tremendous delayed spring flood, drenching the fields and submerging them for so long that the seed was soon ruined. Summer and autumn brought what our hymnbooks call a 'lasting wetness'. Day after day the heavy rain went on falling. We are told how the clothes rotted on peasants' and labourers' bodies as they worked out of doors in the wet weather, under the open sky. No dry hay could be got in; it rotted and moulded in the barns. And the cattle, affected by the ruined fodder, sickened and died in their hundreds. The meat, we are told, 'could not even be used to feed dogs and cats.'

As autumn came and supplies from earlier harvests began to run out, no new grain could be harvested. The bins and pork barrels were empty. People looked for every thinkable or possible substitute for their normal diet. They consumed bark, buds, leaves off the hazel bushes, husks, nettles, hay, straw, and various sorts of roots. They ground up all bones for flour. Their bodies became weak. People became too limp to do heavy work. Lacking even the strength to turn the hand mills in which they were grinding bark for flour, they collapsed where they laboured.

During that winter and the spring that followed, innumerable victims starved to death. Unburied corpses could be found everywhere, both indoors and outdoors, in barns and sheds, under lofts, on roads and paths. Bodies lying out in the open were eaten by stray dogs who had no one to feed them. Corpses were found with fistfuls of hay and tufts of grass stuffed into their mouths.

Thefts occurred daily and hourly. People stole anything edible they could find. The punishment was always the gallows, or the branch of a tree. Everywhere the gallows were strung with corpses of those who had tried to feed themselves with others' food. In an attempt to check such criminality, many new gallows were erected outside the court houses.

The disaster seems to have been, if possible, even more ghastly in Finland than in the mother country. We possess written records of little children who, in their hunger, ate from their own bodies, chewing up their own fingers. On the table of every lower-class home, bark bread was daily bread. A disease, known as '*blodsot*' ('bleeding sickness'), presumably caused by malnutrition, brought many people to the grave. One court roll declares: 'Hunger made men so heavy as if their knees were sunk in the earth'.

Two more years of crop failure followed, though less severe. All parts of the country were affected.

During these years of failed harvests the authorities remitted certain taxes; evidently because they could not do otherwise. There was simply nothing left for them to take. Yet there were some royal bailiffs who still collected their levy – and kept it for themselves.

As always in times of great distress and misery, the countryfolk assembled in their churches to seek help and consolation. And the priests, as always, told their parishioners that it was to punish their sinful lives that God had sent on them these years of famine.

Our forefathers lived close to their animals, closer than anyone does today. They observed their beasts' ways and eating habits, and learnt from them. Instinct guides the beasts of field and forest to their nourishment: elks, deer and hares gnaw the bark off deciduous trees and chew saplings and plants. Horses eat the bark of young spruces, which contains vitamins, and they love the aspen's bark and leaves. A horse's belly can digest cellulose, i.e., wood sugar, indigestible by man.

It is my belief that it was originally the animals who showed humans which food in the forest is edible, and who taught them to flay the trunks of young trees.

For bark bread, only the membrane immediately under the rough bark – the layer which nourishes a tree's growth and forms the annual ring – was used. This inside layer would be scaled off with an iron scraper and collected, after which, before it could be baked, there came a long process of preparing the bark. First it was hung up to dry in the open air until friable; then beaten with a flail or crushed in some other way; then ground into a flour. The bark membrane is very thin, and many trees had to give up their skins before the kneading-trough was filled with dough. Time and patience were needed to collect and produce all this wood-flour; but these people who were seeking nourishment in the forest had time on their hands. Probably whole families, adults and children, went out with their scraping irons and flayed the trees.

Leksand Museum, in Dalarna, contains a remarkable flail, with sharp iron tags to it, once used for preparing bark flour. It is a monument to ancient Dalarna, a part of the country where bark bread was common fare.

The bark was collected in summer, before the end of July and the August mists. Thereafter the trees would be damaged by the scraping irons, and might dry up and wither away. Certain types of tree were chosen for bread, notably the pine which, found in every forest, was also the most plentifully available. Long before the spruce, which was another though lesser source of bread, the pine had spread over Sweden. Among deciduous trees, too, there were three species which yielded bark flour: elm, asp and silver birch. The elm was the greatest favourite of all. Besides being regarded as the most nutritious, its bark was also the easiest to prepare.

The elm family flourishes chiefly in Asia and North America, where there are no fewer than 130 species. Of these, only three grow naturally in Sweden. It was the so-called wood-elm, a tree common in south and central Sweden but very rare in Norrland, which yielded bread.

In his work, referred to above, Troels-Lund tells of the great importance of the elm during the famine years in Scandinavia

1596–98. 'Every man, both poor and rich,' he writes, 'had to nourish himself on bark bread, no grain being available.' People living in the agricultural districts of southern Norway and along the coast used the tasty bark of the elm, whilst those who lived in mountainous districts had to be content with pine. A contemporary chronicler describes the state of affairs: 'He who was then willing to give a poor man an elm in his wood did a deed of charity; but in the end everyone made free to an elm wherever he could find one, therewith to save his life.'

This was in Norway; but there is much to suggest that bark bread was more frequently eaten in Finland than in any other Nordic country. There the villages were even more isolated than in Sweden; help in time of famine was out of the question. In his poem on Pavo the peasant, who lived 'high among the sandy meads of Saarijärvi', the Finnish poet Runeberg [1804–1877] has raised a literary monument to his people, who had to live on bark bread. The poem has no counterpart in Swedish poetry. When he enjoins his wife to 'mix in half bark' into the bread she is to bake to help his neighbour, whose field has fallen victim to frost, Pavo appears to be the very embodiment of a noble soul: and as an image of truly neighbourly feeling within the old village community his helpfulness has a basis in reality. Yet I cannot regard the submissive, patient and contented Pavo as typical of the Finnish peasantry, among whom, I fancy, wrath, grumbling and impatience were not unknown. In Finland, too, peasant risings broke out. Pavo's patience is superhuman. It cannot possibly have been shared by his class as a whole. I see him as an individual portrait.

And indeed, as Runeberg was all too well aware, the history of the Finnish common people still remained to be written:

> What tongue has told the fearful tale,
> The strife this folk has sufferéd,
> When warfare roared from dale to dale
> And winter frosty came, with hunger pale?
> Who measured out the blood it shed
> And all its patient toil?

That the blood shed was immeasurable, we know. As for its patience, it was very likely not so great as Runeberg imagined.

The common man's outlets for his impatience, however, were too few to leave their impact on history.

Even during our 20th-century wars, when food has had to be rationed, the Finns have mingled bark with their bread. A Finnish engineer now living in Sweden has told me how, during the last war, he and his neighbours baked cakes of a flour, 30 per cent of which was the same substance as that used by Pavo's wife.

I have tasted bark bread, baked according to extant recipes. Somewhat sour to the tongue, it is otherwise insipid, i.e., tastes of nothing.

Our ancestors made use of many other ingredients besides bark for their famine bread. As late as in the 19th century the Norrland countryfolk chopped up husks and straw and ground the mixture into a flour, which thus consisted of the leavings otherwise given to horses, cows and pigs. As bread, to quote the expert judgement of those who ate it, it was 'hardly edible'. The sharp tags of straw and the acid husks exacerbated the throat, and were hard to swallow. Of those who ate such bread we are told from Dalarna that they had to drink a mouthful of water to each mouthful of bread even to get it down their gullets.

Mosses of various kinds, chiefly reindeer moss, were also used by the common people. The last time these plants were on the popular menu was in the hard years of the 1860's, Sweden's last great period of famine. In 1868, on instructions from the authorities in Kopparberg County, the country agronomist travelled around Dalarna to show the peasants 'how to bake certain species of moss and lichen.'

My mother told me how, in 1868, as a four-year-old, she went out with her mother into the countryside collecting hazel and heather buds to grind and knead into the dough. Cornflour, if any was left in the bin, would be mingled with this famine bread. Otherwise it consisted wholly of other ingredients. And even a hundred years ago bark bread was everyday fare in the homesteads of these parts of the Swedish countryside which most suffered from crop failure. I also remember my grandmother telling me how she had baked bread of pine bark. The greater admixture of ordinary flour in the dough, the more 'easily eaten' was her loaf.

What effect, then, did this bread, which so often appeared daily on our ancestors' tables, have on the health of the populace? If eaten for long periods at a time, was it harmful to the stomach? Could it make folk feel ill or cause sicknesses?

As far as I know, no one has researched these questions; so, to obtain a reliable and expert opinion, I have asked one of Sweden's leading specialists on diseases of the stomach. Before replying, he consulted experts on timber research, whose knowledge on the composition of wood bark is exhaustive. Whereafter he satisfied my curiosity:

The layer of the bark which was used for baking bread, he tells me, contains cane sugar, fruit and grape sugar. Further, it consists of hemicellulose, a little sebacic acid, and a certain quantity of protein. Of the components of the bark membrane only the cellulose and lignin, substances having no nutritional value whatever, cannot be digested. The irritation caused by bark on the mucous membranes, however, is quite insignificant and we have no reason to suppose it can have had any deleterious effect on the stomach functions, either in old people or in children. This famine bread was therefore perfectly harmless to those who consumed it.

My specialist on stomach disorders sums up: 'Bark bread was only in part worthless. Mainly it was a nourishing addition to people's food, and rich in minerals.'

This positive declaration by the experts surprised me. Like many others, I have always assumed that bark bread mostly served to fill the stomach, give the hungry a feeling of repletion; I have believed that it only temporarily relieved their hunger pangs. In reality this bread, taken from the trees of the forest, was a real source of popular nourishment. So we can assume on good grounds that, during the many famine years which have passed over this people, bark bread has saved numerous Swedes from starving to death.

Among the 'extraordinary destinies of the Swedish people,' as Carl Grimberg called them, none is more extraordinary than that it should have survived them.

Thrice King

THE DECADES AROUND THE MID-15TH CENTURY are one of the most miserable epochs in the whole of our history. They were replete with conflicts within the Union, with civil war and struggles for power among the great families. Regents followed one another in swift succession. Between the death of Engelbrekt in 1436, and 1470, the year when Sten Sture the Elder became regent, the Swedish people had eight different régimes, two Union kings (Kristoffer of Bavaria and Christian I), three regents and, for three separate periods, Karl Knutsson Bonde as their king.

At times such confusion prevailed that the realm seems to have lacked any government at all. The Union party and the Nationalist party were constantly at war. Again and again the Union was renewed 'for all futurity'; and each time it broke up. The monarchy and the aristocracy disputed the right to grant fiefs, a matter of extreme importance. But the Swedish noble families, too, were locked in internecine strife over their estates. In these quarrels Sweden's oldest and most aristocratic families make their appearance, names which are to recur later in our history: the Oxenstiernas, the Vasas, the Bielkes, the Trolles, the Totts and the Axelssons. Of these, several believed themselves called to govern and take over responsibility for the entire kingdom. Such noble families, always at enmity with one another and disputing each other's estates, were often closely interrelated.

The history of this period, therefore, makes depressing reading. Is there any reason why a latter-day reader should devote time to it? I do not think so, and therefore I have decided to give only a summary account of this epoch, presenting some of its more intriguing personalities.

One of the families of magnates, the Bondes, produced a king of

Sweden. He was number eight among the Karls. Three times he became head of state, a record not only among Swedish monarchs but also (as far as I know) in world history.

Karl Knutsson Bonde must be viewed as a characteristic figure of his age. Both temperamentally and intellectually he evinces certain essential late mediaeval qualities. In Sweden he gave a last spurt to the dying flame of chivalry. A hundred and fifty years had passed since it had burned at its brightest. Most mediaeval personages appear to us as having had no inner life of their own; of being carved in wood. Of their qualities as human beings we can form no conception. But we know more about Karl Knutsson than we do about any of his contemporaries. If Engelbrekt, the popular leader of the commons, is an unknown man who in middle life suddenly emerges from the anonymous masses, this man, thrice king, was from the outset in a privileged position. Even as a young man he achieved fame. And since he became the outstanding figure of his age, he deserves a chapter to himself.

To be placed three times on a throne and twice deposed from it suggests a dramatic lifetime amid ever shifting circumstances. It resembles the destiny of that other mediaeval Swedish king, Magnus Eriksson, who was also deposed and driven into exile. The resemblance, however, is only superficial. Unlike Magnus Eriksson, I cannot see Karl VIII as a tragic personality. It is not here his fascination lies. To come by the crown was his goal, and in his struggle to obtain it he was repeatedly frustrated. But there is nothing tragic about the setbacks of the ambitious. A gambler throws the dice and loses – what is there moving about that? Of his own free will he stakes his money in order to win more; if he loses he has no one to blame but himself.

There is a mediaeval rhyme about Karl Knutsson's mutable fate.

While yet my barrel freely flowed
Both man and woman friendship showed;
But when at length it lost its store
Not man nor woman knew me more.

Attributed to the king himself, the rhyme can hardly be historical. Whoever its author, it bespeaks experience of human nature, an experience which has lost none of its validity.

Karl Knutsson's lineage was the highest possible. After the Bielkes and the Natt och Dags, the Bondes are said to be our oldest extant Swedish aristocratic family. They were related to the Folkungs. Persistent research has even traced Karl's lineage back to Saint Erik, and further back than that no one in Sweden can trace the elegance or nobility of his origins – unless, of course, he can prove descent from Odin.

Karl VIII was without question the most brilliant nobleman of his epoch. An educated and travelled man, in his days of power he kept up a scintillating and stately court. Generous to his friends and supporters, for his relative Tord Bonde, according to the 18th-century historian Lagerbring, he paid for a sumptuous and costly wedding where the guests dined off 1,400 silver plates, a wedding present worth a large fortune.

Karl VIII was also our only mediaeval king of whom we possess a portrait. The great contemporary sculptor Bernt Notke, famous for his *St George and the Dragon* group in Stockholm Cathedral, made a statuette of Karl Knutsson in gilded oak. It is said to be a very good likeness. Anatomical examination of his bones has been thought to confirm this. The sculpture, in the gallery at Gripsholm Castle, shows the king on his knees at prayer. Coarsely sculpted, the figure gives an impression of great physical strength, and in fact the sources describe Karl VIII as a most stately knight, magnificent to behold on horseback. The face in Notke's statuette, however, is not notable for its beauty. The cheeks bulge as if he were blowing up a balloon, and the highly characteristic nose resembles a potato. Karl Knutsson's contemporaries' descriptions of him are therefore contradicted by this work of art. Perhaps the discrepancy can be explained by the changes which have taken place in ideals of manly beauty during the lapse of five hundred years.

To his contemporaries, at all events, the model was a manly and handsome man, notably so when compared with Kristoffer, King of the Union. His rival for the throne is described as of stunted stature, an ugly man with a poor posture. Nor did this advantage, possessed by the leader of the Swedish national party over his opponent, lack significance.

At the age of twenty-five Karl Knutsson left his family estate of Fågelvik in the Tjust district of Småland and joined forces with Engelbrekt. Not that he made any important contributions to the war of liberation. Militarily he was more successful in crushing the peasant revolts against him, after Engelbrekt's murder. The means he used to achieve this end have already been described.

Bishop Thomas characterizes the Earl Marshal, as he then was, as follows:

> Many a stiff neck bent he
> That would not suffer his rule . . .

Perhaps when he wrote these words the author of the *Song of Freedom* was thinking of the four captured peasants, 'the worst', whom the Earl Marshal had had burnt outside Västerås Castle, in December 1436. The *Karl Chronicle* fleetingly depicts this event in six lines:

> . . . and the worst of them all
> forth from the mob he did call,
> whom folk declared
> worst blame had dared.
> These bade he confession make,
> and burnt forthwith at the stake.

Having sent the ringleaders to their fiery death Karl Knutsson granted the rest of the insubordinate peasants their lives. According to the *Karl Chronicle*, they thanked him for 'his mercy and great honour', and swore never again to repeat their act of lunacy. The same effective deterrent was applied to the two leaders of the Värmland rising, as the *Karl Chronicle* says in a single line:

> Both were burnt in one fire.

As has already been suggested, Karl Knutsson intended to reign over an obedient and submissive commons.

In the *Chronicle* the man who thrice became king of Sweden is likened to the greatest of all heroes, the Archangel Michael himself, prototype of all crusaders, original ideologist of chivalry. Even so, after King Erik's deposition, the Earl Marshal reached in vain for the crown. In 1441, Kristoffer of Bavaria was elevated to the throne, and Karl had to content himself with the fief of Finland. The *Chronicle*'s comparison between the two candidates is crushing for the Union monarch. At his coronation, the populace, seeing the two men together, cannot comprehend the choice which has been made. In their eyes Kristoffer, small and squat, looks completely insignificant beside the tall and imposing Karl. It is he who bears himself like a king.

This unnatural choice instantly brought its own punishment, in the form of a severe crop-failure. In the last years of the 1430's when the Earl Marshal was governing Sweden, the weather had always been fine and what it should be, alleges his chronicler; but as soon as the Union king had taken over, the weather changed and became dreadful. Each year turned out worse than the last, and famine ensued. It was Kristoffer's sinful and vicious life which was bringing these hard times on the people. The ancient belief in a causal connection between fertility and the lives led by kings was still strong. The king was still held to be responsible for the weather, part of a deeply rooted monarchic superstitition which has survived the millennia.

According to the *Karl Chroncile*, the commons hated Kristoffer:

> peasants and husbandmen all
> him bark-king call.

It was said that, though the people were living on bark bread, the king's train, when he passed through the countryside, was so enormous that five 'lasts' of corn had to be brought together merely to feed his horses. The evils imputed to Kristoffer were too many for the author of the *Chronicle* to enumerate: 'it were too long to write'. The king is depicted as a thoroughly rotten individual, a rake, a gambler and a whoremaster. He drank 'almost every night', and was much given to lechery. He was also a perjurer, whose word could not be trusted. In brief, he was a spirit from hell, for whose sake the people had to bear these sufferings.

In 1448, when Kristoffer lay on his deathbed, Sweden was swept by a monstrous hurricane which laid low the forests. In the Black-friars at Skänninge, Östergötland, the roof of the choir collapsed in the gale and two monks were crushed to death during Mass – so violently did Nature react at the moment when this devil went back to hell where he belonged.

Like Queen Margareta, Kristoffer, the Union king, was persistently denigrated by the Swedish nationalist party; and for a long while this pitch-black image of King Kristoffer was accepted by Swedish historians as true to fact. But modern research has seen him in a considerably kinder light. A Swedish historian, Gottfrid Carlsson, and a Danish, Kristian Elster, are agreed in assessing Kristoffer's reign, though no more than a seven-year interlude, as mainly beneficial.

He made some important judicial reforms. Magnus Eriksson's corpus of laws for the whole realm were reviewed and revised, improving certain aspects of the judiciary; the new version was given Kristoffer's name. Henceforth, in each assize, a general enquiry was to be held every year. Further, an important regulation was introduced into the rules governing the institution of kingship. From now on the king was to take only the advice of indigenous counsellors: foreigners (*utföddan män*) were no longer to sit in the Council of State. Actually this was merely a reversion to a paragraph in the original Union Agreement, whose flouting by King Erik of Pomerania had been one of the causes of the insurrection.

In the 1430's the realm had seen a great increase in deeds of violence. Unable to maintain law and order, the central authority had failed to protect citizens' lives and property. Under a new royal edict subjects were forbidden to take the law into their own hands, to wreak personal revenge or settle their affairs by force of arms. The Strängnäs Decree's ban on bearing weapons, in 1437, had referred only to peasants. Now, in the name of the rule of law, it was extended to apply to noblemen and magnates as well, indeed to all citizens except the king's Council and his officials. In yet another decree – the fifth, if my count is right, within a century – the old ban on exacting 'hospitality' from the commons was once again renewed. Presumably it had no more practical effect than its forerunners.

So Kristoffer, that ugly little fellow, would appear to have done his Swedish subjects a certain amount of good, after all. Here is a final verdict on his reign, as passed by Gottfrid Carlsson, that eminent connoisseur of our later Middle Ages:

'It is hardly going too far to say that no greater misfortune ever befell the idea of a Nordic Union than King Kristoffer's sudden death at the age of only thirty-two.'

No bad passing out mark for the Bavarian! It should also be added that, as far as we know, he never burnt any insubordinate peasant at the stake.

Sweden was an electoral monarchy. In 1448 a new king was to be elected. Karl Knutsson's most dangerous rivals were the Oxenstierna clan, but its representatives, Bengt and Nils, together only received eight votes, as against Karl's sixty-three. And 'then the people cried out aloud that they would have no other king,' writes the 19th-century historian Fryxell. Various portents had also foreshadowed Karl's elevation to the throne – the election took place in the spring, after a long period of severe drought, and fears were entertained for the year's sowing. But on the very day of Karl Knutsson's arrival in Stockholm as a candidate for the throne, it rained cats and dogs and the downpour refreshed the torrid earth: 'the common folk, recognizing therein Karl's accustomed good fortune, believed they saw God to be well pleased, and their devotion to him became all the greater.'

So now Sweden had a wholly Swedish king. The first reign of Karl VIII lasted until 1457. His subjects' devotion to him, however, seems to have grown cooler with every year that passed and after nine, in the provinces of Central Sweden, it had run out altogether. The Uppland peasants revolted and he was overthrown.

This rising was led by no lesser a personage than the Archbishop of Sweden, Jöns Bengtsson Oxenstierna, a prominent figure of the age. If this history were mainly concerned not with the Swedes but with their chieftains, Jöns Bengtsson at this point would deserve a great many of its pages to himself. A highly cultivated man, he had been rector of Leipzig University, one of the most famous seats of European learning. But his interests were extensive. He was also a soldier, as able to wield sword and lance as missal and chalice. Our mediaeval bishops were men of many parts.

As archbishop of Uppsala, Oxenstierna had found cause for grievous displeasure with Karl Knutsson's policies toward the

Church and the nobles' estates. Now he decided to drive out this unchristian king and reinstate the Kalmar Union. For the Church these conflicts between Swedes and Danes were no more than deplorable civil wars within European Christendom. If the commons were displeased with Karl's régime it was mainly because of his fiscal methods, which had become sheer fleecing and extortion 'to bone and marrow'. The peasantry, too, were crying out for a new king, whether Dane or Swede made little odds. All they demanded was some relief from their heavy burdens.

Cleverly exploiting Karl's unpopularity, Jöns Bengtsson, standing before the high altar of Uppsala Cathedral, divested himself of his pontificals, his bishop's mitre and all the rest of his ecclesiastical insignia, and swearing he would not don them again until he had set the country to rights, put on his armour and buckled on his sword, as if arming for a crusade. At the head of a troop of knights this cleric and amateur soldier defeated the king's men-at-arms in a snowstorm on the ice of Lake Mälaren, routing a professional general, experienced in many wars. The duties of Archbishops of Uppsala have subsequently been restricted, but such a combination of bishop with cavalry commander was by no means unique in the Middle Ages.

Chased from his throne, Karl Knutsson fled to Danzig, where he remained for seven years. Taking with him into exile quantities of valuable possessions as well as considerable sums of money – taxes levied from his Swedish subjects – he was spared the exile's usual indigence.

On July 2, 1457, at Mora Stones in Uppland, a new Union monarch, Christian I of Oldenburg, was acclaimed. Before long it became obvious that this Danish king stood in as great need of his subjects' taxes as the Swede had done. Historians are unanimous in finding little difference between Christian's fiscal policies and Karl's. Great though the new king's exactions were, they were always inadequate to his expenses, and his constant financial straits gave him the popular nickname 'Christian-bottomless-empty-pocket'. The commons' written complaints against him also bear witness to his total mendacity. 'At times he lied to the sack', we read in one such document. To 'lie the sack full' is an old popular expression.

After six years of such rule the commons of Sweden had had more than enough of Christian I. Again the Uppland peasants rose, and marching on Stockholm, partly occupied it. An armistice was concluded, but the king broke it and subjected the peasants to a regular bloodbath. E. Hildebrand states that about one thousand men were slain on August 21, 1463; even those who had sought sanctuary in the chapel of a monastery were cut down.

Archbishop Oxenstierna, who had called in the Union king, now became the leader of the opposition against him. Finally he was flung into prison and taken off to Denmark. This triggered off a general Swedish insurrection. Its leader was another cleric of military endowments, Bishop Kettil Karlsson Vasa of Linköping, an ancestor of Gustav Vasa. Christian's army of legionaries was decisively defeated by the Swedish peasant army in battle at Haraker, north of Västerås, in April 1464. In this battle a young squire, Sten Gustavsson Sture, son of King Karl's sister, distinguished himself for his courage and presence of mind. Later he was to become known as Sten Sture the Elder.

'Now,' writes Olaus Petri in his chronicle, 'was made a general outcry among the peasants throughout the land that they would have back King Karl.' The exile was therefore recalled and at an assembly of the whole realm in Stockholm, in August 1464, acclaimed as king for the second time. At this meeting all estates are said to have been represented, which is why Erik Lönnroth is of the opinion that this assembly, more than any other, is entitled to be called the first Swedish parliament.

But Karl VIII's second reign was to be brief: a mere five months, the shortest in Swedish history. His sworn enemy Oxenstierna, released from his Danish prison, came home, and, in alliance with his episcopal colleague Kettil Karlsson, soon succeeded in rendering Karl's position untenable. By January 1465 he was obliged to abdicate, laying down the crown of Sweden before the high altar in Stockholm Cathedral and solemnly undertaking never again to hanker after it.

On this condition Karl was to receive Raseborg and Korsholm in Finland in fief. By way of consolation he was also allowed to retain his royal title.

This time Karl's place of exile lay within the realm. Tradition says he lamented his fate at Raseborg Castle:

When I was lord of Fågelvik
No man could call me poor or weak;
But when of Sweden I was king,
Unhappy, I owned not anything.

The following years of the 1460's were a period of extremely confused government, and the state of affairs almost more than I can describe. Regents succeeded each other at brief intervals, all presumably aspirants to the crown. First, Kettil Karlsson seized power, but as early as August 1465 was relieved of it by Jöns Bengtsson Oxenstierna. Oxenstierna in his turn was succeeded by Erik Axelsson Tott, a new star in the political firmament. The Oxenstiernas belonged to the Union party and enjoyed the support of the Danes; the Totts were opposed to the Union. As so often happens in history when two parties are at odds, victory goes to a third. And that was what happened now, the third party being of course Karl Knutsson Bonde. Recalled from his exile in Finland in November 1467, his promise never more to reach for the crown forgotten, he entered the capital as king for the third time. Oxenstierna attempted one last rising against him, but failed.

This was the fifth change of régime within three years. Those who like to see power changing hands had their fill of such spectacles in the Sweden of the 1460's.

King for the third time, Karl was allowed to retain his throne up to his death, on May 15, 1470. On his death bed he married his concubine in order to legitimize an infant son. He lived to be sixty-two, a ripe old age in mediaeval times. Altogether, between 1448 and 1470, he had only reigned for twelve years.

In his lifetime Karl Knutsson Bonde had taken care to arrange for his posthumous reputation. He was the first Swedish king to appreciate clearly how important propaganda is to those in power. It is the duty of those who govern to enlighten the governed as to the excellence of their régime and their own admirable qualities, and explain to them how catastrophic any other government would be. The *Karl Chronicle* has all the necessary ingredients of such a stroke of propaganda.

As propagandist and demagogue Karl VIII was a precursor of Gustav Vasa and, like his more famous successor, a successful one. Posterity believed the *Karl Chronicle*. Our nationalist historians, almost without exception, have represented Karl Knutsson as the country's bulwark against malevolent and intriguing Swedish prelates. (His propaganda of hatred against the Danes will be studied in my next chapter.) The men who opposed him are represented as faithless, treacherous and unpatriotic.

But in his chronicle, Ericus Olai, one of Karl VIII's contemporaries, is more discriminating. While he presents Engelbrekt as the good and noble leader of his people, of Karl Knutsson even though he was in power at the time when his chronicle was written – Ericus Olai avoids painting too flattering a portrait. Indeed, carefully though he chooses his words, he even dares to insinuate that Karl was an intriguer, at times a timid and even downright cowardly one.

We have seen what cruel treatment Karl Knutsson was capable of meting out to his rebellious subjects. Karl obviously had neither scruples nor inhibitions; but this has always been taken for granted in persons who lust after power, and he was certainly neither as cruel nor as tyrannous as many other mediaeval princes. Approving his political goals – a free and independent Swedish kingdom – our historians have been indulgent toward his methods. Karl Knutsson's patriotic sentiments would appear to have been sincere. It was also his policy to extend the powers of the monarch as against those of the nobility and the Church. But time and time again the Swedes revolted to depose him; obviously they did not regard his régime as beneficial to the people he ruled. In his mediaeval history E. Hildebrand opines that the words on Karl's memorial stone at Mora, *natione suecus* ('born Swedish'), are no empty phrase; but he adds: 'His misfortune was that he did not know how to put his country's interests first'. To a nationalistic historian, of course, to be Swedish is in itself a virtue.

The sources generally describe Karl Knutsson as a charming fellow, who made an agreeable impression on his entourage and who knew how to win friends and influence people. He also behaved in a manner befitting a king, in his subjects' eyes a great point in his favour. It is required of a king that he shall look stately on horseback; and Karl VIII filled the bill perfectly. It has always been a popular requirement that anyone who by the Grace of God occupies a throne shall look the part. Even so latter-day a poet as Verner von Heidenstam [1859–1940] insisted on this; on one occasion he expressed his scorn for kings who walk about in overcoats. Presumably he had been deeply ashamed to see his own king, Oscar II, demean himself by wearing so humiliating and vulgar an article of apparel. Heidenstam would have taken great pleasure in the sight of Karl Knutsson, that truly royal personage, entering Stockholm – several times over – on horseback.

In the *Chronicle* which bears his name, Karl VIII embodies every ideal of kingship; and it is in this light Swedes have been taught to see him in their history books. One might even ask whether even today the last vestiges of the *Chronicle*'s propaganda is not to be found in our school curriculum. The three authors of a school history book published in 1969 make Karl Knutsson out to be neither more nor less than the great liberator of his country. They sum up his achievements as follows: 'At the same time there were many who wanted Sweden to be a free country. The leader of these freedom-loving Swedes was Karl Knutsson'.

From the facts adduced above we can estimate the exact degree of freedom enjoyed by the Swedish commons under the rule of Karl the Liberator.

The epitaph of the man who was thrice king of Sweden is written in the first person singular. That he should posthumously continue the apotheosis of the *Karl Chronicle* is perfectly in style. Amiably he characterizes himself:

> Gladly I did that which was pleasing to God;
> in Stockholm Castle I died. God command
> my soul to eternal rest.

How Swedes Learned to hate Danes

> Swedish men,
> Be watchful then;
> The Dane by nature
> Is a cruel creature.
> (From Hyltén – Cavallius – Stephens: *Sveriges historiska och politiska visor*, 1853)

SWEDEN HAS FOUGHT MORE WARS against Denmark than against any other country. Up to the formation of the Kalmar Union a state of war between the neighbouring peoples had virtually been the norm. During the first Union period, it is true, there had been a long period of peace; but in the 1430's armed conflicts, interrupted by armistices, of which the longest was under Sten Sture the Elder, began again; and the last decades of the Union were one continuous war. Afterwards, between the final break-up of the Union and 1814, Sweden and Denmark fought no fewer than eleven wars: 1563–70, 1611–13, 1644–45, 1657–58, 1659–61, 1674–78, 1700, 1710–21, 1788, 1808–09 and 1814. If we had statistics of the numbers of people, Swedes and Danes, who lost their lives in these eleven wars, they would add up to a horrifying figure.

Century after century the two peoples have been each other's curse and hereditary enemies. How can such a thing have been possible? What was the reason – or reasons – for all these wars?

The answer is to be found, I believe, in the popular hatred of Danes for Swedes, and vice versa, in the Late Middle Ages. It was a hatred, always smouldering, which burst into flame again at every renewed outbreak of hostilities. A hatred which persisted for nearly 400 years. The phenomenon is by no means unique; it has many parallels in world history, for instance in the mutual hatred between the Germans and the French which has flared up again during two wars in our own century.

But such collective feelings of enmity, loathing, rage and resentment, involving whole peoples, cannot be strictly speaking hereditary; are not a fact of nature. Nor are they spontaneous and self-generating. The Swedish peasant had done the Danish peasant no harm, nor had the Danish peasant harmed the Swede; therefore they felt no personal enmity. Not knowing each other they could hardly either love or hate each other. Probably they were wholly indifferent. What is certain is that both wished to be left in peace, had such a thing only been possible. In both kingdoms the peasantry's lot was a hard one – the Danes' being the harder – and this lot was not enhanced by going out to slaughter each other and burn down one another's homesteads. For the peasant, war was above all a recurrent torment.

It has been stated that even as late as the Engelbrekt rising the feelings of the Swedes 'were remarkably free from any hatred for the Danes'. Such hatred can therefore only have come into being at some later date – as a result of extraneous influences. It was the ruling caste which, in the 15th century, during the struggles within the Union, implanted and exploited it as an instrument of policy. It was artificially nourished; the fruit of propaganda.

The Late Middle Ages saw the birth of the political song in Sweden. Most of our 15th-century poetry is anonymous political propaganda. Usually such songs were supposed to be creations of the populace, sprung from its honourable and instinctive loathing for its neighbours to the south. Actually they were commissioned by the authorities, by kings and regents, who salaried their authors. Modern research has established that many of these ditties originated in Karl Knutsson's chancellery.

In these poems the Danes are invariably described as an inherently bad lot. Treacherous, cruel and bestial monsters, they had been fashioned that way by God, and therefore could not help it. The gravest charge against them was that of breaking faith.

From these contemporary writings it is obvious, on the other hand, that the Swedes were invariably true to their word; a virtue most highly esteemed, as we see in the *Gotland Song*, from the mid-century:

> What Swedish men declare,
> that do they stand by;
> no man beguile
> nor rich nor poor;
> this ever was their way.

Against the Swede's unshakeable habit of keeping his word, the Dane's constitutional treachery was contrasted as night to day. This sub-human image of their neighbours was held up to the gaze of an unenlightened and gullible commons, who were in no position to check its truth. The subjects of the Swedish crown had to be incited against the Danes, and the surest instrument for swaying an illiterate peasantry was by easily memorized ditties. As they toiled in the fields and meadows, they passed the time of day humming these songs which were rooting in their minds the myth of the diabolical Dane.

Naturally, both at this time and later, in the 16th century, a corresponding hatred for the Swedes was being implanted in Denmark and exploited in various ways by the powerful, for their own ends. A number of Danish chronicles, too, appeared in print; in them the Swedes, in their turn, were depicted either as monsters of guile and cruelty or else as comically conceited peacocks, strutting about and showing off their gaudy plumage. Such writings no doubt appealed to the famous Danish sense of humour.

Professor Sven Ulric Palme has written an essay on the origins of anti-Danish feeling in Sweden. Whether any corresponding Danish study has appeared on the violently anti-Swedish feeling which flourished in Denmark from the 15th century onwards I do not know.

Hatred for the Danes is one of the leitmotifs of the *Karl Chronicle*. The *Erik Chronicle* has obviously been the author's – or authors' – stylistic model. But whilst the *Erik Chronicle* has great artistic qualities and is on the whole polite and courtly in tone, at points even capable of human sympathy, the *Karl Chronicle* is crude, clumsy and coarse throughout. Saturated with a nasty sadism, it evinces a rabid hatred for Karl's enemies. In it Danes are described as devils from hell, veritable angels of Darkness, whom it is quite simply the duty of every Christian man, and most pleasing in the sight of God, to plague, kill and exterminate.

Its account of how Bishop Arnold Klemedsson met his violent death, in 1434, exemplifies its contents. Arnold, being Danish-born, was of course a damned spirit, whom King Erik against the will of the Swedes had tried to place on the archiepiscopal throne at Uppsala, an action which seems to have precipitated a life-and-death struggle. With sadistic glee the *Chronicle* describes Arnold's wretched and deeply deserved end in his castle:

At Arnö full fearsomely fared he;
And there this spurious bishop died.
In slivers sliced his servants him
And salted into barrels three.
To Denmark then they took away
This damned, accurséd man.

By the last two lines the *Chronicle* presumably means that the bishop, having been righteously treated in Sweden, was now restored to his own proper origins in the underworld.

Thc seed scattered from the *Karl Chronicle* contained many fertile grains of anti-Danish hatred; falling on fertile soil, they brought forth a hundredfold.

Besides being spread abroad in songs and ballads, this devilish image of the Danes was disseminated orally, in documents and in the manifestos read out to the laity at their outdoor gatherings, their assemblies and markets. As an institution the Catholic Church, which controlled everyone's beliefs and modes of thought, favoured peace and the Union; but certain clerics placed themselves in the service of this nationalistic agitation and their sermons on that admirable theme – the noble character of Swedes and the rascality of all Danes – proved a considerable asset.

From his archiepiscopal throne at Uppsala, Johannes Magnus, archbishop and historian, together with Hemming Gadh,* the

* See pp. 94 et seq.

greatest Dane-eater of the age, preached this gospel of hatred. As the most eminent spiritual authority in the realm his position was unique, and he used it to attack Sweden's nearest neighbour. In the ears of this prelate the Danish language sounded extremely funny; it tickled his sense of humour. The Danes, he declared, haven't even the sense to talk like ordinary folk; they cough and splutter out their words, turning and twisting them deep down in their throats, so that they can hardly get them out. Even to speak at all, they are obliged to distort and wrest their mouths, the upper lip to the right and nether lip to the left. This deformation of their features, the archbishop was sure, was sheer vanity. They were so conceited they imagined it became them.

The most important of these 15th-century political propaganda poems are to be found in the collection of songs from which I have taken the quotation at the head of this chapter. Typical of the genre, this Gotland song, probably dating from 1449, is one long orgy of hatred for the Danes. It runs to 28 verses, every one of which ends with the stern warning: 'Swedish men, be watchful still!'

In this poem two characteristics are seen as above all typical of the Danes: cruelty and guile. Danes never keep promises or agreements, and in this they resemble the most poisonous and treacherous of arachnids:

> The scorpion useth to play,
> embraceth with his mouth alway;
> with his tail stingeth;
> so do the Danes
> when they parley.

In a document from the period we are told how the Danes treat the crew of a captured Swedish ship: not content with cutting off their ears and noses, they even chop off their hands and feet, after which they fling them, maimed and limbless, into the sea.

Malicious ridicule of wounded enemies is rife. In *A song of the Battle of Brunkeberg, A.D. 1471* (*En vijsa om Brunchaberg Slagh Anno 1471*) Christian I is held up to cruel mockery, and his name is spat upon. He is ridiculed for having received a ball in his nose – a comic place to be wounded – and also bleeding from the mouth.

With arquebus lead
Four front teeth fled
One after another,
In blood him smother.

Here we are light-years away from any chivalry or gallantry toward a beaten foe. This disdainful poem has been made out to be a genuine soldier's song, composed by one of the combatants at the Battle of Brunkeberg. In point of fact it is a product of Sten Sture the Elder's chancellery.

Of the three Stures, Sten Sture the Younger was the cleverest at propaganda. He travelled through the country inciting the commons against the Danes and all who favoured the Union. At council meetings and in market places he caused manifestos to be read out, accusing members of the Union party of various grave crimes.

These polemics between the two kingdoms, unexcelled in crudity and ferocity, continued during the 16th century, the Vasa period, when, instead of abating, these expressions of an undying hatred grew even more virulent. The Danes for their part disseminated a chronicle libelling the Swedes; and Gustaf Vasa riposted by having one of his henchmen, Bishop Peder Svart, pen a piece which, in crudity and the number of its insults, was fully a match for the enemy's. In the well-known song about King Gustav and his Dalesmen, bucketsful of high-grade calumny are poured over the Danes. Particularly nasty are the wretchedly ineffectual attempts at humourous jibes at the enemy.

During Gustav Vasa's reign the last traces of the tolerant and humane Union spirit, earlier found in both peoples, were finally stifled. A raucous nationalism, always sensitive to questions of prestige, took over.

On either side national feeling, at the least dissension, was easily hurt; even over events from the distant past. Learned men, Swedish and Danish, became involved in long disputes over the numbers of the fallen at the Battle of Lena, in 1208, three and a half centuries earlier. Had it been 5,000 men, or 6,000? This wrangle, though it did not actually lead to war, had other and most tragic consequences. In the 1560's the dispute over the right to use the Union arms, the

Three Crowns, was one of the causes of the Seven Years War. One wonders how deeply the common man in Sweden and Denmark can really have been attached to this national symbol, whose origins were anyway not specifically Scandinavian but European. If anyone had asked him to lay down his life for this emblem, I do not believe he would have been prepared to.

It was during the reign of Gustav Vasa that the fuel for this nationalistic megalomania, which was afterwards to burst out into complete lunacy in the 17th century, was gathered. The chief contributor was Johannes Magnus. In his history of the prehistoric kings of the Swedes and Goths he claimed that the Swedish kingdom had been founded immediately after the earth had dried out after the Flood. As for the antediluvian epoch, even the sharp-eyed Johannes Magnus could not discover any Swedish kings.

That the Swedes should gradually have come to accept this rabid view of the Danes as cruel, treacherous and devilish, implanted in them century after century, is therefore not surprising. 'Even in the lower ranks of society the conception of the Danes as the hereditary enemy became deeply rooted' (E. Hildebrand). And thus it was that a popular hatred, which the enemies of the Union could draw on whenever they needed a war-psychosis, was artificially created. Each successive war heaped new fuel on the flames, which were kept burning down the centuries.

During the wars of the 16th and 17th centuries manifold cruelties and atrocities were committed against the populations of the border provinces. Naturally this provided fresh stuff for propaganda which, exploited to the utmost by either party, renewed the two peoples' mutual hatred. The means used were old and well-proven. Each people was told all about the *enemy's* murders, his acts of pillage, rape and arson, and was given detailed accounts of the *other side's* violent deeds. Afterwards all this lopsided information was mirrored in histories enjoying official sanction in schools as factual and objective. Swedish schoolchildren were told all about what the Danes had done; and what the Swedes had done was duly brought to the knowledge of Danish schoolchildren.

I can speak to the point. Swedish soldiers, as far as I could discover from my history books, both in elementary school and higher institutes of education, have in all our wars never been anything but kindly and humane, or behaved otherwise than decently and correctly. After all, these wars were all justifiable wars, fought in defence of their fatherland. Even when they fought in such distant lands as Denmark, Norway, Germany, Poland and Russia, they were doing no more than defending Sweden. And always they fought honourably, decently, with shining weapons. Never did they commit atrocities, kill their prisoners, commit rape or take the lives of women and children.

By contrast, these history books taught me all about the Danes' monstrous behaviour in Småland, my own part of the country, during border wars. Certainly there was no lack of materials. On the other hand, I was kept in ignorance of my own countrymen's activities on the other side of the border. If they had not committed the same outrages as their enemies, they would have been showing an elevation of spirit utterly unnatural to their age – but it is in Danish, not in Swedish schoolbooks, you can read about these atrocities.

The Kalmar War of 1611–13 is famous for the barbarous cruelties committed by either side – witness a letter written by the 17-year-old Gustavus Adolphus dated February 13, 1612, to his cousin Duke Johan and extant in the State Archives.

With triumphant delight the royal youth describes a successful punitive raid – what we should today call an act of reprisal – which he had just carried out against Skåne. Within a single fortnight he had laid waste and levelled to the ground no fewer than 24 large Skanian parishes. Gustavus Adolfus reports to his cousin how he and his troops had 'rampaged, destroyed, burnt and killed, utterly at our own will.'

Royal words and therefore not to be doubted.

In this letter the king expressly declares that the Swedes 'had met with no resistance' from the 'enemy' – explicitly, the 'enemy' being a defenceless civilian population, including its women and children. How many people, we may ask ourselves, escaped alive from this Skanian Song My of 1612, – in which Gustavus Adolphus's soldiery were allowed to kill 'utterly at their will', 356 years before the Song My in Vietnam?

I first came across this authentic letter in a Danish work on the Kalmar War, and it has somewhat modified the image idea of our great hero-king I was presented with at school. Deeply impressed by our history books' accounts of his deeds I had accepted Gustavus Adolphus as one of my childhood idols, fully on a par with Sitting Bull, Buffalo Bill and Texas Jack. With his noble spirit, his courage, his scorn for death, he had utterly seduced my schoolboy heart. In my games I did my best to emulate Gustavus Adolphus, as I did all our other great warrior kings. In an autobiographical novel I have related how my alter ego tried to tread in the hero-king's footsteps:

'As Gustavus Adolphus he was up in the loft struggling with sheaves of straw which were Tilly's black cavalry, the damned catholics, locked in struggle with Wallenstein's host until, wounded by nine bullets, he lay exhausted. One dark and murky February night Karl X Gustaf storms the icy ramparts of Copenhagen, but after a bloody fray is repulsed – in a frenzy of rage he runs up the roof of the ice-cellar, and though clinging desperately to its roof shingles again and again comes tumbling down.'

How deeply I resented Karl X Gustaf's failure to storm the Danish capital in 1658! He had so nearly captured it. If he had, it would have put paid for ever to our treacherous and untrustworthy neighbours and incorporated their country in our own. Scandinavia, once and for all, would have become one great Swedish kingdom.

Enough of this hatred which had originated in the Middle Ages, and had even survived in 20th-century schoolbooks for a Swedish boy still to think of the Danes as treacherous cowardly people whose word was never to be relied on. Every time Sweden had been involved in some war in other lands the Danes had seized their chance to attack us in the rear. They had done so when we were busy with Poland in 1657; and they had repeated the same treacherous attack in 1788 and 1809, when we had our hands full defending Sweden against the Russians. What the national schoolbooks omitted to mention, however, was that the Danes' attacks on these occasions were paying us out in kind for Field Marshal Lennart Torstensson's attack on Jutland in 1644 and for Karl X Gustaf's unquestionable breach of the Peace of Roskilde in 1658.

Earlier generations of illiterates, I imagine, found it even easier than a 20th-century schoolboy to swallow this propaganda image of the Danes which helped to make possible no fewer than eleven wars between the two peoples. Generation after generation, century after century, such feelings of collective hatred were a heavy legacy on the backs of two neighbouring peoples, racially akin. Many hereditary enemies are known to world history besides the Swedes and the Danes. Indeed, I have never read of two neighbouring peoples who have been hereditary friends. It seems as if only hostility between peoples is hereditary and abiding on this earth.

But at the point of transition between the Middle Ages and the modern era there was a man of immense authority living in Sweden who did not preach this gospel of hatred: Olaus Petri. He took no part in this frenzy against the accursed Danes, which Gustav Vasa during his reign only intensified. Olaus Petri writes of these conflicts between Denmark and his own fatherland with an objectivity remarkable for his time. His judgments on the conflicts of the Union period are nuanced, free from all hatred. Unlike the official propaganda, he drew no distinction between Swedes and Danes. For him the one folk was not made up of good, noble and faithful people, and the other of beasts and turncoats. His history assesses events ethically. It is grounded in Christian morals.

With Olaus Petri viewing history so utterly differently from Gustav Vasa, it is only logical that the king should have discounted the reformer's history of Sweden, regarded it as 'of little worth'. He also had the power to suppress it, and did everything he could to prevent its dissemination. Even in the 16th century Olaus Petri's *Swedish Chronicle* could have been multiplied a thousandfold by Gutenberg's invention; but for more than two and a half centuries it was only available in handwritten copies. Not until 1818 was his work, which opened a new epoch in Swedish history-writing, printed and published in Sweden.

When he writes: 'Full oft hath truth had to stand aside in history', the reformer states an eternal truth. For his part he made an honest attempt to seek it out. No dupe of the hue and cry against our neighbours to the south, he realised the magnitude of the disaster to both peoples inherent in this novel nationalism. Nothing but fresh wars could spring from such a soil. As for the patriotic claptrap of Swedes and Danes – and the Danes were certainly not behind us in boastfulness – he writes in his chronicle:

'Wherefore little doth it behove the Swedes to laud themselves for all they have won in Denmark, no more behoveth it the Danes to boast of what they have gained in Sweden: great dam and ruin hath befallen both parties.'

Words written about the year 1540. Naturally Olaus Petri could form no idea of the 'dam and ruin' or of the sufferings which would be inflicted on both peoples in the course of the eleven wars they would have to fight against each other, up to 1814. But his words about truth which 'full oft hath had to stand aside in history' were confirmed by the fate which befell his own *History*. Not until four years after the commencement of a lasting peace in Scandinavia, in 1818, would the peoples of whom his work treated be able to read it in print.

From age to age, from generation to generation, war has been mankind's ever faithful companion and its most dangerous enemy. Christians have sought its cause in the congenital and inextirpable evil in human nature, that evil whose first-fruit was Cain's murder of his brother Abel, and in their parents' original sin, passed down to ensuing generations. To the Marxist, with his materialistic view of history, no war, in any society, is anything but a class war; an eternal struggle for possession of the land and its natural resources, and one which will continue as long as the economics of capitalism persist in our world. Apparently the Marxist does not even exempt the wars of religion, which cost millions of Europeans their lives in the 16th and 17th centuries. By concrete examples I have tried to demonstrate a third cause of war: nationalistic feeling, inciting the peoples to hate each other.

Compared with our 20th-century instruments the medieval means for fostering such hatred were primitive. The mass media, press, radio, TV are many times more effective than Karl Knutsson's propagandist poems, disseminated in handwritten copies. In the hands of unscrupulous overlords bereft of all conscience our new instruments of propaganda constitute an imminent threat to peace among the peoples of this earth.

Whatever the ultimate causes of war – and they differ from case to case – there appears to be a general consensus as to the truth of a fact so true as to be trivial, indeed banal: if mankind does not abolish war, war will abolish mankind.

The Forests and Popular Liberties

'*—where are great forests, wherein is all their consolation.*'—Gustav Vasa.

Where the plough cannot go,
nor the scythe make its blow,
standeth the forest——.

Old saying.

IN A LETTER to the poet Atterbom, of September 13, 1837, C. J. L. Almquist, poet, novelist, social critic and dramatist, wrote: 'You know I am a declared friend of the peasantry.' Almquist had tried a peasant existence himself, and even if he idealized it in his stories he probably knew better than any other member of the educated classes in his day and age what life was like for the common people. On page 595 of his *Monografi* he lays express emphasis on the peculiar status of the Nordic – Swedish and Norwegian – peasantry in Europe, calling it a unique social phenomenon, which had stirred the amazement of foreign visitors. 'Alone among all the countries of Europe, Scandinavia . . . possesses in its *peasants* a class at the very base of its population who, as long ago as anyone can remember, already enjoyed political rights . . . We who live in Scandinavia and have been accustomed to these peculiarities from our childhood up, perhaps see in them nothing remarkable; but the surprising fact of it appears to the eye of an observer, the more he compares other European peoples with those of Scandinavia.'

In his comparisons between peoples, as in so much else, Almquist is himself a keen observer, superior both in learning and in knowledge. As long as he was able to remain in Sweden he was regarded as possessing the cleverest head in it; but finally to save it from falling on the scaffold, this brilliant author had to emigrate to the United States, accused of poisoning a money-lender.

Almquist overestimated the political freedom enjoyed by the Swedish peasantry, by the commons. Nevertheless it is true that mediaeval feudalism subjected Europe's peasantry to a general serfdom, and this serfdom included the peasants of one Scandinavian country: Denmark. Almquist could also have observed the 'surprising fact of it' in a people whom he does not mention, namely the Swiss. Only in three continental countries – England's position was exceptional – in Sweden, Norway and Switzerland, did the common people escape the full weight of feudal oppression. A crucial reason for this, it seems to me, was the physical nature of these three lands.

In 1291 the original Swiss cantons, Schwyz, Uri and Unterwalden, founded the Swiss League and therewith the Swiss peasant republic, which the Habsburg princes' armies of knights found it impossible to conquer. Already, in the Early Middle Ages, the fresh breezes of liberty were blowing in this Alpine country. The little state was surrounded by mighty powers who time and again sought to conquer it by superior military strength; but behind the magnificent ramparts of their mountains its people defended themselves successfully and preserved their freedom. That this little peasant republic should have come into being in the very midst of these rapacious mediaeval principalities and thereafter survived for almost seven centuries seems utterly miraculous.

In Norway's mountains and deep valleys the Norwegian peasants, too, had dwellings inaccessible to outside interference. Mounted men-at-arms found no roads to advance by. Nor had the country any indigenous nobility; and the Danish nobles were few in number, and thereto extremely remote from their own capital in Copenhagen. To keep the Norwegians under effective surveillance was beyond the power of their Danish overlords.

Sweden, lastly, was a vast, almost uninhabited country, whose forests served her population as Alps the Swiss, and the mountains the Norwegians. The 'surprising fact' noted by Almquist thus comprehends the mountain peasants of Norway and Switzerland and the sylvan Swedes.

Our earliest evidence for the topic now to be discussed dates from the great Roman historians. In his narratives of his own campaigns against the Germans, Caesar refers at several points to the severe obstacles presented by the forests to his troops' advance. Tacitus, too, speaks of the forests as being the breastwork of the Germanic peoples. Caesar writes: 'It is the greatest pride of the German tribes to surround themselves with broad desolate frontier regions. They regard it as evidence of their own strength that their neighbours should have been driven out of their lands and gone away, without anyone daring to settle in their proximity. This makes them, in their own opinion, safe and free from all fear of sudden assaults'. (Caesar: *De Bello Gallico*, IV). Pomponius Mela, too, writes how the Germans did not wage war to gain an empire or to extend their territories, but in order that the countryside all around them should lie untilled and uninhabited. In those days the great forest regions along the frontiers of their realm had constituted part of their defences.

Our first historian to write in the Swedish language, Olaus Petri, is also the first Swede to lay stress in his chronicle on the enormous importance of the forest to the popular liberties of his fatherland: 'Sweden is such a land as swamps, mountains and forests do fortify, on such wise that the commons cannot long be forcibly oppressed, forasmuch as they have great means to oppose their lords'. And they exploited these means. In his history of the Nordic peoples Olaus Magnus describes how a peasant rising begins: 'The manner in which this is done, is that the population or peasantry, to the number of several thousand from the same part of the country, assemble at an agreed time in the forest.'

On many points the views of Gustav Vasa and Olaus Petri differed sharply: but that the Swedish forests were the bulwark of peasant freedom was one on which they were entirely agreed, as we can see from the king's letters during the Dacke rising. Gustav is resentful at the defeats which his troops of noblemen and German men-at-arms are repeatedly suffering at the hands of the rebellious Smålanders. But he finds something to which he can attribute these reverses: the forest. He writes: 'Little could we molest them up there, where are great forests, wherein is all their consolation.'

Not only has the forest been a 'consolation' to the people by affording a refuge in time of war; it has also been a vital condition of their existence, and this long before it became the Swedes' most important source of exports. We have seen how the bark of its tree trunks contributed to their daily bread. Ever since men settled here the forests have also provided them with game for their meat, with grazing and fodder for their cattle, with timber for their dwellings, with fuel to warm them, with tapers to light them, with bark for preparing their leather, and with tar and charcoal.

Quite literally, the products of the forest have accompanied the Swede from cradle to grave. Tools and utensils were all made of wood: the men's harrows and primitive ploughs, the women's spindles, spinning wheels and looms. Wood became the wheels under their wagons and the oars for their boats and skiffs. The first boat which ever floated on the water was hollowed out of the trunk of an oak. From the trunk of the alder were fashioned the wooden clogs which were people's everyday footwear. The trough in which their dough was kneaded and the table from which it was eaten were likewise of wood, and so were all their eating utensils, spoons, ladles, bowls and plates. From the forest, too, came the bench where a man sat in the daytime and the bed he slept in at nights. Of wood was fashioned a cradle for the new-born babe, and a coffin for the old man who had just died. A human being's first resting place, it was also his last.

In this way, from birth to death, the forest followed a man. And of old the forest was everyman's property – and no one's. 'The forest grows as well for the poor as for the rich,' is an old Swedish saw. Our ancestors called the forest 'The poor man's garden'. They also used it as their fortress and bulwark. Olaus Magnus writes that the Norsemen considered it 'right and just to take nature to their aid in crushing cruel enemies'. He devotes a whole chapter of his history to *On Fights in the Forests*, showing how the local population exploited their natural bulwarks offered by the terrain: 'They make deep notches in the trees along the road where the enemy is expected, bind the trees together at their crowns and so arrange their ropes and tackle as easily to pull them down and overthrow the enemy while yet he is afar off; with the outcome that horsemen and footmen, as if stricken by lightning, are slain in heaps on the spot, or else, if by chance they have entered some wretched narrow path, are overwhelmed with stones which are hurled down [on them] as if from the high walls of a fortress.'

There was another simple but effective means of barring an enemy's advance through wooded country. Impassable log-jams were constructed of trees felled criss-cross over roads and paths. These fellings served as forts, from behind which a Fabian defence could be kept up. During the Middle Ages these were primitive frontier fortresses; I have seen traces of them along the old national boundary between Småland and Blekinge.

In a country of deep forests like Sweden foreigners could hardly take a step without going astray. In such a terrain foreign legionaries could not find their way. But the natives knew every inch of it. The foreigners had to contend with an enemy who knew how to make use of natural obstacles and how at any moment to become invisible. The men of the forests, the peasants, struck when it suited them, and hid when it did not. In his letters Gustav Vasa himself bears witness to how his German legionaries, whom he had brought into the kingdom as his indispensable allies against his own Swedish peasants, could not do service in the depths of the great Småland forests. In such terrain they could not fight. Every bush terrified them out of their wits: behind it might be lying a man with a crossbow, ready to let fly a lethal bolt. At home on the plains of Germany, during Thomas Münzer's insurrection of a decade and a half before, these legionaries had had no difficulty at all in cutting his peasants to pieces. But the fighting methods of the inhabitants of Sweden, this land of forests, were strange to them, took them aback.

Here an unsought contrast presents itself with a Danish peasant rising in the 1530's. During the so-called Counts' Civil War, King Christian III suppressed his subjects' insurrection with the aid of German legionaries specially called in for the purpose. The decisive battles were fought on the plainlands of Skåne and Själland, in the open fields, where several thousands of peasants were cut down by the swords and lances of well-equipped corps of mounted cuirassiers. Slaughtered like cattle, they had no chance of escape. Whereafter the impotent Danish peasants were forcibly suppressed, deprived of their liberties. Not until the mid-19th century did they achieve a position comparable to that of their Swedish and Norwegian brothers.

My theory, then, is that the difference between plainlands and forest has deeply affected the liberties of the Scandanavian peoples.

Nowadays we should call this medieval forest warfare 'guerilla warfare'. The term was first used during the Spaniards' revolt against Napoleon, which contributed so much to his fall, and it has been the usual word for resistance and freedom-movements all over over the world ever since. Guerilla warfare is waged by irregulars, without a regular military organization and who observe no conventions of war. Such fighters are sometimes called partisans, sometimes '*franc-tireurs*'.

The Second World War saw resistance movements against the Nazi empire in a number of occupied countries. The most successful were the Jugoslavs, whose mountains and forests were a great asset. Otherwise the partisans consisted partly of regular military forces, hundreds of thousands of undefeated troops hiding in the great forests, where they took a heavy toll of the intruders. During the Winter War of 1939–40 the Finns, too, were greatly assisted by their immense desolate forests, where the Russian invaders could find no roads and, like Gustav Vasa's legionaries, all too easily went astray.

Anyone interested in the subject will find many books on it. Its topicality is obvious. For more than a decade now the wole world has been following the guerilla war being waged in the jungles and swamps of South-East Asia. Nor are forests the partisan's only recourse. There are other parts of the globe which the Creator seems to have designed specially for guerillas.

But the forests not only provided a hiding place for insurgents, where they could gather and prepare their actions undisturbed; whenever war broke out it was also a reliable place of refuge for the fleeing population. As soon as the 'fiery cross' was sent out to sound the alarm at an enemy's approach, the villagers and their families had recourse to the depths of the most impenetrable parts of the forest, taking with them as many of their indispensable belongings as they could. Homes and farmsteads were left to their fate, in most cases a fiery one. When, in due course, the refugees returned, they found only the ashes of their dwellings, in which they began to search for such objects as had escaped the flames.

The marching troops brought violence, robbery and conflagration into the land. The old court rolls contain any amount of incontrovertible evidence of such rapine. They record the peasantry's unending complaints of their sufferings at the hands of troops passing through the countryside. Sometimes such events are called *Durchzug* or *Durch-Marsch*, German words which witness clearly to the nationality of these unbidden guests, speaking their own country's language. From the border wars the provinces of Southern Sweden have preserved numerous accounts of peasant families, men, women and children, who had fled from the legionaries and taken refuge in the forest. They have been passed on from one generation to another, both in local histories and by oral tradition. *When war came to the farmstead* could be their common rubric.

'The blessed forest saved our lives,' writes the rector of Markaryd, a border village, in his notes of the Danish rapine in 1611. Many people, we may assume, owed their lives to the forest, our forefathers' bulwark in time of war.

But in another respect too the forest afforded protection to the individual. For anyone who could not satisfy his need of freedom within the village community it afforded a refuge from society's obligations, laws, rules and customs. Earlier I have stressed the conformism of the old Scandinavian community, and how little elbow-room it left for its deviants. Anyone who differed temperamentally from the majority moved within a narrow framework of tolerance. The peasant liberties inherited from heathen times and from the Early Middle Ages, severely reduced after the introduction of the class society, also imposed their own limits; and these might not be exceeded. Fixed by the interests of family and clan, they were formulated in the interests of the community. Our own age's reasons of state afford a comparison. The general advantage curtailed personal freedom; common interests were opposed to individual ones. If, as we are inclined to believe nowadays, each person's life is a goal in itself, we are here involved in an insoluble contradiction.

Peasant society had originally been based on blood-relationships, on natural family ties. And from this it had developed into an association for mutual peace and protection, opposed to other families and clans, similarly allied. But it was *entirely voluntary in character.* It was based on a social contract, to which the members of that society had acceded of their own free will, and this contract could be annulled by anyone who did not feel disposed to comply with its requirements and statutory duties. The individual was free to leave society and live his own life outside the village community; but thereafter, no longer enjoying society's protection, did so entirely at his own risk. No modern society permits the individual to make such an exit. Against reasons of state he is powerless. But in ancient peasant society this was by no means the case. If displeased with the community, or no longer at home in it, an alternative, not offered by modern society, was always open to him: *the forest.*

All round the inhabited parts of the countryside were immense wildernesses, where as yet no organized community existed. In documents from the village courts these wild tracts are referred to comprehensively as *the forest.* They became an asylum for all who had unilaterally annulled their contract with society. Juridic notions permitted a form of exile, referred to in ancient court rolls as '*skoggång*' ('gone to the forest'), where such voluntary exiles are called '*skogsmän*' ('woodsmen'). Vis-à-vis society they were equal legal entities, with whom it could negotiate.

The subject has been studied in depth in a classic work by G. O. Hyltén-Cavallius, called by Strindberg 'the cornerstone of Swedish ethnography'. On the basis of the 17th-century court rolls this author demonstrates that by no means all these woodsmen were criminals who had fled from justice. To a great extent they were people whom we should today call political refugees. 'That is to say, the Småland woodsmen, notorious in the history of Gustav Vasa, so far from being ordinary border thieves, were often men from the most powerful clans in the country, who had fled to the forest for political reasons. In so doing they were following an immemorial custom of the Gothic peoples, and to this extent were wholly within their rights.'

We can ignore the 'ordinary border thieves'. What has captured my imagination is this other sort of woodsman's motives for abandoning society. In one instance my reasons are purely personal: family reasons, which have also had a bearing on two of my novels.

In the work I quote from above we read the following excerpt from the court rolls:

In 1620, in Algutsboda parish, a certain woodsman by name Åke Duvemåla, together with his mistress, had 'far out in the wilds of the forest, among a heap of fallen timber whither none could well come, dug a hole in the earth, and then away under the earth a goodly way, large as a fair-sized cellar, and before all made a door. Thereafter he had built therein a stove of clay and stone, and dug the chimney up through the soil, with a damper in it. Within he had a bed, benches and all his belongings, pots, dishes and whatever [else] he needed. Some way from the lair was a spring where throughout the winter he had his watering place, on such wise that he rarely went out of his lair for food; but his whore not at all. And those who have seen this lair in the earth, they have said upon oath that they could never have deemed it possible to find such a thieves' hiding place. Item, the neighbours thereabouts do complain that they each year have lost fearfully many small beasts, sheep, goats and other creatures. Many hides too have been found, in sign and evidence that he is guilty of such thieving'.

Duvemåla is a little village in my own native parish, and consists only of three farmsteads. In 1833, my grandmother was born on one of these farms, which has been in the possession of the same family since the 17th century. I ask myself: did this woodsman, Åke of Duvemåla, derive from this homestead? If he did, he may be one of my maternal ancestors. It is this possibility which has aroused my interest in him.

Åke had left his village and was living in a lair in the earth with his 'mistress'. This last expression does not accord with the parlance of those days and must therefore be the editor's circumlocution. In the direct quotation from the court rolls some sentences, further on, call the woman the 'whore'. Åke's motive's for 'going to the forest' cannot be in doubt. Not being legally married, he and his woman could not live together in the village, and therefore had had to take to the woods.

It was this excerpt from the court rolls which gave me my idea for my novel *Mans kvinna*, in which an unmarried peasant falls in love with a married woman, wife of another peasant, and flees with her into the forest. The book ends with their flight. The same motif is revived in another of my novels *Ride To-Night*, in which the peasant Ragnar Svedje takes to the forest to continue the resistance to 'the German lord of Ubbetorp Manor'. This novel describes the life of the woodsmen after they have left the village. For housing I have taken the lair which Åke of Duvemåla furnished for himself and his 'whore' in the oak-clearing. In his lair, though he refuses to join him in his thievery, Svedje lives together with the forest thief Ygge. The court rolls bear witness that Åke of Duvemåla stole small farm animals, sheep and pigs, etc. Short of such thefts he and his woman would not have been able to keep body and soul together.

A number of other judicial cases, in which a man and a woman had sought refuge in the forest because of illicit love, are to be found in 17th-century legal documents. In certain circumstances 'double whoredom', so called, where both parties were guilty of adultery, was – under the harsh laws of those days – punishable by death, The guilty parties are referred to in the court documents as 'runaway fornicators' or as 'runaways from the land, male and female'. At the assize in Allbo hundred, on June 28, 1627, the court dealt with a case of adultery, where an 'old man ready to drop, more than 80 years old, had in his old age escaped across the frontier with his mistress'. Any old man who committed such a mighty deed today would certainly make the headlines.

The flight of lovers to the forest was an understandable reaction to peasant society's inhuman laws against their cohabitation. Otherwise, voluntary flight from society was due, as Hyltén-Cavallius puts it, to 'personal dissatisfaction with the general state of affairs'. Such conflicts between the individual and society which, even as late as the 17th century, found outlet in flight to the woods, are immemorial, timeless.

As a rule tents made of branches seem to have provided the woodsman's dwelling. As for nourishment, the larder of the wilderness was still not exhausted, and much of his food he could take direct from nature. The forests were replete with game, and in the lakes streams and rivers the fish were plentiful. If he need something more tasty to put on his bread, the peasants' farm animals had to be slaughtered where they grazed. Originally an honest man, he necessarily became a robber and a thief. In summer and autumn the wild berries of the forest supplemented his diet. Bread must have been an acute problem, that is if the woodsman was not prepared to content himself with what he could bake from tree bark.

This free life of the woodsman was no romantic or idyllic existence. Dependent on the forest for his board and lodging, he was forced to wage an even harder struggle against hunger and cold. When hurt, or stricken down by some serious disease, he was left to die alone and helpless in his forest lair, like a sick animal.

He must have had strong reasons for putting up with such a life. Defiance was basic to his temperament, and freedom so highly prized that for its sake he renounced the safer existence within the community and all the advantages enjoyed by persons of fixed abode. Words cost nothing; it is actions which have to be paid for, and the woodsman's cost him dear. As Hyltén-Cavallius puts it: 'He lives undefeated and indomitable, still fighting society, and when finally he goes under, still defiant to the last, he dies fearless as he has lived.'

Who can but respect so passionate a love of freedom?

I was born in the middle of a forest, and it has set its stamp on me. All my life I have carried with me my origins. I understand what the forest has meant to the people who have had their home there, and to us who have grown up within its confines.

When I was a child, its spirits of nature were still an everyday reality for many older people. I heard men say how, with their own eyes, they had seen the wood goblin. Once upon a time the forest lands had been densely populated with giants and trolls; but nowadays these were dying out, either struck by lightning or else run over and killed by the trains which had begun to run through the forests on their gleaming rails. For a long time I believed what the older people told me. The tall tree-stumps, with their claw-like branches, were dead and atrophied trolls. But gradually I began to doubt the existence of the beings whom so many people had talked to me about, but which I myself, neither by daylight nor in the dark, had ever seen in real life.

In the daytime, as soon as ever I could I ran out into the paddock, penetrated deep into the gloom among the tree-trunks, but never, though I often got lost during these childhood excursions into the wilds, do I remember being anxious or scared. On the contrary: from those memories of the forest I retain only a sense of security and freedom.

My best hiding places were the densest thickets. There no one could see me. When I was not in the forest, at home and at school, I was exposed to the eyes of others. Always I was being observed and, as often as not, being told off. I was surrounded by adults who wanted to decide over my behaviour. But as long as I was out of everyone's sight I was free to behave as I liked. I could shout at the top of my voice, throw myself down on the mosses, kick my legs and turn somersaults, and no one cared. No matter what I was up to, there was no one there to reprimand me. All round were only trees and bushes, and no matter how crazy my behaviour these did not curse me. Overhead, like a caress, was only the gentle hush of the pines and spruces. The tall trees seemed to be protecting me, to defend my right to autonomy and to behave however I liked. At home and at school there was something known as good or bad behaviour. This was nowhere to be found in the forest.

For all these reasons I was happier as a child in the forest than anywhere else. For me the forest represented security. The child's dawning need for freedom found an outlet in a life close to it; a need which became ever more insistent as I grew older.

Afterwards, when I was still older and became a lumberjack I experienced the forest differently. When I was ten I used to go with my father to his clearings, and from the age of fifteen onwards worked for several winters in my parish's great crown forest. Of all physical work I have ever done, forestry is the hardest and most demanding. But it was also the sort of work I found most to my taste and which gave me real pleasure – work in the fresh air, an air redolent of pine-gum and pine needles, work carried out in utter privacy, free of the foremen who disturb factory work or the farmer's supervision on a farm. In my days felling was done by two-man teams. Each such team chopped away in its own particular tract of the crown forest; piecework, with which one's employer could not interfere. Just two men, working together in the solitude and freedom of the forest, their own masters.

In times past the forest used to be called 'the poor man's winter shirt'. Diffusing warmth from his stove, it also warms men's shivering bodies in other ways. No surer way exists of driving the cold out of one's limbs than to take an axe and fell some great tree. Before many minutes have gone by, great beads of sweat are dropping from one's brow. Though the lumber-jack, quartered in some wretched shack, may sometimes shiver at nights, he need never feel cold by day.

In my autobiographical novel *When I was a Child** I have described how a lumberman experienced the forest while at work:

> 'Walter was back in the forest where he had started life as a seven-year-old. The vast forest which in winter provided cover from the gale and in summer shade from the sun. The lumberman's work was free. He does not have to keep pace with a team or fit in with them. Here he worked at his own speed, quickly or slowly and rested when he liked.
>
> 'Walter attacked the old spruce. His axe bounced off the frozen tree, which flew out in little chips, hard as pebbles. The conifer forest grew lighter or darker as the shadows of clouds flitted over crowns and branches. The trees sighed, cracked and with a last long soughing sigh, the sigh of the dying, fell.'

For me the Swedish countryside means above all the forest. Unchanging it stands there at all times of year, whatever the weather, waiting for me. In winter all waters lie frozen hard under their icy lid. But the forest is always just as open and accessible. In winter its greens are even more vivid than in summer and its scent, for me, even fresher and healthier. The forest, whether I've been working in it or just strolling about, has given me the strength for my never-ending grind at the typewriter, to which I've mostly sat chained like a galley-slave at his oar. Whenever the writer of this history has been utterly weary the forest has been his remedy, his cure. And still is. Which is why he has devoted these pages to it.

Always, from my childhood and youth up, I have associated the forest with *freedom*.

* Orig: *Soldat med brutet gevär*. 1944. Transl. G. Lennestock, Knopf, N.Y. 1956. Heinemann, London.

The Three Stures

Number One

NOT UNTIL AFTER HIS DEATH was the first Sture called 'the Elder'. While he was still alive, of course, no one could know that two more regents of the same name would come after him. When he first took over the government it was under the name of Sten Gustavsson Sture. A nephew of Karl Knutsson, he was keeping the reins of power inside the family.

The tradition which ascribes to Karl the philosophical reflection that, as king, he had 'been a wretched and unhappy man' also avers that on his deathbed he warned his nephew against accepting a crown which brought to its wearer only grief and misery. It is possible that Sten Sture followed his uncle's advice when he accepted and always retained the title of regent (*riksföreståndare*). But his action may also have been based on psychological insight. Sweden was an elective kingdom. Herr Sten was familiar with the mentality of its great men. He knew how hotly they aspired to a royal crown. Many human lives had been sacrificed in the struggle to obtain it and all who could not attain to it were envious of the glory it conferred. In remaining content with the status of regent Sten Sture not only wielded the same real powers as if he had been king, but also protected himself against the envy of his aristocratic brethren.

The Sture family is long ago extinct. Originally it consisted of five different branches, each with its own coat of arms. One branch sported a bull; another a sturgeon; a third an ox's head, between whose horns was a star. It was this branch which was eventually to become the Oxenstierna (Oxe-star) family, perhaps the most famous aristocratic dynasty in Swedish history. Sten Sture the Elder's shield was charged with three water-lily leaves.

A genealogical enquiry into the Stures is without interest to my history; but one indisputable historical fact must nevertheless be discussed here. For half a century after 1470, members of this clan dominated Swedish politics and were largely responsible for the destinies of the Swedes.

On Walpurgis Eve, 1471, a meeting was held at Arboga, to which, Olaus Petri tells us in his *Chronicle*, both burghers and peasants were summoned. At Arboga the Swedish people were to agree on the election of a governor for the whole realm. A 'last' of German beer was 'prepared' for the peasants, after which they gave their votes to 'him who had given the beer they desired'. The outcome of the voting was that those who supported Sten Sture gained the upper hand. He was 'chosen governor'.

Olaus Petri does not mince matters. Herr Sten was elected because he had stood them all that beer. German beer was regarded as a good deal stronger than the Swedish, and a 'last' contains around 290 litres, which means that something in the region of five thousand pints of good strong beer were drunk at the Arboga assembly which appointed Sten Sture the Elder regent. One of the passages in Olaus Petri's history which made Gustav Vasa, Herr Sten's descendant, 'no little wroth' was this tale of the Arboga beer, which he found derogatory to his ancestor's memory. The king was a grandson of the regent's sister.

'It turns sour like Arboga beer' is an old Swedish saying, presumably originating in those barrels which flowed so freely at Arboga on Walpurgis Eve, 1471. Studying the matter on the spot, just five hundred years later, I am able to confirm that a good beer is indeed brewed at Arboga. One, furthermore, which has no disagreeable after-effects.

Herr Sten had gained most votes at the assembly but as regent he did not command the support of a united people, not even of a united peasantry. Before his power could be consolidated, there had to be a military confrontation with Christian I and the Swedish Union party. It took place on October 10, 1471, at Brunkeberg, just outside the gates of Stockholm. After five centuries there is every reason to lay great stress on the true implications of this battle, which actually exemplified a deep split in the nation usually glossed over by historians. A large host of Uppland peasantry together with smaller bodies of Sörmlanders and possibly Västmanlanders, whose leaders were afterwards treated as traitors, fought on the Danish side. That October day, some Swedes fell fighting for the regent, Sten Sture; others for the Danish Union king, Christian I.

Nor did the regent's total victory at Brunkeberg lead to the unification of the Swedish provinces in a national state, as we today understand the term. That day was still far off. In certain parts of the country, such as Dalarna and Småland, a separatist movement survived for another seventy years or so.

In the contemporary *Sture Chronicles*, we read that the three Stures' régime was mild and just, and that for this they were much loved. Under their government, by and large, times were good in Sweden. When, once in a while, the peace was disturbed, it was only because of the infidelity of the Danes, 'false treaties' and the dastardly tricks with which they succeeded in pulling the wool over the eyes of the honest gullible Swedes. These chronicles give a picture of the Sture period which is as lop-sided and touched up as the one the *Karl Chronicle* gives of the immediately preceding epoch.

Historians have drunk deep from the Sture chronicles, and there is little more to be got out of them. Many passages are devoted to the aristocracy's internecine strife. They relate how lords struggled over castles, fortresses, fiefs and estates and the power which goes with property. Somehow I seem to have read all this before. The Sture clan had managed to lay its hands on a sizeable slice of the Swedish soil; but in the Axelssons, the Karlssons, the Trolles and the Vasas they had powerful rivals. The Axelssons, more especially, were landowners of the first order, and up to his fall in 1487 were Herr Sten's most dangerous opponents. Ivar Axelsson, their leader, was son-in-law to Karl Knutsson and therefore related to the regent.

Economic developments in Europe always had implications for Sweden and play a large rôle in our history. During the Later Middle Ages the city burghers had grown much more numerous and important. Capitalists were steadily converting land values into money values. In Sweden, nevertheless, the bourgeoisie's path to power through the money bag was travelled a good deal more slowly than in commercial centres of the continent. In Sweden, arable land still constituted the most important component of wealth or capital. Wealth, indeed, was identical with its possession. Together with the Church it was the aristocracy who were the great landowners and their wealth was retained, secured and increased by continual intermarriage among their families.

Property gives power over men. Throughout history this has been its great, often decisive rôle. But these conflicts between the mediaeval magnate families, sprung from their insatiable greed for power, become trivial and wearisome by eternal repetition, and I hardly think I do my reader a disservice by not going into them in detail. But that they were always going on and exercised an important influence on the course of events must nevertheless be pointed out.

Not that the conditions under which the tillers of the soil, more than nine-tenths of the population, were altered by these changes in land-ownership. Bergkvara, for example, an estate belonging to the Trolles in the heart of Värend (Småland), was one of the largest and most valuable of all south Swedish estates. Even today it comprises 1200 acres of arable soil – and on its domain it had hundreds of peasants and labourers. To these people it mattered not a jot whether the Trolles or some other aristocratic clan were the owners of this immense domain. Either way, they had to put in just as many days of compulsory labour at Bergkvara, days as wearisomely long and as strictly supervised, no matter who lorded it over this noble estate. In their lives nothing ever happened which has been regarded as worthy of note; their lords' struggles for possession of the land, on the other hand, have been extensively recorded for posterity.

But the reading they make is as tedious as it is distasteful.

As a monument to the victory at Brunkeberg the great *Saint George and the Dragon* group was erected in Stockholm Cathedral. This massive oak and elk-horn sculpture is the work of the German artist Bernt Notke, who had already immortalized Karl Knutsson. For Notke's superb young knight, the victor, Herr Sten Sture himself, is supposed to have stood model. His long sword upraised, he is shown in the very act of slaying the dragon, a terrifying and loathsome monster, whom we must suppose to represent King Christian I.

Of Herr Sten the *Rhymed Chronicle* tells us that 'in his time no man was his peer'. Panegyric can hardly go further. Yet comparison between Sten Sture the Elder and other mediaeval Swedish rulers undeniably falls out in his favour. He did not take his enemies' lives; nor did he burn peasants at the stake. Above all, he seems to have been a restorer and preserver of the peace. After four decades of incessant warfare and internecine strife, with Herr Sten's government the realm enters on a period of peace without counterpart since the days of Queen Margareta. Across the Baltic, along the eastern frontier, there were a few disturbances; but in Sweden itself a period of quietude began which lasted for about twenty-five years, a whole quarter of a century, and for this the credit must first and foremost go to the regent.

The people, who were crying out for peace, appreciated the new régime. In 1484, an eloquent Latin inscription was set up over the sacristy door of Kalmar Church, outside Uppsala. It reads: 'Peace flourisheth in Sweden, because Herr Sten ruleth.'

He also made an important contribution to Sweden's national independence, by abrogating the power of the German residents in Sweden's trading cities, in whose councils they had hitherto occupied half the seats. Thereafter the Swedish interests dominated. In cultural matters, too, important progress was made in the first Sture's days. In 1477 Scandinavia's first university was opened at Uppsala and a few months afterwards Copenhagen followed suit with its own seat of learning. In 1483, an immigrant German printer published, in Latin, the first printed book ever to appear in Sweden: an edifying work called *Dialogus creaturarum optime moralisatus*. It was a historic event. Gutenberg's invention had at last made its appearance in a remote, culturally indigent land. The man who was primarily responsible for these cultural developments was Jakob Ulfsson, Archbishop of Uppsala.

As for Herr Sten himself, he has gone down to posterity as the dragon-slaying knight astride his horse in Stockholm Cathedral. On its haunches can be seen the arms of the Sture clan. As a man, however, he is less accessible to us than his uncle, Karl Knutsson. Almost no personal letters can with certainty be attributed to him; no diaries; nor have we a single jotting demonstrably from his hand.

To the 19th-century historian C. T. Odhner, Sten Sture the Elder is 'a man who enjoyed the unreserved confidence of the people, whose rights he protected and who associated familiarly with common men, consulted them in their councils and visited them in their homes.' These verdicts I cite mostly as curiosities of the nationalist school of history-writing. Nevertheless, I believe they do have some basis in reality.

A modern expert, on the other hand, Professor Sven Ulric Palme, has tried to denigrate the traditional dragon-slayer and national hero in a biography which dwells on a hitherto overlooked aspect of the first Sture's activities; namely, his private business affairs.

Palme carefully documents his account. He has dug up deeds, wills, contracts of purchase, papers dealing with matters of inheritance and other incontrovertible documents, and the portrait which transpires from these sources is that of a leading representative of what we should call his day's high finance: a ruthless businessman, an unscrupulous land-speculator and a collector of other men's estates. After the death of Karl Knutsson, he omits to implement the terms of his will, by dishonest transactions acquiring for himself parts of his uncle's property which he withholds from their rightful legatees. Although he already owns many estates and farms, he is always acquiring more. Estate after estate falls into his hands. He speculates in fields and meadows, in mills, in waterfalls and eel-fisheries, at times using methods dubious or even illegal to come by them. In some cases he even seems to have cheated widows out of their husbands' inheritances. On one occasion he even extended his ruthlessness as a businessman to his political activities. He falsified, so it seems, the so-called Treaty of Nöteberg, 1323, which fixed the kingdom's eastern frontier with Russia.

In Palme's work Sten Sture the Elder stands exposed. The *Sture Chronicles* gilded the picture but the gilt has rubbed off. Yet so far from reducing his fascination for us it rather augments it, brings him closer to our own age. In Sten Sture the Elder, certainly one of the most remarkable personalities of 15th-century Sweden, we discover a timeless trait: insatiable acquisitiveness. As a businessman he is seen to have belonged to an undying and most disagreeable race of men: the robber baron and exploiter of landed property, a species which in our own day has proliferated all over Sweden – the lot-jobbers and real-estate sharks who speculate in the rising land-values of our Swedish soil, buying up and parcelling out ancient peasant holdings and selling them off at two hundred per cent profit.

If Palme's work is to be believed, the national interests meant nothing at all to the elder Sten Sture. It was not in the kingdom's interest he was working, but in his own. Palme gives him a place in a rogue's gallery 'of the great popular seducers in our history'.

On the other hand it is obvious to me that Sten Sture enjoyed the commons' confidence, and that it was here, throughout his long reign, that his régime found its abiding support. If, according to Palme, he did not deserve it, but had come by it by demagogy and guile, why – I cannot help asking myself – didn't the people in the course of twenty years see through his blandishments? As far as I can see, it was under the first of their line that the Stures became popular with the commons, a popularity from which his two successors benefited and which lasted far into the 16th century. There must have been some reason for this. As I look for patterns of cause and effect in Swedish history, I cannot help believing there must have been some connection between the first Sture's regency and his clan's abiding reputation with the commons.

One comes closest to the truth, I think, if one describes Sten Sture the Elder as a master of *realpolitik*, with all that this implies of opportunism and time-serving mingled with ruthlessness. Circumstances, he found, altered cases. 'Probably he thought he could best promote the interests of the land and realm', opines Gottfrid Carlson, 'by serving his own'. This is no unique faith among those who yield power. 'Politics is the art of the possible', declared Bismarck. One great and popular 20th-century Swedish statesman, Per Albin Hansson, has agreed with him. Five centuries earlier than our social-democratic prime minister, Herr Sten seems to have reached the same insight – *pari passu* – as he.

Constantly in conflict with his Council of State and other powerful nobles, Herr Sten managed to remain regent for a period of twenty-seven years.

In 1497, however, the Council finally evicted him from office. He was defeated by the Unionist King Hans of Denmark, who the same year made his entry into Stockholm and was there crowned king, his son Christian being simultaneously crowned heir apparent to the Swedish throne – a coronation which was to have fateful consequences two decades later.

After a few years Herr Sten again succeeded in becoming regent. But already in 1503 he departed this life. His death is associated with some curious circumstances which speak volumes about the political state of affairs prevailing in the Sweden of those days. The succession was secured by a bold coup. It is an occurrence from the Swedish Middle Ages that could have been taken from the pages of *The Three Musketeers*.

For a long while King Hans's queen, Kristina, had been courageously defending Stockholm against the Sture party. When the capital finally fell, she was taken prisoner. By and by Sten Sture released her and personally accompanied that great lady on her journey southwards to the Danish frontier. On his way back he suddenly fell dangerously ill.

Immediately, poison – an all too normal cause of sudden death in fashionable circles during the Renaissance – was suspected, the Danish queen's physician being regarded as the culprit. But other suspicions fell on Svante Nilsson's betrothed, a certain Fru Märta, who, it was assumed, had wished to get the regent out of the way in favour of her husband to be, a member of the Sture family. If nothing else, these rumours and suspicions are an index of the confidence placed in one another by the rivals for power.

As he journeyed northwards towards Stockholm the regent grew weaker and had to halt at Jönköping. And there, on December 13, 1503, the first of the Stures died. He was about sixty – his exact age is not known – but still in the prime of life. His death was wholly unexpected.

By its very suddenness it created an extremely serious situation for the Sture party. No one seemed to be left in Sweden to stand in the path of King Hans. who now had an excellent opportunity to make a comeback.

It is at this juncture that Hemming Gadh, one of the most remarkable Swedes of the Later Middle Ages, appears. He was one of the regent's attendants. For twenty years he had been Herr Sten's ambassador in Rome, and thereafter, with the regent's support, had been elected to the Linköping see. Here was another military prelate, who knew as well how to wield a soldier's sword as the sword of the spirit; a reincarnation, it seemed, of Jöns Bengtsson Oxenstierna, who had also lived as intensively in the material world as in the immaterial. To all three Stures Hemming Gadh became an influential adviser, and in this capacity probably contributed more to Swedish history than has ever been appreciated. One of the most virulent anti-Danish partisans of the Sture epoch, he was afterwards imprisoned in Denmark, in company with Gustav Eriksson (the future Gustav Vasa), by Christian II but afterwards went over to the Union king, who rewarded him by cutting his head off. This Swedish nationalist who became a traitor is an enigmatic personality. We shall meet him again in due course.

Doctor Hemming, as he was called, was Herr Sten's faithful friend and supporter, and at his master's sudden demise proved himself to be the man to avert the perils of the situation that had arisen in Jönköping.

What was to be done? Obviously, the regent's death had to be concealed from the Danes and from the Union party. So to gain time and give the Sture party a breathing space in which they could arrange for the election of a successor, the regent's corpse, too, had to be concealed. Doctor Hemming exacted a strict oath of secrecy from all in the dead regent's party who knew what had occurred. After which – it was the depth of winter – Herr Sten's corpse, wrapped and covered in 'a multitude of skins' was laid on a sledge. But Gadh realised, too, that the party could not arrive in the capital without a living regent. Therefore a double had to be found. As it happened, the dead man had a faithful old servant, Lasse Birgersson, Deeply devoted to his master, he also by great good fortune strongly resembled him.

Wearing the deceased's clothes, rings and chain of chivalry,

Lasse Birgersson was placed on his easily recognizable horse. Since there was nevertheless a risk of detection whenever the party halted, the double's eyes were blindfolded, on the pretext that some eye-trouble from which Herr Sten had long been suffering had taken a turn for the worse, and with it his eyesight, so that he was unable to recognize people. All who desired speech with the regent en route were referred to Doctor Hemming Gadh, who had been given plenary powers during his master's unfortunate illness.

In this way the unique funeral procession wound its way to Stockholm with one regent, dead, under a heap of hides, and a living one, blindfolded and on horseback. Since the company was travelling by sleigh, the journey was necessarily a slow one; and Doctor Hemming sent on outriders ahead to Stockholm to inform Svante Nilsson that Sweden temporarily lacked a regent. In this way Svante gained a breathing space in which to summon his supporters to the capital.

On the company's arrival with Herr Sten's corpse an assembly was summoned. Before it met, it was announced that the old regent had suddenly died. Whereupon a successor was elected. Not unexpectedly, he turned out to be Herr Svante Nilsson, who at once began to busy himself with consolidating his own position, immediately occupying Stockholm Castle and other major fortresses throughout the realm.

This political coup, which would make an exhilarating chapter in any adventure story, took place in Stockholm in December, 1503. The man behind it had been the most learned Doctor Hemming Gadh. For two decades he had lived in Rome, no doubt learning such lessons from Pope Alexander VI Borgia's and Machiavelli's Renaissance Italy as were now to come in very handy.

If I have given a brief account of these events it is because they are so typical of that age; a tangible example of events taking a decisive turn as a result of a clever utilization of circumstance. Power was transferred in a fashion which was made to appear wholly fortuitous. Yet events could have turned out quite differently. Power could have gone to some quite different person. It seems to me I have rarely come across any historical event of which I can say with conviction that it happened as it necessarily had to, or that things could not have turned out otherwise. Historiographers may one day discover a law which governs events. Such insight is altogether beyond a layman. To me history seems often both irrational and unpredictable, which is precisely why I find it so fascinating and am consumed with curiosity about it. If history were fated, or followed eternal laws, or were predictable or automatic, I should lose all taste for it.

Number Two

Svante Nilsson is less well-known than the other Stures, and less space has been devoted to him in our history books. He came from another branch of the family than his predecessor, and in his own lifetime is said never to have used the Sture name. At one time an adherent of the Union party, who had been attached to King Hans, he had afterwards gone over to Herr Sten and the Swedish party.

The second Sture does not seem to have been a colourful figure. Compared with his predecessor he makes a faded impression as regent. Nor was it easy for him to assume office. The legacy of the first Sture – the everlasting war against the Danes – was burdensome, and in 1503 the Swedes looked as though they were likely to lose it. The people whom he now had to govern had every reason to ask whether it was ever going to end. The Union dispute was originally to have been decided by force of arms; but almost a century had now gone by and the method had proved fruitless.

In the southern border provinces people were so weary of the war that the peasants were concluding their own peace treaties, as we shall see in my next chapter. In this part of the country the inhabitants were refusing to bear arms against the populations of Blekinge and Skåne, in a solemn letter even going so far, on one occasion, as to inform Svante Nilsson to that effect. What did the regent do about these traitorous subjects? As far as we know, nothing. It was beyond his power.

Such things could happen during that part of the Middle Ages when separatism flourished among the Swedish provinces. The commons were going through one of their active periods, asserting their own independence through the provincial assemblies. When the popular assemblies made difficulties and declined to support the levies against Denmark, the central authorities' military resources were insufficient to exact obedience.

Unable to raise the troops he needed within Sweden, Svante Sture recruited German cavalry and infantry. For we are in the great age of the legionaries, and Herr Svante appears to have been the first national regent to have called in Germans. It is true, they had earlier been employed by King Albrekt; but then, he was a German himself. In recruiting foreign armies the regent was a forerunner of Gustav Vasa, whose national Swedish state could never have been founded without German aid. These professional military men, who killed for pay, came to be hated and detested all over the country for their unruly behaviour and outrages against the population. Whenever their pay was not forthcoming, they plundered the villages. All this foreign soldiery was but one more stone added to the burdens borne by the commons. Since the King of Denmark, too, employed German legionaries, Germans went abroad to kill other Germans on Swedish soil in a war between Swedes and Danes. No better illustration could be found of this utter meaninglessness of the Union wars.

In Svante Sture's time Kalmar, the key to the realm of Sweden on the south-eastern coast and regarded as Scandinavia's strongest fortress, virtually impregnable, was the great bone of contention. At this time Kalmar Castle was being held by the Danes, who defended it against Swedish besiegers for six years, 1503–1509. The commander-in-chief of the besieging army was Doctor Hemming Gadh, now a bishop. He had military capacity but no diocese, the Pope having refused to ratify his appointment to the see of Linköping. Although a man in the autumn of his years – he was sixty – Gadh was more disposed to warfare and affairs of state than episcopal matters. Unquestionably he was adept at the art of siege warfare. Though his attempts to capture Kalmar Castle were not successful, he did the Danes much damage there.

Generally speaking, the second of the Stures tried to continue the policies of his forerunner. In his attempts to play off the commons against the powerful lords of the Council he was less successful than Sten Sture the Elder. Chiefly this was because of the Union war. The Danes had allied themselves with the Hanseatic League. All-puissant in Scandinavian commerce, the League blockaded Swedish harbours, and prevented all salt imports. To the population salt, which was basic to the preservation of meat, butter and fish, was indispensable. Everything else necessary to human life a peasant household could provide for itself. Only salt had to be brought from overseas. It is impossible to exaggerate the crucial importance of salt to the economy in those days. Christian II knew what he was doing in 1520 when, wishing to regain his hereditary Swedish dominions, he gained the goodwill of the peasantry of certain Småland hundreds by giving a bushel – or in some instances a gallon – of salt to each homestead.

This salt shortage, threatening the population with starvation and cunningly exploited by Herr Svante's opponents, became one of his greatest problems of domestic policy. In foreign affairs he achieved ultimate success by signing a treaty with Russia and putting an end to the disturbances along the eastern frontier. But the state of war with Denmark persisted, and as long as he remained regent became the norm.

Svante Sture's régime, however, only lasted eight years (1504–1512) and ended with his death, which was as unexpected as his predecessor's.

A rich silver mine had just been discovered in the Sala district in Bergslagen, and the Västmanland miners had been summoned to a meeting at Västerås to discuss whether the new find might not be of great benefit to the realm. At their assembly on January 2, 1512, the regent was present. But during the meeting 'he fell straitway down and was dead', probably from a stroke. For a few days his death, too, was kept secret, while preparations were being made for the election of his son. To some extent the events which had followed the death of the first Sture at Jönköping were repeated after the death of the second at Västerås.

Number Three

Sten Sture the Younger is a more interesting personage than his father. With him a notably gifted ruler enters the stage. Our older historians have acclaimed him as one of Sweden's greatest heroes, one of the standard-bearers of its liberties; one of those whom the poet acclaims as

> ... noble shades, revered fathers,
> Sweden's heroes and knightly men*

Geijer calls him the 'most noble and chivalrous of the Stures', and *The Last Knight* is the title of Strindberg's play about him. This pride of place derives from the circumstance of his falling in battle, still a young man, at Lake Åsunden, a classical death for any hero.

Sten Sture's chivalrous career had begun at a remarkably early age. At the coronation of King Hans in St Nicholas Church, Stockholm, he had been dubbed a knight at the age of four. The peace treaty between the Swedes and the Union monarch, namely, contained a paragraph under which a certain number of Swedes were to be knighted. Sten Sture's father, Svante Nilsson, who had had a hand in Hans becoming King of Sweden, was one of those to be knighted – so it was only natural that the son, too, should benefit from the king's gracious pleasure. For twenty-seven long years the Swedish throne had lacked an occupant, and the Swedes, for lack of a king, had had no one who could elevate them to the order of knighthood. Naturally, many admirable and highly deserving Swedes had suffered from this long period of kingless government, and had found it a grave shortcoming that they could not be knighted. Now, after so long a period of deprivation and vacuity, they grasped their opportunity. Vanity, that timeless attribute of the human race, was at long last to be gratified.

The sources inform us that many aristocratic ladies, too, were eager for their husbands to become knights. Feminine vanity on a husband's behalf was not peculiar to 15th-century Sweden – even today any Swedish wife whose husband can sport an order on his chest can count on honorable placement at the royal dinner table, and no year goes by without birthday honours in the form of 6,000 orders to Swedish men and women being handed out; a tradition

* Poem by J. H. Kellgren (1751–1795).

going back to our mediaeval coronations, of which one of the most notable was this coronation in 1497. We Swedes need kings for our own vainglory. The need is as immemorial as it is inextirpable.

Concerning the knighting of Sten Sture at the 1497 coronation, Fabian Månsson writes: 'But no knightly dubbing caused so much annoyance as the sight of a four-year-old child being led forward to stammer out his oath of chivalry. The commons, however, laughed at it, and sung ditties, the gist of which was that aristocratic females were crying out to be dubbed knights, inasmuch as they had boy-babies growing in their bellies.'

Svante Nilsson's little son must have been about half as tall as the sword which dubbed him. Whether the four-year-old comprehended anything at all of the important oath he then swore may also be doubted. But in his early years he is supposed to have played with swords and trained himself in warlike arts. For these, during his brief lifetime, he was to find ample use.

At the time of his father's demise Sten Sture the Younger can hardly have reached the age of twenty – his exact date of birth is not certainly known. But he was already married to the 17-year-old Kristina Gyllenstierna, one of the few Swedish women to find a place in our mediaeval history. Sten Sture was a mature, even precocious youth, who knew what he wanted; and that was to succeed his father as the first man in the country. From the outset he showed the will and power for action, not to say the ruthlessness, of a man of ambition. Now he made haste to steal a march on his rivals for the regency.

His father had not used the Sture name, but the younger man, obviously well aware of the weight it carried with the commons, immediately assumed it. In all haste he took over the castles and fortresses commanded by his father's bailiffs and made them his own. Having done this, he travelled round the realm to win the favours of the lower orders on the eve of the election of a new regent. In a word, the third Sture, like the leaders of our modern political parties on the eve of a parliamentary election, went canvassing. In their assemblies, outside their parish churches, in their market places, he spoke to the assembled commons, caused manifestations to be read out, putting the fear of the Dane into them likewise a fear of traitors within the Council of State and the nobility. In short, he spared no efforts to convince the populace that there was only one man fit to defend their liberties and their welfare, namely himself.

The magnates fought young Herr Sten 'with life and power' (*med liv och makt*). Few members of the Council wished to see Svante Nilsson's son succeed him. 'For the council of the realm rarely had the same wishes as the clergy, miners and peasants', writes Fabian Månsson.

But the lords of the Council, for once, did not get their own way. With most of Sweden's fortresses in his hands and a 'benevolent commons' on his side, the younger Sture was altogether too strong for his adversaries. In July, 1512, the Council had to accept him as regent.

But once in power, he fell foul of the Church, a fateful dispute which he tried to resolve by force of arms. Against Archbishop Gustav Trolle, the representative of the Holy See in Sweden, he committed an act of violence which was to have important consequences.

Professor Gottfrid Carlsson has revised the fair image of the 'last of the knights' painted by tradition, and condemns his action against the archbishop. As he sees the matter, Sture's destruction of the archbishop's residence at Stäket near Uppsala and the capture of its occupant was an action almost beyond condoning. Sten Stures' men not only mishandled Gustav Trolle's servants but also the primate himself. As that age saw these things, such an outrage might have been regarded as the most banal of political arguments. But it should also be mentioned that the decision to commit it had been taken at a parliamentary meeting in Stockholm, in 1517.

This dramatic conflict between Sten Sture the Younger and Gustav Trolle was to be bloodily resolved by the infamous Stockholm Bloodbath of November 1520. Our annalists have regarded the regent as the noble hero of the drama and the archbishop as a despicable and treacherous, not to say diabolical, figure, 'the Judas Iscariot of Swedish history'. If Trolle was the instigator of the Stockholm Bloodbath – a point on which historians disagree sharply – he certainly must be regarded as a scoundrel of the first order. Unquestionably he was a hard-hearted man. But after the gross injustice which the Sture party had inflicted on him one can understand his thirst for revenge.

For his attack on the archbishop, Sten Sture was excommunicated by the Pope. In practical politics he had set in motion the schism with Rome which Gustav Vasa was to complete.

The chivalrous young Sture shows a less agreeable face to research when one considers his behaviour toward his stepmother Märta Ivarsdotter, widow of Svante Nilsson. From extant letters it transpires that he stripped her 'without mercy of the entailed estates and fiefs which the regent had given her, and which were her only means of subsistence.'

In the days when I was an admirer of warrior kings and Indian chieftains, 'the last of the knights', too, was one of my boyhood idols. In his *Song of Athens*, Viktor Rydberg* had represented to me what a glorious death would be mine if I fell 'fighting for your land, for your fatherland'. And I was deeply moved by the same exhortation, placed by another poet in the mouth of the young Sture as he parades his peasant army before the Battle of Duvnäs Forest:

Ye honest Dalesmen,
break shields and helmets asunder;
we fear no men . . .

That was the way! That was how brave men should act! And who could scorn death more completely than young Herr Sten? As a hero he has been immortalized by Edvard Bäckström in his ballad in the play *The Prisoner of Kalö* from the late romantic period of the 19th century, when the heroic poetry practised mainly by writers who had proved unfit for military service was still in flower. The first time I remember hearing this ballad sung was by a fine singer around the year 1910, at a volunteer riflemen's celebration. The last verse, more especially, about the hero's death on a sledge on the Mälaren ice, sent thrills of emotion up and down my youthful spine:

When fallen he lay on his bier
And the snowflakes played in his wounds,
Mildly he looked on his own:

* Swedish poet 1828–1895.

'Why pale, ye men, at death?
Fresh courage! when greatest your need
Then God will find his man'.

National romanticism needed to acclaim masters of the craft of war. And in young Sture it made a find. His victories over the Danes at Brännkyrka and Duvnäs revealed his military capacities. He must have been the most consummate Swedish military commander of his day. And Doctor Hemming Gadh supported him in word and deed. Of Herr Sten's courage there can be no doubt. No one knows how the battle on Lake Åsunden might have turned out had he not been wounded at the outset – 'a hand's breadth above the knee' – and had to be carried from the battlefield. The Swedes might well have been victorious. Usually soldiers survive a bullet in the leg, and one wonders what went wrong with his wound. But the art of medicine, as exercised by the surgeon-barbers of those days, was extremely primitive. During his return to Stockholm the wound was probably not looked after properly and infection must have set in. The third Sture died of blood-poisoning.

Some of our chroniclers see in Sten Sture the Younger a statesman. His ambition was probably boundless. We have evidence that in his last years he even aspired to the kingship. Presumably he regarded his victories over the Danes as having amply earned him the crown of Sweden; and indeed no one can begrudge him his ambition. There is much evidence that he had made himself popular among the commons, and doubtless they would have been glad to see him on the throne as King Sten Sture I. Still in the full flush of his youth, only three or four years older than Gustav Eriksson Vasa, he seemed to have the greater part of his life before him.

But a Danish bullet put paid to the twenty-seven-year-old regent's career. We may speculate as to what would have happened in Sweden had he continued to govern it. In liberating the country from the Union and crushing the power of the Church, if not in other respects, Gustav Vasa carried out the young Sture's policies. Nor was Gustav's personality cast in the same mould as his predecessor's. In my view there is a discernible and crucial difference between these two men. Sten Sture was more a man of the people. Gustav was – or afterwards mostly became – the ally of the aristocracy. Nor did the young regent ever have to combat any peasant risings against his régime. Gustav, by contrast, had to suppress five great popular revolts; and to do it accepted the help of the nobility.

What sort of reign might have been King Sten's? So often history seems the sport of chance. It is my belief that if that bullet at Åsunden had had another trajectory or spared the young regent's life, our history from 1520 onwards would have been quite different.

According to Olaus Petri, when King Hans had occupied Stockholm Castle, in 1497, he said to his defeated opponent Sten Sture the Elder; 'Ye have made an evil testament in Sweden, inasmuch as ye have made the peasants, whom God hath created slaves, into masters; and those who should be lords ye have made slaves.'

An effective line for a play. But who can believe there is a word of truth in it? Who can suppose that, in the 1490's, the peasantry of Sweden were the real lords of the realm or were trying to enslave its upper classes? What this remark – if it was ever really made – certainly expresses, concisely and to the point, is the feudal view of a peasant. The king was also indicating the difference between the status of the Swedish commons and of the Danish. The Swedish peasantry enjoyed a considerably greater measure of freedom than their Danish brethren, who lived in a state of feudal servitude which was a relic of their ancient thraldom.

Historians differ widely in their view of the Swedish commons' status during the Sture period. Without summarizing all their views, let me touch on the more extreme. I leave it to my reader to form his own intermediate view. My own will transpire presently.

In a major modern work by E. Ingers, the peasantry under the Stures are made out to have almost become a ruling class. Ingers thinks that, by and large, the Stures realized the programme summed up in the words 'a well-disposed commons'. Ingers heads his chapter on the Sture epoch 'The Great Age of the Swedish Commons'. According to him, all three Stures were concerned with the interests and welfare of the common people, and their policies satisfied its demands. They associated on a familiar and equal footing with the common man, and listened to what he had to say. This work makes out that for the Swedes the Sture epoch was a golden age. After their national state had come into being they bitterly regretted the change, and always hankered after its return.

The state of affairs during this allegedly great age of the commons finds expression in a mural, dated 1482, one among the many which cover the walls and vaults of our Uppland churches. On either side of the arms of Sweden stand a knight and a peasant, together holding up the shield. The knight is wearing his steel helmet; the peasant has taken off his soft round hat and supports the shield on his shoulder. All classes of society are united in striving for the common good. A piece of pictorial propaganda, it is slanted in the same way as the words of the *Sture Chronicles*.

Fabian Månsson,* who had a profounder knowledge of the Sture and early Vasa epochs than any of his contemporaries, was of the opposite opinion. He takes quite a different view of their history. Altogether he wrote six volumes on the subject, 2,640 pages of print. None of our other historians have devoted so much time, so much energy or so many pages of manuscript to this era. Having several times re-read his six books, I am sure no living historian knows more about this subject than Fabian Månsson did. Not, of course, that I uncritically accept all his conclusions.

Though I knew Fabian Månsson personally, our meeting did not take place until 1937–1938, the last year of his life. By then he was a sick and weary man, who knew his days were numbered. By the year of his death, 1938, five of his six historical works had been published. Two parts of his great work on Gustav Vasa and Nils Dacke were already in print, and the third, unfinished, came out in 1948, ten years after his death. He knew very well his remaining strength would not suffice to carry through this demanding work in the short time he had left. I remember how tired his voice sounded, as he said: 'So much work still needs to be done on this period. I can only hope that younger men will come after me to continue my research.'

Fabian Månsson was the son of a poor fisherman and small farmer in the south of Sweden. He was a historian of the people, who

* Fabian Månsson (1872-1938), member of the Swedish Parliament from 1912 to his death, was one of the pioneers of the Swedish labour movement, famous as an orator and for his remarkable achievements as a writer of history.

wrote about the people, for the people – an original blend of historical science and imaginative literature. His works are as stuffed with dialogue as a historical novel; but they also contain great quantities of historical facts, which the author's endless energy and patience has assembled from innumerable sources. Since Fabian did his own research and went direct to the original sources, he is usually to be relied on. Passionately addicted to documented truth, he had a highly developed historical sense. But in the end he had collected so much material that it overwhelmed him. His books overflow with a wealth of detail, are therefore difficult to survey and, as epics, burst at the seams. Fabian Månsson was no master of the art of self-limitation. And this is why his history of the Sture and early Vasa epoch did not gain the popularity it deserved.

Yet no professional Swedish historian, in my opinion, can match his insight into the past, nor his ability to recreate long-vanished times and environments. He had a sixth sense for people's way of seeing their own existence and for the conditions under which they had lived. No one else has given us so graphic or lively a picture, couched in such pithy and powerful language, of the dramatic transition from the Middle Ages to that later epoch to which the Stures and Gustav Vasa have lent their names.

Fabian Månsson's trilogy *Sancte Eriks gård* (Saint Erik's Estate) treats of social and political developments in Sweden between the Engelbrekt rising and the end of the Sture period. The estate in question is none other than Stäket, the archbishop's residence, which Sten Sture the Younger, in 1517, demolished into a heap of ruins and rubble. Månsson's great work has an eloquent sub-title: *The birth pangs of national unity*. Simple and congenial, it exactly fits the contents. Only after an enormously difficult and protracted parturition did the national state of Sweden come into being. This process, so infinitely costly and painful to the Swedish people, took a hundred years. Much blood was shed in its course. And it was the common man, above all the peasant, the tiller of the soil who had to bear these birth pangs and torments, all the miseries of that age when Swedes were becoming one nation.

When at long last it was born, however, the child turned out to be a monarchy, an administrative apparatus which mostly stifled the little freedom and independence as the commons had hitherto enjoyed.

For Fabian Månsson the Sture epoch was far from being the great age of the commons. Rather it was a time of endless trials and tribulations. His thesis is that the great families tried – and indeed often managed – to involve the various provinces' peasantry in their own internecine quarrels, ensnaring the lower classes of the population into a conflict in whose outcome they had no stake whatever. No matter which side won, their lot remained the same. In Fabian Månsson's view, even the three Stures exploited the commons in precisely the same fashion as all the other aristocratic parties, using them as tools for their own power politics. Apart from the Stures, the next most important factor was the Council of State, which was made up of the leading men of the high nobility and the Church. Their cultural attainments have already been limned: several of these lords of the council could neither read nor write.

The historian also attributes the Union wars, the greatest popular burden of all, to the crassly egoistic policies of the upper classes. If one group of magnates wished to preserve the Union, it was merely because they thought it lay in their own private interests. Owning estates in all three Scandinavian countries they could best administer them if the north was at peace. The Sture party, on the other hand, the nationalist nobles, did not want to be subordinate to any Union king. They were opposed to the Union because they desired a free hand to rule their own country as they saw fit. If the commons, the peasantry, all the lower classes of society, were in favour of retaining the Union, it was because they wanted *peace*.

At one point Fabian Månsson defines their motives:

'The peasants thought they would gain greater advantage from the Union, from peace and quiet, than from the endless vendettas and arson which occurred in times of war. This was why, from generation to generation, they sat still and, in their hearts, tacitly acclaimed the Union.'

Both these sentences, in my view, express the basic desires and longings of the Swedish people during the Late Middle Ages. Not that the Swedes were the only people who had to go through the 'birthpangs of national unity' during this epoch. Developments in Sweden must be viewed against the dramatic revolution then taking place everywhere in Europe, a revolution characterized by the dissolution of feudalism and the growth of powerful monarchies. The new rulers who sat on the thrones of Europe were despots. It was a process which, when it reached Sweden in the first decades of the 16th century and was finally implemented by Gustav Vasa, had long been going on in other lands.

Only one continental people had succeeded in defending themselves againt the Hapsburg's armies of mounted knights: the inhabitants of Alpine Switzerland. In their free peasant republic, founded by the Oath of 1291, popular liberties had been preserved; but only by arming the entire population. Fabian Månsson strongly underlines the incontrovertible fact that it had only been by force of arms that the Swiss had escaped princely oppression and serfdom. A historic personage, Didrik Petri, rector of Söderåkra, is obviously the author's own mouthpiece when he declares:

'Only by arming all the commons can a good society be founded. The Swiss Republic shows us that'.

On the other hand, when Didrik Petri goes on to explain the miseries of the Swedish commons as the consequence of their having 'left themselves undefended' he can hardly be a mouthpiece for the author. Fabian Månsson knew very well that the Swedish peasantry, as a whole, had never been disarmed. The many attempts to deprive them of their weapons had only met with temporary and partial success. They had always retained their hunting weapons; and these they also used in war. Furthermore, these arms were home-made; if forced to hand over their crossbows, they immediately made themselves new ones.

The reference to the Swiss Confederation is crucial to Fabian Månsson's view of society and of history. His ideal society was a community of interests, a country of small peasants, subject to no superior state authority or bureaucracy, and one which placed no restrictions on personal freedom – a community which in reality was an ancient form of communism, with its roots in the early Christian Church, whose members had held all things in common.

Obviously his ideal society, with its freedom of the individual and its decentralized popular self-government – which he fancied he saw realised in mediaeval Switzerland – had little in common with the communist states of today.

In Sweden, events took quite another turn and, to my mind, a most regrettable one. The outcome of national unity and all its birthpangs was a royal despotism; a state in which, after Nils Dacke's insurrection, no further revolts were possible. The question of whether such a development was necessary – indeed the whole question of historical necessity – is worthy of close analysis. At this point I for one am assailed by grave doubts as to that mystical law of event known as 'historical necessity'.

On the whole I accept Fabian Månsson's version of the Sture and Vasa epochs. The essence of his interpretation cannot here be detailed in all its amplitude; but in all essentials it seems to hold water. On one point, however, I regard his conclusions as erroneous. His theory that the Stures, too, ruthlessly exploited the commons for power politics and for their own ends, is based on insufficient evidence. Their government, as no one can deny, was less severe and more popular than either that of their forerunner (Karl Knutsson) or of their successor (Gustav Vasa). Unless this is conceded, how explain the Stures' popularity with the commons, to which so many sources bear witness? Some writers represent the Stures as demagogues, seducers of the commons. Is it not strange that the people, thus seduced, should have given them its confidence, and that in certain provinces they were even loved? Surely, in the course of fifty years, it would have occurred to the common man that he had been thoroughly duped and exploited by these three regents – if he really had? Would it not have resulted in an insurrection? Yet, there was no insurrection against them, as far as we know. Why not? The question remains unanswered.

Viewing our history integrally down the centuries, the following can be said: Compared with the two centuries immediately preceding – the two hundred years which had passed since a class society had first come into being in the 13th century – the Sture period, for the Swedish people, represented an improvement. By and large the first Sture, unlike his two successors, succeeded in his pacific policies. And what the common people wanted more than anything else was peace: 'Thus, from generation to generation, they sat still, and in their hearts tacitly acclaimed the Union.'

This movement of the popular mind is the subject of my next chapter.

A Warrior People's Dream of Peace

In his history of the Nordic peoples Olaus Magnas describes the 'terrible struggles' which they had 'ever been obliged to fight'. In words and images he depicts their wars on land, at sea, in valleys and on the hills, in forests and in the fields, in the mountains and on frozen lakes, in every conceivable theatre of war. 'From the very outset hath wars and disturbances ever been on the increase and, sobeit God interveneth not, will never cease in this world, as long as man's nature remaineth that which it now is.'

More than four centuries have passed since these words were written; but as yet, as everyone knows, there has been no sign of any divine intervention.

Olaus Magnus calls the Scandinavian kingdoms the 'abode of the war god'. The Swedes, more especially, had gained a steady European reputation for their bellicosity, a reputation which reached its climax in the 17th century, when Sweden became a great power and Swedes were fighting on most European battlefields. In his letters and despatches, Pierre Chanut, the French ambassador to the court of Queen Christina, describes the Swedes as a notably warlike people. They cannot live without wars, he writes. Without wars Sweden, within a few years, would again become a poor country: 'Sweden needs to keep her people on the move and not let them rest.' When the Peace of Westphalia is signed, in 1648, Chanut is dubious whether this lack of a war will really be to Sweden's advantage.

To me the century when Sweden was a great European power seems to have been our most unhappy and miserable in modern times. Pierre Chanut, too, that clever diplomat, regarded Sweden's political grandeur as transient. 'It had been won with German soldiers and French money'. Concerning this remark, so shocking to all Swedes who may still today entertain fanciful notions of their own greatness, Professor Curt Weibull, in a recently published work, observes: 'Chanut might have added: together with able commanders and a carefully organized and implemented plunder of the countries in which the war was being waged.'

Today no one of unclouded judgment really believes that any people's predestined scene of activity on this earth is a battlefield. Presumably there have at all times been certain individuals born to be soldiers, who have only been able to realize their own destinies by killing their fellow men. But no one will ever convince me that whole nations have been made up of this particular species of brute. As for us Swedes, we have of course been just as well- or ill-suited, just as much or as little destined to warfare, as any other people.

In this history I have only dwelt on those of our wars which appear to have been major calamities. Historically, the Swedes were always regarded as a militant nation. Therefore I shall now devote some space to the pacific nature of this same people.

For six hundred years the inhabitants of what today are the five Swedish provinces of Västergötland, Småland, Halland, Skåne and Blekinge lived along a frontier which, to them, was nothing but a curse and a nuisance. This frontier is supposed to have first been drawn up in 1054. It remained in force, with brief intervals, until 1658. As long as it existed, the outbreak of each successive war between Sweden and Denmark turned the countryside on either side of it into a theatre of hostilities. From the wars of our own time in various parts of the world we know how tragic is the lot of border populations. In the past the men of Västergötland, Småland, Halland, Skåne and Blekinge were all subject to a similarly monstrous fate. The liberal 19th-century historian Fryxell sums it up in a single sentence of his Swedish history. In the end, he says, the poor people along the frontier hid themselves in the depths of the forests, 'in their hearts cursing both Swedes and Danes.'

An original source, witnessing to the manner in which the frontier between Sweden and Denmark was drawn up in 1054, is to be found in the Older Västergötland Law, where we are told that this demarcation of the two kingdoms was done by the King of the Svear,

Emund Slemme, in Uppsala, and by Sven Tjugoskägg ('Twenty Beard') of the Danes, a monarch who is thought to be identical with Sven Estridsson. From the point of junction between Västergötland and Halland in the north, to Brömsebro, on the Blekinge coast in the south, the kings, accompanied by twelve men from either kingdom, erected six frontier stones. Professor Gerhard Hafström has published a remarkable study of the old boundary: in 1934, almost nine hundred years after it had first been erected, he excavated the sixth and last frontier stone at Brömsebro. Today it is protected as a historical monument the local people are proud to show off to visitors. The probable sites of the other stones were also discovered by the same historian.

The *Rhymed Chronicle* immortalizes this event of 1054:

> Twixt Sweden and Denmark these XII men
> Six stones set up, and [they] stand there yet.

Long stretches of the frontier were utterly unnatural. They took no account whatever of the countryside as such, nor of the habitations of those who lived in it. Usually the boundary coincides with lakes and rivers, but in the great forests it is simply the shortest line between two points. In places this frontier between the two realms bisected villages and separated adjacent farms, thereby also separating members of the same family and clan.

Yet no frontier stones could expunge what they had in common, or the friendships existing between their clans and families. They were, and remained, close relatives. Against their will the authorities had drawn up a frontier which they had never desired; and they continued to associate in despite of it. As before, they intermarried, they traded, they bought and sold cattle, bartered services and commodities. In the countryside along the frontier the community of interests remained undisturbed. The border folk needed each other.

Though formally either Swedes or Danes, these were extraneous labels, arbitrarily imposed from without. In their own view of themselves the border folk seem to have remained the same people as they had always been down the centuries, down the millennia. It was quite simply impossible, all of a sudden, to expunge so immemorial a community of interests. The Smålanders had more in common with the Skånians and men of Blekinge than they had with such remote peoples as the Upplanders or Dalesmen.

But the outbreak of each new war turned the border peasantry into enemies. Nothing seems more natural than that they should have opposed such a forcible transformation, nothing more humanly explicable than their reluctance to go over the border and kill their relatives, friends and neighbours. All the border folk desired was to be left in peace and quiet. What advantage could they derive from troubling their neighbours?

In one of my novels (*Förräddarland* 1967) I have written of the commons' predicament along the border in wartime. The action takes place in my own part of the country, on the frontiers of Blekinge and Småland. For many years before I began to write that book I had been preoccupied with this motif, so deeply embedded in the lives of my ancestors and preserved orally in popular tradition. And in my description of the separate peace signed by the peasantry along the frontier in 1522 I drew on material of which I shall now give an account.

These frontiersmen, in my opinion, are among those whom history has overlooked. Little mention is made, in our academic histories, of their separate peace treaties. Nor have I been able to find more than a single study of the subject, an essay by Professor Folke Lindberg in *The Swedish Historical Review* 1928. It has been my main source of information.

This paucity of source materials is explicable. These treaties among the peasantry, being unsanctioned by the central authorities, were not included among official documents. But two documents of importance have nevertheless been preserved for posterity. They relate to the peaces contracted on the border in 1505 and 1525.

Though historians describe these separatist treaties comprehensively as 'peasant peaces' (*bondefreder*) the word is somewhat adventitious, inasmuch as in a number of instances they were signed by both nobles and burghers, and sometimes drawn up by parish priests. The size and kind of the contracting parties, too, varied widely. Treaties of peace were concluded between whole provinces, between hundreds and even between parishes. These last, of course, were strictly local affairs. Usually they have left no documentary trace; may even have been purely oral, in which case they have left posterity in the dark.

As early as the 11th century we know of separate peace treaties being signed between Scandinavian provinces in time of war. The phenomenon is referred to in the history of Snorre. King Olof Skötkonung of Sweden was waging war against St Olaf of Norway, but Ragvald Jarl, on behalf of the Västergötlanders, concluded his own peace with the Norwegians. The king at Uppsala may have disapproved of the Västergötland peasantry's high-handed action, but without the salt they imported from Norway they could not live, and in such straits the province had simply been obliged to sue for peace. Again, during the war of 1381 between Sweden and Denmark, the province of Skåne, independently of Denmark, signed a separate peace with the Swedes. As we have seen, this happened again in 1434 and 1436, when they concluded an armistice with Engelbrekt without asking King Erik of Pomerania's permission. The declaration of neutrality by the five Värend hundreds during the Danish invasion of 1520 was of the same order.

But the great age of peasant peace treaties was the two last decades of the Middle Ages, 1505–1525, a time when Sweden and Denmark were almost continuously at war. Half a score of peace treaties between the frontiersmen are known to history from this time, and two are documented beyond all doubt in extant texts.

Most of these peace treaties were concluded between the Smålanders and the men of Blekinge, who were dependent on their mutual trade across the frontier. The Smålanders could not do without the salt, herring and spices which came from Ronneby, and the men of Blekinge needed meat and butter from the cattle-raising district of Värend. 'The oxen were the peacemakers', is an old popular saying from the borderlands. Gentle and pacific indeed is the ox.

In the history of these peasant peace treaties, Furs Bridge, across the Lyckeby River, a waterway which for six hundred years constituted the boundary between Sweden and Denmark, occupies a prominent position. At Fur, today a railway halt on the Karlskrona-Växjö line, the Lyckeby River crosses an immemorially ancient road leading to Ronneby in Blekinge. The pine forest grows dense along the river banks, whence the bridge's name (*furu*=pine). Down the centuries travellers have halted here to rest at an inn or tavern. In the Middle Ages, Furs Bridge was an important meeting place for the border folk, who assembled here to consult on their common affairs. Originally built of logs, it has been supplanted in our own day by a modern road bridge. But remains of the oaken timbers which used to support the span of the older bridge can still be discerned in the waters of the Lyckeby River.

This old bridge over the waterway which constituted the frontier was neutral territory and therefore a natural venue for meetings and peaceful negotiations. In these timbers which once formed part of the bridge and which five centuries have hardly sufficed to rot away completely, I read a genuine fragment of the history of the Swedish people. Questions of the welfare or otherwise of human beings, matters of life and death, have been decided on them. On Furs Bridge were concluded a number of parish treaties between Vissefjärda parish, on the Swedish side, and Fridlevstad on the Danish. For me these oaken timbers are original documents, the sort which historians call relics, and to which they assign a primary source-value. They are tangible evidence of past occurrences. In them the peace treaties concluded on this bridge come to life and bring me closer to history than any written document.

In 1505, war broke out again between the regent Svante Sture and King Hans of the Union. Once again the borderlands were exposed to all the horrors with which they were so familiar; to passages of men-at-arms and all that this implied of plunder and rapine, fire, devastation and death. But immediately the inhabitants on either side of the border sent representatives to a provincial assembly at Hjortsberga, in Blekinge, to avert this threat by mutual agreement. In August 1505 this meeting bore fruit in a peace treaty between Värend, Möre, Sunnerbo and Västbo hundreds, on the Swedish side, and the province of Blekinge and the Skånian hundred of Göinge, on the Danish. The treaty was put into writing, and its crucial points, modernized, read as follows:

'Notwithstanding that a state of war exists between the crowns of Sweden and Denmark, a state of unbroken peace shall be maintained as hitherto between the parties who are signatories to this treaty.

'The commons shall not follow their lords further than to the boundary of the realm.

'If the lords should prepare raids across the border, the people on that side which is threatened shall receive advance warning.

'Free trade and traffic shall prevail across the frontier, as hitherto.

'The parties shall together combat the bands of robbers in the forests along the border, and he who gives these criminals protection or assistance shall be branded a traitor.'

The treaty was confirmed by the Värend provincial assembly at Växjö, on August 15, 1505. A copy was sent to the regent Svante Sture and duly entered into his copy book, where the document has been preserved for posterity. Clearly and unmistakably it tells us how in times past the common people, on both sides of the border, made a mutual attempt to keep the peace.

Overtly and in writing the men of Skåne, Blekinge and Småland, in thus refusing to cross the border on a violent errand or under arms, had opted out of the war; had become deserters. On either side the signing of this agreement made them guilty of associating with the enemy in time of war. The most remarkable paragraph of all is that in which they undertake to give each other warning of impending attacks across the frontier. To warn the enemy – that is obviously treason, and the penalty for it is death. Even today, if Sweden should go to war, a special law can be brought into force to this effect.

We do not know how the regent reacted or whether he reacted at all. Any reply he may have despatched to the provincial assembly at Växjö has been lost. Probably he resigned himself to a state of affairs beyond his control. As we have already seen in considering his reign, he lacked the military resources to force a recalcitrant peasantry to take the field against the Danes. This being so, the provincial assembly was in a position so strong that the central authorities were no match for it. Nor is it likely that this separate peace treaty, signed at Hjortsberga in August 1505, came as a surprise to Svante Sture. It was by no means unique, as can clearly be seen from the commentary appended to the treaty, according to which the commons 'had made a pact between themselves, now as in the past'. This is a very important item of information: *their peace treaty was in accordance with ancient tradition.* So we have every reason to suppose that other treaties of a similar nature must have been concluded, even though they have left no trace in history.

The other extant document bears witness to a separate peace treaty, concluded between Värend and Blekinge, at Kolshult in Blekinge, on May 18, 1525, and confirmed by Hjortsberga provincial assembly on the 22nd of that month.

In the spring of 1525, the situation was as follows: With forces based on Gotland, the Danish Commander-in-Chief Sören Norrby was fighting energetically for King Christian II of the Union, whom still remained to be finally defeated. Now Norrby was on the point of invading Blekinge. But the men of Blekinge made haste to renew their ancient pact with the inhabitants on the other side of the border, and on St Erik's Day the two neighbouring peoples met at Kolshult. What occurred then is to be seen on a piece of parchment still extant in the Danish archives.

Lengthy quotations from historical documents are likely only to bring a yawn to my reader and cause him to skip my pages; so I refrain from them. But this old fragment of parchment from Kolshult bears such eloquent witness to the pacific nature of these Swedes, that it deserves to be reproduced without abbreviation.

Slightly modernized, it reads as follows:

'We, the common peasantry who build and live in the land of Blekinge, do by this our open letter make it known to all and sundry that in fifteen hundred and twenty-five after the birth of God, on Saint Erik's Day (May 18) we were assembled at Kolshult, together with our good friends who build and live in the land of Värend, concerning the bond and undertaking to which the countries long ago agreed and bound themselves, with letters duly sealed and signed. Now we do promise and aver upon our honour and manhood, that if (the which God forbid) any would anger or do hurt or dam to the land of Värend, then will we follow after to help and console you and stand manly by you to the utmost of our power, as good sworn men of the peasantry should do.

Item, dear friends, should it so be that any rascality or footloose men of the forest make so bold as to cause damage or hurt in the land of Blekinge and then enter your land, then do we request that ye shall capture and seize all such and send them to us. The same are we willing to do unto you, if any should force his way in to the land of Värend.

Item, when we receive sure tidings from you that any danger threatens, then will we come to your rescue and spare neither night nor day, and hope to God you will do the same again for us.

That thus it shall be, and on both sides be kept without breach, and that thus in truth it hath been decided: thereto append we our province's seal beneath this our open letter, written and given at Hjortsberga provincial assembly, Monday next after *Rogacionum for ascensionem Domini*, in this year which is written (May 22, 1525).'

The document, in the Danish archives, still bears the broken seal of the province of Blekinge.

This peace meeting was held on the feast of Erik the Holy, an important date in the peasants' calendar: if this saint granted ears of rye, another, Saint Olov, would grant them rye loaves. That year it fell on a Thursday, and the agreement was already ratified at Hjortsberga assembly on the following Monday. The danger was imminent, and people made haste to protect their own countryside. The document confirms their pacific traditions when it says that 'over a long time past' there had been treaties between the provinces in the form of 'good sealed letters', confirming them. Again we find the promise of mutual assistance 'to the utmost of our power' against all who intend 'hurt or damage' in the countryside. Special mention is made of individual men of violence; but most important of all is the paragraph stipulating messages concerning danger, 'then will we come to your rescue and spare neither night nor day'; a sentence which can only mean that the danger in question lay in Sören Norrby's advancing and pillaging legionaries.

This original document shows, incontrovertibly, how deeply the allied folk along the frontier detested these national wars.

How important to the kingdom as a whole was this provincial separatism, which found expression in these treaties of peace among the peasantry? Whether they had any effect on state policy is hard to say, though in certain instances they obviously bore political fruit. In 1523, a provincial peace treaty between Västergötland and the Skånian provinces obliged Gustav Vasa to cancel an invasion of Skåne.

In January of that year his two commanders, Lars Siggesson Sparre and Bernt von Melen, invaded Skåne in considerable strength. The campaign was 'carefully prepared and extremely costly'. At this time von Melen, a German, was Gustav Vasa's favourite. On his master's account he had enlisted 3,000 German men-at-arms. The rest of his army consisted of a forced levy of Swedish peasants. The attacking troops outnumbered the defenders of Skåne several times over.

Swedes and Germans crossed the Lagan River, the national boundary, but had not advanced very far into Skanian territory before the whole enterprise ground to a halt. After only six weeks in the field, Lars Siggesson and von Melen had to commence their withdrawal, and recrossed the frontier. Notwithstanding the great superiority of the invading army, the whole attempt to conquer Skåne became, from the outset, an inglorious failure.

Von Melen's post facto explanation of his military fiasco was that he had been frustrated by the early spring floods. Overflowing their banks, the rivers in Skåne had become so swollen, he claimed, that his soldiers had been unable to cross them. Actually, his men-at-arms had never even got as far as any Skanian river. They had halted at Markaryd, just inside the frontier. If his army had been able to cross the Lagan, which is broader than any other Skanian river, how can these lesser waters have presented so formidable an obstacle? Von Melen's explanation was nothing but an excuse, as even his contemporaries realised.

The real fate of the campaign transpires in a document still to be found in the archives of the Hanseatic League. It is a report dated February 11, 1523, from one of the League's observers in Sweden to the council at Stralsund. The German observer writes:

'Further, Gustav Eriksson, the leader in Sweden, possesseth upwards of a thousand cavalry, German and Danish, and he hath upwards of 3,000 men-at-arms and innumerable peasants. Further, that he wished this winter to invade Skåne with them and lay it waste by fire; but the peasants of Västergötland, which lieth nearby, would not follow [him], inasmuch as they are leagued with the peasants of Halland and Blekinge, on the Skanian border, so that the one peasant should not harm the other. When His Danish Majesty wished to invade Västergötland and Sweden, plunder and burn, then would the Skanian peasants not support him, but hindered and fought against the royal troops; the same would the Västergötland and Swedish peasants even abide by, according to their treaty.'

So it was not the flooded rivers, after all, which prevented Gustav Vasa from invading Skåne! What had put paid to the invasion was the peace treaty between the commons of the border provinces. On both sides of the frontier hordes of peasants sabotaged the campaign. The peasants of Västergötland refused to follow the German legionaries – what business could they have in Skåne? – and the Danish king's plan for an invasion of Västergötland, too, had to be called off: 'that would the Skanian peasants not support'.

In 1523, an ancient peace treaty between the peasantry on either side came into force and proved effective 'so that the one peasant should not harm the other'. Ten simple words which sum up the sense of these separatist peaces.

'So at all events we have no reason to doubt the existence of a peace treaty between the peasants of Skåne and of Sweden at this time', writes Folke Lindberg; and goes on: 'If, furthermore, we take into account the fact that, at the time in question, the ancient pact between Blekinge and Värend must have been in full force, the picture becomes complete. We gain the impression that what faces us is a gigantic association of the commons in the Skanian provinces and the whole of Southern Sweden.'

Another aspect of the story of the peaceful strivings of the border peasantry was the attempts of the population of Värend in Småland to stay outside the last wars of the Union. In the Sture epoch, indeed, Värend almost seems to have been an independent republic only loosely attached to the rest of the realm. The province had no desire to involve itself in these national wars between Swedes and Danes, and during Christian II's successful invasion of Sweden, a kingdom to which he had a titular right, the Värend peasants lay low. But in 1520 they were alarmed by a letter from the King of the Union demanding that they should recognise him as King of Sweden and swear him fealty.

This put them on the spot. The war's outcome was still uncertain – Stockholm was still holding out against the Danes, who might not be victorious. In opting for the Union king the Värend peasants would have taken sides. On the other hand, it they refused Christian his oath of fealty they would have the Danes to reckon with, and be lumped with the other side. Apparently they could not care less who won, Swedes or Danes, as long as they did not themselves have to join in the struggle. Although in favour of the Union, which had brought their province great blessings, they were loth to recognise Christian as their king. They had no desire at all to become the subjects of so tyrannous a ruler. Later that year their suspicions of the Union king turned out to have been justified: in the summer of 1520 he decreed that the Smålanders should hand over their weapons and this led to a peasant rising against him, centred on the Kalmar district. But neither did the province accept a Swedish tyrant, as later became plain in Nils Dacke's insurrections.

But the king's alarming letter demanded an answer, and a meeting of the provincial assembly was summoned for March 25, 1520. I should give a great deal to see the minutes of that meeting, which had to arrive at so excruciating a decision. As it is, no one knows whether their reply to the king was unanimous. At all events, the people of Värend decided to play for time; before reaching a decision they wanted to wait and see how 'matters and negotiations' fell out in other parts of the country. In their letter to the king, therefore, they declare themselves temporarily neutral. Värend would continue to lie low until Saint Olov's Day, July 29. If by that day Christian had brought the rest of the country under his dominion, Värend too would recognise him.

The Smålanders' opportunist and unheroic attitude is reminiscent of Sweden's neutral policies during the Second World War. But its purpose – the preservation of peace – was as valid and as humanly understandable in the 16th century as it was four hundred years later.

For Gustav Vasa these peasants along the frontier of his state who concluded independent peace treaties were nothing but a pack of traitors; self-opinionated folk who, if he was to feel safe on his throne, would have to be extirpated. Against this powerful Renaissance monarch the provinces could no longer assert their individual autonomy. Though it fought him to the bitter end, after the failure of Dacke's insurrection even Småland was finally incorporated in the realm. And this was the end, once and for all, of the separatism of the so-called 'folk lands'.

Yet even after Gustav Vasa, even, surprisingly enough, far into the 17th century, the commons continued to make peace along the frontier. Gerhard Hafström's book on the old Swedish-Danish frontier (1934) mentions three parish treaties concluded in the 17th century on the historic Furs Bridge, the immemorial meeting place between Smålanders and the men of Blekinge. In 1611, 1644 and 1657, as in the Middle Ages, representatives of the neighbouring parishes of Vissefjärda and Fridlevstad met on the bridge – in each case to sign their own peace treaty in time of war between Sweden and Denmark. At the 1644 and 1657 meetings the Smålanders' spokesman was the Vissefjärda clergyman, Nicolaus Petri, known as Master Bock ('goat'), and the sheriff, Per of Bockabo. At times it seems to have been the custom for parish priests to take the lead at these meetings.

Even later, during Karl XI's 1674–78 war, we have evidence that a parochial peace treaty was concluded on Furs Bridge. The document, drawn up on that occasion by the peasants themselves, is dated 1675 and partially extant. By that time Blekinge had been part of Sweden for almost twenty years, yet some of her population were not prepared to help Denmark recover her lost province. It would have meant the reestablishment of the detested national frontier. In this document we are told that a 'sure and strong peasant peace' has been concluded.

This is the last such treaty on the southern border to be found in the sources.

But several peace treaties were also concluded between the peasantry on either side along the Swedish-Norwegian border, from the Middle Ages up to the mid-17th century. On the Swedish side it was the Värmlanders above all who put out peace feelers to the peasantry across the border in war-time. During the Kalmar War of 1611, for instance, the Värmland peasants invited their Norwegian brethren to a peace meeting, and this led to a pact between them.

A Norwegian history contains an eloquent anecdote from a war between Sweden and Norway, showing the neighbouring peoples' feelings when conscripted to fight each other. Two peasants, musket in hand, met at the border. Amazed, the two men just stood and gaped at each other. Then the Norwegian threw down his weapon and burst out:

'Well I never! If it isn't Ola from Kattbo!'

It *was* Ola from Kattbo. He too also threw down his musket, and the two peasants fell into each others' arms.

The common man's reluctance to go to war extended even to conscripted troops. We know of a great many cases of desertion, evasion and flight, particularly during the century when Sweden was a great European power. During the 1620's, when the men were to be stacked aboard transports and shipped overseas to Poland and Germany, there was a notable increase in such acts of desertion. Not a few conscripts objected to being despatched abroad like so many parcels – the whole transport had been organized by Gustavus Adolphus in person. There were even attempts at mutiny. But our nationalistic historians are extremely gingerly in their treatment of these events.

This right to make peace independently across the frontiers was deeply entrenched in the popular mind, and in the border country the memories of these peasant treaties survived from generation to generation. Remarkable evidence of this is a private member's bill mooted in the Lower Chamber of the Riksdag on January 22, 1869, by a certain Jonas Jonasson, M.P. for Gullaboås in Södra Möre. Objecting to the armaments race in Europe, this M.P. expresses his indignation at 'the enormous sums of money used every year to acquire and maintain materials for the mass-mutilation and destruction of our fellow human beings. Not only do the peoples have to raise these monies by their sweat and toil, they are also forced to sacrifice their very lives and blood.' It is not the peoples who are the cause of wars, asserts this peasant from Gullaboås; on the contrary, they have often resisted them by concluding peace treaties of their own. His bill goes on:

'Within the hundred which I have the honour to represent, mention is often made of how, during the wars between Sweden and Denmark, the commons in this place situated on what was then the frontier concluded a so-called *peasant peace* with their neighbours in Blekinge, leaving it to others to destroy one another, something for which they, for their part, had as little wish as reason; and whilst among the peoples today the idea on which such a peasant peace reposed seems to be steadily developing, those who rule them pay less and less heed to it.'

The idea of peasant peaces, he suggests, could be implemented by all states, thus realizing the dream of universal peace. Since one people must take the first step, and the Swedes, for the past fifty-five years, had been enjoying the blessings of peace and it would be an action worthy of them to be that people. His bill culminates in the proposal 'that the Riksdag shall submit to His Majesty's Government a humble petition that His Majesty's Government will be so gracious as to extend the hand [of friendship] to all the regents and parliaments of Europe in favour of a general disarmament and with the aim to conclude with Sweden an everlasting peace.'

Even two centuries after the cessation of the border treaties with the disappearance of the border, their memory was still very much alive among the commons of Södra Möre.

The traditional image of the Swedes as a notably warlike nation stands in need of revision. Generation after generation, there were these other Swedes. Swedes who nourished an inextirpable love of peace. The border peasantry were the pioneers of peace in Scandinavia – such is my contention; which is why I have devoted so much space to this 'warrior people's' dream of peace.

Tyrant I: Christian II

IN SWEDISH HISTORY Christian II of Denmark, Norway and Sweden, the last king of the Union, appears mainly as the chief butcher of the Stockholm Bloodbath, the wholesale executions with which he tried to secure his position after he had crushed the Swedish resistance. Horrific descriptions of those November days in 1520 have fastened in the minds of Swedes. Christian the Tyrant has lived down the ages as a bloodthirsty sadist. Some chroniclers even seem ashamed of the fact that such a blood-sullied monarch should ever have sat on the Swedish throne at all. Nevertheless, Christian II had been duly crowned in Stockholm on September 7, 1520 and properly acknowledged by the Council and the Estates. A few days after the Stockholm Bloodbath the surviving city burghers even staged a great feast in his honour. It was only after his final defeat that he came to be called Christian the Tyrant, and that was about all there was to be said about him. His features have been limned once and for all. In Swedish history Christian II has been made to stand in the corner – and there he has stood ever since.

But this image of the last king of the Union, whom we see there so clearly standing in the corner, is altogether too summary. The portrait can be complemented from sources which add many lights and shades and show Christian II to have been a most complex and richly endowed personality; an astonishing figure; a man of contradictions. The tyrant who was responsible for the Bloodbath, of course, remains. He is beyond rehabilitation. But he also becomes a tempting subject for psychological study. Christian's reign appears to have been one long series of paradoxical and inexplicable actions, both good and bad. How they can all have been the work of one and the same man is an enigma. Poets, dramatists and novelists, always attracted to history's enigmatic personalities, have found in

Christian II a fascinating theme. In one instance at least he has given rise to a literary masterpiece: Johannes V. Jensen's *Kongens Fald* (1913).

As a human story the life of Christian II, oscillating between greatness and abasement, is without counterpart among our Swedish kings. At the age of six he was crowned heir to the throne in Denmark and Norway. At the age of eighteen he was crowned in Sweden, where, in 1499, we even find him acting as stand-in for his father, King Hans. In 1513, at the age of thirty-two, he is King of Denmark and Norway and, seven years later, of all three Scandinavian countries. He marries a sister of the Emperor Charles V and thus becomes the brother-in-law of the most powerful of all European potentates. Being himself absolute monarch over the three kingdoms of the Nordic Empire, he is himself virtually the Emperor's peer. Christian II's position in fact was more powerful than that of any later Scandinavian monarch. But only three years were to pass before he was stripped of every vestige of authority and driven into a humiliating exile. After an unsuccessful attempt to regain his throne, Christian is flung into prison. There, for twenty-seven long years, he spends the rest of his life as a prisoner of the Danish State; and dies in captivity.

One of his successors on the Swedish throne, Karl XIV Johan* declared proudly on his deathbed: 'No one ever had a career like mine'. Christian II could have said the same, but not as a matter of any pride. Where Karl XIV Johan succeeded, Christian II failed. And the loser who falls on evil days – particularly if he is a highly gifted personality whose every undertaking, however grandiose, ends in disaster – is always a more interesting human figure than the man of success and good fortune. How did it come about?

Even a ruler who has earned the sobriquet 'The Tyrant' has the right to as fair a trial as possible. Usually it has been considered adequate to explain the last Union monarch's evil deeds as being typical of a Renaissance prince. Any ruler who gave vent to violent passions is liable to be saddled with this cliché. Christian, we are told, was a product of his time and place. I am not satisfied with such

* Marshal Bernadotte, summoned by the Estates to be Crown Prince of Sweden in 1810.—*Transl.*

an explanation. I do not believe that people are only the children of the time and environment in which they grow up. Widely differing individuals, leading very different lives, spring from the same age and environment. An epoch is a tree which bears various fruits. The 16th century shows us both good and evil people. It gave birth to tyrants, but also to saints. Christian II and Gustav Vasa were equally 16th-century rulers, and as tyrants they had many peers in Europe. But it was also the century of such great men of the spirit and humanists as Erasmus of Rotterdam, Thomas More and Olaus Petri. They, too, were children of their age and milieu.

Christian II, eldest son of King Hans of Oldenburg, was born on March 8, 1481. The founder of this dynasty had been Christian I, celebrated in Sweden as king of the Union. He was also famous for his unusual stature. Formerly he was supposed to have been well over six-foot tall, though the Danes have measured his skeleton and found it to be less. His father King Hans, we are told, though noted for his firm grasp of practical affairs and eye for realities, suffered from periods of acute melancholy, suggestive of a manic-depressive temperament. He was musical, loved feasts and gaiety, but also evinced a weakness for the fair sex. This king kept a titular mistress, a married woman, Fru Edele Jernskegg.

Christian's mother, Queen Christina, was sister of the Elector of Saxony, Frederik the Wise, who ruled over Luther's native country and therefore has his place in the history of the Reformation. She is described as a God-fearing and pious woman.

Before she gave birth to Christian, her first-born, strange natural phenomena, signs and portents occurred, foreboding the boy's remarkable and dramatic destiny. The 16th-century Danish historian Huitfeldt repeats a contemporary anecdote from the birth. The boy was heard to be weeping aloud in his mother's womb: 'He could clearly be heard'. A natural conclusion: the child was loth to come into the world. And 'at the hour of his birth' the boy came out of his mother's womb with one hand open and the other clasped. When his closed fist was opened by the midwife, it was found to be full of blood and mucous. Whence another conclusion: 'He was to be a bloodthirsty person'.

This anecdote about Christian's birth, however, is posthumous and therefore coloured by what was then known about his life. There is nothing remarkable about a baby being born with blood in his hand, as every doctor and midwife knows. Luckily, not all newborn infants who have blood in their fists at birth turn into bloodthirsty people.

King Hans' and Queen Christina's first-born showed hardly any of the family traits characteristic of his father, grandfather or other relatives. Nor did he outwardly resemble any members of his typically blond and Nordic-looking dynasty. Christian wore the aspect of a dark-haired southerner. In a contemporary portrait now in the Copenhagen Museum of Art, his features are altogether southern. First and foremost an observer cannot help being struck by the dark, strangely veiled eyes. In this painting Christian the Tyrant has the gaze of a dreamer and a seer. He seems absent, lost in thought, withdrawn, unaware of place and moment. Far away in the distance he beholds something which holds him in thrall. But deep in the darkness of his eyes is a dangerous glint. At any moment one imagines it can burst into flame.

Altogether, Christian does not seem really at home in his Danish environment, and various attempts have been made to explain his southern physiognomy. He is supposed to have been a royal bastard, fruit of a liaison between the queen and a Roman aristocrat, a papal legate who had been staying in Copenhagen the year before his birth. Such an Italian father would explain his 'hot blood' and violent temperament. This theory is attractive, but must be rejected as a romantic fancy, and no Danish historian has ever taken it seriously. For the newly married Queen Christina to have had sexual relations with anyone except her husband or borne the king a bastard successor to the throne is a patent absurdity, the more so as she is known to have been a woman who satisfied every requirement of honour and virtue.

For the son of a king, Christian's education was most unusual, As a little boy he was placed in the charge of Hans Meisenheim Bogbinder – 'book-binder' – and his wife. These merchant burghers of Copenhagen, respected and reliable middleclass people, accepted him as if he had been their own son. The king's confidence in them must have been complete to have put them in charge of his son. And presumably the task of bringing up the crown prince of Denmark was accepted by them as a signal honour.

Nothing could have been better for the future ruler than to escape the confines of the royal castle and live among the ordinary run of mankind. He gets to know his future subjects from the inside. In the house of Hans the bookbinder, Christian, during his childhood's impressionable years, gained insight into the conditions under which the popular classes lived. We do not know how long he stayed with his foster-parents, but his stay in the burgher home was to have important consequences for his reign. In this new environment he must have become aware of the great difference which obtained between the various Estates; during his years there he gained experiences which he later exploited as king. As a social reformer and radical legislator he was in a position to base his ideas on a realistic knowledge of the common people.

In works on Christian II we are told that he 'was educated wholly in the principles of humanism' – a remarkable description of the education of a pupil who later became known as The Tyrant. Historical facts prove that the last Union monarch did in fact enjoy an all-round education unusual in those days among the sons of princes. His childhood years in the burgher home, when he associated on an equal footing with craftsmen and their like, were certainly a fruitful part of his apprenticeship.

On reaching the age of twenty-five years, Christian was regarded as mature enough to govern a kingdom. King Hans appointed his son governor of Norway.

That was in 1506. The following year, at Bergen, came the great experience of his life. He met Dyveke.

Sigbrit Willumsdotter, widow of a Dutch merchant, had emigrated to Norway with her young daughter. In Holland both women had been living in extreme poverty, and in their new country were seeking a less intolerable existence. In Bergen, Sigbrit Willumsdotter opened a bakery, selling its products, waffles, various cakes and pastries in the city's market places. Though the mother went unnoticed, the daughter, Dyveke, who was unusually pretty, attracted all the more attention. The young Dutchwoman was a 'wonderfully beautiful girl, of handsome proportions, slim and slender as a reed, with refined features and a mild expression; she was shy and gentle, and her deportment and whole nature were characterized by an extraordinary charm'.

In his book about Christian II, the Danish historian C. F. Allen describes the prince's first meeting with Dyveke. The governor's chancellor, Erik Valkendorf, had seen the girl out with her mother selling cakes in the market. Struck by her extraordinary beauty, he had mentioned her to Christian. This had awakened the young prince's curiosity, with the result that Mother Sigbrit and her daughter were among the guests invited to a banquet given by the city of Bergen for the governor in its Town Hall. During the dancing Christian, 'out of respect for the convenances', had asked one of the city's own daughters for the first dance, but then asked Dyveke to dance with him, and thereafter had neither thoughts nor eyes for any other. She had captivated him utterly, at first sight. The banquet over, Christian resolutely opened negotiations with Mother Sigbrit, and she offered no objections. Her daughter became the twenty-six-year-old governor's mistress.'

In those days a man in Christian's elevated station, a king's son, had little trouble in getting any woman he desired as a sexual partner. He could simply pick and choose. The sequel to that banquet at Bergen in 1507, therefore, was in no way unusual. The governor of Norway took young Dyveke to his bed. What is remarkable is that this was not the prelude to a transient affair, no mere princely caprice; it led to a relationship which has rightly taken its place in history. Here we have the only royal romance in the annals of Scandinavia to have political consequences – because of its effects on the despot's psyche. Christian's love for Dyveke and its tragic ending are thought to have been decisive for his actions on a number of crucial occasions.

Of Dyveke we know little more than that she possessed unusual feminine charm. When she first went to the prince's bed it was probably as Mother Sigbrit's obedient and well brought up daughter. Dyveke herself can hardly have had any say in the matter. But there is evidence to suggest that she came to love her lover. At all events, for her the relationship lasted as long as life itself – i.e. for ten years, until her mysterious death in 1517.

What is certain is that Dyveke was before all others the woman in Christian's life. As long as she lived he was 'wildly passionate' in his devotion to her. That it was not only lust on his part, but true love, is beyond question. As his actions were to prove.

Mother Sigbrit and Dyveke went with the governor of Norway to Oslo, where he had a house built for them in the immediate proximity of his own palace. Later, when Christian succeeded to his father's throne in 1513, both women moved with the new king to Copenhagen, where he also furnished a dwelling for them, hard by his castle.

Dyveke was the king's lover, mistress or concubine – whichever word we use to describe her position, it was no secret. She was his titular mistress, and to keep mistresses was a privilege of princes. Christian was merely following his father's example and the custom in royal houses in those days. An unwritten law, however, required that royal mistresses should preferably be of noble birth; and Christian had had the impudence to choose one from among the lower orders, a woman, furthermore, of foreign birth and of unknown origins. His overt relationship with Dyveke was regarded as a challenge to the Danish nobility, and by the highest circles of Copenhagen society she was ill-seen, even hated.

After Christian's political marriage to Elizabeth, sister of Charles V, Dyveke became an insult to the Emperor himself, and Charles demanded that his brother-in-law should send his concubine away. Christian refused. Resolutely flouting all objections to his love-affair, no matter what their source, he kept his mistress close to him.

Mother Sigbrit's presence at court still further augmented the scandal and it was through the titular mistress's mother that the affair came to assume political proportions. Sigbrit Willumsdotter was a strong-willed, fearless and ambitious woman, a woman to reckon with, who came to exert a great influence over the king. Her flair for business was so great that Christian entrusted her with the realm's affairs, elevating an unknown foreign woman of low birth, a mere bakeress, who had stood selling bread in the public market-places, to a key position in finance and politics. The action was utterly unique in European history. For the blue-blooded arrogant aristocracy it was, of course, a scandal of stupendous proportions. But Mother Sigbrit knew what she was about. Troels-Lund writes of her that she was one of the best finance ministers Denmark has ever had!

Not only was Dyveke's mother a foreigner and an outsider; she also came to be regarded as a witch, who had gained her ascendency over Christian by magic. In her house she was believed to have installed a laboratory and there, experimenting with alchemical pumps and retorts, manufactured gold. The mind of that age was in thrall to an obsession with magic and witchcraft, and there were those who regarded Mother Sigbrit as the real ruler of Denmark, governing the king himself with the Devil's aid; and if the Devil held him fast in his grip, it was in the shape of the beautiful Dyveke. All of a sudden, at Midsummer 1517, the royal mistress died. What she died of was never known. Certain of the symptoms suggest appendicitis. But in the Middle Ages sudden death was always likely to give rise to suspicions of poison. So it did now. A man of high estate, the powerful nobleman Torben Oxe, was believed to be the culprit. Oxe was alleged to have sent Dyveke a basket of summer's first cherries poisoned; of which she, eating, had promptly died.

Christian was wild with grief and lust for revenge. He had Torben Oxe summoned before the Council of State, but for lack of evidence the Council acquitted him. Convinced as he was of the accused's guilt, this only infuriated the king still further. Rejecting the verdict, he appointed a fresh court, consisting this time not of Torben Oxe's own peers but his peasants. Overawed by such royal pressure, they could only condemn him to death. The sentence was carried into effect.

Guilty or not? The question can never be answered. There was no looking into the matter then, and it has never been reviewed afterwards. A case, perhaps, of judicial murder. Torben Oxe was also accused of having sought – perhaps even of having enjoyed – Dyveke's favours. Christian himself believed that he had 'defiled the royal bed'. But on this point research acquits him. The Danish nobles had certainly had strong motives for wishing to get rid of the king's mistress. So much is unquestionable. But they gained nothing by her death. If there is a murder which could have yielded political dividends, surely it was Mother Sigbrit who should have been the victim? As it was, she was still alive, and her status remained unshaken. Indeed, after Dyveke's demise, Christian became even more attached to her mother and her influence over him became all the greater, likewise her power over the realm. Ever since his accession, Christian had been opposed by the aristocracy. Now he conceived a violent hatred for these noblemen who – he was convinced – had deprived him of the woman he loved.

In the life of Christian II the death of Dyveke was, as far as we can see, a turning point. Her loss precipitated an acute psychological crisis.

A Danish psychiatrist, Dr Paul J. Reiter, head of a Copenhagen mental hospital, has devoted a major work to the king's medical and psychological aspects. In it Reiter sheds some light on certain of his traits, hitherto unstudied. Christian, he declares, was a schizoid personality with the asthenic features commonly regarded as characteristic of a 'weak character'. At certain periods in his life, Reiter says, Christian's state of mind was such that he cannot be regarded as responsible for his actions. The first such period, according to Reiter, occurred after Dyveke's death in 1517. It was his life's great and decisive catastrophe. His feelings for the woman he loved are described by this psychiatrist as an erotic possession, a storm of 'raging passion, which the young foreign girl had stirred up in his soul'. Several times previously Christian had acted both precipitately and ruthlessly; but on the whole the balance of his mind had not been disturbed. Now it was different.

Reiter is not inclined to label this king a psychopath: under more favourable circumstances he might have developed into a more integrated personality. But the loss of the woman he loved and his conviction that she had been murdered by his enemies shook him to the very foundations of his soul. All restraint thrown to the winds, his blind passions were unleashed.

In this psychiatrist's opinion it was the Dyveke catastrophe which led Christian II into the paths of violence that culminated in the Stockholm Bloodbath, and to his ever afterwards being nicknamed

Christian the Tyrant. During those fateful November days of 1520 the king, Reiter says, was in a state of acute anxiety and excitement, utterly without self-control. Such were the ultimate roots of what might be called Sweden's St Bartholomew's Eve.

Historically the Stockholm Bloodbath is an enigma, and must ever remain so. Historians are still disputing exactly what happened during those November days in 1520. The same year as I sit writing this, a Swede, Professor Curt Weibull, has been involved in mutual polemics with a Danish colleague, Niels Skyum-Nielsen, on this very question. In brief, three candidates have been advanced as primarily responsible for this blood-letting: Christian II, his demoniac adviser Jens Andersen Beldenacke, and the Swedish archbishop Gustav Trolle. In the last resort, however, guilt for the massacre must obviously rest on the king himself. He could have prevented it if he had wished. Except by his will not a head could have fallen.

The course of events, as far as we know, was more or less as follows. When Christian had been crowned king, great festivities were held in Stockholm Castle, the chief notables of the kingdom and the mayors and council of Stockholm being invited. The king was at his most amiable. Walking about in the halls he lavished his favours on his Swedish guests, who, according to a contemporary record, 'fell to gaiety, dancing and games, and gave themselves up to all kinds of amusements'.

Next day the scene changed. The coronation guests were once more summoned to the castle, where the gate was closed. When the king had mounted his throne, archbishop Trolle stepped forward. He presented to Christian an indictment, demanding the severest penalty of the law upon those who on the occasion of the seizure and demolition of the Archbishop's castle at Stäket in the autumn of 1517 had committed so grave a crime against Holy Church, against himself and all his retainers. The objects of this indictment were in the first place aristocratic members of the Sture party; but also the mayors and council of Stockholm. The next person to speak was Kristina Gyllenstierna, recently widowed wife of Sten Sture. Authoritatively and without mincing her words she maintained that both the action against Stäket and the deposition of Gustav Trolle had been decided upon at a parliament held in Stockholm and must therefore be regarded as wholly legal; measures, moreover, for which all those who had participated in them, indeed all the leading men of the kingdom, had been in a body responsible. In evidence of this she handed the king the document which confirmed the parliament's decision. At that moment one of the leading prelates of Sweden, Bishop Hans Brask of Linköping, got up, as he put it, to 'make his apology'. He had been one of those who had signed the parliamentary decision; his seal, together with all the others, was hanging from the dangerous document. But from his own seal he now produced a capsule within which he had concealed a slip of paper. On this were written the words: 'To this sealing I am compelled and forced'. In this way, in a scene which was to become legendary, the Bishop of Linköping is said to have saved his own skin.

A cross-examination of all the others now began. The questions came thick and fast. The atmosphere became more and more excited. The hours passed. And when darkness had begun to fall, the doors were flung open and a troop of soldiers marched in. The arrests were swiftly made and, Olaus Petri tells us in his *Chronicle*, 'Bishop Vincentius of Skara and Bishop Mattias of Strängnäs, and many of the Swedish nobility, together with their servants and many Stockholm citizens, were seized by the neck and imprisoned, some in the tower, some in the chapel and some elsewhere in the castle. There they passed the night.'

Their fate was decided next day, November 8, when the prisoners were indicted before an ecclesiastical court, in which Gustav Trolle was one of the judges. They were pronounced guilty of heresy, a verdict which at once disencumbered the king of his earlier promise of a general amnesty. It was now up to him to carry out the punishments, and this he did with unerring precision.

The situation best appears in the following little scene: the Stockholm headsman presents himself to Bishop Vincentius, who with justifiable amazement, enquiries: 'What news?' And receives the answer: 'Not exactly good news, Your Grace: I have orders to chop Your Grace's head off.'

The executioner's hour had come. One of the witnesses, no less a person than Olaus Petri, has left us a record of what ensued. His description of the sanguinary drama, in the last pages of his Swedish *Chronicle*, is laconically realistic:

'The king caused the trumpets to be blown and an announcement to be made that all should remain within, where they were. And about midday he caused the Bishop of Skara and the Bishop of Strängnäs, with the knights and knights' retainers and citizens whom he had caused to be taken prisoner, to be led out into the great market place, there to take their lives. And when they thus were come into the market and stood up in a ring, some of the kings' council stood up in the oriel window. Nils Lycke spake unto the people who stood in the market place, and bade them take no horror of that punishment which was there to be inflicted. For his Royal Majesty, quod he, had been implored to implement these punishments by Archbishop Gustav, who thrice falling upon his knees had begged and pleaded that the wrong he had suffered might be punished. Much else he also declared, wherewith to exonerate the king. Then cried Bishop Vincentius up to him under his very eyes and said that he spake not truth, but that his king acted with lies and treachery toward Swedish men. And demanded that the others might have judgment passed upon each for himself, and know wherefore they must die; and mighty hard words spake he against the king, and said that God would be revenged upon such tyranny and injustice. Wherefore Bishop Mattias of Strännäs was the first to be beheaded outside the town court, and his head was laid betwixt his legs, the which befell not any of the others. And next thereafter was Bishop Vincentius beheaded.'

After which the turn came to many lords of the Council and other great men and to the three mayors and all the councillors of Stockholm: likewise to a number of prominent citizens. One expert on the history of Stockholm, Nils Ahnlund, has said that 'the number of victims was stated by the headsman to have been 82, a number therefore certainly reliable'.

Finally, Olaus Petri's *Chronicle* tells us: 'And the dead bodies remained lying in the market from Thursday until Saturday. And full pitiful and sorry a sight it was to see how the blood together with water and excrement ran down in the gutters from the market. Yea, it was a horrible and merciless murder.'

The Stockholm Bloodbath was an event which caused greater indignation in Scandinavia than anything else ever to happen here. No action has been more roundly condemned. Mediaeval people were hardened to violence. The occasional execution stirred them not a jot. But this massive slaughter was too strong even for their stomachs. The beheadings took three hours. Which means one head falling about every other minute.

Even from the despot's own point of view to take the lives of so many people at one and the same time and place was an error of judgment. That day too much blood ran in the gutters. People were sickened. If the executions had been phased out in time and carried out in a number of different places, people would not have been so profoundly shocked. As it was, the horror was concentrated in one spot, and became even more ghastly because of the great coronation banquet which, as we have seen, immediately preceded it. One day it was wine that flowed. The next blood.

Its epilogue, too, was utterly loathsome. On November 10, a couple of days after the bloodbath, the Stockholm burghers staged a banquet in the tyrant's honour. His queen, Elizabeth, had given birth to a daughter. In a city 'still steaming with the blood of its leading citizens' the banquet took place in the City Hall, beautifully adorned for the occasion. On their way to it the guests, crossing the great market place of Stortorget where the bloodbath had taken place, can hardly have failed to notice its traces. Ladies were invited – not only the leading citizens' but also the aristocracy's 'wives and virgins' – to this sumptuous banquet with its 'manifold merry-makings'. The wine flowed, and after it was over 'was delightsome dancing'. The newly crowned king was as gracious as could be, kind and amiable as he had been during the coronation ceremonies before the massacre.

Danish historians have been much bemused and confounded by this feast given in honour of the Tyrant after the massacre. How can the Stockholmers have brought themselves to do such a thing? Only a couple of days had passed since their guest of honour had had many of the capital's leading citizens beheaded. How could their surviving peers acclaim the king so soon afterwards? Many relatives of the victims must have been among the guests. The only explanation can be the terror this orgy of blood had instilled into the Stockholmers' hearts. Trembling for their own lives, they tried to assuage the Tyrant's wrath by a banquet in his honour.

This Swedish St Bartholomew's Eve fell most heavily on the aristocracy, on the Stockholm burghers and on the Church. It did not affect the Swedish commons, whose grief at the death of the leading aristocrats can hardly have been inconsolable. The commons had no very friendly feelings for great men. If the peasants revolted against Christian, it was for quite different reasons. First and foremost they resented his efforts to disarm them. To pay the wages of the great host of German, Scottish and French legionaries, without whom he could not have conquered Sweden, he had also imposed a heavy burden of taxes. As far as Christian was concerned, though he had enjoyed a hereditary right to the realm for more than twenty years, he had been obliged to recover it by force of arms and he regarded the Swedes as owing him the military expenses he had been put to.

In the course of a century Denmark had had only four kings. But Sweden had had no fewer than fifteen kings or regents. By getting rid of so many leading Swedes, all of them potential rebels, Christian hoped to stabilize his own royal authority in Sweden and secure for himself the same position as he enjoyed in Denmark. But the very act by which he imagined he had restored the Kalmar Union had in fact given it its death-blow. It is one of history's tragic ironies that the Stockholm Bloodbath can only be seen as a final settlement of accounts between the Union party and the Swedish nationalists. Even if murder was not an argument viable in law, in those days it was in reality accepted and utilized as such. The real motives were usually disguised. Such political murders were made to wear an air of legality by judicial proceedings before the courts. And this was exactly what happened when alleged heretics were executed under Canon law. In my view Professor Lauritz Weibull comes closest to the historical truth of the matter when he declares in an essay: 'the Bloodbath was not an isolated occurrence. It was the final catastrophe in the long and bitter struggle between the two parties who were then rending Sweden apart'.

*

After he left Sweden for ever at the end of 1520 Christian was only to remain ruler of the North for three more years. But this brief period was marked by a notable achievement, for which he also deserves to be remembered. He became a social reformer. The judiciary, in particular, was radically reformed. Christian devoted the last years of his reign to passing new laws for his subjects. He had set up for himself a great, if at this epoch unattainable, goal: to restructure Scandinavian society.

King Christian II's legislation comprises more laws than that of any other ruler of any of the three kingdoms. And it is here we stumble on the extraordinary contradictions in his nature: the harsh tyrant – the friend of the common people – the Renaissance despot – the democrat before his time – the Devil in human guise – Christian 'beloved of the peasants'.

Danish historians tell me that no book exists which comprehends all Christian II's legislation. After his fall, in 1523, his law books were burnt at the Viborg Assembly. A symbolic gesture, it was the funeral of all his reformist ideas. To learn something of their contents, therefore, I have had to turn to a composite work in several volumes, a collection of documents in Danish history, one volume of which, printed in Copenhagen in 1781, treats of his law books. To go through them all here would take up a hundred pages, so I shall have to summarize their essential content.

The chief impression I have gained from studying them is that the last Union monarch's aim was to establish social equality in mediaeval Danish society. This can be seen most clearly in two laws for the Danish nation; the *Landslagen* and *Stadslagen* (Law for the Country, Law for the Town) dated, in the one instance, late in 1521 and, in the other, January 6, 1522. What he was planning was a thorough-going social revolution.

Christian wished to strip the Danish Church of its enormous privileges. As in Sweden, and indeed everywhere else, the clergy were only subject to canon law. Now a national court was to be set up, before which all bishops and other clerics, in the eyes of Danish law, would be on a par with other citizens. Never a friend of the Church, the king was as little a friend of the nobility. In their well-fortified cannon-proof fortresses the bishops lived like princes. On one occasion Christian is supposed to have observed they could just as well live in barns – a remark which, passing from mouth to mouth, made the 'bishops thoughtful'. Nor, if the king had his way, were they in future to travel sumptuously around the realm with their great trains of several hundred armed men.

Christian's law for the countryside is of the greatest interest to the political history of the Scandinavian commons' long struggle for their liberties. In this code of laws his foresight as a legislator can clearly be discerned. All trace of the ancient Scandinavian institution of thraldom still existing in Denmark in the form of '*vornedskabet*' – i.e. the unfree status of the peasantry vis-à-vis the landowners on their estates – is here abolished. This limitation on the Danish people's freedom, which tied them to their birthplace and prevented them from tilling any soil outside its boundaries, survived until 1702, and in 1733 was replaced by the somewhat milder '*stavnsbaandet*'.

'*Vornedskabet*' was a form of serfdom, under which a peasant was a mere chattel, changing owners with the land he worked. It is this commerce in human beings which is expressly forbidden in Christian's new law: the 'unchristian custom, which hath been in Sjaelland and thereabouts, of selling and giving away poor peasants as other soulless creatures, shall this day henceforth no longer prevail'.

The peasantry's relations with the nobility were regulated in several respects. A Danish nobleman still took the same view of his peasant as the German princes: the peasant had been created a thrall, a serf, a slave. 'Though in the eyes of God he was their equal, the great had no more respect to a poor peasant than to a dog'. That Christian's legislation threw the nobility into a panic and led to an insurrection against him is easy to understand.

A new law for schools, too, stipulates that in instructing their pupils they shall use humanistic text books. Furthermore, the pupils shall no longer stray about and beg at doorways. Even the peasant's children are to go to school, where they shall first and foremost learn to read and write their mother tongue. Hitherto fierce whippings, such as can only be called gross cruelty to children, had been permitted in Danish schools. Christian's new law abolished such barbaric physical punishment. The '*ferle*', a coarse whip or stick with a lump at one end, often used for beating children on their hands, was forbidden.

Such humane paragraphs in Christian's school legislation may seem self-evident to us. In their day and age they were revolutionary.

The new law promulgated for the towns and burghers, too, was intended to bring about a radical transformation of economic life. The country markets were to be abolished and trade concentrated in the cities. Christian also had plans for a great Nordic trading company for his three realms, a common market based on Copenhagen and Stockholm. Here he paid special attention to the Bergslagen ore exports. He intended to put an end to the immense powers of the Hanseatic League which for almost two hundred years had dominated all trade in the North. This far-sighted project envisaged the economic union known today as Nordek. Even today, four and a half centuries after Christian, it remains a utopia.

The king's new laws had many regulatory affects on the economy. Sometimes they almost seem 20th century in character. Designed to improve agriculture, the mother of all industries, they devote great care also to fisheries, where his legislation enters into details. The country exported a great deal of herring. One paragraph forbids excessively small-meshed nets, thus guaranteeing a certain minimum in the size of fish caught.

But what above all characterizes Christian's legislation is the principle of equality. Burghers and peasants were to be the nobility's equals before the law. To 20th-century posterity it seems obvious that this could never have been carried through in 16th-century Scandinavia. Not until the mid-19th could the Danish peasantry finally and completely free themselves from '*vornedskabet*'.

And when the king was deposed and his law book thrown to the flames, this – given the epoch – seems to have been its natural and predestined fate. Erik Arup, a modern Danish historian, who names some of Christian's most dangerous enemies among the nobility, describes their triumphant feelings at that historic burning of the books before the Viborg Assembly. But the future was to vindicate the legislator:

'They might rejoice at the sight of these damnable law books being consumed by the flames. But their action was to fail of its effect; ever afterwards the sublime and human law of men's equality would stand inscribed in the hearts of the Danish people'.

As we have seen, the status of the Swedish commons was freer than that of the Danish, but even in Sweden the last Union monarch's concern for popular liberties has given him the name Christian 'beloved of the peasants'. The old song *The old Eagle, the Hawk and the Little Birds*, which was also sung in Sweden (at least in the provinces bordering on Denmark) is evidence of how he survived in tradition as a friend of the common man. Originally written in old Danish, it was afterwards translated into Swedish and all its twenty verses are to be found in print in a famous 19th-century work on Swedish folklore by Arvid August Afzelius.

The song is a dirge, in which the commons lament the loss of Christian, their royal protector. He has been driven into exile by his uncle Fredrik and the Danish and Holsteiner nobility. Christian, that is to say, is the old Eagle; the new king is the Hawk, and the common people are the Little Birds. It is these poor little birds who 'of the Hawk make great complaint: He strips them both of down and feathers and would drive them from the wood'.

In the course of these twenty verses the whole political situation in Denmark ensuant upon Christian's fall is mirrored in a fable of bird-life. The poor little birds who are being hunted by the cruel Hawk are represented by the dove and the sandpiper. The exiled king is apostrophized in each verse's refrain. Twenty times over we are told: 'But the Eagle is nesting in the mountains.' Christian 'beloved of the peasants' 'knowth neither lee nor lair, where he can build his nest'.

Afzelius makes this comment on the song: 'There is more truth in this song than in the chronicles. King Christian was a friend of the people and hated the nobility. King Fredrik, on the contrary, sacrificed the peasants' rights to gratify the nobles. King Gustav in Sweden was of the same mind as King Fredrik, and was long hated by the common people. For in Sweden, too, "The Hawk sat in the Oak crown", i.e. the nobles were elevated and enriched, but "the little birds grieved". '

It was neither the first nor the last time in history that the commons had recourse to allegory when there was no other way for them to make their voices heard.

The insurrection of the nobility against Christian II, his deposition and his unsuccessful attempt to recover his throne have no place in this book; they belong to Danish history. Finally, in 1532, he walked unsuspectingly into a trap laid for him by his enemies and – against a promise of safe conduct – became their prisoner for the rest of his life. His prison was Sønderborg Castle, except during his last years, when he was transferred to Kalundborg. In 1559, at the age of seventy-eight, after twenty-seven years as a prisoner of the Danish state, he died, one year before his opponent Gustav Vasa.

Obviously this last Union king, who became a prisoner for life, is differently viewed by Danish and Swedish historians; but in his own country too, he has been critically appraised; notably so by older chroniclers, who have even called him a loathsome tyrant. Opinions on his character differ sharply. Whilst C. F. Allen and Paludan-Müller call him a strong personality, Erik Arup regards him as a weak one, and the Swedish historian Lauritz Weibull agrees with Arup. Modern Danish historians have done him justice as a social reformer and praised his remarkable far-sightedness, and today his reign is more discriminatingly assessed.

The most positive characterization of Christian II is the one made by Palle Lauring in the sixth part of his great Danish history. Based on latest research, it is, as a biography, remarkable. Lauring draws a fascinating psychological portrait of Christian, whom he finds to have been a most complex personality. In this portrait the king appears as a man of great spiritual and physical capacities, with a wide range of activities, an imaginative man, capable of grandiose plans. His projects exceed all common measure. At the same time he is far from being the man he would like to be. He is indecisive, given to tergiversation, unsure of himself. Conscious of his own weaknesses, he does his best to conceal them from others. To put his plans into effect is beyond him – they remain a mere longing and a dream. In this account Christian the Tyrant becomes a political visionary.

While not defending the king's evil deeds, Lauring explains them as due to fear and anxiety. And those November days in Stockholm – the days of the Bloodbath – were the most anxious of all. Sheer terror drove him to his bloody settlement of accounts, terror of these Swedes whom he had finally, after a long war defeated. If he takes their lives it is to be quit both of them and of his fear. But Christian himself cannot stand the sight of human blood. Where was the king during the massacre in the Stockholm market place? A question which has never been answered. One source declares that 'he is in his privy'. He locks himself in – for reasons we can surmise.

This latest biographer of Christian, in my opinion, has found a key to the actions of tyrants and potentates, for whom power is everything. They are possessed by an ever-present fear: fear of losing their power. In their terror they grab at every means of retaining it – notably the most ultimate and definitive: violence and murder.

Palle Lauring thinks we misjudge Christian II by giving him so exigent a title as The Tyrant: 'he was certainly not equal to it.' To rule tyrannically calls for force, for authority, for energy and resolute decision-making. But Christian was forever going back on his decisions. Weak and timorous, in critical situations he rarely knew how to act.

As to the king's ultimate fate, Palle Lauring writes: 'Christian II's long years of imprisonment were wholly illegal. He was never indicted, never examined or tried, nor was any sentence ever passed upon him. It is the greatest judicial murder in Danish history. This does not acquit Christian II of responsibility for his acts, but it lies wholly outside the rule of law on which the laws of Denmark and the commitments of Danish kings were based.'

As a social reformer and as a legislator it was the tragic lot of the last king of the Nordic Union to be right – three centuries too soon.

Tyrant II: Gustav I

The clan and its founder

AN EARLY 19th-CENTURY Swedish biographical reference book declares: 'Vasa is the only family name in our annals which may be said to have a place in world history . . . and of which an educated European cannot be ignorant without it being regarded as a gap in his education'.

In Sweden, too, Vasa, more than any other family name, has penetrated our historical awareness. We come across it daily – we take a stroll in the Vasa Park, eat Vasa bread, take part in the Vasa Race*, worship in the Vasa Church and sport the Order of Vasa on our chests. The name appears in streets and cities, in churches and parishes, in associations and clubs, in orders and medals. We find the word used internationally: in Minnesota, USA, Swedish immigrants have called a town Vasa. I have seen Vasa Bread (a genuine Swedish crispbread, known in England and America as 'Rye King') advertised on several countries' TV. German newspapers advertise a Swedish Vasa Coat, said to be an exceptionally hardwearing garment. The name has become a trade mark. There are Vasa Bazaars and Vasa Companies. The name stimulates sales. Sometimes it seems to possess an inherent value, which cannot be called in question.

It is the name borne by the most illustrious and famous of our royal dynasties. Dynasties in Sweden have come and gone, but if any king has been able to show he has a drop of Vasa blood in his veins it has been counted to his honour and advantage: a fluid

* The Vasa Ski Race in March, between Sälen and Mora, commemorates the turning point in the national struggle when two Mora men caught up with Gustav as he fled into Norway after the Stockholm Bloodbath (1520), and prevailed on him to turn back. Some 8,000 skiers participate.—*Translator*.

nowadays so rare that it must not be wasted. Participation in the Vasa heritage means, in Sweden, the very highest lineage.

But where does this family name, the only one in Sweden regarded as entitled to a place in world history, come from? I have visited the place which first had the honour of bearing it. Vasa, the oldest farm belonging to the clan, lies in Skepptuna parish, Uppland. Near the Fyris River, at one time a navigable waterway, it comprises about 300 acres of the most fertile agricultural land in Uppland. Its old castle-like main building burnt down in 1926, and only its two detached wings remain to form the owner's residence. The estate also comprises large areas of woodlands. Today the farm has no cattle; despite its 300 arable acres it buys its milk from the Milk Marketing Board. Since much of the arable land was once river bed, the humus is admirably fertile. Thirty hands used to be employed here – today the owner does his own work, aided by only three.

The proprietor of Sweden's most famous noble estate is not a nobleman. His name is Birger Jansson. These two names, Vasa and Jansson, are symbolic of the changes which have occurred during the five centuries in which Sweden has developed from a semi-feudal society into a democratic one.

We do not know for certain how the estate, and with it the Vasa clan got their name. The old word *vase* means a bunch of twigs laid out in the lake to attract spawning fish, but in the Vasa arms it means a sheaf of corn. This symbol, however, was not adopted until after the hereditary Vasa monarchy had been established at Västerås in 1544. Earlier, the clan had worn a *sceptrum liliatum*, a lilied sceptre resembling the point of a lance, on its coat of arms. Lance head or sheaf of corn – whether the Vasa arms are to be taken as symbolizing war or the peaceful arts of agriculture remains an open question.

Two other great Uppland estates associated with the name of the Vasas once belonged to them: Lindholmen in Orkesta parish, and Rydboholm in Östra Ryd. Like Vasa, they lie in the province's most fertile region. Rydboholm, for instance, consists of seven hundred acres of superb farming land, with deep rich soil. The Vasas certainly had an eye to the finest land and knew how to come by it. In other provinces, too, they owned estates.

At school I was taught that Gustav Vasa was born on Lindholmen farm in Uppland; but subsequently he has acquired another birthplace, Rydboholm Castle, one of whose towers bears his name and where household equipment from the early Vasa period is still to be seen. Obviously, the founder of Sweden's hereditary monarchy need not content himself with a single birthplace. The people of Orkesta assert that he was born at Lindholmen, and a monument on the railway station declares that it was here, on May 12, 1496, that Gustav Vasa came into the world. A mile or so away, on a hillock in the forest, the remains of the main building of the old Lindholmen farm are to be seen, and under a gigantic oak a huge stone has been raised, bearing the name of the first Vasa king and his almost illegible year of birth. Today Lindholmen is owned by the City of Stockholm, which, I am told, is going to convert the ancient seat of the Vasa into a holiday home for its municipal employees – another shift of power from noble to populace.

Various years between 1494 and 1497 have been given for the birth of Gustav I. Everyone agrees that he was born on Ascension Day, in the month of May, when the cuckoo was to be heard; but we do not know in which year.

The Vasas, then, sprang from the soil of the Uppland countryside. At the height of the Middle Ages a family of enterprising and ambitious Roslagen peasants had raised themselves above their brother commoners and become ennobled. Though the sources are familiar with this family of magnates from the mid-14th century onwards, it was not until the 15th that it produced any men of real note. The first was the Earl Marshal, Christer Nilsson Vasa, a contemporary of Karl Knutsson.

Supporters, at first, of the Union party, the Vasas had later become allied by marriage with the Stures and joined the nationalist side. Subsequently their influence grew, especially after Gustav Vasa's grandfather had married one of Sten Sture the Elder's sisters.

Gustav Vasa was the eldest son of Erik Johansson Vasa, lord of Rydboholm, a knight and councillor of State. As father of the founder of the Swedish monarchy he deserves more attention than the fleeting mention given him by our historians. He has been cursorily described as a man of moderate talents, an 'honest and mirthful gentleman'. The portrait is hardly exhaustive. Contemporary documents offer us a good deal more information than this about Erik Johansson. I will try to amplify his portrait.

The court records of the city of Stockholm state that on June 1 1489, Erik Johansson has assaulted and killed a man, by name Peder Arvidsson. Dragging his victim off to his estate at Rydboholm, he there 'unhonestly did away with him'. The enquiry into this manslaughter reveals that Peder Arvidsson was a citizen of Stockholm who had 'cut into' Erik Johansson's forest and fished his waters, an intrusion for which he had paid with his life. The Lord of Rydboholm administered his own rough justice, and Peder Arvidsson was obviously not the only man to fall foul of him; for the court records also inform us that, at a settlement reached with the citizens of Stockholm in the town court on July 19, 1490, Erik Johansson had to 'apologize for not a few deeds of violence.' According to this contemporary source, he promises to change his behaviour towards 'poor citizens of the town, who trespass on his property' – no longer shall he 'beat, hammer and treat them like other soulless beasts'. It seems that he had been in the habit of manacling such trespassers.

Seven years later Erik Johansson Vasa again appears in a contemporary record as a man of violence. Together with his men he plunders Frösunda rectory. The rector of Frösunda, Otto Ingelsson, 'weeping tears', complains of this deed. 'They raped a servant girl, forced her to show them Otto's possessions, chopped up a table, broke chests and doors in pieces, ate flesh of a Friday, and more, which neither Russians nor paynims would have done.' Archbishop Jakob Ulfsson asked the Pope to excommunicate the assailants, but we do not know whether the bull was ever issued. Nor do we ever hear of Erik Johansson being brought to trial for plundering the Frösunda rectory. If he never was, then, the explanation lies no doubt in the fact that it was the criminal himself who was responsible for the administration of justice in the district where his crime had been committed. As early as 1493, Erik Johansson is named as being a district judge at Danderyd and Rydbo, in that part of Uppland to which Frösunda then belonged.

Eighteen years afterwards the Lord of Rydboholm committed his last act of violence known to us from original documents. As late in 1515, when he had been both a Councillor of State and a knight for twenty years, he broke into and plundered a county church on one of the Mälar islands. According to a letter from Bishop Mattias of Strängnäs to Sten Sture the Younger, Erik Johansson's squires, acting on their master's orders, had committed 'deeds of violence' in this church, plundering it of much of its furnishings. The bishop had not excommunicated this Councillor of State and knight, hoping that he would repent what he had done; but he had shown no remorse. In his letter Bishop Mattias expresses a hope that the regent will exhort Erik Johansson to restore the stolen goods and become reconciled to the Church. 'The sources do not tell us how the affair developed'. Presumably the bishop had to content himself with his pious wish. The Lord of Rydboholm was the regent's close associate.

Obviously, the grandsire of the Vasa dynasty had a covetous eye to ecclesiastical property.

Hans Gillingstam, a modern genealogist, calls Erik Johansson a 'crude and violent person', and this is no exaggerated characterization of a man whom contemporary sources make responsible for assault and battery, manslaughter, rape and theft, even though in between whiles he administered justice in his own part of the country. His activities as a criminal alone, however – activities not altogether foreign to the class of mediaeval magnates – would not suffice to give him a place in Swedish history; and he would have been utterly forgotten by posterity had he not begotten a son who was to be the originator of the Swedish monarchy which still exists.

God's miracle-worker

When I was a child Gustav Eriksson Vasa seemed almost a supernatural being in human guise. God himself had sent him down to earth to be the saviour of my fatherland from 'that bloodhound and unchristian tyrant Christian.' Even as a schoolboy, Snoilsky's* poem about him was familiar to me:

* Carl Snoilsky (1841–1903), Swedish poet celebrated above all for his collection *Svenska Bilder* (1886), portraits and scenes from Swedish history in a strong national-democratic vein. The poem on Gustav Vasa quoted below is part of this work.

We read of King Gösta
in chronicle-book
God's wonder-worker who shattered
the Tyrant's yoke.
His locks are like the silver
which Eskil's chamber filled;
From ground to roof our Sweden
his hand alone did build.

Again and again I read the tales in our history books about the young Gustav's adventures in Dalarna – those famous stories about how, having escaped from Danish captivity and after the Stockholm Bloodbath he wandered northward as an outlawed fugitive and by his fiery speeches contrived to win over the Dalecarlian peasants who chose him as their captain and as leader of a national revolt which resulted in the overthrow of King Christian. For sheer excitement these tales were on a par with my Red Indian books and the volumes within whose blood-red covers Nick Carter was the hero. With tense anxiety I followed Gustav's never-ending flight from the Danish soldiers, as Snoilsky had done before me:

For fear our hearts in childhood
had scarcely strength to beat,
as soldiers' lances piercéd
the straw where he lay hid.

After I had left elementary school the subject of my very first school essay was precisely that occasion during the liberator's flight when he hid himself in a hay cart and Sven Elfsson of Isala cut his own horse's foot to explain away the blood flowing from Gustav's knee, pierced by his pursuer's halberds – the animal pathetically sacrificing its own blood for the saviour of the fatherland. In itself, an admirable tale. The only thing wrong with it is that it did not happen in Dalarna in 1520, or even in Sweden: it is a Roman anecdote about a man called Marius who had such an adventure long before the birth of Christ, interpolated into Gustav Vasa's adventures by a 17th-century Uppsala student who had been travelling in Dalarna.

Even as late as the 18th century Gustav was still having fresh Dalecarlian adventures attributed to him. The province's tourist industry has known how to make good use of them. In the Ornäs

House the visitor is still shown the privy through which Barbro Stigsdotter helped her hunted guest, the future saviour of Sweden, to escape – a monument throwing its own light on Swedish history. Again, in a loft in the Rankhyttan ironworks, the visitor is shown the flail which Gustav is supposed to have used for threshing. In reality Anders Persson's loft from 1520 disappeared – either demolished or rotted away – several hundred years ago. And with it also, presumably, his flails. Naturally the tourist trade overlooks such trifles.

Gustav Eriksson Vasa's appearance is more familiar to us than that of any other Swedish king. He was fond of sitting for his portraits, of which he has left us more than any other monarch. Anyone who has ever held a five-kronor note in his hand knows what he looked like. For a century and more Swedes have been thumbing his portrait.

His image with its flowing beard
So worthy and so dear . . .

According to our older history books, Gustav Vasa seized power in Sweden as the result of divine intervention. 'God will find his man' – and when the Almighty eventually found him it was at Rydboholm, in the guise of Gustav Vasa. He was God's miracle-worker – even in the latter part of the last century many historians were still quite sure of that. 'Christian's behaviour was admittedly vile, but God turned it to the benefit of Sweden,' a textbook from 1859 declares. 'Only by the extirpation of the incessant quarrels and warfare among the powerful lords was it possible for Gustav I to reform religion and introduce into the realm the order which was so utterly needful.' That is to say, the Stockholm Bloodbath was a necessary condition of the Reformation. Another author of school history books from the same epoch, describing the bloodbath, draws his own conclusions; 'The people of Sweden were not crushed, but their patience was at an end, and now they rose under the man whom God had appointed to save our fatherland from the hated Danish yoke.'

The same view is found in C. T. Odhner's *History for Upper School Classes* of 1886, after his account of the bloodbath: 'In God's hand Christian's cruelty became an instrument for the rehabilitation of Sweden, to its happiness and honour; the noble instrument which Providence had elected for the redemption of Sweden had already entered upon his high calling'. Odhner had already called the Vikings an 'instrument in the hand of God for the introduction of Christianity'. Now God had supposedly made similar use of Christian the Tyrant, as a tool with which to carry through his plans for Sweden. The older school of Swedish historians based their works on an unshakable certainty that 'our people, led by God, developed in the direction of all which in the true senses is great, noble and good'. Why, one wonders, did Odhner and other historians condemn the Stockholm Bloodbath, if they regarded the last king of the Union as having done Sweden so great a service by arranging it? The answer of course is that without this massacre of nobles God's miracle-worker could not have saved the country.

Gustav Vasa had a motto: 'All power is of God'. Through all his speeches and letters runs the theme that it was the All Highest who had given him the needful means and resources to rehabilitate Sweden and establish his monarchy. None of his rivals for power in the country enjoy this divine support. He alone has been called, is chosen; and therefore has the right to require the confidence of the Swedish people and their support for his policies. It was Gustav Eriksson, himself, who placed himself in the ranks of God's miracle-workers, as the Bible calls them. In several speeches – such as his speech from the throne at the 1544 Västerås riksdag – he likens himself to a new Moses. As Moses had led the Jews out of captivity in Egypt, so had he, Gustav, rescued the Swedes from their thraldom to the Danes. Again, in his farewell speech to the Estates in 1560, he likens himself to David, the insignificant youth and shepherd who overcame the insuperable Goliath, and whom God had raised to royal estate. He reminds them of the time when he 'in forests and shacks, clad in homespun, drank water and ate wretchedly'. But the king gives God the whole glory for his achievement: 'Hath aught been well done, then it is the work of God. Thank Him for it.' Again, when he had filled his treasury in Stockholm Castle with silver treasures, taken from all the poor parish churches of the realm, he had declared that it was God himself who had given these riches into his hands.

It was in elementary school I first made the acquaintance of this father of our country, whose care for his subjects was as tender as if they had been his own beloved children. Even as late as the 1930s Gustav was still being held up as such to Swedish schoolchildren. In Falk-Tunberg's history book of 1931, Gustav I is described as follows: 'In his private life he was providential for his people, God-fearing and pure in his habits. Simple and economical, a good husband and father'.

This image of Gustav Vasa as the Father of his People and God's Miracle-Worker I have long left behind me. It is, in my opinion, false through and through. This king we were told so much about in school was a fairy-tale king, who had never existed in the flesh. The invention quite simply, of Peder Svart and other contemporary chroniclers, an idealized portrait commissioned and in reality painted by none other than the sitter himself. All the time the artists were working away at their easels His Grace was standing behind them, giving them requisite instructions. Yet the portrait was accepted by historians down the centuries as true and genuine.

Not until our own time has it been subjected to critical examination. Twenty-five years ago Professor Erik Lönnroth declared that a certain change had occurred in the view taken by research of Gustav Vasa: 'Though one cannot speak of any radical re-evaluation, there has certainly been a somewhat pronounced modification of lights and shades. In brief, it means that the features of a liberator and father of his country are fading away.'

Lönnroth presents many facts which would have sufficed for a profound revision of our image of this king, and a major work on the topic was expected from him. But though Lönnroth wrote these words a quarter of a century ago, as far as I know he has never returned to the topic. And in the most recently published biography of the king by Doctor Ivan Svalenius (1950), it is largely the same old King Gösta we knew before who reappears. In the main the portrait is conventional; not without nuances, certainly, but insufficient to modify its lineaments as a whole.

Since we are still awaiting a radical re-evaluation of Gustav I by Swedish historians, it is hardly surprising that a foreign historian should have done part of the work which has so long waited upon his Swedish colleagues. The Englishman Michael Roberts, professor at Queen's University, Belfast, has devoted many years to research into Swedish history, specializing in the Vasa period and the 17th century (*The Early Vasas*, 1968.) His book on Gustav is based on incontrovertible facts. and in his account of the man who created the national state of Sweden he is blithely untroubled by such national prejudices as still have the power to inhibit some of our Swedish historians.

Roberts overlooks none of the king's merits as a ruler. His astounding energy, his enormous capacity for hard work, his admirable grasp of practical affairs, all receive ample recognition. But this Englishman's ethical verdict on God's miracle-worker is little short of devastating. Gustav was possessed with an almost pathological greed for power, he was utterly unscrupulous and ruthless and 'his word was decidedly not to be relied on.' He was litigious, but had scant respect for the law, and still less for truth. His mendacity was beyond belief, his greed for wealth bottomless. To put it bluntly, Gustav was a miser. What earlier writers have called his sense of thrift, Roberts calls 'anguished miserliness'; he finds that this quality 'could be pushed even to ignominy'.

With one exception I have been unable to find any counterpart to this portrait of Gustav Vasa by any Swedish historian. Here we have quite another king from the one whom my generation's schoolchildren had to read about at school. It was when I was studying the history of my home district during the Dacke rising that I began to form my own image of Gustav Vasa. I read up on local history as it reflected my forefathers' view of the Father of the Country, and it appeared to be well-grounded. In almost all historical works Gustav Vasa had been represented as the king who had been most beloved by his people. But between the years 1525 and 1543 his subjects' affection had taken the form of five revolts against him; three in Dalarna, one in Västergötland and one in Småland.

Here was something that did not fit the picture!

My new opinion of the founder of the Swedish monarchy became definitive when I read Fabian Månsson's great work, already referred to. And later on this great student of the Vasa period confirmed it for me in person, when we discussed the past of that part of Sweden from which both stemmed. Fabian explained to me that Gustav Vasa had been a ruthless oppressor of our ancestors, who had deeply infringed their ancient liberties and who with his German legionaries, by mass executions and by starving them out, forced them into submission. After crushing their rebellion, of which Dacke was the leader, he had ravaged Värend, the centre of the liberation movement, so thoroughly devastating it that it took two centuries before this part of the country could again recover and reach the standard of living it had enjoyed in the Later Middle Ages.

Naturally I am well aware of the one-sidedness of the picture of Gustav Vasa which now follows. Its purpose is to present the view of God's miracle-worker which found active outlet in the revolts against him. These had historical grounds which have been too little explored. The good which Gustav Vasa did during his reign is well-known. The ills he inflicted on his subjects are less familiar.

As someone who has no scientific reputation to lose, I shall run no risk if I devote myself to this aspect of the matter and write of Gustav I the Tyrant.

The Kalmar Bloodbath

Every Swedish schoolboy has read about Stockholm Bloodbath in his history book. From the same period we have a similar event, but one which has been wholly overlooked by history teachers: the execution of the garrison of Kalmar Castle in July 1525. This massacre, however, though more or less skipped in the history of the kingdom as a whole, has been described in detail by local historians. Among national historians only Emil Hildebrand has paid it some attention. He declares summarily: 'It was a monstrous bloodbath'.

Gustav Eriksson Vasa had been elected King of Sweden in 1523; but even as late as 1525 – and for a good while to come – his position was shaky. He had not succeeded in driving the Danes out of the country by the force of Swedish arms. When faced by fortresses, his peasant levies had proved useless: his siege of Stockholm had been more or less a military fiasco. Not even the Dalesmen, known for their courage during the first phase of the war of liberation and feared for their effective archery, could prevail against this fortress in the capital. And they implored the king 'with the very loudest cries and wailing' to be allowed to go home and sow and reap and till their land. He granted them their wish. They were permitted to go home to Dalarna. But the capital of the kingdom still remained to be subdued. In lieu of his Swedish peasants, therefore, Gustav Vasa recruited German men-at-arms, well trained, militarily efficient folk, with warfare as their profession. From the Hanseatic League he obtained on credit ten men-of-war from Lubeck and a couple of companies of men-at-arms.

The Germans brought the assault on Stockholm to an effective close. Thanks to the foreign aid and after a lengthy siege, the new king of Sweden was able to enter his capital. But Kalmar was an even stronger fortress than Stockholm. Nor could it be taken by Swedish troops. So the king was again obliged to have recourse to foreign assistance. He gave the task of taking the 'key to Sweden' to his chief German commander, Berend von Melen, who had already proved his capacity as a field commander. Von Melen had blamed his own unsuccessful attempt to conquer Skåne for Gustav in 1523 on 'a sudden thaw'; in reality it had not been the consequence of any thaw, but of the peace treaty concluded by the peasantry along the frontier. But von Melen carried out his task at Kalmar to perfection. After astute parleys the garrison was prevailed on to surrender the castle, and von Melen occupied it in the king's name. For this he was amply rewarded by Gustav Vasa: the German soldier was given a seat in the Swedish Council of State, received Kalmar county and Uppvidinge hundred in fief, and Gustav's own second cousin, Margareta Eriksdotter Vasa, to wife. The German who had conquered the 'key to Sweden' became related by marriage to the King of Sweden, and was his favourite. No Swede occupied a comparable position, and among the native nobility the immense and swift success of this foreigner aroused intense envy. Sweden had just been liberated from her Danish overlords. Now the Swedish nobles had every reason to ask: was there to be a new régime of foreigners in the land? Was the king going to replace Danes by Germans in his council and in the highest posts of the realm?

Berend von Melen was every inch an adventurer. A soldier of fortune, he is the very embodiment of a legionary, a type altogether characteristic of that age. All over Europe the great age of the legionaries had begun, and von Melen was a formidable representative of his species. He had served many masters, sometimes even two at once. Earlier, he had served as a colonel under Christian II and taken part in his campaign against the Swedes. Christian's commandant at Stegeborg, upon this fortress being captured by the Swedes, had gone over to them and entered King Gustav's service. The mark of a true legionary was his ability to change masters from one day to another. Such behaviour was hardly regarded in those days as treason, but in much the same light as we view an employee who leaves one firm to take up a better job with another, True, a legionary had to swear an oath of fealty to each new master; but this oath to the colours was nothing but a formality, over in a jiffy, and the cause of no qualms. For in any case he had no intention of keeping it.

And Berend von Melen did not take his oath of fidelity to Gustav seriously, either. Indeed, in view of von Melen's eventful past, it is astonishing that Gustav should have placed such implicit trust in this commander of legionaries. How could he rely on a man who had forthwith abandoned the Danish colours for the Swedish? There can only be one explanation: Gustav stood in such dire need of efficient legionaries and capable military commanders that out of sheer necessity he was obliged to use this German colonel.

And von Melen turned out to be as faithful to him as he had been to Christian. He regarded Kalmar Castle, which he had captured, as his private property. Placing his brother Henrik in command of it, he gave him strict orders on no account whatever to hand it over to the King of Sweden. When Gustav demanded that the castle gates be opened to him, all he got from Henrik von Melen was an apologetic but flat refusal.

By this time the king had already other reasons for suspecting Berend von Melen of guile and treachery. He had sent him to Gotland to seize that island from Sören Norrby, but von Melen had come home empty-handed. Further, it had come to Gustav's ears that while on Gotland von Melen had entered into treasonable negotiations with the enemy. Obviously the legionary was contemplating a fresh change of masters. The King of Sweden had suffered reverses; his new monarchy, only two years old, stood on shaky foundations. Probably the commander of the legionaries was counting on its imminent collapse, and had already begun to reinsure himself against that eventuality. He would not have hesitated for a moment to return to King Christian.

Von Melen can be regarded as a traitor twice over, but Gustav discovered his treachery too late, and this was to cost him dear. Even then he could only proceed cautiously against his military commander. As long as he was in charge of a numerous body of his own countrymen this German was a military factor in the Swedish power game, and a man very dangerous to its king.

In the spring of 1525 von Melen was summoned to Stockholm by King Gustav, who again demanded that the gates of Kalmar Castle should be thrown open to its rightful owner. Expressly promising to hand it over, von Melen set off for Kalmar to fulfil his promise. Naturally, he lost no time in breaking it. Nor had he ever had any intention of letting Kalmar, which he regarded as his own fief, pass out of his hands. This great fortress was in truth worth the keeping. On the eve of a journey to his own country, von Melen therefore required an oath of fidelity from the Swedish and German soldiers of the castle garrison that 'They were to obey and abet him and keep the castle in his possession, and not surrender it, neither to King Gustav nor to anyone else, until such time as he had returned from that journey (to Germany)' – W. Sylvander. And the garrison swore to be faithful to him and defend the fortress to the last man against King Gustav and his people. The man whom von Melen left behind in command of the castle was Henrik Jute, a soldier who had earlier done service under Sten Sture.

Together with his brother Henrik and his own family von Melen went back to Germany, where he joined the king's enemies and for many years to come troubled him with his conspiracies.

But Kalmar had been captured on King Gustav's account and belonged to the Swedish crown. The king's bitterness against this relative by marriage, who had played such a disgracefully double game, was understandable. The legionary had pulled the wool over his eyes. Gustav had showered gifts and rewards on von Melen; and all the thanks he had got was the blackest treachery. Few Swedes of the day were as intelligent as Gustav Eriksson of Rydboholm; but in cunning and dissimulation he had met his match in this German, Berend von Melen. Gustav Vasa is noted for his ability to learn from experience. This time he certainly did.

Beautifully situated on a promontory in Kalmar Sound, Kalmar Castle looks as idyllic as can be. Yet the ground around its walls is certainly more deeply drenched in blood than any other in Scandinavia. Every time war broke out between Sweden and Denmark the fight for the 'key to Sweden' was equally sanguinary. Always the struggle came to be focused on Sweden's strongest frontier fortress, and the side which was in possession of it always had the upper hand. But the fortress was almost impregnable by mediaeval military art. Above the castle gates is inscribed the proud legend: 'never captured by force of arms'. During the Sture epoch it had withstood a number of lengthy sieges, the memory of which has survived in popular tradition.

Von Melen's treason had made it necessary for Gustav Vasa to take the strongest of all Scandinavian fortresses for the second time. In July, 1525, he went down to Kalmar with some choice troops, four companies of footmen, all told about fifteen hundred élite soldiers. Obviously the king was well aware that he was faced with a difficult and costly undertaking: but for his men it became even more costly than he expected. Many hundreds of them paid for the castle with their lives.

In the month of July, 1525, one of the bloodiest chapters in the history of Kalmar Castle was written. Gustav's troops tried to storm the fortress and a horrible slaughter commenced. Faithful to their oath to their master, von Melen's legionaries put up the stoutest and most obstinate resistance. Though outnumbered many times over, they repulsed the storm troops. Again and again the assailants were driven back from the walls leaving behind them enormous losses in killed and wounded. The bodies of Gustav's men filled the moats, and the survivors, attacking across these heaps of corpses, only augmented their numbers.

Peder Svart, who describes the struggle in his chronicle, is of the view that King Gustav lost half his force within a few days: 'A good half part of them lay on their necks, and a great part limbless, some with an arm off, some with a thigh, some both arms and thighs.'

The historian of Kalmar, W. Sylvander writes: 'The king wept tears of grief at the terrible reverse and the loss of so many heroes and so many competent men-at-arms.' And Peder Svart adds: 'King Gustav wept so that he must well-nigh have swooned.'

As far as we know it was a unique situation in Gustav Vasa's life. He is not known to have been a weak, lachrymose or sensitive man, nor do we anywhere else hear of his shedding tears. There is therefore something remarkable about this outburst of grief at Kalmar. If Gustav gave vent to his feelings it was only human – militarily, too, he had reason to grieve. The men he had lost in the moats were his élite soldiers. And he could not spare a man.

His troops seem to have done everything humanly or militarily possible. But contemporary chroniclers also relate how the king, beside himself with rage after the failure of the assaults, called his troops a lot of chicken-hearted cowards. 'Tearing off his royal mantle and donning his armour, he declared he would take part in the assault himself, either to conquer or die, either to take the castle or else perish before it. But his men-at-arms implored him to spare his precious life for the fatherland, and for God's sake not to shame them by personally taking part in the storming operations.' They promised him to try a new assault and not yield, 'even if each and every one of them fell in it'. Whereupon the king withdrew his threat, took off his armour and promised to spare his own life.

This is one of the few occasions when Gustav Vasa makes an appearance in a wholly military context. As a leader of armies he is not to be compared with Sten Sture the Younger, who was a man of real military talent; nor was Gustav a warrior king like his grandson Gustavus Adolphus, who was to lead his own troops in the field. So whether he really had any serious intention of risking his life in the struggle at Kalmar in 1525 is hard to say. Perhaps the threat alone sufficed.

New assaults led to new reverses and fresh losses. But the garrison too was being decimated. Finally, against a promise of free conduct, it offered to capitulate. The castle was surrendered on St Margaret's Day, July 20, 1525. No note of the terms of the capitulation has survived, but it is generally supposed that the defenders reserved their right to depart without let or hindrance. And this – in view of what followed upon their capitulation – is the crux of the matter.

Kalmar's trustworthy historian Sylvander, who has studied the matter more thoroughly than anyone else, writes: 'It is almost incontrovertible that the garrison . . . on the one hand threatened rather to die fighting than surrender at discretion, and that the king, rather than sacrifice any more of his courageous troops, granted the defenders freedom of life and limb. Without question the garrison had not only negotiated their unhindered evacuation of the castle but also their repatriation at the king's expense, *for he had them given victuals and ships in which to return to Germany*. The king obtained the castle by negotiation.'

Other historians have queried this point, and regard the terms of the capitulation as obscure: they doubt whether the king gave the garrison any promise to spare their lives or let them depart. Personally I regard Sylvander's statement as impeccable. Psychologically, too, it is wholly probable. Why else should the soldiers in the castle give up the fight, unless they were afterwards to be granted their lives? The legionary scorns death. That is his character. If it were not, he would not adopt such a profession. These men would certainly have preferred to die honorably, sword in hand, to a dishonorable death on the headsman's block, and would scarcely have capitulated except against the king's express promise of a safe conduct; unless they had thought their lives were safe. Great weight attaches to this psychological argument.

As a result of negotiations, therefore, the survivors inside the castle expected to go free. Their lot was otherwise. Gustav Vasa broke the safe conduct. The men of the garrison were seized and held prisoner, and the king appointed a court-martial, presided over by himself, before which they were brought and tried as traitors. But neither juridically nor morally, as far as we can see, can they have committed treason. After all, they were not in the king's service, were not his troops, and had never sworn fealty to him. Von Melen was their lord; it was to him they had sworn to be faithful, and to him they had demonstrated their fidelity by fighting on to the last. It was Berend von Melen who had been guilty of treason against Gustav Vasa; not his men.

Nevertheless the court-martial condemned them all to death on the wheel, as traitors. The sentence was commuted to decapitation. Whereafter, with the sole exception of two servingmen 'who were graciously granted their lives at the urgent plea of those who afterwards took them into their service', the entire remnant of the garrison were beheaded. All the others had fallen in the siege. We do not know exactly how many soldiers perished on the block in Kalmar. Fabian Månsson gives a figure of between sixty and seventy. Other writers place the figure either higher or lower. A local historian tells how the edge of the executioner's axe finally became so blunted that it could no longer be used, upon which he finished his task by crushing the soldiers' heads with a mace.

The analogy with the Stockholm Bloodbath of five years earlier leaps, of course, to mind. Christian II, too, flouted his own express assurances of an amnesty to his defeated opponents of the Sture party. Gustav I revoked the safe conduct he had promised to the capitulating defenders of Kalmar Castle. The difference in the victims' numbers cannot have been very great.

But in their effects the events in Stockholm and Kalmar were quite disparate. The first bloodbath stirred up an immense storm of indignation. Its political consequences were decisive. The other massacre occurred in obscurity, and historians have noticed it only in a somewhat distrait fashion. The explanation is simple. Among the Stockholm victims were members of the leading and highest families of the realm, noble lords and prelates of the Church, who bore celebrated names, men known and famed throughout the country. Olaus Petri lists 'those whose heads had fallen and whose names were famous'. But at Kalmar it was only ordinary humble soldiers who were beheaded, nameless men. In the one instance the victims' deaths were of great consequence; in the other, of little or none. In all ages different value has been set on different human lives, according to birth, status and property.

Peder Svart, Gustav I's favourite and ever-willing chronicler, though he finds Kalmar Bloodbath horrible, naturally acquits the king of all responsibility for it. He throws all the blame on that vicious traitor von Melen. Had Gustav Vasa cut von Melen's head off, he would have been entirely within his rights. Instead, he executed the rank and file, who had committed no crime. Peder

Svart, that is, discreetly ignores the crux of the matter. As he had to – otherwise Gustav Vasa's sanguinary orgy at Kalmar would have borne too disconcerting a resemblance to Christian the Tyrant's in Stockholm.

And facts only speak out when historians make use of them. What we have here is a concrete instance of how history is falsified by selection. The facts of the Stockholm Bloodbath have spoken down the ages, for four and a half centuries. Those which have all this time been available about the Kalmar Bloodbath have remained dumb. It is high time they were allowed to speak.

The King's Church

Gustav Vasa broke the Roman Catholic Church's economic hegemony in Sweden, stripped it of its enormous wealth, and deprived it of its military limb, the bishops' cavalry – those trains of horsemen who rode through the country demanding board and lodging from the peasantry. Bishop Hans Brask of Linköping was the last in the long line of lords spiritual who united in their person the functions of prelate and a cavalry officer. The Swedes were also relieved of the tax monies which for several centuries they had been paying to the head of the Church in Rome, and of which God's Vicar on Earth had never rendered any account. Had they known how he used these funds they would at times have been deeply shocked, as must any believing Christian who had learnt not to store up riches which moth and rust consume. During the Late Middle Ages and the decadence of the Papal Church the Peter's Pence were often put to such uses. The Church had also sold heaven to her Swedish members in the form of indulgences. Profitable deals in men's salvation after death certainly ought not to have been the business of those who alleged they represented the man who said his kingdom was not of this world. This was the opinion of the Church reformer Olaus Petri; and Gustav shared his view of the matter.

In liberating his kingdom from its dependence on the universal Catholic Church the king did something which in itself was praiseworthy. He also abolished the power of the bishops, succeeding in Sweden where Christian II had failed in Denmark. But according to the Reformation propaganda the Lutheran Church was to meet a great need among Swedes and salve their spiritual anxieties. In point of fact, however, the common man in Sweden had not asked for any novel doctrine. On the contrary, he would have much preferred to keep his old one, to which he and his ancestors had adhered for more than four hundred years. Many generations had died peacefully in the Catholic faith. What really precipitated the Reformation was the king's and the crown's urgent pecuniary needs.

To judge from Olaus Petri's declarations, Gustav's intention seems to have been to provide Swedes with a Church of their own, a national institution, a popular and wholly independent Church, with no supreme head except God Himself. Even to someone who believes as little in the one doctrine as in the other, this seems a change for the better, and one with which one can sympathize. But what was the upshot of the ecclesiastical reformation which Gustav Vasa despotically – setting Olaus Petri aside – took over? After a couple of decades all that had happened was that, instead of a pope, the Swedish church found it had a king as its supreme authority. It became not a popular but a royal institution. As for its property, Gustav Vasa treated it as his own, deciding all its affairs out of hand. It became the king's Church.

It was Gustav I who founded the Swedish State Church, which still exists. But a state Church is an institution offensive to all commonsense. For more than four hundred years the kingdom of Sweden has had a certain definite religion, a certain definite faith: the Evangelical Lutheran. But how can a kingdom believe in something? And even if the kingdom is called a state, its capacity for faith is just as nugatory. The state is not even a figure of folklore, as the Devil is in the view of modern theologians. It is an abstraction and, as such, can neither think nor feel, nor embrace any conviction whatsoever. Only a living human being is blessed with such a faculty.

This new Church was organized subserviently to the king's surveillance and control. The old Church, with its fortified episcopal residences, had acquired almost one-fifth of the land throughout the realm. All this now became crown property. And with the riches of this cavalry-and-estate-owning Church the king should have been content. The poor little parish churches should have been allowed to keep their possessions. Yet they too were stripped of their belongings, plundered of their silver and other ornaments. Not a single parish church was left untouched. Down the centuries, generation after generation, men had made great sacrifices to enhance the temples which were their parish's place of assembly. Now the king's men came and took from them their bridal crowns, their candlesticks, their chalices, their altar cloths, their monstrances, their images of the Virgin and other treasures, sacred to the common people. Through the ages these objects had been inextricably involved in people's holy days and festivals, in their spiritual life. It is calculated that eighty-five per cent of the silver in the parish churches of Småland, 3,700 kilograms, were taken away. The loss of these gleaming treasures, which had helped to brighten their dark churches, left a great gap. Only the bare walls were left.

It was a gross outrage to the piety of the country folk. To anyone who knows at first hand how profoundly serious are the religious feelings of the countryman it seems only natural that this plunder of his churches should have led to insurrections. To me no rising seems more understandable than the church-bell rising in Dalarna in 1531. The people were being deprived of property honestly earned by them. In their eyes the king's proceedings were nothing but barefaced robbery, an act of burglary committed against their temples. Finds made in various parts of Sweden have revealed how people tried to rescue their beloved heirlooms from the royal bailiffs. Silver treasures from churches, buried in the 16th century, have been found in prehistoric cairns.

To rob the people like this was hardly the right way to create the popular Church which should have replaced the cavalry-and-state-owning Church. As far as we can judge, even the reformer Olaus Petri, himself a man of the people, thought it was the wrong way of going about things.

On one occasion; before Gustav Vasa, on June 6, 1523, had been elected king at Strängnäs, he had sworn an oath never to touch the property of the Catholic Church as it existed at that time. This promise formed part of an agreement concluded on July 25, 1521, between himself and Bishop Hans Brask, the Church's chief representative. Gustav had solemnly promised to defend the privileges of Holy Church, her personnel and her possessions 'as long as I live'. Further, the regent, as he then was, bound himself to be the bishop's friend for better or for worse and 'never to desert him'. Before he had lived much longer Gustav had broken his oath in every detail. After a few years the universal Roman Catholic Church in Sweden had been overthrown and Hans Brask had fled into exile.

Gustav Vasa's actions were dictated by the kind of council given by Machiavelli in *The Prince*: 'And therefore a wise prince cannot, nor ought not keep his faith given when the observance thereof turns to disadvantage, and the occasions, that made him promise, are past. – And ordinarily things have been succeeded with him that hath been nearest the Fox in condition'. The king of 1527 saw no reason to keep the promise made by the regent of 1521. The Västerås *riksdag* of that year is more important than almost any other in Swedish history. It was at this assembly that Gustav finally defeated his most dangerous opponent within the realm, Bishop Hans Brask. In doing so he took a decisive step toward setting up his royal dictatorship. If he needed the wealth of the Church, it was in order to exert his own power and implement his plans – and so he simply seized it, using methods again reminiscent of *The Prince*. Lauritz Weibull has summed up the results of the Västerås *riksdag*: 'Gustav Vasa had been granted the tool of power for which he had been striving. He had come by it after a series of machiavellian machinations. With these implements in his hands he could now proceed further!'

King Gustav lost no time in doing so. In his ecclesiatical confiscations he went further than anyone in the kingdom, in 1527, could ever have imagined. In a royal brief dated January 31, 1531, he requires of each church one bell and also the congregation's entire land tithe for that year – all the church's regular income, that is, except the amount needed for the purchase of wax and wine.

Gustav Vasa implemented his policies by setting off one class of the population against another – a method much favoured by rulers. He played off the aristocracy against the commons, the peasants against the burghers, and one province against another. Soon he was consulting none of their representatives before arriving at his decisions: latest research shows that from the early 1530's onwards Gustav Vasa's dictatorship was complete.

After 1529, the king did not again summon a *riksdag* until 1544. He held meetings of the Council; but they were mere formalities. What really mattered and had to be obeyed were the royal decrees, and these he issued arbitrarily. When the *riksdag* finally met again it was simply in order to approve the decisions already made and long ago implemented by the king. The analogy with Hitler's *Kroll-Opera* leaps to mind.

His confiscations of parish plate continued even after he had paid off the kingdom's debt to Lübeck. In 1541–42 he set in motion a systematic plunder of country churches in the Götaland provinces, and this was one of the causes of the Dacke rising. This time Gustav did not even pretend to ask the lords of the Council for their opinion. Probably it was his new German advisers, Konrad von Pyhy and Georg Norman, who had put the idea into his head. On the king's personal orders, his bailiffs abstracted from the poor parish churches all that might be left in them of value. Altar cloths and copes were removed and handed over to Queen Margareta, who used the superb materials to clothe the royal children.

It is estimated that six and a half tons of church silver were gathered into the celebrated St Eskil's chamber, Gustav Vasa's private treasury. This was one imposing result of the Lutheran reformation in Sweden; and to that extent it was a great success. But there was also a religious aspect. The faith hitherto held by Swedes was now found to be utter error. For four centuries they had been baptised into the wrong church, had lived and died in the wrong religion. Now at last the moment had come for the introduction of the true faith. Now it was decided – to use the words of the Västerås *riksdag* – that 'the pure word of God shall be everywhere preached according to God's command, and not according to uncertain miracles, the fables and vain imaginings of men, as hath been heretofore'. It was to be preached in the vernacular, so that the common man should understand the doctrines of the priesthood. In point of religious enlightenment this was a great step forward. The Church of Sweden was purged of the dogmas of the papal Church, together with the worship of saints, the milk of the Virgin

Mary and so forth, by which the people were no longer to be seduced and confused. Holy Writ was to be interpreted and disseminated in such a manner as could be understood by everyone. Thanks to the labours of Olaus Petri, the New Testament was published for the first time in Swedish. It was he who first tried to teach our people to read.

Gradually, however, new dogmas arose, a Lutheran protestant theology, hardly easier for the common man to understand than the doctrines and Latin masses of the Roman Catholic Church had been. Among other things the Reformed Church set in process an intensive and thoroughgoing study of diabolism, one result of which was some statistics over the total number of devils in hell. A 16th-century protestant theologian at a German university made a precise calculation, running into thirteen figures: 2,666,866,764,664, a figure which, even so, only took into account the 'lesser devils'.

In Lutheran doctrine the Lord of Hell, the Devil, became a good deal more terrifying than he had ever been in Catholic doctrine, and after the lake of burning brimstone had been introduced hell became both more realistic and more horrible. It was the new Church which implanted in the psyche of the common man a terror of hell that was to become a monstrous popular torment, which has survived down into our own time. I have myself known several of its victims. On the lips of the common man the prince of the underworld acquired a multitude of new names, over and above the purely conventional 'Satan' and 'Devil', 'The Evil One', 'The Enemy', 'The Dangerous One', under which he had appeared down the centuries. In my own childhood it was The Dangerous One who was used to terrify me. All these new sobriquets taught folk to understand how deeply the Devil was to be feared.

So Sweden officially became an Evangelical Lutheran kingdom, with its own state Church, but a great deal of time was to pass before people were transformed spiritually from Catholics to Protestants. Here was no question of a spontaneous conversion; and it is quite possible that, but for Gustav Vasa's monetary straits, the Swedes would have remained Catholics to this day. I feel we should be sorry for those many people who would have preferred to keep their ancient faith. The nuns of Vadstena, forced to listen to sermons by Lutheran clergy, are famous for their passive resistance. They stuffed their ears with wool and wax.

Popular discontent at the Reformation was fanned by printed Catholic propaganda, and it did not take Gustav Vasa long to realise that freedom of the printed word could be a serious danger to his régime. Through it his subjects had a chance, which they had lacked before the age of the printing press, of spreading nefarious opinions. Closing a Catholic printing works and exiling its printer, he subsidized those printers who published reformist tracts. Even this was not enough; a censorship was necessary. In 1539, Gustav issued an edict, expressly commanding that no 'print' should be placed in the hands of the common people 'without we first have considered and decided therein'. *This was the first law establishing censorship in Sweden*, a law which made possible a total suppression of the free word. Two hundred years later Gustav's successors on the throne were still applying it, right up to the 18th century. All printed matter, as the expression went, had to be 'seen over' before it came to the eyes of the public.

Even in his care for his subjects' reading matter Gustav Vasa was therefore a pioneer and innovator – not that any of his predecessors would not have done the same, had the printer's dangerous art been invented in their day.

The press policies of modern dictators follow ancient precedent.

Sweden's greatest householder

No Swedish king was ever so deeply knowledgeable about agriculture as was Gustav Eriksson Vasa. That he possessed a practical knowledge of farming is certain. During the years when he was growing up at Rydboholm and on the other Vasa farms he had obviously studied the daily life of the peasantry at each season of the year and, even if he had not participated in them himself, had studied their tasks. He knew when the field had to be harrowed, when the grain had to be sowed, when the hay had to be brought in, and when the sheep had to be shorn. When he became king he wrote to the peasantry all over his kingdom, instructing them in the proper cultivation of their homesteads. Such insights are unique in a man in his position; perhaps he is the only Swedish ruler who had an intimate knowledge of farming. I cannot imagine Queen Christina issuing directives for the proper method of pig-breeding, or Gustav III writing letters to the common people on the best season for planting potatoes!

These commands and regulations, always being issued by their king, hardly amused the peasantry. On the contrary, his interference in the cultivation of their farms certainly angered and irritated them. Such matters they thought they understood better than His Grace. And sometimes they really did. The peasants of Öland, in one famous instance, certainly did. In a royal missive Gustav strictly enjoined them to bring in their hay on St Olof's Day (July 29) at the latest. To this letter the addressees could certainly have replied: 'Your Grace! Are we to take in the hay stooks under roof, even if they've been standing in drenching rain for a week? Are we to harvest soaking hay, which will be utterly ruined in the barn?'

The Swedish peasant had of old been in the habit of cultivating his land as he pleased and thought fit. He had no desire to be subjected to the guardianship of an all-puissant king who intervened in his private affairs with directives, regulations and bans, this authoritarian master who even threatened to take his farm away from them if he did not look after it properly. Were free peasant proprietors to put up with such treatment?

From Eli Heckscher's *Economic History of Sweden* it transpires that Swedish agriculture, taken as a whole, increased its yield during the early Vasa period. The number of derelict farms was reduced, output per homestead of grain, meat and butter rose. The king's concern for the mother-industry would therefore appear to have borne fruit, though we must also bear in mind that such an increment was also favoured by the state of peace which, beginning in the mid-1520s, was only interrupted by the civil war of 1541–42.

Another aspect of Gustav I's great interest in agriculture was his enormous personal acquisitions of land, which in due course made him the country's largest private land owner, with estates comprising at his death some 5,000 homesteads.

When Gustav came to power the soil of Sweden is estimated to have been distributed as follows: 3,754 crown homesteads, 14,340

Church homesteads, 13,922 noble homesteads, and 35,239 taxable homesteads – i.e. farms, owned by the peasants themselves. The Church, that is, had owned almost five times as many homesteads as the crown. Forty years later, in 1560, the distribution is utterly different. Now the state owns 18,936 homesteads, the Church none, the nobility 14,175 and the peasants 33,130. All Church estates have passed to the crown; the nobles have retained and somewhat augmented theirs; but the peasantry have lost a couple of thousand homesteads.

That is to say, in 1560 the king and his clan owned so many homesteads that they corresponded to more than a quarter of the crown lands, and to almost one-sixth of all lands belonging to the commons. No Swedish king has ever possessed anything like such great wealth. In mid-16th-century Europe, according to Michael Roberts, stories were circulating of the fabulous wealth of Gustav Vasa.

His miserliness and avarice for land seem to have been pathological. He only had to be seized with desire for some fertile acres, a forest well-stocked with game or some good eel-fisheries, to became immediately possessed of them. In his day the ownership of the soil was not fixed by law, once and for all. Ownership was a matter of interpretation. Gustav never passed up an opportunity to acquire a good homestead. Further, as can be seen from a declaration made by him on April 20, 1542 he claimed that all common lands were crown property. 'Forasmuch as such lands as do lie uncultivated, they belong to God, to us and to the crown of Sweden, and none other'.

But already in the 1550s the notion that the crown was the rightful owner of *all* land, that peasants only had the right to till it, and that this right could in certain cases be taken away from them, had probably been put into Gustav's head by his German advisers. In Sweden it was a revolutionary concept.

Juridically, the crown in Sweden had never owned any peasant lands which were subject to tax. The peasant proprietor had a right to the land he cultivated. And so it had been, up to the reign of Gustav Vasa. But foreign law asserted the view that *all* land had originally belonged to the crown, which had subsequently ceded it, partly to the nobility with *dominium directum* (full ownership rights), and partly to the peasants, who only enjoyed an hereditary right to its use, *dominium utile*.

This idea of the state having plenary rights of land-ownership had originally been the brainchild of an Italian jurist, Johannes Bassarius, who had lived in the 13th century. Applied in feudal Germany, it was therefore probably brought to King Gustav's ears by Konrad von Pyhy, Georg Norman and other Germans. Such an overriding proprietorship of all taxable homesteads fitted in admirably with Gustav Vasa's policies, and the king began applying it in practice. If, in his opinion, any peasant was mismanaging his farm, he was turned off it; and if a homestead had paid no tax for three years, it was seized by the crown.

Gustav Vasa's new view of land ownership is mirrored in two of his letters to his bailiffs and the commons, dated April 15, 1541, and February 4, 1553. Wherever a tax-paying peasant is found to be allowing his land to become derelict or otherwise ruining it, this land belongs to 'us and to the crown of Sweden. May all take note thereof'.

'Us and the crown of Sweden' – the identification is complete. The two are become one flesh.

All of which was to say that any tax-paying peasant who in ancient custom had been held to be the owner of his land should be allowed to cultivate it only as long as the king and the crown permitted. In reality the crown peasant's status was now to be that of a farmer: the landowner could give him notice and turn him out. A century later this view of property rights was to assume weight and importance. In the great battle between the Estates, the nobles and peasants were struggling fiercely for the soil, and there were peasant revolts. The nobility, namely, implementing Gustav Vasa's idea, had seized taxable lands to which they regarded themselves as having been given all rights of ownership by Queen Christina. Whenever a peasant failed to pay his taxes for three successive years, his homestead was declared forfeit; which meant quite simply that the nobleman took it over and the peasant was evicted from his farm, his own and his family's home. (My novel *Ride To-Night*, whose action is placed in the year 1650, treats of this imminent threat to the liberties of the commons).

This order of things which Gustav Vasa attempted to introduce into Sweden was feudal, and as such utterly foreign to all Swedish juridic ideas, as understood by the people. Nor did it strike any lasting root in our country. But historians have overlooked its connection with the struggle a century later, between the Estates.

For insurgents, the block

In the Late Middle Ages, Dalarna was politically Sweden's leading province, almost a realm within the realm. The great age of the Dalesmen had begun with Engelbrekt's assault on the Borganäs bailey on Midsummer Day 1434, and it lasted right up to the day of Gustav Vasa's razzia among the leaders of the church bell rising at Kopparberg in 1533; that is for a century, all but one year.

Bergslagen, the great mining region, the abode of many wealthy mine-masters, included Southern Dalarna. Otherwise, Dalarna was a province where poverty was indigenous. It was rich only in people. It had no nobles, no estates and no large farms. The land was distributed into small parcels, sufficient to support many peasants. Equality between one man and another was therefore greater here than in the provinces dominated by the aristocracy, such as Uppland, Södermanland and Östergötland. If Dalarna's status was unique, it was partly because of her large population. The province could put several thousand armed men into the field, a force utilized more especially by the Stures who always sought, and could always rely on, getting the Dalesmen's support whenever they needed it. Gustav Vasa, too, had come up to Dalarna on the same errand as the Stures before him. Their feat of arms with their home-made weapons had made the Dalesmen a military power-factor to reckon with. Particularly feared by their enemies were their sharp iron-tipped arrows, which they made for their cross-bows and long-bows. Even today the crossed arrows are a prominent feature of the coat of arms of Dalarna.

In the Later Middle Ages, Dalarna, with her poor but unfeudalized population, had also been the chief source of Swedish insurrections. More risings against foreign and native powers had broken out there than in any other part of the country. Even as late as 1743, at the time of the 'great Dalesmen's dance' (the scornful name given to the revolt by those who tragically and bloodily crushed it) this proud tradition lived on and proved to be a source of inspiration to the Dalesmen. And in 1788 Gustav III, who had read the history of Gustav I with close attention, stood up on the wall of Mora churchyard and, dressed in local costume and wearing the ribbon of the Order of the Seraphim on his breast, raised the parishes against the Danes and Russians.

The Dalesmen had done more than any other Swedes to put Gustav Eriksson Vasa on the throne. Subsequently they made even greater efforts to remove him from it. These attempts had begun as early as 1524. Only a year after Gustav had been elected king they were already wanting to get rid of him. In Dalarna it was a time of famine and bark bread. The cost of life's basic necessities had risen sky-high, and people lacked 'honest coin'. They attributed their troubles to all the Lübeckers the king had brought into the country. In exchange for a loan to finance the war against the Danes he had given these foreigners a monopoly of all trade, and they were utilizing it to skin the population of the very province which had most helped him to seize power.

The Dalesmen's first insurrection against Gustav was led by two Catholic prelates, Peder Kansler, known as Sunnanväder, and Master Knut. Both had been evicted by Gustav from their livings. Now they wanted to see the Stures on the throne. The king was reasonable and prepared to negotiate. At a meeting with the discontented and fist-shaking Dalesmen, at Tuna in October, 1525, he promised to set everything amiss to rights, and for the moment the discontent subsided. As for the two leaders of the rebellion, by and by Gustav got them into his clutches and they were sent to the block.

The second rising of the Dalesmen, in 1527–28, was a considerably more serious affair. What was in question this time was the oppressive burden of taxation – that abiding source of insurrection – bearing on the commons. In order to pay off the state's debt to the Lübeckers the king had decreed the imposition of very harsh taxes. This time the Dalesmen had a suitable candidate to replace Gustav Eriksson on the throne, a youth who claimed to be the eldest son of Sten Sture the Younger, a man much loved in Dalarna. To history he is known as the 'Daljunker', but research has not been able to establish his true identity. Since he was no more than sixteen years old, Sten Sture and Kristina Gyllenstierna can hardly have had a son of his age in their marriage. Peder Svart calls the Daljunker an 'angry and desperate rogue' '*arg förtvifflad bof*'. In the king's propaganda against him as leader of the insurrection he is called Jöns Hansson, and declared to be a 'rascal', a stable hand who after robbing his first master had run away from his second. All contemporary witnesses agree, however, that the Daljunker behaved like a man of education and assumed all the airs and graces of a gentleman. Nevertheless his alleged mother, Kristina Gyllenstierna, utterly disavowed him. A statement of doubtful authenticity declares that she was forced to do so under torture. The young man himself declared that his mother was ashamed of him; if she would not recognize him, he said, it was because he was born 'before she was wedded'. Recent research (Folke Lindberg) takes into account the possibility that he may really have been the person he pretended to be.

Not all the Dalecarlian villages supported this alleged scion of the Stures, who unsuccessfully tried to invade Dalarna from Norway. After that King Gustav was able to crush his rebellion. In February, 1528, he summoned the Dalesmen to a meeting at Tuna Mead for a settlement of accounts. They were promised, of course, a safe conduct – and of course Gustav abused it. When the Dalesmen arrived at Tuna they found themselves confronted with the king's men-at-arms, in full panoply of war, who ringed them in in the meadow. 'They were rounded up like cattle'. And now the most effective of all instruments for forcing men into submission was brought out: the headsman's axe. After which their terror could be counted on to bring them to heel. The supposed ringleaders were plucked out of the crowd, led to the block and instantly beheaded. 'When the others saw how blood had begun to flow, another sound came into their barking. They feared desperately for their lives, began to shriek and weep, fell on their knees, imploring and begging the king for God's sake to show mercy, and promising betterment' – to quote Peder Svart's chronicle.

These rebels who died on the block in Tuna Mead are anonymous. Nor do we know their numbers. Gustav Vasa also insisted that sentence of death should be passed on the Daljunker, who had fled to Germany. The same year, in the autumn of 1528, the young man – whoever he was – was beheaded in Rostock city market place.

Tuna Mead or compound is a large open place in the southern part of Dalarna. For centuries it had been the scene of popular assemblies. Long before 1528 it was already historic, and after the king's razzia in that year it became bloodsoaked ground. When I saw it, in 1971, the meadow was under plough. A ring of great stones marks this immemorial meeting place. But that historic event in 1528, when an unknown number of Dalecarlians met their deaths, has still not been commemorated in any way. The event lives, admittedly, in a magnificent poem by one of the great Swedish writers of our time, Erik Axel Karlfeldt. But I lack a monument to these nameless men, on the spot where they perished for the Dalesmen's right to self-determination.

In the following year the Västergötland revolt broke out. It began among the commons of north-west Småland: 'the Smålanders made no little noise' says Peder Svart. Their 'noise' spread to a number of other provinces, but the king managed to splinter the movement and separate the men behind it, and it was soon suppressed. Nor could the noblemen of Västergötland and the Småland peasantry really have had the same aims.

The church bell revolt of 1531, the third and last to be made against Gustav Vasa in Dalarna, occurred chiefly in the parishes around Lake Siljan, always the most restless part of the province. Its centre was at Leksand, and it was there it gestated. It was a brief affair, 'a flame suddenly lit, which hastily went out', according to a local historian. The rising's main importance however, lay in its consequences – chiefly in its horrible epilogue, two years later, when the king held another razzia at Kopparberget, Falun.

The resistance movement began among the enterprising parishioners of Leksand, led by their vicar Herr Evert. Leksand church possessed the largest bell in all Dalarna. In a 'Survey of Dalecarlian bells which were seized in 1531–1533' its weight is stated to be 16 ship-pounds, or about 2,700 kilos. The Leksand peasants resolved never to hand over their bell willingly, and were prepared to defend it by main force. Anders Persson, of Rankhyttan, had advised them to 'deal the king's emissaries as many blows as they could well stand, without any being slain'. And when, in the event, the bailiff Lasse Eriksson and his assistants came to fetch the church bell, the insurrection broke out in Leksand churchyard, one of the most beautiful in Sweden. The king's men were 'beaten and hammered with axe-hammers' and 'treated so piteously that none can fully tell the tale.'

None of the sources say that any of Gustav Vasa's emissaries were killed – the insurgents appear to have followed Anders Persson's advice. As far as we know, therefore, the violence offered by this resistance movement amounted to no more than assault and battery, with grave threat to life. But Gustav Vasa, in revenge, took at least ten lives.

At the moment when the bell rising broke out, Christian II was preparing to recover his lost kingdom by invading from Norway, and at first this exterior threat obliged the king to settle matters with his subjects in a conciliatory spirit. The rising in Dalarna against the church levies had never been general. In the end the king even took the great bell at Leksand, the source of the disturbances. Other rebellious parishes offered to compound for their bells by a payment of 2,000 marks – the price of 200 cows – providing they could keep them and the king overlooked the violence offered to his officers. Gustav Vasa agreed and accepted the money, pardoned the insurgents completely and received them back 'one and all' into his friendship, as the settlement put it.

The wretched Dalesmen took the king at his word. Their gullibility, writes one historian, is astounding: 'they should have remembered how the king had settled accounts in Tuna Mead, three years before.'

For Gustav Vasa was a man with a long memory. He never forgot. Two years after reaching this settlement with his subjects, he came back to Dalarna with his men-at-arms, noblemen in full armour, and at the Kopparberget carried out his inquisition. This was in February 1533. The king alleged that after the settlement the Dalesmen had conspired with King Christian. The allegation is not proven, and I have not been able to find more than one modern historian who is prepared to believe it. All others are more or less sceptical, and I am among the most sceptical of all. In my firm opinion this supposed treason was nothing but a pretext to crush a people who would not submit to him. 'We cannot escape the impression that there was something of the spirit of the Stockholm Bloodbath in this final settlement of accounts', writes a local historian.

Again the Dalesmen were penned in a ring by the soldiers. Some were dragged straight to the block. Others were taken to Stockholm, and there beheaded. Among the executed were two of the king's old friends in Dalarna. When 'the noxious weeds had been plucked out' the rest of the Dalesmen were pardoned.

At Kopparberget 'Dalarna's brilliant history was drowned in blood' – is E. Hildebrand's grim way of putting the matter. And it is correct. It was the headsman's axe which finally suppressed this stiff-necked people, whose only wish had been to manage their own province's affairs.

Before being executed, seven of the leaders were imprisoned for a year in the capital. Peder Svart claims that only Måns Nilsson from Aspeboda, Anders Persson from Rankhyttan and Ingel Hansson were 'cut off' in Stockholm. The other prisoners, he says, were granted their lives. But the king's faithful chronicler is given the lie by the minutes of a court of justice. From this document it transpires that, on February 17, 1534, seven imprisoned Dalesmen were condemned by the Stockholm Court to lose their lives and their property. This sentence was passed on them exactly one year after they had been taken prisoner at Kopparberget.

Peder Svart states that one of the Dalesmen's leaders, Nils from Söderby, was 'cut off' at Kopparberget, he being the fifth, and adds: 'several more were there executed'. According to the chronicler the decapitated heads were placed on a plank. The head of Nils from Söderby, as their 'captain', was placed in the centre, crowned with a 'tall crown of birch-bark'. The heads of four of his comrades, like a bloody wreath, were placed two on either side. The macabre plank with the five insurgents' heads was then affixed to a 'rather tall stake'.

Peder Svart mentions 'several more', as if others besides those whose heads were set up on the plank were also executed. How many could they have been? And how numerous were the other unknown rebels who had been beheaded at Tuna Mead three years before? I have asked several specialists on the reign of Gustav Vasa whether they can say approximately how many victims altogether were claimed by the king's razzias in Dalarna. None have been able to. All we know for certain is that seventeen men perished on the block in the course of his reign. One more should be mentioned: the vicar of Leksand, Herr Evert, leader of the bell rising, who was condemned to death but died in a Stockholm prison before the sentence could be carried out.

In his work on Kopparberget, Professor Bertil Boëthius describes the Dalesmen who were 'cut off' at Tuna and Falun as criminals, and their deeds as 'crimes'. This is a view of history to which I cannot subscribe. Did not the Dalesmen's 'crime' really consist in holding different views as to how they should manage their own affairs, their own society, from those held by the king? But Gustav Vasa could assert his view with an argument which admitted of no answer. The headsman's sword.

Nationalist historians maintain, of course, that what Gustav Vasa was asserting were the interests of the realm as a whole, and that to these the provinces' special interests had to yield. The sufferings and deaths of individuals, that is, are of no consequence where the national state must prevail. And if, compared with the interest of the state, human lives are of so little import that those in power have the right to sacrifice them to it, then Gustav Vasa, in taking the lives of the Dalecarlian rebels, acted rightly. But it is also possible to regard his action as political murder. Unfortunately this concept is never juridically defined. From the point of view of the Swedish nation as a whole Gustav Vasa's execution of the rebels has generally been accepted as justified.

Gustav Vasa and Machiavelli

In the preface to his translation of Machiavelli's *The Prince*, the great Swedish novelist Hjalmar Bergman, known as an authority on Italian history and culture, writes: 'The author has given the reader nothing less than a portrait of the human being – a portrait so crucial that one can say it is coeval with, and will probably only die in the same year as, mankind itself.'

Machiavelli was working on *Il Principe* in 1513 – I have not been able to discover when it was finished. Written in Italian, it was translated into Latin, but not until 1532 was the original edition published in that tongue. Up to then it had been circulating in manuscript copies. Danish historians are of the opinion that Christian II had a copy in his hands as early as about 1520. He commanded Poul Helgesen, a deeply learned cleric, to translate a book the title of which is not given but which on good grounds is believed to have been *Il Principe*. Helgesen translated the beginning of the work, but it was not long before he came to the conclusion that it was an 'evil book' and refused to go on with it. Instead, he translated for the king Erasmus of Rotterdam's *A Christian Prince's Education and Doctrine*, indubitably a somewhat different kind of book from *The Prince*.

It is known that copies of *Il Principe* were being read in the courts of Europe in the 1520's. Palle Lauring is of the view that Christian II may have obtained a copy from the Hapsburg court in Vienna, with which, as brother-in-law to the Emperor, he was in intimate contact. And we certainly have every reason to believe that Christian the Tyrant derived great profit from his reading.

In his dedication of the book to Lorenzo di Medici, Machiavelli explains that in his work he wishes to 'draw up rules for how princes should govern'. In a word, *Il Principe* is a handbook in the art of seizing, exercising and retaining power. The work was written for Renaissance princes, but in the modern age its principles for political action have been applied by virtually all despots, kings, dictators and presidents. Thanks to its influence on them it has had a hand in deciding the destinies of nations.

According to *The Prince*, force, treachery, guile, lies, hypocrisy and dissimulation are all necessary and defensible instruments of policy. Unless he uses them no prince can hope to rule successfully. This is why, among all humane and sensible people, this author has acquired such an evil reputation. But I wonder whether this has not been to do him an injustice? I ask myself: What he gives us here, is it his innermost, sincere view of life? In view of his own fate – Machiavelli was imprisoned and tortured – I cannot believe that he had a very high opinion of princely tyrants; and, when all is said and done, the book concludes with a call to rebellion against the princes who were terrorizing the Italy of his day. Should not *The Prince*, perhaps, be read as a satire on potentates, as an icily logical parody on tyrannical government? At very least the book is double-bottomed, and open to divers interpretations. Its author tells us what this world of ours is like. But does he not really mean it should be otherwise?

Machiavelli presents the human being under two guises: as a wielder of power, and as its victim. His prince exploits all his insights into human nature, all its shortcomings and weaknesses, its cowardice, its fear, its ingratiation, opportunism, selfishness, meanness, vanity – above all its lackey-like soul. Only by cleverly exploiting such knowledge can he keep his power and govern successfully.

The ideal prince described by Machiavelli in *Il Principe* is strikingly like King Gustav I of Sweden. In the main, Gustav Vasa ruled according to the principles of statesmanship expounded in this book, and without a doubt he was a most successful monarch. But did Gustav himself ever read Machiavelli? Though not out of the question, it is hardly likely.

When *Il Principe* first appeared in print, in 1532, Gustav had already been king for nine years and had long been putting its lessons into practice. It is possible of course that a copy of the work had already reached the Stockholm court at an earlier date, though this does not mean the king had necessarily read it. Gustav was no bookworm. What we know about his person – and we know surprisingly much – does not suggest that he had a thirst for self-education. It was not in learning that he was pre-eminent.

Nevertheless in his youth he may well have become acquainted with the spirit and principles of *Il Principe* – through Doctor Hemming Gadh. This hypothesis deserves closer study.

As I have said, Hemming Gadh had come home to Sweden after living in Rome for twenty years as Sten Sture the Elder's envoy. The last decades of the 15th century were the time when the ideas of statesmanship which Machiavelli was later to expand in his books were burgeoning in Italy. Since Doctor Hemming was then continuously resident in that country he must have been familiar with and impressed by these ideas. After his return to his own country he put them into practice, notably on the occasion of the death of Sten Sture the Elder – as I have related before – and later on when he became a traitor to the nationalist party and went over to King Christian. Many of his temperamental letters, preserved in the Sture archives, bear witness to his unscrupulous attitude – in the spirit of Italian Renaissance – toward political problems.

Gustav Vasa had become acquainted with Hemming Gadh when, as a youthful junker, he had entered Sten Sture the Younger's court, some time around 1515. According to Peder Svart, Doctor Hemming became Gustav's tutor. And Gustav appreciated the old and widely experienced politician. Despite his later defection to Christian, Gustav once called him 'a right-thinking and honest Swedish man' – but admittedly not until the Union king had cut Gadh's head off.

It seems perfectly natural, therefore, that Doctor Hemming should have instructed his pupil in the arts of politics and statesmanship, and that in doing so he should have drawn on his own experiences in Italy, where in the course of his long residence he had become acquainted with a thrusting nationalism that had developed into what later came to be called Machiavellianism. Thus it is at least possible, that while Machiavelli was writing *Il Principe* in Italy, its ideas were already being presented orally in Sweden by a man familiar with its author's environment; and he no lesser a person than the tutor of junker Gustav. The spirit of *The Prince*, that is, may have been implanted without either pupil or teacher even being aware of the book's existence. Without ever having read a single word by him, Gustav Vasa may well have become Machiavelli's pupil.

Unfortunately we have no eye-witness accounts of the lessons which Hemming Gadh gave to junker Gustav, and this hypothesis – that he may have influenced the founder of the national state of Sweden with lessons drawn from Machiavelli's Italy – can only remain a hypothesis.

It is also possible that Gustav Vasa was perfectly able to acquit himself without any influence from his teacher or any instruction in political ideology. He may have been born with the traits of character typical of Machiavelli's *Prince* – perhaps he was a natural despot, who had no need at all of any 'rules for how princes should rule'.

Gustav Vasa the man

Of all figures in the history of 16th-century Sweden, Gustav I is the one who is most alive for us. No one else has left to posterity so many documents and eye-witness accounts of himself. He made sure he should be known to future generations. Above all it is in his own letters that we come closest to Gustav Vasa the man.

The State Archives have published *Konung Gustav Den Förstes registratur* containing several thousands of letters in twenty-nine bulky volumes. So far I have not found time to count them, the task would take a couple of days. For Gustav I wrote more letters than any other Swedish ruler – perhaps more than any Swede, whether man or woman, with the possible exception of Strindberg.

Were all these letters dictated by His Grace to his clerks, in person? Besides an amanuensis he probably had several collaborators who assisted in their composition. Nevertheless these thousands of letters show a quite remarkable uniformity of style and expression. As one reads them one gains an overall impression of their being the work of a single author. For the king to have conceived and written so vast a corpus of documents would have called for a super-human capacity for work. That they could have been written from beginning to end by one and the same person is incredible. Can the explanation be that his collaborators gradually came to be so deeply versed in the king's style and manner and they acquired an illusory ability to mimic his own masterly language?

For Gustav Vasa is both a master of the Swedish language and one of its innovators. His letters overbrim with pithy and trenchant expressions, with drastic imagery, striking similes, authentically popular turns of phrase and stock phrases. Often the author of these letters simply takes the speech of the common man, and transfers it on to paper. We are all the time aware of his origins, all the traits of a Roslagen peasant. This king wrote a language his subjects could understand, a faculty which was a great political asset to him when he had to pacify a rebellious and threatening commons. During the Dacke rising, especially, numerous documents were written by him to allay popular discontent; and probably they had the desired effect. He knew how to use words which, when his letters were read out to them, the people understood. We are told that the commons enjoyed being addressed by His Grace in person.

Gustav Vasa is the author of many household sayings and turns of speech which we Swedes still use without knowing where they originated. To educate his subjects he resorted to precepts, germinal ideas, moral *obiter dicta*. He played the schoolmaster. Among his maxims I find this one the best: 'To speak once, and abide by one's words, is better than to speak a hundred times.' Himself, Gustav abided but rarely by his word, but certainly people's confidence in the utterances of our modern politicians would be augmented if they could translate this rule of life into practice.

Gustav Vasa was a forceful personality, of monumental proportions. What did this man not achieve in his forty-year reign! He never lost sight of a goal until he had attained it – as in most cases he did. No methods were beneath him. In *The Prince* rulers are warned against 'misusing leniency'. In the case of the King of Sweden no such warning was needed.

Gustav Vasa exhibits traits both fascinating and imposing – in some instances even likeable. Fabian Månsson is obviously ambivalent in his attitude to the despot. Sometimes, in spite of himself, he admires him. In his novelistic depiction of the young junker Gustav at the court of Sten Sture, Fabian gives us a portrait of which he is half enamoured, a portrait fraught with insight into Gustav's milieu. Gustav, a young nobleman among his peers, joins in the games and pleasures of youth. He is a great favourite with the opposite sex, whether married or not. He is a tall, handsome, imposing young man – 5 ft 7 in in his socks, someone has calculated – with blue eyes the colour of cornflower and 'blooms in his cheeks'. His sister's son, Per Brahe, who once saw his uncle naked, bears witness that his skin was without birthmark or trace of smallpox.

Nowhere on Gustav's 'well-formed' frame was there a blemish large enough to place a needle's point. Arriving in Stockholm to help him drive out the Danes, the German legionaries were delighted at the sight of their new master. To serve such a king was wholly to their taste!

These physical endowments may have contributed to his successes. In social life he was no dullard. On the contrary, he was a charmer. When, on occasion, he let himself go in the society of other people, he was always happy to 'make merry.' For Junker Gustav also played and sang to the lute, may even have been a pioneer of the lute-song as a characteristic Swedish pastime. One experience which made a deep impression on him was probably his captivity. In 1518 he had been one of the hostages at a negotiation outside Stockholm between King Christian and the regent, Sten Sture the Younger. The king had broken his pledge: he forcibly and treacherously brought the hostages on board his ship and sailed for Denmark. This experience very probably left its mark on the young Gustav Eriksson. To some extent it explains the development of his character. Understandably enough it made him hate the Danes even more heartily than before. But it was also a youthful adventure from which he had profited. Since others do not keep their troth with you, neither need you keep yours with them! So says *The Prince*, but the prisoner at Kalö, – the Danish castle where Gustav was kept in captivity between 1518 and 1519 – having himself experienced the truth of this saying, did not need to read it in print.

Gustav Eriksson Vasa was the first of his clan to sit on the throne of Sweden. He was an upstart king, and his colleagues in the neighbouring kingdoms looked down their noses at him. This was why he sought to increase his own prestige by obtaining a real princess of the blood for his queen. First he approached the royal house of Denmark; and was turned down. His next overtures were to the Polish royal family, with the same negative outcome. Gustav was regarded as a usurper, and therefore no peer of such princely families as had inherited their elevated status from many generations of forbears.

As a suitor Gustav I had to bear many humiliations. When, at long last, he managed to get a prince to accept him as a son-in-law he had already been on the throne for eight years; and even then his father-in-law was only a petty German prince of no importance. After long and troublesome negotiations Gustav obtained the hand of Princess Katarina of Saxony-Lauenburg. Though his father-in-law's princely status was of the type of which there were thirteen to the dozen, even he hesitated a long while before he could bring himself to hand over his daughter to a Swedish king who occupied so uncertain and rickety a throne.

Whether or to what extent Gustav suffered from an inferiority complex is impossible to say; but some of his actions must be regarded as a self-made man's imperious need for self-assertion. And assert himself he did. While many of his contemporaries' thrones have long ago collapsed, the monarchy which he established still stands.

How Gustav Vasa was viewed by other princes in his day can be seen in a letter from the Tsar of Russia. Sweden and Russia were just then at war, and the despotic ruler of all the Russians felt it necessary to denigrate and mock his adversary. In his letter he alleges that Gustav Eriksson was the son of a Småland peasant. We do not know how Gustav reacted to this insult, but he could hardly have been more pointedly taunted. Not only was he declared to be the son of a common peasant, but of a Småland peasant to boot! This was after the Dacke rising, and Gustav Vasa's feelings about Smålanders can be surmised. But in a letter of 1575 his son Johan responds to this gross accusation, refuting the Tsar's allegation that his father had been of low birth: 'One of our forefathers of the fifth generation before us, his name was Christer Nilsson, he was of the most noble family, wherefore none knoweth the beginning of His noble lineage and origin or was so highly Esteemed here in the Realm, even as the Constable (*cusabel*) is in France.'

It has been claimed that Gustav killed his first queen, Katarina, in a fit of rage. The rumour was widespread, but is unsupported by any evidence; so the king must be acquitted of this particular charge. At the same time it is interesting to note that he was so famed for his violent temperament and savage moods that people could have believed him capable of such a deed.

His second marriage, to Margareta Leijonhufvud, turned out

happily. The dynasty was secured by numerous children. The marriage also brought Gustav some political advantages. By it he became related to several of the leading families of the Swedish aristocracy. His third marriage, on the other hand, in which he took the sixteen-year-old virgin Katarina Stenbock from her betrothed, comes unpleasantly close to baby-snatching.

All sources agree that in his three marriages Gustav Vasa was and remained an exemplary and faithful husband. No amount of research has ever unearthed a single concubine, not even in his bachelor days before his first marriage. Not that any of his historians have gone so far as to allege that he had remained continent up to his first marriage in 1531, when he was already a man of thirty-five – that would be to put the case too strongly. But, once married, he did his best to bring up his children in the fear of the Lord, in the fashion of his day. Did he exhort his sons Erik and Magnus to follow his example in point of extra-marital relationships? Perhaps. But if so, they certainly did not obey him. Both had many illegitimate offspring by their mistresses.

Several of Gustav's children caused him grief and darkened his old age. His worries for his eldest son Erik, the heir to the throne, are famous. By his inane courtships in Europe, Erik made a fool both of himself and of the new dynasty. At one time he was simultaneously courting a German princess and Queen Elizabeth of England. Such an escapade on the part of a future king of Sweden must have affected his father deeply. Erik was also responsible for the great scandal at Vadstena Castle, when he spied on his sister Cecilia's illicit love affair and arranged matters in such a way that one night the castle guard found a man in her bed. This was no way for a brother to treat his sister, and his father let him know it.

But the king's paternal anxiety must also have been extended to his other son, Magnus. In him the streak of insanity which runs through the Vasa clan – according to genealogists since the beginning of the 15th century – comes out very strongly. Our modern psychiatric experts regard it as likely that Duke Magnus of Östergötland was a schizophrenic. According to contemporary documents he was sometimes 'kept in custody', how or where we are not told. Yet he must have had lucid intervals. Erik XIV tried to exploit his half-brother for his own political ends by presenting him as a suitor to Mary Stuart. There is a remarkable notice concerning Duke Mägnus in an autobiography entitled *Annales*, published by an Italian, Antonio Possevino, in the early years of the 17th century. Possevino was Pope Gregory XIII's envoy to Johan III of Sweden, and one of his tasks was to find out how things stood at Vadstena, after the Reformation the last surviving nunnery in Sweden. In his *Annales* the envoy laments divers acts of violence and outrage against the nunnery's inmates in the reign of Gustav I. Among other matters he wishes to let it be known to all 'that the man who took the lives of three Vadstena nuns after subjecting them to gross violence was King Gustav's son, Duke Magnus'.

Duke Magnus lived until 1595 and was buried with all pomp in the nuns' church at Vadstena, in the presence of the regent, Duke Karl, and members of the Council. He has a magnificent tomb in St Bridget's own church. Heidenstam has written a poem acclaiming his memory. Had the poet realised that in Antonio Possevino's autobiography the man he celebrates is called a rapist and murderer, it is unlikely he would ever have penned it.

The Swedish public's view of Gustav Vasa has been deeply influenced by Strindberg's play about this king. The finest of all Strindberg's historical plays, it is my belief that even historians have been swayed by it. The strong man who appears on the stage with a hammer in his hand had a certain basis in reality, and his utterances are cast in the authentic style of the king's own letters. It all sounds thoroughly genuine. Gustav, in his lifetime, may well have spoken just like this. But in one respect this kingly figure is utterly unhistorical. He thanks the All Highest for having punished him; and this is something utterly untypical of the real Gustav. In none of the sources are we told that he ever felt the least remorse for any of his actions, or regarded himself as deserving to be punished for them. None of his broken oaths, none of his sacred promises or solemn assurances, seem ever to have caused him the least twinge of conscience. And indeed on one occasion he expressly defended his actions when he wrote: 'Necessity knows (*bryter*' – lit. 'breaks') no law; not the law of man and at times not even the law of God'. That is to say, he did not even acknowledge God as his judge or as having the right to punish him.

Even on his deathbed there was nothing of the remorseful penitent about Gustav. When his private chaplain and confessor Master Hans came to his death bed and required him to confess his sins, Gustav sent him packing.

The conscience-stricken king in Strindberg's play, therefore, is no one but the author himself. It is Strindberg, who had just gone through his 'Inferno Crisis' and was still wrestling with God; he uses the king as his mouthpiece.

In his farewell speech to the Estates of the realm, however, Gustav Vasa does concede that his reign *may* have had its faults and shortcomings. He takes into account 'that all things are not conducted ('*drivne*') so right or well as they should be'. If so, 'I will gladly be prayed for: do it for God's sake and forgive me for it'. The king calls on God to witness that it has not 'befallen out of iniquity or reluctance, but from human weakness, that I have not been able or had the strength to better it.'

This speech is the only document I have been able to find in which the king conceded that he is no more than a man; and even this admission is hedged with reservations.

As a modern view of Gustav Vasa, based on scientific research, I will quote Michael Roberts' final words, in which this English historian sums up his reign. As the verdict of a foreign historian I find it to be of peculiar interest: 'But with all the flaws in his character he was indubitably a great king. For he died with most of his objectives realized, and with things achieved which would have appeared incredible in 1523. Of no Swedish monarch can it be said with greater certainty that his reign was a solid success. What he minded he compassed.'

If success is the measure of a king's greatness, it only remains to agree. But there are other footrules, too, and it is these I have mainly used in this chapter.

In Olaus Petri's *Chronicle* these standards were used to measure other kings, even in their own lifetime. There is no book I would more wish to read than an uncensored history of the reign of Gustav I, written by Olaus Petri, the greatest of all 16th-century Swedes.

Life in the Villages

In the first part of my History I have explained how the '*byalag*', or village community, was an independent factor in society. I called it a fortress of popular liberties. Within its own confines the village was a closed community, a little world of prehistoric origins, all on its own. Linguistic research into place names has proved beyond all doubt that the village must have come into being as early as the period of the Great Migrations, about A.D. 500. Within this village community the inhabitants joined forces in order to be able to manage themselves and their own affairs. As long as they stuck together, they could assert themselves against the outside world. The '*byalag*' was based on a natural community of interests, which gave rise to a living village – a form of life which has persisted in Sweden right up to the 20th century, for more than a thousand years.

If I am now to describe what life was like in the old village community, on work days and holy days, my account will presuppose a time when the realm was at peace, when the villagers were allowed to attend to their own tasks without interference from troops extorting board and lodging as they passed through the countryside. It would appear from the source materials, that they were in fact never free from one or another of their great torments: war, crop failure and plague, or indeed from all three at once. Mostly it is the evil events which have been remembered. Yet there were long periods of peace and good harvests, free from pernicious and infectious diseases. At such times, relieved of their three torments, the villagers were able to derive some satisfaction from life. Compared with that of later generations, their existence was austere. They were unenlightened and had none of our material conveniences.

On the other hand, they did not suffer from the lack of things they could not even envisage.

The most positive aspect of the village community was its unwritten laws for mutual aid and assistance. Here their fellowship was without flaw. People behaved above all helpfully toward one another, as if it were the most natural thing in the world. Anyone needing help must at once be given it. 'You help me, and tomorrow I'll help you', was the rule. 'Neighbours are brothers' is an old Swedish saying. Whenever a villager fell ill or suffered an accident, when he could not sow his field or do his haymaking in time, then his neighbours got together and did it for him – without compensation. All they asked in return was themselves to be helped in their turn. Otherwise, cash wages were unknown among the villagers. When some job was finished and had to be paid for, payment was always in kind: food, a loaf of bread maybe, or a piece of pork.

This peasant community knew nothing of the commercialism which has overwhelmed modern society. Neighbour did not exploit neighbour for profit. So their need for joy, one of mankind's eternal longings, was satisfied communally without any individual making a profit on it. The entertainments industry may have had its modest forerunners, but as a major and highly profitable, affair it did not come into being in Sweden until our own century.

One remarkable feature of peasant culture was the long-vanished work feasts. All the villagers' more important tasks were carried out jointly, and within the '*byalag*' troubles and joys, toil and merrymaking, profit and pleasure were rolled into one. These work feasts can be traced back to heathen times. They were rooted in the rational arrangement for carrying out tasks on a basis of mutual help; but in another respect, too, they served the villagers well. Work done jointly was greatly preferable to the thraldom of solitary toil. Any man who did heavy and solitary work in field or meadow was liable to be assailed by melancholy reflections or fall to pondering the sense of his lot in life. But many hands make light work. To be able to chat as one worked was an asset. Anyone who has ever done heavy manual labour knows how contact with one's mates can help offset its monotony. Good comradeship and friendly chat enliven men's spirits, make the long working hours seem shorter. 'With both hand

and mouth we can lend each other a helping hand', says an old Swedish proverb.

The villagers' work feasts had many names, varying from province to province. That the Swedish word for ale ('*öl*') often appears in these names as a suffix witnesses to the crucial position of this most important of mediaeval beverages. There were '*slåtteröl*' (haymaking feast), '*taklagsöl*' (the feast when the roof was completed on a new house), the '*byköl*' (when the laundry had been done) and many others. To these must be added such family occasions as the '*barnsöl*' (on the birth and christening of a child) and '*gravöl*' (funeral feast).

Certainly, most of the village's teamwork was therefore carried out to an accompaniment of food and drink. There was no stinginess toward the participants. Amply regaled, they found relief from the plainness of their everyday fare.

The major feasts were held at the conclusion of some seasonal work. The hay-feast, marking the conclusion of haymaking at the end of July, was one of the greatest events of the peasant year.

In the days of the old village communities more time was devoted to livestock than to agriculture. This was above all true of those parts of the country where the farms were small. Here the meadow meant more than the ploughed field; second only was the peasant a ploughman. Little of the land attached to each farm was arable. But the hayfields, the grazing lands, the watermeads, the swamps, mires and bogs which would have to feed the cattle during the long winter, that was the vital crop. During summer the beasts were let out hoof by hoof to graze on the common lands. The big problem was how to find fodder for them during the six winter months. All grass growing on the farm fields would be cut, dried and brought into barns and sheds erected out in the fields, thence to be brought into the farm as soon as the sledges could run over the snowladen ground.

This was why, of all summer work, haymaking was the most gruelling. The size of a meadow was calculated according to the number of haymakers needed to mow it in a day. To scythe a whole field was slow work. The ground was not only littered with stones but also thick with bushes and shrubs. As a boy I went haymaking with my father every weekday in July. Our small farm measured a sixteenth of a hide ('*mantal*'). Our scythes were for ever striking against loose stones, and this prevented us from swinging them freely. Instead we had to poke about with the point, whose edge became notched and jagged from the stones and frequently had to be rewhetted. But we had time to spare – a whole long month. Every blade of grass was utilized for hay. Once a peasant in our village was bitten by a snake when tearing off grass he could not get at with his scythe.

The days around St Olof's Day saw the last blades of grass fall to the scythe. By St Olof's Mass, the 29th of the haymaking month, all haymaking had to be finished, and in the evening on the last of July the hay feast was held. It was the time of year when the contents of the storehouse were beginning to be exhausted. By then the mistress of the household would be sweeping up the last flour left in the bin and scraping the pork barrel for this great summer feast. For then the workpeople would have to be plenteously regaled with food and drink. Dancing and games in barns or on rock ledges were all part of the feast, which went on all night long. Finally, towards morning and long after sunrise, a flock of weary haymakers went off home to bed. They had been working hard; but also enjoyed themselves. Toil had blended with merry-making.

This great feast of the hay-harvest, which went on all day at the height of summer and continued through the mild warm night has something idyllic about it; an idyll which seems the more golden the further it recedes from us. The village hayfeast has vanished from people's lives – but survives in Swedish literature. Strindberg has devoted a chapter to it in his novel *The People of Hemsö*.

From the grasses of the field the villagers took fodder for their cattle, and therefore food for themselves. From the ploughed field they took their clothing. It was there their garments grew. Flax is one of the oldest cultivated plants in the world. It is known to have been grown before 2,000 B.C. In Egyptian tombs believed to be 4,000 years old, archaeologists have found flax seed. This useful plant had probably reached Scandinavia in the Bronze Age, when it had brought about a revolution in people's clothing. Until the introduction of flax our forefathers had wrapped themselves in skins, first in the furs of beasts of prey, mostly wolves, then in the hides of their slaughtered domestic cattle and sheep. But as soon as they had learnt how to grow and treat flax they began wearing cloth. At about the same time, perhaps, they had learnt how to use sheep's wool and goat-hair for the same purpose.

The flax fields with their blue flowers added a dash of colour to the old village lands and were a splendid sight to the eye. Even in my own childhood such a field was still occasionally to be seen. But to turn this new plant into cloth called for lengthy and troublesome work, not to say a great deal of patience. From the day when the flax seed was sown on the ploughed field to the day when the linen cloth was finally spread out on the ground for bleaching a whole calendar year had passed. The process began one spring and ended the next. Before it could be turned into clothing for the body, or sheets and bolsters for a bed, the flax had to go through a long and complex process. No fewer than eleven different stages were involved – I fancy I can name them all: 1. Sowing, 2. Reaping, 3. Drying, 4. Beating, 5. Breaking, 6. Tawing, 7. Heckling, 8. Spinning, 9. Winding, 10. Weaving, 11. Bleaching.

Both men and women, young and old, took part in the villager's work feasts in connection with the flax's preparation. The flax was treated in a special shed, a '*basta*' where it was broken, scutched, swingled and heckled. Its preparation was mainly woman's work. The men saw to the sowing, reaping and breaking, but the other stages in the process were done by the women. And in the end it was the women who with their needles and thread transformed the linen weave into garments.

These village festivals were not without their magical aspects. The draught animals which participated in the work were decked out with flowers and foliage; leafy twigs were tied to the horses' fore-locks and floral wreaths were hung on the horns of the oxen. Such adornment had originally been a sacrifice to ensure happiness by propitiating and invoking the blessing of fertility gods. Such is still the custom today. The 'roofing feast' ('*taklagsöl*'), still a feature of Swedish life, is held when the roof trusses are raised on a new building. The wreath which is then hung up at the apex has magical significance, though today few workers in the building trade are aware of it.

A singular instance of such immemorially ancient magic is connected with the women's great autumn feast, their cheese-making: This was held at a time when the cows, still on their autumn grazing grounds, were yielding plenty of milk. In order to make many cheeses at one and the same time from a collective milk supply, the women exchanged milk at a feast put on by each in turn in her own farmhouse. The origins of this cheese-making ('*ystmöte*') are demonstrably mediaeval. In his *History* no lesser a writer than Olaus Magnus has left us an initiated description of this feast. He praises the women of Västergötland, more especially, for their gigantic cheeses. It seems they weighed hundreds of kilos:

'Among all the inhabitants of the North the people of Västergötland are most in demand for their cheese-making, wherein none other folk can be called their equals – very often they make such great cheeses, that two strong fellows are hard put to it to carry even one of them a short way. Nevertheless, cheesemaking is never the men's work, but the women's. From divers villages in that province they gather in summer at the home of her, whose intent it is to make cheese. Now the milk is boiled in great kettles, rennet is added, and the content pressed in great wooden forms, mostly four-sided. – But no man is thought worthy to be present at this women's work, and should any beg admittance, it were in vain.'

Sweden's last Catholic archbishop wrote these words in the mid-16th century. In the early years of the 20th I several times helped my mother to carry her milk jugs to the farm where the cheese-makers were to gather. But I was only allowed to carry them as far as the threshold; to enter the house with mother was forbidden. Though I often wondered why, I only came across the explanation in the pages of Olaus Magnus. Naturally, it was because I was of the male sex! The mediaeval historian omits to explain why no man was 'worthy' to be allowed inside, merely states it as a fact. The explanation can only be magical. The presence of a male would have disturbed the influences curdling the milk, and spoiled its coagulation. Men could cause the same damage to the butter-making. If a man came into a house where a woman was churning butter, no butter would appear in the churn until he had gone out again.

All important family events, too, were celebrated with a feast, to which the villagers invited each other. Whether a mournful occasion or a joyful, the whole village had to celebrate it. Theirs was the fellowship of participation. And people took their time over such feasts. As a rule a single day did not suffice. It called for several, and perhaps the nights too. A wedding feast went on day and night, only interrupted by the intermittent need for a few hours' sleep. But lengthiest of all was the feast held when the *byalag* was to change its alderman. The outgoing alderman, who had preserved order in the village, had to be thoroughly thanked and feasted. We are told that an alderman feast in the fertile and wealthy Söderslätt plains of Skåne could last as long at ten or twelve days.

Communal life obeyed an order of things which the village folk had themselves designed and established. Although known in Sweden since the 17th century, this autonomous village law is certainly of considerably older date. Some of its regulations could be harsh; and sometimes it intervened in private matters which should have been no concern of the village as a whole. Evidence exists, for instance, that a village could arrogate to itself the right to forbid anyone living in it to marry outside its confines. Baskemölla village council in Österlen, Skåne, required a fine of any man marrying exogamously. This, though probably exceptional, shows that a village could claim an absurd degree of autonomy and self-sufficiency. No one was yet aware, of course, of the dangers of in-breeding.

But though offences against village custom were punished by a fine, the fines – charmingly enough – went into the council's entertainments account. The offenders were allowed to participate in the feast paid for by their fines, and therefore received a certain rebate on what they had paid.

The village community operated a communal assistance scheme that was greatly to the advantage of anyone who found himself in any of those situations in life where one is most in need of help. If a young man and a girl wished to get married, the village council made a collection to help them set up house. In several Swedish provinces we hear of a '*fästmögång*' – or betrothal round. This meant that the girl who was setting up house went around the village collecting flax, wool and hemp, each household making its contribution, a contribution sanctioned by custom. Meanwhile her fiancé went the round of all the farms, carrying a sack, into which each farm poured half a peck of grain for the new householder to sow his field for the first time.

Finally, when the wedding took place, the village council gave the bridal couple gifts. And again when, in due course, the *barnsöl* was celebrated, the new member of the community also had to receive a gift. A woman in childbirth was an object of special care, and all sorts of attentions were showered upon her, the village community having a tender interest in the continuation of the race. During her confinement the women brought her a particularly tasty porridge boiled from barley-grain with a liberal addition of butter. 'Whenever there was a new-born child, they lived it up for weeks on end', writes one observer of folk-ways. This custom of bringing porridge to a woman in childbirth still survived in the Småland countryside in the 20th century.

The village community followed its members with a helping hand, literally from the cradle to the grave. When someone died, the coffin-bearers assumed their function. The road to the parish churchyard, though many miles long, might be impassable to horse and cart. In that event the coffin had to be carried there by the men of the village, two six-men teams taking over from one another at regular intervals.

The '*byalag*', as a social assistance organization, was always at work. Its care for individuals began at birth and ended only with death.

The closed conformist peasant society, however, had one serious drawback for young marriagables: the narrow choice of partner. Contacts with people outside its little closely-confined world were rare. People living in other parishes were 'foreigners', and regarded with suspicion. For this reason extra-parochial marriages were rare. The elective scope of persons hankering after marriage was limited to perhaps a radius of half a dozen miles. Further, marriage was usually determined by the size of homestead. The parties ought to be approximately each other's equal in respect of property.

The village was therefore the great marriage market within which a man or woman had to find their better half. Gradually, as a result, all the villagers became interrelated. The family groups held the individual within their grasp and dictated his destinies. Young people, especially, had to bow completely to the dictates of village custom. Their freedom of movement was notably restricted.

For the village community was severely moralistic. No young couple not yet betrothed might show themselves publicly arm in arm or even holding hands. If a boy and a girl behaved in this way it roused intense indignation. Only at nights could young people consort with some intimacy, and then in a specially authorized '*natt-frieri*', a term which might be translated – to use the New England expression – 'bundling'. The custom seems once to have been general in all Swedish provinces, but it survived longest in Dalarna and Norrland, where it was still being practised at the close of the 19th century.

This form of nocturnal association made it possible for individuals of the opposite sex to get to know one another with a view to marriage. Indeed, it was the only way for them to make intimate approaches. A boy could visit a girl in her bed and spend the night with her with her parents' knowledge and permission, on condition that both young people should remain fully dressed and that their cohabitation should not lead to any act of a sexual nature. Presumably no limits were set to their caresses; but these might not turn into coitus. If they did, then the concept of sin immediately put in its appearance. Whoredom had been committed, and that was a breach of the Sixth Commandment.

Naturally any young fellow and maiden who found themselves physically attracted to each other were exposed to severe temptation. If they did not have the strength to resist it and the girl became pregnant, then the problem would be solved by a shotgun marriage. The community's morals had been besmirched by a premature birth. Otherwise little harm had been done.

These bundlings, however, had a sensible purpose. Marriages could be entered into on a basis of free choice. Husband and wife had already learnt to be fond of, devoted to, one another.

The Lutheran Church condemned 'this sinful relationship

among the young' and its clergy energetically combated bundling. But the custom, popular and not easily abolished, persisted down the centuries. As late as 1889 the rector of Bjursås in Dalarna got his church council to adopt a resolution, under which 'nocturnal runnings hither and thither should be regarded by all right-thinking people in the parish as shameful'. Probably the right-thinkers were not in a majority. These nightly encounters were a tradition, had always been popularly approved, and the clergyman in his pulpit was powerless against them. Not until they were no longer necessary – i.e., when moralistic attitudes became less severe and the young were at liberty to walk arm in arm through the village in broad daylight – did bundling come to an end.

But there was one night in the year when all the sexual laws of peasant society were suspended. The shortest Midsummer Night. This exception had its roots in the fertility rites of the heathen millennia. In the days when our forefathers still worshipped the god of fertility they had celebrated Midsummer as a festival of nature, with an uninhibited sensual joy. Afterwards it was Christianized – as far as possible. The image of the fertility god was shattered, and the cross raised in his stead. But the Church did not entirely succeed in transforming this festival of nature, with all its magic, into St John the Baptist's Day. In the popular mentality it was altogether too deeply rooted in immemorial custom. Some heathen cults showed a remarkable capacity for survival. Even if their origins have been forgotten they have persisted down the ages.

An unwritten law applied to all young people: no one went to bed on Midsummer Night. And while it lasted actions were permitted which during other nights of the year were strictly forbidden. One of these, in all certainty, was the sexual act. During the night of the solar festival the moral code was suspended. 'Midsummer Night is not long, but it sets many a cradle rocking' says an old saw, certainly justified by experience.

During the village's work feasts, too, relations between the sexes became more free and easy, in a way that apparently deviated from the rules of official morality. A note on one Blekinge parish mentions a custom which obtained at its '*brytegille*': the young man and maiden who in the course of the day's labours had worked on the same '*bråta*' (pile of timber) should pass the night in the same bed. A local history from Västergötland relates the following. At a wedding it was the general custom to make up common beds for the young folk, as for brothers and sisters, during the three nights of the '*brytegille*'. No mention is here made of any requirement that the young people – as in their nightly bundlings – should remain clothed. From Delsbo, the 18th-century theologian Samuel Ödmann tells of a wedding at which he had himself been a guest. Afterwards, together with other young men, he went to a sleeping-cottage ('*sovstuga*') where 'brother-and-sister beds had been made up, and all the girls were already abed, with room for one boy between each'.

As far as I know, no one has yet made a methodical study of sexual life and manners in peasant society; nor indeed is there enough material to entice a thesis-writer. On the other hand, though I believe most writers have romanticized its realities, the subject has been a favourite theme for poets and novelists. In his poem on his forefathers, Erik Axel Karlfeldt has beautifully depicted their love-life. It seems to have been virtually ideal:

> In the springtime of life they kissed their girls.
> One became their faithful bride.

But in his diaries Johannes Rudbeckius, a 17th-century Bishop of Vasterås, gives us a more nuanced picture of the moral state of affairs in the see where Karlfeldt's ancestors had lived. The bishop mentions many offences of whoredom which had occurred among the people of Västmanland and Dalarna. Fornication, i.e., extra-marital intercourse between the sexes, is one of this watchful ecclesiastic's greatest headaches. He notes an astounding number of exceptions to the virtuous life-style for which our poet praises his forefathers.

We have, too, many well-documented cases of assault and battery, drunkenness and fornication in peasant society. Old court rolls mention breaches of the Sixth Commandment, 'Thou shalt not covet another man's wife', more frequently than breaches of the Seventh, 'Thou shalt not steal'. The punishments for fornication were harsh; but legislation against nature's gift of a strong sexual instinct have always been of limited effect. The threat of eternal punishment and the torments of hell, held perpetually over his parishioners' heads by the clergyman, probably had greater effect on people's way of life.

I have already discussed the positive aspects of the village community, and they are worth commemorating. But such a society must not be viewed through a romantic haze. There is no basis for such a view. Nowhere in the past do we find a popular golden age. Our ancestors revealed a hardiness and strength of character in a tough existence which can tempt us to overlook the intermittent crudity of their behaviour. They were primitive people, and their daily life does not yield the stuff of moralistic tales suitable for inclusion in an elementary-school reader. Their way of life was saturated with prejudice and superstition. Nevertheless we must always bear in mind that these were unenlightened folk, a race of illiterates, and that their prejudices and superstition were the fruits of their environment. Their breaches of God's Ten Commandments were numerous. The astonishing thing is that they were not even more common.

I wish neither to praise nor condemn the generations who lived in that peasant society. Only to understand them.

*

'The fundamental notion of human collaboration and common interest on which the *byalag* is based seems to me so timeless that it could well be realised even in our latter-day environments.'

This sentence is to be read in the first part of this work. I wrote it a few years ago. Even before then the *byalag*, in a few tentative instances, had been seeking its modern form in Stockholm and these experiments had turned out successfully. In the three years which have passed since then, the idea has been put into serious practice in many of our cities and communities. It has been the young who have taken the lead in setting up these new *byalag*. To those who are young today and still have life with all its possibilities before them, who want to seize them and make themselves the masters of their own destiny, it is a natural, obvious development.

The generation which is now growing up has begun to be aware of the sort of existence which awaits people in industrialized and mechanized society, a society of technocrats and bureaucrats. The older generation has created for them a society in which cars, killing on an average four people every day, have taken up so much space that in the near future there will soon be no room left in our cities for human beings. Meanwhile our Swedish countryside, perhaps the richest and most varied in Europe, is being irrevocably destroyed for all futurity. In our national anthem we Swedes acclaim Sweden's 'meadows green'; but today the dark clouds of sulphur oxide which hang over these fields forbode their death.

There are many signs that today's youth do not accept the great city as an environment to live in and wish they were back in the little country town or village. This is a healthy reaction. Youth has realised that people can survive without the automobile, but not without breathing unpoisoned air. As a result of this insight the *byalag* has been resurrected in a new form. Its goal is a society at whose centre the human being shall take his rightful place.

In this respect the old peasant village community was a model, especially in the strong human fellowship, both at work and in its feasts, which made life's burdens easier to bear. It knew nothing of environmental ravages; its air was not polluted; nor did it have to combat pollution in its waters. No one had to measure the percentage of poison in the air they breathed. No one was afraid to eat the fish from its clear lake and stream waters. The village council had other pre-occupations than those of its 20th-century successors.

What I wrote about the idea of the *byalag* in Part I has brought in a great number of letters from my readers. Many of my correspondents assert that it is above all in the depopulated areas of Sweden that the idea ought to be applied. Such an association would look after the abandoned, the isolated and the helpless who have no say in the society whose citizens they are – a society arranged in such a way that they no longer understood, or even feel, they have a part to play in what is going on in their own country.

Recent experience of the state of affairs in the Swedish countryside at this moment of writing is suggestive of the tasks awaiting a modern *byalag*.

In 1970, in order to visit historic places in various parts of the country, I toured five provinces, namely Dalarna, Närke, Västmanland, Uppland and Småland, partly by bicycle. My experiences were everywhere identical, or anyway varied little from one province to another. My journey took me mainly through districts with small farms. Never on the road did I meet with a pedestrian; now and then a cyclist. But I was passed by several thousand cars. When I did not know my way there was no one to ask. After all I could not stop the motorists who were rushing past at top speed. Who then, should I enquire from? These roads were bare of any encounters between human beings.

So I had to enquire inside the houses. But everywhere the villagers' dwellings seemed empty and deserted. Out of doors not a soul was to be seen. No one was scything the meadow. The fields with their deciduous trees, once kept alive by cow-muzzle and scythe, had all disappeared. Nor was anyone at work in the ploughed fields, where clumps of spruces were spreading out.

I knock at the front door of the main building of a farmstead.* No one comes to open. I go on knocking – until it dawns on me that the house is uninhabited. Dark eyes of curtainless windows turn away the intruder.

I go on to the next house, and it is the same story. No one opens. No one is at home. At last, in the fourth or fifth cottage, the door opens. So someone must be living there. But from the occupant's speech and clothing I can see at once he is not from the village. Quite right, the man who has opened to me is a summer visitor, knows almost nothing, and can tell me nothing of the roads in the vicinity. In the next house lives another summer visitor. And when I ask these temporary villagers about the natives, the race of people who cultivated the village's lands and occupied it for something like a thousand years, I always get one of two answers: 1. They've abandoned their farmlands and moved out, or 2. They're dead.

Finally, in some other houses, I come across people who really do belong here and are still alive. But these are old men and old women,

* The typical Swedish farm or manor house consists of three buildings set on three sides of a square, detached as a precaution against fire. The '*manbyggnad*', or main building, is in the centre.—*Trans.*

none under sixty, most over seventy. And they tell me: 'We're the last people left in the village. And we're of an age when we can't have many years left. After us there'll be no one.'

When these old people have gone, the village will be quite dead. A thousand-year-old way of life will have vanished.

The Women Outside History

A great many of the people who made history are still visible to us, their latter-day descendants, frozen into bronze or marble. Their image, preserved in these indestructible materials, has escaped annihilation. They are statues, standing there for us to contemplate in their timeless elevation. But once they, too, were people of flesh and blood like ourselves, lived under the same sun as we do. But can we, as we stand in front of these statues, intuit any of life's own warmth or movement? For me these bronze and marble figures exude only the desolate chill of eternity.

Here stand the great dead, those who have done memorable things in various fields of life. The principle upon which these immortals have been selected is itself illustrative of certain approved patterns of greatness, and of each age's way of evaluating actions. But in itself this very mode of selection is almost a reason to ask ourselves: Did humanity in the past consist, then, only of *one* sex?

A year or so ago one of our magazines compiled an inventory of the Swedish capital's statues. It had found 44 statues of men, and only four of women. Eleven times as many men as women, that is, have been accorded the abiding dignity of bronze or marble.

By and large this ratio, 44:4, accurately mirrors the real state of affairs, though I should have thought that 44:2 would have been still nearer the truth. Few women's faces appear in Swedish history. They have not been able to distinguish themselves on the field of battle; nor, unless they have been reigning queens, have they had a seat in the Council of State. Women have been excluded from the council chamber, *riksdag* and government. In a few instances where, regrettably, male heirs to the throne were lacking, we have had to make do with women as our monarchs. Only once was a woman ever elected to the throne – Queen Margareta – and she was a singularly happy choice.

True, two female personalities whose portraits I have already drawn, Saint Bridget and Queen Margareta of the Union, figure in our mediaeval history. To these should be added a third: Kristina Gyllenstierna, wife of Sten Sture the Younger. Not only does she have a niche in our history; she has even had a statue raised to her. After her husband's death she became famous for her brave defence of Stockholm against the Danes. Annalists concede to Fru Kristina a male intelligence, the highest honour, of course, any woman can aspire to.

In our history books her namesake, Queen Christina, has occupied a good deal of space, as she reigned over Sweden for ten years. But a lady like Ebba Brahe only features in Swedish history in a purely feminine capacity and then thanks to a man, King Gustavus Adolphus, who loved her in her youth. Agneta Horn was an unmarried 17th-century aristocrat who kept a remarkable diary that lives on in our literature. In memoirs from the period when Sweden was a great power we also encounter the wives of the fighting men. While their men were occupying important positions abroad they had authoritative tasks to carry out at home. In General Archibald Douglas' biography (1957) of his ancestor, the 17th-century Field Marshal Robert Douglas, we are confronted with a typical and most impressive representative of this class of women – the Field Marshal's wife, Hedvig Mörner. In her husband's absence – he was campaigning in many lands – she had many matters to attend to. After she had become a widow on May 28, 1662, the task of preparing a worthy funeral for her husband, in November of that year, occupied her for six whole months; just one instance of the sort of tasks that devolved on the wives of the military nobles in Sweden's age of political and military greatness.

But generally speaking representatives of the female sex chiefly appear in our history as the wives of kings. As far as we can see from the available sources, the lot of most queens who sat on the throne of Sweden was not a happy one. Gustav Vasa's first marriage was brief and unhappy: his queen died very young in circumstances which gave rise, as we have seen, to horrible rumours; and his third marriage was imposed on a sixteen-year-old girl whom he took away from her betrothed. Queen Maria Eleonora, Gustavus Adolphus' German spouse, was of an hysterical disposition. As the wife of a warrior king who neglected her, she had to pay heavily while allowing her husband 'the hero king' to fulfil his mission on the stage of world history.

Karl X Gustav (1654–1660) devoted himself even less to a calm domestic existence than Gustavus Adolphus did. Hardly had he been betrothed to the eighteen-year-old Princess Hedvig Eleonora of Holstein-Gottorp, than he set out for the war in Poland, in 1656. Nevertheless the couple met now and again; a son was born and the succession secured. The marriage had fulfilled its purpose. After the king's death Hedvig Eleonora survived until 1715, fifty-five years of widowhood. One of her main interests, we are told, was card-playing. As dowager queen she must certainly have found time hang heavy on her hands.

What a soldier-king's marital life could be like can be seen from Karl XI's marriage to the Danish princess Ulrika Eleonora, in 1680. The young king was exceedingly shy and in order to celebrate his wedding in peace and quiet he arranged for it to take place at Skottorp Manor in Halland, in the neighbourhood lay a military encampment, which he had to inspect! But Kärl was France's ally, and the French ambassador, Feuquières, was keeping an eye on his every step. In his despatch to Paris, Feuquières describes the King of Sweden's manner of passing his wedding night. By three in the morning he was out of the bridal bed, donning his uniform to ride out and inspect his troops.

It should be added, however, that Karl XI only fought one war, and that was enough to last him a lifetime. For the last eighteen years of his reign he was a friend of peace.

But his son Karl XII – or to give him his ever-renowned anglicized name Charles the Twelfth – prided himself on being wedded to his army. Such a marriage no doubt brought great happiness to whatever woman might otherwise have become his queen.

A queen who has excited the sympathy of historians is Charles' sister, Ulrika Eleonora. She occupied the throne for two years without leaving any mark on history. In his youth her husband, Fredrik I, had been a soldier, but his military interests subsequently gave place to an intense womanizing, which made people feel sorry for his wife. In his old age he wanted to act as commander-in-chief in a war against Russia, 1741–1743. But the king demanded so many and such costly conveniences for himself in the field – among other impedimenta he wished to take with him his mistress Hedvig Taube – that for economic reasons the government prevailed on him to stay at home. As it turned out, the defeat which followed in this war could hardly have been greater if the king had been permitted to charge at the head of his army.

The Danish-born wife of Gustav III (1771–1792), Sofia Magdalena, too, arouses intense sympathy in the reader. No marriage in which the man, as was the case here, takes no interest in the opposite sex can fail to be unhappily affected. But Gustav III's brother, Karl XIII, so far from being indifferent to women, loved all too many of them. His spouse, Hedvig Elisabeth Charlotta, one of the most neglected of our aristocratic women, consoled herself for her husband's notorious infidelities by keeping a diary, which has become a classic.

Karl XIV Johan – ex-marshal Bernadotte – was Sweden's last soldier king (1818–1844). His married life must have suffered from the circumstances that he had spent the greater part of his time in the field before becoming King of Sweden. Later on, when he had settled down on the Swedish throne, his queen, Désirée, also came to Sweden. After a short while she fled back to her native France, appalled, so we are told, by the Scandinavian climate and by the chill which pervaded the rooms of the palace in Stockholm – a chill, no doubt, not only of the kind measurable by a thermometer. At all events, Désirée stayed away for twelve years, bravely resisting any desire to visit her husband.

With one or two exceptions our Swedish queens have not been Swedes by birth; as a consequence, the Swedes, since the days of Gustav Vasa and his two younger sons, have not had a single king of pure Swedish blood. All our later queens have been imported from foreign dynasties. For the most part it has been German princesses who have been honoured with the task of procreating ours, the last time when this happened being in the 1930's. The women who have sat on the throne of Sweden, therefore, have been strangers in a strange land, with friends and relatives in another. For various reasons, mostly linguistic, they have led an isolated existence in their adopted country. As wives they seem mostly to have been neglected and, as human beings, unhappy.

But these women who, as queens and solely thanks to their husband's position have found a place in our history, are exceedingly few. Let me pass on to the women of the people, the soldiers' wives who stayed at home on the smallholding after their men had been conscripted for the wars. For these women are to be counted in their hundreds upon hundreds of thousands, a nameless mass, a vast unknown segment of the Swedish nation. Historians have ignored them. Swedish schoolchildren and students have never read a word about them in their history books. Nameless women, history has passed them by.

I try to imagine what the women's lot was like in a warlike nation. As I have already suggested in my chapter on the Vikings, their destiny was largely to *wait* – wives who went about their business at home, waiting for the return of their husbands and sons serving in the Swedish armies abroad. For years, for decades they waited. How could they do anything else? They could not vote against the war, or demonstrate – there was absolutely nothing they could do to bring their men home again. All they could do in their loneliness was – wait.

The longest waiting the women of Sweden ever had to endure was during the Great Nordic War, 1700–1721; therefore I will make a leap forward a couple of centuries in time, from the 16th century to the first decades of the 18th. In my journey through our history I take the liberty of moving to and fro across the centuries. That these soldiers' wives who had to stay at home had no contact whatever with their husbands during their long absence is a fact which should be stressed. The common soldier could not usually write letters, nor send any message home to his closest relatives. Year after year the war went on, and on their smallholding his wife had no means even of knowing whether her husband was still alive or not. Probably, once in a while, through the clergyman or the officers' families, she would receive news of the war and its more important events. No doubt in the age of Charles XII she would hear about the Swedes' great victories at Narva, Düna and Klissow, strange foreign-sounding places. But what chiefly interested her can hardly have been the success or otherwise of a campaign. What she wanted to know was – is my husband still alive?

Our military archives have preserved only a single letter from a private soldier. In this document from 1710 trooper Lars Rask of the Life Guards writes from Dorpat in the Baltic States to his wife Brita Johansdotter at Flista, in Götlunda, describing his predicament. He writes about comrades who have fallen. He has himself been seriously ill, but has recovered. Deeply moving is his complaint at having received no reply to his two letters. All his comrades have had news from home:
Since his letter is unique, I shall quote it in full:

> Most honoured D[earest] Wife and
> Most honoured D[earest] Parents.
> God with us.
> As time permits I can
> not let it pass, but I must
> write [to] my D.Wife and my
> M[ost] D[ear] Parents and my Master and Mistress
> And let you know that I am
> in good health God be praised, and
> horse and equipment are still
> intact God be praised, and I
> have been most sick but now
> God be praised am I well and hale;
> and many are sick and many
> are dead, but none in our troop
> other than Jöns Travare was killed at
> the first engagement and Arvas Ryttare of
> Valby died of sickness. 11 troopers are
> shot dead in our company.
> But I have written 2 times
> and never had a word, but
> I believe that God the all highest
> he will help us home to you
> this summer with Jesu's help, and I

intend before midsummer together with
my comrades to be in Sweden.
Greetings to my brother and his M[ost] D[ear] wife
and children and
Jon and his dear Wife.
All the troopers have had letters
except me and Erik.
God give us peace.
Dorpat the 29 March 1701 *Lars Rask.*

This letter-writer's hopes of his comrades and himself being home again 'before midsummer' that year were not to be realised. Trooper Rask could not know that the campaign was still only in its initial stages. His regiment would have far to ride before the enlisted men could return to their smallholdings. Twenty more years, twenty midsummer feasts, would pass by before peace came and they could again see their homeland.

God give us peace – the last words of the only letter home we know of, written by a Swedish private soldier. Comment is supererogatory. As a Carolinian portrait it comes closer to the truth, I believe, than any other.

As I try to find my way back to the past, to my forefathers' destinies and the circumstances under which they lived, I pause before those people who once trod the same soil as myself and who therefore arouse my keenest curiosity. This fellow-feeling for our ancestors first came to me before a 17th-century soldier's cottage which I have discovered. Old enlistment rolls preserved in the War Office archives gave me the name of the soldier who was serving for ward (*rote*)* no. 132 Moshultamåla at the outbreak of the long period of hostilities in 1700. His name was Anders Swensson. And he was the occupant of the soldier's cottage where, two hundred years later, I was born; the same little plot of land on which I took my first steps. Here I shall not write of my own antecedents; but the information we have on this private soldier is documented and

* A *rote* was a unit of one hundred homesteads, together responsible for providing and maintaining one soldier or seaman with his equipment. He lived in a *soldattorp* or soldier's cottage, specially provided for him and his family. *Transl.*

incontrovertible. It is illustrative of the history of the Swedish people.

The earliest of the sources known as the *General Mönster Rulla* (General Muster Roll) are from 1683, the year when Karl XI first inspected the Calmare Regemente – the Kalmar Regiment. It formed a section of the *indelningsverk* – the regional system of recruitment – which the king declared would remain 'unshakable for all futurity'. At the outbreak of war in 1700, No. 132 Swensson, who belonged to the Konga Company of the regiment, was mobilized and put to sea. The navy transported him overseas to Cureland on the East Baltic coast. Afterwards he and his unit took part in Charles XII's triumphal march through Europe, through Poland, Saxony and Russia – until he reached Poltava, where it came to an end. At the battle, which in 1709 put paid to Sweden's imperial epoch, almost every man of the Kalmar Regiment fell. Therefore it had to be recruited afresh. Three days later the few soldiers of the regiment who had survived its annihilation were taken prisoner at Perevolotjna, where the entire army capitulated.

Soldier No. 132, Anders Swensson from Moshultamåla ward, was one of those who escaped with their lives at Poltava. But not with their liberty – his march went on, this time as a prisoner-of-war into Siberia. There he spent thirteen years in captivity. Not until the spring of 1722 did this enlisted man return to his soldier's smallholding. Whereupon he was found to be no longer 'serviceable' and naturally enough, after all he had been through in the last twenty-two years, was classed as 'useless'. He was given his papers and cashiered. The general muster roll which makes note of Anders Swensson, who 'had come home from captivity', adds: 'received the Royal War College's dismissal, 17 Aug. same year' (1722).

Being cashiered, he lost his smallholding, and another enlisted man moved in instead.

And that is all I know about private Anders Swensson, who held the same number in his regiment as my father was to do, almost two hundred years later.

But Anders Swensson had a wife; and about her neither I nor anyone else knows anything at all, not even so much as her name. No military documents record it. The General Muster Roll had no interest in soldiers' wives. Their business in wartime was simply to stay at home, run the smallholding, and look after the children.

But Wife Swensson once lived in a cottage on the hillock in the forest where I first saw the light of day; I know the surroundings and can imagine what life was like for her during the twenty-two years her husband was abroad, defending the fatherland.

One day in 1700, the first year of the new century, she stood on the stone doorstep of the soldier's cottage, bidding Anders farewell. Around them they had their children. She remained standing on the slope where the cottage stands until she had seen her husband disappear along the path up by the meadow. Then she went into the house, shut the door, blew her children's noses as they asked her where father had gone, and told them to pull themselves together. After which she resumed not only her usual chores, but also her husband's. Who else would have?

And she waited. She waited as she worked on the ploughed fields around her cottage where her bread was growing, she waited as she did the haymaking on the great meadow by the Bjurbäcken stream, from which she brought in her cow's winter fodder. In the springtime, when the pike spawned, she fished in the stream. And when the autumns came she picked lingonberries in the fenced woodland meadow and boiled them into a mash. All year round she had the children with her as she worked out of doors. They were too small to be left in the cottage.

In the winters, when the only outdoor work she could do was to chop wood and stack it in the shed and feed and milk the cow, she had time to work indoors. Then she spun flax and tow yarn for the peasants of the ward, which helped her to keep her family alive. Payment was made *in natura*, in bread and something to put on it: perhaps a pound of pork for five times its weight of spun yarn. Women who did such work were called spinstresses, and some of the common people's jingles have survived concerning their terms of payment:

Monday and Tuesday the spinstress span,
Wednesday and Thursday with chips she ran;
Friday and Saturday she ate up her pay;
On Sunday she goes to the church to pray.

During the dark winters there was little daylight for the women to sit at their spinning wheel, and illumination was always a problem. Either they had to sit close to the fireplace and spin by the light from the flames, or else be put to the expense of candles. Another jingle runs:

When the candle's burnt down
And the woman has spun,
Much more she has lost than she's won.

The years passed away, as they had always done since the beginning of time; and as each new year began Wife Swensson thought to herself: 'This year Anders'll be back.'

But no letter ever reached her from her husband, never a word. Knowing he could not write, she expected no letters. It was for him she was waiting.

Sometimes people got news of the war through the parish priest. But it was mostly rumour, and often totally untrue. When the first news of Poltava arrived, the battle – which had put paid to the Swedish Empire – was made out by the royal propaganda to have been a victory. Not until after a long lapse of time was the nation told what had really happened. And not until peace had at last been concluded did the women whose husbands had been in the Kalmar Regiment learn that the regiment had been annihilated, long ago, in 1709, twelve years earlier, and with it their husbands.

In this way Wife Swensson waited for her Anders for twenty-two long years. And many times she looked down the road to see if he was coming along it. Then, one spring day in 1722, here he comes, walking among the trees in the meadow. Since 1700 there has been a great change in his appearance. His thirteen years in Siberia, more especially, have left their mark on him. It is a strange reunion. At first she doesn't even recognize him; she has to look at him again and again. It had been a young man who had left his wife behind. It is an old man who has come back to her.

And the soldier has come home to an old woman.

In defence of his fatherland, his own part of the country, he has been thousands of miles away; even, in the end, deep into the Ukraine. Meanwhile his wife has been living out her solitary lonely life. And now, when at long last he has come home, it is only to be cashiered. Anders is unfit for further military service. So he and his wife are evicted from their home.

Such, amid a warlike people, could be a woman's destiny. How many other families shared the same fate as the Swenssons of Ward 132, Moshultamåla, Konga Company, the Royal Kalmar Regiment?

The history of Sweden's wars, viewed from inside the soldiers' cottages, still remains to be written.

I have paused a moment before a vanished race of people. But in the forest regions which make up the greater part of Sweden we find traces of them in a countryside whose very soil is a state archive of incontrovertible evidence. Its memories of them have never been distorted or falsified. The little hillside cottage, that monument to a long-forgotten habitation, is only susceptible to one interpretation: *Here lived human beings.*

Often, the traces of this extinct race are to be found deep in the forest. In some little glade or on a small hillock a few grey stones, laid out in a rectangle, are still visible above the ground. Long ago these uncut and untrimmed stones were laid out here to provide foundations for a cottage; a primitive shack whose floor, often, was only the bare earth. The rectangle's dimensions enable us to assess the size of the dwelling.

Nearby, usually on the fringe of the forest, can be seen another trace of the cottagers who once lived here: a little cairn, overgrown with moss and nettles. Here the cottagers had their baking oven. But the monument which speaks most vividly to my imagination is a little hollow, not far from the cottage's foundations. Whether dried out or still full of water, it, too, is documentary evidence. Here was the cottagers' well, where they once drew their water. A well-spring in every sense, it gives rise to vivid images of those women's lives and labours.

Water is indispensable to human life. Nothing replaces it. And it was the women, who carried the water home on their shoulders in buckets slung from a yoke. In winter's biting cold they had to trudge through deep snowdrifts, a circlet of icicles forming round the folds of their skirts. Slipping and stumbling on the ice, bowed against the gale, soaked by autumn rains and sweating in the summer heats, or fumbling their way through the winter darkness, they brought up their heavy buckets from the well to the cottage. In youth they walked erect. Shouldering their yoke they went with swift healthy strides down the path and came back again. But under the heavy weight of their wooden pails, the women's backs, as the years went by, became bent and crooked. On ever slower footsteps they went their laborious way, leaving the cottage's warmth for the rain and cold. This brought on rheumatism, pains in limbs and muscles. The torment fell on them. Arms and legs grew stiff. The pail hung ever more heavily from the yoke.

Slowly the young women turned into worn-out old crones who bore their watery burden on trembling swollen legs and painful feet. Silent and taciturn, to and fro they went with their buckets between the well and the cottage, to the end. Calm and reticent they ended their days, and their old bodies, bent and grimed with charcoal, were placed in a coffin and laid to rest in forgotten graves. No monuments have ever been raised to their life-work.

One such half-overgrown hollow, marking the site of a well deep in the forest, moves me more deeply than all the others. Here a cottage once stood. Its occupant was Private Nils Thor, who served for Rörshult ward in my home parish. He was my great grandfather. He was married to Lisa Jakobsdotter, with whom he had ten children. Known in the village as 'Thora-Lisa', his wife is said to have been a '*hurk*' woman, i.e., strong, self-willed and mannish. Hers was the woman's lot I have just depicted. On this spot, during the greater part of her life, she carried her pail from the well to the cottage.

I have also discovered some written evidence about Thora-Lisa Jakobsdotter, my great-grandmother. To the entry giving her date of death the parish register adds a few words: *Found dead on the ground.*

When I think of her it is always on her way from the well, with her pail of water. It is there I imagine she collapsed.

Such a death has nothing glorious about it. Identical with hundreds of thousands of others it was not in the least remarkable, merely the fulfilment of a woman's fate. Indeed it was quite ordinary – all too ordinary, too universal, to attract the interest of historians; too commonplace to be worth recording. Such, in times past, was the lot of altogether too many Swedish women – which is why Wife Swensson, Lisa Jakobsdotter and all their sisters in misfortune have found no place in our history books.

The men went abroad to wreck other men's lives. The women stayed at home to preserve life. But it was the men's exploits which, on wings of fame, flew out across the world. No one noted the women's, no one recorded the names of those who had stayed at home to care for the race.

The Dacke Rising – Our Greatest Popular Revolt

From forest thief to the idol of modern youth

To my chapter heading should be added three words: 'against native oppressors'. The Engelbrekt rising had been a revolt against a foreign power, against the rule of Danish bailiffs. The Dacke rising was a freedom movement aimed at the rule of their Swedish successors; a civil war between two estates, Swede fighting Swede, nobleman against commoner. This difference between the two revolts has been crucial to our historians' way of seeing them. The first rebellion they have regarded as justified. The second, not. In the nationalist view, Engelbrekt's triumphal progress was a blessing; so, seen from the same angle, was Dacke's defeat – for it was against a native overlord, the founder of our Swedish national state, that the Småland peasants revolted. And this has settled their posthumous reputation. 'Incontrovertibly it was fortunate for Sweden that he (Dacke) failed', writes Gottfrid Carlsson.

Our latest professional historian to carry out research into Dacke, Dr. Lars-Olof Larsson, declares that 'surprisingly enough, we have no modern all-round scientific account of the Dacke rising'. But this is perfectly natural, exactly what one would expect from the evaluations which, right up to our own day, have been our historians' lodestone. Not until the last few decades has research demonstrated that this insurrection, led by the crown-cottager Nils Dacke from Flaka, was a real popular revolt, the biggest in Swedish history. Dacke had a majority of the Småland population behind him, as well as a large part of the population of Östergötland, and the struggle lasted for more than a year. Not until Gustav Vasa had mobilized all the nobility's men-at-arms throughout the entire kingdom, called in Danish auxiliaries and recruited 6,000 men in Germany, was he finally victorious. So I should like to ask: Which side were the true nationalists?

Compared with Dacke's freedom movement, the three Dalecarlian revolts against the king seem to have been no more than riots. Only Dacke's insurrection constituted a real threat to Gustav's new monarchy.

Anyone who sets out to write the history of the Dacke rising in terms of an overall new and radical view of history, therefore finds himself on virgin soil. He keeps coming up against a host of unanswered questions and obscure unexplored connections between one fact and another. All this obliges him to do his own research. I have tried to form an independent idea of my own concerning this great popular revolt. As long as I can remember – for natural reasons – the subject has fascinated me; for it was precisely in my own part of the country, in the hundreds of Möre, Konga and Uppvidinge, that the flames of revolt were first lit. As a schoolboy my imagination ran riot around Odhner's account of this rebel who was hunted down through the forests of my own countryside by the king's soldiers, until 'in Rödeby Forest they caught up with him and shot him through with arrows'.

I have tried to understand why my forefathers joined Dacke in his revolt, and I shall try to describe their struggle, their sufferings, and the catastrophe which befell our Småland countryside. Although I have been gathering materials for the task for the last forty years, I am far from happy with the results. Dacke's peasants were mostly illiterate. They have left no records. They composed no chronicles of their struggle. From Dacke's side the documents are few and meagre. It was left to the king's party to write the history of the revolt, and this confronts research with an almost insoluble problem: historians can only hear one party in the case. Nevertheless, in local history, I have found much valuable material not yet exploited by our national historians; likewise in still living folk-tradition; naturally my account is based on the latest professional research.

What really happened? And why, and how? These are the eternal questions always confronting the critic of source materials, questions to which he can never arrive at a certain or unambiguous answer that excludes all others. All he can do is choose between the various *possible truths* offered him by the sources. I have made my own – a layman's – choice. Another writer might well choose otherwise.

The portrait of Nils Dacke to be found in our history books is in the main the portrait drawn by Gustav Vasa and by the three chroniclers who have written about his reign: his nephew Per Brahe, the royal secretary Rasmus Ludvigsson, and Erik Göransson Tegel, son of Göran Persson, King Erik XIV's secretary and adviser, of evil repute. It is the portrait of a forest thief. As the king depicts him, Dacke was not even a human being. He was a beast, a monster: 'a gross beast and forest spirit, little better than a soulless animal.' The word here translated 'forest spirit' ('*skogsäle*') means a heathen spirit created by the Devil and sent out into the world to seduce and destroy Christian men. This monster resided in holes and hiding places in the forest, to the ineffable terror of the population. Its name was therefore the most horrifying label the king could apply to Nils Dacke, the rebel leader.

In the king's first letter, dated July 3, 1542, in which he writes at length about the revolt that had just broken out in Småland, he calls the participants 'a mob of forest thieves'. This way of seeing his rebellious subjects he reinforces, in his later missives, with such expressions as 'scoundrels', 'criminals', 'traitors' and 'murderers'. Hardly an opprobrious epithet exists which Gustav Vasa does not fling at their leader. Not only is Nils Dacke a thief: he is a great scoundrel, a heretic, an assassin, an incestuous whoremonger. Hardly a single major crime exists but the king includes it among his offences. Gustav's repertoire of invective was rich indeed; and he brought it all to bear on Nils Dacke.

By his letters to the peasantry in the restive hundreds the Most Puissant, High-Born Prince and Most Christian Lord, King Gustav I, did his best to inspire loathing for the rebels' leader. But this time, as subsequent events were to show, his eloquent penmanship was to avail him nothing. The peasants of Möre, Konga, Uppvidinge and elsewhere elected to follow the 'forest thief'.

In what follows we shall see Gustav's and the royal chroniclers' lists of Dacke's crimes for what they were: namely, special pleadings. But for almost four centuries more or less all our historians' assessments of the Dacke rising have succumbed to their influence. A victor writes not only his own history but also that of the vanquished. Dacke himself is not permitted to speak. He can neither defend nor explain either his motives or his actions. His tongue has been silenced for ever. The maxim 'truth wins out in the end', as applied to history, is the greatest lie ever printed.

Even if one or another among our older historians feels a certain sympathy for his revolt against Gustav Vasa's régime, most of them see Dacke as a criminal and a rebel. A popular historian like Anders Fryxell, one might have thought, would have judged him less categorically. But even he calls Dacke 'a horribly wicked man'. The fact is, the rebel was also a protagonist of the Catholic cause, and this may have had a certain influence on the Lutheran dean's view of him. In imaginative literature, too, the 'forest thief' has survived up to our own day. At best he becomes a sort of Robin Hood. In literature it was in a novel by Ivar Ljungquist, *Nils Dacke* (1927), that he began to be re-evaluated. Here the Dacke rising is seen in its proper historical context: as a conflict between the province and the kingdom, a struggle of the peasant republic of Småland against the national monarchy, a struggle whose outcome was doomed from the beginning. The Värend folk are crushed by the central authorities in Stockholm. Ljungquist's account is based on a profound knowledge of time and place. Next to Fabian Månsson's works, which appeared later, this is the best book on the subject in our literature, outside the works of the professional historians.

His essay on the life of the peasant leader prior to the insurrection makes Gerhard Hafström, a historian of law, the pioneer of Dacke research. In the new materials presented by Hafström, the footpad and forest thief who lived by murder and plunder disappears and in his stead appears a man of superior peasant stock who, for political reasons, had 'gone to the forest' and whose deeds of violence are a reaction to the insufferable tyranny of bailiffs. This student declares that among the 'woodsmen' were 'men from the district's leading families'. Dacke was no footpad. Materials found by Hafström show him in fact to have sprung from a family of wealthy and powerful border peasants.

A modern historian who has continued this new line in Dacke research in a popular-scientific work is Dr Alf Åberg. He gives the peasant leader the most positive obituary so far. Åberg compares Dacke to the greatest of our freedom-fighters: 'From these materials a free-born peasant, cunning, combative and indomitable, a leader among his peers. A Småland Engelbrekt, steps forth.' As far as I know, Åberg is our only professional historian to see the 'forest thief' in this light.

The latest sizeable scientific study of the Dacke rising is a major academic thesis by Lars-Olof Larsson (*Det medeltida Värend*, 1964), a Lund historian who comes from Dacke's own part of the country. Here appear, for the first time, some hitherto unknown source materials which must considerably change our notions of the insurrection's spread. Many aspects, however, remain to be researched.

Just how controversial a figure in Swedish history Nils Dacke still is can be seen from a dispute which broke out at Växjö in 1955, when it was proposed to raise a monument to him. The city council had allocated funds for a monumental sculpture by Carl Milles.

The statue was to have been erected in the main square, facing the governor's residence. The artist produced a sketch of his monument which showed Dacke reposing under a spruce tree. He called it *Dacke dreaming*. Milles explained that his inspiration was derived from a tale about Dacke's flight, in which he had been 'stripped, had his clothes stolen, and was left lying in the forest. It can be a beautiful sight, to see him lying there, dreaming'. In this vision of the wanted man, resting there under a spruce tree, the sculptor wished to embody mankind's ageless dream of freedom, both in the Middle Ages and today. And this was the interpretation Milles wished people to place on his work.

The upshot was a furious quarrel, partly of a political nature. Conservative voices were heard, protesting loudly that to place a monument to a 'rebel' in front of the governor's residence in the county capital would be an act of provocation, an insult to the King of Sweden. Other opponents to the scheme objected to the work on aesthetic grounds. Scorn was poured on Milles' Dacke, lying there snoring. Milles defended his sketch for his work and told everyone how fine it would look when finished.

In the end the city council allowed the matter to drop, and the work was never carried out. Not long afterwards Carl Milles died.

The following year, however, in 1956, Nils Dacke got his statue. Elsewhere in his own province, in the community of Virserum, he stands erect, battle-axe in hand, his crossbow on his shoulder. It was near this place, in March 1543, his revolt suffered its decisive defeat. Four hundred and thirteen years later he has returned in triumph.

To the authorities, to civil servants, politicians and all who wield power in the kingdom of Sweden, Nils Dacke is still a controversial personage. No jubilees celebrate his insurrection. Nor is his name – unlike Engelbrekt's – considered a suitable citation for official occasions. When the King of Sweden visits Växjö, Kalmar or some other part of Småland no one reminds him that he is in Dacke country, a part of the realm which once revolted.

But for the inhabitants of that countryside Nils Dacke's name is far from controversial, nor has it ever been. True, for a whole century after his revolt (as we see from the court rolls) it was a name uttered only at the speaker's peril. But Dacke's memory was preserved and silently revered by the common man. Dacke found a place in legend and anecdote. In time he became a kind of myth. Today, Nils Dacke's popularity is great among the inhabitants of his own part of the country. Just how highly the district esteems him can be seen in the commercial uses to which his name is being put – we bake Dacke Bread, brew Dacke Beer, make Dacke Sausage, run in the Dacke Race, and play football on the Dacke Field. At Virserum there is a Hotel Dacke, and not far away a Dacke Ski-Jump. Clubs, societies and associations all bear his name. But the Småland Tourist Association has still not exploited the insurgent to the same extent that Dalarna has exploited Gustav Vasa, Dacke's enemy.

Småland students rate him high, something they never used to do. The newspaper published by the Småland Nation* for its

* Students at Swedish universities do not belong to colleges but to mediaeval-style 'nations'. *Transl.*

members at Lund University is called the *Dacke-Kuriren.* The Småland Nation has also built a large and roomy student hostel and named it Dackegården, where it annually holds a Dacke Ball at which evening dress is *de rigeur*. Members of the Småland Nation at Uppsala, too, have opened their own Dacke Night Club, and hope his name will attract clients.

Though not based, perhaps, on any profound knowledge of his great insurrection among the Småland peasantry, there is also an academic cult of Nils Dacke. I have read the script of a play about him, written by a young academic. Here the crown smallholder from Flaka is represented in the guise of a modern communist leader, the prototype being Che Guevara, the Cuban freedom-fighter. Of course there are superficial parallels between the careers of the Cuban and the Swede. Both led freedom movements. Both were defeated. And both sacrificed their own lives in the struggle. But their political goals were utterly different. Che Guevara fought to establish a new society and bring freedom to a people who have never known it. Dacke fought to preserve an old one and to recover the immemorial liberties of his people, of which Gustav Vasa had deprived them. In his extreme peasant individualism Nils Dacke must even seem reactionary. Revolutionary goals change with the passage of time and changing society. Yet the two men do have one quality in common: their indomitable love of freedom.

Parallels between 20th-century political ideologies and this 16th-century Swedish peasant rising can therefore easily seduce us into misunderstanding the latter's nature. It all depends, of course, what one means by 'freedom'. But as a spontaneous liberation movement, as a struggle for elementary human rights, the Dacke rising still possesses actuality, is a timeless revolution.

And this is why Nils Dacke has become popular with today's radical and rebellious youth. His very name suggests the rebel: its hard consonants, suggestive of defiance, indomitable will, every stiff-necked quality one can think of, rings out defiantly.

No figure in Swedish history has been so variously assessed as Nils Dacke. After four hundred years this 'forest thief' has become the idol of the young.

Guerilla fighter and crown-cottager

Who, then, in real life, was Nils Dacke? Of the *person* behind this name our knowledge is extremely scanty. I have already shown how little we know about Engelbrekt. About Dacke we know even less. At least we know that Engelbrekt was short of stature. Concerning the Smålander's appearance, though he has been depicted by a peasant painter on the plank wall of a cottage at Hovby, in Östergötland, we have no certain knowledge at all.

But one fact, at least, has been established by modern research. Dacke was a very different sort of man from the one presented to posterity by Gustav Vasa and the 16th-century chroniclers. Gerhard Hafström calls the king's image of him 'exceedingly doubtful'. Accounts preserved in the Public Record Office reveal that Dacke came from a large peasant family which owned farms on both sides of the Småland-Blekinge frontier, but which was mainly concentrated in the Småland hundred of Södra Möre. One of Nils' uncles, Olof Dacke, owned the homestead of Lindö, in Möre. The leader of the insurrection himself came from the allodiary peasants of Värend – peasants, that is, who owned their lands absolutely, and who in no sense were subject to any landlords. In the Late Middle Ages they had become relatively wealthy from the large-scale export of cattle across the border.

Gustav Vasa alleged against the peasant leader that he was a foreigner, born in Blekinge, where he had his 'traitorous family'; an attempt to exploit anti-Danish feeling. The sources prove that the family had its roots on both sides of the border, and therefore demolish this allegation. Even Per Brahe states that Dacke was a Småland peasant, 'dwelling in Konga hundred'. But the question of which side of the frontier he was born on was utterly irrelevant to the thousands of peasants who joined his revolt. In the border country, as we have seen before, no distinction was drawn between Swede and Dane. It was the same folk who lived on either side of the frontier.

Both our great Swedish rebels, Engelbrekt and Dacke, make very brief appearances in history, the former for little more than two years, the latter for a little more than one. And both died violent deaths, the natural destiny of rebel leaders. We know no more about Dacke's youth and childhood than we do of Engelbrekt's, so we cannot follow his destiny until after he had reached years of manhood.

Two portraits in oils, both supposed to represent Nils Dacke, are extant, but since he did not sit for either they tell us nothing about what the living Dacke looked like. They are pure works of fantasy. Experts who have examined them are of the view that one was painted in the 16th century and the other in the 18th. Mainly they interest us as reflections of two wholly disparate historic views of Nils Dacke. The 16th-century portrait is a picture of a high-ranking chieftain, a knight wearing contemporary dress. He wears both the sword and the chain of chivalry, all knightly emblems. By contrast, in the 18th-century painting, the work of the celebrated court painter Pilo, we see Gustav Vasa's 'forest thief'. Here Dacke's physiognomy is wily and cunning. It is the face of a criminal. A writer in the newspaper *Stockholmsposten* in 1822, who had just seen this painting, declares that Dacke 'looks like a crafty criminal'.

In art, therefore, Dacke has survived both as knight and as bandit.

It is after 1535 or 1536 – the year is uncertain – when Nils Dacke made his first guerilla attack on a bailiff, that we can begin to follow his life in outline. By this time he was married, and his wife – whose name was Gertronsdotter – came from another of the district's respected clans, the Gertrons. During the resurrection the sources speak of him having a son, 'a boy of ten years', who was captured by Gustav Vasa. Dacke may be supposed to have married at about the age of twenty-five, the usual age of first marriage for the sons of peasants. This would mean that when he makes his first appearance on the stage of history he is a man in the prime of life, aged at most thirty-five.

Since Dacke's youth and childhood are obscure, we do not know whether he had any book-learning. The question whether he could read and write – so experts whom I have consulted declare – cannot be decided with certainty. In those days the sons of prosperous peasants were sometimes educated by the parish priest or by the monks in some monastery; and it is possible that the boy Nils, who came from the highly respected Dacke family, attended such a school. But there is no evidence to show he could read and write. Gustav Vasa has left us several thousand letters; Nils Dacke, putatively, only one. But no document survives that bears his signature.

The State Archives do contain a contemporary letter bearing his 'mark'. This typically peasant-like signature with the mark looks like this:

But after the revolt had broken out, its leader had literate persons around him to write his letters. Catholic priests who had joined him for religious reasons were particularly helpful. Lars-Olof Larsson gives the names of three rectors who were his faithful adherents: Thord of Älghult, Karl of Åseda, and Rolf of Nöbbele. But there were many others. So we have no words from Dacke's own hand to help us form an idea of his character, and the utterances attributed to him in the sources, too, are meagre in the extreme. Therefore we can only judge him by his actions. And they yield us a convincing picture of an indomitable rebel.

In a 19th-century reference work we can read of the man 'who shook the throne of Gustav I': 'He was suited to be a popular agitator in an age of savagery and ruin; the worst among the rebels found in him their peer'. Dacke's own men would have taken this assessment as high praise. At the negotiations with the king's commander-in-chief, Gustav Olofsson Stenbock, at Bergkvara in July 1542, the latter demanded that the peasants should hand Dacke over to him. They replied that they had every confidence in their leader and would follow him: 'Dacke was a good man, who always desired the commons' best'. This certificate of the commons for their chieftain is quoted by Rasmus Ludvigsson, whose sympathies cannot have been with the rebel leader.

In his chronicle Per Brahe calls Nils Dacke 'a weak traitor', and the royal party accused him of cowardice 'in open battle'. Yet we know of no occasion when he played the coward. Throughout the rebellion, if the sources are to be believed, Dacke marched at the head of his peasants. Even when he stood alone, abandoned by all, he did not give up the fight.

Without question Nils Dacke had many of the qualities needed in a great popular leader. He could measure the extent of his power in his enemies' fear of him. Just how afraid Gustav Vasa was of Nils Dacke is obvious from all the king's attempts to get him into his clutches, as we shall see shortly. On one occasion the king proposed to his Council that the leader of the insurgents should be got out of the way by assassination. Gustav Vasa was fully aware of Dacke's importance as the very soul of the freedom movement. It was Dacke who kept the forces together, playing the same rôle in the Småland insurrection as Engelbrekt had in his.

So we can understand how great was Gustav Vasa's relief when, one day in August 1543, the news reached him that Nils Dacke was dead.

The Dacke rising seems to have had its origins in the disturbances which occurred in the border country during the so-called Counts' War, in the first years of the 1530's. Even at that date we hear of murders of royal bailiffs, and it has been established that from the middle of the decade onwards Dacke was acting as a guerilla leader. At least this is the best modern expression to describe his activities. He seems to have been the ablest partisan leader, and the most successful, in all Swedish history. But during the great uprising he became more than that. Leading whole armies into pitched battles, he waged a full-scale war. In an essay Professor Arthur Stille, a conservative military historian who has given an account of the military operations during the rising, recognizes Dacke's abilities as a field commander. More especially he praises Dacke for his tactics. As a commander of troops Dacke was a man who had to educate himself from scratch; yet against royalist commanders who were professionals and old hands at the game he acquitted himself admirably. He had received his training as a guerilla fighter. This

Värend peasant had had practical experience of forest warfare. King Gustav's aristocratic colonels had not.

Lurking in the forests, mediaeval guerillas ambushed royal bailiffs and shot them down with their arrows. As a form of warfare it was cruel and ruthless; yet not so cruel as modern warfare in Vietnam where pilots, themselves well protected, are indiscriminately murdering from great heights a defenceless peasant population, millions of men, women and children. The progress of technology has brought war to the utmost limits of barbarism, compared with which mediaeval cruelties seem almost child's play, ham-fisted in their primitivity. But it was the best men could do with the lethal instruments they then possessed.

Six or seven years before the insurrection broke out Nils Dacke had taken part in the murder of a bailiff. This murder has been regarded as a prelude to the revolt. Dacke was then living on Södra Lindö farm in Torsås parish, Möre hundred. In company with Jon Andersson, an allodiary peasant from the border country, he shot down and killed Inge Arvidsson, a royal bailiff, in a forest near the state boundary. Their victim had long been hated by the Möre peasants for his outrages against the commons. Inge Arvidsson, that is to say, did not fall victim to a footpad or lawless poachers: he was killed by two of the district's peasants, two men of standing who came from the landowning peasantry. Their violent deed had been provoked by the bailiff's oppressive behaviour. This fact is important. It gives the Dacke rising its historical character.

After their deed Nils Dacke and Jon Andersson fled to the woods – that immemorial recourse of all men in their predicament. While living in the forest they could cross the frontier at will, into 'the other cottage', as the saying went. In the border forests, groups of discontented Smålanders – partisans – had come into existence. Fleeing from the countryside, they persistently harried the king's men.

Gustav Vasa decided to punish his disobedient and rebellious subjects. In 1537, he instituted a stringent razzia among them. This inquisition was led by no lesser a personage than the Earl Marshal, Lars Siggesson, who proceeded to deal rigorously with the commons of Värend and Möre. All peasants condemned for refusal to pay taxes or other crimes and unable to compound with a fine were seized by the bailiffs and flung into the dungeons of Kalmar Castle. Rasmus Ludvigsson writes: 'By the king's command, the stiff-necked and closely inter-married families along the borders of Blekinge were to be more harshly punished than the others'.

But this punitive expedition did not suffice. Instead of snuffing the flames of revolt it only fanned them, and a year after the king's razzia they burst out again. This time Dacke remained in the background. The leader was Jon Andersson. As yet Gustav Vasa had never so much as heard Dacke's name. In March 1538, the partisans sent the fiery cross into Värend, summoning the peasants to a council on the border. Against this incitement of the populace Ture Trolle, lord of Bergkvara and the chief nobleman of Småland, intervened with vigour and succeeded in suppressing the perilous fiery crosses. Instead, Trolle himself summoned the wrathful peasants to an assembly, and for the time being was successful in pacifying them. This time there was no revolt.

Obviously their attempts to raise a rebellion had failed; and equally obviously this was why Jon Andersson, Nils Dacke and eight others who had been involved in the action sought a reconciliation with the king. In August, 1538, an agreement was reached. Under its terms the rebels were to make good their offence by paying fines. Murder and manslaughter, though among the gravest crimes, did not necessarily entail forfeiture of the offender's life – unlike the theft of a horse or an ox, which usually led straight to the gallows.

According to extant documents specifying the fines paid, Nils Dacke and Jon Andersson now had to pay 40 oxen apiece for the murder, several years earlier, of Inge Andersson. Valued in cash, these expiatory oxen amounted to a heavy fine. The price of an ox at Kalmar was sixteen marks – at Ronneby, in Danish Blekinge, a good deal more. And this means that Dacke had to pay the king 640 marks. This would be about the value of a farm at that time, and was a very large sum indeed for a peasant to have to pay. 'Dacke lost all his property', one source declares.

Already, after his attack on the bailiff, Nils Dacke had 'gone to the woods' for two years, and probably been reduced to poverty. From one document it transpires that it was not Dacke himself who paid the fines on returning to the community, but his relatives. Such was the rule. The clan was responsible for most such expenses, which were known as 'clan fines'. A statement that for a while he had been imprisoned in Kalmar is of doubtful authenticity. Clearly, Dacke moved back to his old farm at Södra Lindö.

But only for a little while. After a year had passed he had left the homestead – probably because he had to – and moved to a crown small-holding on the frontier, where we find him during the last three years before the rising, 1539–42.

Nils Dacke's new abode, in those days called Flaka, today's Flaken, was one of the smallest farms in Torsås parish, an outcropper's smallholding 'newly taken up and built upon'. The spot is incorrectly described as a crown homestead. Actually it was nothing but a crown outcropper's smallholding, so small that it was not even obliged to offer any 'hospitality'. A member of a highly respected family of self-owning peasants, that is to say, had sunk to the economic level of a backwoodsman, tilling rough newly cultivated crown land in the midst of a wilderness.

Flaka lies on the east bank of the Lyckeby river, just south of the point where it widens out into Lake Flakesjön. In Dacke's day the river constituted the frontier between Sweden and Denmark. Flaka being the last habitation on the Swedish side, its occupant could easily cross over to Denmark. The little farmstead is still in use. Flaka being so important and historic a place, and wishing to see for myself what sort of conditions Nils Dacke lived in during the last three years before the outbreak of our greatest popular revolt, I have paid it a visit.

The present owner of Flaken is an elderly farmer. He is keenly aware of the historic character of his homestead, and proud of it. An earlier owner, Gustaf Olsson, who was a juryman, was not. According to one student of local history in these parts, he was even ashamed of it, going so far as to deny that Dacke, that traitor and miscreant, had ever lived in his farmhouse. It was altogether too shameful a blot on his homestead's scutcheon.

The present owner, however, knows all about the Dacke traditions which still live on in the countryside all around. He spoke of Nils Dacke and Jon Andersson as if these men had been his contemporaries and daily associates; as if he had spoken to them only yesterday.

Today Flaken belongs to Rödeby parish, in Blekinge. But this farmer could show me exactly where the old frontier used to run. It had been only a stone's throw from Dacke's cottage. And he was familiar with all the legendary spots along the border mentioned in narratives and tales of the rising. Here had lived Jon Andersson, the rebel leader's neighbour and close friend, though in the end they became enemies. Here in a cave in the forest Dacke had lain hid when on the run from the king's soldiers. A mile or so from Flaken my guide pointed out the very spot where they finally caught up with him and shot him to death. Likewise the ancient cattle track along which, on a wooden sledge, his corpse was dragged to Kalmar.

My informant declared – certainly not quite truthfully – that he had never read a single word in any book about Nils Dacke's rebellion. All his information, he said, had been gleaned orally from old people in the district, who in turn had heard them from people who had been old when they were young, and who had heard them in *their* youth. In this way the story of the insurrection's leader had been passed on down the centuries, from generation to generation. In his own village the 16th-century crown cottager of Flaka is still a living legend.

Even from a cursory inspection of this farm it is obvious that today's Flaken is not a profitable smallholding. Four hundred years ago, when it had only newly been cultivated and had to be tilled by primitive methods, it was certainly even less so. The soil is thin and consists of shallow humus mingled with sand. The small ploughed fields are plentifully sprinkled with stones. This little holding lies in the 'kingdom of stones', as the district is called.

But the occupants of Flaka have been able to supplement their income with fish from the Lyckeby River, which flows close by. The upper reaches of this river flow through my home parish, and when I was a child had plenty of fish in them. In the Middle Ages they certainly had even more. Formerly, eel seems to have been the most important catch. And Professor Hafström has discovered documents from a legal dispute over eel-fishing rights in the Lyckeby River between Nils Dacke and a neighbour on the Danish side, which give us a tangible picture of the life led at Flaka by the future peasant leader.

Eel is a nutritious and much sought-after fish, and could be sold for a good price at the market town of Ronneby. Dacke's neighbour on the Danish side, the peasant Sven of Ledja, claimed a monopoly. But the man who farmed the inhospitable soil of Flaka also needed the eel-fishing, and acted as his own interests dictated. 'When Nils Dacke had dwelt there some while, he had taken unto himself the fishing waters'. A protracted dispute over the eels in the Lyckeby River broke out between him and Sven of Ledja. Finally the court gave its decision and Dacke lost out.

For the crown cottager at Flaka it was a serious setback. Its soil had yielded him only a minimal income, and this legal decision still further reduced his already slim chances of earning a living. Documents from the province show that, somewhere about the beginning of 1542, he surrendered his holding. Rent rolls for the same year show it to have been unoccupied.

Why did Nils Dacke leave his home? The loss of the eel fishing cannot have been the decisive reason which may have lain in his neighbour's claims as a whole – not only to the fishing waters but to the whole of Flaka. According to this theory, Dacke had been deceived by the bailiff who had given him Flaka in the first place. That he was deeply indignant we see from a statement made on oath before Rödeby parish court: 'If the bailiff hath lied to me, I shall tell him the truth.' Whereupon he used the same arguments to settle accounts with the bailiff as he had used before: his cross-bow. His land had been taken from him. Now he committed a new murder*, and again became an outlaw. He went back to the forest.

In Nils Dacke's personal predicament we may have a psychological explanation why he became the leader of the great insurrection. A tiller of the soil, he had found himself obliged to abandon his house and land. He was destitute. What else had he to lose? Nothing. In our day a man in his predicament would be regarded as a member of the agricultural proletariat. Had he lived three hundred years later he could have left the kingdom of stone and emigrated to the United States, *at that time* the home of liberty

* '*dråp*'—strictly speaking manslaughter, second-degree murder. *Transl.*

and a refuge for other countries' rebels. In 1542 no such opportunity existed. America had only just been discovered. Obviously Dacke felt he had no option but to return to his former mode of life. Weapon in hand, he would seize whatever he felt he had a right to. And in the border forests, he knew, were many others who, being in a like predicament, were of the same frame of mind: men who had decided to defend themselves against the bailiffs' oppression by the only means available. Without any doubt they regarded their violent deeds as committed in self-defence.

In May, 1542, Nils Dacke is again referred to in the sources. This time he has gathered around him a partisan force which, emerging from the forest, has commenced a guerilla war. Some time around June 20 – 'just before St John's Day' – it makes an assault on Voxtorp, a bailiff's farm. At the head of his men Dacke attacks the farm, an action which can be regarded as a counterpart to Engelbrekt's attack on that other 'nest of bailiffs', Borganäs, at the same time of the year, one hundred and eight years earlier. The second great rebellion in Swedish history had begun.

In this way one of the poorest crown outcroppers in the realm, a man who had just been obliged to leave his land, 'shook the throne of Gustav I'.

Causes of the rebellion

Concerning the outbreak of the Dacke rising, Strindberg writes in his *Svenska Folket:* 'It did not have its sources in the agitation of a malcontent, for no popular movement can arise unless its causes have sufficiently deep roots. For lack of any proper parliament the peasantry had no other outlet for their dissatisfaction with this new form of personal government, which was infringing their ancient rights and liberties. That the forms taken by their discontent were savage should not surprise us, in view of the savagery prevailing everywhere else'.

A single discontented and embittered man cannot, on his own, make a revolution. Nor can ten, twenty or thirty such men. And it was with only a little force of thirty men that Nils Dacke had attacked the bailiff's castle at Voxtorp. A week or so later, at the head of a thousand, he had invaded Värend and held a '*ting*' at Inglinge Mound, the commons' immemorial place of assembly. Two weeks more, and he is marching on Växjö, the main town in Värend, with a body of three thousand followers. In less than a month his original guerilla group has multiplied itself a hundred times over, and become a host of peasants, men not otherwise given to leaving their homes.

The heartland of the rebellion was Möre, Konga and Uppvidinge, where the fiery cross had called the peasants out of their farmhouses. A contemporary source declares that Dacke 'in a single night' raised the commons of three hundreds. What is more, all these peasants had joined him at what, in this land of cattle-breeders, was the busiest time of year: during the haymaking season when, as we have seen, the most crucial work of the entire year had to be done. Like a great natural force the movement, spontaneous and irresistible, swept over the countryside, borne up on a general deep-rooted discontent. All earlier attempts at revolt had finally been smothered. Now, at last, popular resentment had grown so strong that it had found outlet in action. All the crown cottager of Flaka had done was to precipitate it. No agitation had been necessary. No letters. No inflammatory speeches – his fiery crosses had sufficed.

This is how every revolution worth its name begins – as a perfectly natural unleashing of forces so long dammed up that their final release results in an explosion. But with the Dacke rising the suddenness was only apparent. The popular movement had long existed covertly.

Its causes – its leader's personal motives apart – can be divided into four main groups: political, social, economic and religious. Historians disagree as to which should have most weight attached to it. P. G. Vejde, a leading student of the history of Småland, is of the view that it was the king's ban on all trade across the frontier. Värend supported itself chiefly by cattle breeding. Its people were dependent for their very existence on their cattle exports to the Danish provinces. But in a royal decree of 1532 it had been promulgated: 'None shall hereafter drive oxen or horses out of the realm, whether small or large, at risk of their neck.' That is, the penalty for selling an ox to one's neighbours in Blekinge was death – and this presented a grave obstacle to the Smålanders' economy, which they can only have regarded as a flagrant outrage.

Erik Lönnroth considers the chief cause of the general discontent to have lain in the grievous burden of taxation oppressing the commons in the late 1530's. Alf Åberg, for his part, thinks the rising was primarily a popular reaction to the king's ecclesiastical policies, which were 'a knockout blow to the peasants' own churches, to the congregations' property and the parishes' self-government'. I have already discussed this policy. Around 1541, the king was again plundering parish churches. The small and indigent temples of the Smålanders had been stripped of 3,700 kilos of 'silver, gilt and ungilt,' or about four-fifths of all the precious gleaming metal they had acquired in order to help illumine their murky churches.

Taken together, these causes more than sufficed to precipitate a major popular revolt. But historians draw from them their own conflicting conclusions. To come closest to the truth, perhaps, we should turn to the participants themselves. They, if anyone, should know why, one day in 1542 at the height of their hay-making, they shouldered their crossbows, took up their poleaxes or swords and, knapsack on back, left their cottages to go to war.

We have only one such source, but it is one which in this instance is to be regarded as reliable. Erik Göransson Tegel's chronicle contains a list of the Smålanders' complaints presented to King Gustav's colonels in the autumn of 1542 at the armistice negotiations at Slätbacka, in Skeda parish, Östergötland. The list is a long one. It comprises seventeen articles. Yet Tegel says that it is only a summary.

As it happens, the list agrees remarkably well with the complaints which the peasants of Swabia had made in 1525 during their revolt, seventeen years earlier. At many points indeed the parallels are striking. Was this mere coincidence? Or did Dacke and his clerks know of the German peasants' remonstrance? The question cannot be answered. Between the two revolts there was a difference. Whilst the Swedes were fighting to recover a freedom they had lost, the German commons were fighting for liberties they had hardly known at any time during the Middle Ages. But both lists of complaints were drawn up in the same century, the century of the great peasant revolts, and the points of resemblance between them are sufficient to place the Dacke rising in its European context.

Here is a summary, in modern language, of the original list of shortcomings and complaints, 'in which the men of the Småland commons humbly requested improvement'.

In the first article, the lords and bailiffs are accused of not keeping their promises to the commons. The next attack all the new illegal taxes being exacted by the crown and the nobles. No one asked whether the peasant had anything left when all his dues had been paid and the tax-gatherer had pocketed his share. For a 'very small oak wood', felled for building purposes, a poor man was being taxed 'high above the law'. Acorn-fed pork, too, was subject to a heavy tax: the bailiffs were taking every fifth pig from the peasant. Further, they were exacting 'shirt-linen' ('*skjortelärft*') from poor widows and from sons' and daughters' dowries. The bailiffs certainly had a right to so-called 'lawful hospitality' – viz. board and lodging in the farmhouses. Not content with this, however, they were improperly taking half a peck of corn as well as a man's load of hay. Further, a custom prevailed by which the peasant, over and above the actual tax, had to bribe the tax-gatherer; and anyone who found this beyond his means fared ill. If a poor man fell into debt for 'a paltry bailiff-bribe' he was driven from his farm.

One article is a remonstrance against the plunder of churches. Everything their fathers and forefathers have bequeathed and given to God's honour, it declares, has been taken away from churches and monasteries, so that it will soon be as delightful to walk in a ravaged forest as into a church. Another article demands that the Swedish Mass and other ancient religious rites be reintroduced. As it was, a child would soon know how to whistle a Mass beside a dung cart.

The prevailing state of lawlessness recurs several times. When a poor man suffers damage in some matter and cannot pay his 'bailiff-bribe', he is left no peace either at home, in church or in the monastery; he is neither allowed to compound for it nor reach a compromise. Justice is being weighed out according to the parties' purses – a popular saying from that time which accords well with this remonstrance.

The direst object of complaint is the threat to their very lives which the peasants feel constantly exposed to. The bailiffs are for ever holding the threat of a 'Dalecarlian visitation' over their heads – i.e. that they might suffer the same treatment as had been meted out to the Dalesmen at Tuna and Kopperberget.

The rebel, writes Tegel the chronicler, 'pretended' countless other complaints against the bailiffs and nobles, wherefore he restricts his list to a mere seventeen. On all points betterment was promised.

In this remonstrance the king's ecclesiastical policy occupies only a subsidiary place, two articles only. Yet they are mentioned in all our histories. Nevertheless it is the new taxes, arbitrarily and illegally imposed, which dominate. They are ruining the common man. The peasant is being taxed 'above the law' – so that, after paying his taxes, he hardly has anything left to live on. This accusation is repeated over and over again. Then there are the bailiffs' outrages against persons unable to pay their bailiff-bribe. The remonstrance leaves us with a definite impression that the Smålanders were virtually being stripped of all their rights.

The bailiffs' régime and impoverishment of the commons through taxation were the insurrection's main causes.

Yet these bailiffs were no more than the henchmen of those in power. The ultimate cause of the popular rising was political. It had its roots in the remote past, in this rebellious province's peculiar status in the kingdom. The five hundreds of Värend, 'the heart of Småland', had always been governed by their own assembly. In their declaration of neutrality during the war of 1520, for instance, they had reiterated their rights as an independent peasant republic. Even earlier than that, indeed, the Värend peasants had defied the central authorities in Stockholm. At a provincial assembly of April 7, 1507, they had rejected Svante Sture's demands that they should join in the war against the Danes: 'On no wise were they willing to lie before [i.e. besiege] cities and castles, but rather [preferred to] stay at home and protect and close off their own land. Full oft had their country been exposed to ravages, and none had aided them but themselves.'

Gustav Vasa had the same experience of the disobedient peasants of Värend as Svante Sture. At the very outset of his reign he had tried to bring them to their obedience by force. In 1526, at the head of a strongly armed band of retainers, he had entered Småland and carried out one of his razzias. But the populace had continued to defy the government in Stockholm. Although forbidden, the border traffic had gone on, and the new dues and taxes had not been paid. In 1537, the king had to repeat his visitation, and this led to an attempted rising in the following year. And now Gustav I's attempts to incorporate the popular democracy of Värend into his realm by threats of armed force resulted in the Dacke rising.

A beautiful name for the pre-Gustav Vasa period has survived in this part of Sweden: for the Smålanders it was 'the golden age of the peasantry'.

It was this era which Dacke and his peasants now wished to bring back.

The king and the 'pack of thieves'

Most of the fourteenth and fifteenth volumes of King Gustav I's records, containing his letters for the years 1542–43, are devoted to the Dacke rising. Every second letter either refers to it directly and in detail, or else obliquely in some other context. The king admonishes the commons in those provinces which are still quiet: Let no man be deceived or seduced by the rebellious Smålanders, whom Gustav vilifies as a gang of traitors. Further, he writes to the nobles and the commandants of his fortresses, castles and other strong places, warning them. The nobles he terrifies by describing Dacke's band as a mob of thieves, firebugs and assassins. The nobles are to put their farms into a state of defence, and so support the king until such time as he can 'put down this pack of thieves'.

Gustav Eriksson Vasa had once been an insurgent himself. It was a role in which he had enjoyed great success. After all, it was his insurrection which had put him in power, led to his being elected king. But here all resemblance ended. Gustav's rising had been made at God's express command – such was Gustav's conviction, often expressed. And our older annalists, as we have seen, have agreed with him. One 18th-century historian, Johan Göransson, writes: 'Gustaf Eriksson was raised by a Gracious Heaven to the throne of Sweden'. As God's miracle-worker he had been fully entitled to revolt.

It was a right he conceded to no one else. Gustav Vasa had brought his own war of liberation to a happy conclusion. But Nils Dacke's revolt – from the king's point of view – was utterly reprehensible; it lacked all semblance of divine sanction. The insurrection of the Smålanders and Östergötlanders led by this crown outcropper from Flaka, therefore, constituted a threat to the entire kingdom. It was nothing but an ungodly conspiracy of a mob of thieves and murderers.

In a royal letter to the commons of Kalmar County, dated July 3, 1542, Dacke's folk are persistently described as 'forest thieves and traitors'. In six places this document refers to the rebellious peasants as 'forest thieves', an epithet repeated in the king's ensuing correspondence more times than one can count. Even after their numbers have swollen to tens of thousands, Dacke's peasant army is still nothing but 'the thieving mob'.

On July 3, too, the king gives his version of the assault on the Voxtrop bailiff's farm at midsummer. The bailiff, Nils Larsson, and a courtier, Arvid Västgöte, had been handcuffed, stripped naked, tied to a tree, and shot with arrows – 'as unchristianly and mercilessly to death as other dogs'. Gudmund Slatte, an aged nobleman who was just then breathing his last and who had already 'held candles in his hands', had also been killed by Dacke's men. In all essentials this account of the matter, obviously based on reports from Germund Svensson, the king's commandant at Kalmar, is probably correct. Other sources attribute the deed at Voxtorp to motives of personal vengeance: a few days previously Nils Larsson, the bailiff, had shot to death Nils Dacke's brother-in-law, a peasant of the Gertron family.

The events at Voxtorp are symptomatic.

The revolt which they sparked off was chiefly aimed at the bailiffs and their oppression of the commons. In a letter from the same time – July 6, 1542 – even the king has begun to realise that the revolt does not lack its causes, and he seeks them in his bailiffs' behaviour. He sends the bailiffs Hans Skrifvare and Jören Nilsson a severe reprimand for plundering and ruining the commons. They and others, he says, are skimming the wretched peasantry of everything they possess until, impoverished, they are being obliged to leave their homesteads, wives and children and become forest thieves.

Unbeknown to himself, Gustav Vasa here depicts the personal predicament of the leader of the revolt when he had left Flaka.

This letter must be regarded as an indirect admission that the Småland rising was not without its justifications. Yet for his part the king admits no guilt; he throws the whole responsibility on to his subordinates. Closer investigation, I believe, would reveal that these bailiffs whom he is reprimanding and making an example of had merely been implementing the king's orders and demands. Who, after all, had decreed these taxes which had been the revolt's chief cause?

Even in the 16th century the responsible wielders of power were not above laying the blame for indefeasible actions on their subordinates or civil servants who had done nothing but carry out their orders and implement their will. Among those who hold office today Gustav Vasa has many emulators.

Between King Gustav I of Sweden and King Christian III of Denmark there was a defensive alliance, under which each monarch promised to come to the other's aid against any rebellious subjects. Now Gustav asked for help against the Smålanders; and a Danish force invaded Småland.

In King Gustav's letters we can follow the spread of the rebellion. It is not long before the counter-measures applied by the king prove inadequate. With at most two hundred men Gustav Olofsson Stenbock invades Värend from Västergötland and in the Växjö district joins forces with the Danish auxiliaries under Peder Skram. But Dacke faces them with 2,500 men, and the two monarchs' enterprise ends in a fiasco. On July 22, Stenbock parleys with Dacke at Bergkvara. All the while the king, though apparently ill-informed, seems to be well aware of the situation's gravity. On July 16, he had already written to his bailiffs in Finland, ordering them to recruit 'able fellows' as soldiers; and on July 19 he repeats the same order to his bailiffs in Gästrikland and Hälsingland. On August 2, he thanks the inhabitants of Uppsala for their contributions in men and money against Dacke's peasants. As early as July 6 he had written to Germund Svensson explaining that the basic purpose of these measures is to ravage the rebellious Smålanders and bring them to their obedience and senses again.

At the same time King Gustav mobilizes the entire nobility of the realm and – most important of all – sets in motion new major recruitments of legionaries in Germany. Thus the greater part of the royal army sent against the Swedish peasants consisted of troops of the Swedish aristocracy, a Danish auxiliary army, and German legionaries.

During the summer and autumn of 1542, Nils Dacke enjoyed almost uninterrupted success, and from Gustav Vasa's letters we can see that the royalist side is being hard pressed. On August 6 the letter-writer has received information that the citizens of Ronneby and its mayor Henrik Hoffman have been providing 'the rebellious company at Konga' with weapons and ammunition, billhooks, lead, shot, gunpowder and other things; and that this is causing him deep concern. In September the rebels' successes culminate in their victory at Kisa, where an advancing royal army is caught amid the 'felled trees of the peasants' and perish almost to a man.

Immediately afterward Dacke himself invades Östergötland with his main force and pitches his camp only three miles from Linköping, where the king himself is temporarily stationed. Now the way seems to be open for the rebels to advance into Kolmården, in whose enormous forests they hope to find a base. This possibility troubles the king no end. He knows that the forest is the Smålanders' best ally, and writes of Kolmården as being a district 'where are great forests, wherein is all their consolation'.

By and by Gustav Vasa is obliged to enter into an armistice with the 'pack of thieves'. The situation has become so extremely serious for him that he has no choice. Perhaps it is at this juncture that he tells his nephew Per Brahe, according to the latter's chronicle, that he wants to leave Sweden and buy himself a county in Germany.

The armistice concluded at Linköping on November 8 is confirmed in a royal brief issued by Gustav Vasa on November 25.

According to this document, the truce has been concluded with Nils Dacke and his people – with 'the commons of Småland'. So now the 'pack of thieves' have been transformed into respectable peasants, with whom the king concludes an agreement on an equal footing. Dacke's peasants promise to return to their former allegiance to the king, and he for his part promises to send magistrates and other sensible men into Småland to listen to the commons' complaints, to 'better' all short-comings and see to it that one and all shall be treated 'as is right and reasonable'.

King Gustav, however, is in no hurry to fulfil this promise, the foundation of the whole armistice. In a letter written that very day, November 25, he writes that he does not rely overmuch on this 'hen's treaty' which he has made with the Smålanders. Obviously he has only accepted the truce in order to gain time and rearm against the insurgents. Again he commands the nobility to equip themselves, and in Germany his German chancellor, von Pyhy, is carrying out large-scale recruitments of troops and shipping them in all haste over to Sweden.

In the letters which follow, the commons of Småland reappear as a 'pack of thieves'. Soon Dacke's peasants are being accused of breaking the truce by robbing, burning and plundering the nobles' estates. How far this accusation was true cannot now be determined; but if breaches of the armistice occurred they were demonstrably not sanctioned by the peasant leader. In an order issued from Kronoberg, Nils Dacke had told his people to respect the armistice rigorously.

The king also concerns himself with Dacke's private life. In a letter of March 12, 1543, Dacke is accused of lying with 'two sisters of his own flesh'. Wherever he goes, the king says, he has his lawful wife in bed with him on one side and 'the said lawful wife's niece on the other'. The royal letter-writer's moral indignation knows no bounds: Such is the Christianity and such the divine service practised by this traitor!

On March 31, Gustav again returns to the chief rebel's sex-life, a topic which he still finds of absorbing interest. Wherever Dacke stays he has two women with him in bed, his wife and his wife's niece. Here the letter-writer gives us an interesting picture of the time. Adultery was a very gross crime. The king was trying to arouse the people's loathing for whoremaster Dacke.

Three times during the first phase of the rebellion King Gustav invited its leader to meet him face to face, promising a safe-conduct. The first occasion was on July 25, after the negotiations at Bergkvara, when Dacke was invited under safe conduct to Stockholm. The same invitation was repeated after the military convention reached between the peasant leader and the king's field commanders at Slätbacka on October 7: 'Likewise he (Dacke) was informed that he could freely betake himself to King Gustav at Stegeborg and there negotiate'. Two noblemen were to accompany him, 'for his greater safety sake'. The third invitation to Dacke to avail himself of such a safe-conduct was made in December.

Each time the crown cottager from Flaka declined to meet the king personally, 'well understanding how little such a safe-conduct was to be relied on'. And indeed, in a letter written at Gripsholm on February 21, 1543 Gustav Vasa reveals the real intent behind these invitations. In it the king expounds a plan to have Nils Dacke, with whom he has just signed a treaty of peace, privily assassinated. The letter is addressed to one of his councillors, Herr Måns Johansson. The king proposes to his councillor that either 'a bullet could be put through Dacke or he could be got hold of in some other way. If this could be done without any harm or danger to the assassins, it were not unwelcome'.

To get Dacke into his clutches – such was the simple purpose behind the king's three offers of safe-conduct to the rebel leader.

Gustav Vasa's project for assassinating Dacke if he could not get him into his power in some other way adds nothing to our knowledge of the king's character. It is already quite clear and complete enough. But it does characterize the intended victim. It shows how much Nils Dacke meant personally to the great popular rising. A bullet through the leader – and the revolt would soon be quashed.

Though it took Gustav I a whole year and all the troops he could muster in Sweden and abroad to suppress the liberation movement, according to his own letters it was never a question of opposing a popular rising against his government. In his version of its history the great army of rebellious Smålanders and Östergötlanders was, and remained, nothing but a 'pack of thieves' who were giving him a certain amount of bother. One would have thought a much less sizeable force would have sufficed to deal with such a little band of vagrants.

This disparity between the king's official version of the Dacke rising and its historical realities seems utterly comic. In a royal letter of March 16, 1543, a statement is repeated that 'Dacke is said to be at Jönköping, fourteen thousand men strong.' This figure for Dacke's forces troubles the letter-writer – if it is correct, then 'there will be perils enough'. Even so, this army of 14,000 men is still only referred to as a 'pack of thieves'!

If we are to believe Gustav I's records, that immense collection of royal missives, this would mean that in 1543 the greater part of the male adult population of the province of Småland consisted of criminals.

No one really believes that Gustav Vasa was unaware of the Dacke rising's true character. But in his letters he carried through his lies about the great popular insurrection with admirable persistence and logic. The superb mendacity of rulers is familiar in all ages and all societies. In our own age it has in many quarters reached gigantic dimensions. There are, always have been, régimes which are unable to retain their power without help of the lie official. But in the days of Gustav Vasa political mendacity reached one of its apexes in Swedish history.

Triumphal progress of the rebellion

Nowhere in my history shall I devote space to campaigns and battlepieces. Those already to be found in the pages of our professional historians are quite enough. Therefore I shall restrict myself only to the decisive events of the civil war.

Of course there was no question of a war in the modern sense of the term, a war in which each action was carried out on orders from a headquarters. During the first phase of the insurrection, more especially, bands of Dacke's men operated independently, out of their leader's control. Bailiffs' and noblemens' farms were burned down and plundered. The Swedish commons' long-standing hatred for bailiffs had found violent outlet. There was a hue and cry after the king's tax collectors. They were many. Fabian Månsson states that there were 727 in Kalmar County alone.

Many tales of the popular reaction against the king's servants, 'the red-garbed' men, have survived the centuries. Widespread is the tale of the peasant's wife who received a visit in her farmstead from a royal bailiff, on his usual errand, just when she was making pea soup for dinner. When he claimed some peas as 'tax cover' she replied: 'You shall have them boiled!' Upon which the good wife took her pot, which contained the measure of six tankards, and emptied the pea soup over her guest. Fabian Månsson has a somewhat different version. Here it is the peasant himself who empties the pot over his 'guest'. It is possible that this tale has its root in a legend which had found its way to Sweden from Graubünden in Switzerland. A castle bailiff from Fardün had spat in some pea soup which was getting ready for a peasant, Johannes Calzar, who promptly ducked the bailiff's head in the boiling pot and drowned him, shouting: 'Eat up the soup you've peppered!' This dinner is said to have set in motion a great peasant rising in Graubünden.

For the rebels, the first four months of the rising were an almost unbroken series of triumphs, a campaign which took them from Voxtorp bailey in Småland to Östergötland's capital and cathedral town of Linköping. A latter-day student is amazed at such swift progress. How could a levy of unpractised peasants defeat professional soldiers, their superiors in weaponry, training and general materiel?

That the rising was a sort of forest warfare, where the German legionaries were lost, confused and 'terrified of every bush', I have already explained; and here lies the explanation of the peasants' numerous victories. Further, in his '*sackakarlar*' – as the woodsmen who had been in it from the outset during its guerilla phase, were called – Dacke had a well-trained body of picked men. As the war expanded they made admirable officers for smaller bodies of his peasant troops. In his conduct of his army's movements Dacke revealed an admitted ability, outmanoeuvring the king's field commanders. But the main explanation of his successes seems to me to lie in the good fighting morale of his peasants. The Germans were fighting for their pay; it could even happen that, when the king did not pay them their wages, they mutinied and refused to fight. And what bones could these foreigners have to pick with the commons of Sweden? The Swedish peasants, on the other hand, were fighting for their human rights, for the right to till their own soil, to exploit their forests and their waters, for their economy and for their very existence; for the freedom, which they had always possessed before, to manage their own affairs.

How many men fought under Dacke? No one who has looked into the matter regards himself as able to estimate the total forces under his command. Contemporary chroniclers believe the reports from the king's commanders, and state that Dacke when his strength was at its greatest had as many as 30,000 to 40,000 men under arms. In relation to the total population of the two insurgent provinces these figures do not appear unreasonable. But the king's field commanders, of course, made their statements to explain their defeats at the rebels' hands. Their own numbers were too inferior.

I should be inclined to estimate the number of Smålanders and Östergötlanders who went into the field during the Dacke rising as having been at most 20,000, probably 15,000 men.

During the Late Middle Ages men had invented a new and more efficient means of shortening each other's already brief lives: firearms. Dacke's peasants were the first people's army in Sweden to use them. From helpful friends and supporters in Blekinge, on the other side of the border, the Smålanders received a truly modern armoury, consisting of 'tubes', halberds, arquebuses, powder and shot. But the new firearms could only suffice for a small part of the troops. The greater part had to be content with the peasant's classical weapons originally used during the Swiss commons' wars of liberation, namely the halberd, the spiked mace, the battle scythe, the pitchfork and the pole-axe. Probably their weaponry varied from man to man. But the Värend commons had never been disarmed; all attempts by the authorities to take their weapons from them had proved in vain. The weak point in the peasant army's weaponry was its lack of the defensive armour of those days, the helmets, shields and breastplates supplied to men-at-arms.

But the most effective among their weapons, one which hung on the wall in almost every farmhouse – the crossbow – was made by Dacke's peasants themselves. Olaus Magnus and other mediaeval historians describe it as a powerful weapon, peculiarly well-suited for forest warfare. The Smålanders used a crossbow whose bow was of steel and which shot iron-tipped arrows two feet long and weighing two and a half ounces. Modern experiment with these weapons confirms their efficiency. Experts regard the arrows as being lethal at a distance of 160 yards and that at 110 yards they could pierce any ordinary armour. The crossbow played a great part in the Dacke rising. It was feared both by iron-clad knights on horseback and by other professional soldiers, in spite of their armour.

We have no figures for the numbers who fell in our greatest popular revolt, nor is there any possibility of estimating them. Neither side has left any reliable basis for such a calculation. Per Brahe states that the insurgent army lost about 500 men in the great battle of March 1543, when it suffered decisive defeat. But if we add to those who died in battle – as naturally we must – the numbers of those who died *after* it, then the final figure will certainly be a good deal higher. These people may have survived the battle, but what happened to them afterwards? How were the survivors of a battle looked after?

Here we touch on a field that is altogether unresearched. I have been unable to find a single work on mediaeval military medicine. Perhaps, if no one has dealt with the subject, it is for the simple reason that it did not even exist. A special chaplaincy to the Swedish army began to be established in the 16th century, but no mention is made in the literature of any physical care for the men who were being slaughtered. No field ambulance yet existed. The wounded were handed over to the surgeon-barber, the forerunner of the army surgeon, who in fact had been originally a barber pure and simple. The Swedish name is derived from the German word for a beard. In the Vasa period the 'beard-cutter' served with the royal troops, as we can see from the Kalmar city accounts for 1542, which show that 52 marks had been paid out in wages to surgeon-barbers attending on the burghers and their servants who had fallen fighting Dacke outside their city.

But what befell the wounded from a people's army? An expert on medical history whom I have consulted thinks that most of them, sooner or later, must have died of their wounds. And this, presumably, was the fate of those who survived the battles of the Dacke rising. Most of these encounters took place in desolate woods, where those of the maimed and mutilated who could not move off the field had to be left to lie there in their torments, waiting for the only possible end. Insofar as they received any assistance it was from a folk-medicine which could hardly have made much progress since the Battle of Stiklastad, in 1030, where we are told that the wounded were treated only with boiling water. The only other healing fluids were human spittle and urine. I have myself seen people apply their own urine to fresh wounds, supposing it to have a purificatory effect. The juices of certain herbs were also efficacious. Otherwise people's only recourse was to magic signs, incantations and prayers. When it came to sickness and death, mediaeval people were fatalists. It was not an accident or wound which killed a man, but death itself. And if he recovered it was not thanks to any treatment. 'It was so ordained'.

The 'beard-cutters' used their knives not only for cutting beards, but also for operating on the wounded, from whom they extracted bullets and amputated legs and arms. Not that they could do much to relieve their victims' pain: no real anaesthetics are known to have existed before the mid-19th century. In mediaeval operations, strong men held the patient by his arms and legs and bound him down like a beast on the butcher's block. There were attempts at anaesthesia: like a cow at the butcher's, the victim was knocked out by a violent blow on the head, after which the surgeon had to chop off the limb as swiftly as possible before he came round again. A capable surgeon-barber could amputate an arm or a leg in less than a minute. In wintertime, when the cold was severe, amputations were done out of doors. Fierce cold reduces the body's sensitivity. Alcohol, too, was used as an anaesthetic. During the wars of Charles XII brandy had come into use. When any of the king's soldiers had to lose a limb, the field-surgeon would pour a quart of brandy down his throat before he began sawing off the limb.

The sources tell us absolutely nothing about how the wounded were cared for during the Dacke rising. The royal chronicles represent the peasant leader as being utterly callous to their sufferings. In battle, they say, he had the drums rolled to drown the screams of pain from his wounded. It is possible that monks who knew the art of medicine took charge of Dacke's men when they lay 'limbless' and with mangled bodies after a battle. The monks had been expelled from their monasteries and therefore naturally supported this peasant chieftain who wanted to bring back their Church. Probably the clergy also relieved the souls of the dying by bringing them extreme unction, sprinkling them with holy water, holding up a crucifix before their dying eyes and putting a burning candle into their hands to light their way up to heaven. Long before the Red Cross, the cross of Christ made its appearance on the battlefields.

Those who have painted history's battles have overlooked the fate of those who were left lying on the field after the fight was over. Little on this aspect of the matter is to be found in the annalists' pages. Here we come face to face with a suffering of unimaginable extent. When I try to conceive of all the pain which men have suffered in their wars down the millennia, then the sunlight grows dark for me, the grass is no longer green, the flowers lose their scent and birdsong becomes the whimpering of men in agony.

In early September 1542 the rebels gained their greatest victory. It took place near the present-day community of Kisa, on the border between Östergötland and Småland. A royalist force consisting mainly of German soldiers was about to invade Småland. Hardly had they begun their march before they met their fate. The peasants of Kinda rose to a man. Encircling the invaders in the forest, they trapped them in their barricades of felled trees. The battle ended with the royalist army's virtual annihilation. Only a few fragments escaped and turned up at Linköping on September 15. At least a thousand German legionaries lay dead behind the barricades. Today they sleep their last sleep in the Swedish forest.

Local tradition assigns the place of battle to Slätmon, just north of Kisa, where a ten-foot-high stone has been raised as a monument. It stands in the depths of the forest. There is no text on its mossy face, and none of the locals even know when it was erected. Nearby, an old overgrown road passed between two gigantic boulders. The passage between them is called 'The Gates of Hell'. The boulders form a narrow pass through which the royalists had to march, and where they fell into an ambush.

When I was at Kisa, studying the scene of the insurgents' victory, I fell in with a couple of German tourists. They were much amazed when I told them how close they were to a four-centuries-old mass grave containing the corpses of a thousand or so of their compatriots.

In early October Dacke and his whole main army of Smålanders were encamped three English miles outside Linköping, the king himself being in the neighbourhood. Småland was lost to him; and now he himself writes that 'Östergötland is hanging by a thread'. The possibility that Dacke might go on and reach the immense forests of Kolmården, in the north of Östergötland, only thirty English miles from Linköping, and which form the border with Södermanland, terrified him. The region provided an admirable base. From Kolmården the insurgents could threaten Stockholm.

It was in this strategic situation that the Linköping armistice was concluded. So far Dacke had been victorious. His opponents were hard-pressed and in need of a breathing space to recover their strength. By agreeing to the armistice Dacke gave Gustav just such a respite. And therefore the question arises: Did the peasant leader, in doing so, make his great and decisive mistake, and spoil all his chances of final victory for the rebellion? In the position he was in there seems to be no reason why he should have concluded an armistice. But the royalist side certainly had every reason to: it gave them a chance to mobilize all their resources. Dacke had extended his to the limit. He had reached the peak of his successes. But his opponents could draw on many others still unexploited. When the fighting recommenced, Dacke had lost his chances of advancing into Kolmården, which would have afforded his army such an admirable forest encampment.

Obviously Dacke thought that Gustav might be willing to conclude a definitive peace treaty with him, leaving him to govern Småland and hold it in fief. Today the idea must seem naïve. Seen against the background of the provincial separatism of those days it was not so unrealistic. As we have seen, Småland, in the Later

Middle Ages, had only been loosely attached to the kingdom of Sweden; and Nils Dacke was probably assuming that under his own governorship his part of the country could retain its former liberties.

But nothing could have been more unlike Gustav Vasa than to hand over one of his largest provinces, the one, furthermore, forming his frontier with Denmark, to his rebellious subjects, to a 'pack of thieves'.

The king may have scorned his 'hen's peace' with the Smålanders. Yet the historical fact remains: it was his salvation in an exceedingly troublesome and perilous situation.

The Småland chieftain in Kronoberg Castle

On a little islet off the shore of Lake Helgasjön, four miles from Växjö, stand the ruins of Kronoberg Castle. On this little island a fort had been erected in the mid-14th century which, in the Later Middle Ages, was to become the castle of the bishops of Växjö. After the Västerås *riksdag* Gustav Vasa expelled the last Catholic bishop, Ingemar Petersson, and took over Kronoberg as a royal estate and one of his own castles.

Nils Dacke 'occupied the castle with one thousand men from Konga', and it was from Kronoberg that, in the late autumn and winter of 1542–43, he governed Småland. In less than a year he had exchanged his crown outcropper's holding for a castle.

On November 25, he held a provincial assembly at Växjö, where he declared his peaceful intentions and 'exhorted the commons to stand together in defence of their own interests'. He ruled that the armistice, if the king confirmed and abided by it, must be held inviolate. All further plunder of noble estates was strictly forbidden. The leader summoned local assemblies in the hundreds. In nine of these hundreds he appointed new bailiffs to maintain law and order and ensure that any new legislation which might be promulgated should be obeyed, all this in an attempt to re-establish orderly conditions in the province. No man should now be allowed to take the law into his own hands.

But to put an immediate stop to the immediate deeds of violence being committed by errant bands of insurgents was beyond his power. Ignoring the armistice, they were still wrecking the nobles' farms and estates. And this rapine by local rebel leaders, which was going on in defiance of Dacke's orders, provided Gustav Vasa with his pretext to break the armistice.

'Nils Dacke drank Yule at Kronoberg' we read in old histories; he had also begun to implement his political programme. Dacke restored the Catholic Church which the Smålanders had adhered to for four centuries and which was still so popular with them. During the insurrection Dacke had received strong support from Catholic parish priests who, expelled from their churches, for the past fifteen years had been wandering about as refugees – '*The Shepherd has Fled*' is one of Fabian Månsson's chapter headings. According to Hafström, at least sixteen Småland priests, as well as all the clergy of Öland, supported Dacke. Now they were rewarded by permission once again to hold Masses for their faithful parishioners. The tawdry services of the Lutherans, which the Smålanders had likened to Masses that 'could be whistled at the tail of a dung-cart', were abolished. Once again God was worshipped and invoked as He had always been. Once again the Latin words were being sung and spoken under the vaultings, to the laity's edification and consolation. Småland had reverted to its former faith.

But folk missed the sacred 'furniture' of their churches: their gleaming silver, the images of the Virgin, the candlesticks, the chalices and patens, the chandeliers, the monstrances – all these were now in the king's safe keeping, in St Eskil's Chamber.

The rebellion's main objective, however, had been to gain relief from the insufferable burden of taxation. Nils Dacke announced a considerable reduction in the commons' taxes and re-opened the border. This last measure was of great economic importance, the king's ban on all such commerce, as we have seen, having been a death-blow to the cattle trade, the main source of people's livelihood. Once again a peasant was free to sell his ox at Ronneby, where he could get a much better price for it without having to pay with his neck.

For a few brief months the sky brightened over Småland. 'All should be in accordance with ancient law and custom, whereat the commons rejoiced'. For the population of the oppressed province there was now a prospect of a return to 'the golden age of the peasantry'.

In his letters to the king's commissioners Nils Dacke unfolds his plans for the future. He is counting on receiving Småland in fief from the king; on these terms, as his liege, he will serve him faithfully. In a contemporary satirical epitaph over the fallen rebel leader it is said that he 'wished to become a king'. No contemporary source supports such an allegation. That his ambitions were altogether more modest can be seen from the fact that, even during the most successful phase of his rebellion, he offered the throne to Svante Sture – an act of recklessness in the hour of victory. Everything goes to show that, in installing himself at Kronoberg, Dacke had attained his political goal. So far from aiming at the throne of Sweden, he was perfectly content to be governor of Småland.

In Germany the Swedish peasant rising had caused a sensation. The king still had powerful enemies there, notably Berend von Melen. The German princes' incessant intrigues against Gustav Vasa, especially during the 1550's, have been explored in detail by Ingvar Andersson. On its way to Germany rumour had greatly magnified Dacke's successes. Clearly, the German lords believed his victory to be certain and definitive. And now, from the fruits of Dacke's victory, Berend von Melen, Duke Albrecht of Mecklenburg and Count Fredrik of the Palatinate, together with other feudal princes, wished to take their pickings. What part the Emperor himself played in all this is still somewhat uncertain. In Strindberg's play, Olaus Petri convinces the king that he must reply to a letter from 'that tramp' Nils Dacke, his most effectual argument being that 'even the Emperor has written letters to Dacke' And so Gustav Vasa does, too! The king's reaction has a certain psychological truth about it. Now he was even prepared to stoop so low as to conclude an armistice, on equal terms, with the 'forest thief'.

Until recently this letter from the Emperor has been regarded as dramatic licence by Strindberg; but latest research reveals it to have had a solid basis in fact. Dacke's German connections have long been one of the rebellion's least researched aspects. Gottfrid

Carlsson, however, has devoted an essay to them, and quite recently Gerhard Hafström has lit upon some hitherto unknown and still unpublished source material in the shape of a number of letters from Charles V and Fredrik, the Count Palatine, in which they declare their intention to support Dacke. The world's greatest monarch acted the part of a potential ally of the Småland chieftain! And the crown cottager of Flaka had become a factor in European power politics.

A proclamation to the population of Sweden from the Emperor's Secretary of State, Nicolas Granvella, is already known to historians. It exhorts the Swedes to overthrow Gustav Vasa, who has usurped their throne and replace him with Fredrik, the Count Palatine. Husband of Christian II's daughter (Charles V's niece), Fredrik regarded himself as the legitimate heir to the Swedish crown.

Another fact, too, has long been known. One November day, while Dacke was still in residence at Kronoberg, he received a letter from Duke Albrecht of Mecklenburg. Brought by a burgher of Rostock, it offered him military aid. But the letter also contained a request for money, either ready coin or silver, to pay the legionaries' wages. Obviously the Germans entertained exaggerated notions of the wealth of the Småland peasantry, whom they perhaps imagined kept silver spoons in their homes.

So we find German feudal lords, who were keeping their own peasantry in a state of serfdom, offering auxiliaries to these Swedish peasants who had revolted against *their* overlords. Politically the situation was grotesque. And very properly in view of the armistice he had just concluded with the King of Sweden, Nils Dacke declined their offer. If Gustav Vasa kept his promises toward him, he said, 'he would desire none better lord and king'.

Unlike the King of Sweden, Dacke's peasants never received any military help from Germany. Not that Nils Dacke did not realise that Charles V's and the German princes' offer could be an effective means of bringing pressure to bear on Gustav. In letters written to the king's commander at Christmas time he makes use of it, writing that the Emperor has offered him Småland in fief, and implying, of course, that the King of Sweden should do no less.

But soon Gustav has enough forces at his disposal to retake his lost province. Even in the beginning of 1543 Nils Dacke perceives that he will be obliged to resume the struggle.

But now his triumphs had reached their zenith. Two months of the new year have not gone by before he is on the downward path. When he leaves his residence at Kronoberg he has only six months left to live.

From Kronoberg to Flaka

In early 1543, military operations were resumed on both sides. The royal chroniclers Rasmus Ludvigsson and Tegel accuse the 'false and faithless Dacke' of not abiding by the terms of the armistice. By not keeping the peace, he had obliged the king to resort to arms. Latest research has shown the baseless character of this allegation. 'Contemporary sources provide no evidence that Dacke at this time took any steps inconsistent with the truce', writes a modern scholar. What they do provide is evidence that, in his letters to King Gustav, the governor of Småland repeatedly put forward proposals for a peaceful settlement; but got no answer.

Gustav Vasa had used the respite to rearm; and as the new year began he felt strong enough to settle accounts in quite another fashion. It was the royalist side which broke the truce – on the pretext that the other side had already done so.

Against the rebellious Smålanders the king had now had time to mobilize the troops of the entire Swedish nobility. Resorting to methods which have rightly been called 'a monumental piece of sharp practice', he also prevailed on the Dalesmen to go to war against the Smålanders, playing off one province which had revolted and been crushed against another, which had not. A letter, written in the name of the people of Dalarna but in fact dictated by the king, declares the Smålanders to be traitors, and promises 'their most dear lord and king Gustav' to help him against the 'pack of thieves'. The document's alleged signatories also exhort the commons of other provinces to place men at the king's disposal.

This letter Gustav Vasa despatched to Nils Larsson, his bailiff in Dalarna. Still further to confirm its authenticity, Larsson attached the seal of Dalarna to the forgery and sent some of his own servants through the province, dressed as peasants, to prevail upon their supposed brethren. This time the king's literary gifts had the desired effect. A troop of Dalecarlian peasants joined him against the peasants of Småland – a propaganda coup hardly matched even by the Nazis.

In the critical situation which had arisen for him in the autumn of 1542, King Gustav, under the terms of the agreement reached between the two monarchs at a meeting at Brömsebro in 1541, had applied to King Christian III of Denmark for still more assistance against his rebellious subjects. In a letter of October 15 he urgently appeals to his ally to send him ten companies of men-at-arms, i.e., about 5,000 men. In February 1543, Gustav renews his appeal, and in the late winter a fresh army of Danish auxiliaries prepares to invade Sweden. According to Per Brahe's chronicle, this army consisted of no more than three companies of horse and foot, or about 1,500 soldiers and legionaries. On February 24, commanded by Peder Pedersen, it crossed the frontier and entered Småland. Militarily, its exploits were not remarkable; mostly it is famed for its atrocities against the unarmed country folk.

Meanwhile the king had continued to recruit men in Germany, both during the rebellion and during the armistice, and on a considerably bigger scale than has hitherto been realised. Recent research has shown that during the Dacke rising the number of German soldiers in Sweden was more than doubled. When the insurrection had first broken out, in the summer of 1542, there had been six companies of German legionaries, or about 3,000 men, in the country. After only half a year had gone by, they amounted to thirteen companies of infantry and a company of cavalry. By the late winter of 1543, it is clear that the king was in a position to put a German army of at least 6,000 men into the field.

But as far as we know not a single German soldier fought for Dacke. It was the king who brought in the Germans.

At the resumption of hostilities, therefore, the situation had radically changed, a change wholly to the insurgents' disadvantage. Their time of victories was over. The king had rearmed, and now the peasant host was to face a great army of well-trained professional soldiers, for whom they were no match. Militarily, the royalist side now had the upper hand.

The course of events, in brief, was as follows, In late January Dacke launched an assault on Kalmar Castle, held during the rising for the king by its capable commandant, Germund Svensson. The assault is repulsed; the peasants are no storm-troopers. To scotch the king's invasion of Småland, Dacke invades Östergötland with all the forces he can assemble. Earlier he has gained victories even on the Östergötland plains; but in this new campaign his peasants are no match for the regiments of enemy horse. Dacke, forced to beat a retreat, withdraws into the deeply wooded hundreds of north-east Småland, whose commons had all joined his cause.

The final battle was fought in the neighbourhood of present-day Virserum, the little market town where his statue now stands. It was to be decisive for the insurrection. At the site of the battlefield between Lakes Hjorten and Virserumssjön is one of the most beautiful spots in the district, the landscape forms a narrow pass through which the royal army, advancing from the north, would have to advance; and so it was here, in the forest, that the peasants blocked its path. Even a layman in strategic and tactical matters can appreciate Dacke's choice of a strongly defensive position.

The battle was fought one day around March 20, 1543; according to one source, on Good Friday. The lakes were still frozen, and this must have been to the defenders' disadvantage. Several sources state that the royal army managed to outflank the peasants' position by marching over the ice and taking them in the rear, the struggle taking place partly on the frozen surface of Lake Hjorten.

The result was a total defeat for the insurgents. Per Brahe writes that between four and five hundred Smålanders were left lying on the battlefield. At the very beginning of the fight Dacke was shot 'by a hackbut, two balls through the thigh', and was carried from the field. This loss of their leader probably contributed to the peasants' defeat.

Among Gustav Vasa's infantry in this battle was a troop of Dalesmen, whose numbers are given as five hundred strong. Men from the commons of two provinces fought each other, Dalesmen against Smålander, peasant against peasant. A tragedy was played out, often repeated in history – the tragedy which occurs whenever men of the same class, sharing the same vital interests, go to war and kill one another.

In a letter of April 26, 1543, Gustav Vasa thanks the Dalesmen who had taken part in the campaign against the Smålanders for the 'fidelity and manliness they had shown', and for 'willingly allowing themselves to be used' against the Dacke party. Now they are to have their reward, their cash 'consolation'. The king informs his bailiff in Eastern Dalarna that he has sent two clerks down into the country with 'a large sum of money', to reward and pay off his soldiers.

The inexplicable aspect of this tragedy is that the Dalesmen should already have forgiven the king for Tuna Mead and Kopparberget.

After this battle, in March 1543, Dacke's army broke up into partisan groups, each acting independently and fighting hopeless skirmishes against overwhelming odds. In the Kalmar hundreds two brothers of the Gertron family, the leader's brothers-in-law, attempted new risings; but they were quickly crushed. Soon the countryfolk realised that the rising was a lost cause. Parish after parish, hundred after hundred, negotiated and submitted. In the spring and summer of 1543 Småland became an occupied country. And was treated as such.

The Dacke rising had ended as it had begun: as a guerilla war. In Värend, which had been its heartland, men went on resisting to the bitter end. Two months after the great defeat, fresh fighting broke out in Uppvidinge hundred. It was Dacke himself who lit the flame.

The peasant leader, shot through both thighs, had been tended by faithful followers. Obviously his wounds must have been well nursed during the period from the end of March to May, when he had been in hiding. By May he had recovered and was again ready for the fight. The court rolls of Östra hundred inform us where he had been convalescing: Lars, Rector of Näshult, 'sheltered Dacke around Easter time, 1543'. Further, the rolls inform us, Dacke 'lay in the home of' Gröms of Skärvete during 'the time when he was shot'. A whole flora of legends relate how the faithful villagers kept their wounded chieftain well concealed from the king's men-at-arms.

In May, Nils Dacke, having made his way down to Värend, appeared in Ålghult parish, in the hundred of Uppvidinge. Thord, Rector of Ålghult, was one of his most reliable friends; afterwards he had to pay for his fidelity with his life. Dacke managed to gather together a small body of Uppvidinge peasants for a last stand. He had become a guerilla leader again. At Lenhovda, the place where the men of Uppvidinge held their assemblies, he and his companions attacked a party of royal troops commanded by Colonel Jakob Bagge and put them to flight. The royalist side lost eleven dead.

It was Nils Dacke's last fight; and it was a victory.

But thenceforward all the sources refer to him as a solitary man on the run, abandoned by all. Some of the men who had been closest to him in his days of triumph had abandoned the cause and were prepared to betray their leader to save their own lives. In this way Dacke became the last man to go on fighting in the insurrection to which he had given his name – abandoned by all, it was for his own life he was fighting now.

During these last months of his life Dacke was a fugitive, leading a precarious existence in the forests, hunted down like a wild beast by large troops of the king's men-at-arms. Gustav Vasa went to great lengths to lay his hands on this dangerous man. The coast was watched in order to prevent him escaping by sea. Everyone who had joined in the rising but was now willing to help track him down was promised a free pardon.

Many are the tales, passed down from generation to generation, about Nils Dacke's last days. More than anything else, it is the hunted fugitive who has captured the popular imagination. The legends about his flight are innumerable. In all the border country toward Blekinge there is hardly a wood in which he is not supposed to have hidden, hardly a cave or a hollow beneath some boulder or a cleft in the rocks that was not his hiding place.

It is this Dacke – the man lying beneath the spruce tree – who gave Carl Milles his inspiration for the monument which was never raised to his memory.

From May to August Dacke led this hunted existence, probably in the great border forest which had sheltered him before. What we do know for certain is that in the first days of August he was on the Danish side of the border, in Rödeby Forest, which stretches away there, mile upon mile. For it was here he ended his life.

Nils Dacke had come back to the country round Flaka, whose soil he had tilled and where he was so familiar with the lie of the land. From Kronoberg Castle he had come back to his smallholding.

The circle was complete. His destiny was nearly accomplished.

No other Swede has ever had a destiny which for its ups and downs of fortune have been comparable to his – first, the self-owning peasant – then the crown outcropper – the guerilla leader – the leader of the insurrection – the governor of Småland – the man who negotiated on an equal footing with the King of Sweden – the man in whom the Emperor Charles V, the most powerful man on earth, thought he had found an ally – the leader of the defeated revolt – then the guerilla again – and at the last the solitary fugitive. And all this inside little more than a year!

Nils Dacke fell in the forest not far from Flaka, the little outcropper's farm which had once been his own. We have no reason to doubt the older historians who say so. On the whole they may be relied on. Two of the leader's captains and closest friends, Peder Skrivare and Peder Skegge, are supposed to have betrayed him, purchasing their own lives by leading his enemies to his forest hiding place. According to another source he was 'spied out' by two neighbours, the Hampe brothers, whom Gustav I rewarded by exempting them from taxes. In Rödeby Forest, somewhere near the frontier, King Gustav's soldiers caught up with him, and Dacke met the fate that usually awaits a rebel. All other versions of his end – that he was taken prisoner, or escaped to Germany – can be dismissed as fiction. That he should have surrendered alive contradicts everything his actions tell us of his character. He was the indomitable woodsman, untameable, untamed; the rebel who never bowed his head to the yoke. In all probability he died as he had lived, defiant to the end.

This picture of him agrees furthermore with a statement in Tegel's chronicle: when Dacke 'would not surrender, he was shot to death'.

So this source, too, tells us he died fighting. Or possibly was ambushed.

According to local tradition his corpse, laid on a wooden sled, was dragged along a cattle track to Kalmar: 'the men-at-arms, who were mounted, did not wish to have the dead man hanging across their horse's back'. The animals, that is, would have been infected by the rebel's body.

Original documents from Kalmar Castle show that Nils Dacke's corpse was chopped into four pieces and impaled. In the castle it was 'quartered and in four places was placed on stake and wheel and on his head [was placed] a copper crown'. The castle accounts contain an item requisitioning 130 nails 'for the needs of Nils Dacke and his party'. These long nails were required in order to impale the rebels and nail up the various parts of their bodies. No fewer than 130 nails were needed; corpses of other captured Dacke men were to be impaled with their leader's. That this was indeed done transpires from the still extant receipt issued by the king's counting house: 'To Nils Dacke and his party, nails 130, which were smithed in Kalmar Castle'.

In *Epitaphium Nicolai Dacke*, the victors' sadistic epitaph over the rebel leader, written on the back of a hand-written folio of Laurentius Petri's *Chronicle* and dated 1559, special emphasis is laid on his copper crown. Dacke's head, with this crown on it, is said to have been impaled on Kalmar town wall. It is Dacke himself who is speaking. He calls himself 'the Captain'. In the year of Our Lord fifteen hundred and forty-two he had begun his insurrection:

'Strange was the game I then did play,
To become a King was my way,
And thus at last in truth I fare
sith now at Kalmar this crown I wear.'

Outside the city gates the Smålanders could behold their king.

In the concluding vignette of his *Nils Dacke*, the novelist Ivar Ljungquist draws on this source. In the novel's last sentences the rebel leader's aged mother, herself grievously sick, comes riding to Kalmar on a borrowed horse, to ask after her son. The passage, a poetic interpretation of what had happened, is worth quoting in full: 'One day . . . a little old woman came to the town wall where the rebels' heads had been set up. Twelve were hanging there, and all looked the same, she thought, for eyes and cheeks and all flesh had been pecked off them by the birds and the rest was covered in great swarms of flies. But in the middle was a head with a copper crown on its brow. It could only be his. And as the flies dispersed in a gust of wind and she descried two locks of hair at the dead man's temple, she was sure of it. Such hair had Nils had, brown, soft and shining.

She knelt down close to the wall and prayed for a long while.

Then she went back to her nag and without entering the town rode back the same way she had come. In a cottage by the roadside she was given water, and when its occupants asked her why she, who was so old, was riding abroad alone, she replied:

"I was looking for my son and at last have found him. So now I've only to give back the horse and die before winter comes."

After these words she thanked them for their hospitality and though dusk had begun to fall, rode on her way.'

'*—so that Småland should not be utterly ruined—*'

The news of Nils Dacke's death had reached King Gustav at Stegeborg on August 7, 1543. He had heard it in a letter from Germund Svensson at Kalmar. The same day he replies to his commandant at the castle. He had learned that 'that traitor Dacke has got his wages, albeit he did deserve a worse departure. But had he been taken alive it would have been most serviceable, for the sake of many things'.

We can form a lively idea of the sort of death the rebel leader would have died, had the king's soldiers taken him alive. But the writer of the letter consoles himself with the reflection that what has occurred 'hath befallen of God's will'. Which may be interpreted as meaning: Any further wages which may be outstanding to him are now being drawn by Dacke in hell.

In his letter the king orders his commandant to seek out Dacke's wife and mother – 'that witch his Mother' – and these orders Germund Svensson was strictly to obey. His emissaries were not to return until they had found and captured both the women. The king's men-at-arms are known to have caught Dacke's ten-year-old son, who was taken to Stegeborg. In a letter to Esbjörn Skrivare at that castle, a few months later, the king orders this officer to keep a strict watch on 'the young Dacke' so that he shall not escape or get up to some roguery. Even the ten-year-old was dangerous to Gustav Vasa. According to the chronicle, Dacke's son afterwards 'died from pestilenzia at Stockholm'. Here we may believe what we like. No outbreak of plague is known to have occurred in Stockholm at this time. But one thing may safely be assumed: the king did not let any person bearing the name of Dacke escape with his life.

Dacke's mother is thought to be identical with a peasant wife, Elin Dacke of Hult, who is mentioned in contemporary documents. She too had to tread the path from an independent homestead to a crown smallholding. In the years 1551–59 she was living on the little outcropper's farm of Lönbomåla. According to popular tradition two bailiffs set fire to her cottage. She was burnt to death. It was the wages of witchcraft. Part of the Dacke family was extirpated after the insurrection. The rebel's paternal uncle, Olof Dacke of Lindö, was taken to Stockholm, where he was broken on the wheel, quartered and impaled. Two Gertron brothers, Dacke's brothers-in-law, underwent the same treatment in their own village. But not all the Dackes were exterminated. Just before Christmas, 1546, Gustav Vasa employed one of them, a man by name Gisse Dacke of Djuramåla, in the parish of Vissefjärda, as ward registrar. And again, in 1624, in the days of Gustavus Adolphus, one of Nils Dacke's relatives was to carry on his work during some disturbances among the peasantry. The name of this peasant leader was Jon Stind; he was stated to be 'Niels Tacke's relation.'

In his letters Gustav I had promised to show no mercy to the rebellious commons of Småland. He would punish them in such a fashion 'that they and their children would never forget it.' The king is not noted for keeping his promises; but this one, let it be said to his credit, he fulfilled to the letter, as Fabian Månsson, the man who is our best witness to this fact, has told me. The rebellious hundreds of Värend and Möre were so devastated, ravaged, laid in ruins and in every way tormented that two centuries had to pass by before they again reached the level of subsistence they had enjoyed before the insurrection.

The great popular rebellion and its defeat were the greatest catastrophe ever to befall Småland. The subject is a large one, and many of its crucial aspects remain unresearched. It would require a long chapter to itself. Here a few last details will suffice. They give us an idea of the horrors and sufferings the Smålanders were subjected to in the mid-fifteen-forties, in one year.

Drawing on the court rolls of Uppvidinge hundred from this time, P. G. Vejde describes an assembly at Lenhovda in the summer of 1543, at which the peasantry of my own native hundred were to be punished for their part in the Dacke rising. The flock of 'criminals' are penned in by a strong troop of the king's soldiers, cavalry and German legionaries, under the command of Colonel Jakob Bagge. New gallows had been erected, and on top of a pile of great logs the executioners, holding their axes as they wait for their victims, bide their time. Seated on his horse, Jakob Bagge fulminates against the commons, commanding the people to denounce their leaders and hand them over – whoever obeys will save his own life. Upon which the terrified and bewildered peasants begin betraying each other, and without further ceremony guilty and innocent alike are led to the gallows or the block, where one after another 'justice is done upon them'. In the face of this massacre panic breaks out. People fling themselves on their knees, shrieking promises with upraised hands never again from this day onward to be disobedient to King Gustav or to ignore his edicts.

The pattern is familiar – from the king's razzias in Dalarna. Their rebellion crushed, great numbers of Smålanders had to 'follow in the footsteps of the Dalesmen', as the bailiffs, according to the peasants' demonstrance, had so often threatened.

In letters to his commanders Gustav Vasa gives the military permission to plunder at will those hundreds which have been infected by the rebellion: 'What part they can get from the enemy, that do we give them to plunder'. To the German legionaries, particularly, the king's permission was welcome. All the sources unanimously agree that they exploited it to the uttermost.

The mentality of these men who made war for a wage transpires from a letter quoted by Machiavelli. Written by his friend Francesco Vettori and dated Florence 1526, it describes the German soldiery's progress through Northern Italy: 'compared with them there is no one who does not prefer the Devil himself'. Presumably they did not behave any more humanely toward the population of Småland.

These men from the Germany of the peasant risings were experts at torture; they were 'practicians'. In their own country the so-called 'Emperor's law', promulgated against rebellious peasants, doomed all traitors to the most monstrous death. Before being executed they were broken on the wheel where every limb of their body was crushed. All the Dacke men who were caught by these German experts perished in this monstrous fashion.

Smoke from burning villages marked the royal troops' path through the rebellious province. Burning, plundering, raping and torturing, the king's soldiery passed through Värend and Möre.

When an author is faced with an event so horrible that he can find no words to depict it, he is sometimes obliged to turn aside and say it 'defies description'. It is just such an occurrence I here find myself faced with. Imagination boggles at it. And in the end Gustav Vasa took a step which seems to confirm the monstrous lengths to which it had gone. After a while, according to Tegel's chronicle, he recalled his German legionaries from the rebellious province, '*so that Småland should not be utterly ruined*'.

Further, as I have said before, a hunger blockade was enforced against Småland. No grain or other necessities of life were to be introduced from other provinces. And when, in the very year of the Dacke rising, there was a severe crop failure, the Smålanders' cup of misery brimmed over. Not only this – the peasants lost most of their draught animals. All who were fined for their part in the rising had to pay their fines in cattle. Several thousands of 'propitiatory oxen' were driven in herds to Stockholm.

The defeated Smålanders were starving, ruined, bleeding to death, impotent. Incapable of further resistance, they were utterly in the power of the victor. Anyone who saw any means of saving his own life seized it. They were defeated, and therefore they submitted. What else could they do? They had sacrificed their all to their revolt – and they had lost. No choice was left them. Professional soldiers might fight to the death, to preserve at least their honour. For Dacke's peasants war held no honours. What use could they have had for such figments? Nothing remained for them but to stick it out, bow their necks under the yoke of a silent suffering, and try to save their own ruined lives. To go on living.

And they survived, and gave life to new generations. Only after two centuries had gone by had my ancestors rebuilt their province.

In this way Småland, the last Swedish province ever to raise the standard of revolt, was forcibly incorporated into the kingdom of Sweden.

And in 1544, the year following his victory over the men of Småland, Gustav Vasa, by the Succession Pact at Västerås, founded his hereditary monarchy. The kingdom of Sweden had been saved, largely thanks to the assistance given to its king by his six thousand German legionaries.

'Those who are victorious, no matter how they gain the victory, are never shamed by it before history' – in these words, in Machiavelli's history of Florence, a spokesman for a defeated people utters an eternally valid truth. It will serve to close this chapter on the Dacke rising, our greatest popular revolt.

W9-CAM-396

TUNNELS

TUNNELS

RODERICK GORDON / BRIAN WILLIAMS

Chicken House
Scholastic Inc./New York

Published by Chicken House,
an imprint of Scholastic Inc.,
Publishers since 1920.
CHICKEN HOUSE, SCHOLASTIC,
and associated logos are trademarks and/or
registered trademarks of Scholastic Inc.
www.scholastic.com

Published in the United Kingdom in
2007 by Chicken House,
2 Palmer Street, Frome, Somerset BA11 1DS.
www.doublecluck.com

Attention all readers! The authors, the publisher, and Will Burrows wish it to be made clear that digging underground tunnels is a specialized business, can be very dangerous, and should NOT be attempted by you in your backyard or anyplace else where there's dirt.

Library of Congress Cataloging-in-Publication Data

Gordon, Roderick. [Highfield mole] Tunnels / by Roderick
Gordon and Brian Williams. — 1st American ed. p. cm.

Summary: When Will Burrows and his friend Chester
embark on a quest to find Will's archaeologist father, who
has inexplicably disappeared, they are led to a labyrinthine
world underneath London, full of sinister inhabitants with
evil intentions toward "Topsoilers" like Will and his father.

ISBN-13: 978-0-439-87177-8 • ISBN-10: 0-439-87177-8

[1. Adventure and adventurers—Fiction.
2. Underground areas—Fiction. 3. Archaeology—Fiction.
4. London (England)—Fiction. 5. England—Fiction.]
I. Williams, Brian James, 1958- II. Title.

PZ7.G6591Tu 2008 [Fic]—dc22
2007009169
10 9 8 7 6 5 4 3 08 09 10 11 12

Printed in the U.S.A. 23
First American edition, January 2008

The text type was set in Vendetta.
The display type was set in Squarehouse.

Book design by Leyah Jensen

IN MEMORIAM

Elizabeth Oke Gordon
1837—1919

"Everything unknown is doubted."
—Anonymous

PART 1

BREAKING GROUND

1

SCHLAAK! The pickax hit the wall of earth and, sparking on an unseen shard of flint, sank deep into the clay, coming to a sudden halt with a dull thud.

"This could be it, Will!"

Dr. Burrows crawled forward in the cramped tunnel. Sweating and breathing heavily in the confined space, he began feverishly clawing at the dirt, his breath clouding in the damp air. Under the combined glare of their helmet lamps, each greedy handful revealed more of the old wooden planking beneath, exposing its tar-coated grain and splintery surface.

"Pass me the crowbar."

Will rummaged in a satchel, found the stubby blue crowbar, and handed it to his father, whose gaze was fixed on the area of wood before him. Forcing the flat edge of the tool between two of the planks, Dr. Burrows grunted as he put all his weight behind it to gain some purchase. He then began levering from side to side. The planks creaked and moaned against their rusted fixings until, finally, they bellied out, breaking free with a resounding *crack*. Will recoiled slightly as a clammy breeze bled from the ominous gap Dr. Burrows had created.

Urgently they pulled two more of the planks out of place, leaving a shoulder-width hole, then paused for a moment in silence. Father and son turned and looked at each other, sharing a brief conspiratorial smile. Their faces, illuminated in each other's light beams, were smeared with a war paint of dirt.

They turned back to the hole and stared in wonder at the dust motes floating like tiny diamonds, forming and re-forming unknown constellations against the night-black opening.

Dr. Burrows warily leaned into the hole, Will squeezing in beside him to peer over his shoulder. As their helmet lamps cut into the abyss, a curved, tiled wall came into sharp focus. Their beams, penetrating deeper, swept over old posters whose edges were peeling away from the wall and waving slowly, like tendrils of seaweed caught in the drift of powerful currents at the bottom of the ocean. Will raised his head a little, scanning even farther along, until he caught the edge of an enameled sign. Dr. Burrows followed his son's gaze until the beams of their lamps joined together to clearly show the name.

"'*Highfield & Crossly North*'! This is it, Will, this is it! We found it!" Dr. Burrows's excited voice echoed around the dank confines of the disused train station. They felt a slight breeze on their faces as something blew along the platform and down onto the rails, as if sent into an animated panic by this rude intrusion, after so many years, into its sealed and forgotten catacomb.

Will kicked wildly at the timbers at the base of the opening, throwing up a spray of splinters and hunks of rotting wood, until suddenly the ground below him slid away and spilled into

the cavern. He scrambled through the opening, grabbing his shovel as he went. His father was immediately behind him as they crunched a few paces on the solid surface of the platform, their footsteps echoing and their helmet lamps cutting swathes into the surrounding gloom.

Cobwebs hung in skeins from the roof, and Dr. Burrows blew as one draped itself across his face. As he looked around, his light caught his son, a strange sight with a shock of white hair sticking out like bleached straw from under his battle-scarred miner's helmet, his pale blue eyes flashing with enthusiasm as he blinked into the dark.

Dr. Burrows himself was a wiry man of average height—one wouldn't have described him as tall or, for that matter, short, just somewhere in the middle. He had a round face with piercing brown eyes that appeared all the more intense due to his gold-rimmed glasses.

"Look up there, Will, look at that!" he said as his light picked out a sign above the gap through which they had just emerged. WAY OUT, it read in large black letters. They turned on their flashlights, and the beams combined with those of their weaker helmet lamps, ricocheting through the darkness to reveal the full length of the platform. Roots hung from the roof, and the walls were caked with efflorescence and streaked with chalky lime scale where fissures had seeped moisture. They could hear the sound of running water somewhere in the distance.

"How's this for a find?" Dr. Burrows said with a self-congratulatory air. "Just think, nobody has set foot down here since the new Highfield line was built in 1895." They had emerged onto one end of the platform, and Dr. Burrows now shone his flashlight into the opening of the train tunnel to their side. It was blocked by a mound of rubble and earth. "It'll be just the same down the other end—they would've sealed both tunnels," he said.

"Dad, Dad, over here!" Will called. "Have you seen these posters? You can still read them. I think they're ads for land or something. And here's a good one . . . 'Wilkinson's Circus . . . to be held on the Common . . . 10th day of February 1895.' There's a picture," he said breathlessly as his father joined him.

The poster had been spared any water damage, and they could make out the crude colors of the red big top, with a blue man in a top hat standing in front of it.

They walked farther along, stepping around a mountain of rubble that spilled onto the platform from an archway. "That would've led through to the other platform," Dr. Burrows told his son.

They paused to look at an ornate cast-iron bench. "This'll go nicely in the garden. All it needs is a rubdown and a few coats of gloss," Dr. Burrows was muttering as Will's flashlight beam alighted on a dark wooden door hidden in the shadows.

"Dad, wasn't there an office or something on your diagram?" Will asked, staring at the door.

"An office?" Dr. Burrows replied, fumbling through his pockets until he found the piece of paper he was searching for. "Let me have a look."

Will didn't wait for an answer, pushing at the door, which was stuck fast. Quickly losing interest in his blueprint, Dr. Burrows went to the aid of his son and together they tried to shoulder open the door. It was badly warped in the frame, but on the third attempt it suddenly gave and they tumbled into the room, a downpour of silt covering their heads and shoulders. Coughing and rubbing dust from their eyes, they pushed their way through a shroud of cobwebs.

"Wow!" Will exclaimed quietly. There, in the middle of the small office, they could make out a desk and chair, furred with dust. Will moved cautiously behind the chair and, with his gloved hand, brushed away the layer of cobwebs on the wall to reveal a large, faded map of the railway system.

"Could've been the stationmaster's office," Dr. Burrows said.

Two of the walls were lined with shelves stacked with decaying cardboard boxes. Will selected a box at random, lifted off the misshapen lid, and looked in wonder at the bundles of old tickets. He picked one of them out, but the perished rubber band crumbled, sending a confetti of tickets spewing over the desktop.

"They're blanks—they won't have been printed up," Dr. Burrows said.

"You're right," Will confirmed, never ceasing to be amazed at his father's knowledge, as he studied one of the tickets. But Dr. Burrows wasn't listening. He was kneeling down and tugging at a heavy object on a lower shelf, wrapped in a rotten cloth that dissolved at his touch. "And here," Dr. Burrows announced as Will turned to look at the machine, which resembled an old typewriter with a large pull handle on its side, "is an example of an early ticket-printing machine. Bit corroded, but we can probably get the worst off."

"What, for the museum?"

"No, for *my* collection," Dr. Burrows replied. He hesitated, and his face took on a serious expression. "Look, Will, we're not going to breathe a word about this, any of this, to anyone. Understand?"

"Huh?" Will spun around, a slight frown creasing his brow. It wasn't as if either of them went around broadcasting the fact that they embarked on these elaborate underground workings in their spare time—not that anyone would be seriously interested, anyway. Their common passion for the buried and the as-yet-undiscovered was something they didn't share with anyone else, something that brought father and son together . . . a bond between them.

Because his son hadn't made any sort of response, Dr. Burrows fixed him with a stare and went on.

"I don't have to remind you what happened last year with the Roman villa, do I? That bigwig professor turned up, hijacked the dig, and grabbed all the glory. *I* discovered that site, and what did I get? A tiny acknowledgment buried in his pathetic effort of a paper."

"Yeah, I remember," Will said, recalling his father's frustration and outbursts of fury at the time.

"Want that to happen again?"

"No, of course not."

"Well, I'm not going to be a footnote on this one. I'd rather *nobody* knew about it. They're not going to nick this from me, not this time. Agreed?"

Will nodded in assent, sending his light bouncing up and down the wall.

Dr. Burrows glanced at his watch. "We really ought to be getting back, you know."

"All right," Will replied grudgingly.

His father caught his tone. "There's no real hurry, is there? We can take our time to explore the rest tomorrow night."

"Yeah, I suppose," Will said halfheartedly, moving toward the door.

Dr. Burrows patted his son affectionately on his hard hat as they were leaving the office. "Sterling work, Will, I must say. All those months of digging really paid off, didn't they?"

They retraced their steps to the opening and, after a last look at the platform, clambered back into the tunnel. Twenty feet or so in, the tunnel blossomed out so they could walk side by side. If Dr. Burrows stooped slightly, it was just high enough for him to stand.

"We need to double up on the braces and props," Dr. Burrows announced, examining the expanse of timbers above their heads. "Instead of one every three feet, as we discussed, they're about one in ten."

"Sure. No problem, Dad," Will assured him, somewhat unconvincingly.

"And we need to shift this pile out," Dr. Burrows continued, nudging a mound of clay on the tunnel floor with his boot. "Don't want to get too constricted down here, do we?"

"Nope," Will replied vaguely, not really intending to do anything about it at all. The sheer thrill of discovery resulted all too often in him flouting the safety guidelines his father tried to lay down. His passion was to dig, and the last thing on his mind was to waste time on "housekeeping," as Dr. Burrows called it. And, in any case, his father rarely volunteered to help with any of the digging itself, only making an appearance when one of his "hunches" paid off.

Dr. Burrows whistled abstractedly through his teeth as he slowed to inspect a tower of neatly stacked buckets and a heap of planking. As they continued on their way, the tunnel climbed, and he stopped several more times to test the wooden props on either side. He smacked them with the palm of his hand, his obscure whistling rising to an impossible squeak as he did so.

The passage eventually leveled out and widened into a larger chamber, where there was a trestle table and a pair of sorry-looking armchairs. They dumped some of their equipment on the table, then climbed the last stretch of tunnel to the entrance.

Just as the town clock finished striking seven, a length of corrugated iron sheeting lifted a couple of inches in a corner of the Temperance Square parking lot. It was early autumn, and the sun was just tipping over the horizon as father and son, satisfied the coast was clear, pushed back the sheeting to reveal the large timber-framed hole in the ground. They poked their heads a little way out, double-checking that there was nobody else in the parking lot, then clambered from the hole. Once the sheeting was back in place over the entrance, Will kicked dirt over it to disguise it.

A breeze rattled the billboards around the parking lot, and a newspaper rolled along the ground like tumbleweed, scattering its pages as it gained momentum. As the dying sun silhouetted the surrounding warehouses and reflected off the burgundy-tiled facade of the nearby housing projects, the two Burrowses ambling out of the parking lot looked every inch a pair of prospectors leaving their claim in the foothills to return to town.

On the other side of Highfield, Terry Watkins—"Tipper Tel" to his friends at work—was dressed in pajama bottoms and brushing his teeth in front of the bathroom mirror. He was tired and hoping for a good night's sleep, but his mind was still somersaulting because of what he'd seen that afternoon.

It had been an awfully long and arduous day. He and his demolition team were pulling down the ancient white leadworks to make way for a new office tower for some government department or other. He'd wanted more than anything to go home, but he had promised his boss that he would take out a few courses of brickwork in the basement to try to make an assessment of how extensive its foundations were. The last thing his company could afford was an overrun on the contract, which was always the risk with these old buildings

As the portable floodlight glared behind him, he had swung his sledgehammer, cracking open the handmade bricks, which revealed their bright red innards like eviscerated animals. He swung again, fragments spinning off onto the soot-covered floor of the basement, and swore under his breath because the whole place was just too darned well built.

After further blows, he waited until the cloud of brick dust settled. To his surprise he found that the area of wall he'd been attacking was only one brick thick. There was a sheet of old pig iron where the second and third layers should have been. He belted it a couple of times, and it resounded with a substantial *clang* on each blow. It wasn't going to give up easily. He breathed heavily as he pulverized the bricks around the edges of the metal surface to discover, to his sheer amazement, that it had hinges, and even a handle of some type recessed into its surface.

It was a *door*.

He paused, panting for a moment while he tried to figure out why anyone would want access to what should rightfully be part of the foundations.

Then he made the biggest mistake of his life.

He used his screwdriver to pry out the handle, a wrought-iron ring that turned with surprisingly little effort. The door swung inward with a little help from one of his work boots and clanged flat against the wall on the other side, the noise echoing for what seemed like forever. He took out his flashlight and shone it into the pitch-blackness of the room. He could see it was at least twenty feet across and was, in fact, circular.

He went through the doorway, stepping onto the stone surface just inside it. But on the second step, the stone floor disappeared, and his foot encountered nothing but air. *There was a drop!* He teetered on the very edge, his arms windmilling frantically until he managed to regain his balance and pull himself back from the brink. He fell back against the doorjamb and clung on to it, taking deep breaths to steady his nerves and cursing himself for his rashness.

"Come on, get a grip," he said aloud, forcing himself to get going again. He turned and slowly edged forward, his flashlight revealing that he was indeed standing on a ledge, with an ominous darkness beyond it. He leaned over, trying to make out what lay below—it appeared to be bottomless. He had walked into a huge brick well. And, as he looked up, he couldn't see to the top of the well—the brick walls curved dramatically up into the shadows, past the limits of his little pocket flashlight. A strong breeze seemed to be coming from above, chilling the sweat on the back of his neck.

Playing the beam around, he noticed that steps, maybe a foot and a half wide, led down around the edge of the wall, starting just below the stone ledge. He stamped on the first step to test it and, since it felt sound, began to descend the stairway cautiously, so as not to slip on the fine layer of dust, bits of straw, and twigs that littered it. Hugging the diameter of the well, he climbed down, deeper and deeper, until the floodlit door was just a tiny dot way above him.

Eventually the steps ended, and he found himself on a flagstone floor. Using his flashlight to look around, he could see many pipes of a dull gunmetal color lacing up the walls like a drunken church organ. He traced the route of one of these as it meandered upward and saw that it opened into a funnel, as if it was a vent of some kind. But what caught his attention more than anything else was a door with a small glass porthole. Light was unmistakably shining through it, and he could only think that he had somehow blundered into the subway system, particularly since he could hear the low humming sound of machinery and feel a constant downdraft of air.

He slowly approached the window, a circle of thick glass mottled and scored with time, and peered through. He couldn't believe his eyes. Through its undulating surface, there was a scene resembling a scratchy old black-and-white film. There appeared to be a street and a row of buildings. And, bathed in the light of glowing spheres of slow-moving fire, people were milling around. Fearsome-looking people. Anemic phantoms dressed in old-fashioned clothes.

Terry wasn't a particularly religious man, attending church only for weddings and the odd funeral, but he wondered for a moment if he had stumbled upon some sort of purgatorial theme park. He recoiled from the window and crossed himself, mumbling woefully inaccurate Hail Marys, and scuttled back up the stairs in a blind panic, barricading the door lest any of the demons escape.

He ran through the deserted building site and padlocked the main gates behind him. As he drove home in a daze, he wondered what he would tell the boss the next morning. Although he had seen it with his own eyes, he couldn't help but replay the vision over and over in his mind. By the time he had reached home, he really didn't know what to believe.

2

IN A GRIM turn-of-the-century dentist's chair in the Highfield Museum, Dr. Burrows settled down to his sandwiches, using a display case of early twentieth-century toothbrushes as a makeshift table. He flicked open his copy of *The Times* and gnawed on a limp salami-and-mayonnaise sandwich, seemingly oblivious to the dirt-encrusted dental implements below, which local people had bequeathed to the museum rather than throwing them away.

In the cabinets around the main hall where Dr. Burrows now sat, there were many similar arrangements of spared-from-the-garbage articles. The "Granny's Kitchen" corner featured an extensive assortment of tawdry eggbeaters, apple corers, and tea strainers. A pair of rusty Victorian mangles stood proudly by a long-since-defunct 1950s *Old Faithful Electric* washing machine.

On the "Clock Wall," though, there was one item that caught the eye—a Victorian picture clock with a scene painted on a glass panel of a farmer with a horse pulling a plow—unfortunately the glass had been broken and a vital chunk was missing where the horse's head would have been. The rest of the display was made up of 1940s and 1950s windup and electric wall clocks in dull plastic pastel hues—none of which were working, because Dr. Burrows hadn't quite gotten around to fixing them yet.

Highfield, one of the smaller London boroughs, had a rich past, starting as it had in Roman times as a small settlement and, in more recent history, swelling under the full impact of the Industrial Revolution. However, not much of this rich past had found its way into the little museum, and the borough had become what it was now: a desert of single-room-occupancy apartments and nondescript shops.

Dr. Burrows, the curator of the museum, was also its sole attendant, except on Saturdays, when a series of volunteer retirees manned the fort. And always at his side was his brown leather briefcase, which contained a number of periodicals, half-read textbooks, and historical novels. For reading was how Dr. Burrows occupied his days, punctuated by the odd nap and very occasional clandestine pipe smoking in "The Stacks," a large storage room chock-full of boxed postcards and abandoned family portraits that would never be put out on display due to the lack of space.

Other than the occasional school group desperate for a local outing in wet weather, very few visitors at all came to the museum and, having seen it once, they were unlikely ever to return.

Dr. Burrows, like so many others, was doing a job that had originally been a stopgap. It wasn't as if he didn't have an impressive academic record: A degree in history had been followed up with yet another in archaeology, and then, for good measure, topped off with a doctorate. But with a young child at home and few positions offered in any of the London universities, he had happened to spot the museum job in the *Highfield Bugle* and sent in his résumé, thinking he had better get *something*, and quickly.

Finishing off his sandwich, Dr. Burrows crumpled the wrapper into a ball and playfully launched it at a 1960s orange plastic wastepaper basket on display in the "Kitchen" section. It missed, bouncing off the rim and coming to rest on the parquet floor. He let out a small sigh of disappointment and reached into his briefcase, rummaging around until he retrieved a bar of chocolate. It was a treat he tried to save until midafternoon, to give the day some shape. But he felt particularly forlorn today and willingly gave in to his sweet tooth, ripping off the wrapper in an instant and taking a large bite out of the bar.

Just then, the bell on the entrance door rattled, and Oscar Embers tapped in on his twin walking sticks. The eighty-year-old former stage actor had formed a passion for the museum after donating some of his autographed portraits to the archives.

Dr. Burrows tried to finish his crammed mouthful of chocolate but, chewing manically, he realized that the old thespian was closing in far too quickly. Dr. Burrows thought of fleeing to his office but knew it was too late now. He sat still, his cheeks puffed out like a hamster's as he attempted a smile.

"Good afternoon to you, Roger," Oscar said cheerfully while fumbling in his coat pocket. "Now, where did that thing go?"

Dr. Burrows managed a tight-lipped "*Hmmm*" as he nodded enthusiastically. As Oscar began to wrestle with his coat pocket,

Dr. Burrows managed to get in a couple of crafty chews, but then the old man looked up, still grappling with his coat as if it were fighting back. Oscar stopped trawling his pockets for a second and peered myopically around the glass cases and walls. "Can't see any of that lace I brought you the other week. Are you going to put it on display? I know it was a little threadbare in places, but good stuff all the same, you know." When Dr. Burrows did not answer, he added, "So it's *not* out, then?"

Dr. Burrows tried to indicate the storeroom with a flick of his head. Never having known the curator to be so silent for so long, Oscar gave him a quizzical look, but then his eyes lit up as he found his quarry. He took it slowly from his pocket and held it, cupped in his hand, in front of Dr. Burrows.

"I was given this by old Mrs. Tantrumi—you know, the Italian lady who lives just off the end of Main Street. It was found in her cellar when the gas company was doing some repairs. Stuck in the dirt, it was. One of them kicked it with his foot. I think we should include it in the collection."

Dr. Burrows, cheeks puffed, braced himself for yet another not-quite-antique egg timer or battered tin of used pen nibs. He was taken off guard when, with a magician's flourish, Oscar held up a small, gently glowing globe, slightly larger than a golf ball, encased in a metal cage that was a dull gold in color.

"It's a fine example of a . . . a light . . . thing of some . . . ," Oscar trailed off. "Well, as a matter of fact, I don't know *what* to make of it!"

Dr. Burrows took the item and was so fascinated that he quite forgot Oscar was watching him intently as he chewed his mouthful of chocolate.

"Teeth giving you trouble, my boy?" Oscar asked. "I used to grind them like that, too, when they got bad. Just awful—know exactly how you feel. All I can say is that I'm glad I took the plunge and had them all out in one go. It isn't so uncomfortable, you know, once you get used to one of these." He started to reach into his mouth.

"Oh, no, my teeth are fine," Dr. Burrows managed to say, quickly trying to head off the prospect of seeing the old man's dentures. He swallowed the last of the chocolate in his mouth with a large gulp. "Just a bit dry today," he explained, rubbing his throat. "Need some water."

"Ohhh, better keep an eye on that, y'know. Might be a sign that you've got that diabetes malarkey. When I was a lad, Roger" — Oscar's eyes seemed to glaze over as he remembered— "some doctors used to test for diabetes by tasting your . . ." He lowered his voice to a whisper and looked down in the direction of the floor. ". . . *waters*, if you know what I mean, to see if there was too much sugar in them."

"Yes, yes, I know," Dr. Burrows replied automatically, far too intrigued by the gently glowing globe to pay any attention to Oscar's medical curiosities. "Very strange. I would venture to say, offhand, that this dates from possibly the nineteenth century, looking at the metalwork . . . and the glass I would say is early, definitely hand-blown . . . but I have no idea what's inside. Maybe it's just a luminous chemical of some type—have you had it out in the light for long this morning, Mr. Embers?"

"No, kept it safe in my coat since Mrs. Tantrumi gave it to me yesterday. Just after breakfast, it was. I was on my constitutional—it helps with the old bowel mov—"

"I wonder if it could be radioactive," Dr. Burrows interrupted sharply. "I've read that some of the Victorian rock-and-mineral collections in other museums have been tested for radioactivity. Some pretty fierce specimens were uncovered in a batch up in Scotland—powerful uranium crystals that they had to shut away in a lead-lined casket. Too hazardous to keep out on display."

"Oh, I hope it's not dangerous," Oscar said, taking a hasty step back. "Been walking around with it next to my new hip—just imagine if it's melted the—"

"No, I don't expect it's that potent—it probably hasn't done you any real harm, not in twenty-four hours." Dr. Burrows gazed into the sphere. "How very peculiar, you can see liquid moving inside.... Looks like it's swirling... like a storm...." He lapsed into silence, then shook his head in disbelief. "No, must be the heat from my hand that's making it behave like that . . . you know . . . thermoreactive."

"Well, I'm delighted you think it's interesting. I'll let Mrs. Tantrumi know you want to hang on to it," Oscar said, taking another step back.

"Definitely," Dr. Burrows replied. "I'd better do some research before I put it out, just to make sure it's safe. But in the meantime I should drop Mrs. Tantrumi a line to thank her, on behalf of the museum." He hunted in his jacket pocket for a pen but couldn't find one. "Hold on a sec, Mr. Embers, while I fetch something to write with."

He walked out of the main hall and into the corridor, managing to stumble over an ancient length of timber dug out of the marshes the previous year by some overzealous locals who swore blindly that it was a prehistoric canoe. Dr. Burrows opened the door with CURATOR painted on the frosted glass. The office was dark, because the only window was blocked by crates stacked high in front of it. As he groped for the light on his desk, he happened to uncurl his hand a little from around the sphere. What he saw completely astounded him.

The light it was giving off appeared to have turned from the soft glow he'd witnessed in the main hall to a much more intense, light green fluorescence. As he watched it, he could have sworn that the light was growing even brighter, and the liquid inside moving even more vigorously.

"Remarkable! What substance becomes more radiant the *darker* the surroundings?" he muttered to himself. "No, I must be mistaken, it can't be! It must be that the luminosity is just more noticeable in here."

But it *had* grown brighter; he didn't even need his desk light to locate his pen because the globe was giving off a sublime green light, almost as bright as daylight. As he left his office and returned with his donations ledger to the main hall, he held the globe aloft in front of him. Sure enough, the moment he emerged back into the light, it dimmed again.

Oscar was about to say something, but Dr. Burrows rushed straight past him, through the museum door, and out onto the street. He heard Oscar shouting, "I say! I say!" as the museum door slammed shut behind him, but Dr. Burrows was so intent on the sphere that he completely ignored him. As he held it up in the daylight, he saw that the glow was all but extinguished and that the liquid in the glass sphere had darkened to a dull grayish color. And the longer he remained outside, exposing the sphere to natural light, the darker the fluid inside became, until it was almost black and looked like oil.

Still dangling the globe in front of him, he returned inside, watching as the liquid began to whip itself up into a miniature storm and shimmer eerily again. Oscar was waiting for him with concern on his face.

"Fascinating . . . fascinating," Dr. Burrows said.

"I say, thought you were having an attack of the vapors, old chap. I wondered if maybe you needed some air, rushing out like that. Not feeling faint, are you?"

"No, I'm fine, really I am, Mr. Embers. Just wanted to test something. Now, Mrs. Tantrumi's address, if you'd be so kind?"

"So glad you're pleased with it," Oscar said. "Now, while we're about it, I'll let you have my dentist's number so you can get those teeth seen to, pronto."

3

WILL was leaning on the handlebars of his bicycle at the entrance to a stretch of wasteland encircled by trees and wild bushes. He glanced at his watch yet again and decided he would give Chester another five minutes to turn up, but no more. He was wasting precious time.

The land was one of those forgotten lots you find on the outskirts of any town. This one hadn't yet been covered by housing, probably due to its proximity to the municipal waste station and the mountains of trash that rose and fell with depressing regularity. Known locally as "the Forty Pits," owing to the numerous craters that pitted its surface, some almost reaching ten feet in depth, it was the arena for frequent battles between two opposing teenage gangs, the Clan and the Click, whose members were drawn from Highfield's rougher housing projects.

It was also the favored spot for kids on their dirt bikes and, increasingly, stolen mopeds, the latter being run into the ground and then torched, their carbon black skeletons littering the far edges of the Pits, where weeds threaded up through their wheels and around their rusting engine blocks. Less frequently, it was also the scene for such sinister adolescent amusements as bird or frog hunting; all too often, the creatures' sorry little carcasses were impaled on sticks.

As Chester turned the corner toward the Pits, a bright metallic glint caught his eye. It was the polished face of Will's shovel, which he wore slung across his back like some samurai construction worker.

He smiled and picked up his pace, clutching his rather ordinary, dull garden shovel to his chest and waving enthusiastically to the lone figure in the distance, who was unmistakable with his startlingly pale complexion and his baseball cap and sunglasses. Indeed, Will's whole appearance was rather odd; he was wearing his "digging uniform," which consisted of an oversized cardigan with leather elbow pads and a pair of dirt-encrusted old cords of indeterminate color owing to the fine patina of dried mud that covered them. The only things Will kept really clean were his beloved shovel and the exposed metal toe caps of his work boots.

"What happened to you, then?" Will asked as Chester finally reached him. Will couldn't understand how *anything* could have held up his friend, how *anything* could possibly be more important than this.

This was a milestone in Will's life, the first time he'd ever allowed somebody from school—or anywhere else, for that matter—to see one of his projects. He wasn't sure yet whether he'd done the right thing; he still didn't know Chester that well.

"Sorry, got a flat," Chester puffed apologetically. "Had to drop the bike back home and run over here—bit hot in this weather."

Will glanced up uneasily at the sun and frowned. It was no friend to him: His lack of pigmentation meant that even its meager power on an overcast day could burn his skin.

"All right, let's get straight to it. Lost too much time already," Will said curtly. He pushed off on his bicycle with barely a glance at Chester, who began to run after him. "Come on, this way," he urged as the other boy failed to match his speed.

"Hey, I thought we were already there!" Chester called after him, still trying to catch his breath.

Chester Rawls—almost as wide as he was tall, and strong as an ox, known as Cuboid or Chester Drawers at school—was the same age as Will, but evidently had either benefited from better nutrition or had inherited his weightlifter's physique. One of the less offensive pieces of graffiti in the school bathrooms proclaimed that his father was an armoire and his mother a bowfront desk.

Although the growing friendship between Will and Chester seemed unlikely, the very thing that had helped to bring them together had also been the same thing that singled them out at school: their skin. For Chester, it was severe bouts of eczema, which resulted in flaky and itchy patches of raw skin. This was due, he was told unhelpfully, to either an unidentifiable allergy or nervous tension. Whatever the cause, he had endured the teasing and gibes from his fellow pupils, the worst ones being "'orrible scaly creature" and "snake features," until he could take no more and had fought back, using his physical advantage to quash the taunters with great effect.

Likewise, Will's milky pallor separated him from the norm, and for a while he had borne the brunt of chants of "Chalky" and "Frosty the Snowman." More impetuous than Chester, he had lost his temper one winter's evening when his tormentors had ambushed him on the way to a dig. Unfortunately for them, Will had used his shovel to great effect, and a bloody and one-sided battle had ensued in which teeth were lost and a nose was badly broken.

Understandably both Will and Chester were left alone for a while after that and treated with the sort of grudging respect given to mad dogs. However, both boys remained distrustful of their classmates, believing that if they let their guards down, the persecution would more than likely start all over again. So, other than Chester's inclusion on a number of school teams because of his physical prowess, both remained outsiders, loners at the edge of the playground. Secure in their shared isolation, they talked to no one and no one talked to them.

It had been many years before they'd even spoken to each other, although there'd long been a sneaking admiration between the two for the way they'd both stood their ground against the school bullies. Without really realizing it they gravitated toward each other, spending more and more of their time together during school hours. Will had been alone and friendless for so long, he had to admit that it felt good to have a companion, but he knew that if the friendship was going to go anywhere he'd sooner or later have to reveal to Chester his grand passion—his excavations. And now that time had come.

Will rode between the alternating grassy mounds, craters, and heaps of trash, careering to a halt as he reached the far side. He dismounted and hid his bicycle in a small dugout beneath the shell of an abandoned car, its make unrecognizable as a result of the rust and salvaging it had endured.

"Here we are," he announced as Chester caught up.

"Is this where we're going to dig?" Chester panted, looking around at the ground by their feet.

"Nope. Back up a bit," Will said. Chester took a couple of paces away from Will, regarding him with bemusement.

"Are we going to start a new one?"

Will didn't answer but instead knelt down and appeared to be feeling for something in a thicket of grass. He found what he was looking for—a knotted length of rope—and stood up, took up the slack, then pulled hard. To Chester's surprise, a line cracked open in the earth, and a thick panel of plywood rose up, soil tumbling from it to reveal the dark entrance beneath.

"Why do you need to hide it?" he asked Will.

"Can't have those scumbags messing around with my excavation, can I?" Will said possessively.

"We're not going in there, are we?" Chester said, stepping closer to peer into the void.

But Will had already begun to lower himself into the opening, which, after a drop of about six feet, continued to sink deeper, at an angle.

"I've got a spare one of these for you," Will said from inside the opening as he donned a yellow hard hat and switched on the miner's light mounted on its front. It shone up at Chester, who was hovering indecisively above him.

"Well, are you coming or not?" Will said testily. "Take it from me, it's completely safe."

"Are you sure about this?"

"Of course," Will said, making a show of slapping a support to his side and smiling confidently to give his friend some encouragement. He continued to smile fixedly as, in the shadows behind him and out of Chester's sight, a small shower of soil fell against his back. "Safe as houses. Honest."

"Well . . ."

Once inside, Chester was almost too surprised to speak. A tunnel, several feet wide and the same in height, ran at a slight incline into the darkness, the sides shored up with old timber props at frequent intervals. It looked, Chester thought, exactly like the mines in those old cowboy films they showed on TV on Sunday afternoons.

"This is cool! You didn't do all this by yourself, Will, you can't have!"

Will grinned smugly. "Certainly did. I've been at it since last year—and you haven't seen the half of it yet. Step this way."

He replaced the plywood, sealing the tunnel mouth. Chester watched with mixed emotions as the last chink of blue sky disappeared. They set off along the passage, past stores of planks and shoring timbers stacked untidily against the sides.

"Wow!" Chester said under his breath.

Quite unexpectedly the passage widened out into an area the size of a reasonably large room, two tunnels branching off each end of it. In the middle was a small mountain of buckets, a trestle table, and two old armchairs. The timber planking of the roof was supported by rows of Stillson props, adjustable iron columns scabbed with rust.

"Home again, home again," Will said.

"This is just . . . wild," Chester said in disbelief, then frowned. "But is it really all right for us to be down here?"

"Of course it is. My dad showed me how to batten and prop—this isn't my first time, you know. . . ." Will hesitated, catching himself just in time before he said anything about the train station he'd unearthed with his father. Chester regarded him suspiciously as he coughed loudly to mask the lull in the conversation. Will had been sworn to secrecy by his father, and he couldn't break that confidence, not even to Chester. He sniffed loudly, then went on. "And it's perfectly sound. It's better not to tunnel under buildings—that takes stronger tunnel props and a lot more planning. Also, it's not a good idea where there's water or underground streams—they can cause the whole thing to cave in."

"There's isn't any water around here, is there?" Chester asked quickly.

"Just this." Will reached into a cardboard box on the table and handed his friend a plastic bottle of water. "Let's just chill out for a while."

They both sat in the old armchairs, sipping from the bottles, while Chester looked up at the roof and craned his neck to look at the two branch tunnels.

"It's so peaceful, isn't it?" Will sighed.

"Yes," Chester replied. "Very . . . um . . . quiet."

"It's more than that, it's so warm and *calm* down here. And the smell . . . sort of comforting, isn't it? Dad says it's where we all came from, a long time ago—cavemen and all that—and of course it's where we all end up eventually—underground, I mean. So it feels sort of natural to us, a home away from home."

"Suppose so," Chester agreed dubiously.

"You know, I used to think that when you bought a house, you owned everything under it as well."

"What do you mean?"

"Well, your house is built on a plot of land, right?" Will said, thumping his boot on the floor of the cavern for effect. "And anything below that plot, going right down to the earth's core, is yours as well. Of course, as you get nearer the center of the planet, the 'segment,' if you want to call it that, gets smaller and smaller, until you hit the very center."

Chester nodded slowly, at a loss for what to say.

"So I've always imagined digging down—down into your slice of world and all those thousands of miles that are going to waste, instead of just sitting in a building perched on the very crust of the earth," Will said dreamily.

"I see," Chester said, catching on to the idea. "So if you were to dig down, you could have, like, a skyscraper, but facing the wrong way. Like an ingrown hair or something." He involuntarily scratched the eczema on his forearm.

"Yes, that's exactly right. Hadn't thought of it like that. Good way of putting it. But Dad says you *don't* actually own all the ground under you—the government has the right to build subway lines and things if they want to."

"Oh," Chester said, wondering why they had been talking about it in the first place, if that was the case.

Will jumped up. "OK, grab yourself a pickax, four buckets, and a wheelbarrow, and follow me down here." He pointed to one of the dark tunnels. "There's a bit of a rock problem."

Meanwhile, back up at ground level, Dr. Burrows strode purposefully along as he made his way home. He always enjoyed the chance to think while he walked the mile and a half or so, and it meant he could save on the bus fare.

He stopped outside the newsstand, abruptly halting in midpace, teetered slightly, rotated ninety degrees, and entered.

"Dr. Burrows! I was beginning to think we'd never see you again," the man behind the counter said as he looked up from a newspaper spread open before him. "Thought you might've gone off on a round-the-world cruise or something."

"Ah, no, alas," Dr. Burrows replied, trying to keep his eyes off the Snickers, Milky Ways, and Mars bars that were displayed enticingly in front of him.

"We've kept your backlog safe," the shopkeeper said as he bent below the counter and produced a stack of magazines. "Here they are. *Excavation Today*, *The Archaeological Journal*, and *Curators' Monthly*. All present and correct, I hope?"

"Tickety-boo," Dr. Burrows said, hunting for his wallet. "Wouldn't want you to let them go to anyone else!"

The shopkeeper raised his eyebrows. "Believe me, there isn't exactly an excessive demand for these titles around here," he said as he took a £20 note from Dr. Burrows. "Looks like you've been working on something," the shopkeeper said, spotting Dr. Burrows's grimy fingernails. "Been down a coal mine?"

"No," Dr. Burrows replied, contemplating the dirt encrusted underneath his nails. "I've actually been doing some home repairs in my cellar. Good thing I don't bite them, isn't it?"

Dr. Burrows left the shop with his new reading matter, trying to tuck it securely into the side pocket of his briefcase as he pushed open the door. Still grappling with the magazines, he backed blindly out onto the sidewalk, straight into somebody moving at great speed. Gasping as he rebounded off the short but very heavyset man he'd blundered into, Dr. Burrows dropped his briefcase and magazines. The man, who had felt as solid as a locomotive, seemed totally unaffected and merely continued on his way. Dr. Burrows, stuttering and flustered, tried to call after him to apologize, but the man strode on purposefully, readjusting his sunglasses and turning his head slightly to give Dr. Burrows an unfriendly sneer.

Dr. Burrows was flabbergasted. It was a man-in-a-hat. Of late, he had begun to notice, among the general population of Highfield, a type of person that seemed—well, *different*, but without sticking out too much. Being a habitual people watcher, and having analyzed the situation as he always did, he assumed that these people had to be related to one another in some way. What surprised him most was that when he raised the subject nobody else in the Highfield area seemed to have registered at all the rather peculiarly slope-faced men wearing flat caps, black coats, and very thick dark glasses.

As Dr. Burrows had barged into the man, slightly dislodging his jet-black glasses, he'd had a chance to see a "specimen" at close hand for the very first time. Apart from his oddly sloping face and wispy hair, he had very light blue, almost white, eyes against a pasty, translucent skin. But there was something else: A peculiar smell hung around the man, a *mustiness*. It reminded Dr. Burrows of the old suitcases of mildewed clothes that were occasionally dumped on the museum steps by anonymous benefactors.

He watched the man stride purposefully down Main Street and into the distance, until he was only just in view. Then a passerby crossed the road, interrupting Dr. Burrows's line of sight. In that instant, the man-in-a-hat was gone. Dr. Burrows squinted through his spectacles as he continued to look for him, but although the sidewalks were not that busy, he couldn't locate him again, try as he might.

It occurred to Dr. Burrows that he should have made the effort to follow the man-in-a-hat to see where he was going. But, mild-mannered as he was, Dr. Burrows disliked any form of confrontation and quickly reasoned with himself that this was not a good idea given the man's hostile manner. So any thought of detective work was quickly abandoned. Besides, he could find out on another day where the man, and perhaps the whole family of hatted look-alikes, lived. When he was feeling a little more intrepid.

Underground, Will and Chester took turns at the rock face, which Will had identified as a type of sandstone. He was glad that he'd recruited Chester to help with the excavation, since he really seemed to have a knack for the work. He watched with quiet admiration as Chester swung the pickax with immense force and, once a fissure opened up in the face, seemed to know exactly when to pry out the loose material, which Will quickly shoveled into buckets.

"Need a break?" he suggested, seeing that Chester was beginning to tire. "Let's take a breather." Will meant this literally, because with the entrance to the dig covered up, it all too soon became very airless and stuffy where they were, twenty feet or so from the main chamber.

"If I take this tunnel much farther," he said to Chester as they both pushed loaded wheelbarrows before them, "I'll have to sink a vertical shaft for ventilation. It's just that it's such a drag putting one of those in, when I could be making more headway down here."

They reached the main chamber and sat in the armchairs, drinking the water appreciatively.

"So what do we do with all this?" Chester said, indicating the filled buckets in the wheelbarrows.

"Lug it to the surface and tip it in the gully at the side."

"Is it all right to do that?"

"Well, if anyone asks I just say I'm digging a trench for a war game," Will replied. Taking a swig from his bottle, he swallowed noisily. "What do they care, anyway? To them we're just a bunch of dumb kids with buckets and shovels," he added dismissively.

"They *would* care if they saw this—this isn't what ordinary kids do," Chester said, his eyes flicking around the chamber. "Why *do* you do it, Will?"

"Take a look at these."

Will gently lifted a plastic crate from the side of his chair and onto his lap. He then proceeded to take out a series of objects, leaning across to place them one by one on the tabletop. Among them were Codswallop bottles—Victorian soft-drink bottles with strangely shaped necks that contained a glass marble—and a whole host of medicine bottles of different sizes and colors, all with a beautiful frosty bloom from their time in the ground.

"And these," Will said reverentially as he produced an entire range of Victorian jars of differing sizes with decorative lids and names in swirly old writing that Chester had never seen before. Indeed, Chester seemed to be genuinely interested, picking up each jar in turn and asking Will questions about how old they were and where exactly he'd dug them up. Encouraged, Will continued until every single find from his recent excavations was laid out on the table. Then he sat back, carefully watching his newfound friend's reaction.

"What's this stuff?" Chester asked, probing a small pile of heavily rusted metal with his finger.

"Rosehead nails. Probably eighteenth century. If you look carefully, you can see that each one is different, because they were handmade by—"

But in his excitement Chester had already moved down the table to where something else had caught his eye.

"This is so cool," he said, holding up and turning a small perfume bottle so that the light played through its wonderful cobalt blue and mauve tones. "Incredible that someone just chucked it out."

"Yeah, isn't it?" Will agreed. "You can have it if you want."

"No!" Chester said, astonished by the offer.

"Yeah, go on, I've got another one just like it at home."

"Hey, that's great . . . thanks," Chester said, still admiring the bottle with such rapture that he didn't see Will break into the widest grin imaginable. Will practically lived for the moments he could show his father his latest crop of finds, but this was more than he could have ever hoped for—someone his own age who seemed to be sincerely interested in the fruits of his labors. He surveyed the cluttered tabletop and felt a swell of pride. This was what he lived for. He often pictured himself reaching back into the past and plucking out these little pieces of discarded history. To Will the past was so much nicer a place than the grim reality of the present. He sighed as he began to replace the items in the crate.

"I haven't found any fossils down here yet . . . anything *really* old . . . but you never know your luck," he said, glancing wistfully in the direction of the branch tunnels. "That's the thrill of it all."

4

DR. BURROWS whistled, swinging his briefcase in time with his brisk pace. He rounded the corner at precisely 6:30 P.M., as he always did, and his house came into view. It was one of many crammed into Broadlands Avenue—regimented brick boxes with just enough room for a family of four. The only saving grace was that this side of the road backed onto the Common, so at least the house had views of a big open space, even if one was forced to see them from rooms barely large enough to swing a mouse, let alone a cat.

As he let himself in and stood in the hall, sorting the old books and magazines from his briefcase, his son was not far behind. At breakneck speed Will careened onto Broadlands Avenue on his bicycle, his shovel glinting under the first red glow of the newly lit streetlights. He skillfully slalomed between the white lines in the middle of the road and banked wildly as he shot through the open gate, his brakes reaching a squealing crescendo as he pulled up under the carport. He dismounted, locked up his bicycle, and entered the house.

"Hi, Dad," he said to his father, who was now poised awkwardly just inside the living room, still holding his open briefcase in one hand as he watched something on television.

Dr. Burrows was unarguably the biggest influence in his son's life. A casual comment or snippet of information from his father could inspire Will to embark on the wildest and most extreme "investigations," usually involving ludicrous amounts of digging. Dr. Burrows always managed to be "in at the kill" on any of his son's digs if he suspected there was going to be something of true archaeological value unearthed, but most of the time he preferred to bury his nose in the books he kept down in the cellar, *his* cellar. Here he could escape family life, losing himself in dreams of echoing Greek temples and magnificent Roman colosseums.

"Oh, yes, hello, Will," he answered absentmindedly after a long pause, still absorbed in the television. Will looked past his father to where his mother was sitting, equally mesmerized by the program.

"Hi, Mum," Will said and then left, not waiting for a response.

Mrs. Burrows's eyes were glued to an unexpected and rather fraught turn of events in the *ER*. "Hello," she eventually replied, although Will had already left the room.

Will's parents had first met at college when Mrs. Burrows had been a bubbly media student dead set on a career in television.

Unfortunately, these days television filled her life for a completely different reason. She watched it with an almost fanatical devotion, juggling schedules with a pair of VCRs when her favorite programs, of which there were so very many, clashed.

If one has a mental snapshot of a person, an image that is first recalled when one thinks of them, then Mrs. Burrows's would be of her lying sideways in her favorite armchair, a row of remotes neatly lined up on the arm and her feet resting on a footstool topped with television pages ripped from the newspapers. There she sat, day after day, week after week, surrounded by a haphazard slag heap of videotapes, frozen in the flickering light of the small screen, occasionally twitching a leg just to let people know she was still alive.

As he did every night, Will had beaten a path to the kitchen or, more specifically, the fridge. He was opening the door as he spoke, but didn't so much as glance at the other person in the room as he acknowledged her presence.

"Hi, sis," Will said. "What are we having for dinner? I'm starved."

"Ah, the mud creature returns," Rebecca said to him. "I had the funniest feeling you'd show up about now." She rammed the fridge door shut to stop her brother from nosing inside and, before he had a chance to complain, thrust an empty packet into his hands. "Sweet-and-sour chicken, with rice and some vegetable stuff. It was on sale, two for one, at the supermarket."

Will looked at the picture on the packet and, without comment, passed it back to her.

"So how's the latest dig going?" she asked, just as the microwave gave a *ting*.

"Not great—we've hit a layer of sandstone."

"We?" Rebecca shot him a quizzical glance as she took a dish out of the microwave. "I'm sure you just said *we*, Will. You don't mean Dad's working on it with you, do you? Not during museum hours?"

"No, Chester from school is giving me a hand."

Rebecca had just placed a second dish in the microwave and very nearly trapped her fingers in the door as she was closing it.

"You mean you actually asked somebody to help you? Well, *that's* a first. Thought you didn't trust anybody with your 'projects.'"

"No, I don't usually, but Chester's cool," Will replied, a bit taken aback by his sister's interest. "He's been a real help."

"Can't say I know much about him, except that he's called—"

"I know what they call him," Will cut her off sharply.

At twelve, Rebecca was two years younger than Will and couldn't have been more different from him; she was slim and dainty for her age, in contrast to her brother's rather stocky physique. And with her dark hair and sallow complexion, she wasn't bothered by the sun, even at the height of summer, while Will's skin would begin to redden and burn in a matter of minutes.

The two of them being so completely dissimilar, not just in appearance but also in temperament, their home life had something of the feel of an uneasy truce, and each showed only a passing interest in the other's pursuits.

There weren't the family outings that you would ordinarily expect, either, because Dr. and Mrs. Burrows also had completely divergent tastes. Will would go off with his father on expeditions—a habitual destination was the south coast, where they would go fossil hunting.

Rebecca, on the other hand, would arrange her own vacations—where, or to do what, Will did not know or care. And on the rare occasions Mrs. Burrows ventured out of the house, she would just trudge around the shops in the West End of London or catch the latest films.

Tonight, as was the case most nights, the Burrowses were sitting with their meals on their laps watching an oft-repeated

1970s comedy that Dr. Burrows seemed to be enjoying. No one spoke during the meal except Mrs. Burrows, who at one point mumbled, "Good . . . this is good," which may have been in praise of the microwave food or possibly the finale of the dated sitcom, but nobody made the effort to inquire.

Having wolfed down his food, Will left the room without a word, placing his tray by the kitchen sink before he went bounding up the stairs, a canvas sack of recently discovered items clutched in his hands. Dr. Burrows was the next out, walking into the kitchen, where he deposited his tray on the table. Although she hadn't finished her food yet, Rebecca followed closely behind him.

"Dad, a couple of bills need paying. The checks are there on the table."

"Have we got enough in the account?" he asked as he dashed off his signature on the bottom of the checks, not even bothering to read the amounts.

"I told you last week, I got a better deal on the house insurance. Saved us a few pennies on the premium."

"Right . . . very good. Thanks," Dr. Burrows said, picking up his tray and turning purposefully toward the dishwasher.

"Just leave it on the side," Rebecca said a little too quickly, stepping protectively in front of the dishwasher. Only last week she'd caught him attempting to program her beloved microwave by furiously jabbing at the buttons in random sequences, as if he was trying to crack some secret code, and ever since then she had been making sure she unplugged all the major appliances.

As Dr. Burrows left the room, Rebecca shoved the checks in envelopes and then sat down to prepare a shopping list for the next day. At the tender age of twelve, she was the engine, the powerhouse behind the Burrowses' home. She took it upon herself not just to do the shopping but also to organize the meals, supervise the cleaning lady, and do just about everything else that, in any ordinary household, the parents would have taken responsibility for.

To say Rebecca was meticulous in her organization would have been a gross understatement. A schedule on the kitchen bulletin board listed all the provisions she required for at least two weeks in advance. She kept carefully labeled files of the family's bills and financial situation in one of the kitchen cupboards. And the only times when this smooth operation of the household began to falter were on the occasions that Rebecca was absent. Then the three of them, Dr. and Mrs. Burrows and Will, would subsist on the food Rebecca had left for them in the freezer, helping themselves when they felt like it with all the delicacy of a pack of marauding wolves. After these absences, Rebecca would simply return home and put the house back in order again without protest, as if she accepted that her lot in life was to tidy up after the other members of her family.

Back in the living room, Mrs. Burrows flicked a remote to commence her nightly marathon of soaps and talk shows while Rebecca cleaned up in the kitchen. By nine o'clock, she had completed her chores and, sitting at the half of the kitchen table that wasn't taken up by the numerous empty coffee jars Dr. Burrows kept promising he'd do something with, had finished off her homework. Deciding it was time for bed, she picked up a pile of clean towels and went upstairs with them under her arm. Passing the bathroom, she hesitated as she happened to glance in. Will was kneeling on the floor, admiring his new finds and washing the soil off them using Dr. Burrows's toothbrush.

"Look at these!" he said proudly as he held up a small pouch made of rotten leather, which dripped dirty water everywhere. He proceeded to very gently pry open the fragile flap and lifted out a series of clay pipes. "You usually only find the odd piece . . . bits the farm laborers dropped. But just look at these. Not one of them is broken. Perfect as the day they were made. . . . Think of it . . . all those years ago . . . the eighteenth century."

"Fascinating," Rebecca said, without the vaguest suggestion of any interest. Flicking back her hair contemptuously, she continued across the landing to the linen cupboard, where she put the towels, and then into her room, closing the door firmly behind her.

Will sighed and resumed the inspection of his finds for several minutes, then gathered them up in the mud-stained bathroom mat and carefully conveyed them to his bedroom. Here he thoughtfully arranged the pipes and the still-sopping leather pouch next to his many other treasures on the shelves that completely covered one wall of the room—his museum, as he called it.

Will's bedroom was at the front of the house, Rebecca's at the back, and it must have been about two o'clock in the morning when he was woken by a sound. It came from the garden.

"A wheelbarrow?" he said, immediately identifying it as his eyes flicked open. "A loaded wheelbarrow?" He scrambled out of bed and went to the window. There, in the light of the half-moon, he could make out a shadowy form pushing a barrow down the path. He squinted, trying to see more.

"Dad!" he said to himself as he recognized his father's features and saw the glint of moonlight from his familiar specs. Mystified, Will watched as his father reached the end of the garden and passed through the gap in the hedge and then out onto the Common. Here, Will lost sight of him behind some trees.

"What *is* he up to?" Will muttered. Dr. Burrows had always kept strange hours because of his frequent catnaps in the museum, but this level of activity was unusually lively for him.

Will recalled how, earlier that year, he had helped his father excavate and lower the floor of the cellar by nearly three feet and then lay a new concrete floor to increase the headroom down there. Then, a month or so later, Dr. Burrows had had the bright idea of digging an exit from the cellar up to the garden and putting in a new door because, for some reason or other, he'd decided that he needed another means of entry to his sanctuary at the bottom of the house. As far as Will knew, the job had finished there, but his father could be unpredictable. Will felt a pang of resentment—what was his father doing that meant he had to be so secretive, and why hadn't he asked Will to help him?

Still groggy with sleep and distracted by thoughts of his own underground projects, Will put it from his mind for the time being and returned to bed.

THE NEXT day after school, Will and Chester resumed their work at the excavation. Will was returning from dumping the spoils, his wheelbarrow stacked high with empty buckets as he trundled to the end of the tunnel where Chester was hacking away at the stone layer.

"How's it going?" Will asked him.

"It's not getting any easier, that's for sure," Chester replied, wiping the sweat from his forehead with a dirty sleeve and smearing dirt across his face in the process.

"Hang on, let me have a look. You take a break."

"OK."

Will shone his helmet lamp over the rock surface, the subtle browns and yellows of the strata gouged randomly by the tip of the pickax, and sighed loudly. "I think we'd better stop and think about this for a minute. No point banging our heads on a sandstone wall! Let's have a drink."

"Yeah, good idea," Chester said gratefully.

They went into the main chamber, where Will handed Chester a bottle of water.

"Glad you wanted to do some more of this. It's pretty addictive, isn't it?" he said to Chester, who was staring into the middle distance.

Chester looked at him. "Well, yes and no, really. I said I'd help you get through the rock, but after that I'm not so sure. My arms really hurt last night."

"Oh, you'll get used to it and, besides, you're a natural."

"You think so? Really?" Chester beamed.

"No doubt about it. You could be nearly as good as me one day!"

Chester punched him playfully on the arm and they laughed, but their laughter petered out as Will's expression turned serious.

"What is it?" Chester asked.

"We're going to have to rethink this. The sandstone vein might just be too thick for us to get through." Will knitted his fingers together and rested his hands on top of his head, an affectation he had picked up from his father. "How do you feel about . . . about going under it?"

"Under it? Won't that take us too deep?"

"Nah, I've gone deeper before."

"When?"

"A couple of my tunnels went much farther down than this," Will said evasively. "You see, if we dig under it, we can use the sandstone, because it's a solid layer, for the roof of the new tunnel. Probably won't even need to use any props."

"No props?" Chester asked.

"It'll be perfectly safe."

"What if it isn't? What if it collapses with us underneath?" Chester looked distinctly unhappy.

"You worry too much. Come on, let's get on with it!" Will had already made up his mind and was starting off down the tunnel when Chester called after him.

"Hey, why are we breaking our backs on this. . . . I mean, is there anything on any of the blueprints? What's the point?"

Will was quite taken aback by the question, and it was several seconds before he replied. "No, there's nothing marked on the ordnance surveys or Dad's archive maps," he admitted. He took a deep breath and turned to Chester. "The *digging* is the point."

"So you think there's something buried there?" Chester asked quickly. "Like the stuff in those old garbage dumps you were talking about?"

Will shook his head. "No. Of course the finds are great, but *this* is far more important." He swept his hand extravagantly in front of him.

"What is?"

"All this!" Will ran his eyes over the sides of the tunnel and then the roof above them. "Don't you feel it? With every shovelful, it's like we're traveling back in time." He paused, smiling to himself. "Where no one has gone for centuries . . . or maybe *never* gone before."

"So you've got no idea what's there?" Chester asked.

"Absolutely none, but I'm not about to let a bit of sandstone beat me," Will replied resolutely.

Chester was still flummoxed. "It's just . . . I was thinking, if we aren't heading for anything in particular, why don't we just work on the other tunnel?"

Will shook his head again but offered no further explanation.

"But it would be so much easier," Chester said, a tone of exasperation creeping into his voice as if he knew he wasn't going to get a sensible answer out of Will. "Why not?"

"A hunch," Will said abruptly and was off down the tunnel before Chester could utter another word. He shrugged and reached for his pickax.

"He's crazy. And *I* must be crazy, too. What on earth am I doing here?" he mumbled to himself. "Could be at home, right now . . . on the PlayStation . . . and warm and dry." He looked down at his mud-sodden clothes. "Crazy, crazy, crazy!" he repeated several times.

Dr. Burrows's day had been the same as usual. He was reclining luxuriously in the dentist's chair with a newspaper folded in his lap, on the brink of slipping into his post-lunchtime nap, when the door of the museum burst open. Joe Carruthers, former major, strode purposefully in and scanned the room until he located Dr. Burrows, whose head was lolling drowsily in the dentist's chair.

"Look sharp, Burrows!" he bellowed, almost taking pleasure in Dr. Burrows's reaction as his head jerked up. Joe Carruthers, a veteran of the Second World War, had never lost his military bearing or his brusqueness. Dr. Burrows had given him the rather unkind nickname "Pineapple Joe" because of his strikingly red and bulbous nose—possibly the result of a war injury or, as Dr. Burrows sometimes speculated, more likely due to his consumption of excessive amounts of gin. He was surprisingly sprightly for a man in his seventies and tended to bark loudly. He was the last person Dr. Burrows wanted to see right now.

"Saddle up, Burrows, need you to come and have a look at something for me, if you can spare a mo'? Course you can, see you're not busy here, are you?"

"Ah, no, sorry, Mr. Carruthers, I can't leave the museum unattended. I'm on duty, after all," Dr. Burrows said sluggishly, reluctantly abandoning the last vestiges of sleep.

Joe Carruthers continued to bellow at him from across the museum hall. "Come on, man, this is a *special* duty, y'know. Want your opinion. My daughter and her new hubby bought a house just off Main Street. Been having work done on the kitchen and they found something . . . something funny."

"Funny in what way?" Dr. Burrows asked, still irked by the intrusion.

"Funny hole in the floor."

"Isn't that something for the builders to deal with?"

"Not that sort of thing, old man. Not that sort of thing at all."

"Why?" Dr. Burrows asked, his curiosity roused.

"Better if you come and have a gander for yourself, old chap. I mean, you know all about the history hereabouts. Thought of you immediately. Best man for the job, I told my Penny. This chappie really knows his stuff, I said to her."

Dr. Burrows rather relished the idea that he was regarded as the local historical expert, so he got to his feet and self-importantly put on his jacket. Having locked up the museum, he fell into step beside Pineapple Joe's forced march along Main Street, and they soon turned onto Jekyll Street. Pineapple Joe spoke only once as they turned another corner, into Martineau Square.

"Those darn dogs—people shouldn't let them run wild like that," he grumbled as he squinted at some papers blowing across the road in the distance. "Should be kept on a leash." Then they arrived at the house.

Number 23 was a terraced house, no different from all the others that lined the four sides of the square, built of brick with typical early Georgian features. Although each property was rather narrow, with just a thin sliver of garden at the rear, Dr. Burrows had admired them on the occasions he'd happened to be in the area and welcomed the chance to have a look inside one.

Pineapple Joe hammered on the original four-paneled Georgian door with enough force to cave it in, Dr. Burrows wincing with each blow. A young woman answered the door, her face lighting up at the sight of her father.

"Hello, Dad. You got him to come, then." She turned to Dr. Burrows with a self-conscious smile. "Do come down to the kitchen. Bit of a mess, but I'll put the kettle on," she said, closing the door behind them.

Dr. Burrows followed Pineapple Joe as he stomped over the tarpaulins in the unlit corridor, where the wallpaper had been half stripped from the walls.

Once in the kitchen, Pineapple Joe's daughter turned to Dr. Burrows. "Sorry, how rude, I didn't introduce myself. My name's Penny *Hanson*—I think we've met before." She emphasized her new surname proudly. For an awkward moment, Dr. Burrows looked so totally mystified by this suggestion that she flushed with embarrassment and quickly mumbled something about making the tea, while Dr. Burrows, indifferent to her discomfort, began to inspect the room. It had been gutted and the plaster stripped back to the bare brick, and there was a newly installed sink with half-finished cupboard units along one side.

"We thought it was a good idea to take out the chimney, to give us the space for a breakfast bar over there," Penny said, pointing at the wall opposite the one with the new units. "The architect said we just needed a brace in the ceiling." She indicated a gaping hole where Dr. Burrows could see that a new metal joist had been bedded in. "But when the builders were knocking out the old brickwork, the back wall collapsed, and they found this. I've contacted our architect, but he hasn't called me back yet."

To the rear of the fireplace a heap of soot-stained bricks indicated where the hearth wall had been. With this wall removed, a sizable space had been revealed behind it, like a hidey-hole.

"That's unusual. A second chimney flue?" he said to himself, almost immediately uttering a series of no's as he shook his head. He moved closer and looked down. In the floor was a vent about three feet by a foot and a half in size.

Stepping between the loose bricks, he crouched down at the edge of the opening, peering into it.

"Uh . . . have you got a flashlight handy?" he asked. Penny fetched one. Dr. Burrows took it from her and shone it down into the opening. "Brick lining, early nineteenth century, I would venture. Seems to have been built at the same time as the house," he muttered to himself as Pineapple Joe and his daughter watched him intently. "But what the blazes is it for?" he added. The strangest thing was that as he leaned over and peered down into it, he couldn't see where it ended. "Have you tested how deep it is?" he asked Penny, straightening up.

"What with?" she replied simply.

"Can I have this?" Dr. Burrows picked up a jagged half-brick from the pile of rubble by the collapsed hearth. She nodded, and he turned back to the hole and stood poised to drop it in.

"Now listen," he said to them as he released it over the vent. They heard it knocking against the sides as it fell, the sounds growing quieter until only faint echoes reached Dr. Burrows, who was now kneeling over the opening.

"Is it—?" Penny began.

"Shhh!" Dr. Burrows hissed impolitely, giving her a start as he held up his hand. After a moment he raised his head and frowned at Pineapple Joe and Penny. "Didn't hear it land," he observed, "but it seemed to bounce off the sides for ages. How . . . how can it be *that* deep?" Then, seemingly oblivious to the grime, he lay down on the floor and stuck his head and shoulders into the hole as far as he could, probing the darkness below him with the flashlight in his outstretched arm. He suddenly froze and started to sniff loudly.

"Can't be!"

"What's that, Burrows?" Pineapple Joe asked. "Anything to report?"

"I might be mistaken, but I could swear there's a bit of an updraft," Dr. Burrows said, pulling his head out of the gap. "Why that should be, I just don't know—unless the whole block was built with some form of ventilation system between each house. But I can't for the life of me imagine why it would have been. The most curious thing is that the duct"—he rolled over onto his back and shone his flashlight upward, above the hole—"appears to carry on up, just behind the normal chimney. I presume it also vents as part of the chimney stack, on the roof?"

What Dr. Burrows did not tell them—did not dare tell them, because it would have appeared too outlandish—is that he had smelled that peculiar mustiness again: the same smell he had noticed on his collision with the man-in-a-hat the day before on Main Street.

Back in the tunnel, Will and Chester were finally making progress. They were digging out the soil below the sandstone when Will's pickax hit something solid.

"Drat! Don't tell me the rock carries on down here, too!" he yelled, exasperated. Chester immediately dropped his wheelbarrow and came running in from the main chamber.

"What's the matter, Will?" he asked, surprised at the outburst.

"Blast! Blast! And blast!" Will said, violently hacking at the obstacle with his pickax.

"What? What is it?" Chester shouted. He was shocked. He had never seen Will lose his cool this way before; he was like a boy possessed.

Will increased his attack with the pickax, working at fever pitch as he struck wildly at the rock face. Chester was forced to take a step back to avoid his swings and the torrents of soil and stone he was throwing out behind him.

Suddenly Will stopped and fell silent for a moment. Then, slinging aside his pickax, he sank to his knees to scrape frantically at something in front of him.

"Well, look at that!"

"Look at what?"

"See for yourself," Will said breathlessly.

Chester crawled in and saw what had excited his friend so much. Where Will had cleared away the soil there were several courses of a brick wall visible under the sandstone layer, and he'd already loosened some of the first bricks.

"But what if it's a sewer or railway tunnel or something else like that? Are you sure we should be doing this?" Chester said anxiously. "It might have something to do with the water supply. I don't like this!"

"Calm down, Chester, there's nothing on the maps around here. We're on the edge of the old town, right?"

"Right," Chester said hesitantly, unsure what his friend was getting at.

"Well, this won't have been anything built in the last hundred to hundred and fifty years—so it's unlikely to be a train tunnel, even a forgotten one, way out here. I went through all the old maps with Dad. I suppose it might be a sewer, but if you look at the curvature of the brick as it meets the sandstone, then we're probably near the top of it. It could just be the cellar wall of an old house—or maybe some foundations, but I wonder how it came to be built *under* the sandstone? Very odd."

Chester took a couple of steps backward and said nothing, so Will resumed his efforts for a few minutes and then stopped, aware that his friend was still hovering nervously behind him. Will turned and let out a resigned sigh.

"Look, Chester, if it makes you happy, we'll stop for today, and I'll check with my dad tonight. See what he thinks."

"Yeah, I'd rather you did, Will. You know . . . in case."

■ ■ ■

Dr. Burrows said good-bye to Pineapple Joe and his daughter, promising to find out what he could about the house and its architecture from the local archives. He glanced at his watch and grimaced. He knew it wasn't right to leave the museum closed for so long, but he wanted to look at something before he went back.

He walked around the square several times, examining the terraced houses on all four sides. The whole square had been built at the same time, and each house was identical. But what interested him was the idea that they might all have the mysterious ducts running through them. He crossed the road and went through the gate into the middle of the square, which had at its center a paved area surrounded by some borders of neglected rosebushes. Here he had a better view of the roofs, and he pointed with his finger as he tried to count exactly how many chimney pots there were on each one.

"Just doesn't add up." He frowned. "Very peculiar indeed."

He turned, left the square, and, making his way back to the museum, arrived just in time to close up for the day.

IN THE dead of night, Rebecca watched from an upstairs window as a shadowy figure loitered on the pavement in front of the Burrowses' house. The figure, its features obscured by a hoodie and a baseball cap, glanced furtively both ways along the street, behaving more like a fox than a human. Satisfied that it wasn't being observed, it descended on the garbage bags and, seizing hold of the bulkiest, ripped a hole in it and quickly began to rummage through the contents with both hands.

"Do you really think I'm that stupid?" Rebecca whispered, her breath clouding the glass of her bedroom window. She wasn't the slightest bit concerned. Following warnings about identity theft in the Highfield area, she had been fastidiously destroying any official letters, credit card bills, or bank statements—in fact, anything containing the family's personal details.

In his haste to find something, the man was tossing out trash from the sack. Empty cans, food packaging, and a series of bottles were being strewn across the front lawn. He snatched out a handful of papers and held them close to his face, rotating them in his fist as he scrutinized them under the dim streetlight.

"Go on," she challenged the scavenger. "Do your worst!"

Wiping the grease and old coffee grounds off one piece of

paper with his hand, he twisted around so he could see it more clearly under the streetlight.

Rebecca watched as he feverishly read the letter, then grimaced as he realized it was worthless. He tensed his arm in a gesture of disgust and threw it down.

Rebecca had had enough. She'd been leaning on the windowsill but now she stood up, throwing back the curtains.

The man caught the movement and flicked up his eyes. He saw her and froze, then, twisting around to check both ends of the street again, he slouched off, glancing back at Rebecca as if defying her to call the police.

Rebecca clenched her small fists in fury, knowing she would be the one who'd have to clean up the mess in the morning. Yet another tedious chore to add to the list!

She closed the curtains, pulled back from the window, and went out of her bedroom onto the landing. She stood, listening; there were several staccato snores. Rebecca turned on her slippered feet to face the door of the main bedroom, at once recognizing the familiar sound. Mrs. Burrows was asleep. In the lull that followed she listened even harder, until she was able to discern Dr. Burrows's long nasal breaths, then cocked her head toward Will's bedroom, listening again until she caught the rhythm of his faster, shallower breathing.

"Yes," she whispered with an exultant toss of her head. Everyone was in a deep slumber. She felt instantly at ease. This was *her* time now, when she had the house to herself and could do what *she* wanted. A time of calm before they awoke and the chaos resumed again. She drew back her shoulders and stepped noiselessly to the doorway of Will's room to look in.

Nothing moved. Like a shadow flitting across the room, she whisked over to the side of his bed. She stood there, gazing down at him. He was asleep on his back, his arms splayed untidily above his head. Under the faint moonlight filtering between the half-closed curtains she studied his face. She stepped closer until she was leaning over him.

Well, look at him, not a care in the world, she thought and leaned even farther over the bed. As she did so, she noticed a faint smudge under his nose.

Her eyes scanned the unconscious boy until they settled on his hands. "Mud!" They were covered in it. He hadn't bothered to wash before getting into bed and, even more revolting, must have been picking his nose in his sleep.

"Dirty dog," she hissed quietly. It was enough to disturb him, and he stretched his arms and flexed his fingers. Blissfully unaware of her presence, he made a low, contented noise deep in his throat, wriggling his body a little as he settled again.

"You're a total waste of space," she whispered finally, then turned to where he'd thrown his filthy clothes on the floor. She gathered them up in her arms and left his room, going over to the wicker laundry basket that stood in a corner of the landing. Feeling inside all the pockets as she bundled the clothes into the basket, she came across a scrap of paper in Will's jeans, which she unfolded but could not read in the diminished light. *Probably just trash,* she thought, tucking it away in her bathrobe. As she withdrew her hand from her pocket, she caught a fingernail on the quilted material. She bit thoughtfully at the rough edge and strolled toward the main bedroom. Once inside, she made sure she stepped only on the precise areas where the floorboards under the old and worn shag carpet wouldn't creak and betray her presence.

Just as she had watched Will, she now watched Mrs. and Dr. Burrows, as if she were trying to divine their thoughts. After several minutes, though, Rebecca had seen enough, and picked up Mrs. Burrows's empty mug from the bedside table, giving it an exploratory sniff. Ovaltine again, with a hint of brandy. With mug in hand, Rebecca tiptoed out of the room and went downstairs into the kitchen, navigating her way easily through the darkness. Placing the mug in the sink, she turned and left the kitchen to return to the hallway. Here she stopped again, her head inclined slightly to one side, her eyes closed, listening.

So calm . . . and peaceful, she thought. *It should always be this way*. Like someone in a trance, she remained standing there, unmoving, until finally she drew in a deep breath through her nose, held it for a few seconds, then released it through her mouth.

There was a muffled cough from upstairs. Rebecca glared resentfully in the direction of the staircase. Her moment had been broken, her thoughts disrupted.

"I'm so tired of all this," she said bitterly.

She padded over to the front door, unlatched the safety chain, and then made her way into the living room. The curtains were fully open, giving her a clear view of the back garden, which was dappled in shifting patches of silvery moonlight. Her eyes never once left the scene as she lowered herself into Mrs. Burrows's armchair, settling back as she continued to watch the garden and the hedge that divided it from the Common. And there she remained, relishing the solitude of the night and enshrouded in the chocolatey darkness, until the early hours. Watching.

7

THE NEXT day in the museum, Dr. Burrows was growing weary of his task of arranging a display of some old military buttons. He exhaled loudly with sheer frustration and, hearing a car horn on the road outside, happened to glance up.

Out of the corner of his eye, he caught sight of a man walking on the opposite side of the street. He wore a flat cap, a long coat, and, although the day was distinctly overcast with only intermittent glimpses of the sun, a pair of dark glasses. It might easily have been the man he had bumped into outside the newsstand, but he couldn't be sure, because they all looked so similar.

What was it that was so compelling about these people? Dr. Burrows felt in his bones that there was something special about them, something decidedly incongruous. It was as if they had stepped straight out of another time—perhaps from the Georgian era, given the style of their clothing. For him, this was on a par with finding a piece of living history, like those reports he'd read of Asian fishermen netting coelacanths, or maybe something even more tantalizing than that. . . .

Never a man to rein in his obsessions, Dr. Burrows was well and truly hooked. There had to be a rational explanation for the hatted-man phenomenon, and he was determined to find out what it was.

"Right," he decided on the spot, "now's as good a time as any."

He put down the box of buttons and hurried through the museum to the main door, locking it behind him. As he stepped outside onto the street, he located the man up ahead and, keeping a respectable distance, he followed him down Main Street.

Dr. Burrows kept pace with the man as he left Main Street, turned onto Disraeli Street, and then crossed the road to take the first right onto Gladstone Street, just past the old convent. He was about fifty feet behind him when the man drew to a sudden halt and turned to look directly at him.

Dr. Burrows felt a tremor of fear as he saw the sky reflecting off the man's glasses and, sure the game was up, immediately spun around to face the opposite direction. At a loss to know what else to do, he squatted down and pretended to tie an imaginary shoelace on his slip-on shoe. Without getting up he peered furtively over his shoulder, but the man had completely vanished.

His eyes frantically scanning the street, Dr. Burrows began to walk briskly, then broke into a run as he approached the spot where he had last sighted his quarry. Coming to it, he discovered that there was a narrow entrance between two small buildings. He was slightly surprised that in all the times he'd been this way before he'd never once noticed it. It had an arched opening and ran like a narrow tunnel until it passed beyond the back of the houses and then continued for a short distance as an uncovered alleyway. Dr. Burrows peered in, but the lack of daylight in the passage made it difficult to see very much. Beyond the stretch of darkness, he could make out something at the far end. It was a wall, cutting off the alleyway altogether. A dead end.

Checking the street one last time, he shook his head in disbelief. He couldn't see anywhere else the man might have gone, vanishing as abruptly as he had, so he took a deep breath and started down the passage. He picked his way cautiously, wary that the man might be lying in wait in an unseen doorway. As his eyes adjusted to the shadows, he could see that there were soggy cardboard boxes and milk bottles, mostly broken, scattered across the cobblestones.

He was relieved when he emerged back into the light again, and paused to survey the scene. The alleyway was formed by garden walls to the left and right and was blocked at its far end by the wall of a three-story factory. The old building had no windows until its uppermost story and couldn't possibly have provided the man with any means of escape.

So where the blazes did he go? thought Dr. Burrows as he turned and looked back up the alleyway, to the street, where a car flashed by. To his right, the garden wall had a three-foot-high trellis running along it, which would have made it almost impossible for the man to climb over. The other wall had no such encumbrance, so Dr. Burrows went up to it and peered over. It was a garden of sorts, neglected and barren, peppered with faded plastic dishes containing dark green water.

Dr. Burrows gazed helplessly into the private wasteland and was about to forget the whole thing when he had a sudden change of heart. He slung his briefcase over the wall and rather awkwardly clambered after it. The drop was greater than he'd expected, and he landed badly, his outstretched hand managing to flip over one of the dishes, splattering its contents up his arm and neck. He rose to his feet, swore silently, and brushed off as much of it as he could.

"Blast! Blast! And blast!" he said through clenched teeth as he heard a door open behind him.

"Hello? Who's there? What's going on?" came an apprehensive voice.

Dr. Burrows wheeled around to face an old woman who was standing not five feet away, with three cats around her ankles observing him with feline indifference. The old woman's sight was apparently not good, judging from the way she was moving her head from side to side. She had wispy white hair and wore a floral housecoat. Dr. Burrows guessed she was at least in her eighties.

"Er . . . Roger Burrows, pleased to meet you," Dr. Burrows said, not able to think of anything to explain why or how he had come to be there. The expression on the old woman's face was suddenly transformed.

"Oh, Dr. Burrows, how very kind of you to drop by. What a nice surprise."

Dr. Burrows was himself surprised and not a little confused. "Um . . . not at all," he replied hesitantly. "My pleasure entirely."

"Gets a bit lonely with just my pussycats for company. Would you care for some tea? The kettle's on the boil."

Lost for words, Dr. Burrows simply nodded.

The old woman turned, her entourage of cats darting before her into the kitchen. "Milk and sugar?"

"Please," Dr. Burrows said, standing outside the kitchen door as she bustled around, getting a teacup down from a shelf.

"I'm sorry to turn up unannounced like this," Dr. Burrows said, in an attempt to fill the silence. "This is all so very kind of you."

"No, it's you who is very kind. I should be thanking you."

"Really?" he stuttered, still frantically trying to figure out exactly who the old woman was.

"Yes, for your very nice letter. Can't see as well as I used to, but Mr. Embers read it to me."

Suddenly, it all fell into place, and Dr. Burrows sighed with relief, the fog of confusion blown away by the cool breeze of realization.

"The glowing sphere! It is certainly an intriguing object, Mrs. Tantrumi."

"Oh, good, dear."

"Mr. Embers probably told you I need to get it checked."

She held her head to one side, waiting expectantly for him to continue while she stirred the tea.

". . . well, I was rather hoping you could show me where you found it," he finished.

"Oh, no, dear, wasn't me—it was the gas men. Shortbread or gingersnap?" she said, holding out a battered cookie tin.

"Er . . . shortbread, please. You were saying the gas men found it?"

"They did. Just inside the basement."

"Down there?" Dr. Burrows asked, looking at an open door at the bottom of a short flight of steps. "Mind if I take a look?" he said, pocketing the shortbread as he began to negotiate the mossy brick steps.

Once inside the doorway he could see that the basement was divided into two rooms. The first was empty, save for some dishes of extremely dark and desiccated cat food and loose rubble strewn across the floor. He crunched through to the second room, which lay beneath the front of the house. It was much the same as the first, except that the light was poorer in here and there was an old wardrobe with a broken mirror, tucked in a shadowy recess. He opened one of its doors and was immediately still.

He sniffed several times, recognizing the same musty odor he had smelled on the man in the street and more recently in the duct at Penny Hanson's house. As his eyes became used to the darkness, he could see that inside the wardrobe were several overcoats—black, as far as he could tell—and an assortment of flat caps and other headwear stacked in a compartment to one side.

Beneath the hat compartment, he found a small drawer, which he slid open. Inside were five or six pairs of glasses. Taking one of these and pulling an overcoat from its hanger, he made his way back out into the garden.

"Mrs. Tantrumi," he called from the bottom of the steps. She waddled to the kitchen door. "Did you know there's quite a few things in a wardrobe down here?"

"Are there?"

"Yes, some coats and sunglasses. Do they belong to you?"

"No, hardly ever go down there myself. The ground's too uneven. Would you bring them closer so I can see?"

He went to the kitchen door, and she reached out and ran her fingers over the material of the overcoat as if she were stroking the head of an unfamiliar cat. Heavy and waxy to the touch, the coat felt strange to her. The cut was old-fashioned, with a shoulder cape of heavier material.

"I can't say I've ever seen this before. My husband, God rest his soul, may have left it down there," she said dismissively and returned to the kitchen.

Dr. Burrows examined the dark glasses. They consisted of two pieces of thick and absolutely flat, almost opaque, glass, similar to welders' goggles, with curious spring mechanisms on the arms on either side—evidently to keep them snug against the wearer's head. He was puzzled. Why would the strange people keep their belongings in a forgotten wardrobe in an empty basement?

"Does anyone else come here, Mrs. Tantrumi?" Dr. Burrows said to her as she started to pour the tea with a very shaky hand.

There was a lull in the rattling as she looked confused. "I really don't know what you mean," she said, as if Dr. Burrows was suggesting she had been doing something improper.

"It's just that I've seen some rather odd characters around this part of town—always wearing big coats and sunglasses like these. . . ," Dr. Burrows trailed off, because the old woman was looking so anxious.

"Oh, I hope they aren't those criminal types one hears about. I don't feel safe here anymore—"

"So you haven't seen any people in coats like these—men with white hair?" Dr. Burrows interrupted.

"No, dear, can't say I know what you're talking about." She looked inquiringly at him, then resumed pouring the tea. "Do come in and sit down."

"I'll just put these back," Dr. Burrows said, returning to the basement. Before he left, he couldn't resist another quick look around the place, even resorting to stamping on the ground to see if there was a trapdoor hidden there. He did the same in the small garden, stamping around the lawn while trying to avoid the plastic dishes, all the time watched curiously by Mrs. Tantrumi's cats.

On the other side of town, Chester and Will were back in the Forty Pits tunnel.

"So what did your dad say? What does he think we've found?" Chester asked as Will used a mallet and coal chisel to loosen the mortar between the bricks in the unidentified structure.

"We looked at the maps again, and there's nothing on them." He was lying; Dr. Burrows had not emerged from the cellar before Will had gone to bed and had left the house before Will was up in the morning.

"No water mains, sewers, or anything on this plot," Will went on, trying to reassure Chester. "The brickwork is pretty solid, you know—this thing was built to last." Will had already removed two layers of bricks but hadn't yet broken through. "Look, if I'm wrong about this and anything gushes out, just make sure you get yourself to the far side of the main chamber. The flow should carry you up to the entrance," Will said, redoubling his efforts on the brickwork.

"What?" Chester asked quickly. "A flow . . . carry me up? I don't like the sound of that at all. I'm out of here." He turned to go, paused as if undecided, then made up his mind and began walking toward the main chamber, grumbling to himself all the way.

Will simply shrugged. There was no way he was going to stop, not with the possibility that he could bring to light some fantastic mystery, something so important that it would bowl over his father, and that he'd discovered by himself. And no one was going to stop him, not even Chester. He immediately proceeded to chisel around another brick, chipping away at the wedge of mortar at its edge.

Without warning, part of the mortar exploded with a high pneumatic hiss, and a chunk of it shot straight past Will's gloved hands like a stone bullet and struck the tunnel wall behind him. He dropped his tools and flopped back onto the ground in astonishment. Shaking his head, he pulled himself together and set about the task of removing the brick, which he accomplished in seconds.

"Hey, Chester!" Will called.

"Yeah, what?" Chester shouted gruffly from the main chamber. "What is it?"

"There's no water!" Will shouted back, his voice echoing oddly. "Come and see."

Chester reluctantly retraced his steps. He found that Will had indeed penetrated the wall and was holding his face up to the small breach he'd made, sniffing at the air.

"It's definitely not a sewage pipe, but it *was* under pressure," Will said.

"Could it be a gas pipe?"

"Nope, doesn't smell like it and, anyway, they've never been made of brick. Judging by the echo, it's quite a large space." His eyes flashed with anticipation. "I just knew we were on to something. Get me a candle and the iron rod from the main chamber, will you?"

When Chester returned, Will lit the candle a good distance back from the hole and then carried it slowly before him, nearer and nearer to the opening, watching the flame intently with every step he took.

"What does that do?" Chester asked as he looked on in fascination.

"If there are any gases you'll notice a difference in the way it burns," Will answered matter-of-factly. "They did this when they cracked open the pyramids." There was no change in the flickering flame as he brought it closer, then held it directly in front of the opening. "Looks like we're all clear," he said as he blew out the flame and reached for the iron rod Chester had leaned against the tunnel wall. He carefully lined up the ten-foot pole with the hole and then rammed it through, pushing it all the way in until only a short length protruded from between the bricks.

"It hasn't hit anything—it's pretty big," Will said excitedly, grunting with exertion as he checked the depth by letting the end of the pole swing down. "But I think I can feel what might be the floor. OK, let's widen this a bit more."

They worked together and within moments had removed enough bricks for Will to slither through headfirst. He landed with a muffled groan.

"Will, are you all right?" Chester called.

"Yes. Just a bit of a drop," he replied. "Come in feetfirst, and I'll guide you down."

Chester made it through after a tremendous struggle, his shoulders being broader than Will's. Once he was in, they both began to look around.

It was an octagonal chamber, with each of its eight walls arching up to a central point about twenty feet above their heads. At its apex was what appeared to be a carved stone rose. They shone their flashlights in hushed reverence, taking in the Gothic beading set into the perfectly laid brickwork. The floor was also constructed from bricks laid end on end.

"Awesome!" Chester whispered. "Who'd have ever expected to find anything like this?"

"It's like the crypt of a church, isn't it?" Will said. "But the strangest thing is . . ."

"Yes?" Chester shone his flashlight at Will.

"It's absolutely bone-dry. And the air's sort of sharp, too. I'm not sure—"

"Have you seen this, Will?" Chester interrupted, flicking his light around the floor and then over the wall nearest to him. "There's something written on the bricks. All of them!"

Will immediately swiveled around to study the wall closest to him, reading the elaborate Gothic script carved into the face of every brick. "You're right. They're names: James Hobart, Andrew Kellogg, William Butts, John Cooper . . ."

"Simon Jennings, Daniel Lethbridge, Silas Samuels, Abe Winterbotham, Caryll Pickering . . . there must be thousands in here," Chester said.

Will pulled his mallet from his belt and began to knock on the walls, taking soundings to see if there was any sign of a hollow or adjoining passage. He had methodically tapped away at two of the eight walls when for no apparent reason he suddenly stopped. He clapped a hand to his forehead and swallowed hard.

"Do you feel that?" he asked Chester.

"Yeah, my ears popped," Chester agreed, sticking a gloved finger roughly into one of his ears. "Just like when you take off in a plane."

They were both silent, as if waiting for something to happen. Then they felt a tremor, an inaudible tone, somewhat akin to a low note played on an organ—a throbbing was building, seemingly within their skulls.

"I think we should get out." Chester looked at his friend blankly, swallowing now not because of his ears but because of the waves of nausea welling up inside him.

For once Will did not disagree. He gulped a quick yes, blinking as spots appeared before his eyes.

They both clambered back through the gap in double-quick time, then made their way to the armchairs in the main cavern and slumped down in them. Although they had said nothing of it to each other at the time, the inexplicable sensations had ceased almost immediately after they were outside the chamber.

"What *was* that in there?" Chester asked, opening his mouth wide to flex his jaw and pressing the palms of his hands against his ears.

"I don't know," Will replied. "I'll get my dad to come and see it—he might have an explanation. Must be a pressure buildup or something."

"Do you think it's a crypt, from where a church once stood . . . with all those names?"

"Maybe," Will replied, deep in thought. "But somebody—craftsmen, stonemasons—built it very carefully, not even leaving any debris behind as they went, and then just as carefully sealed it up. Why in the world would they go to all that trouble?"

"I didn't think of that. You're right."

"And there was no way in or out. I couldn't find any sign of connecting passages—not a single one. A self-contained chamber with names, like some sort of memorial or something?" Will pondered, completely befuddled. "What *are* we on to here?"

HAVING learned that Rebecca could be very unforgiving, and that it was really not worth incurring her wrath—not just before mealtimes, at any rate—Will shook himself down and stamped the worst of the mud from his boots before bursting in through the front door. Slinging his backpack to the floor, he froze in astonishment, the tools inside still clattering against one another.

A very odd scene greeted him. The door to the living room was closed, and Rebecca was crouched down beside it, her ear pressed to the keyhole. She frowned the moment she saw him.

"What—" Will's question was cut short as Rebecca rose swiftly, shushing him with a forefinger to her lips. She seized her bemused brother by the arm and pulled him forcibly into the kitchen.

"What's going on?" Will demanded in an indignant whisper.

This was all very odd indeed. Rebecca, the original Little Miss Perfect, was in the very act of eavesdropping on their parents, something he would never have expected from her.

But there was something even more remarkable than this: the living-room door itself. It was *closed*. Will turned his head to look at it again, not quite believing his eyes.

"That door has been wedged open for as long as I can remember," he said. "You know how she hates—"

"They're arguing!" Rebecca said momentously.

"They're *what*? About what?"

"I'm not sure. The first thing I heard was Mum shouting at him to shut the door, and I was just trying to hear more when you barged in."

"You must have heard *something*."

Rebecca didn't answer him immediately.

"Come on," Will pressed her. "What did you hear?"

"Well," she started slowly, "she was screaming that he was a *royal failure* . . . and that he should stop wasting his time on *complete nonsense*."

"What else?"

"Couldn't hear the rest, but they were both very angry. They were sort of growling at each other. It must be really important—she's missing *Friends*!"

Will opened the fridge and idly inspected a container of yogurt before putting it back. "So what could it be about, then? I don't remember them ever doing this before."

Just then the living-room door was flung open, making both Will and Rebecca jump, and Dr. Burrows stormed out, his face bright red and his eyes thunderous as he made a beeline for the cellar door. Fumbling with his key and muttering incomprehensibly under his breath, he unlocked it and then banged it shut behind him.

Will and Rebecca were still peering around the corner of the kitchen door when they heard Mrs. Burrows shouting.

"YOU'RE GOOD FOR NOTHING, YOU PATHETIC FOSSIL! YOU CAN STAY DOWN THERE AND ROT FOR ALL I CARE, YOU STUPID OLD RELIC!" she shrieked at the top of her lungs as she slammed the living-room door with an almighty crash.

"That can't be good for the paintwork," Will said distantly.

Rebecca was so intent on what was happening, she didn't appear to have heard him.

"God, this is so freakin' annoying. I really need to talk to him about what we found today," he continued, grumbling.

This time she did hear him. "You can forget that! My advice is to just stay out of the way until things blow over." She stuck out her chin with great self-importance. "*If* they ever do. Anyway, the food's ready. Just help yourself. In fact, you can help yourself to the whole thing . . . I don't think anyone else is going to have an appetite."

Without a further word, Rebecca spun around and left the room. Will moved his eyes from the empty doorway where she'd been to the oven and gave a small shrug.

He wolfed down two and a half of the oven-ready meals and then made his way upstairs in the now uncannily quiet house. There weren't even the usual strains of the television coming from the living room below as, sitting up in his bed, he meticulously polished his shovel until it gleamed and sent reflections rippling across the ceiling. Then he leaned over to lay it gently on the floor, switched off the light on his bedside table, and slid under his blankets.

WILL woke with a lazy yawn, looking blearily around the room, until he noticed the light creeping in at the edges of the curtains. He sat up sharply as it dawned on him that something was not quite right. There was a surprising lack of the usual morning hubbub in the house. He glanced at his alarm clock. He'd overslept. The events of last night had completely thrown him and he'd forgotten to set it.

He found some relatively clean items of his school uniform in the bottom of his closet and, quickly throwing them on, went across to the bathroom to brush his teeth.

Emerging from the bathroom he saw that the door to Rebecca's room was open, and he paused outside to listen for a moment. He'd learned not to blunder straight in; this was her inner sanctum, and she had berated him for entering unannounced several times before. Because there were no signs of life, he decided to take a look. It was as spotless as ever—her bed immaculately made and her home clothes laid out in readiness for her return from school—everything clean and shipshape and in its place. He spotted her little black alarm clock on her bedside table. *Why didn't she get me up?* he thought.

He then saw that his parents' door was ajar, too, and he couldn't resist putting his head around the corner. The bed hadn't been slept in. This was not right at all.

Where were they? Will reflected on the previous evening's argument between his parents, the gravity of which now began to sink in.

Although he'd never stopped to give it much thought, Will was aware that his home life was pretty strange, to say the least. All four members of the family were so different, as if they'd been thoughtlessly thrown together by circumstances beyond their control, like four complete strangers who happened to share the same car on a train. Somehow it had hung together; each knew his or her place, and the end result, if not entirely happy, had seemed to have found its own peculiar equilibrium. But now the whole thing was in danger of coming crashing down. At least that was how it felt to Will that morning.

As he stood in the middle of the landing, he listened to the disquieting silence again, glancing from bedroom door to bedroom door. *This was serious.*

"It *would* have to happen now . . . just when I've found something so amazing," he muttered to himself. He longed to speak to Dr. Burrows, to tell him about the Pits tunnel and the strange chamber that he and Chester had stumbled upon. It was as if it all meant nothing without his approval, his "Well done, Will," and his fatherly smile of pride in his son's achievement.

As he tiptoed downstairs, Will had the oddest feeling of being an intruder in his own home. He glanced at the living-room door. It was still closed. *Mum must have slept in there,* he thought as he went into the kitchen. On the table was a single bowl; from the few remaining Rice Krispies clinging to it, he could tell that his sister had already had her breakfast and left for school. The fact that she hadn't cleaned up after herself, and the absence of his father's cornflakes bowl and teacup on the table or in the sink, caused vague alarm bells to ring in his head. This frozen snapshot of everyday activity had become the clue to a mystery, like the little pieces of evidence at a crime scene, which, if read in the right way, would give him the answer to what exactly was going on.

But it was no good. He could find no answers here, and he realized he had to be on his way.

"This is like a bad dream," he grumbled to himself as he hastily poured his Wheaties into a bowl. "Total cave-in," he added, glumly crunching on the cereal.

10

CHESTER lounged in one of the two broken-down armchairs in the main chamber of the Forty Pits tunnel. He formed yet another little marble of clay between his fingertips, adding it to the growing pile on the table next to him. He then began to aim them halfheartedly, one after another, at the neck of an empty water bottle that he had balanced precariously on the rim of a nearby wheelbarrow.

Will was long overdue, and as Chester threw the little projectiles he wondered what could have possibly gotten in the way of his friend's arrival. This alone wasn't of great concern, but he was anxious to tell Will what he'd discovered when he had first entered the excavation site.

When Will finally appeared, he was walking at a snail's pace down the incline of the entrance tunnel, his shovel resting on his shoulder and his head hung low.

"Hi, Will," Chester said brightly as he lobbed a whole handful of the clay balls at the defiant bottle. All of them predictably failed to hit the mark. There was a moment of disappointment before Chester turned to Will for a response. But Will merely grunted, and when he did look up, Chester was disturbed by the marked lack of sparkle in his friend's eyes. Chester had noticed something wasn't right over the past couple of days at school—Will seemed to be avoiding him, and when Chester had caught up with him, he had been withdrawn and uncommunicative.

An uneasy silence grew between them in the chamber until Chester, unable to stand it any longer, blurted out, "There's a block—"

"My dad's gone," Will cut him off.

"What?"

"He locked himself in the cellar, but now we think he's gone."

Suddenly, it became clear to Chester why his friend's behavior had been odder than usual. He opened his mouth and then shut it again. He had absolutely no idea what to say.

As if exhausted, Will slumped down in the other armchair.

"When did this happen?" Chester asked awkwardly.

"Couple of days ago—he had some sort of fight with Mum."

"What does she think?"

"Hah, nothing! She hasn't said a word to us since he went," Will answered.

Chester glanced at the tunnel branching off the chamber and then at Will, who was contemplatively rubbing a smear of dried mud from the shaft of his shovel. Chester took a deep breath and spoke hesitantly. "I'm sorry, but . . . there's something else you should know."

"What's that?" Will said quietly.

"The tunnel's blocked."

"What?" Will said. In a flash, he became animated again. He sprang out of the armchair and dashed into the mouth of the tunnel. Sure enough, the entrance to the peculiar brick room was impassable—in fact, only half of the passage still remained.

"I don't believe it." Will stared helplessly at the tightly packed barrier of soil and stone that reached right up to the roof of the tunnel, closing it off completely. He tested the props and stays immediately in front of it, tugging at them with both hands and kicking their bases with the steel toe cap of his work boot. "Nothing wrong with those," he said, squatting down to test several areas of the spoil from the pile with his palms. He cupped his hand, scooped up some of the earth, and examined it as Chester watched, admiring the way his friend was investigating the scene.

"Weird."

"What is?" Chester asked.

Will held the dirt up to his nose and sniffed it deeply. Then, taking a pinch of the soil, he discarded the rest of it. He continued to rub it slowly between his fingertips for several seconds and then turned to Chester with a frown.

"What's up, Will?"

"The props farther into the tunnel were completely sound—I gave them a once-over before we left last time. And there hasn't been any rain recently, has there?"

"No, I don't think so," Chester replied.

"No, and this dirt doesn't feel nearly damp enough to cause the roof to slip in—there's no more moisture than you'd expect. But the weirdest thing is all this." He reached down, plucked out a chunk of stone from the pile, and tossed it over to Chester, who caught and examined it with a bewildered expression.

"I'm sorry, I don't understand. What's important about this?"

"It's *limestone*. This infill has bits of limestone in it. Feel the surface of the rock. It's chalky—totally the wrong texture for sandstone. That's *particulate*."

"Particulate?" Chester asked.

"Yes, much more grainy. Hang on, let me check to make sure I'm right," Will said as he produced his penknife and, folding out the largest blade, used it to pick at the clean face of another piece of the rock, talking the whole time. "You see, they're both sedimentary rocks, and they look pretty much the same. Sometimes it's quite hard to tell the difference. The tests you can use are to drop acid on it—it makes limestone fizz—or look at it with a magnifying glass to see the coarser quartz grains you only get in sandstone. But this is the best method by far. Here we go," Will announced as he took a minute flake of the stone he'd pried from the sample and, to Chester's amazement, slipped it off the blade and into his mouth. Then he began to nibble it between his front teeth.

"What are you *doing*, Will?"

"Mmmm," Will replied thoughtfully, still grinding it. "Yes, I'm pretty sure this is limestone. . . . You see, it breaks down into a smooth paste. . . . If it was sandstone, it'd be crunchier, and even squeak a little as I bit it."

Chester winced as he heard the sounds coming from his friend's mouth. "Are you serious? Doesn't that crack your teeth?"

"Hasn't yet." Will grinned. He reached into his mouth to reposition the flake and chewed on it for a little longer. "Definitely limestone," he finally decreed, spitting out what was left of the flake of rock. "Want a taste?"

"No, I'm fine, really," Chester replied without a moment's hesitation. "Thanks anyway."

Will waved his hand in the direction of the roof over the cave in. "I don't believe there'd be a deposit—an isolated pocket of limestone—anywhere near here. I know the geology of this area pretty well."

"So what are you getting at?" Chester asked with a frown. "Someone came down here and blocked up the tunnel with all this stuff?"

"Yes . . . no . . . oh, I don't know," Will said, kicking the edge of the huge heap in frustration. "All I do know is that there's something very funny about all this."

"It might've been one of the gangs. Could it be the Clan?" Chester suggested, adding, "Or maybe even the Click?"

"No, that's not likely," Will said, turning to survey the tunnel behind him. "There'd be other signs that they'd been here. And why would they just block up this tunnel? You know what they're like—they would've wrecked the whole excavation. No, it doesn't make sense," he said, bemused.

"No," Chester echoed.

"But whoever it was, they really didn't want us to go back in there, did they?"

Rebecca was in the kitchen doing her homework when Will returned home. He was just slotting his shovel into the umbrella stand and hanging his yellow hard hat on the end of it when she called to him from around the corner.

"You're back early."

"Yeah, we had some trouble in one of the tunnels and I couldn't be bothered to do any digging," he said as he slumped down dejectedly in the chair on the opposite side of the table.

"No digging?" Rebecca said with mock concern. "Things must be worse than I thought!"

"We had a roof fall in."

"Oh, right . . . ," she said remotely.

"I can't figure out what happened. It couldn't be seepage, and the really odd thing was that the infill . . . ," he trailed off as Rebecca rose from the table and busied herself at the kitchen sink, clearly not listening to a word he was saying. This didn't bother Will unduly; he was used to being ignored. He wearily rested his head in his hands for a moment, but then raised it with a start as something occurred to him.

"You don't think he's in trouble down there, do you?" he said.

"Who?" Rebecca asked as she rinsed out a saucepan.

"Dad. Because it's been so quiet, we've all assumed he's gone somewhere, but he could still be in the cellar. If he hasn't eaten for two whole days, he might have collapsed." Will rose from his chair. "I'm going to take a look," he said decisively to Rebecca's back.

"Can't do that. No way," she said, spinning around to face him. "You know he doesn't let us go down there without him."

"I'm going to get the spare key." With that, Will hurried out of the room, leaving Rebecca standing by the sink, clenching and unclenching her fists in her yellow rubber gloves.

He reappeared seconds later. "Well, are you coming or not?"

Rebecca made no move to follow him, turning her head to look out the kitchen window as if mulling something over.

"Come on!" A flash of anger suffused Will's face.

"Fine . . . whatever," she agreed as she seemed to come to again, snapping off her gloves and placing them very precisely on the drainer at the side of the sink.

They went to the cellar door and unlocked it very quietly, so their mother wouldn't hear. They didn't need to worry, though, since the sound of a barrage of gunfire was coming thick and fast from inside the living room.

Will turned on the light and they descended the varnished oak stairs he had helped his father fix into place. As they stood on the gray-painted concrete floor, they both looked around in silence. There was no sign of Dr. Burrows. The room was crammed with his belongings, but nothing was that different from the last time Will had seen it. His father's extensive library covered two walls, and on another were shelves housing his "personal" finds, including a railwayman's lamp, the ticket machine from the disused railway station, and a careful arrangement of primitive little clay heads with clumsy features. Against the fourth wall stood a workbench, on which his computer sat, with a half-consumed candy bar in front of it.

As Will surveyed the scene, the only thing that seemed out of place was a wheelbarrow filled with dirt and small rocks by the door to the garden.

"I wonder what that's doing in here," he said.

Rebecca shrugged.

"It's funny . . . I saw him taking a load out to the Common," Will went on.

"When was that?" Rebecca asked, frowning thoughtfully.

"It was a couple of weeks ago . . . in the middle of the night. I suppose he could have brought this in for analysis or something." He reached into the wheelbarrow, took some of the loose soil into his palm, and examined it closely, rolling it around with his index finger. Then he held it up to his nose and breathed in deeply. "High clay content," he pronounced and sunk both hands deep into the soil, lifting out two large fistfuls, which he squeezed and then released, sprinkling them slowly back into the barrow. He turned to Rebecca with a quizzical expression.

"What?" she said impatiently.

"I was just wondering where this could have come from," he said. "It's . . ."

"What are you talking about? He's obviously not here, and none of this is going to help us find him!" Rebecca said with such unnecessary vehemence that Will was left speechless. "Come on, let's go back upstairs," she urged him. Not waiting for Will to respond, she stomped up the wooden steps, leaving him alone in the cellar.

"Women!" Will muttered, echoing a sentiment his father often imparted to him. "Never know where you are with them!" Rebecca in particular had always been a total mystery to Will—he couldn't decide whether she said the things she did on a whim, or if there was really something much deeper and more complex going on inside that well-groomed head of hers, something he couldn't even begin to understand.

Whatever it was, it was no use worrying about that now, not when there were other, more important things to consider. He blew dismissively and rubbed his hands together to get the soil off, then stood motionless in the center of the room until his inquisitiveness got the better of him. He went over to the bench, flicking casually through the papers on top of it. There were photocopied articles about Highfield, pictures of old houses in faded sepia tones, and ragged sections of maps. One of these caught his eye—comments had been scribbled on it in pencil. He recognized his father's spidery handwriting.

Martineau Square—the key? Ventilation for what? Will read, frowning as he traced the network of lines drawn in pencil through the houses on each side of the square. "What was he up to?" he asked himself out loud.

Peering under the bench, he found his father's briefcase and emptied out its contents, mostly magazines and newspapers, onto the floor. In a side pocket of the briefcase, he found some loose change in a small brown paper bag and a clutch of empty chocolate bar wrappers. Then, crouching down, he began to check through the archive boxes stored under the bench, sliding each one out and flicking through its contents.

His search was cut short by his sister's insistence that he come and eat his supper before it got too cold. But before returning upstairs, he made a short detour over to the back door to check the coats hanging there. His father's hard hat and overalls were gone.

Back up in the hallway, he passed a cacophony of applause and laughter from behind the closed living-room door as he went into the kitchen.

The two of them ate in silence until Will looked up at Rebecca. She had a fork in one hand and a pencil in the other as she did her math homework.

"Rebecca, have you seen Dad's hard hat or his overalls?" he asked.

"No, he always keeps them in the cellar. Why?"

"Well, they're not there," Will said.

"Maybe he left them at a dig somewhere."

"Another dig? No—he would've told me about it. Besides, when would he have had the chance to go off and do that? He was always here or at the museum—he never went anywhere else, did he? Not without telling me . . . ," Will trailed off as Rebecca watched him intently.

"I know that look. You've thought of something, haven't you?" she said suspiciously.

"No, it's nothing," he replied. "Really."

11

THE NEXT day, Will awoke early and, wanting to forget about his father's disappearance, donned his work clothes and ran energetically downstairs, thinking he would grab a quick breakfast and maybe meet up with Chester to excavate the blocked tunnel at the Forty Pits site. Rebecca was already lurking in the kitchen; by the way she collared him the moment he turned the corner, it was obvious she'd been waiting for him.

"It's up to us to do something about Dad, you know," she said as Will looked at her with a slightly startled expression. "Mum's not going to do anything—she's lost it."

Will just wanted to get out of the house; he was desperately trying to pretend to himself that everything was normal. Since the night of the argument between his parents, he and Rebecca had been getting themselves to school as usual. The only break from the norm was that they had been eating their meals in the kitchen without their mother. She had been stealing out to help herself to whatever was to be found in the fridge and had been eating it, predictably enough, in front of the television. It was clear what she'd been up to, because pies and chunks of cheese had gone missing, along with whole loaves of bread and tubs of margarine.

They had seen her on a couple of occasions in the hallway as she shambled to the bathroom in her nightgown and her slippers with the backs trodden down. But the only acknowledgment Will or Rebecca received on these chance encounters was a vague nod.

"I've decided something. I'm going to call the police," Rebecca said, standing in front of the dishwasher.

"Do you really think we should? Maybe we ought to wait a while," Will said. He knew the situation didn't look good, but he wasn't quite ready to take that step yet. "Anyway, where do you think he could have gone?" he asked.

"Your guess is as good as mine," Rebecca answered sharply.

"I went by the museum yesterday and it was all closed up." It hadn't been open for days now—not that anyone had called to complain.

"Maybe he just decided he'd had enough of . . . of everything," Rebecca suggested.

"But why?"

"People go missing all the time. Who knows *why*?" Rebecca shrugged her slim shoulders. "But we're going to have to take the matter in hand now," she said resolutely. "And we have to tell Mum what we're going to do."

"All right," Will agreed reluctantly. He glanced at his shovel with longing as they entered the hallway. He just wanted to get away from the house and back to something he understood.

Rebecca knocked on the living-room door and they both shuffled in. Mrs. Burrows didn't seem to notice them; her gaze didn't waver from the television for an instant. They both stood there, unsure what to do next, until Rebecca went up to

Mrs. Burrows's chair, took the remote from where it rested on the arm, and turned off the television.

Mrs. Burrows's eyes remained exactly where they had been on the now-blank screen. Will could see the three of them reflected in it, three small, unmoving figures trapped within the bounds of the darkened rectangle. He drew in a deep breath, telling himself *he* was the one who should take charge of the situation, not his sister as usual.

"Mum," Will said nervously. "Mum, we can't find Dad anywhere and . . . it's been four days now."

"We think we should call the police . . . ," Rebecca said, quickly adding, ". . . unless you know where he is."

Mrs. Burrows's eyes dropped from the screen to the video recorders below it, but they could both see that she wasn't focusing on anything and that her expression was terribly sad. She suddenly seemed so very helpless; Will just wanted to ask her what was wrong, what had happened, but couldn't bring himself to.

"Yes," Mrs. Burrows replied softly. "If you want to." And that was it. She fell silent, her eyes still downcast, and they both filed out of the room.

For the first time, the full implications of his father's disappearance came home to Will. What was going to happen to them without him around? They were in serious trouble. All of them. His mother most of all.

Rebecca called the local police station, and two officers arrived several hours later, a man and a woman, both in uniform. Will let them in.

"Rebecca Burrows?" the policeman asked, looking past Will into the house as he removed his hat. He took out a small notebook from his breast pocket and flipped it open. Just then, the radio on his lapel issued a burp of unintelligible speech, and he slid the switch on its side to silence it. "Sorry 'bout that," he said.

The female officer spoke to Rebecca. "You made the call?"

Rebecca nodded in response, and the woman gave her a comforting smile. "You mentioned your mother was here. Can we talk to her, please?"

"She's in here," Rebecca said, leading the way to the living room and knocking lightly on the door. "Mum," she called softly, opening the door for the two officers and then standing to one side to let them through. Will started to follow them in, but the policeman turned to him.

"Tell you what, son, I could murder a cup of coffee."

As the policeman shut the door behind him, Will turned to Rebecca with an expectant look.

"Oh, all right, I'll make it," she said irritably and headed for the kettle.

Waiting in the kitchen, they could hear the low drone of adult conversation coming from behind the door, until—several cups of coffee and what felt like an eternity later—the policeman emerged alone. He walked in and placed his cup and saucer on the table next to them.

"I'm just going to take a quick look around the place," he said. "For clues," he added with a wink, and had left the kitchen and gone upstairs before either of them could react. They sat there, peering up at the ceiling as they listened to his muffled footsteps moving from room to room on the floor above.

"What does he think he's going to find?" Will said. They heard him come downstairs again and walk around the ground floor, and then he appeared back in the kitchen doorway. He fixed Will with an inquiring look.

"There's a basement, isn't there, son?"

Will took the policeman down into the cellar and stood at the bottom of the oak steps while the man cast his eye over the room. He seemed to be particularly interested in Dr. Burrows's exhibits.

"Unusual things your dad has. I suppose you've got receipts for all these?" he said, picking up one of the dusty clay heads. Noticing Will's startled expression, he continued, "Only joking. I understand he works in the local museum, doesn't he?"

Will nodded.

"I went there once . . . on a school trip, I think." He spotted the dirt in the wheelbarrow. "So what's all that?"

"I don't know. Could be from a dig that Dad's been doing. We usually do them together."

"Dig?" he asked, and Will nodded in reply.

"I think I'd like to take a look outside now," the policeman announced, his eyes narrowing as he studied Will intently and his demeanor taking on a sternness that Will hadn't seen before.

In the garden, Will watched as he systematically searched the borders. Then he turned his attention to the lawn, crouching down every so often to examine the bald patches where one of their neighbor's cats was accustomed to relieving itself, killing off the grass. He spent a little time peering at the Common over the ramshackle fence at the end of the yard before coming back into the house. Will followed him in, and as soon as they entered, the officer put his hand on his shoulder.

"Tell me, son, no one's been doing any digging out there recently, have they?" he asked in a low voice, as if there was some dark secret that Will was dying to share with him.

Will merely shook his head, and they moved into the hall, where the policeman's eyes alighted on his gleaming shovel in the umbrella stand. Noticing this, Will tried to maneuver himself in front of it and block his view.

"Are you *sure* you—or any members of your family—haven't been digging in the garden?" the policeman asked again, staring at Will suspiciously.

"No, not me, not for years," Will replied. "I dug a few pits on the Common when I was younger, but Dad put a stop to that—said someone might fall in."

"On the Common, eh? Big holes, were they?"

"Pretty big. Didn't find anything much there, though."

The policeman looked at Will strangely and wrote something in his notebook. "Much like what?" he asked, frowning with incomprehension.

"Oh, just some bottles and old junk."

At that point, the policewoman came out of the living room and joined her colleague by the front door.

"All right?" the policeman said to her, tucking his notebook back into his breast pocket. He gave a last penetrating look at Will.

"I got everything down," the policewoman replied, and then turned to Will and his sister. "Look, I'm sure there's nothing to worry about, but per standard procedure we'll make some inquiries about your father. If you hear anything or need to talk to us—about anything at all—you can contact us at this number." She handed Rebecca a printed card. "In many of these cases, the person just comes back—they just needed to get away, have some time to think things over." She gave them a reassuring smile and then added, "Or calm down."

"Calm down about what?" Rebecca ventured. "Why would our father need to calm down?"

The officers looked a little surprised, glancing at each other and then back at Rebecca.

"Well, after the disagreement with your mother," the policewoman said. Will was waiting for her to say more, to explain exactly what the argument had been about, but she turned to the other officer. "Right, we'd better be off."

"Ridiculous!" Rebecca said in an exasperated tone after she had shut the door behind them. "*They* obviously haven't got the faintest idea where he's gone or what to do about it. Idiots!"

12

"WILL? Is that you?" Chester said, shielding his eyes from the sun as his friend emerged from the kitchen door into the cramped backyard behind the Rawlses' house. He had been whiling away the time that Sunday morning by swatting bluebottles and wasps with an old badminton racket, easy targets as they grew lazy in the noonday heat. He cut a comical figure in flip-flops and a beanie hat, his oversized frame accentuated by baggy shorts and his shoulders reddened by the sun.

Will stood with his hands in the back pockets of his jeans, looking a little preoccupied. "I need a hand with something," he said, checking behind him that Chester's parents weren't in earshot.

"Sure, what with?" Chester replied, flicking the mutilated remains of a large fly off the frayed strings of his racket.

"I want to take a quick look around the museum tonight," Will replied. "At my dad's things."

He had Chester's undivided attention now.

"To see if there are any clues . . . in his office," Will went on.

"What, you mean break in?" Chester said quietly. "I'm not . . ."

Will cut him short. "I've got the keys." Taking his hand from his pocket, he held them up for Chester to see. "I just want to have a quick look, and I need somebody to watch my back."

Will had been completely prepared to go it alone but, when he stopped to think about it, it seemed natural to enlist the help of his friend. Chester was the only person Will could turn to now that his father had gone. He and Chester had worked very effectively together in the Forty Pits tunnel, like a real team—and, besides, Chester seemed genuinely concerned about Will's father's whereabouts.

Lowering his racket to his side, Chester thought for a moment as he gazed at the house and then back at Will again. "All right," he agreed, "but we'd better not get caught."

Will grinned. It felt good to have a real friend, someone other than his family he could trust, for the first time in his life.

After it had grown dark, the boys stole up the museum steps. Will unlocked the door and they slipped in quickly. The interior was just visible in the zigzag shadows thrown by interlacing bands of weak moonlight and the yellow neon from the street lamps outside.

"Follow me," Will whispered to Chester and, crouching low, they crossed through the main hall toward the corridor, dodging between the glass cabinets and grimacing as their sneakers squeaked on the parquet flooring.

"Watch the—"

"Ouch!" Chester cried as he tripped over the marsh timber lying on the floor just inside the corridor and went sprawling. "What's that doing there?" he said angrily as he rubbed his shin.

"Come on," Will whispered urgently.

Near the end of the corridor, they found Dr. Burrows's office.

"We can use the flashlights in here, but keep your beam down low."

"What are we looking for?" Chester whispered.

"Don't know yet. Let's check his desk first," Will said in a hushed voice.

As Chester held his flashlight for him, Will sifted through the piles of papers and documents. It wasn't an easy task; Dr. Burrows was clearly as disorganized at work as he was at home, and there was a mass of paperwork spread across the desk in arbitrary piles. The computer screen was all but obscured by a proliferation of curling yellow Post-it notes stuck around it. As they searched, Will focused his efforts on anything that was written on loose-leaf pages in his father's barely legible scrawl.

Finishing the last of the piles of papers, they found nothing of note, so they each took one side of the desk and started searching the drawers.

"Wow, look at this." Chester produced what appeared to be a stuffed dog's paw fixed to an ebony stick from among a load of empty tobacco tins. Will simply looked at him and frowned briefly before resuming his search.

"Here's something!" Chester said excitedly as he was investigating the middle drawer. Will didn't bother to look up from the papers in his hand, thinking it was another obscure object.

"No, look, it's got a label with writing on it." He handed it to Will. It was a little book with covers of purple and brown marbling and a sticker on the front that read *Ex Libris* in ornate and swirling copperplate lettering, with a picture of an owl wearing massive round glasses.

"*Journal*," Will read. "That's definitely my dad's writing." He opened the cover. "Bingo! It looks like a diary of some sort." He fanned through the pages. "He's written something on quite a few of these." Pushing it into his bag, he asked, "Are there any others?"

They hurriedly searched the remainder of the drawers and, finding nothing else, decided it was time to leave. Will locked up, and the boys made their way toward the Forty Pits, because it was close by and they knew they wouldn't be interrupted there. As they slunk through the streets, ducking behind cars when anyone appeared, they felt alive with the thrill of the forbidden mission at the museum and couldn't wait to look at the journal they'd unearthed. Reaching the Pits, they descended into the main chamber, where they arranged the cage lights and made themselves comfortable in the armchairs. Will began to pore over the pages.

"The first entry is not long after we discovered the lost train station," he said, looking up at Chester.

"What train station?"

But Will was too engrossed in the journal to explain. He recited slowly, in broken sentences, as he struggled to decipher his father's writing.

I have recently become aware of a small and . . . in . . . incongruous grouping of interlopers coming and going among the general populace of Highfield. A group of people who have a physical appearance that sets them apart. Where they come from or what their purpose is I have yet to ascertain but, from my limited observation of them, I believe that all is not what it seems. Given their apparent numbers (5+?) . . . homogeneity of their (racial?) appearance . . . I suspect they may cohabit or at the very least . . .

He trailed off as he scanned the rest of the page. "I can't quite make out the rest," he said, looking up at Chester. "Here's something," he said, flicking over the page. "This is clearer."

Today a rather intriguing and baffling artifact came into my possession by way of a Mr. Embers. It may well be linked to these people, although I have yet to . . . substantiate this. The object is a small globe held in a cage of some type of metal, which, at the time of this writing, I have not been able to identify. The globe emits light of varying intensity depending on the degree of background illumination. What confounds me is that the relationship is directly inverse—the darker the surroundings, the brighter the light it emits. It defies any laws of physics or chemistry with which I am familiar.

Will held up the page so that Chester could see the rough sketch his father had made.

"Have you actually seen it?" Chester inquired. "This light thing?"

"No, he kept all this to himself," Will replied thoughtfully. Turning the page, he began to read again.

Today I had the opportunity to . . . scrutinize, albeit for a brief moment, one of the pallid men at close quarters.

"Pallid? As in pale?" Chester said.

"Suppose so," Will answered, and then read out his father's description of the mysterious man. He went on to the episode with Pineapple Joe and the inexplicable duct in the house, and his father's thoughts and observations on Martineau Square. There followed a large number of pages debating the likely structure within the terraced houses that lined the square; Will leafed through these until he came to a photocopied extract from a book, stapled into the journal.

"It says *Highfield's History* at the top of the page, and it seems to be about someone called Sir Gabriel Martineau," Will read:

Born in 1673, he was the son and heir of a successful cloth dyer in Highfield. In 1699, he inherited the business, Martineau, Long & Co., from his father and expanded it considerably, adding a further two factories to the original premises on Heath Street. He was known to be a keen inventor and was widely recognized for his expertise in the fields of chemistry, physics, and engineering. Indeed, although Hooke (1635–1703) is generally credited with being the architect behind what is essentially the modern air pump, there are a number of historians who believe that he built his first prototype using Martineau's drawings.

In 1710, during a period of widespread unemployment, Martineau, a deeply religious man who was renowned for his philanthropic and paternal attitude toward his workforce, began to employ a substantial number of laborers to build dwellings for his factory workers, and personally designed and oversaw the construction of Martineau Square, which still stands today, and Grayston Villas, which was destroyed in the Blitz. Martineau soon became the largest employer in the Highfield district, and it was rumored that Martineau's Men (as they became known) were engaged in digging a substantial underground network of tunnels, although no evidence of these remains today.

In 1718, Martineau's wife contracted tuberculosis and died, aged thirty-two. Thereafter Martineau sought solace by joining an obscure religious sect and was rarely seen in public for the remaining years of his life. His home, Martineau House, which formerly stood on the edge of what is now Highfield's historic district, was destroyed by a fire in 1733, in which Martineau and his two daughters are believed to have perished.

Underneath, Dr. Burrows had written:

Why is there no trace of these tunnels now? What were they for? I haven't been able to find any mention of them in the town hall records or the borough archives or anywhere. Why, why, why?

Then, scrawled with such gusto the paper was wrinkled and even ripped in places, were large, crude capitals in blue ballpoint:

FACT OR FICTION?

Will frowned and turned to Chester. "This is incredible. Have you ever heard of this Martineau?"

Chester shook his head.

"Very weird," Will said, slowly rereading the photocopied extract. "Dad never mentioned any of this, not once. Why would he have kept something like this from me?"

Will chewed his lip, his expression transforming from exasperation to one of deep preoccupation. Then he suddenly jerked his head up, as if he had been elbowed in the ribs.

"What is it?" Chester said.

"Dad was onto something that he didn't want anyone to nick from him. Not again. That's it!" Will cried, remembering the time when the professor from London University had pulled rank on his father and taken the Roman villa dig away from him.

Chester was about to ask what Will was talking about when, in a flurry, Will began flipping forward through the journal.

"More stuff about these *pallid* men," Will said, continuing on until he came to a part of the notebook where there were only the ragged stubs of missing pages. "These have been torn out!"

He thumbed through a few more pages to the final entry. Chester saw him hesitate.

"See the date," Will said.

"Where?" Chester leaned in.

"It's from last Wednesday . . . the day he had the fight with Mum," Will said in a quiet voice, then took a deep breath and read aloud:

Tonight's the night. I have found a way in. If this is what I think it is, my hypothesis, wild as it may seem, will be proved correct. This could be it! My chance, my last chance, to make my mark. My moment! I have to follow my instincts. I have to go down there. I have to go through.

"I don't understand—" Chester began.

Will held up his hand to silence his friend and continued:

It could be dangerous, but it's something I have to do. I have to show them—if my theory is right, they'll see! They'll have to. I am not just a bumbling curator.

And then Will read the final sentence, which was underscored several times.

I will be remembered!

"Wow!" Will exclaimed, sitting back in the damp armchair. "This is incredible."

"Yes," Chester agreed somewhat halfheartedly. He was beginning to think that Will's father had perhaps not been completely sane. It sounded to him suspiciously like the ramblings of someone who was losing it, big-time.

"So what was he onto? What was this *theory* he was talking about?" Will said, flipping back to the ripped-out pages. "I'll bet this is where it was. He didn't want anyone to steal his ideas." Will was buzzing now.

"Yes, but where do you think he's actually gone?" Chester asked. "What does he mean by *go through*, Will?"

This took the wind out of Will's sails. He looked blankly at Chester.

"Well," he began slowly, "two things have been bugging me. First is, I saw him working on something at home very early one morning—'bout two weeks before he disappeared. I figured he was digging on the Common . . . but that doesn't stack up."

"Why?"

"Well, when I saw him, I'm sure he was pushing a barrowload of spoil *to* the Common, not *away* from it. Second thing is, I can't find his overalls or hard hat anywhere."

13

"**OI, SNOWFLAKE,** I hear your old man's done a runner," a voice shouted at Will as soon as he entered the classroom. There was an immediate hush as everyone turned to look at Will, who, gritting his teeth, sat down at his desk and started to take his books out of his bag.

It was Speed, a vicious, skinny kid with greasy black hair who was the self-appointed leader of a gang of similarly unpleasant characters.

"Can't blame him, can you? Probably got sick of you!" Speed sneered, his voice dripping with derision.

Hunched doggedly over his desk, Will did his best to pretend he was searching for a page in his textbook.

"Sick of his *freak* of a son!" Speed shouted, in that horribly guttural yet slightly squeaky way that only someone whose voice is in the process of breaking can do.

The fury welled up inside Will. His pulse raced and his face felt hot; he hated that it would be betraying his anger. As he remained with his eyes fixed steadfastly on the absolutely meaningless page before him, he experienced, just for a fraction of a second, a moment of incredible self-doubt and guilt. Maybe Speed was right. Maybe it was his fault. Maybe he was partly to blame for his father's departure.

He dismissed the thought almost immediately, telling himself that it couldn't have been because of him. Whatever the reason, his father wouldn't have just walked out. It must have been something serious . . . something deadly serious.

"And *totally* over your *mental* mum!" Speed bawled on even more loudly. At this, Will heard gasps and the random giggle around him in the otherwise completely silent classroom. So it was already general knowledge about his mother. . . .

Will gripped his textbook with such force that the cover was beginning to buckle. He still didn't look up, but he shook his head slowly. This was only going one way. . . . He didn't want to fight, but the little creep was pushing it too far. It was a matter of pride now.

"Hey, Vanilla Ice, I'm talking to you! Are you or are you not fatherless? Are you or are you not a b—"

That did it! Will suddenly stood up, sending his chair shooting back. It scraped across the wooden floor and then toppled over. He locked eyes with Speed, who also rose from his desk, his face contorted with spiteful relish as he realized he'd hit the bull's-eye with his gibes. Simultaneously three of Speed's gang leaped excitedly out of their chairs with predatory glee.

"Has Snow White had enough?" Speed sneered, moving with a swagger between the desks toward Will, his cackling entourage in tow.

Reaching Will, Speed stood close to him, his fists clenched by his sides. Although Will wanted to take a step back, he knew he had to stand his ground.

Speed pushed his face even closer, so that it was inches away from Will's, then arched his back like a second-rate boxer.

"Well, . . . have . . . you?" he said, emphasizing each word with a finger jab at Will's chest.

"Leave him alone. We've all had enough of *you*." Chester's imposing bulk suddenly moved into view as he positioned himself behind Will.

Speed glanced uneasily at him, then back at Will.

Aware the whole class was watching him, and that he was expected to make the next move, Speed could only think of hissing dismissively through his teeth. It was a lame attempt to save his pride, and everyone knew it.

Fortunately at that very moment the teacher entered and, realizing what was afoot, cleared his throat loudly to let them know he was in the room. It did nothing to deflate the standoff between Will, Chester, and Speed, and he had to march over and order them in no uncertain terms to sit down.

Will and Chester took their places and, after a few seconds, Speed and his followers skulked back to their desks, too. Will leaned back in his chair and smiled at Chester. Chester was a true friend.

Returning from school later that day, Will stole into the house, taking pains not to alert his sister that he was home. Before he opened the cellar door, he paused in the hallway to listen. He heard the strains of "You Are My Sunshine": Rebecca was singing to herself as she did the housework upstairs. He quickly descended into the cellar and unbolted the door to the garden, where Chester was waiting.

"Are you sure it's all right for me to be here?" he asked. "Feels sort of . . . well . . . wrong."

"Don't be stupid, course it is," Will insisted. "Now, let's see what we can find in here."

They searched through everything stored on the shelves and then in the archive boxes that Will had already made a start on the last time. Their efforts were fruitless.

"Well, that was a complete waste of time," Will said despondently.

"So where d'you think the dirt came from?" Chester asked, going over to the wheelbarrow to examine it more closely.

"Haven't figured that out yet. I suppose we could search the Common. See if he was up to something there."

"Big area," Chester said, unconvinced. "Anyway, why would he bring that dirt down here?"

"Don't know," Will replied as he happened to run his eyes over the bookshelves one last time. He frowned as he noticed something at the side of one of the units.

"Hang on a minute . . . that's odd," he said as Chester ambled over.

"What is?"

"Well, there's a plug in a socket down here, but I can't see where the cord goes." He flipped the switch next to the outlet and they both looked around; it didn't appear to have had any effect.

"What's it for, then?" Chester said.

"It's definitely not an outside light."

"Why's that?" Chester asked.

"Because we don't have any," Will replied as he went to the other end of the shelves, peering into the dark corner between the two units, then stepping back and regarding them thoughtfully. "Funny. The cord doesn't seem to come out again on this side."

Taking the stepladder from beside the garden door, he set it up in front of the bookshelves and climbed up to inspect the top of the unit.

"No sign of it here, either," he said. "This just doesn't make sense." He was about to climb down when he stopped and ran his hand over the top of the shelves.

"Anything?" Chester asked.

"Lots of brick dust," Will replied. He hopped down from the ladder and immediately tried to pull the end of the shelf unit away from the wall.

"There's definitely a bit of give. Come on, lend me a hand," he said.

"Maybe it's just badly attached," Chester suggested.

"Badly attached?" Will said indignantly. "*I* helped put these up."

They both pulled together with all their strength and, although a thin sliver opened up at the rear of the unit, the shelves appeared to be firmly secured at the top.

"Let me check something," Will said as he mounted the stepladder again. "There seems to be a loose nail lodged in this bracket." He yanked it out and let it fall onto the concrete floor by Chester's feet. "We used screws to secure this to the wall, not nails," he said, looking down at Chester with a bewildered expression.

Will leaped down from the ladder, and they both pulled on the unit again. This time, shuddering and creaking, it swung out from the wall to reveal that it was hinged on one side.

"So that's what the cord's for!" Will exclaimed as both of them stared at the rough-hewn opening in the bottom half of the wall. The bricks had been removed to form a hole approximately three feet square. Inside, a passage was visible, illuminated by a motley array of old neon strip lights burning along its length.

"Wow!" Chester gasped, his face a picture of surprise. "A secret passage!"

Will smiled at Chester. "Let's check this out." Before Chester had time to say anything, Will ducked into the passage and was crawling along it at a steady pace. "There's a bend here," came his muffled voice.

As Chester watched, Will started to go around the corner and then, very slowly, came back into view again. He sat back and turned his head to Chester, his face disconsolate in the glow of the strip lights. "What is it?" Chester asked.

"The tunnel's blocked. It's caved in," Will said.

Will slowly crawled back out of the passage, then clambered through the hole in the wall and into the cellar again. He straightened up and sloughed off his school blazer, dropping it where he stood. It was only then that he noticed his friend's grim expression.

"What is it?"

"The cave-in . . . you don't think your dad's under it, do you?" Chester said almost in a whisper, barely able to contain a shudder as he pictured the horrific possibility. "He might have been . . . crushed," he added ominously.

Will looked worriedly away from his friend and thought for a moment. "Well, there's only one way to find out."

"Shouldn't we tell someone?" Chester stammered, taken aback by his friend's seeming detachment. But Will wasn't listening. His eyes had narrowed with the look of preoccupation that meant his mind was churning away, formulating a plan of action.

"You know, the infill is exactly the same as in the Pits tunnel—it's all wrong. There are lumps of limestone again," he said, loosening his tie and pulling it over his head before discarding it next to the crumpled blazer on the floor. "This is too much of a coincidence." He returned to the mouth of the passage and leaned in. "And did you notice the props?" he said, running his hand over one that was just within reach. "This was no accident. This has been hacked at and pulled in on purpose."

Chester joined his friend at the opening and examined the props, which had deep notches sliced into them. They were cut almost clear through in places, as if someone had been swinging an ax at them.

"Blimey, you're right," he said.

Will rolled up his sleeves. "Better get started, then. No time like the present." He ducked into the passage, dragging behind him a bucket he'd found just inside the opening.

Chester looked down at his school uniform. He opened his mouth to say something, but then thought better of it, removed his blazer, and hung it neatly on the back of a chair.

14

"GO!" SAID Will in an urgent whisper as he crouched low within the shadows of the hedge bordering the Common at the bottom of the garden.

Chester growled with the effort as he heaved the overladen wheelbarrow into motion and then weaved precariously between the trees and shrubs. Reaching open ground, he veered off to the right toward the gullies they were using to dump the spoil. From the mounds of fresh earth and small cairns of rock already deposited there, it was evident to Will that his father had been using these gullies for the very same purpose.

Will kept a watchful eye open for any passersby as Chester swiftly emptied the barrow at the top of the gully. He deftly spun it around for the return journey, while Will remained behind to push in any large pieces of rock or clumps of soil and clay.

Once that was done, Will caught up with Chester. As they were retracing the well-trodden route back to the garden, the wheel on the old barrow began to squeal piercingly, perhaps protesting the countless trips it had been forced to make. The noise cut through the peaceful calm of the balmy autumn evening.

Both boys froze abruptly in their tracks, looking around to check whether it had attracted any attention from the nearby houses.

Trying to catch his breath, Chester bent forward with his hands resting on his knees as Will stooped to examine the offending wheel.

"We'll have to oil that stupid thing again."

"Duh, do you think so?" Chester puffed sarcastically.

"I think you'd better carry it back," Will replied coldly as he straightened up.

"Do I have to?" Chester groaned.

"Come on, I'll give you a hand," Will said as he grabbed hold of the front of the barrow.

They lugged it the remaining distance, grunting and cursing under their breath but maintaining a strict silence as they crossed the backyard. They trod lightly as they negotiated the small ramp down to the rear entrance into the cellar.

"My turn at the face, I suppose." Will gasped as they both flopped with exhaustion onto the concrete floor. Chester didn't answer.

"You all right?" Will asked him.

Chester nodded groggily, then squinted at his watch. "I think I should be getting home."

"S'pose so," Will said as Chester slowly pulled himself to his feet and began to gather his things. Will didn't say so, but he was very relieved that Chester had decided to call it a day. They were both dog tired after the intensive digging and tipping, to the point that he could see Chester was a little unsteady on his feet from fatigue.

"Same time tomorrow, then," Will said quietly, flexing his fingers and then stretching one shoulder in an effort to reduce the stiffness.

"Yeah," Chester croaked in reply, without even looking at Will as he shuffled out of the cellar by the back door.

They went through this same ritual every evening after school. Will would very carefully open the garden door, without making a sound, to let Chester in. They would get changed and immediately begin working for two or three hours at a stretch. The excavation was particularly slow and tortuous, not only because of the limited space in the tunnel and the fact that they couldn't let anyone above hear them, but because they could tip the excavated material onto the Common only under cover of nightfall. At the end of every evening, after Chester had gone home, Will made sure that the shelf unit was pushed back into place and secured and the floor swept.

This night he had an additional task: As he saturated the axle of the noisy wheel with oil, he wondered how much farther it was to the end of the tunnel and, not for the first time, whether there would be anything there. He was concerned that they were running out of supplies; without his father's help with materials, he had been forced to salvage as much timber as he could from the Forty Pits, so as the tunnel beneath the house progressed, the other one became more and more precarious.

Later, as he sat hunched over the kitchen table, eating yet another dinner that had gone stone-cold, Rebecca appeared in the doorway as if from nowhere. It made Will start, and he swallowed noisily.

"Just look at the state of you! Your uniform is filthy—do you expect me to wash everything *again*?" she said, folding her arms aggressively.

"No, not really," he replied, avoiding her eyes.

"Will, what exactly are you up to?" she demanded.

"I don't know what you mean," he said, ramming in another mouthful.

"You've been sneaking off somewhere after school, haven't you?"

Will shrugged, pretending to examine a dry slice of beef curling on the tip of his fork.

"I know you're up to something, all right, because I've seen that big ox sneaking around in the backyard."

"Who?"

"Oh, come on, you and Chester have been tunneling somewhere, haven't you?"

"You're right," Will admitted. He finished his mouthful and, taking a breath, tried to lie as convincingly as he could. "Over by the town dump," he said.

"I knew it!" Rebecca announced triumphantly. "How can you even *think* of digging another of your useless holes at a time like this?"

"I miss Dad, too, you know," he said as he took a bite out of a cold roasted potato, "but it's not going to help any of us if we just mope around the house, feeling sorry for ourselves . . . like Mum."

Rebecca stared at him distrustfully, her eyes shining with anger, then turned on her heel and walked out of the room.

Will finished the congealed meal, staring into space as he slowly chewed each mouthful, ruminating on the events of the past month.

Afterward, up in his bedroom, he took out a geological map of Highfield, first marking the spot where he thought the house stood, and then the direction he calculated his father's tunnel in the cellar was taking, and, while he was at it, the locations of Martineau Square and Mrs. Tantrumi's house. Will looked long and hard at the map, as if it were a puzzle he could solve, before he finally put it aside and climbed into bed. Within minutes he'd slipped into an uneasy and fitful slumber, in which he dreamed of the sinister people his father had described in his journal.

In the dream he was dressed in his school uniform, but it was covered in mud and tattered and torn at the elbows and knees. He'd lost his socks and shoes and was walking barefoot down a long, deserted terraced street, which felt familiar though he couldn't quite place where he knew it from. As he glanced up at the low sky, which was yellowy gray and formless, he fidgeted anxiously with the ragged material of his sleeves. He didn't know if he was late for school or for supper, but he was certain he was supposed to be somewhere or doing something—something vitally important.

He kept to the center of the street, wary of the houses on both sides. They stood ominous and dark; no light shone from behind their dusty windows, nor did any smoke rise from their precariously tall and twisted black chimney stacks.

He was feeling so very lost and alone when, far off in the distance, he spotted someone crossing the street. He knew instantly that it was his father, and his heart leaped with joy. He began to wave, but then stopped as he sensed that the buildings were watching him. There was a brooding malevolence to them, as if they harbored an evil force, like a tightly coiled spring, holding its breath and lying in wait for him.

Will's fear grew to an unbearable pitch, and he broke into a trot toward his father. He tried to call to him, but his voice was thin and ineffectual, as though the air itself were swallowing his words the instant they left his lips.

He was running at full tilt now, and with every stride the street was becoming narrower, so that the houses on either side were closing in on him. He could now clearly see that there were shadowy figures lurking threateningly in their dark doorways, and that they were beginning to spill out onto the street as he passed them.

Terrified out of his wits, he was tripping and sliding on the slick cobblestones as the figures amassed behind him in such numbers that they were indiscernible from one another, sweeping into a single blanket of darkness. Their fingers extended like wisps of animated black smoke, clutching at him as he desperately tried to elude them. But the shadowy figures had hold of him; they were tugging him back with their inky tendrils until he was forced to a complete standstill. Catching a last brief glimpse of his father in the distance, Will screamed a silent scream. The jet-black blanket folded over him; he was all at once weightless and falling into a pit. He hit the bottom with such impact that it knocked the air from his lungs and, gasping for breath, he rolled onto his back and saw for the first time the stern and disapproving faces of his pursuers as they peered down at him.

He opened his mouth, but before he knew what was happening, it was filled with dirt—he could taste it as it smothered his tongue, and stones dashed and scratched against his teeth. He was being buried alive—he couldn't breathe.

■ ■ ■

Gagging and retching, Will awoke, his mouth dry and his body dripping with cold sweat as he sat up. In a panic he fumbled for his bedside light. With a click, its comforting yellow glow bathed the room in reassuring normality. He glanced at his alarm clock. It was still the middle of the night. He fell back onto his pillow, staring at the ceiling and breathing heavily, his body still trembling. The memory of the soil clogging his throat was as fresh and vivid in his mind as if it had really happened. And as he lay there, catching his breath, he was plagued by a renewed and even more acute sense of loss for his father. However hard he tried, he just couldn't shake off the overwhelming hollowness, and in the end he gave up any pretense of sleep, watching as the cold light of dawn began to lick around the edges of the curtains and finally stole into the room.

15

THE WEEKS passed, until finally a police inspector came by to speak to Mrs. Burrows about her husband's disappearance. He wore a dark blue raincoat over a light gray suit and was well spoken, if a little brusque, as he introduced himself to Will and Rebecca and asked to see their mother. They showed him into the living room, where she sat waiting.

As they followed the policeman they gasped, thinking that somehow they must have entered the wrong room. The television, that eternal flame that burned in the corner, was silent and dark, and—just as remarkable—the room was incredibly neat and tidy. During the time when Mrs. Burrows had led her hermitlike existence and neither Will nor Rebecca had set foot inside, both had assumed it had degenerated into an unholy mess, and they pictured it littered with half-consumed food, empty wrappers, and dirty plates and cups. They couldn't have been more wrong. It now looked spotless—but what was more astounding was their mother herself. Instead of her drab couch-potato garb of bathrobe and slippers, she had changed into one of her best summer dresses, done her hair, and even put on some makeup.

Will stared at her in sheer disbelief, wondering what in the world could have brought about this abrupt transformation.

He could only think that she was imagining she was playing a part in one of the TV murder mystery series she so adored, but this didn't make the scene before him any more explicable.

"Mum, this is . . . this is . . . ," he spluttered.

"Detective Chief Inspector Beatty," his sister helped him out.

"Please do come in," Mrs. Burrows said, rising from her armchair and smiling pleasantly.

"Thank you, Mrs. Burrows . . . I know this is a difficult time."

"No, not at all." Mrs. Burrows beamed. "Rebecca, would you please put the kettle on and make us all a nice cup of tea?"

"That's very kind, thank you, ma'am," Inspector Beatty said, hovering awkwardly in the center of the room.

"Please." Mrs. Burrows motioned toward the sofa. "Please, make yourself comfortable."

"Will, you can give me a hand," Rebecca said, grabbing her brother by the arm as she tried to shepherd him toward the door. He didn't move, still rooted to the spot by the sight of his mother who, it seemed, was once more the woman she hadn't been for years.

"Uh . . . yeah . . . oh, yes . . . ," he managed.

"Do you take sugar?" Rebecca asked the detective, still tugging at Will's arm.

"No, white and no sugar, thank you," he replied.

"Right, milk, no sugar—and, Mum, just the two sweeteners?"

Her mother smiled and nodded at her, and then at Will, as if she was amused by his bewilderment. "And maybe some cookies, Will?"

Will snapped out of his trance, turned, and accompanied Rebecca into the kitchen, where he stood in wide-mouthed disbelief, shaking his head.

While Will and Rebecca were out of the room, the detective spoke to Mrs. Burrows in a low, serious voice. He said that they had been doing everything they could to locate Dr. Burrows, but since there was no news at all of his whereabouts they had decided to step up the investigation. This would entail circulating the photograph of Dr. Burrows more widely and conducting a "detailed interview," as he put it, with her down at the station. They also wanted to speak to anyone else who'd had contact with Dr. Burrows just prior to his disappearance.

"I'd like to ask you a few questions now, if that's all right. Let's start with your husband's job," the detective said, looking at the door and wondering when his tea was going to arrive. "Did he mention anyone in particular at the museum?"

"No," Mrs. Burrows replied.

"I mean, is there someone there he might have confided in . . . ?"

"About where he's gone?" Mrs. Burrows completed the sentence for him, and then laughed coldly. "You won't have any luck with that line of investigation, I'm afraid. That's a dead end."

The detective sat up in his chair, a little baffled by Mrs. Burrows's response.

She continued, "He runs the place single-handed; there isn't any other staff. You might consider interviewing the old codgers that hung out with him, but don't be surprised if their memories aren't what they used to be."

"No?" Inspector Beatty said, a small smile showing at the edges of his mouth as he wrote in his notebook.

"No, most of them are in their eighties. And why, may I ask, do you want to interview me and my children? I have already told the police everything I know. Shouldn't you be putting out an APB?"

"An APB?" The detective grinned broadly. "We don't use that term here in England. We put emergencies out over the radio—"

"And my husband isn't an emergency, I suppose?"

At that moment, Will and Rebecca appeared with the tea, and the room went quiet as Rebecca put the tray on the coffee table and passed around the mugs. Will, clutching a plate of cookies, also entered the room and, since the detective didn't seem to object to either him or Rebecca remaining there, they both sat down. The silence grew uneasily. Mrs. Burrows was glaring at the detective, who was looking into his tea.

"I think we may be getting ahead of ourselves here, Mrs. Burrows. Can we just focus on your husband again?" he said.

"I think you will find that we are all *very* focused on him. It's you I'm worried about," Mrs. Burrows said tersely.

"Mrs. Burrows, you have to realize that some people don't . . . ," the detective began, ". . . don't *want* to be found. They want to disappear because, maybe, life and its pressures have become too much for them to handle."

"Too much to handle?" Mrs. Burrows echoed furiously.

"Yes, we have to take that possibility into consideration."

"My husband couldn't take pressure? What pressure, exactly? The problem was that he never *had* any pressure at all—or drive, for that matter."

"Mrs. B—" The detective tried to get a word in, glancing helplessly at Will and Rebecca, who were both looking back and forth from him to their mother as if they were spectators watching a rally in a particularly savage tennis match.

"Don't think I don't know that most murders are committed by family members," their mother proclaimed.

"Mrs. Burr—"

"That's why you want to question us at the station, isn't it? To find out whether we *dunnit*."

"Mrs. Burrows," the detective began again quietly, "nobody's suggesting that a murder has been committed here. Do you think we might start over, see if we can get off on the right foot this time?" he proposed, valiantly trying to regain control of the situation.

"Sorry. I know you're only doing your job," Mrs. Burrows said in a calmer voice, then sipped her tea.

Inspector Beatty nodded, grateful she had stopped her tirade, and took a deep breath as he glanced down at his notebook. "I know it's a difficult thing to think about," he said, "but did your husband have any enemies? Maybe from business dealings?"

At this, much to Will's surprise, Mrs. Burrows put her head back and laughed out loud. The detective muttered something about taking that as a no as he scribbled in his little black notebook. He seemed to have regained some of his composure.

"I have to ask these questions," he said, looking straight at Mrs. Burrows. "Did you ever know him to drink excessively or take drugs?"

Again Mrs. Burrows unleashed a loud hoot of laughter. "Him?" she said. "You've got to be joking!"

"Righto. So what did he do in his spare time?" the detective asked in a flat voice, trying his very best to get the questions over and done with as quickly as he could. "Did he have any hobbies?"

Rebecca immediately shot a glance at Will.

"He used to do excavations . . . archaeological digs," Mrs. Burrows answered.

"Oh, yes." The detective turned to Will. "I understand you helped him out, didn't you, son?" Will nodded. "And where did you do all this digging?"

Will cleared his throat and looked at his mother, and then at Inspector Beatty, who was waiting, pen held expectantly in hand, for an answer.

"Well, all over, really," Will said. "Near the edge of town, at garbage dumps and places like that."

"Oh, I thought they were official undertakings," the detective said.

"They *were* real digs," Will said firmly. "We found the site of a Roman villa once, but mostly it was eighteenth- and nineteenth-century stuff we were after."

"Just how extensive . . . I mean, how *deep* were the holes you dug?"

"Oh, just pits, really," Will said evasively, willing the detective not to pursue this line of questioning.

"And were you engaged in any such activities around the time of his disappearance?"

"No, we weren't," Will said, very aware of Rebecca's eyes burning into him.

"You're sure he wasn't working on anything, maybe without your knowledge?"

"No, I don't think so."

"OK, then," the detective said, putting away his notebook. "That's enough for now."

The next day, Chester and Will didn't hang around outside school for long. They spotted Speed and one of his faithful followers, Bloggsy, loitering a little distance beyond the gates.

"I think he's looking for a rematch," Will said, glancing over at Speed, who glared straight back at him until Chester caught his eye. At this point, Speed contemptuously turned his back on them, muttering something under his breath to Bloggsy, who simply sneered in their direction and gave a harsh, derisory laugh.

"Couple of jerks," Chester growled as he and Will set off, deciding to take the shortcut home.

Leaving their school behind them, a sprawling modern yellow-brick-and-glass job, they sauntered across the road and entered the adjoining housing projects. Built in the 1970s, the projects were known locally as Roach City, for obvious reasons, and the infested blocks that made up the development were in a constant state of disrepair, with many of the apartments abandoned or burned out. This in itself didn't cause the boys any hesitation, but the trouble with the route was that it took them right through the home turf of the Click, who made Speed and his gang look like Girl Scouts.

As they walked side by side through the projects, the weak rays of the sun glinting off broken glass on the blacktop and in the gutters, Will slackened his pace almost imperceptibly, but enough that Chester noticed.

"What's up?"

"I don't know," Will said, glancing up and down the road and peering apprehensively into a side street as they passed by.

"Come on, tell me," Chester asked, looking quickly around. "I really don't fancy getting jumped in here."

"It's just a feeling; it's nothing," Will insisted.

"Speed's got you all paranoid, hasn't he?" Chester replied with a smile, but nevertheless he sped up, forcing Will to do likewise.

As they left the projects behind them, they resumed a more normal pace. Very soon they reached the start of Main Street, which was marked by the museum. As Will did every evening, he glanced at it in the vain hope that the lights would be burning, the doors open, and his father back in attendance. Will just wanted everything to be normal again—whatever that was—but once again the museum was closed, its windows dark and unfriendly. The town council had evidently made the decision that for now it was cheaper to simply shut it rather than look for a temporary stand-in for Dr. Burrows.

Will looked up at the sky; heavy clouds were beginning to pull across and blank out the sun.

"Should go well tonight," he said, his mood lifting. "It's getting dark earlier, so we won't have to wait as long to start tipping."

Chester had begun to talk about how much faster the proceedings would be if they could do away with all this cloak-and-dagger subterfuge when Will mumbled something under his breath.

"Didn't catch that, Will."

"I said: Don't look now, but I think there's somebody following us."

"You what?" Chester replied and, not being able to stop himself, immediately turned to look behind.

"Chester, you prat!" Will snapped.

Sure enough, thirty feet or so behind them was a short, stocky man in a trilby, black glasses, and a dark, tentlike overcoat that reached almost to his ankles. His head was facing in their direction, although it was difficult to tell if he was actually looking at them.

"Rats!" Chester whispered. "I think you're right. He's just like the ones your dad wrote about in his journal."

Despite Will's previous instruction to Chester not to look at the man, he now couldn't stop himself from peering back for another glimpse.

"A 'man-in-a-hat'?" Will said with a mixture of wonder and apprehension.

"But he's not after *us*, is he?" Chester asked. "Why should he be?"

"Let's slow down a little and see what he does," Will suggested.

As they reduced their speed, the mysterious man did likewise. "OK," Will said, "how about if we cross the road?"

Again the man mirrored their actions, and when they increased their pace again, he quickened his, to maintain the distance between them.

"He's definitely following us," Chester said, the panic audible in his voice for the first time. "Why, though? What does he want?

I don't like this—I think we should take the next right and make a run for it."

"I don't know," Will said, deep in thought. "I think we should confront him."

"You've got to be *joking*! Your dad disappeared off the face of the planet not long after seeing these people and, for all we know, this man could be responsible. He might be part of the gang or something. I say we get out of here and call the police. Or get help from someone."

They were silent for a moment as they looked around.

"No, I've got a better idea," Will said. "What if we turn the tables? Trap him. If we split up, he can only follow one of us, and when he does, the other can come up behind him and . . ."

"And what?"

"Like a pincer movement—sneak up from behind and nobble him." Will was getting well into his stride now as the plan of action firmed up in his mind.

"He could be dangerous, totally *postal* for all we know. And what are we going to nobble him *with*? Our school bags?"

"Come on, there's two of us and only one of him," Will said as the shops on Main Street came into view. "I'll distract him while you tackle him—you can do that, can't you?"

"Oh, great, thanks," Chester said, shaking his head. "He's freakin' huge—he'll make hamburger meat of me!"

Will looked into Chester's eyes and smiled mischievously.

"All right, all right." Chester sighed. "The things I do . . . ," he said as he looked quickly back and then made to cross the road.

"Whoa! Scratch that," Will said. "I think they've got the jump on us!"

"They?" Chester gasped as he rejoined his friend. "What do you mean, *they*?" he asked, following Will's gaze to a point farther up the street.

There in front of them, some twenty paces ahead, was another of the men. He was almost identical to the first one, except that he sported a flat cap pulled down low over his forehead so that his dark glasses were only just visible under its peak. He also wore a long, voluminous coat, which was flapping gently in the wind as he stood in the middle of the sidewalk.

There was now no question in Will's mind that these two men were after them.

As Will and Chester drew level with the first of the shops on Main Street, they both stopped and peered around. On the opposite side of the street two old ladies were chatting to each other as they bundled along with their wicker shopping carts creaking on their wheels. One was dragging behind her a recalcitrant Scottish terrier decked out in a tartan dog coat. Apart from that, there were only a few people, off in the distance.

Their minds were racing with thoughts of shouting for help or flagging down a car if one happened to pass by when the man in front started toward them. As the two men closed in, Will and Chester both realized they were rapidly running out of options.

"This is too weird, we're well and truly snookered, who the heck *are* these guys?" Chester said, his words running into one another as he stared back over his shoulder at the man in the trilby hat. As he advanced toward them, the heavy thud of his boots on the pavement sounded like a pile driver. "Any bright ideas?" Chester asked desperately.

"Right, listen, we hoof it across the road straight toward the one in the flat cap, fake right, then cut left and duck into Clarke's. Got it?" Will said breathlessly as the flat-capped man in front of them loomed closer and closer. Chester hadn't got the remotest idea what Will was proposing, but under the circumstances he was ready to agree to anything.

Clarke Brothers was the main grocery store on Main Street, with a brightly striped awning and immaculately arranged stalls of fruits and vegetables at either side of its entrance. Now that the daylight was beginning to dwindle, the glare spilling out from the shop windows beckoned to them invitingly, like a beacon. The man in the flat cap was caught in its glow, his wide, muscular form almost blocking the entire width of the sidewalk.

"Now!" Will shouted, and they charged into the street. The two men swept in to intercept the boys, who were sprinting down the road at top speed, their school bags bouncing wildly on their backs. The men moved much faster than either Will or Chester had anticipated, and their plan quickly turned into a chaotic game of tag as the two boys dodged and weaved between the lumbering men, who tried to snatch at them with huge, outstretched hands.

Will squawked as one of them caught hold of him by the scruff of his neck. Then, more by accident than design, Chester hurtled straight into the man. The impact knocked off his dark glasses to reveal bright pupils, shining devilishly like two black pearls under the brim of his hat. As he turned in surprise, Will took the opportunity to push himself away, putting both hands against the man's chest. The collar of Will's blazer ripped off with a rending tear as he did so.

The man, momentarily distracted by the impact with Chester, growled and whipped around to Will again. Slinging away the detached collar, he lunged in a renewed effort to grab him.

In a blind panic, Chester, his head down and his shoulders bunched up, and Will, half falling and half whirling like an uncoordinated dervish, somehow made it to the door of Clarke's as the man wearing the trilby lurched forward, took a last swipe at them, and missed.

Will's and Chester's momentum carried them straight through the door, squashed together between the jambs as the bell above rang like a demented hall monitor. They ended up in an unruly heap on the floor of the store, and Chester, coming to his senses, immediately twisted around and slammed the door shut, holding it closed with both feet.

"Boys, boys, boys!" said Mr. Clarke the younger, teetering perilously on a stepladder as he arranged a display of imported coconuts on a shelf. "What's all the pandemonium? A sudden desperate yearning for my exotic fruits?"

"Um, not exactly," Will said, trying to catch his breath as he picked himself up from the floor and made an attempt to act natural, despite the fact that Chester was now standing somewhat awkwardly with his shoulder braced against the door behind him.

At this point, Mr. Clarke the elder rose from behind the counter like a human periscope.

"What was that terrible racket?" he asked, clutching papers and receipts in both hands.

"Nothing for you to worry about, brother dear." Mr. Clarke junior smiled at him. "Don't let us distract you from your paperwork. It's just a couple of ruffians in search of some rather special fruit, I'll wager."

"Well, I hope they don't want kumquats; we are all out of kumquats at the moment," Mr. Clarke senior said in a dour voice as he slowly retracted below the counter again.

"Then kumquat may!" Mr. Clarke junior laughed in a singsong voice, at which Mr. Clarke senior groaned from behind the counter.

"Don't you mind my older brother; he always gets in such a tizzy when he's doing the books. Paper, paper everywhere, and not a drop to ink," Mr. Clarke junior declaimed, adopting a theatrical pose in front of an imagined audience.

The Clarke brothers were a neighborhood institution. They had inherited the business from their father, as he had from his father before him. For all anybody knew, there had probably been a Clarke in business when the Romans invaded, selling turnips or whatever vegetables were in vogue at the time. Mr. Clarke junior was in his forties, a flamboyant character with a penchant for hideously garish blazers that he had custom-made by a local tailor. Dazzling lemon-yellow, puce-pink, and powder-blue stripes danced between the tables of sensibly red tomatoes and downright soberly green cabbages. With his infectious high spirits and seemingly endless repertoire of quips and puns he was a great favorite of the ladies of the borough, both young and old, yet oddly enough he had remained a confirmed bachelor.

On the other hand, Mr. Clarke senior, the elder brother, couldn't have been more different. A staunch traditionalist, he frowned upon his brother's exuberance, both in appearance and in manner, insisting on the somber, time-honored dress code: the old shop coat his forefathers had sported. He was painfully clean and neat; his clothes could have been ironed while he was wearing them, such was the crispness of his mushroom brown shop coat, white shirt, and black tie. His shoes were so beautifully polished, and his hair, cut short at the back and sides, was oiled flat with such a glistening sheen, that from behind one would have had a hard time telling which way up he was.

The two brothers, within the shady green interior of the shop, were not unlike a caterpillar and a butterfly trapped within a shared cocoon. And with their constant bickering, the flippant joker and his straitlaced brother resembled a comedy team in constant rehearsal for a performance that would never take place.

"Expecting a rush on my lovely gooseberries, are you?" Mr. Clarke junior said in a mock Welsh accent and smiled cheekily at Chester, who, still propped against the door, made no effort at a response, as if struck dumb by the whole situation. "Ah, the strong, silent type," Mr. Clarke junior whispered with a wink as he danced down the stepladder and whirled in a flourish to come face to face with Will.

"It's young Master Burrows, is it not?" he said, his expression suddenly becoming serious. "I am so sorry to hear about your dear father. You've been in our thoughts and in our prayers," he continued, placing his right hand softly on his heart. "How is your mother bearing up? And that delightful sister of yours . . . ?"

"Fine, fine, both fine," Will said distractedly.

"She's a regular here, you know. A valued customer."

"Yes," Will blurted, a little too quickly, as he tried to pay attention to Mr. Clark junior while still keeping an eye on the door against which Chester remained buttressed as if his life depended on it.

"A highly valued customer," the invisible Mr. Clarke senior echoed from behind his counter, accompanied by the rustle of papers.

Mr. Clarke junior nodded and smiled. "Indeedy, indeedy. Now, you boys just park your pretty selves there while I get a little something for you to take home to your mother and sister." Before Will could utter a word, he had spun gracefully on his heel and practically tap-danced into the stockroom at the rear of the shop. Will took the opportunity to go over to the window to check on the whereabouts of their two pursuers. He recoiled with surprise.

"They're still there!" he said.

The two men were standing on the sidewalk, one directly in front of each window, staring in over the display tables of fruits and vegetables. It had now turned quite dark outside, and their faces glowed like ghostly white balloons under the illumination from the shop's interior. They were both still wearing their impenetrable glasses, and Will could make out their bizarre hats and the waxy shine of their angular coats with the unusual shoulder mantles. Their craggy, slanting faces and their clenched mouths looked uncompromising and brutal.

Chester spoke in a strained, low voice: "Get them to call the police." He gestured with his head at the counter, where they could hear Mr. Clarke senior grumbling as he thumped so forcefully on a stapler that it sounded like he was using a jackhammer.

Just then, Mr. Clarke junior waltzed back into the shop carrying a basket piled high with an impressive array of fruits, a large pink bow tied to its handle. He offered it to Will with both hands outstretched, as if he were about to break into an aria.

"For your mother and sister and, of course, you, old chap. A little something from me and the old codger over there, as a token of our sympathy for your predicament."

"Better a codger than an upstart," came the muffled voice of Mr. Clarke senior.

Pointing at the windows, Will opened his mouth to explain about the mysterious men.

"All clear," Chester said loudly.

"What's that, dear boy?" Mr. Clarke junior asked, looking past Will at Chester, who was now standing in front of one of the windows and peering up and down the street.

"What's all clear?" Mr. Clarke senior sprung up like a deranged jack-in-the-box.

"Papers!" Mr. Clarke junior ordered in the voice of an angry librarian, but his brother remained above the counter.

"Uh . . . just some kids," Will lied. "We were being chased."

"Boys will be boys!" Mr. Clarke junior giggled. "Now please do remember me to your dear sister, Miss Rebecca. You know, she really has such a good eye for quality produce. A gifted young lady."

"I will." Will nodded and forced a smile. "And thanks for this, Mr. Clarke."

"Oh, think nothing of it," he said.

"We do hope that your father returns home soon," Mr. Clarke senior said dolefully. "You shouldn't worry; these things happen from time to time."

"Well . . . it's like that Gregson boy . . . terrible thing, that," Mr. Clarke junior said with a knowing look and a sigh. "And then there was the Watkins family. . . ." Will and Chester watched him as he seemed to focus on a point somewhere between the ranks of the carrots and the cucumbers. "Such nice people, too. No one's seen hide nor hair of them since they—"

"It's not the same thing, not the same at all," Mr. Clarke senior interrupted his brother sharply, then coughed uneasily. "I don't think this is the time or place to bring that up, Junior.

A little unsympathetic, do you not think, given the situation?"

But "Junior" wasn't listening; he was in full flow now and not to be stopped. Crossing his arms and with his head tilted to one side, he took on the aura of one of the old biddies he habitually gossiped with. "Like the flippin' lost colony of Roanoke it was, when the police got there. Empty beds, the boys' uniforms all laid out for school the next day, but they were nowhere to be found, none of them. Mrs. W had ordered half a pound of our green beans that very morning, if I recall, and a couple of watermelons. Anyway, no sign of any of them anywhere."

"What . . . the watermelons?" Mr. Clarke senior asked in a deadpan voice.

"No, the *family*, you silly sausage," Mr. Clarke junior said, rolling his eyes.

In the silence that ensued, Will looked from Mr. Clarke junior to Mr. Clarke senior, who was staring daggers at his wistful sibling. He was beginning to feel as Alice must have when she'd stepped through the looking glass.

"*Ho-hum*, better get on," proclaimed Mr. Clarke junior with a last lingering look of sympathy at Will, and he tiptoed back up his stepladder, singing, "Beetroot to me, *mon petit chou* . . ."

Mr. Clarke senior had sunk out of sight once again and the sound of rattling papers resumed, accompanied by the whir of an old-fashioned adding machine. Will and Chester cautiously opened the shop door halfway and peeked nervously into the street.

"Anything?" Chester asked.

Will moved out onto the pavement in front of the shop.

"Nothing," he replied. "No sign of them."

"We should've called the police, you know."

"And told them what?" Will said. "That we were chased by two weirdos in sunglasses and silly hats and then they just disappeared?"

"Yes, exactly that," Chester said, irritated. "Who knows what they were after?" He suddenly looked up as the thought reoccurred to him. "What if they *were* the gang that took your dad?"

"Forget it—we don't know that."

"But the police . . . ," Chester said.

"Do you really want to go through all that hassle when we've got work to do?" Will interrupted him sharply, scanning Main Street up and down and feeling more at ease now that more people were around. At least they would be able to call for help if the two men turned up again. "The police would probably think we're just a couple of kids goofing around. It's not as if we've got any witnesses."

"Maybe," Chester agreed grudgingly as they started toward the Burrowses' house. "There's no shortage of nuts around here," he said, looking back at the Clarke brothers' shop, "that's for sure."

"It's safe now, anyway. They're gone, and if they do come back, we'll be ready," Will said confidently.

Strangely enough, the incident had not deterred him in the slightest. As he thought about it, quite the opposite was true: It confirmed to him that his father *had* been onto something, and now he was on the right track. Although he didn't mention any of this to Chester, his resolve to continue with the tunnel and his investigations hardened even further.

Will had begun to pick at the grapes in the garish basket,

and the pink ribbon, now undone, flapped in the breeze behind him. Chester appeared to have gotten over his misgivings and was looking expectantly at the basket, his hand poised to help himself.

"So do you want to bail? Or are you still going to help me?" Will quizzed him in a teasing voice, moving the basket tantalizingly out of his reach.

"Oh, all right, then, hand me a banana," his friend replied with a smile.

16

"ALL THIS evidence points to a deliberate dismantling," Will said, squatting next to Chester on a pile of rubble in the cramped confines of the workface.

They had now reclaimed about twenty feet of the tunnel, which had begun to dip down in a sharp decline, and found they were running critically short of timber. Will had hoped they would be able to salvage some of the original props and planking from the tunnel itself. What confounded them both was that very little of it was still there, and that much of the timber they did find was damaged beyond use. They had already stripped out every last piece they could from the other tunnel over at the Forty Pits, as well as removing the Stillson props, without bringing the whole excavation crashing down.

Will patted the work face, looking at it with a frown. "I just don't get it," he said.

"So what do you really think happened? That your dad pulled it in behind him?" Chester asked as he, too, looked at the plug of soil and solidly compacted rock that they had yet to remove.

"Backfilled it? No, that's impossible. And even if somehow he had, where are the struts? We'd have found more of them.

No, none of this makes any sense," Will said. Leaning forward, he picked up a handful of gravel. "Most of this is virgin infill. It's all been lugged here from somewhere else—precisely the same thing that happened at the Pits."

"But why go to all the trouble of filling it in when you could simply collapse the whole thing?" Chester asked, still mystified.

"Because then you'd have trenches opening up under people's houses or across their yards," Will replied despairingly.

"Oh, right," Chester agreed.

They were both exhausted. The last section had been particularly hard going, made up mostly of sizable chunks of rock, some of which even Chester found difficult to manhandle into the wheelbarrow by himself.

"I just hope we haven't got far to go." Chester sighed. "It's really beginning to get to me."

"Tell me about it." Will rested his head in his hands, staring vacantly at the tunnel wall opposite them. "You do realize, don't you, there might be nothing at all at the end of this? A dead end?"

Chester looked at him but was too tired to say anything. So they sat there in silence, deep in their own thoughts, and after a while Will spoke. "What was Dad thinking, doing all this and not telling us what he was up to? *Me*, especially," he said, with a look of sheer exasperation. "Why would he do that?"

"He must have had a good reason," Chester offered.

"But all the secrecy; keeping a secret journal. I don't understand it. We were never a family that kept things . . .

important things . . . from each other like that. So why wouldn't he have told me what he was up to?"

"Well, you had the Pits tunnel," Chester interjected.

"Dad knew about that. But you're right. I never bothered to tell Mum, because she's just not interested. I mean, we weren't exactly a . . ." Will hesitated, searching for the right word. ". . . *perfect* family, but we all got along and everyone sort of knew what everyone else was up to. Now everything's so messed up."

Chester rubbed some soil out of his ear. He looked at Will thoughtfully. "My mum thinks people shouldn't keep secrets from each other. She says they always have a way of coming out and causing nothing but trouble. She says a secret's just the same as a lie. That's what she tells my dad, anyway."

"And now I'm doing exactly that to Mum and Rebecca," Will said, bowing his head.

After Chester had gone and Will finally emerged from the cellar, he made straight for the kitchen, as he always did. Rebecca was sitting at the kitchen table opening the mail. Will noticed right away that his father's hoard of empty coffee jars, which had cluttered up the table for months, had vanished.

"What've you done with them?" he demanded, looking around the room. "With Dad's jars?"

Rebecca studiously ignored him as she scrutinized the postmark on an envelope.

"You threw them out, didn't you?" he said. "How could you do that?"

She glanced up at him briefly, as if he were nothing more than a tiresome gnat that she couldn't quite be bothered to swat, and then continued with the mail.

"I'm starving. Anything to eat?" he said, deciding it wasn't wise to ruffle her feathers by pursuing the matter, not so close to mealtime. As he passed her on the way to the fridge, he stopped to examine something lying to the side. "What's this?"

It was a package neatly wrapped in brown paper.

"It's addressed to Dad. I think we should open it," he said without a moment's hesitation, snatching up a dirty butter knife left on a plate by the sink. Cutting into the brown paper, he excitedly tore open the cardboard box inside, then ripped away a cocoon of bubble wrap to reveal a luminous sphere, glowing from its time in the darkness.

He held it up before him, his eyes sparkling with both excitement and the waning light emanating from the sphere. It was the object he'd read about in his father's journal.

Rebecca had stopped reading the telephone bill and had risen to her feet. She was looking at the sphere intently.

"There's a letter in here as well," Will said, reaching into the ravaged cardboard box.

"Here, let me see it," Rebecca said, her hand snaking toward the box. Will took a step back, holding the sphere in one hand while he shook open the letter with the other. Rebecca withdrew her hand and sat back down, watching her brother's face carefully as he leaned on the counter by the sink and began to read the letter aloud. It was from University College's physics department.

Dear Roger,

It was wonderful to hear from you again after all these years—it brought back warm memories of our time together at college. It was also good to catch up on your news—Steph and I would love to visit when convenient.

As regards the item, I apologize for taking so long to respond, but I wanted to be sure I had collated the results from all concerned. The upshot is that we are well and truly stumped.

As you specified, we did not breach or penetrate the glass casing of the sphere, so all our tests were noninvasive in nature.

On the matter of the radioactivity, no harmful emissions registered when it was tested—so at least I can put your mind at rest on that one.

A metallurgist carried out an MS on a microscopic shaving from the base of the metal cage, and he agreed with your view that it's Georgian. He thinks the cage is made out of pinchbeck, which is an alloy of copper and zinc invented by Christopher Pinchbeck (1670–1732). It was used as a substitute for gold and only produced for a short while. Apparently, the formula for this alloy was lost when the inventor's son, Edward, died. He also told me that genuine examples of this material are scarce, and it's hard to find an expert who can give an unequivocal identification. Unfortunately, I haven't yet been able to get the cage carbon dated to confirm its precise age—maybe next time?

What is particularly interesting is that an X-ray revealed a small, free-floating particle in the center of the sphere itself that does not alter its position even after rigorous agitation—this is puzzling, to say the least. Moreover, from a physical inspection, we agree with you that the sphere appears to be filled with two distinct liquid factions of differing densities. The turbulence you noted in these factions does not correspond to temperature variations, internal or external, but is unquestionably photoreactive—it only seems to be affected by a lack of light!

Here's the rub: The crew over in the chemistry department have never seen anything like it before. I had a fight on my hands to get it back from them—they were dying to crack the thing open in controlled conditions and run a full analysis. They tried spectroscopy when the sphere was at its brightest (at maximum excitation its emissions are in the visible spectrum—in layman's terms, not far off daylight, with a level of UV within acceptable safety parameters), and the "liquids" appeared to be predominantly helium- and silver-based. We can't make any more progress on this until you allow us to open it.

One hypothesis is that the solid particle at the center may be acting as a catalyst for a reaction that is triggered by the absence of light. We can't confirm how, at this juncture, or come up with any comparable reactions that would occur over such a long period of time, assuming the sphere really does date from the Georgian era. Remember, helium was not discovered until 1895—this is at odds with our estimate for the date of the metal casing.

In short, what we have here is a real conundrum. We would all very much welcome a visit from you for a multifaculty meeting so that we can schedule a program for further analysis of the item. It may even be useful for some of our team to drop into Highfield for a quick investigation into the background.

I look forward to hearing from you.

With kindest regards,

Tom

Professor Thomas Dee

Will put the letter on the table and met Rebecca's stare. He examined the sphere for a moment, then went over to the light switch and, shutting the door to the kitchen, flicked off the lights. They both watched as the sphere grew in brightness from a dim greenish luminescence to something that indeed approached daylight, all in a matter of seconds.

"Wow," he said in wonder. "And they're right, it doesn't even feel hot."

"You knew about this, didn't you? I can read you as easily as a comic book," Rebecca said, staring fixedly at Will's face, which was lit by the strange glow.

Will didn't respond as he turned on the lights but left the door shut. They watched as the sphere dulled again. "You know how you said no one was doing anything about finding Dad?" he said eventually.

"So?"

"Chester and I came across something of his and we've been . . . um, making our own inquiries."

"I knew it!" she said loudly. "What have you found out?"

"*Shh,*" Will hissed, glancing at the closed door. "Keep it down. I'm *certainly* not going to bother Mum with any of this. Last thing I want to do is get her hopes up. Agreed?"

"Agreed," Rebecca said.

"We found a book Dad was keeping notes in—a sort of journal," Will said slowly.

"Yes, and . . . ?"

As they sat at the kitchen table, Will recounted what he had read in the journal and also their encounter with the strange pallid men outside the Clarkes' shop.

He stopped short of telling her about the tunnel under the house. To him, that was just a *little* secret.

17

IT WAS a week later when Will and Chester finally made the breakthrough. Dehydrated from the heat at the work face, and with muscles that were cramped and fatigued by the relentless cycle of digging and tipping, they were on the verge of wrapping up for the day when Will's pickax struck a large block of stone and it tipped backward. A pitch-black opening yawned before them.

Their eyes locked onto the hole, which exhaled a damp and musty breeze into their tired and dirty faces. Chester's instincts screamed at him to back away, as if he were about to be sucked into the opening. Neither of them said a word; there were no great cheers or exultations as they gazed into the impenetrable darkness, with the dead calm of the earth all around them. It was Chester who broke the spell.

"I suppose I'd better be getting home, then."

Will turned and looked at him with incredulity, then spotted the flicker of a smirk on Chester's face. Filled with an immense sense of relief and accomplishment, Will couldn't help but erupt into a peal of hysterical laughter. He picked up a clod of dirt and hurled it at his grinning friend, who ducked, a low chuckle coming from beneath his yellow hard hat.

"You . . . you . . . ," Will said, searching for an appropriate word.

"Yeah, what?" Chester beamed. "Come on, then, let's have a look-see," he said, leaning into the gap next to Will.

Will shone his flashlight through the opening. "It's a cavern. . . . Can't make out much in there. . . . Must be pretty big. I think I can see some stalactites and stalagmites." Then he stopped. "Listen!"

"What is it?" whispered Chester.

"Water, I think. I can hear water dripping." He turned to Chester.

"You're kidding," Chester said, his face clouding with concern.

"No, I'm not. Could be a Neolithic stream. . . ."

"Here, let me see," said Chester, taking the flashlight from Will.

Tantalizing as it was, they decided against any further excavation there and then. They would resume the following day when they were fresh and better prepared. Chester went home; he was tired but quietly elated that their work had borne fruit. It was true that they were both badly in need of sleep, and Will was even, unusually, considering taking a bath as he swung the shelves back into position. He did the usual sweep-up and made his way lethargically upstairs to his room.

As he passed Rebecca's door, she called out to him. Will grimaced and held as still as a statue.

"Will, I *know* you're out there."

Will sighed and pushed open her door. Rebecca was lying on her bed, where she'd been reading a book.

"What's up?" asked Will, glancing around her room. He never ceased to be amazed at how infuriatingly clean and tidy she kept it.

"Mum said she needs to discuss something with us."

"When?"

"As soon as you came in, she said."

"Great, what now?"

Mrs. Burrows was in her usual position as they entered the living room. Slumped to one side in her armchair like a deflated mannequin, she raised her head dozily as Rebecca coughed to get her attention.

"Ah, good," she said, pushing herself into a more normal sitting position and, in the process, knocking a couple of remote controls onto the floor. "Oh, drat!" she exclaimed.

Will and Rebecca sat down on the sofa while Mrs. Burrows rummaged feverishly through the mound of videotapes at the base of her chair. Eventually coming up with both remotes, her hair hanging forward in straggles and her face flushed from the effort, she positioned them very precisely on the arm of her chair again. Then she cleared her throat and began.

"I think it's time we faced the possibility that your father isn't coming back, which means we have to make some rather crucial decisions." She paused and glanced at the television. A model in a spangled evening dress was revealing a large letter *V* on the game-show wall, where several other letters were already revealed. Mrs. Burrows muttered, "The Invisible Man," under her breath as she turned back to Will and Rebecca. "Your father's salary was stopped a few weeks ago and, as Rebecca tells me, we are already running on empty."

Will turned to Rebecca, who simply nodded in agreement, and their mother continued. "All the savings are gone and what with the mortgage and all the other expenses, we're going to have to cut our cloth. . . ."

"Cut our cloth?" asked Rebecca.

"'Fraid so," their mother said distantly. "There won't be anything coming in for a while, so we're going to have to downscale—sell whatever we can, including the house."

"What?" Rebecca said.

"And *you'll* have to take care of it. I'm not going to be around for a while. I've been advised to spend a little time in a . . . well . . . sort of hospital, somewhere I can rest and get myself back on form."

At this, Will raised his eyebrows, wondering just what "form" his mother could be referring to. She had been set in her current form for as long as he could remember.

His mother went on. "So while I'm gone you two will have to go and stay with your auntie Jean. She's agreed to look after you."

Will and Rebecca glanced at each other. An avalanche of images fell through Will's mind: the housing projects where Auntie Jean lived, its public spaces crammed with garbage bags and disposable diapers, and its graffitied elevators reeking of urine. The streets filled with burned-out cars and the endlessly screaming motorcycles of the gangs and small-time drug dealers. The sorry groups of drunks who sat on the benches, squabbling ineffectually among themselves as they downed their brown-bagged "Trampagne." "No way!" he suddenly blurted out as if waking from a nightmare, making Rebecca jump and his mother sit bolt upright, once again knocking the remotes off the arm of her chair.

"Drat!" she said again, craning her neck to see where they had fallen.

"I'm not going to live there. I couldn't stand it, not for a second. What about school? What about my friends?" Will said.

"What friends?" Mrs. Burrows replied spitefully.

"You can't really expect us to go there, Mum. It's awful, it smells, the place is a pigsty," Rebecca piped up.

"*And* Auntie Jean smells," Will added.

"Well, there's nothing I can do about that. I have to get some rest; the doctor said I'm very stressed, so there's no debate. We've got to sell the house, and you're just going to have to stay with Jean until—"

"Until what? You get a job or something?" Will put in sharply.

Mrs. Burrows glared at him. "This is not good for me. The doctor said I should avoid confrontation. This conversation is over," she snapped suddenly, and turned on her side again.

Back out in the hall, Will sat on the bottom step of the stairs, numb, while Rebecca stood with her arms folded, leaning against the wall.

"Well, that's an end to it all," she said. "At least I'm going away next week—"

"No, no, no . . . not now!" Will bellowed at her, holding up his hand. "Not with all this going on!"

"Yeah, maybe you're right," she said, shaking her head. Then they both lapsed into silence.

After a moment, Will stood up decisively. "But I know what I have to do."

"What?"

"Take a bath."

"You need one," Rebecca said, watching him climb wearily up the stairs.

18

"MATCHES."

"Check."

"Candles."

"Check."

"Swiss Army knife."

"Check."

"Spare flashlight."

"Check."

"Balls of string."

"Check."

"Chalk and rope."

"Yep."

"Compass."

"Umm . . . yep."

"Extra batteries for the helmet lights."

"Check."

"Camera and notebook."

"Check, check."

"Pencils."

"Check."

"Water and sandwiches."

"Ch—planning a long stay, are we?" Chester asked as he looked at the absurdly large packet wrapped in aluminum foil. They were carrying out a last-minute equipment check down in the Burrowses' cellar, using a list Will had made at school earlier that day during his home ec class. After ticking them off, they stowed each item in their backpacks. When they were finished, Will closed the flap on his and shrugged it onto his back.

"OK, let's do it," he said with a look of sheer determination on his face as he reached for his trusty shovel.

Will drew back the shelves and, once both he and Chester were inside, pulled them shut again and secured them by means of a makeshift latch he'd rigged up. Then Will squeezed past Chester to lead the way, moving swiftly ahead on all fours.

"Hey, wait for me," Chester called after him, quite taken aback by his friend's enthusiasm.

At the work face, they dislodged the remaining blocks of stone, which fell away into the darkness and landed with dull splashes. Chester was about to speak when Will preempted him.

"I know, I know, you think we're about to be swept away in a flood of raw sewage or something." Will peered through the enlarged opening. "I can see where the rocks fell—they're sticking up out of the water. It can only be about ankle deep."

With that, he turned around and started to climb backward through the hole. He paused on the brink to grin at Chester, then ducked out of sight, leaving his friend dumbfounded for an instant, until Chester heard Will's feet land in the water with a loud splash.

There was a drop of about six feet. "Hey, pretty cool," Will said as Chester scrambled through after him. Will's voice echoed eerily around the cavern, which was approximately ten feet in height and at least thirty feet long, and, as far as they could make out, crescent shaped, with much of the floor submerged. They had entered near one end, and so were only able to see as far as the curve of the wall allowed.

Stepping out of the water, they shone their flashlights around for a few seconds, but when the beams came to rest on the side of the cavern nearest to them they were both immediately transfixed. Will held his flashlight steady on the intricate rows of stalactites and stalagmites, all of varying sizes, from the width of pencils to much larger ones as thick as the trunks of young trees. The stalactites speared down as their counterparts reached up, some meeting to form columns, and the ground was covered with overlapping swells of the encrusted calcite.

"It's a grotto," Will said quietly, reaching out to feel the surface of an almost translucent milky white column. "Isn't it just beautiful? Looks like icing on a cake or something."

"I think it looks more like frozen snot," Chester said in a whisper, also touching a small column, as if he didn't believe what he was seeing. He drew back his hand and rubbed his fingers together with an expression of distaste.

Will laughed, ramming the heel of his hand against a stalactite with a soft thud. "Hard to believe it's actually rock, isn't it?"

"And the whole place is made of it," Chester said, turning to look farther along the wall. He shivered slightly from the chill air and scrunched up his nose. The whole chamber smelled dank and stale—not very pleasant at all. But to Will it was the sweet smell of success. He'd always dreamed of finding something important, but this grotto surpassed his wildest expectations. So strong was his exhilaration, Will almost felt intoxicated.

"Yes!" he said, triumphantly punching the air. At that instant, standing there in the grotto, he was the great adventurer he'd always dreamed of being, like Howard Carter in Tutankhamen's burial chamber. He whipped his head this way and that, trying to take in everything at once.

"You know, it probably took thousands of years for all this to grow. . . ." Will was babbling as he took a step backward, stopping short as his foot snagged on something. He bent down to see what it was; a small object protruded from the flowstone. Dark and flaking, its color had seeped into the pale whiteness around it. He tried to work it free, but his fingers slipped off. It was stuck solid.

"Shine your light on this, Chester. It feels like a rusty bolt or something. But it can't be."

"Uh . . . you might want to look at this . . . ," Chester replied, his voice a little shaky.

At the center of the grotto, in the deepest part of the clouded pool that lay there, stood the remains of a massive machine of some description. The boys' flashlights revealed ranks of large red-brown cogwheels that were still held together within what remained of a shattered cast-iron frame so tall that in places the stalactites growing from the rock ceiling above touched it. It was as if a locomotive had been mercilessly disemboweled and then left there to die.

"What the heck is it?" Chester asked as Will stood silently beside him, examining the scene.

"Beats me," Will answered. "And there are bits of metal all over the place. Look!"

He was shining his flashlight around the margins of the water, following them as far he could into the deepest reaches of the cavern. Will's first thought had been that the banks were streaked with minerals or something similar, but on closer inspection he discovered they were littered with more bolts like the one he'd just found, all with chunky hexagonal heads. In addition to these, there were spindles and countless pieces of jagged cast-iron shrapnel. The red oxide from these intermingled with darker, inky streaks, which, from their appearance, Will took to be oil spills.

As they stood there in amazed silence and surveyed this worthless treasure trove, they became aware of a faint scratching sound.

"Did you hear that?" Chester whispered as they trained their lights in the direction of the sound.

Will moved a little farther into the cavern, treading carefully on the uneven floor, now invisible beneath the water.

"What was it?" gasped Chester.

"*Shh!*" Will stopped and they both listened, peering around.

A sudden movement and a small splash made them jump. Then a sleek white object leaped from the rippling water and streaked along one of the metal members, stopping still on the top of a huge gearwheel. It was a large rat with a glistening, perfectly white coat and big, bright pink ears. It wiped its snout with its paws and flicked its head, spraying droplets into the air. Then it reared up on its hind legs, its whiskers twitching and vibrating in their flashlight beams as it sniffed the air.

"Look! It doesn't have any eyes," Will hissed excitedly.

Chester shuddered in response. Sure enough, where there should have been eyes there was not even the tiniest break in the sleek, snowy fur.

"Yuck, that's disgusting!" Chester exclaimed as he took a step back.

"Adaptive evolution," Will replied.

"I don't care what it is!"

The animal twitched and arched its head in the direction of Chester's voice. Then, the next instant, it was gone, diving into the water and swimming to the opposite bank, where it scurried away.

"Great! He's probably gone to get his friends," Chester said. "This place will be swarming with them in a minute."

Will laughed. "It's only a stupid rat!"

"That was no normal rat—whoever heard of *eyeless* rats?"

"Come on, you big baby. Don't you remember the Three Blind Mice?" Will said with a wry grin as they began to move around the crescent bank, playing their beams into the nooks and crannies in the walls and up to the ceiling above them. Chester was stepping apprehensively between the rocks and iron debris, constantly peering behind him for an imagined army of sightless rats. "I hate this," he grumbled.

As they approached the shadows at the far end of the grotto, Will increased his pace. Chester did likewise, determined not to be left behind.

"Whoa!" Will stopped in his tracks, Chester bumping into him. "Just look at that!"

Set into the rock was a door.

Will's flashlight flicked over its dull, scarred surface—it looked ancient but substantial, with rivet heads like halves of golf balls spaced around its frame and three massive handles down one side. He reached forward to touch it.

"Hey! No!" Chester fretted.

But Will paid him no heed and tapped lightly on the door with his knuckles. "It's metal," he said, running his palm over the surface—shiny, black, and uneven, like burned molasses.

"So what? You're *not* thinking of going in there, are you?"

Will turned to him, his hand still resting on the door. "This is the only way my dad could've gone. Dead straight I am!"

With that he reached up, grasped the topmost handle, and tried to pull down on it. It refused to budge. He thrust his flashlight at Chester and then, using both hands, tried again, heaving down with all his weight. Nothing happened.

"Try the other way," suggested Chester resignedly.

Will tried again, this time pushing upward. It creaked a little at first and then, to his surprise, swiveled smoothly until it clunked decisively into what he assumed was the open position. He did the same with the other two handles, then stood back. Retrieving his flashlight from Chester, he placed one hand against the center of the door, ready to push it open.

"Well, here goes," he said to Chester, who for once did not raise any objection.

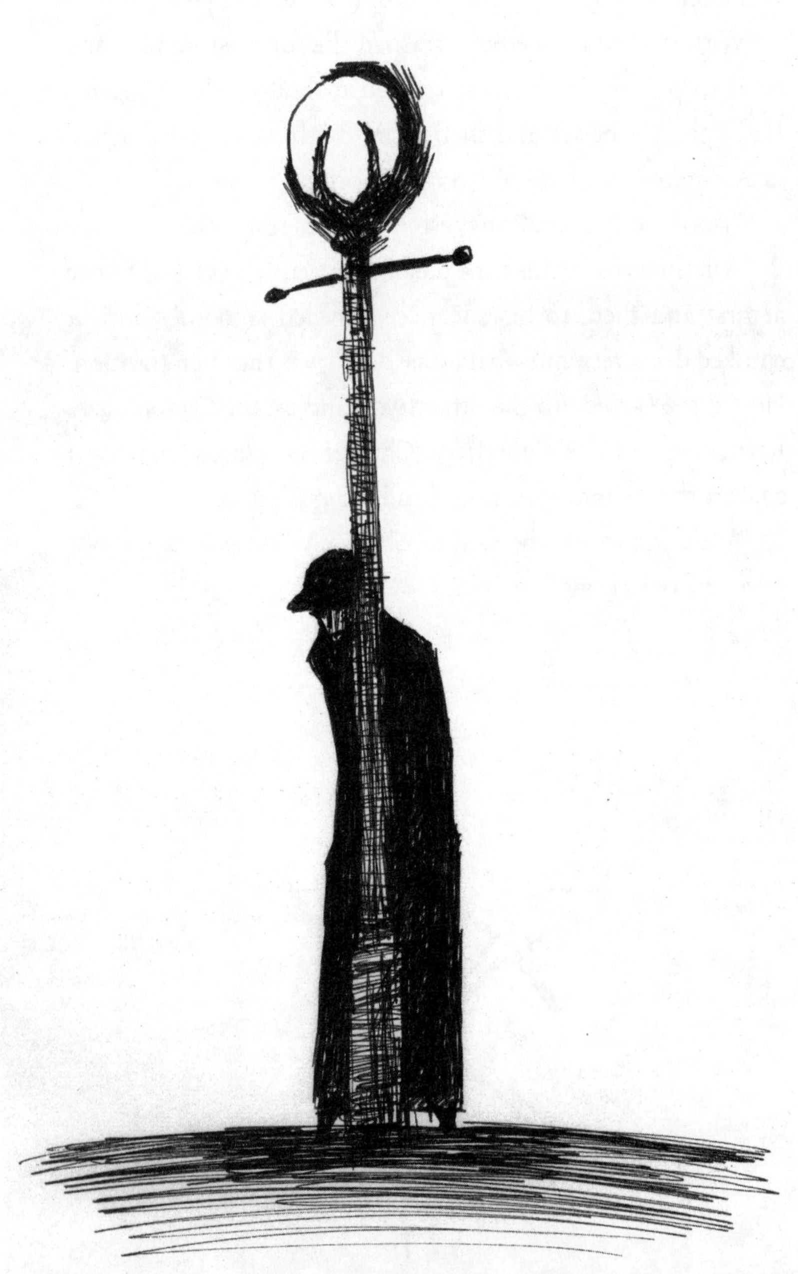

PART 2

THE COLONY

19

THE DOOR swung open with a subdued metallic groan. Will and Chester paused for a moment, adrenaline coursing through their veins as they directed their lights into the dark space beyond. They were both ready to turn and flee in an instant but, hearing and seeing nothing, they stepped carefully over the metal lip at the base of the door frame, holding their breath while their hearts pounded in their ears.

Their flashlight beams licked unsteadily around the interior. They were standing in an almost cylindrical chamber, no more than ten feet long, with pronounced corrugations along its length. In front was another door, identical to the one they had just come through except for a small panel of misty glass held within a riveted frame, like a small porthole.

"Looks like some sort of air lock," Will observed as he moved farther into the chamber, his boots thudding on the grooved iron flooring. "Get a move on," he said unnecessarily to Chester, who had followed him in and, without being asked, was closing the door behind them, turning the handles so all three were engaged again.

"Better leave everything as we find it," Chester said. "Just in case."

Having tried to see through the opaque porthole with no success, Will cranked open the three handles on the second door and pushed it outward. There was a small hiss, as if air were leaking from a tire valve. Chester threw Will a questioning look, which he ignored as he ventured into the short adjoining room. About ten feet square, it had walls like the keel of an old boat, a patchwork quilt of rusting metal plates held together with crude welds.

"There's a number on here," Chester observed as he locked up the handles on the second door. Peeling and yellowing with age, there was a large figure 5 painted on the door beneath the murky porthole.

As they moved cautiously forward, their lights picked out the first details of something in front of them. It was a trellis of interwoven metal bars, running from floor to ceiling and completely blocking the way. Will's light projected jerky shadows against the surfaces beyond as he pushed on the trellis with his hand. It was solid and unyielding. He tucked his flashlight away and, gripping the damp metal, pulled himself as close as he could.

"I can see the walls, and I think I can see the roof, but . . . ," he said, twisting his head around, ". . . but the floor is—"

"A long way down," Chester interjected, the brim of his hard hat scraping against the trellis as he tried to get a better view.

"I can tell you there's nothing remotely like this on the town plans. Do you think I'd have missed something like this!" Will said, as if to dispel any self-doubt that he might have indeed overlooked something so remarkable on the maps.

"Wait, hang on, Will! Look at the cables!" Chester said loudly as he spied the chunky matte lines through the trellis. "It's an elevator shaft," he added enthusiastically, his spirits suddenly buoyed by the thought that, far from being something inexplicable and menacing, what they had encountered was recognizable and familiar. *It was an elevator shaft.* For the first time since they had left the relative normality of the Burrowses' cellar, Chester felt safe, imagining that the shaft must descend to something as ordinary as a railway tunnel. He even dared to let himself think that this could mean the end of their half-baked expedition.

He looked down to his right, located a handle, and, yanking on it, slid the panel across. It grated horribly on its runners. Will took a step back in surprise: In his haste, he'd failed to notice that the barrier was in fact a sliding gate, and he now watched as it opened before them. Once Chester had pushed it all the way back they had an unobstructed view of the dark shaft. Their helmet lamps played on the heavy greased cables running down the middle of the shaft into the darkness below. Into the abyss.

"It's one heck of a drop." Chester shivered, gripping the edge of the old elevator gate tightly as his gaze was swallowed up by the vertiginous depths. Will turned his attention from the shaft and began to look around the iron chamber behind them. Sure enough, attached to the wall at his side he found a small box made of dark wood with a tarnished brass button protruding from its center.

"Yes!" he cried triumphantly and, without a word to Chester, pressed the button, which felt greasy beneath his fingertip.

Nothing happened.

He tried again.

And once more, *nothing.*

"Chester, close the gate, close it!" he shouted, unable to contain his excitement.

Chester rammed it across, and Will jabbed at the button again. There was a distant vibration, and a clank reverberated from deep inside the shaft. And then the cables jerked into life and began to move, the shaft filling with a loud, whining groan from the winching equipment, which must have been housed not far above them. They listened to the clanging echoes of the approaching elevator.

"Bet it's the way down to a subway station." Chester turned to Will, a look of anticipation on his face.

Will frowned with annoyance. "No way. I *told* you there's nothing here. This is something else altogether."

Chester's optimism evaporated, his face falling as they both approached the gate again, pushing their heads against it so their helmet lamps flicked into the black shaft.

"Well, if we don't know what this is . . . ," Chester said, ". . . there's still time to go back."

"Come on, we can't give up. Not now."

They both stood listening to the approaching elevator for a couple of minutes, until Chester spoke. "What if there's someone in it?" he said, drawing back from the gate and starting to panic again.

But Will couldn't tear himself away. "Hang on, I can't quite . . . It's still too dark . . . Wait! I can see it, I can see it! It's like a miners' cage lift!" Staring hard at the elevator as it inched ponderously toward them, Will found he was able to see through the grille that formed its roof. He turned to Chester. "Relax, will you? There's nobody in it."

"I didn't really think there was," Chester retorted defensively.

"Yeah, right, you big wuss."

Satisfying himself that it was empty, Chester shook his head and sighed with relief as the elevator arrived at their level. It shuddered to a clangorous halt, and Will lost no time pulling back the gate and taking a few steps in. Then he turned to Chester, who was hovering on the brink, looking decidedly uncomfortable.

"I don't know, Will, it looks pretty risky," he said, his gaze shifting around the car's interior. It had cage walls and a scratched steel-plate floor, and the whole thing was covered with what looked like years of oily grime and dust.

"Come on, Chester, this is the *big time*!" Not for a second did Will stop to consider there was any way to go but down. If he'd been filled with exhilaration at the discovery of the grotto, then this surpassed even his wildest expectations. "We're going to be famous!" he laughed.

"Oh sure, I can see it now . . . *Two dead in elevator disaster!*" Chester rejoined morosely, stretching his hands in front of him to indicate the newspaper headline. "It just doesn't look safe . . . probably hasn't been serviced in ages."

Without a moment's hesitation Will jumped up and down a couple of times, his boots clanging on the metal floor. Chester looked on, terrified, as the cage rattled.

"Safe as houses." Will grinned impishly and, resting his hand on the brass lever inside the car, looked Chester in the eye. "So are you coming . . . or are you going back to fight the rat?"

That was enough for Chester, who immediately moved into the car. Will slid the gate shut behind him, and, when he pushed and held down the lever, the elevator once again shuddered into motion and began to descend. Through the caging, interrupted every so often by the dark mouths of other levels, they saw the rock face slowly sweeping by in muted shades of browns and blacks and grays, ochres and yellows.

A damp breeze blew around them, and at one point Chester shone his flashlight through the grille above them, up into the shaft and onto the cables, which looked like a pair of dirty laser beams fading into deep space.

"How far down do you think it goes?" Chester asked.

"How should I know?" Will replied gruffly.

In fact, it was almost five minutes before the elevator finally came to a stop with an abrupt and bone-shaking bump that made them fall against the sides of the cage.

"Maybe I should have let go of the lever a bit earlier," Will said sheepishly.

Chester threw his friend a blank look, as if nothing really mattered anymore, and then they both stood there, their lights throwing giant diamond silhouettes from the elevator cage onto the walls beyond.

"Here we go again," Chester sighed as he slid back the gate, and Will pushed impatiently past him into another metal-plate room, rushing through it to get to the door at the far end.

"This is just like the one above," Will noted as he busied himself with the three handles on the side of the door. This one had a large zero painted on it.

They took a few tentative steps into the cylindrical room, their boots ringing out against the undulating sheet-metal flooring and their flashlight beams illuminating yet another door in front of them.

"Seems we only have one way to go," Will said, striding toward it.

"These chambers look like something out of a submarine," Chester muttered under his breath.

Standing on tiptoe, Will looked through the small glass porthole, but couldn't make out anything on the other side. And when he tried to shine his flashlight through it, the grease and the scratches on the ancient surface only refracted the beam, so that the glass became more opaque than ever.

"Useless," he said to himself.

Passing his flashlight to Chester, he rotated the three handles and then pushed against the door. "It's stuck!" he grunted. He tried again without success. "Give me a hand, will you?"

Chester joined in, and with their shoulders braced against the door they pushed and shoved with all their might. Suddenly it burst open with a loud hiss and a massive rush of air, and they stumbled through into the unknown.

Their boots now ground on cobblestones as they regained their footing and straightened up. Before them was a scene that they both knew, for as long as they lived, they would never forget.

It was a street.

They found themselves in a huge space almost as wide as a highway, which curved off into the distance to their left and right. And looking across to the opposite side, they saw the road was lit by a row of tall street lamps.

But what stood beyond these lights, on the far side of the cavern, was what really took their breath away. Stretching as far as they could see, in both directions, were *houses*.

As if in a trance, Will and Chester moved toward this apparition. As they did so, the door slammed shut behind them with such force that they both wheeled around.

"A breeze?" Chester asked his friend, with a baffled expression.

Will shrugged in response—he could definitely feel a faint draft on his face. He put his head back and sniffed, catching the stale mustiness in the air. Chester was shining his flashlight at the door and then began to play it over the wall above, illuminating the huge blocks of stone that formed it. He raised the circle of light, higher and higher, and their eyes were compelled to follow the wall up into the shadows above, where it met the opposing wall in a gentle arch, like the vaulted roof of a huge cathedral.

"What is all this, Will? What is this place?" Chester asked, grabbing him by the arm.

"I don't know—I've never heard about anything like this before," Will replied, staring wide-eyed around the huge street. "It's truly awesome."

"What do we do now?"

"I think we . . . we should have a look around, don't you? This is just incredible," Will marveled. He struggled to order his thoughts, infused with the first heady flush of discovery and consumed with the irresistible urge to explore and to learn more. "Must record it," he muttered as he hoisted out his camera and began to take photographs.

"Will, don't! The flash!"

"Oops, sorry." He slung the camera around his neck. "Got a little carried away there." Without another word to Chester, he suddenly strode across the cobblestones toward the houses. Chester followed behind his fellow explorer, half crouched and grumbling under his breath as he scanned up and down the road for any sign of life.

The buildings appeared to be carved out of the very walls themselves, like semi-excavated architectural fossils. Their roofs were fused with the gently arching walls behind, and where one might have expected chimneys there was an intricate network of brick ducts sprouting from the tops, which ran up the walls and disappeared above, like petrified smoke plumes. As they reached the sidewalk, the only sound apart from their footfalls was a low humming, which seemed to be coming from the very ground itself. They paused briefly to inspect one of the streetlights.

"It's like the—"

"Yes," Will interrupted, unconsciously touching his pocket where his father's luminescent orb was carefully wrapped in a handkerchief. The glass sphere of the streetlight was a much larger version of this, almost the size of a soccer ball, and held in place by a four-pronged claw atop a cast-iron post. A pair of snow-white moths circled erratically about it like epileptic moons, their dry wings fluttering against the surface of the glass.

Will stiffened abruptly and, lifting his head back, sniffed again—looking not unlike the eyeless rat on the cogwheel.

"What's up?" Chester asked with trepidation. "Not more trouble?"

"No, just thought . . . I smelled something. It was kind of like . . . ammonia . . . something sharp. Didn't you notice it?"

"No." Chester sniffed several times. "I hope it's not poisonous."

"Well, it's gone now, whatever it was. And we're fine, aren't we?"

"Suppose so. But do you think anyone really lives here?"

Chester replied as he looked up at the windows of the buildings. They turned their attention to the nearest house, silent and ominous, as if daring them to approach.

"I don't know."

"Well, what's it all doing here, then?"

"Only one way to find out," Will said as they crept gingerly toward the house. It was simple and elegant, constructed of sandstone masonry, almost Georgian in style. They could just make out heavily embroidered curtains behind the twelve-paned windows on either side of the front door, which was painted with thick green gloss and had on it a door knocker and bell push of deeply burnished brass.

"One sixty-seven," Will said in wonder as he spotted the digits above the knocker.

"What *is* this place?" Chester was whispering as Will caught a faint flicker of light in a chink between the curtains. It shimmered, as if it came from a fire.

"*Shhh!*" he said as he crept over and crouched down below the window, then slowly rose above the sill and peered with one eye through the small gap. His mouth gaped open in silent awe. He could see a fire burning in a hearth. Above this was a dark mantelpiece on which there were various glass ornaments. And as the light from the fire danced around the room, he could just make out some chairs and a sofa, and the walls, which were covered in framed pictures of varying sizes.

"Come on, what's there?" Chester said nervously, continually looking back at the empty street as Will squashed his face against the dirty pane of glass.

"You won't believe this!" Will replied, moving aside to let

his friend see for himself. Chester eagerly pressed his nose against the window.

"Wow! It's a real room!" he said, turning to look at Will, only to find him already on the move, working his way along the front of the house. He stopped as he reached the corner of the building.

"Hey! Wait for me," Chester hissed, terrified he was going to be left behind.

Between this building and the next one in the row, a short alley ran straight back to the tunnel wall. Will poked his head around the corner and, once he was satisfied it was clear, beckoned to Chester that they should move on to the next house.

"This one's number 166," Will said as he examined its front door, which was almost identical to the one on the first house. He tiptoed to the window but was unable to see anything at all through the dark panes.

"What's there?" Chester asked.

Will held a finger to his lips, then retraced his steps back to the front door. Looking at it closely, a thought occurred to him and his eyes narrowed. Recognizing the look, Chester reached out to try to stop him, spluttering, "Will, no!"

But it was too late. Will had barely touched the door when it swung inward. They exchanged glances and then both inched slowly inside, twinges of excitement and fear simultaneously surging through them.

The hallway was spacious and warm, and they both became aware of a potpourri of smells—cooking, fire smoke—and of human habitation. It was laid out just like any normal house; wide stairs started halfway down the corridor, with brass carpet rails at the base of each riser. Waxed wood paneling ran up to a handrail, above which was wallpaper of light and dark green stripes. Portraits in ornate, dull-gold-colored frames hung on the walls, depicting sturdy-looking people with huge shoulders and pale faces. Chester was peering at one of these when a terrible thought struck him.

"They look just like the men who chased us," he said. "Oh, great, we're in a house that belongs to one of those nutters, aren't we? This is freaking nuttytown!" he added as the awful realization hit him.

"Listen!" Will hissed. Chester stood riveted to the spot as Will cocked an ear in the direction of the stairs, but there was nothing, only an oppressive silence.

"I thought I heard . . . no . . . ," he said and moved toward the open doorway to their left, then looked cautiously around the corner. "This is awesome!" He couldn't help himself—he had to go in. And by this time, Chester was also being swept along by the need to know more.

A cheery fire crackled in the hearth. Around the walls were small pictures and silhouettes in brass and gilt frames. One in particular caught Will's eye: THE MARTINEAU HOUSE, he read on the inscription below. It was a small oil painting of what appeared to be a stately home surrounded by rolling grasslands.

By the fireplace were chairs upholstered in a dark red material with a dull sheen. There was a dining table in one corner and in another a musical instrument that Will recognized as a harpsichord. In addition to the light from the fire the room was lit by two tennis-ball-size spheres suspended from the ceiling in ornate pinchbeck cages. The whole thing brought to Will's mind a museum his father had taken him to with a display called "How We Used To Live." As he looked around, he reflected that this room wouldn't have been out of place there.

Chester sidled up to the dining table, where two plain white bone-china cups sat in their saucers.

"There's something in these," he said with an expression of sheer surprise. "Looks like tea!"

He hesitantly touched the side of one of the cups and looked up at Will, even more startled.

"It's still warm. What's going on here? Where are all the people?"

"Don't know," Will replied. "It's like . . . like . . ."

They looked at each other with dumbfounded expressions.

"I honestly don't know what it's like," Will admitted.

"Let's just get out of here," Chester said, and they both bolted for the door. As they reached the sidewalk again, Chester collided with Will as he stopped dead.

"What are we running for?" Will asked.

"Uh . . . The . . . Well . . . ," Chester blathered in confusion as he struggled to put his concerns into words. For a moment they lingered indecisively under the sublime radiance of a streetlight. Then Chester noticed with dismay that Will was staring intently at the road as it curved into the distance. "Come on, Will. Let's just go home." Chester shivered as he glanced back at the house and up at the windows, certain someone was there. "This place gives me the creeps."

"No," Will replied, not even looking at his friend. "Let's follow the road for a bit. See where it goes. Then we can leave.

I promise—all right?" he said, already striding off.

Chester stood his ground for a moment, looking longingly across the road at the metal doorway through which they had first come. Then, with a groan of resignation, he followed Will along the line of houses. Many had lights in their windows, but as far as they could tell there were no signs of any occupants.

As they came to the last house in the row, where the road curved off to the left, Will paused for a moment, deliberating whether to go on or call it a day. His voice squeaking with desperation, Chester started pleading that enough was enough and that they should turn back when they became aware of a sound behind them. It began like the rustling of leaves but quickly grew in intensity to a dry, rippling cacophony.

"What the—" Will exclaimed.

Shooting down from the roof, a flock of birds the size of sparrows dived down toward them like living tracer bullets. Will and Chester instinctively ducked, raising their arms to shield their faces as the pure white birds whirled around them in synchronized agitation.

Will began to laugh. "Birds! It's only birds!" he said, swatting at the mischievous flock but never making contact. Chester lowered his arms and began to laugh, too, a little nervously, as the birds darted between them. Then, as quickly as they'd appeared, the birds swept upward and vanished around the bend in the tunnel. Will straightened up and staggered a few steps after them, then froze.

"Shops!" he announced with a startled voice.

"Huh?" Chester said.

Sure enough, down one side of the street stretched a parade

of bowfronted shops. Without speaking, they both began to walk toward them.

"This is unreal," Chester muttered as they reached the first shop, with windows of handblown glass that distorted the wares inside like badly made lenses.

"Jacobson Cloths," Chester read from the shop sign, then peered at the rolls of material laid out in the eerie, green-lit interior.

"A grocer's," Will said as they moved on.

"And this one's some sort of hardware shop," Chester observed.

Will gazed up at the arching roof of the cavern. "You know, by now we must nearly be under Main Street."

Peering into the windows and soaking up the strangeness of the ancient shops, they kept walking, driven by their careless curiosity, until they came to a place where the tunnel split into three. The center fork appeared to descend into the earth at a steep angle.

"OK, that's it," Chester said resolutely. "We're leaving now. I'm *not* going to get lost down here." All his instincts were screaming that they should turn back.

"All right," Will agreed, "but—"

He was just stepping off the sidewalk onto the cobbled road when there was an earsplitting crash of iron on stone. In a blinding flash, four white horses bore down on him, sparks spraying from their hooves, breathing hard and pulling behind them a sinister black coach. Will didn't have time to react, because at that very instant they were both yanked off their feet and hoisted into the air by the scruffs of their necks.

A single man held them both, dangling helplessly, in his huge gnarled hands. "Interlopers!" the man shouted, his voice fierce and gravelly as he lifted the pair up to his face and inspected them with a look of repugnance. Will tried to bring his shovel up to beat him off, but it was wrested from his grasp.

The man was wearing a ridiculously small helmet and a dark blue uniform of coarse material that rasped as he moved. Beside a row of dull buttons, Will caught sight of a five-pointed star of orange-gold material stitched onto the coat. Their massive, menacing captor was clearly some sort of policeman.

"Help," Chester mouthed silently at his friend, his voice deserting him as they were buffeted about in the man's viselike grip.

"We've been expecting you," the man rumbled.

"What?" Will stared at him blankly.

"Your father said you'd be joining us before long."

"My father? Where's my father? What have you done with him? Put me down!" Will tried to swivel around, kicking out at the man.

"No use wriggling." The man hoisted the struggling boy even higher in the air and sniffed at him. "Topsoilers. Disgusting!"

Will sniffed back.

"Don't smell too good yourself."

The man gave Will a look of withering scorn, then held up Chester and sniffed at him, too. In sheer desperation, Chester tried to head-butt the man. He jerked his face away, but not before Chester, with a wild swing of his arm, had swiped his helmet. It spun from his head, exposing his pale scalp, which was covered with short tufts of wispy white hair.

The man shook Chester violently by the collar and then, with a horrible growl, knocked the boys' heads together. Although their hard hats protected them from any injury as they crashed noisily against each other, they were so shocked by his ferocity that they immediately abandoned any further thoughts of resistance.

"Enough!" the man shouted, and the stunned boys heard a chorus of bitter laughter from behind him, becoming aware for the first time of the other men who were peering at them with pale, unsmiling eyes.

"Think you can come down here and break into our houses?" the man growled as he swept them toward the center fork, where the road descended.

"It's the clink for you two," snarled someone behind them.

They were frog-marched unceremoniously through the streets, which were now filling with people emerging from various doorways and alleys to gawp at this unfortunate pair of strangers. Half dragged and half stumbling, each time they lost their footing the boys would be yanked savagely to their feet by the enormous officer. It was as if he was playing to the audience and making a big show of how he had complete control over the situation.

In all their confusion and panic, Will and Chester looked frantically around in the vain hope that they might find an opportunity for escape, or that someone would come to their rescue. But their faces drained of blood as this hope receded, and they realized the futility of their plight. They were being dragged deeper into the bowels of the earth, and there was absolutely nothing they could do about it.

Before they knew it, they were heaved around a bend in the tunnel, and the space around them opened up. They were struck dumb by a dizzying confusion of bridges, aqueducts, and raised walkways crisscrossed above a lattice of cobbled streets and lanes, all bordered with buildings.

Dragged on at an impossible rate by the policeman, they were watched by huddled groups of people, their wide faces curious and yet impassive. But not all the faces were like those of their captor or the men who had pursued them up in Highfield, with their wan skin and washed-out eyes. If it hadn't been for their old-fashioned dress, some would have appeared quite normal and could easily have passed unnoticed in any English street.

"Help, help!" Chester cried hopelessly as he halfheartedly resumed his efforts to extricate himself from the policeman's grip. But Will hardly noticed any of this. His attention had been seized by a tall, thin individual standing beside a lamppost, whose hard face was set atop a stark white collar and a long dark coat that reflected the light as if it was made from polished leather. He stood out strikingly from the squat people around him, his shoulders slightly bent over like a highly strung bow. His whole being emanated evil, and his dark eyes never left Will's, who felt a wave of dread wash over him.

"I think we're in real trouble here, Chester," he said, unable to tear his gaze from the sinister man, whose thin lips were twisted into a sardonic smile.

20

WILL and Chester stumbled and tripped as they were hauled up a small flight of stairs into a single-story building nestling between what Will took to be drab offices or factories. Once inside, the policeman pulled them to an abrupt halt and, spinning them around, roughly yanked their bags off their backs. Then he literally hurled the two boys at a slippery oak bench, its surface dipping here and there with polished indentations, as if years of wrongdoers had rubbed along its length. Will and Chester gasped as their backs slammed against the wall and the breath was knocked out of them.

"Don't you move!" the policeman roared, positioning himself between them and the entrance. By craning his neck forward, Will could just see past the man and through the half-windowed doors into the street outside, where a mob had gathered. Many were jostling for a view, and a few started to shout angrily and wave their fists as they caught sight of Will. He quickly sat back and tried to catch Chester's eye, but his friend, frightened out of his wits, was staring fixedly at the floor in front of him.

Will noticed a bulletin board next to the door, on which a large number of black-rimmed papers were pinned. Most of the writing was too small to decipher from where he sat, but he could just make out handwritten headings such as ORDER or EDICT, followed by strings of numbers.

The walls of the station were painted black from the floor up to a handrail, above which they were an off-white color, peeling in places and streaked with dirt. The ceiling itself was an unpleasant nicotine yellow with deep cracks running in every direction, like a road map of some unidentified country. On the wall directly above him was a picture of a forbidding-looking building, with slits for windows and huge bars across its main entrance. Will could just make out the words NEWGATE PRISON written under it.

Across from the boys ran a long counter, on which the policeman had placed their backpacks and Will's shovel, and beyond that was an office of some sort, where three desks were surrounded by a forest of narrow filing cabinets. A number of smaller rooms led off this main room, and from one came the rapid tapping of what could have been a typewriter.

Just as Will was looking into the far corner of the room, where a profusion of burnished brass pipes ran up the walls like the stems of an ancient vine, there was a screeching hiss that ended with a solid clunk. The noise was so sudden that Chester sat up and blinked like a nervous rabbit, stirred from his anxious torpor.

Another policeman emerged from a side room and hurried over to the brass pipes. There he glanced at a panel of antiquated dials from which a cascade of twisted wires spiraled down to a wooden box. Then he opened a hatch in one of the pipes, prying out a bullet-shaped cylinder the size of a small rolling pin. Unscrewing a cap from one end of it, he extracted a scroll of paper that crackled as he straightened it out to read it.

"Styx on their way," he said gruffly, striding over to the counter and opening up a large ledger, not once looking in the boys' direction. He also had an orange-gold star stitched onto his jacket, and although his appearance was much like that of the other officer, he was younger and his head was covered with a neatly cut stubble of white hair.

"Chester," Will whispered. When his friend didn't react, he stretched over to nudge him. In a flash, a truncheon lashed out, smacking sharply across his knuckles.

"Desist!" the policeman next to them barked.

"Ouch!" Will jumped up from the bench, his fists clenched. "You fat . . . ," he shouted, his body trembling, trying to control himself. Chester reached out and grabbed hold of his arm.

"Be quiet, Will!"

Will angrily shook off Chester's hand and stared into the policeman's cold eyes. "I want to know why we're being held," he demanded.

For a horrible moment they thought the policeman's face was going to explode, it turned such a livid red. But then his huge shoulders began to heave, and a low, grating laugh rumbled up, which grew louder and louder. Will threw a sidelong glance at Chester, who was eyeing the policeman with alarm.

"ENOUGH!" The voice of the man behind the counter cracked like a whip as he looked up from the ledger, his gaze falling on the laughing policeman, who immediately fell silent. "YOU!" The man glowered at Will. "SIT DOWN!" His voice held such authority that Will didn't hesitate for a second, quickly taking his place next to Chester again. "I," the man continued, puffing out his barrel chest self-importantly, "am the First Officer. You are already acquainted with the Second Officer." He nodded in the direction of the policeman standing by them.

The First Officer looked down at the roll of paper from the message tube. "You are hereby charged with unlawful entry and trespass into the Quarter under Statute Twelve, Subsection Two," he read in a monotone.

"But . . . ," Will began meekly.

The First Officer ignored him and read on. "Furthermore, you did uninvited enter a property with the intent to pilfer, contrary to Statute Six, Subsection Six," he continued matter-of-factly. "Do you understand these charges?" he asked.

Will and Chester exchanged confused looks, and Will was about to reply when the First Officer cut him off.

"Now what have we here?" he said, opening their backpacks and emptying the contents onto the counter. He picked up the foil-wrapped sandwiches Will had prepared and, not bothering to open them, merely sniffed at them. "Ah, swine," he said with a flicker of a smile. And from the way he briefly licked his lips and slid it to one side, Will knew he'd seen the last of his packed lunch.

Then the First Officer turned his attention to the other items, working his way through them methodically. He lingered on the compass but was more taken by the Swiss Army knife, levering out each of its blades in turn and squeezing the little scissors with his thick fingers before he finally put it down. Casually rolling one of the balls of string on the countertop with one hand, he used the other to flick open the dog-eared geological map that had been in Will's bag, giving it a cursory inspection. Finally, he leaned over and smelled the map, wrinkling his face with a look of distaste, before moving on to the camera.

"Hmmm," he muttered thoughtfully, turning it in his banana-like fingers to consider it from several angles.

"That's mine," Will said.

The First Officer completely ignored him and, putting down the camera, picked up a pen and dipped it in an inkwell set into the counter. With the pen poised over a page of the open ledger, he cleared his throat.

"NAME!" he bellowed, throwing a glance in Chester's direction.

"It's, er, Chester . . . Chester Rawls," the boy stammered.

The First Officer wrote in the ledger. The scratching of the nib on the page was the only sound in the room, and Will suddenly felt utterly helpless, as if the entry in the ledger was setting in motion an irreversible process, the workings of which were quite beyond his understanding.

"AND YOU?" he snapped at Will.

"He told me my father was here," Will said, bravely stabbing his finger in the direction of the Second Officer. "Where is he? I want to see him now!"

The First Officer looked across at his colleague and then back to Will. "You won't be seeing anyone unless you do as you are told." He shot another glance at the Second Officer and frowned with barely disguised disapproval. The Second Officer averted his gaze and shifted uneasily from foot to foot.

"NAME!"

"Will Burrows," Will answered slowly.

The First Officer picked up the scroll and consulted it again. "That is not the name I have here," he said, shaking his head and then fixing Will with his steely eyes.

"I don't care what it says. I know my own name."

There was a deafening silence as the First Officer continued to stare at Will. Then he abruptly slammed the ledger shut with a loud slap, causing a cloud of dust to billow up from the counter's surface.

"GET THEM TO THE HOLD!" he barked apoplectically.

They were dragged to their feet and, just as they were being pushed roughly through a large oak door at the end of the reception area, they heard another long hiss followed by a dull clunk as a further message arrived in the pipe system.

The connecting corridor of the Hold was about fifteen feet long and dimly lit by a single globe at the far end, beneath which stood a small wooden desk and chair. A blank wall ran along the right-hand side, and on the wall opposite were four dull iron doors set deep into solid brick surrounds. The boys were pushed along to the farthest door, on which the number four was marked in Roman numerals.

The Second Officer opened it with his keys and it swung back silently on its well-greased hinges. He stepped aside. Looking at the boys, he inclined his head toward the cell and as they hovered uncertainly on the threshold, he lost patience and shoved them in with his large hands, slamming the door behind them.

Inside the cell, the clang of the door reverberated sickeningly off the walls, and their stomachs turned as the key twisted in the lock. They tried to make out the details of the dark and dank cell by feeling their way around, Chester managing to send a bucket clattering over as he went. They discovered there was a three-foot-wide, lead-covered ledge along the length of the wall that directly faced the door, and, without a word to each other, both sat down on it. They felt its rough surface, cold and clammy, under their palms as their eyes gradually adjusted to the only source of light in the cell, the meager illumination that filtered through an observation hatch in the door. Finally Chester broke the silence with a loud sniff.

"Oh, man, what *is* that smell?"

"I'm not sure," said Will as he, too, sniffed. "Puke? Sweat?" Then he sniffed again and pronounced, with the air of a connoisseur, "Carbolic acid and . . ." Sniffing once more, he added, "Is that sulfur?"

"Huh?" his friend muttered.

"No, cabbage! Boiled cabbage!"

"I don't care what it is, it stinks," Chester said, making a face. "This place is just gross." He turned to look at his friend in the gloom. "How are we going to get out of here, Will?"

Will drew his knees up under his chin and rested his feet on the edge of the ledge. He scratched his calf but said nothing. He was quietly furious with himself, and didn't want his friend to pick up any sense of what he was feeling. Maybe Chester, with his cautious approach and his frequent warnings, had been right all along. He clenched his teeth and balled his fists in the darkness. Stupid, stupid, stupid! They had blundered in like a couple of amateurs. He'd allowed himself to get totally carried away. And how was he ever going to find his father now?

"I've got the most awful feeling about all this," Chester continued, now looking desolately at the floor. "We're never going to see home again, are we?"

"Look, don't you worry. We found a way in here, and we're dead straight going to find a way out again," Will said confidently, in an effort to reassure his friend, while he himself couldn't have felt more uncomfortable about their current predicament.

Neither of them felt much like talking after that, and the room was filled with the sound of the ever-present thrumming and the erratic scuttling of unseen insects.

Will woke with a start, catching his breath as if coming up for air. He was surprised to find he had actually dozed off in a half-sitting position on the lead sill. How long had he slept? He looked blearily around the shadowy gloom. Chester was standing with his back pressed against the wall, staring wide-eyed at the cell door. Will could almost feel fear emanating from him. He automatically followed Chester's gaze to the observation hatch: Framed in the opening was the leering face of the Second Officer, but owing to the size of his head only his eyes and nose were visible.

Hearing the keys jangle in the lock, Will watched as the man's eyes narrowed, and then the door swung open to reveal the officer silhouetted in the doorway, like a monstrous cartoon illustration.

"YOU!" he said to Will. "OUT, NOW!"

"Why? What for?"

"MOVE IT!" the officer barked.

"Will?" Chester said anxiously.

"Don't worry, Chester, it'll be all right," Will said weakly as he stood up, his legs cramped and stiff from the damp. He stretched them as he walked awkwardly out of the cell and into the corridor. Then, unrequested, he began to make his way to the main door of the Hold.

"Stand still!" snapped the Second Officer as he locked the door again. Then, grabbing Will's arm in a painful grip, he steered him out of the Hold and down a succession of bleak corridors, their footfalls echoing emptily around the flaking whitewashed walls and bare stone floors. Eventually, they turned a corner into a narrow stairwell that led into a short, dead-ended passage. It smelled damp and earthy, like an old cellar.

A bright light issued from an open door about halfway down. A sense of dread was growing in the pit of Will's stomach as they approached the doorway, and sure enough, he was pushed into the well-lit room by his escort and brought to an abrupt halt. Dazzled by the brightness, Will squinted as he peered around him.

The room was bare except for a bizarre chair and a metal table, behind which two tall figures were standing, their thin bodies bent over so that their heads were almost touching as they talked quietly in urgent, conspiratorial whispers. Will strained to catch what they were saying, but it didn't seem to be in any language he recognized, punctuated as it was by an alarming series of the most peculiar high-pitched, scratchy noises. Try as he might, he couldn't make out a single word; it was completely unintelligible to him.

So, with his arm still held tight in the officer's crushing grip, Will stood and waited, his stomach knotting with nervous tension as his eyes became accustomed to the brightness. From time to time the strange men glanced fleetingly at him, but Will didn't dare utter a word in the presence of this new and sinister authority.

They were dressed identically, with pristine, stark white collars at their necks. These were so large that they draped over the shoulders of their stiff, full-length leather coats, which creaked as the men gesticulated to each other. The skin of their gaunt faces, the color of new putty, only served to emphasize their jet-black eyes. Their hair, shaved high at the temples, was oiled back against their scalps so that they looked as though they were wearing shiny skullcaps.

Quite unexpectedly, they stopped what they were doing and turned to face Will.

"These gentlemen are the Styx," said the Second Officer behind him, "and you will answer their questions."

"Chair," said the Styx on the right, his black eyes staring unwaveringly at Will.

He pointed with a long-fingered hand at the strange chair that stood between the table and Will. Overcome by a sense of foreboding, Will didn't protest as the officer sat him down. From the back of the chair rose an adjustable metal bar with two padded clamps at the top to hold the occupant's head firmly in place. The officer adjusted the height of the bar, then tightened the clamps, pressing them hard against Will's temples. He tried to turn his head to look at the officer, but the restraints held him fast. While the officer continued to secure him, Will realized he had absolutely no choice but to face the Styx, who were poised behind the table like avaricious priests.

The officer stooped. Out of the corner of his eye Will saw him pull something from underneath the chair, then heard the old leather straps creak and the large buckles rattle as each of his wrists was strapped to the corresponding thigh.

"What's this for?" Will dared to ask.

"Your own protection," the officer said as, crouching down, he proceeded to loop further straps around Will's legs, just below the knees, fastening them to the legs of the chair. Both of Will's ankles were then secured in a similar fashion, the officer pulling the bindings so taut that they bit mercilessly and made Will writhe with discomfort. He noticed with some dismay that this appeared to amuse the Styx. Finally a strap some four inches thick was drawn tightly across his chest and arms and fastened behind the back of the chair. The officer then stood at attention until one of the Styx nodded mutely to him and he left the room, closing the door behind him.

Alone with them, Will watched in terrified silence, transfixed like an animal caught in car headlights, as one of the Styx produced an odd-looking lamp and placed it in the center of the table. It had a solid base and a short curved arm topped with a shallow conical shade. This held what appeared to be a dark purple bulb; it reminded Will of an old sunlamp he'd seen in his father's museum. A small black box with dials and switches was placed next to it, and the lamp was plugged into this by means of a twisted brown cable. The Styx's pale finger jabbed at a switch, and the box began to hum gently to itself.

One Styx stepped back from the table as the other continued to lean over the lamp, manipulating the controls behind the

shade. With a loud click, the bulb flared a dim orange for an instant, then appeared to go out again.

"Going to take my picture?" Will asked in a weak attempt at humor, trying to steady the tremor in his voice. Ignoring him, the Styx turned a dial on the black box, as if he were tuning a radio.

Alarmingly, an uncomfortable pressure began to build up behind Will's eyes. He opened his mouth in a silent yawn, trying

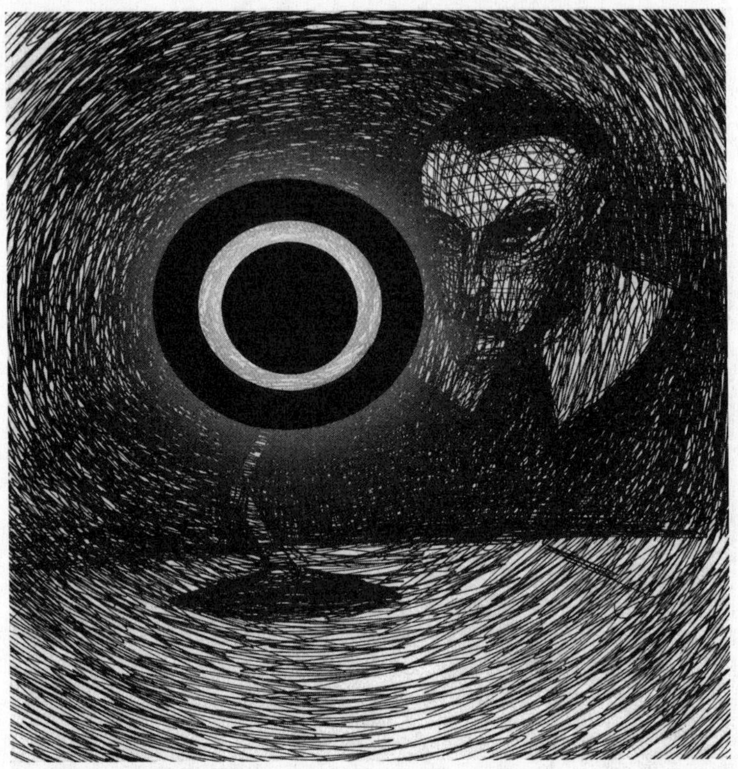

to relieve this strange tension in his temples, when the room began to darken, as if the device was literally sucking all the light from it. Thinking he was going blind, Will blinked several times and opened his eyes as wide as he could. With the greatest difficulty he could just make out the two Styx silhouetted by the dim light reflecting off the wall behind them.

He became aware of an incessant pulsing drone, but for the life of him he couldn't pinpoint where it was coming from. As it grew more intense, his head began to feel decidedly strange, as if every bone and sinew were vibrating. It was like a plane flying too low overhead. The resonance seemed to form into a spiked ball of energy in the very center of his head. Now he *really* began to panic, but, not being able to move a muscle, he could do nothing to resist.

As the Styx manipulated the dials, the ball appeared to shift, slowly sinking through his body into his chest and then circling his heart, causing him to catch his breath and cough involuntarily. Then it was moving in and out of his body, sometimes coming to a rest and hovering a little distance behind him. It was as if a living thing were homing in and searching for something. It shifted again, and now floated half in and half out of his body, at the nape of his neck.

"What's going on?" Will asked, trying to summon up some bravado, but there was no response from the ever-darkening figures. "You're not scaring me with all this, you know."

They remained silent.

Will closed his eyes for a second, but when he reopened them, he found he couldn't even distinguish the outlines of the Styx in the total darkness that now confronted him. He began struggling against his bonds.

"Does the absence of light unsettle you?" asked the Styx on the left.

"No, why should it?"

"What is your name?" The words cut into Will's head like a knife out of the darkness.

"I told you, it's Will. Will Burrows."

"Your real name!" Again the voice caused Will to wince with pain—it was as if each word were setting off electric shocks in his temples.

"I don't know what you mean," he answered through gritted teeth.

The ball of energy began to edge into the center of his skull, the humming growing more intense now, the throbbing pulse enveloping him in a thick blanket of pressure.

"Are you with the man called Burrows?"

Will's head was swimming, waves of pain rippling through him. His feet and hands were tingling with intense pins and needles. This horrible sensation was slowly enveloping his whole body.

"He's my dad!" he shouted.

"What is your purpose here?" The precise, clipped voice was closer now.

"What have you done to him?" Will said in a choked voice, swallowing back the rush of saliva flooding into his mouth. He felt like at any moment he was going to be sick.

"Where is your mother?" The measured but insistent voice now seemed to be emanating from the ball inside his head. It was as though both Styx had entered his cranium and were searching feverishly through his mind, like burglars ransacking drawers and cupboards for valuable items.

"What is your purpose?" they demanded again.

And Will again tried to struggle against his bonds, but realized he could no longer feel his body. In fact, it felt as if he had been reduced to nothing but a floating head, cast adrift into a fog of darkness, and he couldn't fathom which way was up or down anymore.

"NAME? PURPOSE?" The questions came thick and fast as Will felt all his remaining energy seep out of him. Then the incessant voice became fainter, as if Will were moving away from it. From a great distance, words were being shouted after him, and each word, when it finally arrived, set off small pinpricks of light at the edge of his vision, which swam and jittered until the darkness before him was filled with a boiling sea of white dots so bright and so intense that his eyes ached. The entire time, the scratchy whispers swept around him, and the room spun and pitched. Another deep wave of nausea overwhelmed him, and a burning sensation filled his head to the bursting point. White, white, blinding white, cramming into his head until it felt as if it were going to explode.

"I'm going to be sick . . . please . . . I'm going to be . . . I feel faint . . . please," and the light of the white space seared into him and he felt himself growing smaller and smaller, until he was a tiny fleck in the huge white emptiness. Then the light began to recede, and the burning sensation grew less and less, until everything was black and silent, as if the universe itself had gone out.

He came to as the Second Officer, supporting him under one arm, turned the key in the cell door. He was shaky and weak. Vomit was streaked down the front of his clothes, and his mouth was dry with an acrid metallic taste that made him gag. His head was pounding with pain, and as he tried to look up it was as though part of his vision were missing. He couldn't stop himself from groaning as the door was pulled open.

"Not so cocky now, eh?" the officer said, letting go of Will's arm. He tried to walk, but his legs were like jelly. "Not after your first taste of the Dark Light," the officer sneered.

After a couple of steps, Will's legs gave way and he fell heavily onto his knees. Chester dashed over to him, panic-stricken at his friend's condition.

"Will, Will, what have they done to you?" Chester was frantic as he helped him over to the ledge. "You've been gone for hours."

"Just tired . . . ," Will managed to mumble as he slumped down on the ledge and rolled up in a ball, grateful for the coolness of the lead lining against his aching head. He shut his eyes . . . he just wanted to sleep . . . but his head was still spinning, and waves of nausea were breaking over him.

"YOU!" the officer bellowed. Chester jumped up from beside Will and turned to the officer, who beckoned to him with a thick forefinger.

"Your turn."

Chester looked down at Will, who now lay unconscious.

"Oh, no."

"NOW!" the officer ordered. "Don't make me ask you again."

Chester reluctantly came out into the corridor. After locking the door, the officer took him by the arm and marched him off.

"What's a Dark Light?" Chester said, his eyes glazed with fear.

"Just questions." The officer smiled. "Nothing to worry about."

"But I don't know anything. . . ."

Will was woken by the sound of a hatch being pulled back at the base of the door.

"Food," a voice announced coldly.

He was starving. He lifted himself up onto one arm, his body aching dully, as if he had the flu. Every bone and muscle complained when he tried to move.

"Oh God!" he groaned, and then suddenly thought of Chester. The open food hatch shed a little more illumination than usual into the cell and, as he looked around him, there on the floor at the base of the lead-covered ledge was his friend, lying in a fetal position. Chester's breathing was shallow, his face pale and feverish.

Will staggered up onto his legs and, with difficulty, carried the two trays back to the ledge. He inspected the contents briefly. There were two bowls with something in them and some liquid in battered tin cups. It all looked terribly unappetizing, but at least it was hot and didn't smell too bad.

"Chester?" he said, crouching down by his friend. Will felt awful—he, and he alone, was responsible for everything that was happening to both of them. He began to shake Chester gently by the shoulder. "Hey, are you all right?"

"Urgh . . . wha . . . ?" his friend moaned and tried to lift his head. Will could see that his nose had been bleeding; the blood was caked and smudged across his cheek.

"Food, Chester. Come on, you'll feel better once you've eaten something."

Will pulled Chester into a sitting position, propping his back against the wall. He moistened his sleeve with the liquid from one of the cups and began to dab at the blood on Chester's face with it.

"Leave me alone!" Chester objected weakly, trying to push him away.

"That's an improvement. Here, eat something," Will said, handing a bowl to Chester, who immediately pushed it away.

"I'm not hungry. I feel terrible."

"At least drink some of this. I think it's some sort of herbal tea." Will handed the drink to Chester, who cupped his hands around the warm mug. "What did they ask you?" Will mumbled through a mouthful of the gray mush.

"Everything. Name . . . address . . . your name . . . all that stuff. I can't remember most of it. I think I fainted. . . . I really thought I was going to die," Chester said in a flat voice, staring into the middle distance.

Will began to chuckle quietly. Strange as it might seem, his own suffering seemed to be relieved somewhat by hearing his friend's complaints.

"What's so funny?" Chester asked, outrage in his voice. "It's not funny at all."

"No." Will laughed. "I know. Sorry. Here, try some of this. It's actually pretty good."

Chester shuddered with disgust at the gray slurry in the bowl. Nevertheless, he picked up the spoon and poked at it, somewhat suspiciously at first. Then he sniffed at it.

"Doesn't smell too bad," he said, trying to convince himself.

"Just eat it, would you?" Will said, filling his mouth again. He felt his strength begin to return with each mouthful. "I keep thinking I said something about Mum and Rebecca to them, but I'm not sure if I didn't dream it." He swallowed, then was silent for several seconds, biting the inside of his mouth as something began to trouble him. "I just hope I haven't gotten them in trouble, too." He took another mouthful and, still chewing, continued speaking as another recollection came back to him. "And Dad's journal—I keep seeing it in my mind, clear as anything—as if I'm there, watching, as their long white fingers open it and turn the pages, one by one. But that can't have happened, can it? It's all mixed up. What about you?"

Chester shifted a little. "I don't know. I might have mentioned the cellar in your house . . . and your family . . . your mum . . . and Rebecca . . . yes . . . I could have told them something about her . . . but . . . oh God, I don't know . . . it's all a jumble. It's like I can't remember if it's what I *said* or what I *thought*." He put down his mug and cradled his head in his hands while Will leaned back, peering up at the dark ceiling.

"Wonder what time it is . . . ," he sighed, ". . . up there."

Over what must have been the next week, there followed more interrogations with the Styx, the Dark Light leaving both of them with the same awful side effects as before: exhaustion, a befuddled uncertainty about just what it was that they had told their tormentors, and the appalling bouts of sickness that ensued.

Then came a day when the boys were left alone. Although they couldn't be certain, they both felt that surely the Styx must have gotten all they wanted for now, and hoped against hope that the sessions were finally over.

And so the hours passed, and the two boys slept fitfully, mealtimes came and went, and they divided their time between pacing the floor, when they felt strong enough, and resting on the ledge, even occasionally shouting at the door, but to no avail. And in the constant, unchanging light, they lost all sense of time and of day or night.

Beyond the walls of their cell, serpentine processes were in play: Investigations, meetings, and chatterings, all in the scratchy secret language of the Styx, were deciding their fate.

Ignorant of this, the boys worked hard to keep up their spirits. In hushed tones, they talked at length about how they might escape, and whether Rebecca would eventually piece it all together and lead the authorities to the tunnel in the cellar. How they kicked themselves for not leaving a note! Or maybe Will's father was the answer to their problems—would he somehow get them out of there? And what day of the week was it? And more important, not having washed for some time now, their clothes must have taken on a decidedly funky aroma, and that being the case, why did they not smell any worse to each other?

It was during one particularly lively debate, about who these people were and where they had come from, that the inspection hatch shot back and the Second Officer leered in. They both immediately fell silent as the door was unlocked and the grim, familiar figure all but blotted out the light from the corridor. *Which of them was it to be this time?*

"Visitors."

They looked at each other in disbelief.

"Visitors? For us?" Chester asked incredulously.

The officer shook his massive head, then looked at Will. "You."

"What about Ches—"

"You, come on. NOW!" the officer shouted.

"Don't worry, Chester, I won't go anywhere without you," Will said confidently to his friend, who sat back with a pained smile and nodded in silent affirmation.

Will stood up and shuffled out of the cell. Chester watched as the door clanged shut. Finding himself once more alone, he looked down at his hands, rough and ingrained with dirt, and longed for home and comfort. He felt the increasingly frequent sting of frustration and helplessness, and his eyes filled with hot tears. No, he wouldn't cry, he would not give them the satisfaction. He knew Will would work something out, and that he'd be ready when he did.

"Come on, stupid," he said quietly to himself, wiping his eyes with his sleeve. "Drop and give me twenty," he mimicked his soccer coach's voice as he got down on the floor and began to do push-ups, counting as he did so.

Will was shown into a whitewashed room with a polished floor and some chairs arranged around a large oak table. Sitting behind this were two figures, still a little bleary to him because his sight hadn't yet adjusted from the darkness of the Hold. He rubbed his eyes and then glanced down at his front. His shirt was filthy and, worse still, specked with dried traces of his vomit. He brushed at it feebly before his attention was drawn to an odd-looking hatch or window on the wall to his left. The surface of the glass, if it *was* glass, had a peculiar blue-black depth to it. And this matte and mottled surface didn't seem to be reflecting any of the light from the orbs in the room.

For some reason, Will couldn't take his eyes off the surface. He felt a sudden twinge of recognition. A new, yet familiar, feeling swept over him: *They* were behind there. *They* were watching all this. And the longer he stared, the more the darkness filled him, just as it had with the Dark Light. He felt a sudden spasm in his head. He pitched forward as though he was about to faint, and his left hand groped wildly and found the backrest of the chair in front of him. The officer, seeing this, caught him by his other arm and helped him to sit down, facing the pair of strangers.

Will took some deep breaths, and the light-headedness passed. He looked up as someone coughed. Opposite him sat a large man and, at his side but a little behind him, a young boy. The man was much like all the others Will had seen—it could easily have been the Second Officer in civilian clothing. He was staring fixedly at Will with barely concealed contempt. Will felt too drained to care, and numbly returned the stranger's gaze.

Then, as chair legs grated loudly on the floor and the boy moved closer to the table, Will focused his attention on him. The boy was looking at Will with an expression of wonder. He had an open and friendly face, the first friendly countenance Will had seen down there since he had been arrested. Will estimated that the boy was probably a couple of years younger than he was. His hair was almost white and closely cropped, and his soft blue eyes shimmered with mischievousness. As the corners of the boy's mouth curled into a smile, Will thought that he seemed vaguely familiar. He tried desperately to remember where he'd seen him before, but his mind was still too cloudy and unclear. He narrowed his eyes at the boy and tried again to figure out where he knew him from, but it was no use. It was as if he were casting around in a murky pool, trying to find something precious with only his sense of touch to guide him. His head began to spin, and he clenched his eyes shut and kept them that way.

He heard the man clear his throat. "I am Mr. Jerome," he said in a flat and perfunctory tone. It was clear from his voice that he was uncomfortable with the situation and very resentful at being there. "This is my son. . . ."

"Cal," Will heard the boy say.

"Caleb," the man quickly corrected.

There was a long and awkward pause, but Will still didn't open his eyes. He felt insulated and safe with them shut. It was oddly comforting.

Mr. Jerome looked testily at the Second Officer. "This is useless," he grunted. "A total waste of time."

The officer leaned forward and brusquely prodded Will's shoulder. "Sit up and be civil to your family. Show some respect."

Startled, Will's eyes snapped open. He swiveled in his chair to look at the officer in amazement.

"What?"

"I said be civil"—he nodded to Mr. Jerome—"to your *family,* like."

Will swiveled back to face the man and boy.

"What are you talking about?"

Mr. Jerome shrugged and looked down, and the boy frowned, his gaze switching between Will, the officer, and his father, as if he didn't quite understand what was happening.

"Chester's right, you're all totally mental down here," Will exclaimed, then flinched as the Second Officer took a step toward him with his hand raised. But the situation was defused by the boy as he spoke out.

"You must remember this?" he said, delving into an old canvas bag on his lap. All eyes were on him as he finally produced a small object and placed it on the table in front of Will. It was a carved wooden toy, a rat or a mouse. Its white painted face was chipped and faded, and its little formal coat was threadbare; yet its eyes glowed eerily. Cal looked expectantly at Will.

"Grandma said it was your favorite," he continued as Will failed to react. "It was given to me after you went."

"What are you . . . ?" Will asked, perplexed. "After I went where?"

"Don't you remember anything?" Cal asked. He looked deferentially at his father, who was now sitting back in his chair with his arms crossed.

Will reached out and picked up the little toy to examine it more closely. As he tipped it back, he noticed that the eyes closed, a tiny shutter counterbalancing in the head to extinguish the light. He realized that there must be a minuscule light orb within its head, which gave out light through the glass beads that were the animal's eyes.

"It sleeps," Cal said, then added, "You had that very toy . . . in your cot."

Will dropped it on the table as abruptly as if it had bitten him. "What are you talking about?" he snapped at the boy.

There was a moment of uncertainty on everyone's part, and once again an unnerving silence descended over the room, broken only by the Second Officer, who began to hum quietly to himself. Cal opened his mouth as if about to speak, but seemed to be struggling to find the words. Will sat looking at the toy animal, until Cal took it off the table and put it away again. Then, looking up at Will, he frowned.

"Your name is Seth," he said, almost resentfully. "You're my brother."

"Hah!" Will laughed dryly in Cal's face and then, as all the bitterness from his treatment at the hands of the Styx welled up inside him, he shook his head and spoke to him harshly. "Yeah. Right. Anything you say." Will had had just about enough of this charade. He knew who his family was, and it wasn't this pair of imposters before him.

"It's true. Your mother was my mother. She tried to run away with both of us. She took you Topsoil, but left me with Grandma and Father."

Will rolled his eyes and twisted around to face the Second Officer. "Very clever. It's a good trick, but I'm not buying it."

The officer pursed his lips, but said nothing.

"You were taken in by a family of Topsoilers . . . ," Cal said, raising his voice.

"Sure, and I'm not about to be *taken in* by a family of stark, raving loonies down here!" Will replied angrily, really starting to lose it.

"Don't waste your breath on him, Caleb," said Mr. Jerome, putting a hand on his shoulder. But Cal shook it off and continued, his voice beginning to crack with despair.

"They're not your *real* family. We are. We're your flesh and blood."

Will stared at Mr. Jerome, whose reddened face exuded nothing but loathing. Then he looked again at Cal, who had now sat back despondently, his head bowed. But Will was unimpressed. It was all some sick joke. *Do they really think I'm so stupid that I'd be taken in by this?* he said to himself.

Buttoning his coat, Mr. Jerome rose hastily to his feet. "This is going nowhere," he said.

And Cal, rising with him, spoke quietly. "Grandma always said you'd come back."

"I don't have any grandparents. They're all dead!" Will shouted, jumping up from his chair, his eyes now burning with anger and brimming with tears. He tore over to the glass window in the wall and pressed his face against the surface.

"Very clever!" he yelled at it. "Nearly had me going there!" He shielded his eyes from the light of the room in an effort to see beyond the glass, but there was nothing, only an unrelenting darkness. The Second Officer grabbed his arm and pulled him away. Will did not resist—the fight had gone out of him for now.

21

REBECCA lay on top of her bed, staring at the ceiling. She'd just taken a hot bath and was dressed in her acid green robe, her hair up in a towel turban. She was humming softly along to the classical music station on her bedside radio as she mulled over the events of the last three days.

It had all kicked off when she was woken very late one evening by a frantic knocking and ringing at the front door. She'd had to get up and answer it, since Mrs. Burrows, on the strong sleeping pills she'd recently been prescribed, was dead to the world. A drunken brass band couldn't have roused her if they'd tried.

When Rebecca had opened the front door, she'd almost been knocked off her feet by Chester's father as he burst into the hallway and immediately began to bombard her with questions.

"Is Chester still here? He hasn't come home yet. We tried to phone, but no one answered." His face was ashen, and he was wearing a crumpled beige raincoat with the collar askew, as if he'd put it on in a great hurry. "We thought he must've decided to stay over. He *is* here, isn't he?"

"I'm not . . . ," she started to say as she happened to look into the kitchen and realized that the plate of food she'd left out on the side for Will hadn't been touched.

"He said he was helping Will with a project, but . . . is he here? Where's your brother . . . can you get him, please?" Mr. Rawls's words tripped over each other as he glanced anxiously down the hall and up the stairs.

Leaving the man fretting to himself, Rebecca ran up to Will's room. She didn't bother to knock; she already knew what she would find. She opened the door and turned on the light. Sure enough, Will wasn't there, and his bed hadn't been slept in. She turned out the light and closed the door behind her, returning downstairs to Mr. Rawls.

"No, no sign of him," she said. "I think Chester *was* here, though, last night; but I don't know where they might've gone. Maybe—"

On hearing this, Mr. Rawls became almost incoherent, gabbling something about checking their usual haunts and getting the police involved as he tore out the front door, leaving it open behind him.

Rebecca remained in the hallway, chewing her lip. She was furious with herself that she hadn't been more vigilant. With all his secretive behavior and the skulking around with his new bosom buddy, Will had been up to something for weeks—there was no question about that. *But what?*

She knocked on the living-room door and, getting no answer, entered. The room was dark and stuffy, and she could hear regular snoring.

"Mum," she said with gentle insistence.

"Urphh?"

"Mum," she said more loudly, shaking Mrs. Burrows's shoulder.

"Wha? Nnno . . . smmumph?"

"Come on, Mum, wake up. It's important."

"Nah," said an obdurate, sleepy voice.

"Wake up. Will's missing!" Rebecca said urgently.

"Leave . . . me . . . alone," grumbled Mrs. Burrows through an indolent yawn, swinging an arm to warn Rebecca off.

"Do you know where he's gone? And Chester . . ."

"Oh, go awaaaay!" her mother screeched, turning on her side in the chair and pulling the old afghan right over her head. The shallow snoring resumed as she returned to her state of hibernation. Rebecca sighed with sheer frustration as she stood next to the shapeless form.

She went into the kitchen and sat down. With the detective's number in her hand and the cordless phone lying on the table in front of her, she deliberated for a long time over what to do next. It wasn't until the small, predawn hours that she actually made the call and, getting only the answering service, left a message. She returned upstairs to her bedroom and tried to read a book while she waited for a response.

The police turned up at precisely 7:06 A.M. After that, events took on a life of their own. The house was filled with uniformed officers searching every room, poking around every closet and chest of drawers. Wearing rubber gloves, they began in Will's room and worked through the rest of the house, ending in the cellar, but apparently found nothing much of interest. She was almost amused when she saw they were retrieving articles of Will's clothing from the laundry basket on the landing and meticulously sealing each item in its own polyethylene bag before carrying it outside. She wondered what his dirty tighty whities could possibly tell them.

At first, Rebecca busied herself by straightening up the mess the searchers had left behind, using the activity as an excuse to move around the house and see if she could glean anything from the various conversations that were taking place. Then, as no one seemed to be taking the slightest bit of notice of her, she dropped the pretense of tidying and just strolled around wherever she wanted, spending most of her time in the hallway outside the living room, where the chief inspector and a female detective were interviewing Mrs. Burrows. From what Rebecca could catch, she seemed to be detached and disturbed by turns and wasn't able to shed any light at all on Will's current whereabouts.

The searchers eventually decamped to the front of the house, where they stood around smoking and laughing among themselves. Shortly afterward, the chief inspector and the female detective emerged from the living room, and Rebecca followed them to the front door. As the chief inspector walked down the path to the row of parked squad cars, she couldn't help but overhear his words.

"That one's a few volts short of a full charge," he said to his colleague.

"Very sad," the female detective said.

"You know . . . ," the chief inspector said, pausing to glance back at the house, ". . . to lose one family member is unfortunate . . ." His colleague had nodded.

". . . but to lose two is downright iffy," the chief inspector continued. "*Very* suspicious, in my book."

The female detective nodded again, a grim smile on her face.

"We'd better do a sweep of the Common, just to be sure," Rebecca heard him say before he was finally out of earshot.

The next day the police had sent a car for them, and Mrs. Burrows was interviewed for several hours, while Rebecca was asked to wait in another room with a woman from Social Services.

Now, three days later, Rebecca's mind was running over the chain of events again. Closing her eyes, she recalled the deadpan faces down at the police station and the exchanges she'd overheard.

"This won't do," she said, glancing at her watch and seeing the time. She got up from her bed, unwound the towel from her head, and dressed quickly.

Downstairs, Mrs. Burrows was ensconced in her armchair, curled up fully clothed under the afghan that was tucked around her like a drab tartan cocoon. The only light in the room came from a muted public television program, the cool blue light pulsing intermittently and causing the shadows to jump and jerk, lending a sort of animation to the furniture and objects in the room. She was sleeping deeply when a noise in the room brought her awake: a deep murmur, like a strong wind combing through the branches of the trees in the garden outside.

She opened her eyes a fraction. In the far corner of the room, by the half-opened curtains of the French windows, she could make out a large, shadowy form. For a moment she wondered if she was dreaming, as the shadow shifted and changed in the light cast by the television. She strained to make out just what was there. She wondered if it could be an intruder. *What should she do? Pretend to be asleep? Or lie quite still so the intruder wouldn't bother her?*

She held her breath, trying to control her rising panic. The seconds felt like hours as the shape remained stationary. She began to think that maybe it was just an innocent shadow after all. A trick of the light and an overactive imagination. She let the air out of her lungs, opening her eyes fully.

All of a sudden there was a snuffling sound and, to her horror, the shadow split into two distinct ghostlike blurs and closed in on her with blinding speed. As her senses reeled in shock and terror, a calm and collected voice in her head told her with absolute conviction, *They are not ghosts.*

In a flash, the figures were upon her. She tried to scream, but no sound came out. Rough material brushed against her face as she smelled a peculiar mustiness, something like mildewed clothes. Then a powerful hand struck her, and she curled up in pain, winded and struggling for air, until, like a newborn baby, she caught her breath and let out an unholy shriek.

She was powerless to resist as she was scooped out of her chair and borne aloft into the hallway. Now, howling like a banshee, bucking and straining, she glimpsed another figure looming from the doorway of the cellar, and a huge damp hand was clapped over her mouth, stifling her screams.

Who were they? What were they after? Then a terrible thought sprung to mind. Her precious TV and video recorders! That was it! That's what they'd come for! The sheer injustice of it all. It was just too much to take, on top of everything else she'd had to put up with. Mrs. Burrows saw red.

Finding energy from nowhere, she summoned the superhuman strength of the desperate. She wrestled one of her legs free and instantly kicked out. This caused a flurry of activity as her assailants tried to seize it, but she kicked out again and again as she twisted around. One of the faces of her attackers appeared within reach; she saw her chance and lunged forward, biting down as hard as she could. She found that she had it by its nose, and she shook her head like a terrier with a rat.

There was a bloodcurdling wail, and its hold on her relaxed for a moment. That was enough for Mrs. Burrows. As the figures lost their grip on her and fell backward against one another, she found the ground with her feet and swung her arms behind her like a downhill skier. With a yell, she hurtled away from them and into the kitchen, leaving them grasping only the blanket that had been wrapped around her, like the discarded tail of a fleeing lizard.

In the blink of an eye, Mrs. Burrows was back. She swooped into the midst of the three hulking forms. Utter chaos ensued.

Rebecca, from her vantage point at the top of the stairs, was perfectly placed to watch as it all unfolded. In the half-light of the hallway below, something metallic flashed back and forth and from side to side, and she saw a wild face. Mrs. Burrows's face. Rebecca realized that she was wielding a frying pan, swinging it left and right like a cutlass. It was the new one with the extra-wide base and the special nonstick surface.

Time and time again the shadowy forms renewed their attack on her, but Mrs. Burrows stood her ground, repelling them with multiple blows, the pan resounding satisfyingly as it connected with a skull here or an elbow there. In all the confusion, Rebecca could see the streaks of movement as the salvo of blows continued at an incredible rate, boinging away to a chorus of grunts and groans.

"DEATH!" screamed Mrs. Burrows. "DIE, DIE!"

One of the shadowy figures reached out in an attempt to grab Mrs. Burrows's pan arm as it wheeled around in a figure eight, only to be walloped by a tremendous bone-shattering swipe. He let out a deep howl like a wounded dog and staggered back, the others falling back with him. Then, as one, they turned on their heels, and the three of them scuttled out through the open front door. They moved with startling speed, like cockroaches caught in the light, and were gone.

In the stillness that followed, Rebecca crept down the stairs and flicked on the hall light. Mrs. Burrows, her bedraggled hair hanging like limp horns in dark wisps across her white face, immediately shifted her maniacal gaze to Rebecca.

"Mum," Rebecca said softly.

Mrs. Burrows raised the pan above her head and lurched toward her. The feral look of wild-eyed fury on her face made Rebecca take a step back, thinking she was about to turn on her.

"Mum! Mum, it's me, it's all right, they're gone . . . they're all gone now!"

A look of odd self-satisfaction spread across Mrs. Burrows's face as she checked herself and nodded slowly, appearing to recognize her daughter.

"It's all right, Mum, really." Rebecca tried to pacify her. She ventured closer to the rapidly panting woman and gently eased the frying pan from her grip. Mrs. Burrows didn't put up any resistance.

Rebecca sighed with relief and, looking around, noticed some dark splatters on the hall carpet. It could have been mud or—she looked closer and frowned—blood.

"If they bleed," Mrs. Burrows intoned, following Rebecca's gaze, "I can kill them." She drew her lips back, revealing her teeth as she let out a low growl, then started to laugh horribly, an unnatural, grating cackle.

"How about a nice cup of tea?" Rebecca asked, forcing a smile as Mrs. Burrows quieted down again. Putting her arm around Mrs. Burrows's waist, she steered her in the direction of the living room.

22

WILL was rudely awoken by the cell door crashing back and the First Officer hauling him to his feet. Still thick with sleep, he was bundled out of the Hold, through the reception area of the station, out of the main entrance, and onto the top of the stone stairs.

The officer let go of him, and he tottered down a couple of steps until he found his footing. There he stood, groggy and more than a little disoriented. He heard a thump next to him as his backpack landed by his feet, and without a word the officer turned his back and went into the station.

It was a strange feeling, standing there bathed in the glow of the streetlights after being confined in that gloomy cell for so long. There was a slight breeze on his face—it was damp and muggy but, all the same, it was a relief after the airlessness of the Hold.

What happens now? he thought, scratching his neck under the collar of the coarse shirt he'd been given by one of the officers. His mind still befuddled, he started to yawn, but stifled it as he heard a noise: A restless horse brayed and stamped a hoof against the damp cobbles. Will immediately looked up and saw a dark carriage a little way down on the other side of the road, to which two pure white horses were hitched. At the front, a coachman sat holding the reins. The carriage door swung open, and Cal jumped out and crossed the street toward him.

"What's this?" Will asked suspiciously, backing up a step as Cal approached.

"We're taking you home," Cal replied.

"Home? What do you mean, home? With you? I'm not going anywhere without Chester!" he said resolutely.

"*Shhhh,* don't. Listen!" Cal now stood close to him and spoke with urgency. "They're watching us." He inclined his head down the street, his eyes never leaving Will's.

On the corner was a sole figure, dark as a disembodied shadow, standing stock-still. Will could just make out the white collar.

"I'm not leaving without Chester," Will hissed.

"What do you think will happen to him if you *don't* come with us? Think about it."

"But —"

"They can be easy on him or not. It's up to you." Cal looked pleadingly into Will's eyes.

Will glanced back at the station one last time, then sighed and shook his head. "All right."

Cal smiled and, picking up Will's pack for him, led the way over to the waiting carriage. He held the door open for Will, who followed grudgingly, his hands in his pockets and his head down. He didn't like this at all.

As the carriage pulled away, Will studied the austere interior. It certainly wasn't built for comfort. The seats, like the side panels, were made of a hard, black-lacquered wood, and the whole thing smelled of varnish with a faint hint of bleach, somewhat reminiscent of a gymnasium on the first day of school. Still, anything was better than the cell in which he'd been locked up for so many days with Chester. Will felt a sudden pang as he thought of his friend, still incarcerated and now alone in the Hold. He wondered if Chester had even been told that he'd been whisked away, and he swore to himself that he'd find a way to get his friend out of there if it was the last thing he did.

He slumped back dejectedly in his seat and put his feet up on the opposite bench, then pulled back the leathery curtain and stared through the open window of the carriage. As the coach rattled through the cavernous, deserted streets, bleak houses and unlit shopfronts passed with monotonous regularity. Copying Will, Cal also settled back and rested his feet on the seat in front of him, occasionally giving Will sidelong glances and smiling contentedly to himself.

Both boys remained silent, lost in their own thoughts, but it wasn't long before Will's natural inquisitiveness began to revive slightly. He made a concerted effort to take in the murky sights passing him by, but after a short while his eyelids grew heavier and heavier as his extreme weariness and the seemingly endless underworld got the better of him. Finally, lulled by the rhythmic beat of the horses' hooves, he nodded off, occasionally waking with a start when the carriage's buffeting roused him. With a somewhat startled expression, he would look around self-consciously, much to Cal's amusement, and then his head would droop and he'd succumb to his fatigue again.

He didn't know if he'd been asleep for minutes or even hours when the driver cracked his whip, waking him again.

The carriage surged forward, and the lampposts flicked past the window at less regular intervals. Will assumed they must be reaching the outskirts of the town. Wider areas opened up between the buildings, carpeted by dark green, almost black, beds of lichens or something similar. Then came strips of land at either side of the road, which were divided into plots by rickety-looking fences and contained beds of what appeared to be some sort of large fungi.

At one point, their speed dropped as they crossed a small bridge spanning an inky-looking canal. Will stared down into the slow and torpid water, flowing like crude oil, and for some reason it filled him with an inexplicable dread.

He had just settled back into his seat and was beginning to doze off again when the road suddenly dipped down a steep incline and the carriage veered left. Then, as the road leveled out once more, the driver shouted "Whoa!" and the horses slowed to a trot.

Will was wide awake now and stuck his head out the window to see what was going on. There was a huge metal gate blocking the way, and to the side of this a group of men huddled around a brazier as they warmed their hands. Standing apart from them in the middle of the road, a hooded figure held a lamp high and was waving it from side to side as a signal for the coachman to stop. As the carriage ground to a halt, to Will's horror he spotted the instantly recognizable figure of a Styx emerging from the shadows. Will quickly yanked the curtain shut and ducked back into the carriage. He looked questioningly at Cal.

"It's the Skull Gate. It's the main portal to the Colony," Cal explained in a reassuring tone.

"I thought we were already in the Colony."

"No," Cal replied incredulously, "that was only the Quarter. It's sort of . . . like an outpost . . . our frontier town."

"So there's more beyond this?"

"More? There's *miles* of it!"

Will was speechless. He looked fearfully at the door as the clipped sound of boot heels on cobblestones drew nearer. Cal grabbed his arm. "Don't worry, they check everyone who goes through. Just say nothing. If there's a problem, I'll do all the talking."

At that very moment, the door on Will's side was pulled open and the Styx shone a brass lamp into the interior. He played the beam across their faces, then took a step back and shone it up at the coachman, who handed him a piece of paper. He read it with a cursory glance. Apparently satisfied, he returned to the boys once more, directed the dazzling light straight into Will's eyes, and, with a contemptuous sneer, slammed the door shut. He handed the note back to the driver, signaled to the gateman, turned on his heel, and walked away.

Hearing a loud clanking, Will warily lifted the hem of the curtain and peered out again. As the guard waved them on, the light from his lantern revealed that the gate was in fact a portcullis. Will watched as it rose jerkily into a structure that made him blink with astonishment. Carved from a lighter stone and jutting from the wall above the portcullis, it was an immense toothless skull.

"That's pretty creepy," Will muttered under his breath.

"It's meant to be. It's a warning," Cal replied indifferently as the coachman lashed his whip and the carriage lurched through the mouth of the fearsome apparition and into the cavern beyond.

Leaning out the window, Will watched the portcullis shuddering down behind them again until the curve of the tunnel hid it from sight. As the horses picked up speed, the carriage turned a corner and raced down a steep incline into a giant tunnel hewn out of the dark red sandstone. It was completely devoid of buildings and houses. As the tunnel continued to descend, the air began to change—it began to smell of smoke—and for a moment the ever-present background hum grew in intensity until it rattled the very fabric of the carriage itself.

They made a final sharp turn, and the humming lessened and the air grew cleaner again. Cal joined Will at the window as a massive space yawned before them. On either side of the road stood rows of buildings, a complex forest of brick ducts running over the cavern walls above them like bloated varicose veins. In the distance, dark stacks vented cold blue flames and streamed vertical plumes of smoke, which, largely undisturbed by air currents, rose to the roof of the cavern. Here the smoke accumulated, rippling slowly and resembling a gentle swell on the surface of an inverted brown ocean.

"This is the Colony, Will," said Cal, his face next to Will's at the narrow window. "This is . . ."

Will just stared in wonder, hardly daring to breathe.

". . . home."

23

AROUND the same time that Will and Cal were arriving at the Jerome house, Rebecca was standing patiently beside a lady from Family Welfare on the thirteenth floor of Mandela Heights, a dreary, run-down apartment building on the seamier side of Wandsworth. The social worker was ringing the bell of number 65 for the third time without getting a reply, while Rebecca looked around her at the dirty floor. With a low, remorseful moan, the wind was blowing through the broken windows of the stairwell and flapping the partially filled trash bags heaped in one corner.

Rebecca shivered. It wasn't just because of the chill wind, but because she was about to be delivered to what she considered one of the worst places in the world.

By now, the social worker had given up pressing the grimy doorbell and had started knocking loudly. There was still no reply, but the sound of the television could clearly be heard from within. She knocked again, more insistently this time, and stopped as she finally heard the sound of coughing and a woman's strident voice from the other side of the door.

"All right, all right, for gawd's sake, giv'us a chance!"

The social worker turned to Rebecca and tried to smile reassuringly. She only managed something approaching a pitying grimace.

"Looks like she's in."

"Oh, good," Rebecca said sarcastically, picking up her two small suitcases.

They waited in awkward silence as, with much fumbling, the door was unlocked and the chain removed, accompanied by mutterings and curses and punctuated by intermittent coughing. The door finally swung open, and a significantly disheveled middle-aged woman, cigarette hanging from her bottom lip, looked the social worker up and down suspiciously.

"What's all this about?" she asked, one eye squinting from the smoke streaming from her cigarette, which twitched with all the vigor of a conductor's baton as she spoke.

"I've brought your niece, Mrs. Boswell," the social worker announced, indicating Rebecca standing beside her.

"You what?" the woman said sharply, shedding ash on the social worker's immaculate shoes. Rebecca cringed.

"Don't you remember . . . we spoke on the phone yesterday?"

The woman's watery gaze settled on Rebecca, who smiled and leaned forward a little to come within her limited field of vision.

"Hello, Auntie Jean," she said, doing her best to smile.

"Rebecca, my love, of course, yes, look at you, 'aven't you grown. Quite the young lady." Auntie Jean coughed and opened the door fully. "Yes, come in, come in, I've got something on the boil." She turned and shuffled back into the small hallway, leaving Rebecca and the social worker to survey the haphazard piles of curling newspapers stacked along the walls, and the huge number of unopened letters and pamphlets littering the filthy carpet. Everything was covered with a fine film of dust, and the corners of the hallway were festooned with cobwebs. The whole place stank of Auntie Jean's cigarettes. The social worker and Rebecca stood in silence until the social worker, as if pulling herself out of a trance, abruptly bade Rebecca good-bye and good luck. She seemed in a great haste to leave, and Rebecca watched her as she made for the stairs, pausing on the way to glance at the elevator doors as if she was hoping that by some miracle it was back in service and she wasn't facing the long trek down.

Rebecca gingerly entered the apartment and followed her aunt into the kitchen.

"I could do with some 'elp in 'ere," Auntie Jean said, picking out a packet of cigarettes from among the debris on the table.

Rebecca surveyed the tawdry vision that lay before her. Shafts of sunlight cut through the ever-present fog of cigarette smoke that hung around her aunt like a personal storm cloud. She wrinkled her nose as she caught the acrid taint of yesterday's burned food lacing the air.

"If you're going to be staying in my gaff," her aunt said through a fit of coughing, "you're going to 'ave to pull your weight."

Rebecca didn't move; she feared any motion, however slight, would result in her being covered in the grime that coated every surface.

"C'mon, Becs, put down your bags, roll up your sleeves. You can start by putting the kettle on." Auntie Jean smiled as she sat down at the kitchen table. She lit a fresh cigarette from the old one before stubbing out its glowing stump directly on the Formica tabletop, completely missing the overflowing ashtray.

The interior of the Jerome household was surprisingly rich and comforting, with subtly patterned carpets, burnished wood surfaces, and walls of deep greens and burgundies. Cal took Will's backpack from him and set it down by a small table on which an oil lamp with an opaque glass shade stood on a creamy linen doily.

"In here," Cal said, indicating that Will should follow him through the first door leading off the hallway. "This is the drawing room," he announced proudly.

The atmosphere in the room was warm and muggy, with tiny gusts of fresh air coming from a dirt-encrusted grille above where they now stood. The ceiling was low, with ornate plaster moldings turned an off-white by the smoke and soot from the fire that even now roared in the wide hearth. In front of this, sprawled on a worn Persian rug, was a large, mangy-looking animal asleep on its back with its legs in the air, leaving little doubt as to its gender. "A dog!" Will was slightly stunned to see a domestic pet down here. The animal was the color of rubbed slate; it was almost completely bald, with just the odd patch of dark stubble or tuft of hair erupting here and there from its loose skin, which sagged like an ill-fitting suit.

"Dog? That's Bartleby, he's a cat, a Rex variant. An excellent hunter."

Astonished, Will looked again. *A cat?* It was the size of a well-fed, badly shaved Doberman. There was nothing the slightest bit feline about the animal, whose large rib cage slowly rose and fell with its regular breathing. As Will bent over to examine it more closely, it snorted loudly in its sleep, and its huge paws twitched.

"Careful, he'll take your face off."

Will swung around to see an old woman in one of two large leather wing chairs positioned on either side of the fireplace. She had been sitting well back when he had come in, and he hadn't seen her.

"I wasn't going to touch him," he answered defensively, straightening up.

The old woman's pale gray eyes twinkled and never left Will's face.

"He doesn't have to be touched," she said, then added, "He's very instinctive, is our Bartleby." Her face glowed with affection as she glanced at the luxuriating and oversized animal.

"Grandma, this is Will," Cal said.

Once again the old lady's knowing gaze returned to Will, and she nodded. "Of that I am well aware. He's a Macaulay from head to toe and has his mother's eyes, no mistake about it. Hello, Will."

Will was struck dumb, transfixed by her gentle manner and the vibrant light dancing in her old eyes. It was as though some part of him, a vague memory, had been lit, just as a dying ember is rekindled by a faint breeze. He felt immediately at ease in her presence. *But why?* He was naturally wary when meeting adults for the first time, and down here in this strangest of places he couldn't afford to let his guard drop. He'd decided to go along with these people, to play their game, but he wasn't about to trust any of them. However, with this old woman it was different. It was as if he *knew* her. . . .

"Come and sit yourself down, talk to me. I'm sure there's lots of fascinating tales you can tell me from your life up there." She lifted her face momentarily toward the ceiling. "Caleb, put the kettle on, and let's have some fancies. Will's going to tell me all about himself," she said, motioning toward the other leather chair with a delicate yet strong hand. It was the hand of a woman who'd had to work hard all her life.

Will perched on the edge of the seat, the lively fire warming and relaxing him. Although he couldn't explain it to himself, he felt as if he'd reached a place of safety at last, a sanctuary.

The old lady looked intently at him, and he unself-consciously looked straight back at her, the warmth of her attention every bit as comforting as the fire in the hearth. All the horror and the trials of the past week were forgotten for the moment, and he sighed and sat back, regarding her with mounting curiosity.

Her hair was fine and a snowy white, and she wore it in an elaborate bun at the top of her head, held in place by a tortoiseshell comb. She was dressed in a plain blue long-sleeved gown with a white ruffled collar high up on the neck.

"Why do I feel as though I know you?" he asked suddenly. He had the oddest feeling that he could say whatever was on his mind to this complete stranger.

"Because you do." She smiled. "I held you as a baby; I sang you lullabies."

He opened his mouth, about to protest that what she'd said couldn't be true, but he stopped himself. He frowned. Once again, from deep within him came a glimmer of recognition. It was as if every fiber of his body were telling him that she was speaking the truth. There was just something so familiar about the old lady. His throat tightened and he swallowed several times, trying to control his feelings. The old woman saw the emotion welling up in his eyes.

"She would've been so proud of you, you know," Grandma Macaulay said. "You were her firstborn." She inclined her head toward the mantelpiece. "Would you hand me that picture? There, in the middle."

Will stood up to examine the many photographs in frames of different shapes and sizes. He didn't immediately recognize any of the subjects; some were grinning preposterously, and some had the most solemn faces. They all had the same ethereal quality as the daguerreotypes—old photographs showing the ghostlike images of people from the distant past—that he'd seen in his father's museum in Highfield. As the old lady had asked, he reached for the largest photograph of them all, which held pride of place in the very center of the mantelpiece. Seeing that it was of Mr. Jerome and a younger version of Cal, he hesitated.

"Yes, that's the one," the old woman confirmed.

Will handed it to her, watching as she turned it over on her lap, unclipped the catches, and lifted off the back. There was another picture concealed within it, which she levered out with her fingernails and passed to him without comment.

Turning it to catch the light, he studied the print closely. It showed a young woman in a white blouse and a long black skirt. In her arms, the woman held a small bundle. Her hair was the whitest of whites, identical to Will's, and her face was beautiful, a strong face with kind eyes and a fine bone structure, a full mouth, and a square jaw . . . *his* jaw, which he now touched involuntarily.

"Yes," the old lady said softly, "that's Sarah, your mother. You're just like her. That was taken mere weeks after you were born."

"Huh?" Will gasped, nearly dropping the picture.

"Your real name is Seth . . . that's what you were christened. That's you she's holding."

He felt as though his heart had stopped. He peered at the bundle. He could see it was a baby, but couldn't make out its face clearly because of the swaddling. His mind raced and his hands trembled as his feelings and thoughts bled into one another. But through all this, something definite emerged and *connected*, as if he'd been wrestling with a hitherto insoluble problem and suddenly discovered the answer. As if, buried deep in his subconscious, there had been a tiny question hidden away, an unadmitted suspicion that his family, Dr. and Mrs. Burrows and Rebecca, all he'd known for his life, were somehow different from him.

He was having problems focusing on the picture and forced himself to look at it again, scouring it for details.

"Yes," Grandma Macaulay said in a gentle voice, and he found himself nodding. However irrational it might seem, he knew, knew with absolute certainty, that what she was saying was true. That this woman in the photograph, with the monochrome and slightly blurry face, was his *real* mother, and that all these people he'd so recently met were his *true* family. He couldn't explain it even to himself; he just knew.

His suspicions that they were trying to deceive him, and that this was all some elaborate trick, evaporated, and a tear ran down his cheek, drawing a pale, delicate line on his unwashed face. He hurriedly brushed it away with his hand. As he passed the photograph back to Grandma Macaulay, he was aware that his face was flushing.

"Tell me what it's like up there—Topsoil," she said, to spare him his embarrassment. He was grateful, still standing awkwardly by her chair as she put the frame together again, then held it out for him to replace on the mantelpiece.

"Well . . . ," he began falteringly.

"You know, I've never seen daylight or felt the sun on my face. How does that feel? They say it burns."

Will, now back in his chair, looked across at her. He was staggered. "You've never seen the sun?"

"Very few here have," Cal said, coming back into the room and squatting down on the hearth rug at his grandmother's feet. He began gently kneading the loose and rather scabby flap of skin under the cat's chin; almost at once a loud, throbbing purr filled the room.

"Tell us, Will. Tell us what it's like," Grandma Macaulay said, her hand resting on Cal's head as he leaned against the arm of her chair.

So Will started to tell them, a little hesitantly at first, but then, as if a torrent had been unleashed, he found he was almost babbling as he spoke about his life above. It astounded him how easy it was, and how very natural it felt, to talk to these people whom he'd only known for such a brief time. He told them about his family and his school, regaling them with stories about the excavations with his father—or rather, the person he'd believed was his father until this moment—and about his mother and his sister.

"You love your Topsoiler family very much, don't you?" Grandma Macaulay said, and Will could only bring himself to nod in response. He knew that none of this, none of these revelations that he might have a *real* family down here in the Colony, would change the way he felt about his father. And no matter how difficult Rebecca had made his life, he had to admit to himself that he missed her terribly. He felt a tremendous surge of guilt, knowing that by now she'd be racked with worry about what had happened to him. Her small and well-ordered world would be unwinding around her. He swallowed hard. *I'm sorry, Rebecca, I should have told you, I should have left a note!* He wondered if she'd called the police after it was discovered that he was missing, the same ineffective procedure they'd put into motion when their father had disappeared. But all this was pushed aside in an instant when the image of Chester, alone and still incarcerated in that awful cell, flashed before him.

"What will happen to my friend?" he blurted out.

Grandma Macaulay didn't answer, staring absently into the fire, but Cal was quick to respond.

"They'll never let him go back . . . or you."

"But why?" Will asked. "We'll promise not to say anything . . . about all this."

There were a few seconds of silence, and then Grandma Macaulay coughed gently.

"It wouldn't wash with the Styx," she said. "They couldn't have anyone telling the Topsoilers about us. It might bring about the Discovery."

"The Discovery?"

"It's what we're taught in the Book of Catastrophes. It is the end of all things, when the people are ferreted out and perish at the hands of those above," Cal said flatly, as if reciting a verse.

"God forbid," the old lady murmured, averting her eyes and staring into the flames again.

"So what will they do with Chester?" Will asked, dreading the answer.

"Either he'll be put to work or he might be Banished . . . sent on a train down to the Deeps and left to fend for himself," Cal replied.

Will was about to ask what the Deeps were when out in the hall the front door was flung open with a bang. The fire flared and threw up a shower of sparks, which glowed briefly as they were drawn up the chimney. Grandma Macaulay peered around the side of her armchair, smiling as Cal and Bartleby both leaped to their feet. A powerful man's voice bellowed, "HELLO IN THERE!"

Still sleep-ridden, the cat blundered sideways against the underside of an occasional table, which crashed to the ground at the same instant that the drawing-room door burst open. A massive, thickset man entered the room like dirty thunder, his pale yet ruddy-cheeked face beaming with undisguised excitement.

"WHERE IS HE? WHERE IS HE?" he shouted, and locked his fierce gaze on Will, who rose apprehensively from his chair, uncertain what to make of this human explosion. In two strides, the man had crossed the room and clasped Will in a bear hug, hoisting him off his feet as if he weighed no more than a bag of feathers. Letting out a deafening roar of a laugh, he held Will at arm's length with his feet dangling helplessly in midair.

"Let me look at you. Yes . . . yes, you're your mother's boy, no mistake; it's the eyes, isn't it, Ma? He's got her eyes, and her chin . . . the shape of her handsome face, by God, ha-ha-ha!" he bellowed.

"Do put him down, Tam," Grandma Macaulay said.

The man lowered Will back down to the floor, still staring intently into the startled boy's eyes and grinning and shaking his head.

"It's a great day, a great day indeed." He stuck out a huge ham of a hand toward Will. "I'm your uncle Tam."

Will automatically held out his hand and Tam took it into his giant palm, shook it in an iron grip, and pulled Will in toward him, ruffling his hair with his other hand and sniffing at the top of his head loudly in an exaggerated manner.

"He's awash with Macaulay blood, this one," he boomed. "Wouldn't you say so, Ma?"

"Without a doubt," she said softly. "But don't you be frightening him with your horseplay, Tam."

Bartleby was rubbing his massive head against Uncle Tam's oily black pant legs and insinuating his long body between his and Will's, all the while purring and making an unearthly low whining sound. Tam glanced briefly down at the creature and then up at Cal, who was still standing next to his grandmother's chair, enjoying the spectacle.

"Cal, the magician's apprentice, how are you, lad? What do you think of all this, eh?" He looked from one boy to the other. "By God, it's good to see you two under the same roof again." He shook his head in disbelief. "Brothers, hah, brothers, my nephews. This calls for a drink. A *real* drink."

"We were just about to have some tea," Grandma Macaulay intervened quickly. "Would you care for a cup, Tam?"

He swung around to his mother and smiled broadly with a devilish glint in his eye. "Why not? Let's have a cup of tea and catch up."

With that the old woman disappeared into the hall, and Uncle Tam sat down in her vacated chair, which groaned under his weight. Stretching out his legs, he took a short pipe from the inside of his huge overcoat and filled it from a tobacco pouch. Then he used a taper from the fireside to light the pipe, sat back, and blew a cloud of bluish smoke up at the ornate ceiling, all the while looking at the two boys.

For a time, all that could be heard was the crackling of the burning coal, the intrusive purring of Bartleby, and the distant sounds of the old woman busy in the kitchen. No one felt the need to talk as the flickering light played on their faces and threw trembling shadows over the walls behind. Eventually Uncle Tam spoke.

"You know your Topsoiler father passed through here?"

"You saw him?" Will leaned toward Uncle Tam.

"No, but I talked to them that did."

"Where is he? The policeman said he was safe."

"Safe?" Uncle Tam sat forward, yanking the pipe from his mouth, his face becoming deadly serious. "Listen, don't you believe a word those spineless scum say to you; they're all snakes and leeches. The poisonous toadies of the Styx."

"That's quite enough, Tam," Grandma Macaulay said as she entered the room rattling a tray of tea in her unsteady hands and a plate laden with some "fancies," as she called them—shapeless lumps topped with white icing. Cal got up and helped her, handing cups to Will and Uncle Tam. Then Will let Grandma Macaulay have his chair and sat next to Cal on the hearth rug.

"So, about my dad?" Will asked a little sharply, unable to contain himself any longer.

Tam nodded and relit his pipe, unleashing voluminous shrouds of smoke that enveloped his head in a haze. "You only missed him by a week or so. He's gone to the Deeps."

"Banished?" Will sat bolt upright, his face filled with concern as he remembered the term that Cal had used.

"No, no," Tam exclaimed, gesticulating with his pipe. "He wanted to go! Curious thing, by all accounts he went willingly . . . no announcements . . . no spectacle . . . none of the usual Styx theatricals." Uncle Tam drew a mouthful of smoke and blew it out slowly, his brow furrowed. "I suppose it wouldn't have been much of a show for the people, no ranting and wailing from the condemned." He stared into the fire, his frown remaining as if he was profoundly baffled by the whole affair. "In the days before he left, he'd been seen wandering around, scribbling in his book . . . bothering folk with his foolish questions. I reckon the Styx thought he was a little . . ." Uncle Tam tapped the side of his head.

Grandma Macaulay cleared her throat and looked at him sternly.

". . . harmless," he said, checking himself. "Reckon that's why they let him roam around like that. But you can bet they watched his every move."

Will shifted uneasily where he sat on the Persian rug; it felt wrong to be demanding answers from this good-natured and friendly man, this man who was purportedly his uncle, but he couldn't help himself.

"What exactly *are* the Deeps?" he asked.

"The inner circles, the Interior." Uncle Tam pointed with the stem of his pipe at the floor. "Down below us. The Deeps."

"It's a bad place, isn't it?" Cal put in.

"Never been there myself. It's not somewhere you'd choose to go," Uncle Tam said with a measured look at Will.

"But what's there?" Will asked, desperate to learn more about where his father had gone.

"Well, five or so miles down, there are other . . . I suppose you could call them settlements. That's where the Miners' Train stops, where the Coprolites live." He sucked loudly on his pipe. "The air's sour down there. It's the end of the line, but the tunnels go farther—miles and miles, they say. Legends even tell of an inner world down deep, at the center, older towns and older cities, larger than the Colony." Uncle Tam chortled dismissively. "Reckon it's a load of codswallop, myself."

"But has anyone ever been down these tunnels?" Will asked, hoping in his heart of hearts that someone had.

"Well, there've been stories. In the year two twenty or thereabouts, they say a Colonist made it back after years of Banishment. What was his name . . . Abraham something?"

"Abraham de Jaybo," Grandma Macaulay said quietly.

Uncle Tam glanced at the door and lowered his voice. "When they found him at the Miners' Station, he was in a terrible state, covered in cuts and bruises, his tongue missing—cut out, they say. He was almost starved to death, like a walking corpse. He didn't last long; died a week later from some unknown disease that made his blood boil up through his ears and mouth. He couldn't speak, of course, but some say he made drawings, loads of them, as he lay on his deathbed, too afraid to sleep."

"What were the drawings of?" Will was wide-eyed.

"All sorts, apparently: infernal machines, strange animals and impossible landscapes, and things no one could understand. The Styx said it was all the product of a diseased mind, but others say the things he drew really exist. To this very day the drawings are kept under lock and key in the Governors' vaults . . . though no one I know's ever seen them."

"God, I'd give anything to look at those," Will said, spellbound.

Uncle Tam gave a deep chuckle.

"What?" Will asked.

"Well, apparently, that Burrows fellow said the selfsame thing when he was told the tale . . . the *selfsame* words, he used."

24

AFTER all the talk, the tea, the "fancies," and the revelations, Uncle Tam finally rose with a cavernous yawn and stretched his powerful frame with several bone-chilling clicks. He turned to Grandma Macaulay.

"Well, come on, Ma, high time I got you home."

And with that, they bade their farewells and were gone. Without Tam's booming voice and infectious guffaws to fill it, the house suddenly seemed a very different place.

"I'll show you where you'll be sleeping," Cal said to Will, who only mumbled in response. It was as though he were under some kind of spell, his mind teeming with new thoughts and feelings that, try as he might, he couldn't keep from rising to the surface like a shoal of hungry fish.

They wandered out into the hallway, where Will perked up slightly. He began to study the succession of portraits hanging there, working his way gradually along.

"I thought your granny lived in this house," he asked Cal in a distant voice.

"She's allowed to visit me here." Cal immediately looked away from Will, who wasn't slow in noticing there was more to this than Cal was letting on.

"What do you mean, 'allowed to'?"

"Oh, she's got her own place, where Mother and Uncle Tam were born," Cal said evasively, with a shake of his head. "C'mon, let's go!" He was halfway up the stairs with the backpack hooked over his arm when, to his exasperation, he found Will wasn't following him. Peering over the banister, Cal saw that he was still hovering by the portraits, his curiosity piqued by something at the end of the hallway.

Will's hunger for discovery and adventure had taken hold of him again, sweeping aside his sheer fatigue and his preoccupation with all he'd so recently learned. "What's through here?" he asked, pointing at a black door with a brass handle.

"Oh, it's nothing. Just the kitchen," Cal replied impatiently.

"Can I have a quick look?" Will said, already heading for the door.

Cal sighed. "Oh, all right, but there's really nothing to see," he said in a resigned tone and descended the stairs, stowing the pack at the bottom. "It's *just* a kitchen!"

Pushing through the door, Will found himself in a low-ceilinged room resembling something from a Victorian hospital. And it not only looked but smelled like one, too, a strong undercurrent of carbolic blending with indistinct cooking smells. The walls were a dull mushroom color, and the floor and work surfaces were covered with large white tiles, crazed with a myriad of scratches and fissures. In places, they had been worn into dappled hollows by years of scrubbing.

His attention was drawn to the corner, where a lid was gently clattering on one of a number of saucepans being heated on an antiquated stove of some kind, its heavy frame swollen and glassy with burned-on grease. He leaned over the nearest saucepan, but its simmering contents were obscured by wisps of steam as it gave off a vaguely savory aroma. To his right, beyond a solid-looking butcher's block with a large-bladed cleaver dangling from a hook above, Will spotted another door leading off the kitchen.

"Where does that go?"

"Look, wouldn't you rather . . . ," Cal's voice trailed off as he realized it was futile to argue with his brother, who was already nosing into the small adjoining room.

Will's eyes lit up when he saw what was in there. It was like an alchemist's storeroom, with shelf upon shelf of squat jars containing unrecognizable pickled items, all horribly distorted by the curvature of the thick glass and discolored by the oily fluid in which they were immersed. They resembled anatomical specimens preserved in formaldehyde.

On the bottom shelf, laid out on dull metal trays, Will noticed a huddle of objects the size of small soccer balls that had a gray-brown dusty bloom to them.

"What are these?"

"They're pennybuns—we grow them all over, but mostly in the lower chambers."

"What do you use them for?" Will was crouching down, examining their velvety, mottled surfaces.

"They're mushrooms. You eat them. You probably had some in the Hold."

"Oh, right," Will said, making a face as he stood upright. "And that?" he said, pointing at some strips of what appeared to be beef jerky hanging from racks above.

Cal smiled broadly. "You should be able to tell what it is."

Will hesitated for a moment and then leaned a little closer to one of the strips; it was definitely meat of some description. It looked like elongated sinews and was the color of new scabs. He sniffed tentatively, then shook his head.

"No idea."

"Come on. The smell?"

Will closed his eyes and sniffed again, "No, it doesn't smell like anything I—" His eyes snapped open and he looked at Cal. "It's rat, isn't it?" he said, both pleased that he was able to identify it and, at the same time, kind of appalled by the finding. "You eat rat?"

"It's delicious . . . there's nothing wrong with that. Now, tell me what *kind* is it?" Cal asked, reveling in Will's evident disgust. "Pack, sewer, or sightless?"

"I don't *like* rats, let alone eat them. I haven't got the slightest idea."

Cal shook his head slowly, with an expression of mock disappointment.

"It's easy, this is sightless," he said, lifting the end of one of the lengths with his finger and sniffing it himself. "More gamey than the others—it's a bit special. We usually have it on Sundays."

They were interrupted by a loud, machine gun–like humming behind them, and both spun around at the same time. There, purring with all his might, sat Bartleby, his huge amber eyes fixed on the meat strips and drops of anticipatory saliva dripping off his bald chin.

"Out!" Cal shouted at him, pointing at the kitchen door. The cat didn't move an inch, but sat resolutely on the tiled floor, completely mesmerized by the sight of the meat.

"Bart, I said get out!" Cal shouted again, making to close the door as he and Will entered the kitchen again. The cat snarled threateningly and bared his teeth, a pearly stockade of viciously sharp pegs, as his skin erupted with a wave of goose pimples.

"You insolent mutt!" Cal snapped. "You know you don't mean that!"

Cal aimed a playful kick at the disobedient animal, which dodged sideways, easily avoiding the blow. Turning slowly, Bartleby gave them both a slightly scornful look over his shoulder, then padded lethargically away, his naked, spindly tail flicking in a gesture of defiance behind him.

"He'd sell his soul for rat, that one," Cal said, shaking his head and smiling.

After the brief tour of the kitchen, Cal showed Will up the creaking wooden staircase to the top floor.

"This is Father's room," he said, opening a dark door halfway down the landing. "We're not supposed to go in here. There'll be big trouble if he catches us."

Will quickly glanced back down the stairs to assure himself the coast was clear before following. A huge four-poster bed dominated Mr. Jerome's room, so tall it almost touched the dilapidated ceiling that sagged ominously down toward it. The space around it was bare and featureless, and a single light burned in one corner.

"What was here?" Will asked, noticing a row of lighter patches on the gray wall.

Cal looked at the ghostly squares and frowned. "Pictures—there used to be lots of them before Father stripped the room out."

"Why'd he do that?"

"Because of Mother—she'd furnished it, it was her room, really," Cal replied. "After she left, Father . . ." He fell silent, and because he didn't seem inclined to volunteer any more on the subject, Will felt he shouldn't probe further—for the moment, anyway. He certainly hadn't forgotten how the photograph Grandma Macaulay had shown him of his mother had been inexplicably hidden away. None of these people—Uncle Tam, Grandma Macaulay, or Cal—were divulging the whole story. Even if they were indeed his true family—and Will once again found himself questioning the fantastical notion that they were—there was evidently more to all this than he was being told. And he was determined to find out what it was.

Back out on the landing, Will paused to admire an impressive light orb supported by a ghostly bronze hand protruding from the wall.

"These lights, where do they come from?" he asked, touching the cool surface of the sphere.

"I don't know. I think they're made in the West Cavern."

"But how do they work? Dad had one looked at by some experts, but they didn't have a clue."

Cal regarded the light with a noncommittal air. "I don't really know. I do know that it was Sir Gabriel Martineau's scientists who discovered the formula—"

"Martineau?" Will interrupted, recalling the name from the entry in his father's journal.

Cal carried on, regardless: "No, I couldn't really tell you what makes them work—I think they use Antwerp glass, though. It has something to do with how the elements mix under pressure."

"There must be thousands of these down here."

"Without them we couldn't survive," Cal replied. "Their light is like sunlight to us."

"How do you turn them off?"

"Turn them off?" Cal looked at Will quizzically, the illumination bathing his pale face. "Why in the world would you want to do that?"

He started down the landing, but Will stayed put. "So are you going to tell me about this Martineau?" he demanded.

"Sir Gabriel Martineau," Cal said carefully, as if Will was showing a distinct lack of respect. "He's the Founding Father—our savior—he built the Colony."

"But I read he died in a fire in . . . um . . . well, several centuries ago."

"That's what they'd have you Topsoilers believe. There was a fire, but he didn't die in it," Cal replied with a scornful curl of his lip.

"So what happened, then?" Will shot back.

"He came down here with the Founding Fathers to live, of course."

"The Founding Fathers?"

"Yes, the Founding Fathers, OK?" Cal said in exasperation. "I'm not going into all that now. You can read about it in the Book of Catastrophes, if you're so interested."

"The Book . . . ?"

"Oh, just come on already," Cal snapped. He stared at Will and ground his teeth with such irritation that Will refrained from asking any farther questions. They continued down the landing and went through a door.

"This is my room. Father arranged another bed when he was told you had to stay with us."

"Told? Who by?" Will asked in a flash.

Cal raised his eyebrows as if he ought to know better, so Will just looked around the simple bedroom, not much larger than his own back home. Two narrow beds and a wardrobe almost filled it, with very little space in between. He perched on the end of one of the beds and, noticing a set of clothes left on the pillow, glanced up at Cal.

"Yes, they're yours," Cal confirmed.

"I suppose I could do with a change," Will muttered, looking down at the filthy jeans he was wearing. He opened the bundle of new clothes and felt the fabric of the waxy trousers. The material was rough, almost scaly to the touch—he guessed it was a coating to keep out the damp.

While Cal lay back on his bed, Will began to get changed. The clothes felt strange and cold next to his skin. The pants were stiff and scratchy, and they fastened with metal buttons and a belt tie. He wrestled into the shirt without bothering to undo it, and then slowly wriggled his shoulders and arms as if trying to get a new skin to fit. Last of all, he shrugged on the long jacket with the familiar shoulder mantle that they all wore. Although glad to be out of his filthy clothes, the replacements felt stiff and restrictive.

"Don't worry, they loosen up once they're warm," Cal said, noticing his discomfort. Then Cal got up and clambered across

Will's bed to get to the wardrobe, where he knelt down and slid out an old Peek Freans cookie tin from beneath it.

"Have a look at these." He put the tin on Will's bed and pryed off the lid.

"This is my collection," he announced proudly. He fished around in the tin, taking out a battered cell phone, which he handed to Will, who immediately tried to turn it on. It was dead. *Neither use nor ornament:* Will remembered the oft-used phrase his father would trot out on such occasions, which was ironic considering most of Dr. Burrows's prize possessions didn't fit into either category.

"And this." Cal produced a small blue radio and, holding it up to show Will, he clicked on the switch. It crackled with tinny static as he swiveled one of the dials.

"You won't pick up anything down here," Will said, but Cal was already taking something else out of the tin.

"Look at these, they're fantastic."

He straightened out some curling car brochures, mottled with chalky spots of mildew, and passed them to Will as if they were priceless parchments. Will frowned as he surveyed them.

"These are very old models, you know," Will said as he browsed through the pages of sports cars and family sedans. "The new Capri," he read aloud and smiled to himself.

He glanced at Cal and noticed the look of total absorption on the boy's face as he lovingly arranged a selection of chocolate bars and a bag of cellophane-wrapped candies in the bottom of the tin. It was as if he was trying to find the perfect composition.

"What's all the chocolate for?" Will asked, actually hoping that Cal might offer him some.

"I'm saving it for a very special occasion," Cal said as he lovingly handled a bar of Mars Bar. "I just love the way it smells." He drew the bar under his nose and sniffed extravagantly. "That's enough for me . . . I don't need to open it." He rolled his eyes in ecstasy.

"So where did you get all this stuff?" Will asked, putting down the car brochures, which curled slowly back into a disheveled tube. Cal glanced warily at the bedroom door and moved a little closer to Will.

"Uncle Tam," he said in a low voice. "He often goes beyond the Colony—but you mustn't tell anyone. It would mean Banishment." He hesitated and glanced at the door again. "He even goes Topsoil."

"Does he now?" Will said, scrutinizing Cal's face intently. "And when does he do that?"

"Every so often." Cal was speaking so softly that Will had difficulty hearing him. "He trades things that . . ." He faltered, realizing that he was overstepping the mark. ". . . that he finds."

"Where?" Will asked.

"On his trips," Cal said obliquely as he packed the items back into the tin, replaced the lid, and pushed it once again under the wardrobe. Still kneeling, he turned to Will.

"You're going to get out, aren't you?" he asked with a sly grin.

"Huh?" Will said, taken aback by the abruptness of the question.

"Come on, you can tell me. You're going to escape, aren't you? I just know it!" Cal was literally vibrating with excitement as he waited for Will's response.

"You mean back to Highfield?"

Cal nodded energetically.

"Maybe, maybe not. I don't know yet," Will said guardedly. Despite his emotions and everything he felt for his newfound family, he was going to play it safe for now; a small voice in his head was still warning him that this could be part of an elaborate plan to ensnare him and keep him here forever, and that even this boy who claimed to be his brother could be working for the Styx. He wasn't quite ready to trust him yet, not completely.

Cal looked directly at Will.

"Well, when you do, I'm coming with you." He was smiling, but his eyes were deadly serious. Will was taken completely unawares by this suggestion and didn't know how he was going to answer, but at that point was saved by a gong sounding insistently from somewhere in the house.

"That's dinner, Father must be home. Come on." Cal leaped up and ran out the door and down the stairs to the dining room, Will following closely behind. Mr. Jerome was already seated at the head of a deep-grained wooden table. As they entered, he didn't look up, his eyes remaining fixed on the table in front of him.

The room couldn't have been more different from the sumptuous drawing room Will had seen earlier. It was spartan and the furniture basic, appearing to be constructed from wood that had endured centuries of wear. On closer inspection, he could see that the table and chairs had been fabricated from a mishmash of different woods of conflicting shades and with grains at odds to each other; some parts were waxed or varnished, while others were rough with splintery surfaces.

The high-backed dining chairs looked particularly rickety and archaic, with spindly legs that creaked and complained when the boys took their places on either side of the sullen-faced Mr. Jerome, who barely gave Will a glance. Will shifted in his seat, trying to get comfortable and wondering idly how the chairs could accommodate someone of Mr. Jerome's impressive bulk without giving up the ghost.

Mr. Jerome cleared his throat loudly and without any warning he and Cal leaned forward, their eyes closed and their hands folded on the table in front of them. A little self-consciously, Will did likewise.

"The sun shall no longer set, nor shall the moon withdraw itself, for the Lord will be your everlasting light and the dark days of your mourning will be ended," Mr. Jerome droned.

Will couldn't stop himself from peeping at the man through his half-closed eyes. He found all this a little odd—no one would have *ever* thought of saying grace in his house. Indeed, the closest they ever got to anything resembling a prayer was when his mother yelled, "For God's sake, shut up!"

"As it is above, so it is below," Mr. Jerome finished.

"Amen," he and Cal said in unison, too quickly for Will to join in. They sat up, and Mr. Jerome tapped a spoon on the tumbler in front of him.

There was a moment of uncomfortable silence during which no one at the table looked at anyone else. Then a man with long greasy hair shambled into the room. His face was deeply lined and his cheeks were gaunt. He was wearing a leather apron, and his tired and listless eyes, like dying candle flames in cavernous hollows, lingered briefly on Will and then quickly turned away.

As Will watched the man make repeated trips in and out of the room, shuffling to each of them in turn to serve the food, he came to the conclusion that he must have endured great suffering, possibly a severe illness.

The first course was a thin broth. From its steamy vapors, Will could detect a spiciness, as if copious amounts of curry powder had been ladled into it. This came with a side dish of small white objects, similar in appearance to peeled gherkins. Cal and Mr. Jerome wasted no time in starting on their soup and, between loud exhalations, they both made the most outrageous noises as they sucked the liquid from their spoons, splashing large amounts of it over their clothes and simply ignoring the mess. The symphony of slurps and loud gulps reached such a ridiculous crescendo that Will couldn't stop himself from staring at both of them in utter disbelief.

Finally, he picked up his own spoon and was just at the point of taking his first tentative mouthful when, out of the corner of his eye, he saw one of the white objects on his side plate twitch. Thinking he'd imagined it, he emptied the contents of his spoon back into his bowl and instead used the utensil to roll the object over.

With a shock he found it had a row of tiny, dark brown pointed legs neatly folded beneath it. It was a grub of some kind! He sat bolt upright and watched with horror as it curved its back, its minuscule spiky legs rippling open in an undulating wave, as if to greet him.

His first thought was that it had gotten there by mistake, so he glanced at Mr. Jerome's and Cal's side plates, wondering if he should say something. At that very moment, Cal picked up one of the white objects from his own plate and bit into it, chewing it with gusto. Between his thumb and forefinger, the remaining half of the grub twitched and writhed, oozing a clear fluid over his fingertips.

Will felt his stomach heave, and he dropped his spoon in his soup dish with such a crash that the serving man came in and, finding that he was not wanted, promptly exited again. As Will tried to quell his nausea, he saw that Mr. Jerome was looking straight at him. It was such a hateful stare that Will immediately averted his eyes. As for Cal, he was intent on finishing the still-writhing half-grub, sucking it into his mouth as if he was devouring a very fat strand of spaghetti.

Will shuddered; there was absolutely no way he could bring himself to drink his soup now, so he sat there feeling distinctly unnerved and out of place until the serving man cleared the bowls away. Then the main course appeared, a gravy-soaked mush just as indeterminate as the broth. Will prodded suspiciously at everything on his plate just to make sure that nothing was still alive. It seemed harmless enough, so he began to pick at it without enthusiasm, quailing involuntarily with each mouthful, all the while accompanied by his fellow diners' gastronomic cacophony.

Although Mr. Jerome hadn't said a single word to Will during the whole meal, the unbridled resentment radiating from him was overwhelming. Will had no idea why this was, but he was vaguely beginning to wonder if it had something to do with his real mother, the person no one seemed to be prepared to talk about. Or perhaps the man simply despised Topsoilers like him? Whatever it was, he wished the man would say something, anything at all, just to break the agonizing silence. From Mr. Jerome's demeanor, Will knew full well that it wouldn't be pleasant when it came; he was prepared for that. He just wanted to get it over with. He began to sweat and tried to loosen the starched collar of his new shirt by running his finger inside it. It seemed to Will as if the room were filling with a chilled and poisonous aspic; he felt suffocated by it.

His reprieve finally came when, finishing his plate of mush, Mr. Jerome downed a glass of murky water and then abruptly got up. He folded his napkin twice and tossed it carelessly onto the table. He reached the door just as the wretch of a serving man was entering with a copper bowl in his hands. To Will's horror, Mr. Jerome elbowed him brutally aside. Will thought the man was going to fall as he lurched against the wall. He fought to regain his balance as the contents of the bowl tipped out, and apples and oranges rolled around the floor and under the table.

As if Mr. Jerome's behavior was nothing out of the ordinary, the serving man didn't so much as murmur. Will could see a cut on his lip and blood trickling down his chin as the unfortunate man crawled around the base of his chair, retrieving the fruit.

Will was flabbergasted, but Cal seemed to be ignoring the incident altogether. Will watched the pathetic man until he left the room and then, deciding there was nothing he could do, turned his attention to the bowl of fresh fruit—there were bananas, pears, and a couple of figs in addition to the apples and oranges. He helped himself, grateful for something familiar and recognizable after the first two courses.

At that moment the front door slammed with such a crash that the casement windows shook. Will and Cal listened as Mr. Jerome's footsteps retreated down the front path. It was Will who broke the silence.

"Doesn't like me much, does he?"

Cal shook his head as he peeled an orange.

"Why—" Will stopped short as the servant returned and stood submissively behind Cal's chair.

"You can go," Cal ordered rudely, not even bothering to look at the man, who slipped quietly out of the room.

"Who was that?" Will inquired.

"Oh, that was just Watkins."

Will didn't speak for a moment, then asked, "*What* did you say his name was?"

"Watkins . . . Terry Watkins."

Will repeated the name to himself several times. "I'm sure I know that from somewhere." Although he couldn't quite put his finger on it, the name triggered a sense of foreboding in him.

Cal continued eating, enjoying Will's confusion, and then Will remembered with a start. "They went missing, the whole family!"

"Yes, they certainly did."

Taken aback, Will quickly looked across at Cal. "They were snatched!"

"They had to be, they were a problem. Watkins stumbled onto an air channel, and we couldn't have him telling anybody."

"But that can't be Mr. Watkins—he was a big man. I've seen him . . . his sons went to my school," Will said. "No, that can't be the same person."

"He and his family were put to work," Cal said coldly.

"But . . . ," Will stuttered as he juggled the mental image of Mr. Watkins as he used to appear with how he looked now, ". . . he looks a hundred years old. What happened to him?" Will couldn't help but think of his own predicament, and of Chester's. So was that to be their fate? Forced into slavery for these people?

"Just as I said, they were all put to work," Cal repeated, lifting a pear to smell its skin. Noticing there was a smear of Mr. Watkins's blood on it, he polished it on his shirt before taking a bite.

Will was regarding his brother now with renewed scrutiny, trying to figure him out. The warmth he'd been beginning to feel toward him had all but evaporated. There was a vindictiveness, a hostility even, evident within the younger boy that Will didn't understand or very much care for. One moment he was saying he wanted to escape from the Colony, and the next he was acting as if he was completely at home here.

Will's train of thought was broken as Cal glanced over at his father's empty chair and sighed. "This is very hard on Father, but you have to give him time. I suppose you bring back too many memories."

"About *what*, exactly?" Will shot back, not feeling an ounce of sympathy for the surly old man. That was where the notion of his newfound family fell apart—if he never saw Mr. Jerome again, it would be too soon.

"About Mother, of course. Uncle Tam says she always was a bit of a rebel." Cal sighed again, then fell silent.

"But . . . did something bad happen?"

"We had a brother. He was only a baby. He died from a fever. After that, she ran away." A wistful look came into Cal's eyes.

"A brother," Will echoed.

Cal stared at him, any hint of his usual grin absent from his face. "She was trying to get both of us out when the Styx caught up."

"So she escaped?"

"Yes, but only just, and that's why I'm still here." Cal took another mouthful of pear and was still chewing when he spoke again. "Uncle Tam says she's the only one he knows of who got out and stayed out."

"She's still alive?"

Cal nodded. "As far as we know. But she broke the laws, and if you break the law the Styx never let go, even if you make it Topsoil. It doesn't end there. One day they *will* catch up with you, and then they *will* punish you."

"Punish? How?"

"In Mother's case, execution," he said succinctly. "That's why you have to tread very carefully."

Somewhere in the distance, a bell began to toll. Cal got to his feet and glanced through the window. "Seven bells. We should go."

Once they were outside, Cal forged ahead, and Will found it difficult to keep up, his new pants chafing against his thighs with every stride. It was as though they'd stepped into a river of people. The streets heaved with them, all dashing frantically in different directions as if they were late for something. It looked and sounded like a confused flock of leathery birds taking flight. Will followed Cal's lead, and after several turns they joined the end of a line outside a plain-looking building that resembled a warehouse. In front of each of the studded wooden doors at the entrance a pair of Styx stood in their characteristic poses, arched over like vindictive principals about to strike. Will bowed his head, trying to blend in with the crowd and avoid the jet-black pupils of the Styx, which he knew would be upon him.

Inside, the hall was deceptively big—around half the size of a football field. Large flagstones, shiny with dark patches of damp, formed the floor. The walls were roughly plastered and whitewashed. Looking around, he could see elevated platforms in the four corners of the hall, crude wooden pulpits, each with a Styx in place, hawkishly scrutinizing the gathering.

Halfway down the left and right walls were two huge oil paintings. Because of the sheer mass of people in the way, Will didn't have a clear view of the painting on the right, so he turned to examine the one nearer to him. In the foreground was a man dressed in a black coat and a dark green vest, sporting a top hat above his somewhat lugubrious and mutton-chopped face. He was studying a large sheet of paper, which might have been a plan, spread open in his hands. And he appeared to be standing in the midst of some kind of earthworks. Huddled at his sides were many other men with pickaxes and shovels, all of them looking at him with rapt admiration. For no particular reason, it brought to Will's mind pictures he'd seen of Jesus and his disciples.

"Who's that?" Will asked Cal, motioning toward the painting as people bustled past them.

"Sir Gabriel Martineau, of course. It's called the *Breaking of the Ground.*"

With the ever-increasing crowds of people milling around in the hall, Will had to jig his head from side to side to make out more of the painting. Other than the main figure, who Will now knew was Martineau himself, the ghostly faces of the workmen fascinated him. Silvery rays of what could have been moonlight radiated from above and fell on their faces, which glowed with a soft, saintly luminosity. And adding to this effect, many of them appeared to have an even brighter light directly above their heads, as if they had halos.

"No," Will murmured to himself, realizing with a start that they weren't halos at all, but that it was their white hair.

"Those others?" he said to Cal. "Who are they?"

Cal was about to reply when a portly Colonist barged rudely into him, spinning him almost completely around. The man continued determinedly on his way without so much as an apology, but Cal didn't seem to be the slightest bit annoyed by the man's conduct. Will was still waiting for an answer as Cal wheeled back to face him again. He spoke as if he were addressing someone who was irretrievably stupid.

"They're our ancestors, Will," he said with a sigh.

"Oh."

Despite the fact that Will was burning with curiosity about the picture, it was hopeless—his view was now almost completely blocked by the massing crowd. Instead, he turned to the front of the hall, where there were ten or so carved wooden pews, packed with closely seated Colonists. Going up on tiptoes to try to see what was beyond them, he caught sight of a massive iron crucifix fixed to the wall—it seemed to be made from two sections of railway track, bolted together with huge round-headed rivets.

Cal tugged him by the sleeve, and they pushed their way through the gathering to a position closer to the pews. The doors thudded shut, and Will realized that the hall had been crammed to capacity in scarcely any time at all. He found it stifling, squashed against Cal on one side and bulky Colonists on the others. The room was warming up quickly, and wraithlike wisps of steam were beginning to rise from the damp clothes of the crowd and encircle the hanging lights.

The hubbub of conversation died down as a Styx mounted the pulpit by the side of the metal cross. He wore a full-length black gown, and his shining eyes lanced through the fuggy air. For a brief moment, he closed them and inclined his head forward. Then he slowly looked up, his black gown opening, making him look like a bat about to take flight as he extended his arms toward the congregation and started to speak in a sibilant monastic drone. At first, Will couldn't quite catch what he was saying, even though from the four corners of the room the voices of the other Styx were reiterating the words of the preacher in scratchy whispers, a sound not unlike the massed tearing of dry parchments. Will listened more intently as the preacher raised his voice.

"Know this, brethren, know this," he said, his gaze scything through the congregation as he drew breath melodramatically.

"The surface of the earth is beset by creatures in a constant state of war with one another. Millions perish on either side, and there is no limit to the brutality of their malice. Their nations fall and rise, only to fall again. The vast forests have been laid low by them, and the pastures defiled with their poison." All around him Will heard mumbled words of agreement. The preacher Styx leaned forward, grasping the edge of the pulpit with his pale fingers.

"Their gluttony is matched only by their appetites for death, affliction, terror, and banishment of every living thing. And, despite their iniquities, they aspire to rise to the firmament . . . but, *mark this*, the excessive weight of their very sins will weigh them down." There was a pause as his black eyes scanned the flock and, raising his left arm above his head, a long, bony index finger pointing upward, he continued.

"Nothing remains on the soil or in the great oceans that shall not be hunted, disturbed, or despoiled. To the living things slain in droves, these defilers are both the sepulchre and the means of transition.

"And when the judgment comes"—he lowered his arm now and pointed forebodingly at members of the congregation through the hazy atmosphere—"and mark these words, it will . . . then they will be hurled into the abyss and forever lost to the Lord . . . and on that day, the truthful, the righteous, we of the true way, will once again return to reclaim the surface, to begin again, to build the new dominion . . . the new Jerusalem. For this is the teaching and the knowledge of our forefathers, passed down to us through the ages by the Book of Catastrophes."

A hush filled the hall, absolute and unbroken by a single cough or shuffle. Then the preacher spoke again, in a calmer, almost conversational tone.

"So let it be known, so let it be understood." He bowed his head.

Will thought he glimpsed Mr. Jerome seated in the pews, but couldn't be sure because he was so completely hemmed in.

Then, without warning, the whole congregation joined in with the Styx's monotone: "The earth is the Lord's, and the followers thereof, the earth and all that dwell therein. We give our eternal gratitude to our Savior, Sir Gabriel, and the Founding Fathers for their shepherdship and for the flowing together into one another, as all that happens in God's earth is also on the highest level, the Kingdom of God."

There was a moment's pause, and the Styx spoke again. "As above, so below."

The voices of the congregation boomed amens as the Styx took a step back, and Will lost sight of him. He swung around to Cal to ask him a question, but there was no time as the congregation immediately started to file toward the doorway, leaving the hall as swiftly as it had collected. The boys were swept along in the tide of people until they found themselves back on the street, where they stood watching them depart in all directions.

"I don't get this 'As below, so above' stuff," Will told Cal in a low voice. "I thought everybody hated Topsoilers."

"*Above* isn't *Topsoil*," Cal replied, so loudly and in such a petulant tone that several burly men in earshot turned to regard Will with snarls of disgust. He winced—he was beginning to wonder if having a younger brother was all it was cut out to be.

"But how often do you have to do that—go to church?" Will ventured when he had recovered sufficiently from Cal's last response.

"Once a day," Cal said. "You go to church Topsoil, too, don't you?"

"Our family didn't."

"How strange," Cal said, looking shiftily around to check that no one could overhear him. "Load of drivel, anyway," he sneered under his breath. "C'mon, we're going to see Tam. He'll be at the tavern in Low Holborn."

As they reached the end of the street and turned off it, a flock of white starlings spiraled above them and swung into a barrel roll toward the area of the cavern where the boys were now heading. Appearing from nowhere, Bartleby joined them, flicking his tail and wobbling his bottom jaw at the sight of the birds, and giving a rather sweet and plaintive mew that was totally at odds with his appearance.

"Come on, you crazy beast, you'll never catch them," Cal said as the animal sauntered past, his head held high as he hankered after the birds.

As the boys walked, they passed hovels and small workshops: a smithy where the blacksmith, an old man, backlit by the blaze from his furnace, hammered relentlessly on an anvil, and places with names like Geo. Blueskin Cartwrights and Erasmus Chemicals. Of particular fascination to Will was a dark, oily-looking yard full of carriages and broken machinery.

"Shouldn't we really be getting back?" Will asked, stopping to peer through the wrought-iron railings at the strange contraptions.

"No, Father won't be home for a while yet," Cal said. "Hurry up, we should get a move on."

As they progressed toward what Will assumed was the center of the cavern, he couldn't stop himself from looking all around at the amazing sights and the packed houses, huddled together in seemingly endless rows. Until now he hadn't fully appreciated just how huge this place was. And looking up he saw a shimmering haze, a shifting, living thing that hung like a cloud above the chaos of rooftops, fed by the collective glow of the light of all the orbs below.

For a moment, it reminded Will of Highfield during the summer doldrums, except that where there should have been sky and sunlight, there were only glimpses of an immense stone canopy. Cal quickened his pace as they passed Colonists who, from their lingering glances, evidently knew who Will was. A number crossed the road to avoid him, muttering under their breath, and others stopped where they stood, glowering at him. A few even spat in his direction.

Will was more than a little distressed by this.

"Why are they doing that?" he asked quietly, falling back behind his brother.

"Ignore them," Cal replied confidently.

"It's like they hate me or something."

"It's always the same with outsiders."

"But . . . ," Will began.

"Look, really, don't worry about it. It'll pass, you'll see. It's because you're new and, don't forget, they all know who your mother is," Cal said. "They won't do anything to you." All of a sudden, he drew to a halt and turned to Will. "But through here keep your head down and keep moving. Understand? Don't stop for *anything*."

Will didn't know what Cal was talking about until he saw the entrance by the other boy's side: It was a passage barely more than shoulder-width. Cal slipped in, with Will reluctantly following behind. It was dark and claustrophobic, and the sulfurous stench of old sewage hung in the air. Their feet splashed through unseen puddles of unidentifiable liquids. He was careful not to touch the walls, which were running with a dark, greasy slime.

Will was grateful when they finally emerged into the dim light, but then he gasped as he beheld a scene that was straight out of Victorian London. Buildings loomed on either side of the narrow alleyway, slanting inward at such precarious angles that their upper stories almost met. They were timber-framed and in a terrible state of disrepair. Most of their windows were either broken or boarded up.

Although he couldn't tell where they originated, Will heard the sound of voices and cries and laughter coming from all around. There were odd snatches of music, as if scales were being played on a strangled zither. Somewhere a baby was wailing persistently and dogs were barking. As they strode quickly past the badly deteriorated facades, Will caught whiffs of charcoal and tobacco smoke and, through open doorways, glimpsed people huddled at tables. Men in shirtsleeves hung out of windows, staring at the ground listlessly as they smoked their pipes. There was an open channel in the middle of the alley, down which a sluggish trickle of raw sewage ran through vegetable waste and other filth and detritus. Will nearly blundered into it, but stepped sharply to the edge of the alleyway to avoid it.

"No! Watch yourself!" Cal warned quickly. "Keep away from the sides!"

As they hurried along Will hardly let himself blink as he feasted his eyes on everything he saw around him. He was murmuring, "Just fantastic," over and over again to himself, wondering if his father had come across this place, a piece of living history, when his attention was caught by something else. There were people in the narrow passageways that branched off on either side. Mysterious shadowy outlines were stirring within them, and he heard hushed voices, snatches of hysterical muttering, and even, at one point, the far-off sound of someone screaming in agony.

From one of these passageways a dark figure lurched. It was a man with a black shawl over his head, which he hoisted up to reveal his gnarled face. It was covered with a sickly layer of sweat, and his skin was the color of old bone. He grabbed at Will's arm with his hand, his rheumy yellow eyes looking deep into the startled boy's.

"Ah, what is it you're after, my sweet thing?" he wheezed asthmatically, his lopsided smile revealing a row of jagged brown stumps for teeth. Bartleby snarled as Cal hurriedly pushed himself between Will and the man, yanking Will from the man's grasp and not letting go of him through several twists and turns of the alley until at last they were out and back onto a well-lit street again. Will breathed a sigh of relief.

"What *was* that place?"

"The Rookeries. It's where the paupers live. And you only saw the outskirts—you really wouldn't want to find yourself in the middle of it," Cal said, dashing ahead so quickly that Will had to work to keep up. He was still feeling the aftereffects of the ordeal in the Hold; his chest ached and his legs were leaden. But he wasn't about to let Cal see any weakness, and forced himself on.

While the cat bounded ahead into the distance, Will doggedly followed Cal's lead as he leaped over the larger pools of water and skirted around the occasional gushing downpour. Falling from the shadows of the cavern roof above, these torrents seemed to spring from nowhere, like upturned geysers.

They wound their way through a series of broad streets jam-packed with narrow terraced houses until, in the distance, Will spotted the lights of a tavern at the apex of a sharp corner where two roads met. People thronged outside it in various states of intoxication, laughing raucously and shouting, and from somewhere a woman's voice was singing shrilly. As he got closer, Will could make out the painted sign, THE BUTTOCK & FILE, with a picture of the weirdest-looking locomotive he had ever seen, which had, it appeared, an archetypal devil as its driver, scarlet-skinned and replete with horns, trident, and arrow-tipped tail.

The frontage and even the windows of the tavern were painted black and covered in a film of gray soot. People were so tightly packed in that they were overflowing onto the sidewalk outside. To a man, they were drinking from dented pewter tankards, while a number smoked either long clay pipes or turnip-shaped objects, which Will didn't recognize but which reeked of chronically soiled diapers.

As he stuck close behind Cal, they passed a top-hatted man standing at a small folding table. He was calling, "Find the painted lady! Find the painted lady!" to a couple of interested onlookers as he deftly cut a pack of cards using only a single hand. "My good sir," the man proclaimed as one of the onlookers stepped up and slapped a coin down on the green baize of the table. The cards were dealt, and Will was sorry not to see the outcome of the game, but there was absolutely no way he was going to become separated from his brother as they pushed deeper into the midst of the throng. Surrounded by all these people he felt very vulnerable, and was just debating whether he could persuade Cal to take him home when a friendly voice boomed out.

"Cal! Bring Will over here!"

There was an immediate lull in the chatter around them, and in the silence all heads turned toward Will. Uncle Tam emerged from a group of people and extravagantly waved over the two boys. The faces in the crowd outside the tavern were varied: curious, grinning, blank—but for the most part sneering with unbridled hostility. Tam seemed not the slightest bit bothered by this. He threw his thick arms around the boys' shoulders and turned his head to face the crowd, staring back at them in mute defiance.

The cacophony continued inside the tavern, only serving to make the yawning silence outside, and the rising tension that accompanied it, even more intense. This horrible hush filled Will's ears, crashing and swelling and drowning everything out.

Then an earsplitting belch, the longest and loudest Will had ever heard, ripped from someone in the crowd. As the last echoes rang back from the neighboring buildings, the spell was broken, and the whole crowd exploded into peals of harsh laughter, intermingled with cheers and the random wolf whistle.

It wasn't long before all this merriment subsided and people settled down again, the chatter resuming as a small man was widely congratulated and patted on the back so forcibly that he had to cover his drink with his hand to prevent it from slopping onto the pavement.

Still acutely self-conscious, Will kept his head bowed. He couldn't help noticing when Bartleby, stretched out under the bench where the men sat, jerked suddenly, as if some parasite or other had bitten him. Doubling up, the cat began to lick his nether regions with a hind leg pointing heavenward, looking remarkably like a badly plucked turkey.

"Now that you've met the great unwashed," Uncle Tam said, his eyes briefly flicking back over the crowd, "let me introduce you to royalty, the crème de la crème. This is Joe Waites," he said, maneuvering Will face to face with a wizened old man. His head was topped with a tightly fitting skullcap that seemed to compress the upper half of his face, making his eyes bulge out and hoisting his cheeks up into an involuntary grin. A solitary tooth protruded from his top jaw like an ivory tusk. He proffered his hand to Will, who shook it reluctantly, somewhat surprised to find it warm and dry.

"And this"—Tam inclined his head to a dapper man sporting a tawdry checkered three-piece suit and black-rimmed glasses— "is Jesse Shingles." The man bowed gracefully and then chuckled, raising his thick eyebrows.

"And, not least, the one and only Imago Freebone." A man with long, dank hair plaited into a biker's ponytail shot out a mittened hand, his voluminous leather coat flapping open to reveal his immense deep-chested barrel of a body. Will was so intimidated by the sheer mass of the man, he almost took a step back.

"Deeply pleased to meet such a hallowed legend, we being such 'umble personages," Imago said, bending his bulk forward and tugging a nonexistent forelock with his other hand.

"Uh . . . hello," Will said, uncertain what to make of him.

"Knock it off," Tam warned with a grimace.

Imago straightened up, offering his hand again, and in a normal voice said, "Will, very good to meet you." Will shook it again. "I shouldn't tease," Imago added earnestly. "We all know what you've been through, only too well." His eyes were warm and sympathetic as he continued to clasp Will's hand between both of his, finally releasing it with a comforting squeeze. "I've had the pleasure of the Dark Light myself several times, courtesy of our dear friends," he said.

"Yeah, gives you the most god-awful heartburn," Jesse Shingles said with a smirk.

Will was more than a little daunted by Uncle Tam's associates and their strange appearances, but, looking around, it struck him that they weren't that different from most of the revelers outside the tavern.

"I got you both a quart of New London." Tam handed the two tankards to the boys. "Go easy on it, Will, you won't have tasted anything like that before."

"Why? What's in it?" Will asked, eyeing with suspicion the grayish liquid with a thin froth on top.

"Ya don't wanta know, my boy, really, ya don't," Tam said, and his friends laughed; Joe Waites made peculiar birdlike noises, while Imago threw back his head and gave an extravagant but completely silent laugh, his great shoulders heaving violently. Under the bench, Bartleby grunted and noisily licked his chops.

"So you've been to your first service," Uncle Tam asked. "What did you make of it?"

"It was, um . . . interesting," Will said noncommittally.

"Not after years of it, it ain't," Tam said. "Still, it keeps the White Necks at bay." He took a deep swig from his tankard, then straightened his back and let out a contented sigh. "Yep, if I had a florin for every 'As above, so bloody below' I've said, I'd be a rich man today."

" 'As yesterday, so tomorrow,' " Joe Waites said in a weary, nasal voice, mimicking a Styx preacher. " 'So sayeth the Book of Catastrophes.' " He gave a huge exaggerated yawn, which afforded Will a rather unsettling view of his pink gums and the sad, lone tooth.

"And if you've heard one catastrophe, you've heard them all." Imago nudged Will in the ribs.

"Amen," chorused Jesse Shingles and Joe Waites, knocking their tankards together and laughing. "Amen to that!"

"Now, now, it brings comfort to them that don't have minds of their own," Tam said.

Will looked out of the corner of his eye at Cal and saw that he was joining in and laughing with the rest of them. This puzzled Will; at times his brother appeared to be filled with a religious zeal, but at others he didn't stint at showing a total lack of respect, even a contempt, for it.

"So, Will, what do you miss most about life up top?" Jesse Shingles suddenly asked, jerking his thumb toward the rock roof above their heads. Will looked uncertain and was about to say something when the little man went on. "I'd miss the fish and chips, not that I've ever tasted them." He winked conspiratorially at Imago.

"That's enough of that." Tam's brow creased with concern as he cast his eyes over the people milling around them. "Not the time nor the place."

Cal had been happily supping his drink but noticed Will was being a little reticent with his. He wiped his mouth with the back of his hand and turned to his brother, gesticulating toward his so-far-untouched tankard. "Go on, try it!"

Will tentatively took a mouthful of the chalky fluid and held it in his mouth for a moment before gulping it down.

"Well?" Cal inquired.

Will ran his tongue around his lips. "Not bad," he said. Then it bit. His eyes widened and watered as his throat began to burn. He spluttered, trying vainly to stifle the coughing fit that followed. Uncle Tam and Cal grinned. "I'm not old enough to drink this stuff," Will gasped, putting the tankard back on the table.

"Who's to stop you? Whole different set of rules down here. As long as you stay within the law, pull your weight, and attend their services, nobody minds if you let off a little steam. It's nobody's business, anyway," Tam said, slapping him gently on the back.

As if to show their agreement, the assembled group raised their tankards and clanked them together with salutations of "Up yer cludgy!"

And so it went, drink after drink, until about the fourth or fifth round—Will had lost count. Tam had just finished telling a convoluted and unfathomable joke about a flatulent policeman and a blind orb-juggler's daughter that Will could make neither head nor tail of, although all the others found it hilarious.

Picking up his tankard and still chuckling, Tam suddenly peered into his drink and, with his thumb and forefinger, pulled something out of the froth. "I got the bloody slug again," he said as the others burst once more into fits of uncontrolled laughter.

"You'll be married within the month if you don't eat it!" Imago roared.

"In that case . . . !" Tam laughed and, to Will's amazement, placed the limp gray object on his tongue. He moved it around inside his mouth before chewing and then swallowing it, to shouts of applause from his friends.

In the lull that followed, Will felt sufficiently emboldened with Dutch courage to speak up.

"Tam—Uncle Tam—I need your help."

"Anything, lad," Tam said, resting his hand on Will's shoulder. "You only have to ask."

But where did he start? Where did he begin? He had so many concerns swirling through his befuddled mind . . . finding his father . . . and what about his sister . . . and his mother . . . but *which* mother? Through this haze, one pressing thought crystallized—one thing, above all else, that he had to do.

"I have to get Chester out," Will blurted.

"*Shhh!*" Tam hissed. He glanced nervously around. They all drew together to encircle him in a secretive huddle.

"Have you any idea what you're asking?" Tam said under his breath.

Will looked at him blankly, not sure how to respond.

"And where would you go? Back to Highfield? Think you'd ever be safe there again, with the Styx hunting you? You wouldn't last a week. Who'd protect you?"

"I could go to the police," Will suggested. "They'd—"

"You're not listening. They have people everywhere," Tam reiterated forcefully.

"And not just in Highfield," Imago interjected in a low voice. "You can't trust anyone Topsoil, not the police . . . not *anyone*."

Tam nodded in agreement. "You'd need to lose yourself somewhere they'll never think of looking for you. Do you know where you might go?"

Will didn't know whether it was fatigue or the effect of the alcohol, but he was finding it hard to fight back the tears. "But I can't just do *nothing*. When I needed help to find my dad," he said hoarsely, his throat tightening with emotion, "the one person I could rely on was Chester, and now he's stuck in the Hold . . . because of me. I owe it to him."

"Have you any idea what it's like to be a fugitive?" Tam asked. "To spend the rest of your years running from every shadow, without a single friend to help you because you're a danger to anyone you're around?"

Will swallowed noisily as Tam's words sank in, aware that all eyes in their little group were on him.

"If I were you, I'd *forget* about Chester," Tam said harshly.

"I . . . just . . . can't," Will said in a strained voice, looking into his drink. "No . . ."

"It's the way things are down here, Will . . . you'll get used to it," Tam said, shaking his head emphatically.

The high spirits of only a few minutes earlier had completely evaporated, and now Cal's face and those of Tam's men, gathered closely around Will, were stern and unsympathetic. He didn't know if he'd put his foot in it and said totally the wrong thing, but he couldn't just leave it at that—his feelings were too strong. He lifted his head and looked Tam straight in the eye.

"But why do you all stay down here?" he asked "Why doesn't everyone just get out . . . escape?"

"Because," Tam began slowly, "all said and done, this is *home*. It might not be much, but it's all most people know."

"Our families are here," Joe Waites put in forcefully. "Do you think we could just take off and leave them? Have you any idea what would happen if we did?"

"Reprisals," Imago said in a voice that was barely a croak. "The Styx would slaughter the lot of them."

"Rivers of blood," Tam whispered.

Joe Waites pressed even closer to Will. "Do you really think we'd be happy living in a strange place where everything is so completely foreign to us? Where would we go? What would we do?" he gushed, trembling with agitation as he spoke. It was obvious he was extremely upset by Will's questions, only beginning to regain his composure when Tam laid a comforting hand on his shoulder.

"We'd be out of place . . . out of time," Jesse Shingles said.

Will could only nod, cowed by the sheer intensity of emotion he'd aroused in the group. He sighed shakily.

"Well, whatever, I have to get Chester out. Even if I have to do it myself," he said.

Tam regarded him for a moment and then shook his head. "Stubborn as a mule. Talk about like mother, like son," he said, a grin returning to his face. "D'you know, it's uncanny how much you sound like her. Once Sarah set her mind on something there was no budging her." He ruffled Will's hair with his large hand. "Stubborn as a bloody mule."

Imago tapped Tam's arm. "It's him again."

Relieved that he was no longer the center of attention, Will was a little slow to catch on, but when he did he observed that across the street a Styx was talking to a hefty man who had wiry white hair and long sideburns and wore a shiny brown coat with a grimy red neckerchief coiled around his stubby neck. As he watched, the Styx nodded, turned, and walked away.

"That Styx has been dogging Tam for a long time now," Cal whispered to Will.

"Who is he?" Will asked.

"Nobody knows their names, but we call him the Crawfly, on account he can't so easily be shaken off. He's on a personal vendetta to bring down Uncle Tam."

Will watched as the figure of the Crawfly dissolved into the shadows.

"He's had it in for your family ever since your ma gave the White Necks the slip and went Topsoil," Imago said to Will and Cal.

"And till my dying day I'll swear he did in my pa," Tam said, his voice flat and oddly lacking in any emotion. "He killed him, all right . . . that was no accident."

Imago shook his head slowly. "That was a horrible thing," he agreed. "A *horrible* thing."

"So what's he cooking up with that scum over there?" Tam said, frowning as he turned to Imago.

"Who was he talking to?" Will asked, peering at the other man, who was now crossing the road toward the crowd outside the tavern.

"Don't look at him . . . that's Heraldo Walsh. A cutthroat . . . nasty piece of work," Cal warned.

"A burglar, lowest of the low," Tam growled.

"But what's he doing talking to a Styx, then?" Will said, totally confused.

"Wheels within wheels," Tam muttered. "The Styx are a devious bunch. A belt becomes a snake with them." He turned to Will. "Look, I may be able to help you with Chester, but you've got to promise me one thing," he whispered.

"What's that?"

"If you get caught, you'll never implicate Cal, me, or any of us. Our lives and our families are here and, like it or not, we have to stay in this place with the White Necks . . . the Styx. That's our lot. And I'll say it again: They'll never let it rest if you cross them . . . they will do *everything* they can to catch up with you—" Suddenly, Tam broke off.

Will saw the alarm in Cal's eyes. He spun around. Heraldo Walsh was standing not five feet away. And behind him a throng of drunkards had parted fearfully to allow a phalanx of brutish-looking Colonists through. They were clearly Walsh's gang—Will saw the fiery hatred in their faces. His blood ran cold. Tam immediately stepped to Will's side.

"What do you want, Walsh?" Tam said, his eyes narrowed and his fists clenched.

"Ah, my old friend, Tamfoolery," Heraldo Walsh said with a vile, gappy grin. "I just wanted to see this Topsoiler for myself."

Will wished the ground would open up and swallow him.

"So you're the type of scum that chokes our air channels and pollutes our houses with your foul sewage. My daughter died because of your kind." He took a step closer to Will, raising his hand threateningly, as if he was going to grab at the petrified boy. "Come 'ere, you stinking filth!"

Will cowered. His first impulse was to run, but he knew his uncle wasn't about to let anything happen to him.

"That's far enough, Walsh." Tam took a step toward the man to block his approach.

"You're fraternizing with the godless, Macaulay," Walsh yelled, his eyes never leaving Will's face.

"And what do *you* know of God?" Tam retorted, stepping fully in front of Will to shield him. "Now, you drop it! He's family!"

But Heraldo was like a dog with a bone—he wasn't about to let go. Behind him, his supporters were egging him on and cursing.

"You call *that* family?" He thrust a dirt-stained finger at Will. "Sarah Jerome's mongrel?"

At this, several of his men let out wild howls and whoops.

"He's the filthy offspring of that traitorous woman who ran for the sun," Heraldo snapped.

"That's it," Tam hissed through his clenched teeth. He slung the dregs of his beer at the man, hitting him square in the face, dousing his hair and sideburns with the watery gray fluid.

"Nobody insults my family, Walsh. Step up to the scratch," Tam scowled.

Heraldo Walsh's coterie began to chant, "Milling, milling, milling!" and very soon cheers filled the air as everyone out on the sidewalk joined in. Others came rushing out of the tavern door to see what all the commotion was about.

"What's going on?" Will asked Cal, terrified out of his wits as the huge crowd hemmed them in. Right in the center of the closely packed, overexcited rabble, Tam stood resolutely in front of the dripping Heraldo Walsh, locked in an angry staring match.

"A fistfight," Cal said.

The pub owner, a stocky man in a blue apron, with a sweaty red face, pushed through the tavern doors and threaded his way through the mob until he reached the two men. He barged in between Tam and Heraldo Walsh and kneeled down to fix shackles to their ankles. As they both took a step back, Will saw that the shackles were connected by a length of rusty chain, so that the two fighters were bound together.

Then the owner reached into his apron pocket and brought out a piece of chalk. He drew a line on the pavement halfway between them.

"You know the rules." His voice boomed melodramatically, as much for the benefit of the crowd as for the two men. "Above the belt, no weapons, biting, or gouging. It stops on a KO or death."

"*Death?*" Will whispered shakily to Cal, who nodded grimly.

Then the pub owner ushered everyone back until a human boxing ring had been squared off. This wasn't an easy task, because people were jostling against one another as they vied for a view of the two men.

"Step up to the mark," the man said loudly. Tam and Heraldo Walsh positioned themselves on either side of the chalk line. The pub owner held their arms to steady them. Then he released them with the shouted order: "Commence!" and quickly retreated.

In an attempt to knock his opponent off balance, Walsh immediately swung his foot back and the length of chain—six feet or so long—snapped taut, yanking Tam's leg forward.

But Tam was ready for the maneuver and used the forward momentum to his advantage. He leaped toward Walsh, a huge right fist flying at the shorter man's face. The blow glanced off Walsh's chin, drawing a gasp from the crowd. Tam continued with a fast combination of blows, but his opponent avoided them with apparent ease, ducking and diving like a demented rabbit, as the chain between them rattled noisily on the pavement amid the shouts and cries.

"By Jove, he's quick, that one," Joe Waites observed.

"But he don't have Tam's reach, do he?" Jesse Shingles countered.

Then Heraldo Walsh, crouching low, shot up under Tam's guard and landed a blow on his jaw, a sharp uppercut that jarred Tam's head. Blood burst from his mouth, but he didn't hesitate in his retaliation, bringing his fist down squarely on the top of Walsh's skull.

"The pile driver!" Joe said excitedly and then shouted, "Go on, Tam! Go on, you beauty!"

Heraldo Walsh's knees buckled and he reeled backward, spitting with anger, and came back immediately with a frenzied salvo of punches, clipping Tam around the mouth. Tam moved back as far as the limits of the chain would allow, colliding with the crowd. As people stepped on those behind to give the two fighters more room, Walsh pursued him. Tam used the time to collect himself and reorganize his guard. As Walsh closed in, his fists swiping the air in front of him, Tam ducked down and exploded back into his opponent with a combination of crushing blows to his rib cage and stomach. The noise of the thudding wallops, like bales of hay being thrown on the ground, could be heard over the shouts and jeers of the spectators.

"He's softening him up," Cal said gleefully.

Sporadic skirmishes were breaking out among the mob as arguments raged between the supporters of the two fighters. From his vantage point, Will saw heads bobbing up and down, fists flailing, and tankards flying, beer going everywhere. He also noticed that money was changing hands as bets were feverishly taken—people were holding up one, two, or three fingers and swapping coins. The atmosphere was carnivalesque.

Suddenly, the crowd let out a deep *"Oooh!"* as, without warning, Heraldo Walsh landed a mighty right hook on Tam's nose. There was a dramatic lull in the shouting as the crowd watched Tam drop to one knee, the chain snapping tightly between them.

"That's not good," Imago said worriedly.

"Come on, Tam!" Cal shouted for all he was worth. "Macaulay, Macaulay, Macaulay . . . ," he yelled, and Will joined in.

Tam stayed down. Cal and Will could see blood running from his face and dripping onto the cobblestones of the street. Then Tam looked across at them and winked slyly.

"The old dog!" Imago said under his breath. "Here it comes."

Sure enough, as Heraldo Walsh stood over him, Tam rose up with all the grace and speed of a leaping jaguar, throwing a fearful uppercut that smashed into Walsh's jaw, forcing his teeth together in a bloodcurdling crunch. Heraldo Walsh staggered back, and Tam was on him, pounding him with deadly precision, striking the face of the smaller man so rapidly and with such force that he had no time to mount any form of defense.

Something covered with spittle and blood shot from Heraldo Walsh's mouth and landed on the cobblestones. With a shock Will saw it was a large part of a shattered tooth. Hands reached into the ring in an attempt to snatch it away. A man in a moth-eaten trilby was the fastest off the mark, whisking it away and then vanishing into the throng behind him.

"Souvenir hunters," Cal said. "Ghouls!"

Will looked up just as Tam closed on his opponent, who was now being held up by some of his followers, exhausted and gasping for breath. Spitting out blood, his left eye swollen shut, Heraldo Walsh was pushed forward just in time to see Tam's fist as he landed a final, crushing blow.

The man's head snapped back as he fell against the crowd, which this time parted and watched him as he danced a slow, drunken, bent-leg jig for a few agonizing moments. Then he simply folded to the ground like a sodden paper doll, and the crowd fell silent.

Tam was bent forward, his raw knuckles resting on his knees as he tried to catch his breath. The pub owner emerged from the throng and nudged Heraldo Walsh's head with his boot. He didn't move.

"Tam Macaulay!" the owner yelled out to the silent mob, which suddenly erupted with a roar that filled the cavern and must have rattled the windows on the other side of the Rookeries.

Tam's shackle was removed, and his friends ran over to him and helped him to the bench, where he sat down heavily, feeling his jaw as the two boys took their places on either side of him.

"Little runt was faster than I thought," he said, looking down at his bloodied knuckles as he flexed them painfully. He was handed a full tankard by someone who slapped him on the back and then disappeared into the tavern.

"The Crawfly's disappointed," Jesse said as they all turned to see the Styx at the end of the street, his back to them as he strolled away, drumming a pair of peculiar eyeglasses on his thigh as he went.

"But he got what he wanted," Tam said despondently. "The word will go around that I've been in another brawl."

"Don't matter," Jesse Shingles said. "You were justified. Everyone knows it was Walsh who started it."

Tam looked at the sorry, limp figure of Heraldo Walsh, left where he'd dropped. Not one of his cronies had come forward to move him off the street.

"One thing's for sure—he'll feel like a Coprolite's dinner when he wakes up," Imago chortled as a barman threw a bucket of water over the poleaxed figure and then returned inside the tavern, laughing as he went.

Tam nodded thoughtfully and took a huge mouthful of his drink, wiping his bruised lips with his forearm.

"That's if he wakes up at all," he said quietly.

25

REBECCA'S room was filled with the heavy rumble of Monday morning traffic, car horns hooting impatiently from the streets thirteen floors below. A slight breeze ruffled the curtains. She wrinkled her nose disdainfully as she smelled the stale stench of cigarettes from Auntie Jean's nonstop smoking the night before. Although the door to her bedroom was firmly shut, the smoke nosed its way into every nook and cranny, like an insidious yellow fog searching out new corners to taint.

She got up, slipped on her bathrobe, and made her bed as she trilled the first couple of lines of "You Are My Sunshine." Lapsing into vague *la-las* for the rest of the song, she carefully arranged a black dress and a white shirt on the top of the bedspread.

She went over to the door and, placing her hand on the handle, stopped completely still, as if she had been struck by a thought. She turned slowly and retraced her steps to her bed. Her eyes alighted on the pair of little silver-framed photographs on the table beside it.

Taking them in her hands she sat on her bed, looking between the two. In one, there was a slightly out-of-focus photograph showing Will leaning on a shovel. In the other, a youthful Dr. and Mrs. Burrows sat on stripy deck chairs on an unidentified beach. In the picture, Mrs. Burrows was staring at an enormous ice cream, while Dr. Burrows appeared to be trying to swat a fly with a blurred hand.

They had all gone their separate ways—the family had fallen apart. Did they seriously think she was going to stick around to babysit Auntie Jean, someone even more slothful and demanding than Mrs. Burrows?

"No," Rebecca said aloud. "I'm done here." A thin smile flickered momentarily across her face. She glanced at the photographs one last time and then drew a long breath.

"Props," she said, and threw them with such vehemence that they struck the discolored baseboard with a tinkle of breaking glass.

Twenty minutes later she was dressed and ready to leave. She put her little suitcases next to the front door and went into the kitchen. In a drawer next to the sink was Auntie Jean's "cig stash." Rebecca tore open the ten or so packs of cigarettes and shook their contents into the sink. Then she started on Auntie Jean's bottles of cheap vodka. Rebecca twisted off the screw caps and poured them, all five bottles, into the sink, dousing the cigarettes.

Finally she picked up the box of kitchen matches from beside the gas stove and slid it open. Taking out a single match, she struck it and set light to a crumpled-up sheet of newspaper.

She stood well back and chucked the flaming ball into the sink. The cigarettes and alcohol went up with a satisfying *whoosh*, flames leaping out of the sink over the fake-chrome faucet and the chipped floral tiles behind them. Rebecca didn't stay to savor it. The front door slammed, and she and her little suitcases were gone. With the sound of the smoke alarm receding behind her, she made her way across the landing and into the stairwell.

Since his friend had been spirited away, Chester, in the permanent night of the Hold, had passed beyond the point of despair.

"One. Two. Thre . . ." He tried to straighten his arms to complete the push-up, part of the daily training routine he'd started in the Hold.

"Thre . . ." He breathed deeply and tensed his arms without any real enthusiasm.

"Thre . . ." He exhaled hollowly and sank down, defeated, his face coming to rest against the unseen filth on the stone floor. He slowly rolled over and sat up, glancing at the observation hatch in the door to make sure he wasn't being watched as he brought his hands together. *Dear God* . . .

To Chester, praying was something from the self-conscious, cough-filled silences at school assemblies . . . something that followed the badly sung hymns, which, to the glee of their giggling confederates, some boys salted with dirty lyrics.

No, only nerds prayed in earnest.

. . . *please send someone* . . .

He pressed his hands together even harder, no longer feeling any embarrassment. What else could he do? He remembered the great-uncle who had one day appeared in the spare room at home. Chester's mother had taken Chester to one side and told him that the funny little twiglike man was having radiation treatments at a London hospital and, although Chester had never set eyes on him before, she said he was "family" and that that was important.

Chester pictured the man, with his *Racing Post* pamphlets and his harsh "I don't eat any of that foreign filth" when he was presented with a perfectly good plate of spaghetti bolognese. He remembered the rasping cough punctuating the numerous "rollies" he still insisted on smoking, much to the exasperation of Chester's mother.

In the second week of car trips to the hospital the little man had gotten weaker and more withdrawn, like a leaf withering on a branch, until he didn't talk of "life up north" or even try to drink his tea. Chester had heard, but never understood why, the little man had cried out to God in their spare room in horrible wheezing breaths, in those days before he died. But he understood now.

. . . help me, please . . . please . . .

Chester felt lonely and abandoned and . . . and why, oh why, had he gone with Will on this ridiculous jaunt? Why hadn't he just stayed at home? He could be there now, tucked up warm and safe, but he *wasn't*, and he *had* gone with Will . . . and now there was nothing he could do but mark the passage of days by the two depressingly identical bowls of mush that arrived at regular intervals and the intermittent periods of unfulfilling sleep. He had now grown used to the continual thrumming noise that invaded his cell—the Second Officer had told him it was due to machinery in the "Fan Stations." He had actually begun to find it kind of comforting.

Of late, the Second Officer had mellowed slightly in his treatment of Chester and occasionally deigned to respond to his questions. It was almost as though it didn't matter anymore whether or not the man maintained his official bearing, which left Chester with the dreadful feeling that he might be there forever, or, on the other hand, that something was just around the corner, that things were coming to a head—and not for the better, he suspected.

This suspicion had been further heightened when the Second Officer slung open the door and ordered Chester to clean himself up, providing him with a bucket of dark water and a sponge. Despite his misgivings, Chester was grateful for the opportunity to wash, although it hurt like crazy as he did it because his eczema had flared up like never before. In the past it had been limited to his arms, only very occasionally spreading to his face, but now it had broken out all over, until it seemed that every inch of his body was raw and flaking. The Second Officer had also chucked in some clothes for him to change into, including a pair of huge pants that felt as if they were cut from sackcloth and made him itch even more, if that was possible.

Other than this, time tottered wearily by. Chester had lost track of how long he'd been alone in the Hold; it might have been as much as a month, but he couldn't be sure.

At one point he got very excited when he discovered that by gently probing with his fingertips he could make out letters scratched into the stone of one of the cell walls. There were initials and names, some with numbers that could have been dates. And at the very bottom of the wall someone had gouged in large capitals: *I DIED HERE—SLOWLY.* After finding this, Chester didn't feel like reading any more of them.

He'd also found out that by standing on his toes on the lead-covered ledge, he could just reach the bars on a narrow slit window high up on the wall. Gripping these bars, he was able to pull himself up so he could see the jail's neglected kitchen garden. Beyond that there was a stretch of road leading into a tunnel, lit by a few ever-burning orb lampposts. Chester would stare relentlessly at the road where it disappeared into the tunnel, in the forlorn hope that maybe, just maybe, he might catch a glimpse of his friend, of Will returning to save him, like some knight-errant galloping to his rescue. But Will never came, and Chester would hang there, hoping and praying fervently, as his knuckles turned white with the strain, until his arms gave out and he would fall back into the cell, back into the shadows, and back into despair.

26

"WAKEY, wakey!"

Will was rudely woken from a deep and dreamless sleep by Cal shouting and shaking his shoulder mercilessly.

Will's head throbbed dully as he sat up in his narrow bed. He felt more than a little fragile.

"Get up, Will, we have duties."

He had no idea what time it was, but he was certain it was very early indeed. He burped and, as the taste of the ale from the night before soured his mouth, he groaned and lay back down on his narrow bed.

"I said get up!"

"Do I have to?" Will protested.

"Mr. Tonypandy's waiting, and he's not a patient man."

How did I end up here? His eyes firmly shut, Will lay still, longing to go back to sleep. It felt to him exactly like the first day of school all over again, such was the sensation of dread that flooded through him. He had absolutely no idea what they had in store for him, and he wasn't in the mood to find out.

"Will!" Cal shouted.

"All right, all right." With sickening resignation he got up and dressed and followed Cal downstairs, where a short, heavyset man with a severe expression stood on the doorstep. He regarded Will with a look of overt disgust before turning his back on him.

"Here, put these on quickly." Cal handed Will a heavy black bundle. Will unfolded it and struggled into what could only be described as ill-fitting oilskins, uncomfortably tight under the arms and around the crotch. He looked down at himself and then at Cal, who was dressed in the same clothing.

"We look ridiculous!" he said.

"You'll need them where you're going," Cal replied tersely.

Will presented himself to Mr. Tonypandy, who didn't utter a word. He stared blankly at Will for a moment and then flicked his head to indicate that he should follow.

On the street, Cal headed off in a different direction altogether. Although he was also on a work detail, it was in another quadrant of the South Cavern, and Will was seized with trepidation that he wouldn't be accompanying him. As irksome as Will sometimes found his brother, Cal was his touchstone, his keeper in this incomprehensible place with its primitive practices. He felt terribly vulnerable without him by his side.

Following unenthusiastically behind, Will stole occasional glances at Mr. Tonypandy as he walked slowly along with a pronounced limp, his left leg heaving waywardly in its own orbit and his foot beating the cobbles with a soft thwack at each step. Practically as broad as he was tall, he wore a peculiar black ribbed hat that was pulled down almost to his eyebrows. It looked as though it was made of wool but, on closer inspection, appeared to be woven from a fibrous material, something similar to coconut hair. His short neck was as wide as his head, and it suddenly occurred to Will that, from behind, the whole thing resembled a big thumb sticking out of an overcoat.

As they progressed along the street, other Colonists fell in behind them until the troop was a dozen or so in number. They were mostly young, between the ages of ten and fifteen, Will estimated. He saw that many of them were carrying shovels, while a few had a bizarre long-handled tool that looked vaguely like a pickax, with a spike on one side but a long, curved scoop on the other. From the wear on the leather-bound shaft handles and the state of the ironwork, Will could see that the tools had evidently been put to a great deal of use.

Curiosity overcame him, and he leaned over to one of the boys walking beside him and asked in a low voice, "Excuse me, what's that thing you've got there?"

The boy glared charily at him and muttered, "It's a pitch cleaver, of course."

"A pitch cleaver," Will repeated. "Uh, thanks," he added as the boy deliberately slowed his pace, dropping back from him. At that point, Will felt more alone than he could ever remember and was suddenly overwhelmed by the strongest yearning to turn around and go back to the Jerome house. But he knew he had no alternative but to do what he was told down here in this place. He had to toe the line.

Eventually they entered a tunnel, the tramping of their boots echoing around them. The tunnel walls had diagonal veins of a shiny black rock running through them, like strata of obsidian or even, as he looked more closely, polished coal. *Was that what they were on their way to do?* Will's head immediately filled with images of miners stripped to the waist, crawling into narrow seams and hacking away at the dusty black coal face. His mind swam with apprehension.

After a few minutes they crossed through into a cavern, smaller than the one they had just left. The first thing Will noticed was that the air was different in here; the humidity had increased to the point that he could feel the moisture collect on his face and mingle with his sweat. Then he noticed that the cavern walls were shored up with huge slabs of limestone. Cal had told him that the Colony was made up of an interlinking series of chambers, some naturally formed and others, like this one, man-made with partially reinforced walls.

"I hope Dad's seen this!" Will said under his breath, longing to stop and savor his surroundings, perhaps even to do a sketch or two to record it. But he had to be content with taking in as much as he could as they tramped quickly along.

There were fewer buildings in this cavern, giving it an almost rural feel, and a little farther on they marched by some oak-beamed barns and single-story houses like little bungalows, some freestanding but most built into the walls. As for the residents of the cavern, he saw only a handful of people carrying bulky canvas bags on their backs or pushing loaded wheelbarrows.

The troop followed Mr. Tonypandy as he veered off the road and down into a deep trench, the bottom of which was full of sodden clay. Slippery and treacherous, it clung to their boots, hampering their progress as they weaved their way through a meandering course. Soon the trench opened into a sizable crater at the base of the cavern wall itself, and the work party drew up beside two crude stone-built structures with flat roofs. The boys seemed to know that they should just wait, leaning against their shovels and pitch cleavers as Mr. Tonypandy began a lively discussion with two older men who had emerged from one of the buildings. The boys in the troop joked and chatted noisily together, sometimes giving Will sidelong glances as he stood apart from them. Then Mr. Tonypandy left, limping off in the direction of the road, and one of the older men shouted over at Will.

"You're with me, Jerome. Go to the huts."

The man had a livid red scar in the shape of a crescent across his face. It began just above his mouth and ran up across his left eye and forehead, parting the man's snow-white hair and ending somewhere at the back of his head. But for Will, the man's eye, permanently weeping and shot through with a mottled cloudiness, was the most distressing aspect of his appearance. The eyelid over it was so torn and ragged that each time the man blinked, it was like a defective windshield wiper struggling to function.

"In there! In there!" he barked as Will failed to acknowledge the order.

"Sorry," Will answered quickly. Then he and two other youngsters followed the scar man into the nearest building.

The interior was dank and, except for some equipment in the corner, appeared to be empty. They stood idly around as the scar man kicked at the dirt floor as if looking for something he'd lost. He began to swear wildly under his breath until his boot finally struck something solid. It was a metal ring. He pulled at it with both hands, and there was a loud creaking as a steel plate lifted to reveal an opening three feet square.

"OK, down we go."

One by one they filed down a wet, rusty stepladder, and once they had all reached the bottom, the scar man took the lantern from his belt and played it around the brick-lined tunnel. It wasn't quite high enough to stand up in and, judging by the state of the masonry, was clearly eroded and badly in need of repointing where the chalky mortar had crumbled away. Will guessed that it must have been in use for decades, if not centuries.

Five inches or so of brackish water stood in the bottom of the tunnel, and it wasn't long before it plunged over the tops of Will's boots as he tagged behind the others. They had sloshed along for about ten minutes when the scar man stopped and turned to them again.

"Under here . . ." The man spoke condescendingly to Will while the others watched. It was as if he were explaining something to a young child. ". . . are boreholes. We remove the sediment . . . we unblock them. Yes?"

The scar man swung the lantern to illuminate the tunnel floor, which was heavily silted with little island aggregations of flint and limestone shards rising out of the water. He slipped several coils of rope off his shoulder, and Will watched as each boy in turn took an end from him and tied it securely around his waist. The scar man tied the other end of each rope around himself, so that they were connected like a group of mountaineers.

"Topsoiler," the scar man snarled, "we tie the rope around ourselves . . . we tie it well." Will didn't dare to question why as he took the rope and looped it around his waist, knotting it as best he could. As he tugged at it to test it, the man held out a battered pitch cleaver for him.

"Now we dig."

The two boys began to hack away at the floor of the tunnel, and Will knew he was meant to do likewise. Probing with the unfamiliar tool, he edged his way along the brick lining under the swilling waters until he came to a softer patch of compacted sediment and stones. He hesitated, glancing at the other boys to reassure himself he was doing the right thing.

"We keep digging, we don't stop," the scar man shouted as he shone the lantern on Will, who immediately began to dig. It was hard going, both because of the cramped conditions and because the tool he was using, the pitch cleaver, was unfamiliar. And the job wasn't made any easier by the water, which, however fast he worked, would keep washing back into the deepening hole after every stroke.

It wasn't long before Will had come to grips with this new tool and mastered his technique. Now well into his stride, it felt good just to be digging again, and all of his worries seemed to be forgotten, even if only for a short while, as he threw load after load of stone and sopping soil out of the hole. With the water rushing in after every scoopful, he was soon thigh-deep in the borehole, and the other boys had to work furiously just to keep up with him. Then, with a bone-shaking judder, his pitch cleaver jarred against something immovable.

"We dig around it!" the scar man snapped.

With sweat running down his dirty face and stinging his eyes, Will glanced at the scar man and then back at the water lapping against his oilskins, trying to work out the reason for their task. He knew he'd get short shrift from the scar man if he asked, but his curiosity was getting the better of him.

He was just looking up to pose a question when there was an urgent cry, cut off almost as soon as it started.

"BRACE!" the scar man screamed.

Will turned just in time to see one of the other boys completely vanish with a loud gurgling as the water gushed down into what now looked like a huge drain the size of a manhole. The rope yanked tight, cutting into Will's waist and jerking with the fallen boy's desperate movements. The scar man leaned back and dug his boots into the grit and debris of the tunnel floor. Will found he was pinned to the edge of his borehole.

"Pull yourself up!" the scar man shouted in the direction of the swirling hole. Will watched with alarm until he saw grimy fingers snaking up the rope as the boy heaved himself out against the flow. As he got to his feet again, Will saw the terrified look on his mud-streaked face.

"One hole down. Now the rest of you get a move on," the scar man said, lounging back against the wall behind him as he took out a pipe and began to clean its bowl with a pocketknife.

Will stabbed away blindly at the tightly compacted sediment around the object wedged in the hole, until most of it had been removed. He couldn't tell what it was, but when he jabbed at the obstruction itself, it felt spongy, as if it were waterlogged timber. As he drove his heel down in an attempt to loosen it, there was a sudden *whoosh* as it dislodged, and the surface beneath his feet literally gave way. There was nothing he could do, he was in free fall, water sluicing down around him with a cascade of gravel and slurry. His body banged against the sides of the borehole, his hair and face drenched and covered in grit.

He twitched like a marionette as the rope broke his fall. In less than a second, he'd gathered his wits; he guessed he'd dropped almost twenty feet, but he had no idea what lay below him in the blackness.

Now's my chance. It occurred to him in a flash.

He desperately groped under his oilskins, in his pants pockets, his hand closing on the penknife.

. . . *to escape* . . .

He peered below him into the absolute darkness of the unknown, calculating the odds, the rope tensing as the others began to pull.

. . . *and Dad's down here* . . . *somewhere* . . . The idea blinked through his mind as brightly as a neon sign.

. . . *down here, down here, down here* . . . it repeated, flashing on and off with the irksome buzz of an electrical discharge.

. . . *water, I can hear water* . . .

"CLIMB THE ROPE, BOY!" he heard the scar man bellowing from somewhere above. "CLIMB THE ROPE!"

Will's mind raced as he tried to catch the sounds below him; faint splashes and the gurgle of moving water were just audible over the pendulum creaks of the thick rope that bit into his waist, his lifeline back to the Colony above.

. . . *but how deep is it?*

There was water below, that much was certain, but he didn't know if it was sufficient to cushion his fall. He flicked open the blade and pressed it against the rope, poised to cut it.

Yes . . . no?

If the water wasn't deep enough, he'd be jumping to his death in this godforsaken, lonely place. He pictured jagged shards of rock, razor-sharp and deadly, like a line drawing from a comic book . . . the next frame was his lifeless body, impaled and broken as his blood pumped out of him, mingling with the darkness.

But he felt rash and daring. He drew the blade against the rope, and the first braid of fibers separated beneath it.

A daring escape! flashed in his mind, even brighter than before, like a byline from some Hollywood adventure. The words were proud and brave, but then the image of Chester's face, laughing and happy, reared up, shattering it into a million fragments. Will shivered from the cold, his body drenched and plastered with mud.

The muted hollering of the scar man once again drifted from above, as vague and confused as a yodeler down a drainpipe, wrenching Will from his thoughts. He knew he should start pulling himself back up the rope, but he couldn't bring himself to do it. Then he sighed, and all the courage and bravado were gone. In their place was the cold certainty that if not now, there'd be another opportunity to escape later, and he *would* take it next time.

He tucked away the penknife, twisted himself upright, and began the laborious climb back to the others.

Seven long hours later he'd lost count of how many boreholes they'd cleared as they progressed farther and farther into the tunnel. Finally glancing at his pocket watch under the light of the lantern, the scar man told them they were finished for the day. They trudged back toward the stepladder, and Will set off alone for the journey home, his hands and back aching horribly.

As he climbed out of the trench and made his way slowly along the road, he spotted a circle of Colonists outside a building with a pair of large garage-type doors. They were surrounded by banks of stacked crates.

As one of the men stepped back from the gathering, Will heard a high-pitched laugh. Then he saw something that made him blink and rub his eyes. A man in a puce-pink blazer and straw boater pranced in the middle of the group.

"Can't be! No! It is! It's Mr. Clarke junior!" he said aloud, without meaning to.

"What?" came a voice from behind. It was one of the boys who had been working with Will in the tunnel. "You know him?"

"Yes! But . . . but . . . what in the world is he doing here?" Will was dumbfounded as he thought of the Clarkes' shop on Main Street and struggled with the displaced apparition of Mr. Clarke junior down here, still cavorting within the circle of stocky Colonists. As he watched, Will saw that he was picking things from the boxes with little theatrical flourishes and displaying them to his audience, sweeping them along his sleeve like a crooked watch salesman before placing them delicately on a trestle table. Then the other shoe dropped.

"Don't tell me he's selling fruit!" Will said.

"And vegetables." The boy looked curiously at Will. "The Clarkes have been trading with us for as long as—"

"My God, what's *that*?" Will interrupted him, pointing at an outlandish figure that had stepped into view from the shadow of a towering stack of fruit boxes. Apparently ignored, it stood outside the huddle of Colonists and inspected a pineapple as if it were a rare artifact while the exchange continued with the gesticulating Mr. Clarke junior.

The boy followed Will's finger to the stationary figure, which appeared to be human, with arms and legs, but was swathed in some kind of bloated diver's suit, which was a dull bone color. It was bulbous, like a caricature of a fat man, and the head and face were completely obscured by a hoodlike extension. Its large goggles glinted as they caught the light of a street lamp. It looked like a man-shaped slug or, rather, a slug-shaped man.

"Don't you know anything?" The boy laughed with undisguised scorn at Will's ignorance. "It's only a Coprolite."

Will frowned. "Oh, right, a Coprolite."

"From down there," the boy said, flicking his eyes toward the ground as he walked away. Will lingered behind for a moment to watch the strange being—it moved so slowly it reminded Will of the leeches that inhabited the sludge at the bottom of the school fish tank. It was an improbable scene, the pink-jacketed Mr. Clarke junior peddling his wares to the crowd while the Coprolite examined a pineapple, both deep in the bowels of the earth.

He was deliberating whether to go over to talk to Mr. Clarke junior when he spotted two policemen at the edge of the crowd. He left quickly and went on his way, nagged by a question that elbowed all other thoughts aside. *If the Clarkes knew about the Colony, then how many others in Highfield were leading double lives?*

■ ■ ■

As the weeks passed, Will was assigned to further work details in other parts of the Colony. It gave him an insight into the functionings of this subterranean culture, and he was determined to document as much of it as he could in his journal. The Styx were at the very top of the pecking order and a law unto themselves, and next came a small governing elite of Colonists, to which Mr. Jerome was privileged to belong. Will had no idea what he or these Governors actually did, and, on detailed questioning, it appeared that Cal didn't, either. Then there were the ordinary Colonists and finally an underbelly of unfortunates, who either could not work or refused to do so, and they were left to rot in ghettos, the largest of which was the Rookeries.

Every afternoon, after Will had swabbed dirt and sweat off himself using the basic facilities in the so-called bathroom of the Jerome house, Cal would watch as he sat on his bed and jotted down meticulous notes, adding the occasional sketch where he felt it was warranted. Perhaps it would be of children working at one of the garbage dumps. It was quite a scene; these tiny Colonists, little more than toddlers, so adept at scavenging the huge mounds of litter and taking so much care to sort everything into hoppers for processing.

"Nothing goes to waste," Cal had told him. "I should know, I used to do it!"

Or it might be a picture of the stark fortress in the farthermost corner of the South Cavern where the Styx lived, which had a huge iron stockade enclosing it. This drawing had been by far the greatest challenge for Will because he hadn't had an opportunity to get very close. With sentries patroling the neighboring streets, it wouldn't do to be caught showing too much interest in it.

Cal was at a loss to understand why Will took such great pains to write in his journal. He persistently badgered Will, asking him what the point of it all was. Will had replied that it was something his father had taught him to do whenever they found anything during their excavations.

And there it was again, his father. Dr. Burrows was still his father as far as he was concerned, and Mr. Jerome, even if he was Will's *real* father—though he still wasn't wholly convinced of that—came a poor second in Will's estimation. And his deranged Topsoil mother, and his sister, Rebecca, still felt like family. Yet he felt such affection for Cal, Uncle Tam, and Grandma Macaulay that sometimes his loyalties churned in his head with the ferocity of a stoppered tornado.

As he put the finishing touches on a sketch of a Colony house, his mind wandered and he began to daydream again about his father's journey into the Deeps. Will was eager to discover what lay down there and knew that one day soon he would follow. However, every time he tried to imagine what the future might hold for him, he was brought back to bitter reality with a bump, to the plight of his friend Chester, still confined in that abysmal Hold.

Will stopped drawing and rubbed the peeling calluses on the palms of his hands together.

"Sore?" Cal asked.

"Not as bad as they were," Will replied. His mind flashed back to the work detail earlier that day: clearing stone channels in advance of draining a huge communal cesspit. He shuddered. It had been the worst task he'd been designated so far. With aching arms he resumed his notes, but then his concentration was broken by the urgent wailing of a siren, the hollow and eerie sound filling the entire house. Will stood up, trying to pinpoint where it was coming from.

"Black Wind!" Cal jumped off the bed and rushed over to close the window. Will joined him and saw people in the street below running pell-mell in all directions, until it was completely deserted. Cal pointed excitedly, then drew back his hand, looking at the hairs rising on his forearm from the rapid buildup of static in the air.

"Here it comes!" He tugged at his brother's sleeve. "I love this."

But nothing seemed to be happening. The siren's haunting wail continued as Will, not knowing what to look for, scanned the empty street for anything out of the ordinary.

"There! There!" Cal shouted, peering farther down into the cavern. Will followed his gaze, trying to make out just what it was, but it seemed as though something was wrong with his vision. It was as if his eyes weren't focusing properly.

Then he saw why.

A solid cloud billowed up the street like ink diffusing through water, rolling and churning and obscuring everything in its wake. As Will looked down from the window he could see the streetlights bravely trying to burn even more brightly as the sooty fog almost blotted them out. It was as if nocturnal waves were closing over the submerged lights of a doomed ocean liner.

"What is it?" Will asked, enthralled. He pressed his nose against the windowpane to get a better view of the dark fog spreading quickly along the rest of the street.

"It's a sort of backwash from the Interior," Cal told him. "It's called a Levant Wind. It rises from the lower Deeps—a bit like a burp." He giggled.

"Is it dangerous?"

"No, just dust and stuff, but people think it's bad luck to breathe it. They say that it carries germules." He laughed and then adopted a mock Styx monotone. "*Pernicious to those that it encounters, it sears the flesh.*" He giggled again. "It's great, though, isn't it?"

Will stared, transfixed. As the street below was obliterated from view, the window turned black, and he felt an uncomfortable pressure in his ears. His flesh seemed to be buzzing, and all his hairs were standing on end. For several minutes, the dark cloud billowed by, filling their bedroom with the smell of burned ozone and a deadening silence. Eventually it began to thin out, the street lamps flickering through the swirling dust like the sun breaking through clouds, and then it was gone, leaving just a few diffuse gray smudges hanging in the air, as if the scene had been swept by a watercolorist's brush.

"Now watch this!"

"Sparklers?" Will asked, not believing what he was seeing.

"It's a static storm. They always follow a Levant," Cal said, quivering with sheer excitement. "They give you one heck of a belt if you get in the way."

Will watched in astounded silence as a host of fireballs spun out of the dispersing clouds all along the street. Some were the size of tennis balls, while others were as large as beach balls, all fizzing fiercely as bright sparks sprayed from their edges, as if a gang of delinquent pinwheels had gone on a flaming rampage.

The two boys stood mesmerized as, right in front of them, a fireball as large as a melon, its vibrant light illuminating their young faces and reflecting in their wide eyes, abruptly went into a downward spiral, around and around, casting off sparks as it plummeted toward the ground, shrinking to the size of an egg. As it hovered just above the cobblestones, the dying fireball seemed to flicker that much more intensely before, in the blink of an eye, it sputtered out.

Will and Cal were unable to tear themselves away from where it had been, the traces of its last seconds still imprinted on their retinas in little ecstatic tracks, like optical pins and needles.

27

FAR BELOW the streets and houses of the Colony, a lone figure stirred.

The wind had been a gentle breeze at first but rapidly built to a terrifying gale that spat grit in his face with all the ferocity of a sandstorm. He'd wound his spare shirt around his face and mouth as it grew even more intense, threatening to knock him off his feet. And the dust had been so dense and impenetrable that he hadn't been able to see his hands in front of him.

There was nothing else to do but wait until it passed. He'd dropped to the ground and curled up into a ball, his eyes clogged and burning with the fine black dust. There he had remained, the wailing howl blasting out his thoughts until, frail from hunger, he fell into a half-sleeping, half-waking torpor.

Sometime later, he shuddered awake and, not knowing how long he'd been curled up on the floor of the tunnel, lifted his head for a tentative look around. The strange darkness of the wind had gone, save for a few lingering clouds. Coughing and spitting, he sat up and shook the dust from his clothes. With a stained handkerchief he wiped his watering eyes and cleaned his spectacles.

Then, on all fours, Dr. Burrows crawled around, scrabbling about in the dry grit, using the light of a luminescent orb to find the little pile of organic matter that he'd gathered for kindling before the dust storm had hit. Eventually locating it, he picked out something that resembled a curling fern leaf. He squinted at it curiously—he had no idea what it was. Like everything in the last five miles of tunnel, it was as dry and crisp as old parchment.

He was becoming increasingly worried about his supply of water. As he'd boarded the Miners' Train, the Colonists had thoughtfully provided him with a full canteen, a satchel of dried vegetables of some type, some meat strips, and a packet of salt. He could ration the food, but the problem was definitely the water; he hadn't been able to find a fresh source from which to replenish his canteen for two whole days now, and he was running perilously low.

Having rearranged the kindling, he began to knock two chunks of flint together until a spark leaped into it and a tiny flickering flame took hold. With his head resting on the grit floor, he gently blew on the flame and fanned it with his hand, nurturing it until the fire caught, bathing him in its glow. Then he squatted down next to his open journal, sweeping the layer of dust from the pages, and resumed his drawing.

What a find! A circle of regular stones, each the size of a door, with strange symbols cut into their faces. Carved letters collided with abstract forms—he didn't recognize these characters from all his years of study. They were unlike any hieroglyphs he'd ever seen before. His mind raced as he dreamed of the people who had made them, who had lived far below the surface of the earth, quite possibly for thousands of years, yet had the sophistication to build this subterranean monument.

Thinking he heard a noise, he suddenly stopped drawing and sat bolt upright. Controlling his breathing, he held completely still, his heart pounding in his chest, as he peered into the darkness beyond the fire's illumination. But there was nothing, just the all-pervading silence that had been his companion since the start of his journey.

"Getting jumpy, old man," he said, relaxing again. He was reassured by the sound of his own voice in the confines of the rock passage. "It's just your stomach as usual, you stupid old fool," he said, and laughed out loud.

He unwound the shirt from around his mouth and nose. His face was cut and bruised, his hair was matted, and a straggly beard hung from his chin. His clothes were filthy and torn in places. He looked like an insane hermit. As the fire crackled, he picked up his journal and concentrated on the circle of stones once again.

"This is truly exceptional—a miniature Stonehenge. What an incredible discovery!" he exclaimed, completely forgetting for the moment how hungry and thirsty he was. His face animated and happy, he continued with his sketching.

Then he put down his journal and pencil and sat unmoving for a few seconds as a faraway look crept into his eyes. He got to his feet and, taking the light orb in his hand, backed away from the fire until he was outside the stone circle. He began to stroll slowly around it. As he did so, he held the orb to the side of his face like a microphone. He pursed his lips and dropped his voice a tone or two in an attempt to mimic a television interviewer.

"And tell me, Professor Burrows, newly appointed Dean of Subterranean Studies, what does the Nobel Prize mean to you?"

Now walking more quickly around the circle, a jaunty spring in his step, his voice reverted to its normal tone and he moved the light orb to the other side of his face. He adopted a slightly surprised manner with pantomime hesitancy.

"Oh, I . . . I . . . I must say . . . it was truly a great honor and, at first, I felt that I was not worthy to follow in the footsteps of those great men and women—" At that very moment his toe caught against a piece of rock, and he swore blindly as he stumbled for a few paces. Regaining his poise, he began to walk again, simultaneously continuing with his response. "—the footsteps of those great men and women, that exalted list of winners who preceded me."

He swung the orb back to the other side of his face. "But, Professor, the contributions you have made to so many fields—medicine, physics, chemistry, biology, geology, and, above all, archaeology—are inestimable. You are considered to be one of the greatest living scholars on the planet. Did you ever think it would come to this, the day you began the tunnel in your cellar?"

Dr. Burrows gave a melodramatic "ahem" as the orb changed sides again. "Well, I knew that there was more for me . . . much more than my career in the museum back in . . ."

Dr. Burrows's voice trailed off as he ground to a halt. His face fell and became devoid of any expression. He pocketed the orb, plunging himself into the shadows cast by the stones as he thought of his family and wondered how they were getting along without him. Shaking his bedraggled head, he slowly shuffled back into the circle and slumped down by his journal, staring blankly into the flickering flames, which grew more blurred as he watched them. Finally he removed his spectacles and rubbed the moisture from his eyes with the heels of his hands.

"I have to do this," he said to himself as he put his spectacles back on and once again took up his pencil. "*I have to.*"

The firelight radiated out from between the stones in the circle, projecting shifting spokes of gentle light onto the floor and walls of the passage. In the center of this wheel, totally absorbed, the cross-legged figure grumbled quietly as he rubbed out a mistake in his journal.

He didn't have a thought for anyone in the world at that moment; he was a man so obsessed that nothing else mattered, nothing at all.

28

AS A FIRE spluttered in the hearth, Mr. Jerome reclined in one of the wingback armchairs, reading his newspaper. From time to time, the heavily waxed pages flopped waywardly, and he flicked his wrists reflexively to straighten them up again. Will couldn't make out a single headline from his vantage point at the table; the blocky newsprint bled into the paper to such an extent that it looked as though a swarm of ants had dipped their feet in black ink and then stampeded across the pages.

Cal played another card and waited expectantly for his brother's response, but Will was finding it impossible to keep his concentration on the game. It was the first time he'd been in the same room as Mr. Jerome without being on the receiving end of hostile glances or a resentful silence. This in itself represented a landmark in their relationship.

There was a sudden crash as the front door was flung open, and all three looked up.

"Cal, Will!" Uncle Tam bellowed as he blundered in from the hallway, shattering the scene of apparent domestic bliss. He straightened himself up when he saw Mr. Jerome staring daggers at him from his chair.

"Oh, sorry, I . . ."

"I thought we had an understanding," Mr. Jerome growled as he rose and folded the paper under his arm. "You said you wouldn't come here . . . when I'm at home." He walked stiffly past Tam without so much as a glance.

Uncle Tam made a face and sat down next to Will. With a conspiratorial wave of his hand, he indicated to the boys to come closer. He waited until Mr. Jerome's footsteps had receded into the distance before he spoke.

"The time has arrived," Tam whispered, extracting a dented metal canister from inside his coat. He flipped off the cap from one end, and they watched as he slid out a tattered map and laid it over their cards on the tabletop, smoothing out the corners so that it lay flat. Then he turned to Will.

"Chester is to be Banished tomorrow evening," he said.

"Oh God." Will sat up as if he'd been shocked with an electric current. "That's too sudden, isn't it?"

"I only just found out—it's planned for six," Tam said. "There'll be quite a crowd. The Styx like to make a spectacle out of these things. They believe a sacrifice is good for the soul."

He turned back to the map, humming softly as he searched the complex grid of lines, until finally his finger came to rest on a tiny dark square. Then he looked up at Will as if he'd just remembered something.

"You know, it's not a difficult thing . . . to get *you* out, alone. But Chester, too, that's a very different kettle of fish. It's taken a lot more thought, but"—he paused, and Will and Cal stared into his eyes—"I think I might have cracked it. There's only one way you escape to the Topsoil now . . . and that's through the Eternal City."

Will heard Cal gasp, but as much as he wanted to ask his uncle about this place, it didn't seem appropriate as Tam went on. He proceeded to talk Will through the escape plan, tracing the route on the map as the boys listened raptly, absorbing every detail. The tunnels had names like Watling Street, The Great North, and Bishopswood. Will interrupted his uncle only once, with a suggestion that, after some considerable thought, Tam incorporated into the plan. Although on the exterior he was composed and businesslike, Will felt excitement and fear building in the pit of his stomach.

"The problem with this," Tam said with a sigh, "is the unknowns, the variables, that I can't help you with. If you hit any snags when you're out there, you'll just have to play it by ear . . . do the best you can." At this point, Will noticed that some of the sparkle had gone out of Tam's eyes—he didn't look like his normal confident self.

Tam ran through the whole plan from beginning to end once again and, when he'd finished, he fished something out his pocket and passed it over to Will. "Here's a copy of the directions once you're outside the Colony. If they catch up with you, heaven forbid, eat the darn thing."

Will unfolded it carefully. It was a piece of cloth the size of a handkerchief when completely opened. The surface was covered with a mass of infinitesimally small lines in brown ink, like an unruly maze, each representing a different tunnel. Although Will's route was clearly marked in a light red ink, Tam quickly took him through it.

Tam watched as Will refolded the cloth map and then spoke in a low voice. "This has to go like clockwork. You'd put *all* your kin in the very worst danger if the Styx thought for one second I'd had a hand in this . . . and it wouldn't just end with me; Cal, your grandmother, and your father would all be in the firing line." He grasped Will's forearm tightly across the table and squeezed it to emphasize the gravity of his warning. "Another thing: When you're Topsoil, you and Chester are going to have to disappear. I haven't had time to arrange anything, so—"

"What about Sarah?" Will blurted as the idea occurred to him, although her name still felt a little odd on his lips. "My *real* mother? Couldn't she help me?"

A suggestion of a smile dropped into place on Tam's face. "I wondered when you'd think of that," he said. The smile disappeared, and he spoke as if choosing his words carefully. "If my sister is still alive—and nobody knows that for sure—she'll be well and truly hidden." He glanced down at the palm of his hand as he rubbed it with the thumb from the other. "One plus one can sometimes add up to zero."

"What do you mean?" Will asked.

"Well, if by some miracle you did happen to find her, you might lead the Styx her way. Then *both* of you would end up feeding the worms." He raised his head again and shook it just once as he fixed Will with a thoughtful stare. "No, I'm sorry, but you're on your own. You're going to have to run hard and long, for all our sakes, not just yours. Mark my words, if the Styx get you in their clutches, they *will* make you spill your guts, sooner or later, and that would endanger us all," he said ominously.

"Then we'd have to get out, too, wouldn't we, Uncle Tam?" Cal volunteered, his voice full of bravado.

"You've got to be kidding!" Tam turned sharply on him. "We wouldn't stand a chance. We wouldn't even see them coming."

"But . . . ," began Cal.

"Look, this isn't some game, Caleb. If you cross them once too often, you won't be around long enough to regret it. Before you know it, you'll be dancing Old Nick's Jig." He paused. "You know what that is?" Tam didn't wait for an answer. "It's a lovely little number. Your arms are stitched behind your back"—he shifted uncomfortably in his seat—"with copper thread, your eyelids are stripped off, and you're dropped in the darkest chamber you can imagine, full of Red Hots."

"Red *whats*?" Will asked.

Tam shuddered and, ignoring Will's question, went on. "How long do you think you'd last? How many days of knocking into the walls in the pitch-black, dust burning into your ruined eyes, before you collapsed from exhaustion? Feeling the first bites on your skin as they start to feed? I wouldn't wish that on my worst . . ." He didn't finish the sentence.

The two boys both swallowed hard, but then Tam's expression brightened up again. "Enough of that," he said. "You've still got that light, haven't you?"

Still stunned by what he'd just heard, Will looked at him blankly. He pulled himself together and nodded.

"Good," Tam said as he took out a small cloth bundle from his coat pocket and put it on the table in front of Will. "And these might come in handy."

Will touched the bundle tentatively.

"Well, go on, have a look."

Will untied the corners. Inside, there were four knobbly brown-black stones the size of marbles.

"Node stones!" Cal said.

"Yes. They're rarer than slugs' boots." Tam smiled. "They're described in the old books, but nobody 'cept me and my boys has ever seen one before. Imago found this lot."

"What do they do?" Will asked, looking at the strange stones.

"Down here, it's not like you're going to beat a Colonist or, worse still, a Styx in a straight fight. The only weapons you have are *light* and *flight*," Tam said. "If you get in a tight corner, just crack one of these things open. Chuck it against something hard and keep your eyes shut—it'll give a burst of the brightest light you can imagine. I hope these are still good," he said, weighing one in his hand. He looked at Will. "So you think you're up to this?"

Will nodded.

"Right," the big man said.

"Thanks, Uncle Tam. I can't tell you how . . . ," Will said falteringly.

"No need, my boy." Tam ruffled his hair. He looked down at the table and didn't speak for a few seconds. It was totally unexpected; silence and Uncle Tam didn't go together. Will had never before seen him like this, this gregarious and massive man. He could only think that he was upset and trying to hide it. But when Tam raised his head, the broad smile was there and his voice rumbled as it always did.

"I saw all this coming . . . it was bound to happen sooner or later. The Macaulays are loyal, and we will fight for those we love and believe in, no matter what the price. You would've tried to do something to save Chester, and gone after your father, whether I'd helped you or not."

Will nodded, feeling his eyes fill with tears.

"Thought as much!" Tam boomed. "Like your mother . . . like Sarah . . . a Macaulay through and through!" He grabbed Will firmly by his shoulders. "My head knows you have to go, but my heart says otherwise." He squeezed Will and sighed. "Pity is . . . we could have had some times down here, the three of us. Some high times indeed."

Will, Cal, and Tam talked well into the early hours, and when he finally got to bed, Will hardly slept a wink.

Early in the morning, before there was a stir in the house, Will packed his bag and tucked the cloth map Uncle Tam had given him into the top of his boot. He checked that the node stones and light orb were in his pockets, then went over to Cal and shook him awake.

"I'm off," Will said in a low voice as his brother's eyes flickered open. Cal sat up, scratching his head.

"Thanks for everything, Cal," Will whispered, "and say good-bye to Granny from me, won't you?"

"Course I will," his brother replied, then frowned. "You know I'd give anything to come, too."

"I know, I know . . . but you heard what Tam said: I have a better chance by myself. Anyway, your family is here," he said finally, and turned to the door.

Will tiptoed down the stairs. He felt exhilarated to be on the move again, but this was tempered by an unexpected pang of sadness that he was leaving. Of course, he could stay here, somewhere where he actually belonged, if he chose, rather than venturing out into the unknown and risking it all. It would be so easy just to go back to bed. As he reached the hallway, he could hear Bartleby snoring somewhere in the shadows. It was a comforting sound, the sound of home. He would never hear that sound again if he went now. He stood by the front door and hesitated. No! How could he ever live with himself if he chose to leave Chester to the Styx? He would rather die trying to free him. He took a deep breath and, glancing behind him into the still house, slipped the heavy catch on the door. He opened it, stepped over the threshold, and then closed it gently behind him. He was out.

He knew he had a considerable distance to cover, so he walked quickly, his bag thumping a rhythm on his back. It took him a little under forty minutes to reach the building at the edge of the cavern that Tam had described. There was no mistaking it as, unlike most structures in the Colony, it had a tiled rather than a stone roof.

He was now on the road that led to the Skull Gate. Tam had said that he had to keep his wits about him because the Styx changed sentries at random intervals, and there was no way of knowing whether one was just about to appear around the corner.

Leaving the road, Will climbed over a gate and sprinted through the yard that lay in front of the building, a ramshackle farm property. He heard a piglike grunting coming from one of the outlying buildings and spotted some chickens penned up in another area. They were spindly and malnourished but had perfectly white feathers.

He entered the building with the tiled roof and saw the old timber beams leaning against the wall just as Tam had described. As he crept in under them, something moved toward him.

"What—?"

It was Tam. He immediately silenced Will by putting a finger to his lips. Will could hardly contain his surprise. He looked at Tam questioningly, but the man's face was grim and unsmiling.

There was hardly enough room for both of them under the beams, and Tam squatted awkwardly as he slid a massive paving slab along the wall. Then he leaned in toward Will.

"Good luck," he whispered in his ear, and literally pushed him into the jagged opening. Then the slab grated shut behind Will, and he was on his own.

In the pitch-darkness he fumbled in his pocket for the light orb, to which he'd already attached a length of thick string. He knotted this around his neck, leaving his hands free. At first, he moved along the passage with ease, but then, after about thirty feet, it pinched down to a crawlway. The roof of the tunnel was so low that he ended up on his hands and knees. The passage angled upward, and as he heaved himself painfully over jagged plates of broken rock, his backpack kept snagging on the roof.

He caught sight of a movement in front of him and froze on the spot. With some trepidation he lifted the light orb to see what it was. He held his breath as something white flashed across the passage and then landed with a soft thump no more than five feet ahead of him. It was an eyeless rat the size of a well-fed kitten, with snowy fur and whiskers that oscillated like butterfly wings. It stood up on its hind legs, its muzzle twitching and its large, glistening incisors in full view. It showed absolutely no sign that it was afraid of him.

Will found a stone on the tunnel floor and threw it as hard as he could. It missed, glancing off the wall next to the animal, which didn't even flinch. Will's indignation that a mere rat was holding him up welled over, and he lunged toward the animal with a growl. In a single effortless bound it leaped at him, landing smack on his shoulder, and for a split second neither boy nor rat moved. Will felt its whiskers, as delicate as eyelashes, brush his cheek. He shook his shoulders frantically and it launched itself off, springing once on the back of Will's leg as it sped away in the opposite direction.

Will spat a few choice curses at the retreating rodent, then took a deep breath to steady his nerves before setting off again.

He crawled for what seemed like hours, his hands becoming cut and tender from the razor-sharp shards strewn across the floor. Much to his relief, the passage increased in height, and he was almost able to stand up again. Now that he could move at full speed, he became almost euphoric, and felt an irrepressible urge to sing as he negotiated the bends in the tunnel. But he thought better of it when it occurred to him that the sentries at the Skull Gate probably weren't very far from his current position and might somehow be able to hear him.

Eventually he reached the end of the passage, which was cloaked with several layers of stiff sacking, dirtied up to camouflage them against the stone. He brushed them aside and drew his breath as he saw that the tunnel had come out just under the roof of a cavern, and that there was nearly a one-hundred foot drop to the road below. He was proud that he'd gotten this far, past the Skull Gate, but he felt certain that this couldn't be right. He was at such a dizzying height that he immediately assumed he must be in the wrong place. Then Tam's words came back to him: *"It'll look impossible, but take it slowly. Cal managed it with me when he was much younger, so you can do it."*

He leaned over to scan the array of ledges and nooks in the rock wall below him. Then he cautiously clambered out over the edge of the tunnel lip and began the descent, checking and rechecking each shaking hand- and foothold before he made the next move.

He'd climbed no more than twenty feet when he heard a noise below. A desolate groan. He held still and listened, his heart thudding in his ears. It came again. He had one foot on a small ridge with the other dangling in midair, while his hands gripped an outcrop of rock at chest height. He slowly twisted his head and peered down over his shoulder.

Swinging a lantern, a man was strolling in the direction of the Skull Gate with two emaciated cows a couple of paces in front of him. He shouted something at them as he drove them along, completely unaware of Will's presence above him.

Will was totally exposed, but there was nothing he could do. He held absolutely still, praying that the man wouldn't stop and look up. Then just the thing Will was dreading happened: The man came to an abrupt halt.

Oh, no, this is it!

With his bird's-eye view, Will could clearly make out the man's shiny white scalp as he took something out of a shoulder bag. It was a clay pipe with a long stem, which he loaded with tobacco from a pouch and lit, puffing out little clouds of smoke. Will heard him say something to the cows, and then he started on his way again.

Will breathed a silent sigh of relief and, checking that the coast was clear, quickly finished the descent, crisscrossing from ledge to ledge until he was safely back on the ground. Then he dashed as fast as he could along the road, on either side of which were fields of impossibly proportioned mushrooms, their bulbous, ovoid caps standing on thick stalks. He now recognized these as pennybuns and, as he went, the motion of his light bobbing around his neck threw a multitude of their shifting shadows over the cavern walls behind them.

Will slowed his pace as he developed a painful stitch in his side. He took a series of deep breaths to try to ease it, then forced himself to speed up again, aware that every second counted if he was going to reach Chester in time. Cavern after cavern fell behind him, the fields of pennybuns eventually gave way to black carpets of lichen, and he was relieved when he spotted the first of the lampposts and the hazy outline of a building in the distance. He was getting closer. Suddenly, he found himself at a huge stone archway hewn into the rock. He went through it, into the main body of the Quarter. Soon the dwellings were crowding the sides of the road, and he was becoming more and more nervous. Although nobody seemed to be around, he kept the sound from his boots to a minimum by running on his toes. He was terrified that someone was going to appear from one of the houses and spot him.

Then he saw what he'd been looking for. It was the first of the side tunnels that Tam had mentioned.

"You're going to take the backstreets." He remembered his uncle's words. *"It's safer there."*

"Left, left, right." As he went, Will repeated the sequence Tam had drummed into him.

The tunnels were just wide enough for a coach to pass through them. *"Go quickly through these,"* Tam had said. *"If you bump into anyone, just brass it out, like you're supposed to be there."*

But there was no sign of anyone as Will ran with all his might, his bag crashing on his back at every step. By the time he reemerged in the main cavern, he was sweating and out of breath. He recognized the squat outline of the police station between the two taller structures on either side, and slowed to a walk to give himself a chance to cool off.

"Made it this far," he muttered to himself. The plan had seemed feasible when Tam had described it, but now he was wondering if he'd made a dreadful mistake. *"You haven't got time to think,"* Tam had said, pointing a finger at him to emphasize his words. *"If you hesitate, the momentum will be lost—the whole thing will go cockeyed."*

Will wiped the sweat from his forehead and steeled himself for the next stage.

As he drew nearer, the sight of the police station's entrance brought back memories of the first time he and Chester had been dragged up its steps and the grueling interrogations that had followed. It all came flooding back, and he tried to put the thoughts out of his mind as he slipped into the shadows by the side of the building and heaved off his backpack. He dug out his camera, checking it quickly before he put it into his pocket. Then he hid his backpack and headed for the steps. As he climbed them, he took a deep breath, then pushed through the doors.

The Second Officer was reclining in a chair with his feet on the counter. His eyes swiveled to regard the newcomer, his movements dull, as if he'd been dozing. It took him almost a second to recognize who was standing before him, and then a confounded expression crept over his beefy face.

"Well, well, well, Jerome. What in the world are you doing back here?"

"I've come to see my friend," Will replied, praying that his voice didn't crack. He felt as if he were edging out on the branch of a tree, and the farther he went, the thinner and more precarious the branch became. If he lost his balance now, the fall could be fatal.

"So who let you come back here?" the Second Officer said suspiciously.

"Who d'you think?" Will tried to smile calmly.

The Second Officer pondered for a moment, looking him up and down. "Well, I suppose . . . if they let you through the Skull Gate, it must be all right," he reasoned aloud as he lumbered slowly to his feet.

"They told me I could see him," Will said, "one last time."

"So you know it is to be tonight?" the Second Officer said

with the suggestion of a smile. Will nodded and saw that this had dispelled any doubts in the man's mind. At once the officer's manner was transformed.

"Didn't walk the whole way, did you?" he asked. A friendly, generous smile creased his face like a gash in a pig's belly. Will hadn't seen this side of him before, and it made it all the more difficult for him to do what he had to.

"Yes, I had an early start."

"No wonder you look hot. Better come with me, then," the Second Officer said as he lifted up the flap at the end of the counter and came through, rattling his keys. "I hear you're fitting in well," he added. "Knew you would . . . the moment I first laid eyes on you. 'Deep down he's one of us,' I told the First Officer. 'Looks the part,' I said to him."

They went through the old oak door into the gloom of the Hold. The familiar smell gave Will the creeps as the Second Officer swung back the cell door and ushered him in. It took a moment for his eyes to adjust, then he saw him: Chester was sitting in the corner on the ledge, his legs drawn up under his chin. His friend didn't react immediately but stared emptily at Will. Then, with a flash of recognition and sheer disbelief, he was on his feet.

"Will?" he said, his jaw dropping. "Will! I can't believe it!"

"Hi, Chester," Will said, trying to keep the excitement from his voice. He was elated to see him again, but at the same time his whole body was shaking with adrenaline.

"Have you come to get me out, Will? Can I leave now?"

"Uh . . . not quite." Will half turned, aware that the Second Officer was just behind him and could hear every word.

The Second Officer coughed self-consciously. "I have to lock you in, Jerome. Hope you understand—it's the regulations," he said as he shut the door and turned the key.

"What is it, Will?" Chester asked, sensing that something was wrong. "Is it bad news?" He took a step away from Will.

"You all right?" Will replied, too preoccupied to answer his friend as he listened to the Second Officer leave the Hold through the oak door and close it firmly. Then he took Chester into the corner of the cell and they huddled together while Will explained what they had to do.

Minutes later came the sound that Will was dreading: The Second Officer was walking back into the Hold toward them. "Time, gentlemen," he said. He turned the key and opened the door, and Will made his way out slowly.

"Bye, Chester," he said.

As the Second Officer began to close the door, Will put his hand on the man's arm.

"Just a second, I think I left something in there," he said.

"What's that?" the man asked.

The Second Officer was looking directly at him as Will brought his hand out of his pocket. He saw that the little red light was on: The camera was ready. Thrusting it at the man, Will clicked the shutter.

The flash caught the policeman full in the face. He howled and dropped his keys, clapping his hands over his eyes as he sank to the floor. The flash had been so bright compared with the sublime glow of the light orbs that even Will and Chester, who had both shielded themselves from it, felt the aftershock of its brilliance.

"Sorry," Will said to the groaning man.

Chester was standing motionless in the cell, a stupefied look on his face.

"Get a move on, Chester!" Will shouted as he leaned in and yanked him past the Second Officer, who was starting to fumble his way to the wall, still moaning horribly.

As they entered the reception area, Will happened to glance over the counter.

"My shovel!" he exclaimed as he ducked underneath and grabbed it from against the wall. Will was on his way back when he saw the Second Officer stagger out from the Hold. The man snatched blindly at Chester, and before Will knew what was happening he had gotten hold of him around the neck.

Chester let out a strangled yelp and tried to wrestle free.

Will didn't stop to think. He swung the shovel. With a bone-crunching clang, it connected with the Second Officer's forehead, and he crumpled to the floor with a whimper.

Chester wasn't so slow off the mark this time. He was right behind Will as they bolted out of the station, pausing just long enough for Will to retrieve his backpack before they both turned down the stretch of road that Chester had spent so many hours watching from his cell. Then they veered off down a side tunnel.

"Is this the right way?" Chester said, breathing heavily and coughing.

Will didn't answer but kept on running until they reached the end of the tunnel.

There they were, just as Tam had described them, three partially demolished houses on the perimeter of a circular cavern as large as an amphitheater. The rich, loamy surface was springy underfoot as they tramped over it, and the air reeked of old manure. The walls of the cavern caught Will's attention. What at first he'd taken to be clusters of stalagmites were, in fact, petrified tree trunks, some broken halfway down and others twisted around each other. These fossilized remains stood like a carved stone forest in the shadows.

Will felt increasingly uneasy, as if something unwholesome and threatening was radiating from between the ancient trees. He was relieved when they reached the middle house and pushed through the front door, which opened crookedly on a single hinge.

"Through the hall, straight ahead . . ."

Chester shouldered the door shut behind them as Will entered the kitchen. It was roomier than the one in the Jerome house. As they crossed the tiled floor, a thick carpet of dust was stirred into life. It whipped up into a miniature storm, and in the glow of the light orb every movement they made left a trace in the airborne motes.

"Locate the wall tile with the painted cross."

Will found it and pushed. A small hatch clicked open under his hand. Inside was a handle. He twisted it to the right, and a whole section of the tiled wall opened outward—it was a cleverly disguised door. Behind was an antechamber with boxes stacked on either side and a further door set into its far wall. But this was no ordinary door—it was made of heavy iron studded with rivets, and there was a handle by its side to crank it open.

"It's airtight—keeps the germules out."

There was an inspection porthole at head height, but no light was visible through the clouded glass.

"Get going on that while I find the breathing apparatus," Will ordered Chester, pointing at the crank. His friend leaned on the handle, and there was a loud hiss as the thick rubber seal at the base of the door lifted from the ground. Will found the masks Tam had said would be left there, old canvas hoods with black rubber pipes attached to cylinders. They resembled some sort of ancient diving equipment.

Then, from the dark outside, Will heard a plaintive mew. He knew what it was even before he'd turned around.

"Bartleby!" The cat scampered in through the hallway. His paws scrabbling excitedly in the dust, he went straight to the secret door, shoving his muzzle into the gap and sniffing inquisitively.

"What is *that*?" Chester was so flabbergasted by the vision of the oversized cat that he let go of the crank handle. It spun freely as the door trundled down on its runners and slammed shut. Bartleby leaped back.

"For heaven's sake, Chester, just get that door open!" Will shouted.

Chester nodded and began again.

"Need a hand?" Cal asked, moving into vi*-ew.

"No! Not you, too! What the heck are you doing here?" Will gasped.

"Coming with you," Cal replied, taken aback by his brother's reaction.

Chester stopped turning the crank and glanced rapidly from one brother to the other and back again. "He looks just like you!"

Will had reached a point at which the whole situation had taken on an insanity all its own, a random and hopeless insanity. Tam's plan was falling apart before his very eyes, and he had the most awful feeling that they were all going to be caught. He had to get things back on track . . . somehow . . . and *quickly*.

"FOR GOODNESS' SAKE, GET THAT DOOR OPEN, WILL YOU!" he bawled at the top of his voice, and Chester meekly resumed the cranking. The door was now a foot and a half off the ground, and Bartleby stuck his head under for an exploratory look, dropped low, and then slid through the opening, disappearing from sight altogether.

"Tam doesn't know you're here, does he?" Will grabbed his brother by his coat collar.

"Of course not. I decided it was time to go Topsoil, like you and Mother."

"You're not coming," Will snarled through gritted teeth. Then, as he saw the hurt in his brother's face, he let go of his coat and softened his voice. "Really, you can't . . . Uncle Tam would kill you for being here. Go home right—" Will never finished the sentence. Both he and Cal had smelled the strong pulses of ammonia rippling through the air.

"The alarm!" Cal said, with panic-stricken eyes.

They heard a commotion outside, some shouting, and then the crash of breaking glass. They ran to the kitchen window and peered through the cracked panes.

"Styx!" Cal gasped.

Will estimated there were at least thirty of them drawn up in a semicircle in front of the house, and those were just the ones he could see from his limited vantage point. How many there were in total, he shuddered to think. He ducked down and shot a glance at Chester, who was frenziedly cranking the door, the opening now high enough for them to get through.

Will looked at his brother and knew there was only one thing to do. He couldn't leave him at the mercy of the Styx.

"Go on! Get under the door," he whispered urgently.

Cal's face lit up and he started to thank Will, who shoved the breathing apparatus into his hands and propelled him toward the door.

As Cal slithered through the gap, Will turned back to the window to see the Styx advancing on the house. That was enough—he launched himself at the door, frantically shouting at Chester to grab a mask and follow him. As he heard the front door to the house smash open, he knew there was just enough time for them both to get away.

Then one of those terrible things happened.

One of those events that, afterward, you replay in your mind over and over again . . . but you know, deep down, there was nothing you could have done.

That was when they heard it.

A voice they both knew.

29

"SAME old Will," she said, rooting them to the spot.

Will was halfway under the door, his hand gripping Chester's forearm, ready to pull him in, when he glanced at the kitchen entrance and froze.

A young girl walked into the room, two Styx flanking her.

"Rebecca?" Will gasped, and shook his head as if his eyes were deceiving him.

"Rebecca!" he said again, incredulously.

"Where are we going, then?" she said coolly. The two Styx edged forward a fraction, but she held up her hand and they halted.

Was this some trick? She was wearing their clothes, their uniform—the black coat with the stark white shirt. And her jet-black hair was different—it was raked back tightly over her head.

"What are you . . . ?" was all Will managed to say before words failed him.

She'd been captured. That must be it. Brainwashed, or held hostage.

"Why do we keep doing these things?" She sighed theatrically, raising one eyebrow. She looked relaxed and in control. Something wasn't right here; something jarred.

No.

She was one of them.

"You're . . . ," he gasped.

Rebecca laughed. "Quick, isn't he?"

Behind her, more Styx were entering the kitchen. Will's mind reeled, his memories playing back at breakneck speed as he tried to reconcile Rebecca, his sister, with this Styx girl before him. Were there signs, any clues he'd missed?

"How?" he cried.

Reveling in his confusion, Rebecca spoke. "It's really very simple. I was placed in your family when I was two. It's the way with us . . . to rub shoulders with the Heathen. . . . It's the training for the elite."

She took a step forward.

"Don't!" Will said, his mind starting to work again, and his hand surreptitiously reaching inside his coat pocket. "I can't believe it!"

"Hard to accept, isn't it? I was put there to keep an eye on you—and, if we were lucky, flush your mother into the open . . . your *real* mother."

"It's not true."

"It doesn't matter what you believe," she replied curtly. "My job had run its course, so here I am, back home again. No more role-playing."

"No!" Will stuttered as he closed his hand around the little cloth package that Tam had given him.

"Come on, it's over," Rebecca said impatiently. With a barely perceptible nod of her head, the Styx on either side of her lurched forward, but Will was ready. He slung the node stone across the kitchen with all his might. It soared between the two advancing Styx and struck the dirty white tiles, breaking into a tiny snowstorm of fragments.

Everything stopped.

For a split second, Will thought nothing was going to happen, that it wasn't going to work. He heard Rebecca laugh, a dry, mocking laugh.

Then there was a whooshing sound, as if air was being sucked from the room. Each tiny splinter, as it sprinkled to the ground, flared with a dazzling incandescence, loosing beams that blasted the room like a million searchlights. These were so intense that everything was shot through with an unbearable, searing whiteness.

It didn't seem to bother Rebecca in the slightest. With the light ablaze around her, she stood out like some dark angel, her arms folded in her characteristic pose as she clucked with disapproval.

But the two advancing Styx stopped in their tracks and let out screams like fingernails being dragged down a blackboard. They staggered back blindly, trying to cover their eyes.

This gave Will the opportunity he was looking for. He yanked Chester over, pulling him from the crank handle.

But already the light was dwindling, and another two Styx were pushing aside their blinded comrades. They lunged at Will, their clawlike fingers raking out toward him. As he continued to pull on one of Chester's arms both Styx had latched on to the other. It turned into a tug-of-war between Will and the Styx, with the terrified, whimpering Chester caught in the middle. Worse still, now that nobody was bracing the crank handle, it was whirring wildly around as the massive door sank slowly down on its runners. And Chester was right in its path.

"Push them off!" Will cried.

Chester tried to kick out, but it was no use; they had too strong a hold on him. Will wedged himself against the door in a vain attempt to slow its progress, but it was just too heavy and nearly unbalanced him. There was no way he could do anything about it and save Chester at the same time.

As the Styx grunted and strained, and Chester tried with all his might to resist, Will knew the Styx couldn't be beaten. Chester was slipping out of his hands and screaming in pain as the Styx's fingernails bit deep into the flesh of his arm.

Then, as the door continued its relentless descent, the realization hit Will—Chester was going to be crushed unless he let go.

Unless he released Chester to the Styx. The crank handle was spinning madly. The door was now little more than three feet from the ground, and Chester was doubled over—its entire weight pressing down on his back. Will had to do something, and quick.

"Chester, I'm sorry!" Will screamed.

For an instant, Chester stared with horror-stricken eyes into those of his friend, and then Will let go of his arm and he flew straight back into the Styx, the momentum bowling them over in a tumbling confusion of arms and legs. Chester shouted Will's name once as the door clanged down with a terrible finality. Will could only watch numbly through the milky glass of the porthole as Chester and the Styx came to rest in a heap against the wall. One of the Styx immediately picked himself up and raced back toward the door.

"JAM THE HANDLE!" Cal's shout galvanized Will. As Cal held a light orb, Will set to work on the mechanism by the side of the door. He whipped out his penknife and, using the largest blade, attempted to wedge the gear wheels with it.

"Please, please work!" Will begged. He tried several places before the blade slipped in between two of the largest gear wheels and stayed in place. Will took his hands away, praying it would do the trick. And it did, the little red penknife quivering as the Styx applied pressure to the handle on the other side.

Will glanced through the porthole again. Like some macabre silent film, he couldn't help but watch the desperation on Chester's face as he valiantly battled with the Styx. He'd somehow managed to get hold of Will's shovel and was trying to beat them off with it. But he was overpowered by their sheer numbers as they swarmed over him with the insect intent of devouring locusts.

But then one face blocked out everything else as it loomed in the porthole.

Rebecca's face. She pursed her lips sternly and shook her head at Will, as if she was telling him off. Just like she'd done for all those years in Highfield. She was saying something, but it was inaudible through the door.

"We have to go, Will. They'll get it open," Cal said urgently. Will tore his eyes away with difficulty. She was still mouthing something at him. And with a sudden, chilling realization, he knew just what it was. *Exactly* what it was. She was singing to him.

" 'Sunshine . . . !' " he said bitterly. " '*You are my sunshine!*' "

They fled down the rock passage with Bartleby bringing up the rear, and eventually came to a dome-shaped atrium with numerous passages leading off it. Everything was rounded and smoothed, as if eons of flowing water had rubbed away any sharp edges. It was dry now, every surface coated in an abrasive silt, like powdered glass.

"We've only got one mask," Will said suddenly to Cal, as the realization hit him. He took the canvas and rubber contraption from his brother and examined it.

"Oh, no!" Cal's face dropped. "What do we do now? We can't go back."

"The air in the Eternal City," Will said, "what's wrong with it?"

"Uncle Tam says there was some sort of plague. It killed off all the people. . . ."

"But it's not still there, is it?" Will asked quickly, dreading the answer.

Cal nodded slowly. "Tam says it is."

"Then you're using the mask."

"No way!"

In a flash, Will whipped the mask over Cal's head, muffling his protests. Cal struggled, trying to take it off, but Will wouldn't let him.

"I mean it! You're going to wear it," Will insisted. "I'm the oldest, so I get to choose."

At this Cal stopped resisting, his eyes peeking anxiously through the glass strip as Will made sure the hood was seated correctly on his shoulders. Then he buckled up the leather strap to secure the pipes and stubby filter around his brother's chest. He tried not to think what the implications of letting Cal have the mask might be for himself, and could only hope that the plague was yet another of the Colonists' superstitions, of which there seemed to be so many.

Then Will slipped out the map Tam had given him from inside his boot, counted the tunnels in front of them, and pointed to the one they were to take.

"How did the Styx girl know you?" Cal's voice was indistinct through the hood.

"My sister." Will lowered the map and looked at him. "That was my sister"—he spat contemptuously—"or so I used to think."

Cal didn't show any sign of surprise, but Will could see just how frightened he was by the way he kept glancing at the stretch of tunnel behind them. "The door won't hold them for long," his brother added, looking nervously at Will.

"Chester . . . ," Will began hopelessly, then fell silent.

"There was nothing we could've done to help him. We were lucky to get out of there alive."

"Maybe," Will said as he rechecked the map. He knew he didn't have time to think about Chester, not right now, but after all the risks he'd taken to save his friend the whole exercise had failed horribly, and he was finding it hard to focus on what to do next. He took a deep breath. "I guess we should go, then."

And so the two boys, with the cat trailing behind, broke into a steady trot, penetrating deeper into the complex of underground tunnels that would eventually lead them to the Eternal City—and then, Will hoped, out into the sunlight again.

PART 3

THE ETERNAL CITY

30

ONE TWO, *one two, one, one, one two.*

As they jogged along, Will had settled into the easy rhythm he frequently used for the more strenuous bouts of digging back in Highfield. The tunnels were dry and silent; there wasn't the slightest sign that anything lived down here. And as their feet tramped over the sandy floors, not once did Will catch sight of any airborne dust or motes behind them in the beam of his light orb. It was as if their passage had gone completely unnoticed.

But it wasn't long before he began to spot the faintest scintillations before his eyes, smears of light that materialized and then, just as abruptly, vanished from his field of vision. He watched, fascinated, until it dawned on him that something was not quite right. At the same time a dull ache gripped his chest, and a clammy sweat broke out on his temples.

One two, one two, one . . . one . . . one two . . .

He slowed his pace, feeling the resistance as he drew breath. It was peculiar; he couldn't quite put his finger on what was wrong. At first he thought it was simply exhaustion, but no, it was more than that. It was as if the air, having lain undisturbed in these deep tunnels, maybe ever since prehistoric times, was behaving like a sluggish fluid.

One two, one . . .

Will came to an abrupt halt, loosening his collar and massaging his shoulders under the straps of his backpack. He had an almost irresistible urge to throw the weight off his back—it made him feel constricted and uneasy. And the walls of the passage bothered him—they were too close, they were smothering him. He backed away into the middle of the tunnel, where he leaned on his knees and took in several gulps of air. After a while, he felt a little better and forced himself to straighten up.

"What's wrong?" Cal asked, eyeing him worriedly through the glass slit of his mask.

"Nothing," Will replied as he fumbled in his pocket for the map. He didn't want to admit to any weakness, certainly not to his brother. "I . . . I just need to check our position."

He'd taken it upon himself to navigate their route through the many twists and turns, aware that a single mistake would lose them in this subterranean maze of such extraordinary complexity. He remembered how Tam had referred to it as the "Labyrinth" and likened it to pumice stone with innumerable interlocking pores worming randomly through it. At the time, Will hadn't thought much about his uncle's words, but he now knew precisely what he'd meant. The sheer scale of the area was daunting, and although they had been making good time as they were moving rapidly through the passages, Will figured they had a long way yet to go. They were helped considerably by a gentle downward gradient, but this in itself caused him some consternation; he was only too aware that every foot they descended now would have to be climbed again before they reached the surface.

He glanced from the map to the walls. They had a pinkish hue to them, probably due to the presence of iron deposits, which could explain why his compass was worse than useless down here. The needle dithered lazily around the dial, never settling in the same position long enough to give any sort of reading.

As Will looked around him, he reflected that the passages could have been formed by gas trapped under a solidified plug of some kind, as it tried to escape through the still-molten volcanic rock. Yes, that could be the reason there weren't any vertical tunnels. Or possibly they'd been formed by water exploiting lines of weakness in the millennia after the rock cooled. *I wonder what Dad would make of this,* he thought before he could stop himself, his face falling as he realized that he'd probably never see his father again. Not now.

And try as he might, he couldn't stop remembering that last glimpse of Chester as he'd rolled helplessly across the floor, straight back into the clutches of the Styx. Will had let him down yet again. . . .

And Rebecca! There it was, incontrovertible, he'd seen it with his own eyes. She was a Styx! Despite the fact that he felt so weak, Will's blood boiled. He wanted to laugh out loud as he thought back to how worried he'd been about her.

But there was no time to reflect now—if he and Cal were going to get through this alive, he had to make sure they didn't stray off course. He took one last glance at the map and refolded it before they resumed their journey.

One two, one two, one, one, one two.

As their feet crunched in the fine red sand, Will longed for a change, a landmark, *anything* to break the monotony, to confirm that they were still on the right track. He began to despair that they were ever going to reach the end. For all he knew, they could be going around in circles.

He was thrilled when they eventually came across what looked like a small headstone, with a flat face and a rounded top, set against the passage wall. With Cal looking on, he crouched down to brush the sand from its surface.

A sweep of his hand revealed a symbol carved into the pink rock about halfway down the face. It was comprised of three diverging lines, which fanned out like rising rays or the prongs of a trident. Below were two rows of angular lettering. The symbols were unfamiliar and made no sense to him at all.

"What's this? Some kind of marker or milestone?" Will looked up at his brother, who shrugged his shoulders unhelpfully.

Several hours later, the going had become slow and laborious. They came to fork after fork in the tunnel, and Will had to consult the map even more frequently. They'd already taken one wrong turn; luckily they hadn't gone too far before Will realized his mistake and they had painstakingly retraced their steps and found their way back to the correct path again. Once there, they had flopped onto the sandy floor, stopping just long enough to catch their breath. Although he was trying to fight it, Will felt unusually tired, as if he were running on empty. And when they resumed their journey, he felt weaker than ever.

Whatever state he was in, though, Will didn't want Cal to suspect anything was wrong. He knew they must keep going; they must keep ahead of the Styx; they had to get out. He turned to his brother beside him.

"So what does Tam do in this Eternal City?" he said, breathing heavily. "He was very cagey when I asked him about it."

"He searches for coins and stuff like that, gold and silver," Cal said, then added, "most of it from graves."

"Graves?"

Cal nodded. "In the burial grounds."

"So people really lived there?"

"A long time ago. He thinks that several races occupied it, one after the other, each building on top of the last. He says there are fortunes just waiting to be found."

"But who were the people?"

"Tam told me the Bruteans were the first, centuries ago. I think he said they were Trojans. They constructed it as a stronghold or something, while the Topsoil London was built above."

"So the two cities were connected?"

Cal's mask nodded ponderously. "In the beginning. Later the entrances were blocked up, and the stones marking them were lost. . . . The Eternal City was just *forgotten*," he said, puffing noisily through the air filter. He looked nervously back up the tunnel, as if he'd heard something.

Will immediately followed his glance, but all he could see was the shadowy form of Bartleby as he loped impatiently from one side of the tunnel to the other. It was clear that he wanted to go faster than the two boys, and from time to time he would speed past them but then stop to sniff at a crevice or the ground up ahead, often becoming visibly agitated and letting out a low whine.

"At least the Styx will never find us in this place," Will said confidently.

"Don't count on it. They'll be following us, all right," Cal said. "And then there's still the Division in front of us."

"The *what*?"

"The Styx Division. They're sort of a . . . well . . . border guard," Cal said, searching for the right words. "They patrol the old city."

"What for? I thought it was empty."

"There's talk that they're rebuilding whole areas and patching up the cavern walls. It's said that the whole Colony might be moved there, and there's rumors of work parties of condemned prisoners, toiling like slaves. It's only rumors, though—no one knows for sure."

"Tam never mentioned anything about more Styx." Will didn't attempt to hide the alarm in his voice. "Bloody brilliant," he said angrily, kicking a rock in his path.

"Well, maybe he didn't think it would be a problem. We didn't exactly leave the Colony quietly, did we? Don't get too worried, though; it's a huge area to cover and there'll only be a handful of patrols."

"Oh, great! That's a real comfort!" Will replied as he imagined what might be in store for them ahead.

They wandered on for several hours, eventually scrabbling down a steep incline, their feet slipping and sliding in the red sand until they finally reached a level area. Will knew that if he'd been reading the map correctly they should be approaching the end of the Labyrinth. But the tunnel narrowed before them and appeared to end in a blind alley.

Fearing the worst, Will raced ahead, stooping as the roof lowered. To his relief, he found that there was a small passage to one side. He waited until Cal caught up, and they looked apprehensively at each other as Bartleby sniffed the air. Will hesitated, looking repeatedly from Tam's map to the opening and back again. Then he met Cal's eyes and smiled broadly as he edged into the narrow passageway. It was bathed in a subdued green light.

"Careful," Cal warned.

But Will was already at the corner. He became aware of a familiar sound: the patter of falling water. He moved his head until just one eye was peering around the edge. He was struck dumb by what he glimpsed, and inched slowly into the open, into the bottle-green glow, to get a better view. From Tam's description, and the pictures his imagination had conjured up, he was expecting something out of the ordinary. But nothing could have prepared him for the sight that met his eyes.

"The Eternal City," he whispered to himself as he began to move down a huge escarpment. As he looked up, his wide eyes scrutinizing the roof of the immense domed space, water splashed onto his upturned face and made him flinch.

"Underground rain?" he muttered, immediately realizing how ridiculous that sounded. He blinked as it dripped into his eyes, stinging them.

"It's seepage from above," Cal said, coming to a halt behind him.

But Will wasn't listening. He was finding it hard to come to terms with the titanic volume of the cavern, so massive that its farthest reaches were hidden by fog and the mists of distance. The drizzle continued to fall in slow, languorous swathes as they set off again down the escarpment.

It was almost too much to take in. Basaltic columns, like windowless skyscrapers, arced down from the mammoth span of the roof into the center of the city. Others speared upward from the outlying ground in mind-bending curves, encasing the city with gigantic undulating buttresses. It dwarfed any of the Colony's caverns with its scale, and brought to Will's mind the image of a gargantuan heart, its chambers crisscrossed by huge heartstringlike columns.

He pocketed the light orb and instinctively sought the source of the emerald green glow that gave the scene a dreamlike quality. It was as though he were looking at a lost city in the depths of an ocean. He couldn't be sure, but the light seemed to be coming from the very walls themselves—so subtly that at first he thought they were simply reflecting it.

He crossed over to the side of the escarpment and examined the cavern wall more closely. It was covered in a wild growth of tendrils, dark and glistening with moisture. It was algae of some kind, made up of many trailing shoots and thickly layered, like ivy on an old wall. As he held up the palm of his hand, he could feel the warmth radiating from it and, yes, he could see that there was indeed a very dim glow coming from the edges of the curled leaves.

"Bioluminescence," he said aloud.

"Mmmmph?" came the vague response from under Cal's canvas hood, which was twitching absurdly from side to side as he kept watch for the Styx Division.

As he continued down the incline, Will switched his attention back to the cavern, focusing on the most wondrous sight of all, the city itself. Even from this distance his eyes hungrily took in the archways, impossible terraces, and curving stone stairways sweeping up into stone balconies. Columns, Doric and Corinthian, sprang up to support dizzying galleries and walkways. His intense excitement was tinged with a sadness that Chester wasn't seeing all this with him as he should rightly have been. And as for Will's father, it would have blown his mind! It was just too much to absorb all at once. In every direction Will looked there were the most fantastic structures: colosseums and ancient domed cathedrals in beautifully crafted stone.

Then, as he came to the bottom of the escarpment, the smell hit him. It had been deceptively gentle at first, like old pond water, but with each step they'd descended, the more pungent it had become. It was rancid, catching in Will's throat like a mouthful of bile. He cupped a hand over his nose and mouth and looked at Cal in desperation.

"This is just gross!" he said, gagging on the stench. "No wonder you need to wear one of those things!"

"I know," Cal said flatly, his expression hidden by the breathing mask as he pointed to the gully by the foot of the escarpment. "Come over here."

"What for?" Will asked as he joined his brother. He was astonished to see him thrust his hands into the molasses-like slurry that lay stagnating there. Cal lifted out two handfuls of the black algae and rubbed it over his mask and his clothes. Then he grabbed Bartleby by the scruff of the neck. The cat let out a low howl and tried to get away, but Cal streaked him from head to tail. As the filth dripped over his naked skin, Bartleby arched his back and trembled, looking at his master balefully.

"But the stink is worse than ever now! What the heck are you doing?" Will demanded, thinking his brother had taken leave of his senses.

"The Division uses stalker dogs—bloodhounds—around here. Any whiff of the Colony on us and we're as good as dead. This slime will help cover our scent," he said, scooping up fresh handfuls of the brackish vegetation. "Your turn." Will braced himself as Cal doused the fetid weed over his hair, chest, and shoulders and then down each of his legs.

"How can you smell anything over this?" Will asked irately, looking at the oily patches on his clothes. The reek was overpowering. "Those dogs must have *some* sense of smell!" It was all he could do to stop himself from being sick.

"Oh, they do," Cal said as he shook his hands to rid them of the tendrils, then wiped them on his jacket. "We need to get out of sight."

Crossing one by one, they passed swiftly over a stretch of boggy ground and into the city. They went under a tall stone arch with two malevolent gargoyle faces glaring down contemptuously at them, and then into an alley with high walls on either side. The dimensions of the buildings, the gaping windows, arches, and doorways, were huge, as if they'd been built for incredibly tall beings. At Cal's suggestion, they slipped through one of these openings, at the base of a square tower.

Now out of the green light, Will needed his orb to study the map. As he pulled it out from under his coat, it illuminated the room, a stone chamber with a high ceiling and several inches of water on the floor. Bartleby scampered into one corner and, finding a heap of something rotten, he investigated it briefly before lifting a leg over it.

"Hey," Cal said abruptly. "Just look at the walls."

They saw skulls—row upon row of carved death's heads covered the walls, all with toothy grins and hollow, shadowy eyes. As Will moved the orb, the shadows shifted and the skulls appeared to be turning to face them.

"My dad would've loved this. I bet this was a—"

"It's grisly," Cal interrupted, shivering.

"These people were pretty spooky, weren't they?" Will said, unable to suppress a wide grin.

"The ancestors of the Styx."

"What?" Will looked at him questioningly.

"Their forebears. People believe a group escaped from this city at the time of the Plague."

"Where to?"

"Topsoil," Cal replied. "They formed some sort of secret society there. It's said that the Styx gave Sir Gabriel the idea for the Colony."

Will didn't have the chance to question Cal any further because suddenly Bartleby's ears pricked up and his unblinking eyes fixed on the doorway. Although neither of the boys had heard anything, Cal became agitated.

"Come on, quick, check the map, Will."

They left the chamber, cautiously picking their way through the ancient streets. It gave Will an opportunity to inspect the buildings at close range. Everywhere around them the stone was decorated with carvings and inscriptions. And he saw the decay; the masonry was crumbling and fractured. It cried out with abandonment and neglect. Yet the buildings still sat proudly in all their magnificence—they had an aura of immense power to them. Power, and something else—an ancient and decadent menace. Will was relieved that the city's inhabitants weren't still in residence.

As they jogged down lanes of ancient stone, their boots scattered the murky water on the ground and churned up the algae, leaving faintly glowing blotches in their wake like luminous stepping stones. Bartleby was agitated by the water and pranced through it with the precision of a performing pony, trying not to splash himself.

Crossing a narrow stone bridge, Will stopped briefly and looked over the eroded marble balustrade at the slow-moving river below. Slick and greasy, it snaked lazily through the city, crossed here and there with other small bridges, its waters lapping turgidly against the massive sections of masonry that formed its banks. On these, classical statues stood watch like water sentinels; old men with wavy hair and impossibly long beards, and women in flowing gowns, held out shells and orbs—or just the broken stumps of their arms—toward the water, as if offering up sacrifices to gods that no longer existed.

They came to a large square surrounded by towering buildings but held back from entering it, taking refuge behind a low parapet.

"What is that?" Will whispered. In the middle of the square was a raised platform supported by an array of thick columns. On top of the platform were human forms: chalky statues in twisted postures of frozen agony, some with their features obliterated and others with limbs missing. Rusting chains wound around the contorted figures and the posts next to them. It looked like a sculpture of some long-forgotten atrocity.

"The Prisoners' Platform. That's where they were punished."

"Gruesome statues," Will said, unable to take his eyes off it.

"They're not statues, they're real people. Tam said the bodies have been calcified."

"No!" Will said, staring even more intently at the figures and wishing he had time to document the scene.

"*Shhhhh,*" Cal warned. He grabbed Bartleby and pulled him to his chest. The cat kicked out, but Cal wouldn't let go.

Will looked at him inquiringly.

"Get down," Cal whispered. Ducking behind the parapet, he cupped his hand over the cat's eyes and clasped the animal even more tightly.

As he followed suit, Will caught sight of them. At the far end of the square, as silent as ghosts, four figures appeared to float on the surface of the waterlogged ground. They wore breathing masks over their mouths, and goggles with large, circular eyepieces, making them appear like nightmarish man-insects. Will could tell from their outlines that they were Styx. They wore leather skullcaps and long coats. Not the lustrous black ones Will had seen in the Colony; these were matte, and camouflaged with streaky green and gray blocks of dark and light hues.

With easy military efficiency, they were advancing in a line, as one controlled an immense dog straining on a leash. Vapor was blowing from the muzzle of the inconceivably large and ferocious animal—it was unlike any dog Will had ever seen before.

The boys cowered behind the parapet, acutely aware that they had nowhere to run if the Styx came their way. The hoarse panting and snorting of the dog was growing louder—Will and Cal looked at each other, both thinking that at any moment the Styx would appear from around the edge of the parapet. They angled their heads, straining to catch the least sound of the Styx approaching, but there was only the hushed gurgle of running water and the unbroken patter of cavern rain.

Will's and Cal's eyes met. All the signs were that the Styx had gone, but what should they do? *Had the patrol moved on or was it lying in ambush for them?* They waited and, after what seemed like an age, Will tapped his brother on the arm and pointed upward, indicating he was going to take a look.

Cal shook his head violently, his eyes flaring with alarm behind the half-fogged glass; they pleaded with Will to stay put. But Will ignored him and raised his head a fraction over the parapet. The Styx had vanished. He gave the thumbs-up, and Cal rose slowly to see for himself. Satisfied the patrol had moved on, Cal let go of Bartleby and he sprang away, shaking himself down and then glowering resentfully at both of them.

They skirted cautiously around the side of the square and chose a lane in the opposite direction from the one they assumed the Styx had taken. Will was feeling increasingly tired, and it was getting harder for him to catch his breath. His lungs were rattling like an asthmatic's, and a dull ache gripped his chest and rib cage. He summoned up all his energy, and they darted from shadow to shadow until the buildings ran out and the cavern wall was in front of them. They ran alongside it for several minutes until they came to a huge stone staircase cut into the rock.

"That was too close by half," Will panted, glancing behind them.

"You can say that again," Cal agreed, then peered at the staircase. "Is this the one?"

"I think so." Will shrugged. At that point, he didn't much care; he just wanted to put as much distance between them and the Styx Division as possible.

The base of the stairs was badly damaged by a massive pillar that had crashed down and shattered it, and at first the boys were forced to clamber up several broken sections. Once they had reached the steps, it wasn't much better; they were slick with black weed, and the boys nearly lost their footing more than once.

They climbed higher and higher up the stairway and, forgetting for the moment how ill he felt, Will stopped to take in the view from above. Through the haze, he caught sight of a building topped with a huge dome.

"That's the spitting image of St. Paul's Cathedral in London," he puffed, getting his breath back as he peered at the magnificent domed roof in the distance. "I'd love to have a closer look," he added.

"You've got to be kidding," Cal replied sharply.

As they continued, the stairs eventually disappeared into a jagged arch in the rock wall. Will turned for a last glance at the emerald strangeness of the Eternal City, but as he did so he slipped from the edge of the step, tottering forward onto the one below. For a heartbeat he faced the sheer drop in front of him and cried out, thinking he was about to plunge down it. He clutched frantically at the black tendrils covering the wall. Handful after handful broke off, then he finally managed to get a grip and steady himself again.

"Hey, are you all right?" Cal said, now at his side. When Will didn't answer him, he became increasingly concerned. "What's the matter?"

"I . . . I just feel so dizzy," Will admitted in a wheezing voice. He was panting in small, shallow breaths—it was as if he were breathing through a clogged straw. He climbed a few steps but came to a standstill again as he broke into a racking cough. He thought the coughing fit was never going to stop. Doubled over, Will hacked away and then spat. He clutched his forehead, soaked with rain and clammy with an unhealthily cold sweat, and knew there was no way he could hide it from his brother any longer.

"I need to rest," he said hoarsely, using Cal for support as the coughing subsided.

"Not now," Cal said urgently, "and not here." Grabbing Will's arm, he helped him through the archway and into the gloomy stairway beyond.

31

THERE is a point at which the body is spent, when the muscles and sinews have nothing left to give, when all that remains is a person's mettle, his sheer single-mindedness.

Will had reached that point. His body felt drained and worthless, but still he slogged on, driven by the responsibility he felt toward his brother and his duty to get him to safety. At the same time, gnawing away at him was the unbearable guilt that he'd let Chester down, let him fall into the Colonists' hands for a second time.

I'm useless, completely useless. The words ran in a loop through Will's mind, over and over again. But neither he nor his brother spoke as they climbed, grinding their way up the never-ending spiral staircase. At the very limits of his endurance, Will pushed himself on, step after painful step, flight after flight, his thighs burning as much as his lungs. Slipping and sliding on water-drenched stone treads and the stringy weeds that clung to them, he fought to suppress the dread realization that they still had far to go.

"I'd like to stop now," he heard Cal pant.

"Can't . . . don't think . . . I'd ever . . . get going . . . again," Will grunted in time with his plodding steps.

The excruciating hours crawled by, until he had lost track of how long they'd been climbing, and nothing in the world existed or mattered to him except the grueling notion that he had to take the next step, and the next, and so on . . . and just when Will thought he'd reached his limits and that he couldn't go any farther, he felt the faintest of breezes on his face. He knew instinctively it was untainted air. He stopped and sucked at the freshness, hoping to lift the leaden weight from his chest and relieve the interminable rattle in his lungs.

"Don't need it," he said, pointing at Cal's mask. Cal removed it from his head and tucked it in his belt, the sweat running down his face in rivulets and his eyes rimmed with red.

"*Phew,*" he exhaled. "Hot under that thing."

They resumed the climb, and it wasn't long before the steps ended and they entered a sequence of narrow passages. Every so often they were forced to scramble up rusted iron ladders, their hands turning orange as they tested each precarious rung.

Eventually they reached a steeply angled shaft no more than three feet wide. They hauled themselves up its pockmarked surface using the thick, knotted rope they discovered hanging there (Cal was certain his uncle Tam had rigged it up). Hand over hand they went, their feet finding purchase in the shallow cracks and fault lines as they climbed. The incline became steeper, and they had a heck of a job to scrabble over the remaining stretch of slime-covered stone, but despite losing their footing a few times, they finally reached the top, hauling themselves up into a circular chamber. Here there was a small vent in the floor. Leaning into it, Will could see the remnants of an iron grating, long since rusted away.

"What's down there?" Cal panted.

"Nothing, can't see a darn thing," Will said despondently, squatting down to rest on his haunches. He brushed the sweat from his face with a raw hand. "I suppose we do what Tam said. We climb down."

Cal looked behind and then to his brother, nodding. For several minutes neither of them made a move, immobilized with fatigue.

"Well, we can't stay here forever." Will sighed and swung his legs into the vent and, with his back pressed against one side and feet hard against the other, he began to ease himself down.

"What about the cat?" Will shouted after he had gone a short distance. "Is Bartleby going to be able to cope with this?"

"Don't worry about him," Cal said with a smile. "Anything we can do—"

Will never heard the rest of Cal's sentence. He slipped. The sides of the vent shot by, and he landed with a large splash—he was submerged in an icy coldness. He thrashed out with his arms, then his feet found the bottom, and he stood up and blew out a mouthful of freezing liquid. He found he was chest-deep in water, and after he'd wiped it out of his eyes and pushed back his hair, he looked around. He couldn't be certain, but there seemed to be a dim light in the distance.

He heard Cal's frantic shouts from above. "Will! Will! Are you all right?"

"Just had a quick dip!" Will shouted, laughing weakly. "Stay there, I'm going to check something out." His exhaustion and discomfort were ignored for the moment as he stared at the faint glow, trying to make out the vaguest detail of what lay ahead.

Soaked to the skin, he clambered out of the pool and, stooping under the low roof, crept slowly toward the light. After a couple of hundred yards, he could clearly see the circular mouth of the tunnel and, with his heart racing, he sped toward it. Dropping more than three feet off a ledge he'd failed to notice, he landed roughly, finding himself under a jetty of some kind. Through a forest of heavy wooden stanchions, draped with weeds, he could see the dappled reflections of light on water.

Gravel crunched underfoot as he walked into the open. He felt the invigorating chill of the wind on his face. He breathed deeply, drawing the fresh air into his aching lungs. It was such sweetness. Slowly he took stock of the surroundings.

Night. Lights reflected off a river in front of him. It was a wide river. A two-tiered pleasure boat chugged past—bright flashes of color pulsed from its two decks as indistinct dance music throbbed over the water. Then he saw the bridges on either side of him and, in the distance, the floodlit dome of St. Paul's. The St. Paul's he knew. A red double-decker bus crossed the bridge closest to him. This wasn't any old river. He sat down on the bank with surprise and relief.

It was the *Thames.*

He lay back on the bank and closed his eyes, listening to the droning hubbub of traffic. He tried to remember the names of the bridges, but he didn't really care—he'd gotten out, he'd escaped, and nothing else mattered. He'd made it. He was home. Back in his own world.

"The sky," Cal said with awe in his voice. "So that's what it's like." Will opened his eyes to see his brother craning his neck this way and that as he stared at the stray wisps of cloud caught in the amber radiation of the streetlights. Although Cal was sopping from his immersion in the pool, he was smiling broadly, but then he wrinkled up his nose. "*Phew,* what's that?" he asked loudly.

"What do you mean?" Will said.

"All those smells!"

Will propped himself up on one elbow and sniffed. "What smells?"

"Food . . . all sorts of food . . . and . . ." Cal grimaced. ". . . sewage—lots of it—and chemicals . . ."

As Will sniffed the air, thinking again how fresh it was, it occurred to him that he hadn't once considered what they were going to do next. Where were they going to go? He'd been so intent on escaping, he hadn't given anything beyond it a second thought. He stood up and examined his sodden, filthy Colonists' clothes and those of his brother, and the unfeasibly large cat that was now nosing around the bank like a pig searching for truffles. A brisk winter wind was picking up, and he shivered violently, his teeth starting to chatter. It struck him that neither his brother nor Bartleby had experienced the relative extremes of Topsoil weather in their sheltered, subterranean lives. He had to get them moving. And quickly. But he didn't have any money on him—not a penny.

"We're going to have to walk home."

"Fine," Cal replied unquestioningly, his head back as he stared at the stars, losing himself in the canopy of the sky.

"At last I've seen them," he whispered to himself.

A helicopter drifted across the horizon.

"Why's that one moving?" he asked.

Will felt too tired to explain. "They do that," he said flatly.

They set off, keeping close to the bank so as not to be noticed, and almost immediately came upon a set of steps leading up to the walkway above. It was next to a bridge. Will knew then where they were—it was Blackfriars Bridge.

A gate blocked the top of the steps, so they hastily clambered over the broad wall beside it to reach the walkway. Dripping water on the pavement and freezing in the night air, they looked around them. Will was seized by the dreadful thought that even here the Styx might have spies watching out for them. After seeing one of the Clarke brothers in the Colony, he felt that he couldn't trust anybody, and he regarded the few people in the immediate area with mounting suspicion. But nobody was close, with the exception of a young couple walking hand in hand. They strolled past, so involved with each other that they didn't seem to pay the boys or their huge cat the least bit of attention.

With Will taking the lead, they climbed the steps to the bridge itself. Arriving at the top, Will saw that the IMAX cinema was to their right. He immediately knew they didn't want to be on that side of the river. To him, London was a mosaic of places, each familiar to him from museum visits with his father or school expeditions. The rest, the interconnecting areas, were a complete mystery to him. There was only one thing to do: trust in his sense of direction and try to head north.

As they turned left and quickly traversed the bridge, Will spotted a sign to King's Cross and knew instantly that they were heading the right way. Traffic passed them as they arrived at the end of the bridge, and Will paused to look at Cal and the cat under the glow of a streetlight. Talk about three suspicious-looking lost souls—they stuck out a mile. Although it was dark, Will was painfully aware that a pair of young boys soaked to the skin and wandering the streets of London at this late hour, with or without a giant cat, were likely to attract attention, and the last thing he needed now was to be picked up by the police. He made an attempt at concocting a story, rehearsing it in his mind, just in case it happened.

'ello, 'ello, 'ello, the pair of fictitious policemen said. *What 'ave we 'ere, then?*

Uh . . . just out walking the . . . the . . . Will's imagined response came to a faltering stop. No, that wouldn't do, he had to be better prepared than that. He started again: *Good evening, officers. We're just taking the neighbor's pet for a walk.*

The first policeman leaned in to peer curiously at Bartleby, his eyes narrowing as he grimaced in open distaste. *Looks dangerous to me, son. Shouldn't it be on a leash?*

What is it, exactly? the second imaginary policeman chimed in.

It's a . . . , Will began. What could he say? Ah yes . . . *It's very rare . . . a very rare hybrid, a cross between a dog and a cat called a . . . a Dat,* Will informed them helpfully.

Or is it a Cog, perhaps? the second policeman suggested drily, the glint in his eye telling Will he wasn't buying a word of it.

Whatever it is, it's bloody ugly, his partner said.

Shhh! You'll hurt his feelings. Suddenly, Will realized he was wasting his time with all of this. The reality was that the policemen would simply ask for their names and addresses, then radio in to double-check them. And they'd probably be found out even if they tried to give false ones. So that would be it. They'd be taken back to the station and held there. Will suspected he was probably wanted for abducting Chester, or something equally ridiculous, and would likely as not end up in a juvenile detention center. As for Cal, he would be a real conundrum—of course, there wouldn't be a record of him anywhere, no Topsoil identity whatsoever. No, they'd have to avoid the police at all costs.

Perversely, as he contemplated the future, there was a part of him that almost wanted them to be stopped. It would remove the dreadful burden that at the moment lay squarely on his shoulders; he glanced at the cowed figure of his brother. Cal was a stranger, a freak in this cold and inhospitable place, and Will had no idea how he was going to protect him.

But Will knew if he turned himself in to the authorities and tried to get them to investigate the Colony—that's if they believed a runaway teenager in the first place—he could be risking countless lives, his *family's* lives. Who knew how it would end? He shuddered at the thought of the Discovery, as Grandma Macaulay had called it, and tried to imagine her being led out into the daylight after her long subterranean life. He couldn't do that to her—couldn't even bear the thought of it. It was too big a decision for him to take alone, and he felt so terribly alone and isolated.

He pulled his damp jacket around himself and hustled Cal and Bartleby down into the underpass at the end of the bridge.

"It reeks of pee down here," his brother commented. "Do all Topsoilers mark their territories?" He turned to Will inquiringly.

"Uh, no . . . not usually. But this *is* London."

As they emerged from the underpass and back onto the pavement, Cal seemed confused by the traffic, looking this way and that. Coming to a main road, they stopped at the curb. Will gripped his brother's sleeve with one hand and the cat's hairless scruff with the other. Crossing when there was a lull, they made it to the traffic island. He could see people peering curiously at them from the passing cars, and a white van slowed down almost to a halt right beside them, the driver talking excitedly into his cell phone. To Will's relief, it sped off again. They crossed the remaining two lanes and, after a short distance, Will steered them into a dimly lit side street. His brother stood with one hand on the brick wall beside him—he looked completely disoriented, like a blind man in unfamiliar surroundings.

"Foul air!" he said vehemently.

"It's only car fumes," Will replied as he untied the thick string from his light orb and fashioned a slipknot leash for the cat, who didn't seem to mind one bit.

"It smells wrong. It must be against the laws," Cal said with complete conviction.

"'Fraid not," Will answered as he led them down the street. He would have to stay off the main roads and keep to the backstreets as far as possible, even though it would make their journey even more difficult and circuitous.

And so the long march north began. On their way out of central London they only saw a single police car, but Will was able to usher them around a corner in the nick of time.

"Are they like Styx?" Cal asked.

"Not quite," Will replied.

With the cat on one side and Cal twitching nervously on the other, they trudged along. From time to time his brother would stop dead in his tracks, as if invisible doors were being slammed in his face.

"What is it?" Will asked on one of these occasions when his brother refused to move.

"It's like . . . anger . . . and fear," Cal said in a strained voice as he glanced nervously up at the windows over a storefront. "It's so strong. I don't like it."

"I can't see anything," Will said as he failed to make out what was troubling his brother. They were just ordinary windows, a sliver of light showing between the curtains in one of them. "It's nothing, you're imagining it."

"No, I'm not. I can smell it," Cal said emphatically, "and it's getting stronger. I want to go."

After several miles of tortuous ducking and diving, they came to the brow of a hill, at the bottom of which was a busy main road with six lanes of speeding traffic.

"I recognize this—it's not far now. Maybe a couple of miles, that's all," Will said with relief.

"I'm not going near it. I can't—not with that stench. It'll kill us," Cal said, backing away from Will.

"C'mon, don't be stupid," Will said. He was just too tired for any nonsense, and his frustration now turned to anger. "We're so close."

"No," Cal said, digging in his heels. "I'm staying right here!"

Will tried to pull the boy's arm, but he yanked it away. Will had been fighting his exhaustion for miles and was still struggling to breathe; he didn't need this. All of a sudden, it became too much for him. He thought he was actually going to break down and cry. It just wasn't fair. He pictured the house and his welcoming clean bed. All he wanted to do was lie down and sleep. Even as he was walking, his body kept going loose, as if he were dropping through a hole into a place where everything was so comforting and warm. Then he would yank himself out of it, back to wakefulness, and urge himself on again.

"Fine!" Will spat. "Suit yourself!" He set off down the hill, tugging Bartleby by the leash.

As he reached the road, Will heard his brother's voice over the din of the traffic.

"Will!" he yelled. "Wait for me! I'm sorry!"

Cal came hurtling down the hill—Will could see that he was genuinely terrified. He kept jerking his head to look around him, as if he were about to be attacked by some imagined assassin.

They crossed the road at the lights, but Cal insisted on pressing his hand over his mouth until they were a good distance from it. "I can't take this," he said glumly. "I liked the idea of cars when I was in the Colony . . . but the brochures didn't say anything about the way they smell."

"Got a light?"

Startled by the voice, they whirled around. They'd stopped for a minute's rest and, as if he had appeared from nowhere, a man was standing very close behind them, a lopsided grin on his face. He wasn't terribly tall, but he was well dressed in a tightly fitting dark blue suit and a shirt and tie. He had long black hair, which he kept stroking back at the temples and tucking behind his ears, as if it was bothering him. "Left mine at home," he continued, his voice deep and rich.

"Don't smoke, sorry," Will replied, quickly edging away. There was something forced and sleazy in the man's smile, and alarm bells were ringing in Will's head.

"You boys all right? You look beat. I've got a place you can warm up. Not far from here," the man said ingratiatingly. "Bring your doggy, too, of course." He held out a hand toward Cal, and Will saw that the fingers were stained with nicotine and the fingernails black with filth.

"Can we really?" Cal said, returning the man's smile.

"No . . . very kind of you, but . . . ," Will interrupted, glaring at his brother but failing to get his attention. The man took a step toward Cal and addressed him, completely ignoring Will, as if he wasn't there.

"Something hot to eat, too?" he offered.

Cal was at the point of replying when Will spoke.

"Must go, our parents are waiting just around the corner. Come on, Cal," he said, a note of urgency creeping into his voice. Cal looked perplexedly at Will, who shook his head, frowning. Realizing that something wasn't quite right, Cal fell into step beside his brother.

"Shame. Maybe next time?" the man said, his eyes still locked on Cal. He made no move to follow them, but pulled a lighter from his jacket pocket and lit a cigarette. "Be seeing you!" he called after them.

"Don't you look back," Will hissed through his teeth as he walked rapidly away with Cal in tow. "Don't you *dare* look back."

An hour later they entered Highfield. Will avoided Main Street in case he was recognized, taking the back alleys and side roads until they turned onto Broadlands Avenue.

There it was. The house, completely dark, with a real estate agent's sign in the front yard. Will led them around the side and under the carport into the back garden. He kicked over a brick where the spare back-door key had always been hidden and muttered a muted prayer of thanks when he saw it was still there. He unlocked the door, and they took a few wary paces into the dark hallway.

"Colonists!" Cal said right away, recoiling as he continued to sniff the air. "They've been here . . . and not long ago."

"For heaven's sake." It merely smelled a little fusty and unoccupied to Will, but he couldn't be bothered to argue. Not wanting to alert the neighbors, he left the lights off and used his orb to check each room, while Cal remained in the hall, his senses working overtime.

"There's nothing . . . no one here at all. Satisfied?" Will said as he returned downstairs. With some consternation, his brother edged farther into the house with Bartleby at his heels, and Will shut and locked the door behind them. He shepherded them into the living room and, making sure the curtains were tightly closed, turned on the television. Then he went to the kitchen.

The fridge was completely bare except for a tub of margarine and an old tomato, which was green and shrunken. For a moment, Will stared uncomprehendingly at the bare shelves. To him this was unprecedented, confirming just how far things had gone. He sighed as he shut the door and spotted a scrap of lined paper taped to it. It was in Rebecca's precise hand; one of her shopping lists.

Rebecca! The fury suddenly rose in him. The thought of that imposter masquerading as his sister for all those years made him rigid with anger. She had changed everything. Now he couldn't even think back to the comfortable and predictable life he'd been leading before his father went missing, because she had been there, watching and spying. Her very presence tainted all his memories. Hers was the worst kind of betrayal—she was a Judas sent by the Styx.

"Evil!" he shouted, tearing off the list, crumpling it up, and slinging it to the floor.

As it came to rest on the pristine linoleum that Rebecca had mopped week in and week out with mind-numbing regularity, Will looked at the stopped clock on the wall and sighed. He shuffled over to the sink and filled glasses with water for himself and Cal, and a bowl for Bartleby, then returned to the living room. Cal and the cat were already curled up asleep on the sofa, Cal with his head resting drowsily on his arm. He could see that they were both shivering, so he grabbed a couple of blankets from the beds upstairs and draped them over their slumbering forms. The house didn't have its central heating on and it was cold, but not that cold. He'd been right in thinking that they just weren't used to these lower temperatures, and made a mental note to sort out some warm clothes for them in the morning.

Will drank the water quickly and climbed into his mother's chair, wrapping himself in her afghan. His eyes barely registered the death-defying snowboarding stunts on the television as he curled up, precisely as his mother had done for so many years, and fell into the deepest of sleeps.

32

TAM STOOD silent and defiant. He was determined not to show any sign of his trepidation as he and Mr. Jerome faced the long table, their hands clenched behind their backs as if standing at attention.

Behind the table of highly polished oak sat the Panoply. These were the most senior and powerful members of the Styx Council. At either end of the table sat a few high-ranking Colonists: representatives from the Board of the Governors, men that Mr. Jerome had known all his life, men that were his friends. He quaked with shame as he felt the disgrace wash over him, and couldn't bring himself to look at them. He'd never thought it would come to this.

Tam was less intimidated; he'd been carpeted before and always managed to get off by the skin of his teeth. Although these allegations were serious, he knew his alibi had passed their scrutiny. Imago and his men had made sure of that. Tam watched as the Crawfly conferred with a fellow Styx and then leaned back to speak to the Styx child who stood half hidden behind the high back of his chair. Now *that* was irregular. Their children were usually kept well out of sight and far away from the Colony; the newborn were never seen, while the older offspring, it was said, were closeted away with their masters in the rarefied atmosphere of their private schools. He'd never heard of them accompanying their elders in public, let alone being present at meetings such as these.

Tam's thoughts were interrupted as a scratchy outburst of intense debate ran back and forth through the Panoply. Whispers rippled from one end to the other as skinny hands communicated in a series of harsh gestures. Tam glanced quickly at Mr. Jerome, whose head hung low. He was quietly mumbling a prayer as sweat coursed from his temples. His face was puffy and his skin an unhealthy pink. All this was taking its toll on him.

The commotion abruptly ceased amid nods and staccato words of agreement, and the Styx settled back in their seats, a chilling silence descending over the room. Tam readied himself. A pronouncement was about to be delivered.

"Mr. Jerome," the Styx to the left of the Crawfly intoned. "After due consideration and a full and proper investigation"—he fixed his beady pupils on the quivering man—"we will allow you to step down."

Another Styx promptly took over. "It is felt that the injustices brought upon you from specific of your family members, past and present, are unjust and unfortunate. Your honesty is not in question, and your reputation has not been tarnished. Unless you would like to speak for the record, you are unconditionally discharged."

Mr. Jerome bowed dolefully and backed away from the table. Tam heard his boots scuffing on the flagstones but dared not turn to watch him leave. Instead his gaze flicked to the ceiling of the stone hall, then to the ancient wall hangings behind the Panoply, alighting on one depicting the Founding Fathers digging a perfectly round tunnel in the side of a verdant hill.

He knew that all eyes now rested on him.

Another Styx spoke. Tam immediately recognized the Crawfly's voice and was obliged to face his avowed enemy. *He's loving every minute of this,* Tam thought.

"Macaulay. You are a different kettle of fish. Though not yet proven, we believe that you did aid and abet your nephews, Seth and Caleb Jerome, in their foiled attempt to liberate the Topsoiler Chester Rawls and then to escape to the Eternal City," said the Crawfly with evident relish.

A second Styx continued. "The Panoply has recorded your plea of not guilty and your continuing protestations." With a single disapproving shake of his head he fell silent for a moment. "We have reviewed the evidence submitted in your defense, but at this time we are unable to reach a resolution. Accordingly we have decreed that the investigation will remain open, and that you are to be held on remand and your privileges revoked until further notice. Do you understand?"

Tam nodded somberly.

"We said, do you understand?" snapped the Styx child, stepping forward.

An evil grin flicked across Rebecca's face as her icy glare drilled into Tam. There was a stir of hushed astonishment from the Colonists that the minor had dared to speak, but not the smallest indication from the Styx that anything out of the ordinary had taken place.

To say Tam was staggered would be a rank understatement. Was he really supposed to respond to this mere child? When he didn't answer right away, she repeated the question, her hard little voice as sharp as a whip crack.

"WE SAID, DO YOU UNDERSTAND?"

"I do," Tam muttered, "only too well."

Of course, it wasn't a final ruling by any means, but it meant he would live in limbo until they decided either that he was cleared or . . . well . . . the alternative was too horrifying to think about.

As a surly Colonist officer escorted him away, Tam couldn't help but notice the smarmy look of self-congratulation that passed between Rebecca and the Crawfly.

Well, I'll be blowed! Tam thought. *It's his daughter!*

Aroused from his sleep by the booming sound of the television, Will sat up in the armchair with a start. He automatically groped for the remote control and clicked down the volume a couple of notches; it was only when he looked around that he fully realized where he was and remembered how he'd gotten there. He was home, and in a room he knew so well. Although he was surrounded by uncertainty about what he was going to do next, for the first time in a long time he felt that he had a measure of control over his destiny, and it felt good.

He flexed his stiff limbs and took several deep breaths, coughing sharply. Despite the fact that he was ravenous, he felt a little better than he had the day before; the sleep had done him some good. He scratched, then tugged vaguely at his matted hair, its usual whiteness discolored with dirt. Clambering out of the chair, he stumbled over to the curtains and parted them a couple of inches to let the morning sun into the room. Real light. It was such a welcome sight that he pulled them wider.

"Too bright!" Cal screeched repeatedly, burying his face in a cushion. Bartleby, roused by Cal's cries, flicked his eyes open. He immediately shied away from the glare, his long legs propelling him backward until he tumbled off the rear of the sofa. There he remained, hiding from the light and making noises somewhere between hisses and low meows.

"Oh, yikes, I'm sorry," Will stuttered, kicking himself as he hurriedly yanked the curtains shut again. "I completely forgot."

He helped his brother into a sitting position. He was moaning quietly behind the cushion, and Will could see that it was already soaked with his tears. He wondered if Cal's and Bartleby's eyes would ever adjust to natural light. It was just one more problem Will had to contend with.

"That was *so* stupid of me," he said helplessly. "I'll . . . um . . . I'll find some sunglasses for you."

He began to search through a chest of drawers in his parents' room, only to find that it had been emptied. As he was checking the last drawer, he picked out a little bag of lavender languishing on the cheap Christmas gift wrap that his mother had used as a paper liner and held it up to catch the familiar scent. He closed his eyes as the smell conjured up a vivid picture of her. Wherever they'd sent her to recuperate, she'd be lording it over the other patients by now. He was willing to bet she'd commandeered the best chair in the television room and had cajoled someone into bringing her regular cups of tea. He smiled. In a way, she was probably happier now than she'd been for years. And maybe a little safer, too, if the Styx decided to pay a visit.

For no reason in particular, as he rummaged through a bedside cupboard, he thought of his real mother. He wondered where she was right at that very moment, if indeed she was still alive at all. The only person in the long history of the Colony ever to evade the Styx and survive. He set his jaw with a determined look as he caught his reflection in a mirror. Well, now there were going to be two more Jeromes with that distinction.

On a high shelf in his mother's closet he found what he was looking for, a pair of bendy plastic sunglasses she wore on the rare occasions she ventured out in the summer. He went back to Cal, who was squinting at the television in the darkened room, completely absorbed by the midmorning talk show on which the perma-tanned and obsequious host, oozing sincerity, was comforting the inconsolable mother of a teenage drug addict. Cal's eyes were a little red and still wet with tears, but he said nothing and indeed did not shift his gaze once from the screen as Will placed the glasses on his head, looping an elastic band around the arms to hold them firmly in place.

"Better?" Will asked.

"Much better, yes," Cal said, adjusting them. "But I'm really hungry," he added, rubbing his stomach. "And I'm so cold." He rattled his teeth together dramatically.

"Showers first. That'll warm you up," Will said as he lifted his arm to sample the accumulated odor of many days' sweat. "And some clean clothes."

"Showers?" Cal peered at him blankly through the sunglass lenses.

Will managed to get the boiler fired up and went first, the hot water stinging his flesh with painful relief as the clouds of steam enveloped him in an ecstasy of forgetfulness. Then it was Cal's turn. Will showed his fascinated brother how the shower worked and left him to it. From the closet in his bedroom he dug out clean sets of clothes for himself and Cal, although his brother's needed a little adjustment to make them fit.

"I'm a real Topsoiler now!" Cal announced, admiring the baggy jeans with rolled-up cuffs and the voluminous shirt with two sweaters on top of it.

"Yeah, very trendsetting," Will said with a laugh.

Bartleby was more problematic. It took much coaxing by Cal to even get the shivering animal as far as the bathroom door, and then they had to push him from the rear, like a recalcitrant donkey, to get him in. As if he knew what was in store in the steamy room, he leaped away and tried to hide under the sink.

"Come on, Bart, you stinker, into the bath!" Cal ordered, finally running out of patience, and the cat grudgingly crept into the bath and looked at them with the most hangdog of expressions. He let out a warbled, low whine when the water first trickled over his sagging skin, and, deciding he'd had enough, his paws scrabbled on the plastic of the tub as he tried to get out. But with Will holding him down they managed to finish the task, although all three of them were completely drenched by the end of the exercise.

Once out of the bath, Bartleby ricocheted around the bedrooms like a whirling dervish while Will took great pleasure in ransacking Rebecca's room. As he chucked all her incredibly neatly folded clothes onto the floor, he wondered how in the world he was going to find anything that was remotely suitable to dress a giant cat. But in the end some brown legwarmers were cut down to size for the animal's hind legs and an old purple sweater took care of his top half. Will found a pair of Bugs Bunny sunglasses in Rebecca's desk drawer, and these stayed in place on the cat's head once a yellow-and-black-striped Tibetan hat was pulled firmly down.

Bartleby looked quite bizarre in his new outfit. Out on the landing, the two brothers stood back to admire their handiwork, promptly falling into hysterics.

"Who's a pretty boy, then?" Cal chuckled between outbursts of breathless laughter.

"Better-looking than most around here!" Will said.

"Don't you worry, Bart," Cal said soothingly, patting the peeved animal on the back. "Very . . . uh . . . striking," he managed to say before they both lapsed once again into uncontrolled laughter. Behind the pink-tinted lenses, the indignant Bartleby watched them sideways out of his large eyes.

Fortunately, Rebecca, much as Will cursed her, had left the freezer in the utility room well stocked. He read the microwave instructions and heated up three beef dinners complete with dumplings and green beans. They wolfed these down in the kitchen, Bartleby standing with both paws on the table, his tongue rasping against the plastic dish as he hungrily devoured every last scrap of the meat. Cal thought it was just about the best thing he'd ever tasted, but claimed he was still hungry, so Will retrieved another three meals from the freezer. This time, they had pork dinners with roasted potatoes. They washed this down with a bottle of Coke, which sent Cal into fits of rapture.

"So what happens next?" he said finally, tracing the rising bubbles on the side of his glass with a finger.

"What's the mad rush? We'll be all right for a while," Will replied. He hoped that they would be able to hole up there, even if for just a few days, to give him time to figure out their next move.

"The Styx know about this place—someone's already been here, and they'll be back. Don't forget what Uncle Tam said. There's absolutely no way we can stay put."

"I suppose so," Will agreed reluctantly, "and we could be spotted by the real estate agents if they show people around." He gazed in an unfocused way at the net curtains over the kitchen sink and spoke decisively. "But I still have to get Chester out."

His brother looked aghast. "You don't mean go back? I can't go back, not now, Will. The Styx would do something terrible to me."

Cal was not alone in his fear of returning underground. Will could barely contain his terror at the prospect of facing the Styx again. He felt as though he had pushed his luck as far as it would go, and to imagine he could carry out some audacious rescue attempt was sheer lunacy.

On the other hand, what would they do if they remained Topsoil? Go on the run? When he really thought about it, it just wasn't realistic. Sooner or later they'd be apprehended by the police, and he and Cal would probably be separated and placed in foster care. Worse than that, he'd live the rest of his life under the shadow of Chester's death and with the knowledge that he could have joined his father in one of the greatest adventures of the century.

"I don't want to die," Cal said in a faint voice. "Not like that." He pushed his glass away and looked pleadingly into Will's eyes.

This wasn't getting any easier. Will couldn't cope with much more pressure. He shook his head. "What am I supposed to do? I can't just leave him there. I can't. I won't."

Later, while Cal and Bartleby lounged in front of the television watching children's programs and eating potato chips, Will couldn't resist going into the cellar. Just as he expected, when he swung the shelves out, there wasn't a trace of the tunnel—they had even gone to the trouble of painting the newly laid brickwork to blend in with the rest of the wall. He knew that behind it would be the usual backfill of stone and soil. They'd done the job thoroughly. No point in wasting any further time there.

Back in the kitchen, he balanced on a stool while he hunted through the jars on top of the cupboards. He found his mother's video money in a porcelain cookie jar—there was about £20 in loose change.

He was in the hallway on his way to the living room when he began to see tiny dots of light dancing before his eyes, and all over his body pinpricks of heat broke out. Then, without any warning, his legs went out from under him. He dropped the jar, which glanced off the edge of the hall table and shattered, scattering the change all over the floor. It was as if he were in slow motion as he collapsed, a fierce pain burning through his head until everything turned black and he lost consciousness.

Cal and Bartleby came rushing out of the living room at the noise. "Will! What's the matter?" Cal cried, kneeling next to him.

Will slowly came around, his temples throbbing painfully. "I don't know," he said feebly. "Just felt awful, all of a sudden." He started to cough, and had to hold his breath in order to stop.

"You're burning up," Cal said, feeling his forehead.

"Freezing . . ." Will could barely talk as his teeth rattled together. He made an effort to get up, but didn't have the strength.

"Oh, no." Cal's face was creased with concern. "It could be something from the Eternal City. Plague!"

Will was silent as his brother pulled him over to the bottom step of the staircase and propped his head on it. He grabbed the afghan and put it around him. After a while, Will directed Cal to the bathroom to get some aspirin. He swallowed them down with a sip of Coke and, after a brief rest, managed to get shakily to his feet with assistance from Cal.

Will's eyes were feverish and unfocused, and his voice trembled. "I really think we should get help," he said, mopping the sweat from his brow.

"Is there anywhere we can go?" Cal asked.

Will sniffed, swallowed, and nodded, his head feeling as though it were about to burst. "There's only one place I can think of."

"Get yerself out here!" the Second Officer bawled into the cell, his head pushed so far forward that the tendons in his bull-like neck stood proud, like knotted lengths of rope.

From the shadows came several sniffs as Chester did his best to control his terrified sobbing. Ever since he had been recaptured and brought back to the Hold, the Second Officer had been treating him brutally. The man had taken it upon himself to make Chester's life a living nightmare, withholding his meals and waking him up if he happened to nod off on the ledge by emptying a bucket of ice-cold water over his head or by screaming threats through the inspection hatch. All this probably had something to do with the thick bandage wound around the Second Officer's head—Will's blow with the shovel had knocked him out cold—and, what was worse, when he came to, the Styx had spent the best part of a day interrogating him over the accusation that he had been negligent in his duties. So to say that the Second Officer was now very bitter and vindictive would be putting it mildly.

Chester, half starved and exhausted to the point of collapse, wasn't sure how much more of this treatment he could take. If life had been hard for him before the botched escape attempt, it was that much worse now.

"Don't make me come in there and get you!" the Second Officer was yelling. Before he'd finished, Chester shuffled barefoot into the wan light of the corridor. Shielding his eyes with one hand, he lifted his head. It was streaked gray with ingrained dirt, and his shirt was torn.

"Yes, sir," he mumbled subserviently.

"The Styx want to see you. They've got something to tell you," the Second Officer said, his voice distorted with malice, and then he began to chortle. "Something that'll fix you good and proper." He was still laughing as, unbidden, Chester started down the corridor toward the main door to the Hold, the soles of his feet rasping sluggishly across the gritty stones.

"Shift it!" the Second Officer snapped, thrusting his bunch of keys into the small of Chester's back.

"*Ow,*" Chester complained in a pitiful voice.

As they went through the main door, Chester had to cover his eyes altogether, he was now so unused to the light. He continued to shuffle along, heading on a course that would have taken him through to the front desk of the police station if the Second Officer hadn't stopped him.

"And where do you think you're off to? You don't think you're going home, do you?" The man started to guffaw and then became deadly serious again. "No, you go *right,* into the corridor, you do."

Chester, lowering his hands and trying to see through his scrunched-up eyes, made a slow quarter turn and then froze, rooted to the spot.

"The Dark Light?" he asked fearfully, not daring to turn his face toward the Second Officer.

"No, we're past all that now. This is where you get your comeuppance, you worthless little squit."

They passed through a series of corridors, the Second Officer chivying Chester along with further jabs and shoves, chuckling to himself all the way. He quieted down as they rounded a corner and came in sight of an open doorway. From this an intense light streamed out, illuminating the whitewashed wall opposite.

Although Chester's movements were languid and his expression blank, inwardly his fears were raging. Frantically he debated with himself whether he should make a run for it and bolt down the corridor ahead. He didn't have the slightest idea where it led, or how far he'd get, but it would, at the very least, put off facing whatever was waiting for him in that room. For a while, anyway.

He slowed even further, his eyes hurting as he forced himself to look directly at the blaze of light flooding from the doorway. He was getting closer. He didn't know what was waiting inside—another of their exquisitely horrible tortures? Or maybe . . . maybe *an executioner.*

His whole body stiffened, every muscle wanting to do anything but carry him into that dazzling light.

"Nearly there," the officer said over Chester's shoulder, and Chester knew that he had no alternative but to cooperate. There were going to be no miraculous reprieves, no timely escapes.

He was dragging his heels so much that he was barely moving at all when the Second Officer gave him such a hefty shove that he was knocked clean off his feet and sent flying through the doorway into the light. Skidding over the stone floor on his front, he came to a rest and lay there, a little stunned.

The light was all around him, and he was blinking rapidly in its harsh glare. He heard the door slam and, from a rustle of papers, he knew at once there was someone else in the room. He immediately imagined who it—or they—would be: two tall Styx, most likely looming behind a table, just as there'd been during the Dark Light sessions.

"Stand up," ordered a reedy, nasal voice.

Chester did so, and slowly raised his eyes to the source. He couldn't have been more astonished by the sight that greeted him.

It was a single Styx, and he was wizened and small, his thinning gray hair pulled back at the temples and his face crisscrossed with so many lines and wrinkles that he looked like a bleached raisin. Hunched sharply over a tall desk with a slanted top, he resembled an ancient schoolmaster.

Chester was completely disarmed by this apparition with the sheer light all around it. This was not what he'd been expecting at all. He was beginning to feel relieved, telling himself that perhaps things were going to turn out better than he'd thought after all, when his eyes met those of the old Styx.

They were the coldest, darkest eyes Chester had ever seen. They were like two bottomless wells that drew him toward them and by some unnatural and unwholesome power pulled him down into their voids. Chester felt a chill descend over him as if the temperature had plummeted in the room, and he shivered violently.

The old Styx dropped his eyes to the desk, and Chester swayed unsteadily on his feet, as if he'd been abruptly released from something that had had him in its relentless grip. He let out his breath in a rush, unconscious until now that he'd been holding it in. Then the Styx began to read in a measured tone.

"You have been found guilty," he said, "under Order Forty-two, Edicts Eighteen, Twenty-four, Forty-two . . ."

The numbers went on, but it meant nothing to Chester until the Styx paused and, very matter-of-factly, said the word *sentence*. Chester really began to listen at this point.

"The prisoner will be taken from this place and conveyed by train to the Interior, and there be Banished, relinquished to the forces of nature. So be it," the old Styx finished, clapping his hands and holding them pressed hard together, as if he were wringing something out. Then he slowly raised his head from his papers and said, "May the Lord have mercy on your soul."

"What . . . what do you mean?" Chester asked, reeling under the Styx's icy gaze and the implications of what he'd just heard.

Without needing to consult the papers before him, the Styx simply reiterated the punishment and then fell silent again. Chester grappled with the questions that were racing through his head, moving his lips but emitting no sound at all.

"Yes?" the old Styx asked, in such a way that suggested he'd been in this situation many times before and found it thoroughly tiresome to have to converse with the lowly prisoner before him.

"What . . . what does that mean?" Chester eventually got out.

The Styx stared at Chester for several seconds and, with total impassivity, said, "Banished. You will be escorted as far as the Miners' Station, many fathoms down, and then left to do as you will."

"Taken *deeper* into the earth?"

The Styx nodded. "We have no need for your kind in the Colony. You attempted to escape, and the Panoply takes a dim view of that. You are not worthy of service here." He clapped his hands together again. "Banished."

Chester suddenly felt the immense weight of all the millions of tons of dirt and rock above, as if they were pressing directly down on him, squeezing out his lifeblood. He staggered backward.

"But I've done *nothing*. I'm not *guilty* of anything!" he cried, holding out his hands and pleading with the emotionless little man. He felt as if he were being buried alive and that he would never again see home, or the blue sky, or his family . . . everything he loved and yearned for. The hope he had clung to ever since he'd been captured and locked up in that dark room gushed out of him like air from a burst balloon.

He was doomed.

This hateful little man didn't give a hoot about him. . . . Chester saw that in the Styx's impassive face and in his frightful eyes—reptilian, inhuman eyes. And Chester knew that there was absolutely no point in trying to persuade him, or beg for his life. These people were savage and merciless, and they had arbitrarily condemned him to the most awful fate: *an even deeper grave.*

"But why?" Chester asked, tears wetting his face as he wept openly.

"Because it is the law," the old Styx answered. "Because I am sitting here, and you are standing there." He smiled without the remotest trace of any warmth.

"But—" Chester objected with a howl.

"Officer, take him back to the Hold," the old Styx said, gathering up his papers with his arthritic fingers, and Chester heard the door creak open behind him.

33

WILL was thrown forward as a fist landed squarely in the middle of his back. Staggering drunkenly for a few steps, he rebounded off the handrail and turned slowly around to face his assailant.

"Speed?" he said, recognizing the school bully's scowling face.

"Where've you sprung from, Snowdrop? Thought you'd snuffed it. People said you were dead or something."

Will didn't reply. He was deep in the insulated cocoon of the unwell; he felt as though he were looking at the world from behind a frosted sheet of glass. It was all Will could do to stand there, his body quivering as Speed pushed his snarling face just inches in front of his. Out of the corner of his eye, Will glimpsed Bloggsy closing in on Cal a little farther down the sloping path.

They had been on their way to the subway station, and right now a fight was the last thing Will wanted.

"So where's Fat Boy?" Speed crooned, the moisture on his breath clouding in the cold air. "Bit different without your bodyguard, ain't it, dipstick?"

"Oi, Speed, check this out, it's Mini Me!" Bloggsy said, looking from Cal to Will and back again. "What's in the bag, gimp?"

At Will's insistence, Cal had been carrying their dirty Colonists' clothes in one of Dr. Burrows's old expedition duffel bags.

"Payback time," Speed shouted and simultaneously jabbed a fist in Will's stomach. Winded, Will slumped to his knees and then toppled over, curling up with his arms wrapped protectively around his head as he hit the ground.

"This is too easy," Speed crowed, and kicked Will in the back several times.

Bloggsy was making ludicrous whooping noises and crouching in a mock kung-fu-fighting stance as he prodded two fingers at Cal's sunglasses. "Prepare to meet your maker," he said, his other arm drawn back and ready to throw a punch.

Everything happened too quickly for Will after that. There was a streak of purple and brown lightning as Bartleby landed smack in the middle of Bloggsy's shoulders. The impact knocked the boy away from Cal and sent him tumbling untidily down the slope, the cat still latched onto his back. As Bloggsy came to rest facedown on the ground, he was writhing and trying to use his elbows to beat off the flurry of pearl white canines and barbaric-looking claws, all the while letting out the most awful high-pitched cries and screaming for someone to help.

"No," Will shouted weakly. "Enough!"

"Stop it, Bart!" Cal yelled.

The cat, still on top of Bloggsy, spun his head around to look at Cal, who shouted another command.

"Sic 'im!" Cal pointed at Speed, who had remained standing over Will through all this, not believing what he was seeing. Speed's jaw dropped, and a look of sheer horror crept over his face. Bartleby fixed his eyes on the new quarry through the bizarre pink sunglasses, the Tibetan hat now slightly askew on his head. With a loud hiss, he bounded back up the slope toward the startled bully.

"Call it off! Call it off!" Speed shrieked as he started to run up the path as if his life depended on it—which it did. In the blink of an eye, the cat had caught up with him. Sometimes at his side, sometimes blocking his way, Bartleby circled around him like a playful whirlwind, attacking his ankles and slashing at his thighs through his school pants, lacerating his skin. The terrified boy stumbled and tottered in a spasmodic, comic dance as he frantically tried to escape, his feet sliding hopelessly on the pavement.

"I'm sorry, Will, I'm sorry! Just get it off me! Please!" Speed was gibbering, his pants reduced to tatters.

With a look from Will, Cal stuck two fingers into his mouth and whistled. The cat stopped instantly and allowed Speed to run away. Not once did he turn to look back.

Will glanced past Cal to the bottom of the slope, where Bloggsy had picked himself up and was half running, half falling in his haste to make an escape.

"I think we've seen the last of them," Cal said with a laugh.

"Yes," Will agreed faintly as he slowly got to his feet. Wave upon wave of the fever ebbed through him, and he felt as if he was going to pass out again. He could quite happily have lain back down, opened his coat to the cold, and gone to sleep right there and then on the icy sidewalk. The only way Will could get down the remaining stretch of the slope was with Cal supporting him, but they eventually made it to the bottom and into the subway station.

"So even Topsoilers like to go underground," he said, looking at the dirty old station, long overdue for renovation. His manner was instantly transformed; he seemed genuinely at ease for the first time since they had emerged onto the banks of the Thames—relieved that there was a tunnel around him rather than open sky.

"Not really," Will said listlessly as he started to feed change into the ticket machine while Bartleby slavered over a lichenlike patch of freshly deposited chewing gum on the tiled floor. Will's shaking fingers fumbled with the coins, then he stopped and leaned against the machine. "It's no use," he gasped. Cal took the change from him and, as Will told him what to do, he finished paying for the tickets.

Down on the platform, it wasn't long before a train arrived. Once aboard, neither boy spoke. As the southbound train gained speed, Cal watched the cables rippling along the tunnel sides and played with his ticket. Licking his paws, Bartleby was propped on his haunches in the seat next to Cal. There weren't many people in the car, but Cal was aware that they were attracting some pretty curious glances.

Opposite Cal and Bartleby, Will was sitting slumped against the side of the car, soothed by the chill glass on his temple as his head lolled against the window. Between stops, he drifted in and out of a fitful sleep, and during a period of wakefulness saw that a pair of old women had taken the seats across the aisle from them. Snatches of their conversation drifted into his consciousness and mixed with the platform announcements like voices in a confused dream.

"Just look at him . . . disgraceful . . . feet all over the seats . . . MIND THE GAP . . . funny-looking child . . .

LONDON UNDERGROUND APOLOGIZES . . ."

Will forced his eyes open and looked at the two women. He realized immediately that it was Bartleby who was the cause of their apparent distress. The one who was doing all the talking had purple-rinsed hair and wore translucent white-framed bifocals that rested crookedly on her poppy red nose.

"*Shhh!* They'll hear you," her companion whispered, eyeing Cal. She either had badly dyed hair or was wearing a wig that had seen better days. They both held identical shopping bags on their laps, as if they were some form of defense against the miscreants sitting opposite them.

"Nonsense! Bet they don't speak a word of English. Probably got here on the back of a truck. I mean, look at the state of their clothes. And that one—he don't look too bright to me. He's probably on drugs or something." Will felt their rheumy eyes linger on him.

"Send them all back, I say."

"Yes, yes," the old ladies said in unison, and with a mutual nod of agreement fell to discussing, in morbid detail, the ill health of a friend. Cal glowered furiously at them while they gabbled away, now apparently too preoccupied to pay further attention to anyone else. The train came to a stop, and as the old ladies were getting up from their seats Cal lifted the ear flap of Bartleby's Tibetan hat and whispered something into his ear. Bartleby suddenly reared up and hissed in their faces so forcefully that Will was shocked from his feverish stupor.

"Well, I never!" the red-nosed woman cried out, dropping her shopping bag. While she retrieved it, her companion bustled and pushed her from behind, trying to hurry her up.

In a flap, both women struggled off the train, shrieking.

"Horrid urchins!" the red-nosed lady huffed from the platform. "You blasted animals!" she screamed through the doors as they slid shut.

The train moved out, and Bartleby kept his eyes fixed demonically on the flustered twosome as they stood on the platform, still puffing with indignation.

His curiosity getting the better of him, Will leaned over to his brother.

"Tell me . . . what did you say to Bartleby?" he asked.

"Oh, nothing much," Cal replied innocently, smiling proudly at his cat before he turned to look out the window again.

Will was dreading the last half-mile to the housing projects. He staggered along like a sleepwalker, resting whenever it became too much for him.

When they finally reached the apartment building, the elevator was out of order. Will peered into the graffiti-strafed grayness with quiet desperation. That was the last straw. He sighed and, steeling himself for the climb, stumbled toward the squalid stairwell. After a stop on each landing to allow him to catch his breath, they eventually reached the right floor and made their way through the obstacle course of discarded garbage bags.

There was no response when Cal rang the bell, so he had resorted to hammering on the door with his fist when Auntie Jean suddenly opened it. She clearly hadn't been up for long—she looked as tired and crumpled as the moth-eaten overcoat that she'd evidently been asleep in.

"What is it?" she said indistinctly, rubbing the nape of her neck and yawning. "I didn't order nothing, and I don't buy nothing from salesmen."

"Auntie Jean, it's me . . . Will," he said; the blood drained from his head and the image of his aunt blanched, as if all the colors had been washed out of it.

"Will," she said vaguely, and cut another yawn short as it sank in. "Will!" She lifted her head and eyed him disbelievingly. "Thought you'd gone missing." She peered at Cal and Bartleby, adding, "Who's this?"

"Uh . . . cousin . . . ," Will gasped as the floor began to tip and sway, and he was forced to take a step forward to steady himself against the doorjamb. He was aware of the cold sweat trickling from his scalp. ". . . south . . . from down south."

"Cousin? Didn't know you—"

"Dad's," Will said huskily.

She surveyed Cal and Bartleby with suspicion and not a little distaste. "Your 'orrid sister was 'ere, you know." She glanced past Will. "Is she wiv you?"

"She . . . ," Will began to say in a shaky voice.

"Cos the little brat owes me money. Should've seen what she did to my—"

"She's *not* my sister, she's a vile . . . scheming . . . evil . . . she's a . . ." With that, Will keeled over in a dead faint before a very surprised Auntie Jean.

Cal stood at the window of the darkened room. He peered down at the streets below, with their dotted lines of amber lampposts and sweeping cones of car headlights. Then, with foreboding, he slowly raised his head and looked up at the moon, its shining silver spread out against the icy sky. Not for the first time he struggled to grasp, to comprehend, the vast space that yawned before him, the likes of which he'd never before seen in his life. He gripped the windowsill, barely able to control the mounting sense of dread. The soles of his feet clenched involuntarily and almost ached with vertigo.

On hearing his brother moan, Cal tore his eyes from the window and went to sit by the shivering form that was stretched out on the bed with just a sheet over it.

"How's 'e doing, then?" Cal heard Auntie Jean's anxious voice as she appeared in the doorway.

"He's a little better today. I think he's cooling down a bit," Cal said as he doused a washcloth in a bowl of water clunking with ice cubes and dabbed it to Will's forehead.

"Do you want to get someone in to see 'im?" Auntie Jean asked. "'E's been like this for a long time."

"No," Cal said firmly. "He said he didn't want that."

"Don't blame 'im, don't blame 'im at all. I've never 'ad no time for quacks—or them shrinks, neither, for that matter. Once you're in their clutches, there's no telling what—" She stopped short as Bartleby, who had been curled up asleep in the corner, woke with a protracted yawn, then ambled over and started to lap at the water in the bowl.

"Stop that, you stupid cat!" Cal said, pushing him away.

" 'E's just thirsty," Auntie Jean said, then assumed the most preposterous baby voice. "Poor puss, are you a liccle firsty?" She took hold of the astounded animal by the scruff of his neck and began to lead him toward the door. "You come with Mummy for a treat."

A lava flow moves portentously in the distance, its heat so fierce on Will's exposed skin that he can hardly bear it. Silhouetted by the vertical wall of streaming crimson behind him, Dr. Burrows frantically indicates something sprouting out of a massive slab of granite. He shouts excitedly, as he always does when he makes a discovery, but Will isn't able to catch the words due to the deafening white noise intercut with the cacophonous babble of many voices, as if someone is randomly scanning the airwaves on a damaged radio.

The scene shifts into close-up. Dr. Burrows is using a magnifying glass to examine a thin stalk with a bulbous tip that rises a foot and a half or so out of the solid rock. Will sees his father's lips moving but can only understand brief snatches of what he is saying.

". . . a plant . . . literally digests rock . . . silicon-based . . . reacts to stim— . . . observe . . ."

The image cuts to extreme close-up. Between two fingers, Dr. Burrows plucks the gray stalk from the rock. Will feels uneasy as he sees it writhe in his father's hand and shoot out two needlelike leaves that entwine around his fingers.

". . . gripping me like iron . . . feisty little . . . ," Dr. Burrows says, frowning.

There are no more words, they are replaced by laughter, but his father seems to be screaming as he tries to shake the thing off, its leaves piercing his hand and threading straight through the flesh of his palm and wrist and carrying on up his forearm, the skin bruising, bruising and bursting open and becoming smeared with blood as they twist, interweaving in a snakelike waltz. They cut tighter and tighter into his forearm, like two possessed wires. Will tries to reach out to his father, to help him as he battles hopelessly against this horrific attack, as he fights his own arm.

"No, no . . . Dad . . . Dad!"

"It's all right, Will, it's all right," came his brother's voice from a long way away.

The lava glow was gone. In its place was a shaded lamp, and he could feel the soothing coolness of the washcloth Cal was pressing against his forehead. He sat up with a start.

"It's Dad! What happened to Dad?" he cried, and looked around wildly, unsure of where he was.

"You're all right," Cal said. "You were dreaming."

Will slumped back against the pillows, realizing he was lying in bed in a narrow room.

"I saw him. It was all so clear and real," Will said, his voice breaking. He couldn't stem the flood of tears that suddenly filled his eyes. "It was Dad. He was in trouble."

"It was just a nightmare." Cal spoke softly, averting his eyes from his brother, who was now sobbing silently.

"We're at Auntie Jean's, aren't we?" Will said, pulling himself together as he saw the floral wallpaper.

"Yes, we've been here for nearly three days."

"Huh?" Will tried to sit up again, but it was too much for him; he rested his head back against the pillow once more. "I feel so weak."

"Don't worry, everything's fine. Your aunt's been great. Taken quite a shine to Bart, too."

■ ■ ■

Over the ensuing days, Cal nursed Will back to health with bowls of soup or baked beans on toast and seemingly endless cups of oversugared tea. Auntie Jean's sole contribution to his convalescence was to perch at the foot of his bed and burble on incessantly about the "old days," though Will was so exhausted he fell asleep before she could bore him senseless.

When Will finally felt strong enough to stand, he tested his legs by trying to walk up and down the length of the small bedroom. As he hobbled around with some difficulty, he noticed something lying discarded behind a box of old magazines.

He stooped down and picked up two objects. Shards of broken glass dropped to the floor. He recognized the pair of buckled silver frames right away. They were the ones Rebecca had kept on her bedside table. Looking at the photograph of his parents, and then the one of himself, he slumped back onto the bed, breathing heavily. He was distraught. He felt as though someone had stuck a knife into him and was very slowly twisting it. But what did he expect from her? Rebecca wasn't his sister, and never had been. He remained on the bed for some time, staring blankly at the wall.

A little later he got to his feet again and staggered down the hall into the kitchen. Dirty plates sat in the sink, and the garbage bin was overflowing with empty cans and torn microwave-ready food boxes. It was a scene of such carnage that he barely registered the plastic tops of the faucet, melted and brown, and the flame-blackened tiles behind them. He grimaced and turned back into the hall, where he heard Auntie

Jean's gruff voice. Its tones were vaguely comforting, reminding him of the holidays when she would come to visit, chatting to his mother for hours on end.

He stood outside the door and listened as Auntie Jean's knitting needles rattled away furiously while she spoke.

"Dr. bloomin' Burrows . . . soon as I laid eyes on 'im, I warned my sister . . . I did, you know . . . you don't want to be getting 'itched to some overeducated layabout . . . I mean, I ask you, what good's a man who grubs around in 'oles in the ground when there's bills to pay?"

Will peered around the corner as Auntie Jean's needles stopped their metronomic clicking and she took a sip from a tumbler. The cat was looking adoringly at Auntie Jean, who looked back at him with an affectionate, almost loving, smile. Will had never seen this side of her before—he knew he should say something to announce his presence, but somehow he couldn't bring himself to break the moment.

"I tell you, it's nice to 'ave you 'ere. I mean, after my little Sophie passed on . . . she was a dog and I know you don't much like them . . . but at least she was there for me . . . that's more than you can say for any man I ever met."

She held up her knitting in front of her, a garishly colored pair of pants, which Bartleby sniffed curiously. "Nearly done. In just a mo' you can try 'em on for size, my lovely." She leaned over and tickled Bartleby under the chin. He lifted his head and, closing his eyes, began to purr with the amplitude of a small engine.

Will turned to make his way back to the bedroom and was resting against the wall in the hallway when there was a crash behind him. Cal was standing just inside the front door, two bags of dropped shopping spilling open in front of him. He had a scarf wrapped around his mouth and was wearing Mrs. Burrows's sunglasses. He looked like the Invisible Man.

"I can't take much more of this," he said, squatting down to retrieve the groceries. Bartleby padded out from the living room, followed by Auntie Jean, a cigarette perched on her lip. The cat was wearing his newly knitted pants and mohair cardigan, both a strident mix of blues and reds, topped off with a multicolored balaclava from which his scabby ears stuck comically. Bartleby looked like the survivor of an explosion in a Salvation Army shop.

Cal glanced at the outlandish creature before him, taking in the shocking display of colors, but didn't comment. He appeared to be in the depths of despondency. "This place is full of hate—you can smell it everywhere." He shook his head slowly.

"Oh, it is that, love," Auntie Jean said quietly. "Always 'as been."

"Topsoil isn't what I expected," Cal said. He thought for a moment. "And I can't go home . . . can I?"

Will stared back as he searched for something to say to console his brother, some form of words to quell the boy's anxiety, but he was unable to utter a word.

Auntie Jean cleared her throat, bringing the moment to an end.

"Suppose this means you're all going?"

As she stood there in her scruffy old coat, Will saw for the first time how very vulnerable and frail she seemed.

"I think we are," he admitted.

"Righto," she said hollowly. She put her hand on Bartleby's neck, tenderly caressing the loose flaps of his skin with her thumb. "You know you're all welcome 'ere—anytime you want." Her voice became choked, and she turned quickly away from them. "And do bring kitty back wiv you." She shuffled into the kitchen, where they could hear her trying to stifle her sobs as she rattled a bottle against a glass.

Over the next few days, they planned and planned. Will felt himself growing stronger as he recovered from the illness, his lungs clearing and his breathing returning to normal. They went on shopping expeditions: an army surplus shop yielded gas masks, climbing rope, and a water bottle for each of them; they bought some old flash camera units in a pawnshop; and, since it was the week after Guy Fawkes's night, several large boxes of remaindered fireworks from the local deli. Will wanted to make sure they were ready for any eventuality, and anything that gave off a bright light might come in useful. They stocked up on food, choosing lightweight but high-energy provisions so as not to weigh themselves down. After the kindness his aunt had shown them, Will felt bad that he was dipping into her grocery money to pay for it all, but he didn't have any alternative.

They waited until lunchtime to leave Highfield. They donned their now-clean Colonists' clothes and said their good-byes to Auntie Jean, who gave Bartleby a tearful cuddle; then they took the bus into central London and walked the rest of the way to the river entrance.

34

CAL WAS still pressing a handkerchief to his face and muttering about the "foul gases" as they left Blackfriars Bridge and took the steps down to the Embankment. Everything looked so different in the daylight that for a moment Will had doubts they were even in the right place. With people bustling all around them on the walkway, it all seemed so fanciful to suppose that somewhere below them was an abandoned and primitive London, and that the three of them were going to go back down there.

But they were in the right place, and it was only a short walk to the entrance of that strange other world. They stood by the gate and peered down, watching the brown water lapping lazily below.

"Looks deep," Cal remarked. "Why's it like that?"

"Duh!" Will groaned, thumping his palm against his forehead. "The tide! I didn't think of the tide. We'll just have to wait for it to go out."

"How long will that be?"

Will shrugged, checking his watch. "I don't know. Could be hours."

There was no alternative but to kill time by pacing the backstreets around the Tate Modern and return to the bank

every so often to check the water, trying not to attract too much attention in the process. By lunchtime they could see the gravel breaking through.

Will decided they couldn't hang around any longer. "OK, all systems go!" he announced.

They were in full view of many passersby on their lunch breaks, but hardly anyone took any notice of the motley-looking trio, eccentrically dressed and laden with backpacks, as they clambered over the wall and onto the stone steps. Then an old man in a woolly hat and matching scarf spotted them and began to shout, "Ruddy kids!" wagging his fist furiously at them. One or two people gathered around to see what the fuss was all about, but they quickly lost interest and moved on. This seemed to dampen the old man's outrage, and he, too, shuffled off, muttering loudly to himself.

At the bottom of the steps, the water splashed up around the boys' legs as they galloped with all their might along the partially submerged foreshore, only letting up when they were out of sight under the jetty. Without any hesitation, Cal and Bartleby clambered into the mouth of the drainage tunnel.

Will paused for a moment before following. He took a last lingering look at the pale gray sky through the gaps in the planking and inhaled deeply, savoring his last breaths of fresh air.

Now that he'd recovered his strength, he felt like a completely different person—he was prepared for whatever lay ahead. As if the fever had purged him of any doubts or weaknesses, he was feeling the resigned assurance of the seasoned adventurer. But as he lowered his eyes to the slow-moving river, he experienced the deepest pang of loss and melancholy, aware he might never see this place again. Of course, he didn't have to go through with it, he could stay here if he chose, but he knew it would never be the same as before. Too much had changed, things that could never be undone.

"Come on," he said, shaking himself from his thoughts and entering the tunnel, where Cal was waiting for him, impatient to get going. With a single glance, Will could read conflicting emotions in his brother's face: Although the anxiety was plain to see, there was also a hint of something else, a deep sense of relief brought about by the promise of an imminent return to the underworld. It was his home, after all.

Although circumstances had forced his hand, Will reflected on what a terrible mistake it had been to bring Cal with him to the surface. Cal would need time to adjust to Topsoil life—and that was one luxury they didn't have. Like it or not, Will's destiny lay in rescuing Chester and finding his father. And Cal's destiny was inextricably bound to his.

It irked Will that he'd lost so many days to the fever—he had no idea if he was too late to save Chester. Had he already been exiled to the Deeps or come to some unimaginable end at the hands of the Styx? Whatever the truth might be, he had to find out. He had to go on believing Chester was still alive; he had to go back. He could never live with that hanging over him.

They found the vertical shaft, and Will reluctantly lowered himself into the pool of freezing water below it. Cal climbed onto Will's shoulders so he could reach the shaft, then shimmied up it, trailing a rope behind him. When his brother was safely at the top, Will knotted the other end of the rope around Bartleby's chest, and Cal began to hoist him up. This proved to be completely unnecessary because, once in the vent, the animal used his sinewy legs to scrabble up with startling agility. Then the rope was dropped for Will, who hauled himself into the shadows above. Once there, Will jumped up and down to shake off the water and warm himself.

Then they slid down the convex ramp on the seats of their pants, landing with a thump on the ledge that marked the beginning of the rough stairs. Before proceeding, they carefully removed Bartleby's knitted clothes and left them on a high ledge—they couldn't afford to carry any dead weight now. Will didn't really have any idea what he was going to do once they were back in the Colony, but he knew he had to be completely practical . . . he had to be like Tam.

The boys put on their army surplus gas masks, looked at each other for a moment, nodded an acknowledgment, and with Cal leading the way they began the long descent.

The going was arduous at first, the stairs hazardous from the constantly seeping water and, farther down, the carpet of black algae. With Cal taking the lead, Will found he had very little recollection of their previous passage through, realizing that this must have been because the mysterious illness had already gotten a hold on him by then.

In what seemed like no time at all, they had arrived at the opening to the cavern wall of the Eternal City.

"What the heck is *this*?" Cal exclaimed the moment they walked out onto the top of the huge flight of steps, their eyes quickly sweeping down its dark course. Something was very wrong. Approximately a hundred feet below, the steps vanished from view.

"That's what I believe they call a real pea souper," Will said quietly, his glass eyepieces glinting with the pale green glow.

From their vantage point high above the city, they looked out on what appeared to be the undulating surface of a huge opaline lake. The thickest of fogs covered the entire scene, suffused by an eerie light, as if it were one immense radioactive cloud. It was very daunting to think that the vast extent of the huge city lay obscured beneath this opaque blanket.

Will automatically scrabbled in his pockets for the compass.

"This is going to make life a little difficult," he remarked, frowning behind his mask.

"Why?" Cal retorted. His eyes crinkled behind his eyepieces as a broad smile spread across his face. "They won't be able to see us in all that, will they?"

But Will's demeanor remained grim. "True, but we won't see them, either."

Cal held Bartleby still while Will tied a rope leash around his neck. They couldn't risk him wandering off under these conditions.

"You'd better hold on to my backpack so you don't get lost. And whatever you do, don't let go of that cat," Will urged his brother as they took their first steps in the fog, descending slowly into it, like deep-sea divers sinking beneath the waves. Their visibility was immediately reduced to no more than a foot and a half—they couldn't even see their boots, making it necessary to feel for the edge of each step before venturing to the next.

Thankfully they reached the bottom of the stairway without incident, and at the start of the mud flats they repeated the black-weed ritual, wiping the stinking goo all over each other, this time to mask the Topsoil smells of London.

Traversing the edge of the marshland, they eventually bumped into the city wall and followed it around. If anything, the visibility was getting even worse, and it took them forever to find a way in.

"An archway," Will whispered, stopping so abruptly that his brother nearly fell over him. The ancient structure briefly solidified before them, and then the fog closed up, obscuring it again.

"Oh, good," Cal replied without an ounce of enthusiasm.

Once inside the city walls, they had to grope their way through the streets, practically walking on top of each other so that they wouldn't become separated in the impossible conditions. The fog was almost tangible, sucking and rolling like sheets in the wind, sometimes parting to allow them the briefest glimpse of a section of wall, a stretch of water-sodden ground, or the glistening cobbles underfoot. The squelch of their boots on the black algae and their labored breathing through their masks sounded unnervingly loud to them. The way the fog was twisting and playing with their senses made everything feel so intimate and yet, at the same time, so removed.

Cal grabbed Will's arm, and they stood stock-still. They were beginning to notice other noises all around them that weren't of their making. At first vague and indistinct, these sounds were growing louder. As they listened, Will could have sworn he caught a scratchy whispering, so close that he flinched. He pulled Cal back a couple of steps, convinced that they'd already done the very thing he was dreading, they'd stumbled headlong into the Styx Division. However, Cal swore he hadn't heard anything at all, and after a while they nervously resumed their journey.

Then from the distance came the bloodcurdling baying of a dog—there was no question about it this time. Cal tightened his grip on Bartleby's leash as the cat raised his head high, his ears pricking up. Although neither boy said anything to the other, they were both thinking the same thing: The need for them to get through the city as rapidly as they could had become all the more pressing.

Creeping along, their hearts were pounding as Will referred to Tam's map and repeatedly checked his compass with his shaking hands in an attempt to fix their position. In truth, the visibility was so poor he had only the roughest idea where they were. For all he knew, they could be wandering in circles. They seemed to be making no headway at all, and Will was at his wits' end. What a great leader he was turning out to be!

He finally brought them to a halt, and they huddled down in the lee of a crumbling wall. In low whispers they debated what to do next.

"If we start running it won't matter if we come across a patrol. We can easily shake them off in this," Cal suggested quietly, his eyes darting left and right under the moisture-spotted lenses of his gas mask. "We just keep running."

"Yeah, right," Will replied. "So you *really* think you could outrun one of those dogs? I'd like to see that."

Cal *humphed* angrily in response.

Will went on. "Look, we don't have a clue where we are, and if we have to make a run for it, we'll probably hit a dead end or something. . . ."

"But once we're in the Labyrinth, they'll never catch us," Cal insisted.

"Fine, but we've got to get there first, and for all we know it's still a long way off." Will couldn't believe his brother's absurd suggestion. It dawned on him that a couple of months ago *he* might have been the one advocating the crazy dash through the streets of the city. Somehow, he'd changed. Now he was the sober one, and Cal was the impulsive, headstrong youngster, chock-full of madcap confidence and willing to risk all.

The furious whispered exchange continued, growing more and more heated until Cal finally relented. It was to be the softly-softly approach; they would inch their way to the far edge of the city, keeping the sounds of their footsteps to a minimum and melting into the fog if anyone, or anything, came close.

As they stepped over hunks of rubble, Bartleby's head was jerking in all directions, scenting the air and the ground, when all of a sudden he stopped. Despite Cal's best efforts to pull on the leash, the cat refused to move—he'd lowered his body as if he were hunting something, his wide head close to the ground and his skeletal tail sticking straight out behind him. His ears were pointing and twitching like radar dishes.

"Where are they?" Cal whispered frantically. Will didn't answer but instead reached into the side pockets of Cal's backpack and yanked out two large firecrackers. He also took out Auntie Jean's little plastic disposable lighter from an inner pocket in his jacket and held it ready in his hand.

"Come on, Bart," Cal was whispering into the cat's ear as he knelt beside him. "It's all right."

What little hair Bartleby had was bristling now. Cal managed to draw the cat around, and they tiptoed in the opposite direction as if walking on eggshells, Will at the rear with the firecrackers poised in his hands.

They followed a wall as it curved gently around, Cal feeling the coarse masonry with his free hand as if it were some incomprehensible form of Braille. Will was walking backward, checking behind them. Seeing nothing but the forbidding clouds, and coming to the conclusion that it was futile to try to place any reliance on sight in these conditions, he spun around only to blunder into a granite plinth. He recoiled as the leering face of a huge marble head reared out of the parting mist. Laughing at himself, he warily stepped around it and found his brother waiting only a few feet ahead.

They had gone about twenty paces when the fog mysteriously folded back to reveal a length of cobbled street before them. Will hastily wiped the moisture from his eyepieces and let his gaze ride with the retreating margins of the fog. Bit by bit the edges of the street and the facades of some of the nearest buildings came into view. Both boys felt an immense flood of relief as their immediate surroundings were tantalizingly revealed for the first time since they had entered the city.

Then their blood turned cold.

There, not thirty feet away, only too real and horribly clear, they saw them. A patrol of eight Styx were fanned out across the street. They stood motionless as predators, their round goggles watching the boys as they dumbly looked back.

They were like specters from some future nightmare in their gray-green striped long coats, strange skullcaps, and sinister breathing masks. One held a ferocious-looking stalker dog on a thick leather strap—it was straining against its collar, its tongue lolling obscenely out of the side of its monstrous maw. It sniffed sharply and immediately whipped its head in the boys' direction. The black pebbles of its beady eyes sized them up in an instant. With a deep, rumbling snarl it curled back its lips to reveal huge yellowing teeth dripping with saliva. Its leash slackened as it crouched down, preparing to pounce.

But nobody made a move. As if time itself had stopped, the two groups merely stood and stared at each other in horrible, mute anticipation.

Something snapped in Will's head. He screamed and spun Cal around, knocking him from his shocked inertia. Then they were running, flying back into the fog, their legs pumping frantically. They ran and ran, unable to tell how much ground they were covering through the shrouds of mist. Behind them came the savage barking of the stalker and the crackling shouts of the Styx.

Neither boy had a clue where they were heading. They didn't have time to think, their minds frozen with blind panic.

Then Will came to his senses. He yelled at Cal to keep going

as he slowed to light the blue fuse on a huge Roman candle. Not really certain if he'd lit it, he quickly propped it against a chunk of masonry, angling it in the direction of their pursuers.

He ran ahead several feet, then stopped again. He flicked the lighter, but this time the flame refused to come. Swearing, he struck it desperately again and again. Nothing, just sparks. He shook it just like he'd seen the Grays do so often at school when lighting their illicit cigarettes. He took a deep breath and once again spun the tiny wheel. Yes! The flame was small but enough to ignite the fuse of the firecracker, an air-bomb battery. But now the snarling and barking and voices were closing around him. He lost his nerve and simply slung the firecracker to the ground.

"Will, Will!" he heard up ahead. As he homed in on the shouts, he was furious that Cal was making so much noise, though he knew he would never have found him otherwise. Will was running at full tilt when he caught up with his brother and almost bowled him over. They were sprinting furiously as the first firework went off. It screamed out in all directions, its bright primary colors bleeding through the texture of the fog before it ended with two deafening thunderclaps.

"Keep going," Will hissed at Cal, who had crashed headfirst into a wall and was acting a little stunned. "Come on. This way!" he said, pulling his brother by the arm, not allowing him any time to dwell on his injury.

The fireworks continued, exploding fireballs of light high into the cavern or in low arcs that ended in the city itself, momentarily silhouetting the buildings like the scenery in a shadow play. Each iridescent streak culminated in a dazzling flash and a cannon-shot explosion, echoing and rumbling back and forth through the city like a raging storm.

Every so often, Will stopped to light another firecracker, picking out Roman candles, air bombs, or rockets, which he positioned on pieces of masonry or threw to the ground in the hope of confusing the patrol as to their position. The Styx, if they were still following, would be bearing the brunt of this onslaught, and Will hoped that at the very least the smell of the smoke might put the stalker off their scent.

As the last of the fireworks exploded in a cavalcade of light and sound, Will was praying he'd bought them enough time to reach the Labyrinth. They slowed to a jog to allow themselves to catch their breath, then stopped altogether to listen out for any sign of their pursuers, but there was nothing now. They appeared to have shaken them off. Will sat down on a wide step of a building that looked like it could have been a temple and took out his map and compass while Cal kept watch.

"I've no idea where we are," he admitted, tucking the map away. "It's hopeless!"

"We could be anywhere," Cal agreed.

Will stood up, looking left and right. "I say we carry on in the same direction."

Cal nodded. "But what if we end up right back where we started?"

"Doesn't matter. We've just got to keep moving," Will said as he set off.

Once again the silence crowded in on them, and the mysterious shapes and shadows appeared and softened as if the buildings were pulling in and out of focus in this invisible city. They'd made tortuously slow progress through a succession of streets when Cal came to a standstill.

"I think it's clearing a little, you know," he whispered.

"Well, that's something," Will replied.

Once again Bartleby stiffened and crouched down low, hissing as the margins of the fog rolled back before them. The boys froze, their eyes feverishly raking the milky air.

As if veils were being lifted to reveal it, there, not twenty feet away, a dark, shadowy form was hunched menacingly. They both heard a low, guttural growl.

"A stalker!" Cal gulped.

Their hearts stopped with awful realization. They could only watch as it rose up, its muscular forelegs tensing into life as it pawed the ground, then began to move, accelerating forward at a bewildering speed. There was absolutely nothing they could do. There was no point in running; it was too close. Like an infernal steam engine, the black hound was pounding toward them, condensation spewing from its flaring nostrils.

Will didn't have time to think. As he saw the dog spring, he dropped his backpack and shoved Cal out of the way.

The stalker soared through the air and slammed heavily against Will's chest. Its clublike paws knocked him flat on his back, his head thwacking the algae-covered ground with a hard slap. Half stunned, Will reached up and grasped the monster's throat with both hands. His fingers found its thick collar and hung on to it as he tried to hold the brute away from his face.

But the animal was just too powerful. Its jaws snapped at his mask, then caught on to it and bit down. Will heard the squeal of its fangs tightening on the rubber as the mask was crushed against his face, and then a pop as one of the eyepieces shattered. He smelled the putrid breath of the stalker, like warm, sour meat, as the animal continued to wrench and twist the mask, the straps behind Will's head stretched almost to the breaking point.

Praying the mask would stay in place, he tried with all his might to turn his head away. The stalker's jaws slid off the wet rubber, but Will's success was short-lived. The dog pulled back slightly, then immediately lunged again. Screaming, and still hanging on to its thick collar with all his might,

Will was barely managing to keep it away from his face, his arms at the very limit of their strength. The collar was cutting into his fingers—he couldn't believe how heavy the beast was. Time after time, Will whipped his head away, only just evading the snapping teeth, like the jaws of a powerful trap clapping shut.

Then the animal contorted and twisted its body.

One of Will's hands lost its grip, and with nothing to hinder it the animal quickly sought out a more rewarding target. It caught hold of Will's forearm and bit down hard. Will cried out from the pain, his other hand involuntarily opening and letting go of the collar.

There was nothing to stop it now.

The animal instantly scrabbled over him and sank its incisors into his shoulder. Amid the growling and biting he heard the cloth of his jacket rip as the huge teeth, like twin rows of daggers, penetrated and tore into his flesh. Will wailed again as the animal shook its head, snarling loudly. He was helpless, a rag doll being shaken this way and that. With his free arm, he punched weakly at the animal's flanks and head, but it was no use.

Then suddenly the dog detached itself from his shoulder and reared up over him, its huge weight still pinning him down. As its frenzied eyes fixed on his, he could see its slathering jaws just inches from his face, strings of its drool dripping into his eyepieces. Will was aware that Cal was doing all he could to help; he was quickly lunging in to pummel and kick at the beast, then just as quickly pulling back. Each time he did this, the dog merely half turned to snarl at him, as if it knew Cal posed no threat. Its small, savage brain was fixed on only one thing: the *kill* that was completely and utterly at its mercy.

Will tried desperately to roll over, but the creature had him pinned to the floor. He knew he was no match for this unstoppable hellhound that seemed to be made from huge slabs of muscle as hard and unyielding as rock.

"Go!" he yelled at Cal. "Get away!"

Then, from out of nowhere, a fleshy bolt of gray catapulted at the stalker's head.

For one instant, it was as though Bartleby was suspended in midair, his back arched over and his claws extended like cutthroat razors just above the stalker's head. The next, he'd dropped, and there was a shocking frenzy of movement. They heard the wet slicing of flesh as Bartleby's teeth found their first mark. A dark fountain of blood was jetting over Will from a livid gash where the dog's ear had been. The beast let out a low-pitched yelp and immediately bucked and leaped off Will, Bartleby still clamped to its head and neck, blitzing it with bites and savage flesh-tearing slashes from his raking hind feet.

"Get up! Get up!" Cal was shouting as he helped Will to his feet with one hand and retrieved his backpack with the other.

The boys retreated to a safe distance, then stopped, compelled to stay and watch. They were rooted to the spot, transfixed by this brute battle between cat and dog as both writhed in mortal combat, their shapes melting together until they became an indistinguishable whirlwind of gray and red, punctuated by flashing teeth and claws.

"We can't stay here!" Will yelled. He could hear the shouts of the approaching patrol, which was quickly homing in on the fight.

"Bart, leave it! C'mere, boy!"

"The Styx." Will shook his brother. "We have to go!"

Cal reluctantly moved on, peering back to see if his cat was following through the mist. But there was no sign of Bartleby, only the distant hisses and yelps and screeches.

Shouts and footfalls were now echoing all around. The boys ran blindly, Cal grunting with the effort of carrying both packs, and Will trembling with shock, his whole arm throbbing dully with pain. He could feel the blood streaming down his side and was alarmed to find that it was running over the back of his hand in small rivulets and dripping from the ends of his fingertips.

Out of breath, the boys hastily agreed on a direction, hoping against hope it would take them out of the city and not straight back into the arms of the Styx. Once on the marshy perimeter, they would make their way around the edge of the City until they found the mouth of the Labyrinth. And if worse came to worst and they missed it completely, Will knew they would eventually come to the stone staircase again and could quickly return Topsoil.

From the sounds they were hearing, the patrol seemed to be zeroing in on them. The boys were dashing at full speed, but then they blundered headlong into a wall. Had they inadvertently strayed down a blind alley? The terrible thought struck both of them at the same time. They frantically felt along the wall until they found an archway, its sides crumbled away and the keystone missing at its apex.

"Thank God," Will whispered, glancing at Cal with relief. "That was close."

Cal merely nodded, panting heavily. They peered briefly behind them before passing through the ruined archway.

With lightning speed, strong hands grabbed them roughly from either side of the opening, yanking them off their feet.

35

USING his good arm, Will lashed out with all the strength he could summon, but his knuckles just grazed ineffectually off a canvas hood. Their captor cursed sharply as Will followed with another blow, but this time his fist was caught and trapped in the iron grip of a huge hand, forcing him back effortlessly until he was pinioned against the wall.

"That's enough!" the man hissed. "*Shhh!*"

Cal suddenly recognized the voice and began pushing in between Will and his hooded assailant. Will was completely baffled. What was his brother doing? Feebly he tried to lash out again, but the man held him fast.

"Uncle Tam!" Cal shouted joyously.

"Keep it down," Tam rebuked.

"Tam?" Will repeated, feeling all at once very stupid and very relieved.

"But . . . how . . . how did you know we'd be . . . ?" Cal stuttered.

"We've been keeping an eye out since the escape went off the rails," their uncle cut in.

"Yes, but how did you know it was *us*?" Cal asked again.

"We just followed the light and the noise. Who else but you

two would use those bloody fool pyrotechnics? They probably heard it Topsoil, let alone in the Colony."

"It was Will's idea," Cal replied. "It sort of worked."

"Sort of," Tam said, looking with concern at Will, who was steadying himself against the wall, the rubber of his mask scored with deep gouges and one of his eyepieces shattered and useless. "You all right, Will?"

"I think so," he mumbled, holding his blood-soaked shoulder. He felt a little woozy and detached, but couldn't tell if this was because of his wounds or because of the overwhelming sense of relief that Tam had found them.

"I knew you'd not be able to rest with Chester still here."

"What's happened to him? Is he all right?" Will asked, perking up at the mention of his friend's name.

"He's alive, at least for the time being—I'll tell you all about it later, but now, Imago, we'd better make ourselves scarce."

Imago's massive form slipped into sight with unexpected fleetness, his baggy mask twisting furtively this way and that, like a partially deflated balloon caught in the wind, as he scrutinized the murky shadows. He swung Will's pack over one shoulder as if it weighed nothing, and then he was off. It was all the boys could do to keep up with him. Their flight now turned into a nerve-racking game of follow the leader, with Imago's shadow piloting them through the miasma and unseen obstacles while Tam brought up the rear. But the boys were so very grateful to be back under Tam's wing that they almost forgot their predicament. They felt safe again.

Imago cupped a light orb in his hand, allowing just enough light to spill from it so they could negotiate the difficult terrain. They jogged through a series of flooded courtyards, then left the fog behind as they entered a circular building, racing at a staggering pace along corridors lined with statues and flaking murals. They slid in the mud on the cracked marble floors of abandoned rooms and halls strewn with broken masonry until they found themselves hurtling up stairs of black granite. Climbing higher and higher, they were suddenly out in the open again. Traversing fractured stone walkways that had long sections of their balustrades missing, Will was able to look down from giddying heights and catch views of the city below between the meshing clouds. Some of these walkways were so narrow Will feared that if he hesitated for a second he might plunge to his death in the foggy soup that masked the sheer drops on either side. He kept going, putting his trust in Imago, who didn't waver for an instant, his unwieldy form driving relentlessly ahead, leaving little eddies of fog in its wake.

Eventually, after haring down several staircases, they entered a large room echoing with the sound of gurgling water. Imago came to a halt. He appeared to be listening for something.

"Where's Bartleby?" Tam whispered to Cal as they waited.

"He saved us from a stalker," Cal said despairingly, and hung his head. "He never came after us. I think he may be dead."

Tam put his arm around Cal and hugged him. "He was a prince among animals," he said. He patted Cal on the back consolingly before moving forward to confer with Imago in hushed tones.

"Think we should lie low for a while?"

"No, better to make a break for it." Imago's voice was calm and unhurried. "The Division knows the boys are still here somewhere, and the whole place'll be riddled with patrols in no time at all."

"We keep going, then," Tam concurred.

The four of them filed out of the room and traveled along a colonnade until Imago vaulted over a low wall and slid down a slimy bank into a deep gulley. As the boys followed him, the stagnant water came up to their thighs, and thick fronds of glutinous black weed hampered their movements. They waded laboriously through, lethargic bubbles rising up and clumping together on the surface. Even though they were wearing masks, the putrid stench of long-dead vegetation caught in their throats. The gulley became an underground channel, and they were plunged into darkness, their splashes echoing around them until, after what felt like an eternity, they emerged into the open again. Imago motioned for them to stop, then scuttled up the side of the channel, squelching off into the fog.

"This is a risky stretch," Tam warned them in a whisper. "It's open ground. Keep your wits about you and stay close."

Before long, Imago returned and beckoned to them. They clambered out of the water and with sodden boots and pants crossed the boggy ground, the city finally behind them. They went up a slope and then seemed to reach a plateau of sorts. Will's spirits leaped as he spotted the openings in the cavern wall ahead. They had reached a way back into the Labyrinth. They'd made it.

"Macaulay!" a harsh, thin voice called out.

They all stopped dead in their tracks and wheeled around. The fog was patchier here on the higher ground, and through the thinning wisps they saw a lone figure. It was a single Styx. He stood there, tall and arrogant, with his arms folded across his narrow chest.

"Well, well, well. Funny how rats always use the same runs . . . ," he shouted.

"Crawfly," Tam replied coolly as he pushed Cal and Will toward Imago.

". . . leaving their grease and stinking spoor on the sides. I knew I'd get you one day; it was just a matter of time." The Crawfly uncrossed his arms and then snapped them like whips. Will's heart missed a beat as he saw two shining blades appear in the Styx's hands. Curved and about ten inches long, they looked like small scythes.

"You've been a thorn in my side for too long!" the Crawfly yelled.

Will glanced at Tam and was surprised to see he was already armed with a brutal-looking machete he seemed to have conjured from nowhere.

"It's time I righted a few wrongs," Tam said in a low, urgent voice to Imago and the boys. They could see the look of grim determination in his eyes. He turned in the direction of the Crawfly. "Get going, you lot, and I'll catch up to you," he called back to them as he began to advance.

But the saturnine figure with swathes of fog curling around it didn't give an inch. Brandishing the scythes with an expert flourish and crouching a little, the Styx had the appearance of something horribly unnatural.

"This isn't right. He's too bloody confident," Imago muttered. "We should make ourselves scarce." He drew the boys back protectively to one of the tunnel mouths of the Labyrinth as Tam closed in on the Crawfly.

"Oh, no . . . no . . . ," Imago drew in his breath.

Will and Cal turned, searching for the source of his alarm. A mass of Styx had appeared through the mists and were spreading out in a wide arc. But the Crawfly held up one glinting scythe and they came to an abrupt halt a little distance behind him, swaying and fidgeting impatiently.

Tam stopped, pausing for a moment as if weighing the odds. He shook his head just once, then drew himself up defiantly. He tore off his hood and took a large breath, filling his lungs with the foul air.

In reply, the Crawfly yanked off his goggles and breathing apparatus, dropping them at his feet and kicking them aside. Tam and the Crawfly both stepped closer, then stopped. They faced each other like two opposing champions, and Will shuddered as he spotted the cold, sardonic smile on the thin face of the Styx.

The boys held their breath. It had grown so deathly quiet in that place, as if all the sound had been sucked from the world.

The Crawfly made the first move, his arms whipping over each other as he lunged forward. Tam jerked back to avoid the barrage of steel and, stepping to the side, brought up his machete in a defensive move. The two men's blades met and scraped off each other with a shrill metallic scream.

With incredible dexterity, the Crawfly spun around as if performing some ritual dance, darting toward Tam and back again, slashing and slashing with his twin blades. Tam retaliated with thrusts and parries, and the two opponents attacked and defended and attacked in turn. Each sally was so blisteringly fast, Cal and Will hardly dared blink. Even as they watched, there came another salvo of silver and gray, and the two men were suddenly so close they could have embraced, the razor-sharp edges of their weapons grinding coldly against each other. Almost as quickly, they fell back, breathing heavily. There was a lull while each man's eyes remained fixed on the other's, but Tam seemed to be listing slightly and clutching his side.

"This is bad," Imago said under his breath.

Will saw it, too. Between Tam's fingers and down his jacket seeped dark ribbons of liquid, which looked more like harmless black ink under the green light of the city. He was wounded and bleeding badly. He drew himself slowly up and, apparently recovering, in a flash had swung his machete at the Crawfly, who sidestepped effortlessly and swiped him across the face.

Tam flinched and staggered back. Imago and the boys saw the patch of blackness now spreading down his left cheek.

"Oh my God," Imago said quietly, holding on to the boys' collars so tightly that Will could feel his arms tensing as the fight resumed.

Tam attacked yet again, the Crawfly whirling backward and forward, this way and that, in his fluid and stylized dance. Tam's swipes and thrusts were decisive and skillful, but the Crawfly was too fast, the machete blade time and time again meeting with nothing but misty air. As Tam was twisting around to face his elusive opponent, he lost his footing. Trying to straighten up, his boots were slipping hopelessly. He was off balance, in a vulnerable position. The Crawfly couldn't miss this opportunity. He lunged at Tam's exposed flank.

But Tam was ready. He'd been waiting for this moment. He ducked forward and rose inside his opponent's guard, bringing up the machete in a flash, so smartly that Will missed the devastating slash to the Crawfly's throat.

The air between the two combatants filled with dark spume as the Crawfly reeled back. The Styx let both of his scythes tumble to the ground and gave out a bloody, hissing gurgle as he clutched his severed windpipe.

Like a matador delivering the killing blow, Tam stepped forward, using both his hands for the final thrust. The blade sank up to the hilt in the Crawfly's chest. He let out a bubbling hiss and grabbed Tam's shoulders to steady himself. He looked down with sheer disbelief at the rough wooden handle protruding from his sternum, then raised his head. For a moment they stood there absolutely motionless, like two statues in a tragic tableau, staring at each other in silent recognition.

Then Tam braced one foot against the Crawfly and wrenched out his machete. The Styx teetered on the spot, like a puppet suspended by unseen wires, his mouth shaping empty, breathless curses.

They watched as the mortally wounded man spluttered a last choking snarl at Tam and, tottering backward, collapsed to the ground in a lifeless heap. Excited whispers passed down the lines of Styx, who seemed paralyzed, unsure of what they should do next.

Tam wasted no time in such hesitation. Holding his injured side and grimacing with the pain, he sprinted back to join Imago and the boys. This in turn mobilized the Styx, who scuttled forward to form a ring around the body of their fallen comrade.

Tam was already leading Imago and the boys down a Labyrinth passage. But they had hardly gone any distance when he lurched to one side and sought out the wall for support. He was breathing hard and sweat was pouring off him. It streamed down his face, mingling with the blood from his lacerations and dripping from his bristly chin.

"I'll hold them off," he panted, looking back at the tunnel opening. "It'll buy you some time."

"No, I'll do it," Imago said. "You're wounded."

"I'm finished anyway," Tam said quietly.

Imago looked down at the blood welling out of the gaping flap on Tam's chest, and their eyes met for a fraction of a second. As Imago handed him his machete, it was clear the decision had been made.

"Don't, Uncle Tam! Please come with us," Cal begged in a choked voice, knowing full well what this meant.

"Then we'd all lose, Cal," Tam said, smiling wanly and hugging him with one arm. He reached into his shirt and yanked something from around his neck and pressed it into Will's hand. It was a smooth pendant with a symbol carved into it.

"Take this," Tam said quickly. "It might come in useful where you're going." He let go of Cal and took a step away, but then grabbed hold of Will, his eyes never leaving the younger boy. "And watch out for Cal, won't you, Will?" Tam tightened his grip on him. "Promise me that."

Will felt so numb that before he could find any words, Tam had turned away from him.

Cal began to shout frantically.

"Uncle Tam . . . come . . . come with us. . . !"

"Get them away, Imago," Tam called as he strode back toward the mouth of the tunnel, and as he did so the full horror of the approaching Styx army hove into view.

Cal was still calling Tam's name and showing not the slightest intention of going anywhere when Imago grasped hold of his collar and bundled him forcefully before him in the tunnel. The distraught boy had absolutely no choice but to do what Imago wanted, and his shouts immediately gave way to great howls of anguish and uncontrollable sobbing. Will received similarly rough treatment, with Imago repeatedly slapping him on the back to drive him forward. Imago only let up for the briefest moment as they rounded a sharp bend and he seemed to hesitate. The three of them, Will, Cal, and Imago, turned to catch a last glimpse of the big man, his outline dark against the green of the city as he held the two machetes in readiness at his sides.

Then Imago pushed them on again, and Tam was forever lost from view. But burned onto their retinas was that final scene, that final picture of Tam standing proud and defiant in the face of the approaching tide. A single figure before a bristling field of drawn scythes.

Even as they fled they could hear his urgent, shouted curses and the clash of blades, which grew fainter with every twist and turn of the tunnel.

36

THEY ran, and Will held his arm tightly to his side, his shoulder throbbing painfully with each stride. He had no idea how many miles they'd traveled when, at the end of a long gallery, Imago finally slowed the pace to allow them to catch their breath. The width of the tunnels meant they could have walked side by side, but instead they chose to remain in single file—it gave them some solitude, some privacy. Even though they hadn't exchanged a single word since they'd left Tam behind in the Eternal City, each knew only too well what the others were thinking in the wretched silence that hung like a pall over them. As they plodded mechanically along in their mournful little column, Will thought how much like a funeral procession it felt.

He just couldn't believe that Tam was really dead—the one person in the Colony who was so much larger than life, who had accepted him back into the family without a moment's hesitation. Will tried to get his thoughts into some sort of order and deal with the sense of loss and the hollowness that overwhelmed him, but he wasn't helped by Cal's frequent bouts of muffled weeping.

They took innumerable turns down lefts and rights, every new stretch of tunnel as identical and unremarkable as the last.

Imago didn't once refer to a map but seemed to know precisely where they were going, muttering to himself under his mask every so often, as if endlessly reciting a poem, or even a prayer. Several times Will noticed that he would shake a dull metal sphere the size of an orange as they turned yet another corner, but he had no idea why Imago was doing this.

It came as some surprise when Imago drew them to a halt by what appeared to be a small fissure in the ground and looked warily up and down the tunnel on either side of them. Then he started to agitate the metal sphere with vigor around the mouth of the fissure.

"What's that for?" Will asked him.

"It masks our scent," Imago answered brusquely and, tucking the sphere away, he unslung Will's backpack and dropped it into the gap. Then he lowered himself to his knees and squeezed headfirst into the opening. It was a tight fit, to say the least.

For about twenty feet the fissure descended almost vertically, then it began to level off, narrowing even further into a tight crawl space. Progress was slow as Will and Cal followed behind, the sounds of Imago's grunting and wriggling reaching them from up ahead as he desperately struggled through, pushing Will's backpack before him. Will was just wondering what they would do if Imago got stuck when they reached the end and were able to stand again.

At first, Will couldn't make out much through his ruined mask, with one of its eyepieces shattered and the other fogged with condensation. It was only when Imago pulled off his mask and told the boys to remove theirs that Will saw where they were.

It was a chamber, little more than thirty feet across and almost perfectly bell-shaped, with rough walls the texture of Carborundum. A number of small grayish stalactites hung down in the middle of the chamber, directly over a circle of dusty metal, which was set into the center of the floor. As they shuffled around the edges of the chamber, their boots scattered clusters of smooth spheres, which were dirty yellow in color and varied from the size of peas to large marbles.

"Cave pearls," Will muttered, recalling the pictures he'd seen of them in one of his father's textbooks. Despite the way he felt, he immediately cast his eye around for any sign of running water, which would have been necessary for their formation. But the floor and walls appeared to be as dry and arid as the rest of the Labyrinth. And the only way in or out that Will could see was the crawl space they'd just come through.

Imago had been watching him, and answered his unuttered question.

"Don't worry . . . we'll be safe here, Will, for a while," he said, his broad face smiling reassuringly. "We call this place the Cauldron."

As Cal stumbled wearily to the far side of the chamber and slid down against the wall with his head slumped forward onto his chest, Imago spoke to Will again.

"I should take a look at that arm."

"It's nothing, really," Will replied. Not only did he want to be left alone, he was also too terrified to discover just how severe his injuries might be.

"Come on," Imago said firmly, waving him over. "It could get infected. I need to dress it."

Gritting his teeth, Will took a deep breath and, stiffly and awkwardly, removed his jacket and let it slide to the ground. The material of his shirt was firmly stuck to the wounds, and Imago had to work it free little by little, starting at the collar and gently peeling it back. Will watched queasily, wincing as several of the damp scabs were pulled off and he saw fresh blood well out and run down his already stained arm.

"You got off lightly," Imago said. Will glanced at Imago's unsmiling face, wondering if he really meant what he was saying, as he nodded and went on. "You should count yourself lucky. Stalkers usually go for more vulnerable body parts."

Will's forearm had some livid welts, and two semicircles of puncture wounds on both sides, but there was little or no bleeding from these now. He inspected the redness on his chest and abdomen, then felt his ribs, which only hurt if he inhaled deeply. No real damage there either. But his shoulder was a different matter altogether. The animal's teeth had sunk deeper there, and the flesh had been badly mauled by the shaking of the stalker's head. In places it was so raw and torn it looked like it could have been inflicted by a shotgun blast.

"*Eyshh!*" Will exhaled loudly, turning his head away quickly as rivulets of blood seeped down his arm. "It looks awful." Now that he'd actually seen it, he tensed up and couldn't stop himself from trembling, realizing just how much his injuries were hurting him. For a moment all his strength deserted him, and he felt so very weak and vulnerable.

"Don't worry, it looks worse than it is," Imago said reassuringly as he poured a clear liquid from a silver flask over a piece of cloth. "But this is going to sting," he warned Will, then set about cleaning the wounds. When he'd finished, he pushed the flap of his coat open and reached inside to unbutton one of the many pouches on his belt. He pulled out a bag of what looked like pipe tobacco and proceeded to sprinkle it liberally over Will's wounds, concentrating on the lacerations to his shoulder. The small, dry fibers stuck to the lesions, absorbing the blood. "This might hurt a little, but I'm nearly done," Imago said as he packed more of the material on top, patting it down so that it formed a thick mat.

"What's that?" Will asked, daring to look at his shoulder again.

"Shredded rhizomes."

"Shredded *what*?" Will said with alarm. "I hope you know what you're doing."

"I'm the son of an apothecary. I was taught to dress a wound when I was not much older than you are."

Will relaxed again.

"You don't need to worry, Will . . . it's been a while since I lost a patient," Imago said, looking askance at him.

"Huh?" A little slow on the uptake, Will stared at him with alarm.

"Only joking," Imago said, ruffling Will's hair and chuckling. But despite Imago's attempt to lighten the mood, Will could read the immense sadness in the man's eyes as he continued to tend to Will's shoulder. "There's an antiseptic in this poultice. It'll stop the bleeding and deaden the nerves," Imago said as he reached into another pouch and pulled out a gray roll of material, which he began to unwind. He bound this expertly around Will's shoulder and arm and, tying the ends securely in a bow, stood back to admire his handiwork.

"How's that feel?"

"Better," Will lied. "Thanks."

"You'll need to change the dressing every once in a while—you should take some of this with you."

"What do you mean, with me? Where are we going?" Will asked, but Imago shook his head.

"All in good time. You've lost a lot of blood and need to get some fluids in you. And we should all try to eat something." Imago glanced across at the slumped form of Cal. "Come on. Get yourself over here, boy."

Cal obediently heaved himself to his feet and wandered over as Imago sat his bulk down, his legs stretched out in front of him, and began to produce numerous dull metal canisters from his leather satchel. He unscrewed the lid of the first one and proffered it at Will, who regarded the sloppy gray slabs of fungi with unconcealed revulsion. "I hope you don't mind," Will said, "but we brought our own."

Imago didn't seem to mind at all. He simply resealed his canister and waited expectantly as Will unloaded the food from his backpack. Imago fell upon it with evident relish, sucking noisily on slices of honey-roasted ham, which he held delicately in his dirty fingers. As if trying to make the experience last forever, he rolled the meat noisily around in his mouth with his tongue before chewing it. And when he did finally swallow, he half closed his eyes and let out huge, blissful sighs.

In contrast, Cal hardly touched a thing, picking unenthusiastically before withdrawing again to the other side of the chamber. Will didn't have much of an appetite, either, particularly after witnessing Imago's performance. He pulled out a can of Coke and had just started sipping it when he suddenly thought about the jade green pendant that Tam had given him. He found it in his jacket and took it out to examine its dull surface. It was still smeared with Tam's blood, which had congealed within the three indentations carved into one of its faces. He stared at it and ran his thumb across it lightly.

He was certain he'd seen the same three-pronged symbol somewhere before. Then he remembered. It had been on the milestone in the Labyrinth.

While Imago was working his way through a bar of plain chocolate, savoring each mouthful, Cal spoke from the other side of the chamber, his voice flat and listless.

"I want to go home. I don't care anymore."

Imago choked, spitting out a hail of half-chewed chocolate globs. He spun his head around to face Cal, his horsetail braid whipping into the air. "And what about the Styx?"

"I'll talk to them, I'll make them listen to me," Cal replied feebly.

"They'll listen, all right, while they're cutting out your liver or hacking you limb from limb!" Imago rebuked him. "You little idiot, d'you think Tam gave his life just so you could chuck yours away?"

"I . . . no . . ." Cal was blinking with fright as Imago continued to shout.

Still holding the pendant tightly, Will pressed it to his forehead, covering his face with his hand. He just wanted everyone to shut up; he didn't need any of this. He wanted it all to stop, if only for a moment.

"You selfish, stupid . . . what are you going to do, get your father or Granny Macaulay to hide you . . . and risk their lives, too? This is going to be bad enough as it is!" Imago was yelling.

"I just thought—"

"No, you didn't!" Imago cut him off. "You can never go back, d'you understand? Get that into your thick head!" Casting the rest of the chocolate bar aside, he strode to the opposite end of the chamber.

"But I . . . ," Cal started to say.

"Get some sleep!" Imago growled, his face rigid with anger. He wrapped his coat tightly around him and, using his satchel as a pillow, he lay down on his side with his face to the wall.

There they remained for the better part of the next day, alternately eating and sleeping with hardly a word passing between them. After all the horror and excitement of the past twenty-four hours, Will welcomed the opportunity to recuperate, and spent much of the time in a heavy, dreamless sleep. He was eventually woken by Imago's voice, and lethargically opened one eye to see what was going on.

"Come over and give me a hand, will you, Cal?"

Cal quickly jumped up and joined Imago, who was kneeling by the center of the chamber.

"It weighs a ton." Imago grinned.

As they slid aside the metal circle in the ground, it was patently obvious Imago could have managed by himself and that this was his way of patching things up with Cal. Will opened his other eye and flexed his arm. His shoulder was stiff, but his injuries didn't hurt nearly as much as they had.

Cal and Imago were now lying full-length on the ground, peering down into the circular opening as Imago played his light into it. Will crawled over to see what they were looking at. There was a well a good three feet across and then a murky darkness below it.

"I can see something shining," Cal said.

"Yes, railway tracks," Imago replied.

"The Miners' Train," Will realized as he saw the two parallel lines of polished iron glinting in the pitch-blackness.

They pulled back from the hole and sat around it, waiting eagerly for Imago to speak.

"I'm going to be blunt, because we don't have much time," he said. "You have two choices. Either we lie low up here for a while and then I get you Topsoil again, or—"

"No, not there," said Cal right away.

"I'm not saying it's going to be easy to get you there," Imago admitted. "Not with three of us."

"No way! I couldn't take it!" Cal raised his voice until he was almost shouting.

"Don't be so hasty," Imago warned. "If we did make it Topsoil, at least you could try to lose yourselves somewhere the Styx can't find you. Maybe."

"No," repeated Cal with absolute conviction.

Imago was now looking directly at Will. "You should be aware . . ." He clammed up, as if what he was about to say was so terrible that he didn't quite know how to put it. "Tam thinks"—he quickly corrected himself with a grimace—"*thought* that the Styx girl who passed herself off as your Topsoiler sister"—he coughed uneasily and wiped his mouth—"is the Crawfly's daughter. So Tam just killed her father back there in the City."

"Rebecca's father?" Will asked in a nonplussed voice.

"Oh, great," Cal croaked.

"Why's that important? What does—?" Will managed, before Imago cut him short.

"The Styx don't leave be. They will pursue you, anywhere you go. Anyone who gives you shelter—Topsoil, in the Colony, or even in the Deeps—is in danger, too. You know they have people all over the surface." Imago scratched his belly and frowned. "But if Tam was right, it means that as bad as your situation was before, it's worse now. You're in the very greatest danger. You are *marked* now."

Will tried to absorb what he'd just been told, shaking his head at the unfairness, the injustice of it all.

"So you're saying that if I go Topsoil, I'm on the run. And if I went to Auntie Jean's, then . . ."

"She's dead." Imago shifted uneasily where he sat on the dusty rock floor. "That's the way it is."

"But what are *you* going to do, Imago?" Will asked, finding it impossible to grasp the situation he was in.

"I can't go back to the Colony, that's for sure. But don't you worry 'bout me; it's you two that need sorting out."

"But what should I do?" Will asked, glancing over at Cal, who was staring at the opening in the floor, and then back to Imago, who just shrugged unhelpfully, leaving Will feeling even worse. He was at a total loss. It was as though he were playing a game where you were only told the rules after you made a mistake. "Well, I suppose there's nothing Topsoil for me, anyway. Not now," he mumbled, bowing his head. "And my dad's down here . . . somewhere. '

Imago pulled over his satchel and rummaged inside it, fishing out something wrapped in an old piece of burlap, which he passed to Will.

"What's this?" Will muttered, folding back the cloth. With so many thoughts racing through his head, he was in a state of confusion, and it took him several seconds to appreciate just what he'd been given.

It was a flattened and solid glob of paper, which easily fit into his fist. With torn and irregular edges, it had evidently been immersed in water and then left to dry, the pieces clumped together in a crude papier-mâché. He glanced inquiringly at Imago, who offered no comment, so he began to pick away at the outer layers, much as one might peel the desiccated leaves from an ancient onion. As he scratched at their furred edges with a fingernail, it didn't take him long to separate the pieces of paper. Then he laid them out to inspect them more closely under his light.

"No! I don't believe it! This is my dad's writing!" Will said with surprise and delight as he recognized Dr. Burrows's characteristic scrawl on a number of the fragments. They were mud-stained and the blue ink had run, making very little of it legible, but he was still able to decipher some of what was written.

" *'I will resume,'* " Will recited from one fragment, quickly moving on to the others and scrutinizing each of them in turn. "No, this piece is too smudged," he mumbled. "Nothing here, either," he continued, and "I don't know . . . some odd words . . . doesn't make any sense . . . but . . . ah, this says *'Day 15'*!" He continued to scour several more fragments until he stopped with a jerk. "This piece," he exclaimed excitedly, holding the particular scrap up to the light, "mentions me!" He glanced across at Imago, a slight waver in his voice. " *'If my son, Will, had,'* it says!" With a puzzled expression, he flicked it over to check the reverse side but found it was blank. "But what did

Dad mean? What didn't I do? What was I *meant* to do?" Will again looked to Imago for help.

"Search me," the man said.

Will's face lit up. "Whatever he was saying, he's still thinking about me. He hasn't forgotten me. Maybe he always hoped that somehow or other I'd try to follow after him, to find him." He was nodding vigorously as the notion built to a crescendo in his head. "Yes, that's it . . . that must be it!"

Something else occurred to him at that moment, deflecting his thoughts. "Imago, this has to be from my dad's journal. Where did you get it?" Will was immediately imagining the worst. "Is he all right?"

Imago rubbed his chin contemplatively. "Don't know. Like Tam told you, he took a one-way on the Miners' Train." Sticking a thumb in the direction of the hole in the floor, he went on. "Your father's down there somewhere, in the Deeps. Probably."

"Yes, but where did you get this?" Will demanded impatiently, closing his hand over the scraps of paper and holding them up in his palm.

" 'Bout a week after your dad arrived in the Colony, he was wandering around on the outskirts of the Rookeries and was attacked." Imago's voice became slightly incredulous at this point. "If the story's to be believed, he was stopping people and asking them things. Round those parts they don't take kindly to anyone, least of all Topsoilers, nosing about, and he got a good kicking. By all accounts, he just lay there, didn't even try to put up a fight. Probably saved his life."

"Dad," Will said with tears welling in his eyes as he pictured the scene. "Poor old Dad."

"Well, it can't have been too bad. He walked away from it." Imago rubbed his hands together, and his tone changed, becoming more businesslike. "But that's neither here nor there. You need to tell me what you want to do. We can't stick around here forever." He looked pointedly at each boy in turn. "Will? Cal?"

They were both silent for a while, until Will spoke up.

"Chester!" He couldn't believe that with everything else that had been going on, he'd completely forgotten about his friend. "Whatever you say, I've got to go back for him," he said resolutely. "I owe it to him."

"Chester will be all right," Imago said.

"How can you know that?" Will immediately shot back at him.

Imago simply smiled.

"So where is he?" Will asked. "Is he really all right?"

"Trust me," Imago said cryptically.

Will looked into his eyes and saw the man was in earnest. He felt a huge sense of relief, as if a crushing weight had been lifted from his shoulders. He told himself that if anyone could save his friend, then it would be Imago. He drew a long breath and lifted his head. "Well, in that case, the Deeps it is."

"And I'm going with you," Cal put in quickly.

"You're both absolutely sure about this?" Imago asked, looking hard at Will. "It's like hell down there. You'd be better off Topsoil; at least you'd know the lay of the land."

Will shook his head. "My dad is all I have left."

"Well, if that's what you want." Imago's voice was low and somber.

"There's nothing for us Topsoil, not now," Will replied with a glance at his brother.

"Okeydokey, it's decided, then," Imago said, checking his watch. "Now try to get some shut-eye. You're going to need all your strength."

But none of them could sleep, and Imago and Cal ended up talking about Tam. Imago was regaling the younger boy with stories of his uncle's exploits, even chuckling at times, and Cal couldn't help but join in with him. Imago was clearly drawing comfort from reminiscing about the stunts he, Tam, and his sister had pulled in their youth, when they had run rings around the Styx.

"Tam and Sarah were as bad as each other, I can tell you. Pair of wildcats." Imago smiled sadly.

"Tell Will about the cane toads," Cal said, egging him on.

"Oh dear God, yes . . ." Imago laughed, recalling the incident. "It was your mother's idea, you know. We caught a barrel load of the things over in the Rookeries—the sickos there raise them in their basements." Imago raised his eyebrows. "Sarah and Tam took the toads to a church and let them out just before the service got underway. You should have seen it . . . a hundred of the slimy little beggars hopping all over the place . . . people jumping and shrieking, and you could hardly hear the preacher for all the croaking . . . *burup, burup, burup.*" The rotund man rocked with silent laughter, then his brow furrowed and he was unable to continue.

With all the talk about his real mother, Will had been trying his hardest to listen, but he was far too tired and preoccupied. The seriousness of his situation was still foremost in his mind, and his thoughts were heavy with apprehension about what he'd just committed himself to. A journey into the unknown. Was he really up to it? Was he doing the right thing, for himself and his brother?

He broke from his introspection as he heard Cal suddenly interrupt Imago, who had just started on another tale. "Do you think Tam might have made it?" Cal asked. "You know . . . escaped?"

Imago looked away from him quickly and began drawing absently in the dust with his finger, clearly at a loss for words. And in the silence that ensued, intense sorrow flooded Cal's face again.

"I can't believe he's gone. He was everything to me."

"He fought them all his life," Imago said, his voice distant and strained. "He was no saint, that's for sure, but he gave us something—hope—and that made it bearable for us." He paused, his eyes fixed on some distant point beyond Cal's head. "With the Crawfly dead there'll be purges . . . and a crackdown the likes of which hasn't been seen for years." He picked up a cave pearl and examined it. "But I wouldn't go back to the Colony even if I could. I suppose we're all homeless now," Imago said as he flicked the pearl into the air with his thumb and, with absolute precision, it fell into the dead center of the well.

37

"PLEASE!" Chester whimpered inside the clammy hood, which stuck to his face and neck with his cold sweat. After they had dragged him from his cell and down the corridor to the front of the police station, they had pushed something over his head and bound his wrists. Then they'd left him standing there, enveloped in stifling darkness, with muffled sounds coming from all around.

"Please!" Chester shouted in sheer desperation.

"Shut up, will you!" snapped a gruff voice just inches behind his ear.

"What's happening?" Chester begged.

"You're going on a little journey, my son, a little journey," said the same voice.

"But I haven't done anything! Please!"

He heard boots grinding on a stone floor as he was pushed from behind. He stumbled and fell to his knees, unable to rise up again with his hands tied behind his back.

"Get up!"

He was hauled to his feet and stood swaying, his legs like jelly. He'd known that this moment was looming, that his days were numbered, but he'd had no way of finding out what it would be like when it did come. Nobody would speak to him in the Hold, not that he made much of an effort to ask them, so petrified was he of provoking any further retribution from the Second Officer and his fellow wardens.

So Chester had lived as a condemned man who could only guess at the form of his eventual demise. He'd clung on to every precious second he had left, trying not to let them go, and dying a little inside as one after another they slipped away. Now the only thing he could find solace from was the knowledge that he had a train journey before him—so at least he had *some* time left. But then what? What were the Deeps like? What would happen to him there?

"Move it!"

He shambled forward a few paces, unsure of his footing and unable to see a thing. He bumped into something hard, and the sound around him seemed to change. Echoes. Shouts, but from a distance, from a larger space.

Suddenly, there came the clamor of many voices.

Oh, no!

He knew without a shred of doubt exactly where he was—he was outside the police station. And what he was hearing was the baying of a large crowd. If he'd been frightened before, it was worse now. *A crowd*. The jeering and catcalls grew louder, and he felt himself being lifted under each arm and hoisted along. He was on the main street; he could feel the irregular surface of the cobbles when his feet were allowed to touch the ground.

"I haven't done anything! I want to go home!"

He was panting hard, struggling to breathe through the coarse material of the hood. Sopping with his own saliva and tears, it sucked into his mouth with every inhalation.

"Help me! Someone!" His voice was so anguished and distorted that it was almost unrecognizable to him.

Still the crazed shouts came from all around.

"TOPSOIL FILTH!"

"STRING 'IM UP!"

One repeated shout with many voices took form. It went over and over again.

"FILTH! FILTH! FILTH!"

They were shouting at him—so many people were shouting at him! His stomach churned with the stark realization. He couldn't see them, and that made it worse. He was so terrified he thought he was going to be sick.

"FILTH! FILTH! FILTH!"

"Please . . . please stop . . . help me! Please . . . please help me . . . please." He was hyperventilating and crying at the same time—he couldn't help it.

"FILTH! FILTH! FILTH!"

I'm going to die! I'm going to die! I'm going to die!

The single thought pulsed through his head, a counterpoint to the repeated chant of the crowd. They were so close to him now—close enough that he could smell their collective stench and the foul reek of their collective hatred.

"FILTH! FILTH! FILTH!"

He felt as if he were in the bottom of a well, with a vortex of noises and shouts and vicious laughter swirling around him.

He couldn't take it anymore. He had to do something. He had to escape!

In blind terror he tried to break free, struggling and twisting his body, convulsing against his captors. But the huge hands only gripped him even more savagely, and the rabble's cries and laughter reached fever pitch at this new spectacle. Exhausted and realizing it was futile, he moaned, "No . . . no . . . no . . . no . . ."

A sickly, intimate voice came from so close that he felt the speaker's lips brush his ear. "C'mon now, Chester, pull yourself together! You don't want to disappoint all these good ladies and gentlemen, do you?" Chester realized it was the Second Officer. He must have been relishing every second of this.

"Let them have a look at you!" said someone else. "Let them see you for what you are!"

Chester felt numb . . . bereft . . . *I can't believe this. I can't believe this.*

For a moment it was as if all the jeering and chanting and catcalls had stopped. As if he were in the eye of the storm, as if time itself had stopped. Then hands took hold of his ankles and legs, guiding them onto a step of some kind.

What now? He was heaved onto a bench and shoved hard against its back, in a sitting position.

"Take him away!" someone barked. The crowd cheered, and there were rapturous yelps and wolf whistles.

Whatever he had been put on lurched forward. He thought he heard the plunging of horses' hooves. *A carriage? Yes, a carriage!*

"Don't make me go! This isn't right!" he implored them.

He began to gibber, his words making no sense.

"You're going to get exactly what you deserve, my boy!" said a voice to his right, in an almost confidential tone. It was the Second Officer again.

"And it's too good for you," came another he didn't recognize from his left.

Chester was now shaking uncontrollably.

This is it, then! Oh God! Oh God! This is it!

He thought of his home, and the memories of watching television on so many Saturday mornings popped into his head. Happy and cherished moments of normality with his mother in the kitchen cooking breakfast, the smell of food in the air, and his father calling from upstairs to see if it was ready yet. It was like another life he was remembering, someone else's life, from another time, another century.

I will never, ever see them again. They're gone . . . it's all gone . . . finished . . . forever!

His head sank to his chest. He went limp as the stone-cold realization that it was all over spread through his whole body.

I am FINISHED.

From the soles of his feet to the top of his head he was filled with a crushing hopelessness. As if he'd been paralyzed, his breath slowly left his lips, pulling with it an involuntary animal sound, a half whine, half moan. An awful, dread-filled sound of resignation, of abandonment.

For what seemed like an eternity, he didn't breathe at all, his mouth gaping, closing, opening, like that of a stranded fish. His empty lungs burned from the lack of air until finally his whole body jerked. He sucked in a painful breath through the clogged weave of the hood. Forcing his head up, he let go a final cry of utter and final despair.

"WWWWWWWIIIIIILLLLLL!"

Will was surprised to find he'd dozed off again. He awoke, disoriented and with no idea how long he'd actually been asleep, as a dull, far-off vibration roused him. He couldn't pinpoint what it was, and in any case the cold, hard reality of the choice to go into the Deeps came flooding back to him. It was as if he'd awoken into a nightmare.

He saw Imago crouching by the well, inclining his head toward the sound, listening. Then they all heard it plainly; the distant rumbling grew louder with every second until it began to reverberate around the chamber. At Imago's direction, Will and Cal shimmied over to the opening in the floor and readied themselves. As they both sat with their legs dangling from the edge, beside them Imago was leaning his head and shoulders into the well, hanging down as far as he could.

"Slows around the corner!" they heard him shout, and the noise grew more and more intense, until the whole chamber was vibrating around them. "Here she comes. Bang on time!" He pulled himself out, still watching the tracks below as he kneeled between the boys.

"You're sure this is what you want?" he asked them.

The boys looked at each other and nodded.

"We're sure," Will said. "But Chester . . . ?"

"I told you, don't worry 'bout him," Imago said with a dismissive smile.

The chamber was shaking now with the sound of the approaching train, as if a thousand drums were beating in their heads.

"Do exactly as I say—this has to be timed to perfection—so when I say jump, you jump!" Imago told them.

The chamber filled with the acrid taint of sulfur. Then, as the roar of the engine reached a crescendo, a jet of soot shot up through the opening like a black geyser. It caught Imago square in the face, spraying him with smut and making him squint. They all coughed as the thick, pungent smoke flooded the Cauldron, engulfing them.

"READY . . . READY . . . ," Imago screamed, pitching the backpacks into the darkness below them. "CAL, JUMP!"

For a split second Cal hesitated, and Imago suddenly pushed him. He dropped into the well, howling with surprise.

"GO, WILL!" Imago screamed again, and Will tipped himself off the edge.

The sides flashed past, and then he was out and tumbling into a vortex of noise, smoke, and darkness, his arms and legs flailing. His breath was knocked from him as he landed with a jarring crunch, and a pure white light burst around him, one he couldn't even begin to understand. Points of illumination seemed to be leaping over him like errant stars and, for the briefest of moments, he really wondered if he'd died.

He lay still, listening to the percussive beat of the engine somewhere up ahead and the juddering rhythm of the wheels as the train picked up speed. He felt the wind on his face and watched the long wisps of smoke pass above him. *No, this wasn't some industrial heaven: He was alive!*

He resolved not to move for a moment while he mentally checked himself over, making sure he didn't have any broken bones to add to his already burgeoning list of injuries. Incredibly, other than a few additional grazes, everything seemed to be intact and in working order.

He lay there. If this wasn't death, what was the bright, fluxing light he still saw all around him, like a miniature aurora? He pulled himself up onto one elbow.

Countless light orbs the size of large marbles were rolling around the gritty floor of the car, colliding and rebounding off one another in random paths. Some became trapped in the runnels in the floor and would dim slightly as they touched, until they became unseated and scampered off on their ways again, flaring into brilliance once more.

Then Will looked behind him and found the remains of the crate and the straw packing. It all became clear. His fall had been broken by a box of light orbs, which had smashed open when he landed on it. Thanking his luck, he felt like cheering, but instead helped himself to several handfuls of the lights, stuffing them into his pockets.

He got to his feet, bracing himself against the motion of the train. Although the foul-smelling smoke streamed thickly around him, the loose orbs lit up the car to such effect that he was able to see it in detail. It was massive. It must have been nearly a hundred feet long and half that in width, much larger and more substantial than any train he'd ever seen Topsoil. It was constructed from slablike plates of iron, crudely welded together. The side panels were battered and rusted away, and their tops worn and buckled, as if the car had seen eons of hard use.

He dropped down again and, his knees grinding in the grit on the floor, the movement of the car buffeting him around, he went in search of Cal. He came across several other crates made from the same thin wood as the one he'd landed on, and then, near the front of the car, he spotted Cal's boot propped up on another line of boxes.

"Cal, Cal!" he shouted, crawling frantically toward him. In the midst of a mass of splintered wood, his brother was lying still, too still. His jacket was splattered with a wet darkness, and Will could see there was something wrong with his face.

Fearing the worst, Will shouted even louder. Not wanting to knock against Cal in case he was badly hurt, he clambered rapidly across the top of the crates alongside him. Dreading what he was about to see, he slowly held a light orb up to Cal's head. It didn't look good. His face and hair were slick with a red pulp.

Will reached out gingerly and was touching the watery redness on his brother's face when he noticed the broken green forms scattered around him. And there were seeds stuck to Cal's forehead. Will drew back his hand and tasted his fingers. *It was watermelon!* At Cal's side was another damaged crate. As Will shoved it away to make more room, tangerines, pears, and apples spilled out. His brother had evidently had a soft landing, smashing into crates of fruit.

"Thank goodness," Will repeated as he shook Cal gently by the shoulders, trying to stir his limp form. But his head flopped lifelessly from side to side. Not knowing what else to do, Will took his brother's wrist to check his pulse.

"Get off me, will you!" Cal yanked his arm away from Will

as he sluggishly opened his eyes and moaned self-pityingly. "My head hurts," he complained, rubbing his forehead tenderly. He brought up his other arm and glanced bemusedly at the banana in his hand. Then he caught the fragrant smell of the lush fruit all around him and looked uncomprehendingly at Will.

"What happened?" he shouted over the din of the train.

"Lucky duck, you fell in the restaurant car!" Will chuckled.

"Huh?"

"Doesn't matter. Try to sit up," Will suggested.

"In a minute." Cal was groggy but otherwise appeared to be unharmed, except for a few cuts and bruises and a liberal dousing of melon juice, so Will crawled back over the crates and began to investigate. He knew he should be retrieving their backpacks from the cars in front of them, but there was no hurry. Imago had said it would be a long trip and, anyway, his curiosity was getting the better of him.

"I'm going to . . . ," he shouted over at Cal.

"What?" Cal cupped a hand to his ear.

"Explore," Will motioned.

"OK!" Cal yelled back.

Will scrambled through the weird sea of light orbs at the rear of the car and pulled himself up on the end panel. He peered down at the coupling in between the cars and the polished sheen of the well-used rails shooting hypnotically underneath. Then he looked across to the next car, only a few feet away and, without stopping to think, hoisted himself over the edge. With the motion of the train it was awkward, but he managed to reach across and straddle both end panels, then had no option but to jump.

He dropped into the next car and rolled uncontrollably over the floor until he came to rest against a pile of canvas sacks. There was nothing much of note here except for some more crates halfway down, so he crawled to the back of the section and got to his feet again. He tried to see to the very end of the train, but the combination of smoke and darkness made this impossible.

"How many are there?" Will shouted to himself as he went to clamber over the end wall. As he repeated the process over successive cars, he finally got the hang of it and found he could hop over and steady himself before he went tumbling. He was consumed with a burning curiosity to find the end of the train but at the same time wary about what he might come across there. He'd been warned by Imago that it was more than likely there'd be a Colonist in the guard's carriage, so he had to play it carefully.

He'd dropped over the edge of the fourth car and was just crawling across a loose tarpaulin when something stirred beside him.

"What the—" Terrified he'd been caught, Will drove his heel into the shadows as hard as he could. Off balance, the kick wasn't as effective as he'd hoped, but he definitely struck something under the tarpaulin. He readied himself to strike again.

"Leave me alone!" a voice complained weakly, and the tarpaulin flew back to reveal a hunched form in the corner. Will immediately held up his light orb.

"Hey!" the voice squeaked, trying to shield its face from the illumination.

He blinked at Will, tearstains etched through the film of grime and coal smut on his cheeks. There was a pause and a gasp of recognition, and his face split into the broadest grin imaginable. It was a tired face, and had lost much of its healthy chubbiness, but it was unmistakable.

"Hi, Chester," Will said, slumping down next to his old friend.

"Will?" Chester cried, not quite believing what he was seeing; then, at the top of his lungs, he cried out again. "Will!"

"Didn't think I'd let you go by yourself, did you?" Will shouted back. Will realized now what Imago had had in mind. He knew Chester was to be Banished, sent to the Deeps on this very train. The sly old rogue had known all along.

It was impossible to talk with all the noise from the speeding engine up ahead, but Will was content just to be reunited with Chester. Will grinned the widest of grins, luxuriating in a wave of relief that his friend was safe. He leaned back against the end panel of the car and shut his eyes, filled with the most intense feeling of elation that, finally, from the throes of the nightmarish situation he'd found himself in, something good had emerged, something had turned out right. *Chester was safe!* That meant the world to him.

And to top it all, he was being borne toward his father, on the greatest adventure of his life, on a journey into undiscovered lands. In his mind, Dr. Burrows was the only part of his past life he could cling to. Will was determined that he would find him, wherever he was. And then everything would be all right again. They'd all be all right: he, Chester, and Cal, all together, with his father. This notion shone in his thoughts like the brightest of beacons.

All of a sudden, the future didn't seem so daunting.

Will opened his eyes and leaned toward Chester's ear: "No school tomorrow, then!" he shouted.

They both burst into helpless laughter, which was drowned out by the train as it continued to gather speed, spewing dark smoke behind it, carrying them away from the Colony, away from Highfield, and away from everything they knew, accelerating into the very heart of the earth.

EPILOGUE

The gentle heat of the sun filtered down on a beautiful day early in the New Year, so balmy it could have been spring. Unobstructed by tall buildings, the perfect blue canvas of the sky was marred only by the specks of gulls falling and rising on thermals in the distance. If it hadn't been for the occasional intrusion of traffic swerving past on the canal-side road, one might have imagined it was somewhere on the coast, perhaps a sleepy fishing village.

But this was London, and the wooden tables outside the pub were beginning to fill up as the lure of the fine weather became too tempting. Three dark-suited men with the anemic faces of office workers swaggered out through the doors and sat down with their drinks. Leaning over the table, each tried to outdo the other as they talked too loudly and laughed raucously, like squabbling crows. Next to them was a very different group, college students in jeans and faded T-shirts who hardly made any noise at all. They were almost whispering to one another as they supped their beers and rolled the occasional cigarette.

Alone on a wooden bench in the shade of the building, Reggie sipped his pint, his fourth that lunchtime. He felt slightly woozy, but since he had nothing planned for the afternoon, he'd decided to indulge himself. He took a handful of whitebait from the bowl beside him and munched on the little fish thoughtfully.

"Hiya, Reggie," one of the barmaids said, her arms full of precariously stacked glasses as she collected the empties.

"Hi there," he replied hesitantly, never very good at remembering any of the bar staff's names.

She smiled pleasantly at him, then pushed open the door with her hip as she headed back inside. Reggie had been turning up on and off for years, but he had recently become a firm regular, dropping in nearly every day for his favorites, a bowl of whitebait or cod and chips.

He was a quiet man who kept to himself. Other than the fact that he was overgenerous with his tips, what made him stand out from the run-of-the-mill customers was his appearance. He had the most striking white hair. Sometimes he wore it like an aging biker, braided into a bleached snake down his back, but on other occasions it ran wild, fluffed up like a newly shampooed poodle. He was never without his heavily tinted sunglasses, whatever the weather, and his clothes were arcane and old-fashioned, as if he had borrowed them from a theatrical costumer. Given his eccentric appearance, the bar staff came to the conclusion that he must be an out-of-work musician, a retired actor, or even an undiscovered artist, of which there were many in the area.

He leaned back against the wall, sighing contentedly as a slim young girl with a pleasant face and a flowery cotton scarf over her head appeared. Carrying a rattan basket, she went from table to table, trying to sell little sprigs of heather with foil wrapped around their stems. It was a scene that could have been lifted from Victorian times. He grinned, thinking how quaint it was that street gypsies still peddled such innocent wares when all around the big companies were promoting their brands so relentlessly on the billboards.

"Imago."

The name drifted toward him as a breeze picked up and a battered car swerved recklessly around the corner, its wheels squealing. He shivered, and looked suspiciously at an old man as he struggled along the pavement with his walking stick. The man's cheeks were covered with spiky gray stubble, as if he'd forgotten to shave that morning.

As the girl selling the heather brushed past with her basket, Imago looked away from the old man and studied the people at the tables again. No, he was just a little jumpy. It was nothing. He must have imagined it.

He put the bowl of whitebait on his lap and helped himself to another handful, washing it down with some beer. This was the life! He smiled to himself and stretched out his legs.

Nobody saw as he was thrown back against the wall by a sudden spasm and then pitched forward from the bench, his face locked into a grotesque contortion. As he hit the ground, his eyes swiveled up into their sockets and his mouth opened, just once, then closed for the last time.

It was all over long before the ambulance arrived. Because he might have rolled off the stretcher, the two ambulance men decided instead to carry the rigid corpse, one on each side. The crowd of onlookers gasped at the spectacle, muttering among themselves as Imago's body, frozen like a statue in a sitting position, was manhandled into the back of the ambulance. And there was absolutely nothing the paramedics could do about the bowl still grasped in the corpse's hand, so tightly they couldn't lever it out.

Poor old Reggie. A pretty insensitive bunch when it came to the welfare of their clientele, the bar staff were genuinely disturbed by his death. Particularly so when the kitchen was closed and several of them lost their jobs. They were later told there'd been an obscure lead-based compound in his food; it was a freak occurrence, a poisoned fish in a million. His body had simply shut down, his blood clotting like quick-setting cement due to overwhelming toxic shock.

At the inquest, the coroner wasn't too forthcoming about the nature of the poison. Indeed, he was rather baffled by the traces of complex chemicals that had never been recorded before.

Only one person, the girl watching the ambulance from across the road, knew the truth. She took off her scarf and threw it into the gutter, shaking out her jet-black hair with a self-satisfied smile as she put on her sunglasses and inclined her head toward the bright sky. As she walked away, she began singing softly, "You are my sunshine. . . . My only sunshine . . ."

She wasn't done yet. . . .

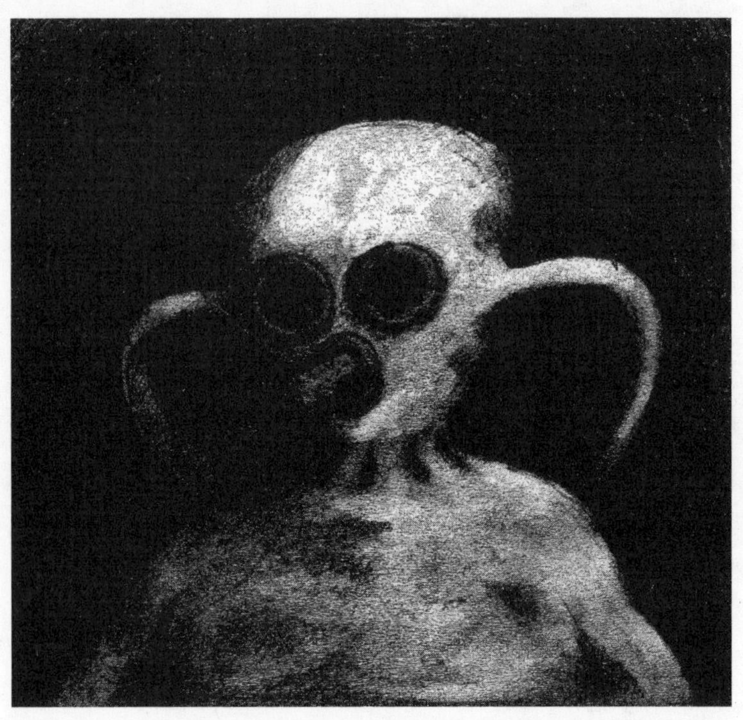

ACKNOWLEDGMENTS

We dedicate this book to our long-suffering families and friends, who have put up with us through our prolonged obsession; and to Barry Cunningham and Imogen Cooper at the Chicken House for their endless encouragement and for keeping us on the straight and narrow; and to Peter Straus at Rogers, Coleridge and White for helping a couple of guys who happened to wander in out of the rain; and to Kate Egan and Stuart Webb; and to our friend Mike Parsons, who has shown bravery beyond belief.

East Hampton Public Library
East Hampton, CT 06424
2280 115509 0